Organizational Behavior
and Management
a
contingency approach

revised
edition

Organizational Behavior and Management
a
contingency approach

Edited by

Henry L. Tosi
Michigan State University

W. Clay Hamner
Duke University

John Wiley & Sons
New York • Chichester • Brisbane • Toronto

To Rosemary and Ellen

First Printing, July 1977
Second Printing, March 1978

**Organizational Behavior and Management
A Contingency Approach**

Revised Edition

Library of Congress Catalog Card Number 77-77475
ISBN 0-471-06239-1

Cover design by H. B. Smith

Printed in the United States of America
10 9 8 7 6 5 4 3 2

Preface to the Revised Edition

As in its first edition, this book is designed to bring present and potential managers into first-hand contact with the past decade's vast increase in information about organizational and environmental influences on performance and satisfaction in industry. The primary objective remains to provide students with a basis for analyzing how the determinants of individual and group behavior enable individuals to accommodate to different and varying types of organizational environments and also with a basis for analyzing the managerial implications of different modes of accommodation.

Readings have been selected from contemporary sources to present a wide range of concepts and to treat important areas in the field of organizational behavior. We have attempted to arrange the material in such a way that the student can relate each reading to the topic under consideration, and we have—with one or two exceptions—eliminated empirical data so that the emphasis of the book will be upon the power of theory and concepts. Our hope is that we have provided a conceptual view that will be useful to students as a foundation for more advanced study or as a basis for creative management practice.

In this revised edition we have, we hope, tightened the theoretical structure of the book by replacing some of the selections with more appropriate choices for given topics than were in print when the first edition was published. We hope that the revisions make the book even more useful than it has already proved itself to be for courses in management, organization theory, organizational behavior, and industrial psychology (the presumption being that the student has had introductory work in management and the behavioral sciences).

We wish to express our gratitude to Andre L. Delbecq, Steven Kerr, Jonathan S. Monat, George Strauss, Charles E. Summer, and A. Thomas Hollingsworth, all of whom have reviewed plans for this book and offered valuable suggestions. Kay Bartol, Joe Champoux, Bob Duncan, and Barry Staw are some who have used the book in the classroom and have been helpful in suggesting changes for this revision.

H. L. T.
W. C. H.

Contents

A Contingency Model
of Organization Behavior

The contingency approach to managing assumes that an organization is a system, or unit, of behavior composed of subsystems, or subunits. The boundaries of these subsystems are identifiable, as is the boundary of the total organizational system.

The specific forms of the subsystems and, logically, the system itself are shaped by the context, or the environment in which the organization exists. To survive, the organization must respond, adapt, and cope with the environment. This response—an adaptation—is "contingent" on the environment. Hence a contingency approach to organizational behavior and management is one in which the structure of each department and the interrelationship between them are, in large part, dependent on the type of customer (or client) served, the nature of societal requirements, or other particular demands or pressures on the organization.

In this book we discuss three levels of systems: individuals as they behave in groups, groups as they operate within the organization, and the organization as it behaves within a society. An underlying concept is that the behavior which occurs is in large part a consequence of the larger context within which the system exists. We seek, therefore, to understand and explain the interrelationship within, and among, the various subunits in an organization as well as between the organization and its environment. This perspective is shown in figure 1, outlining a general contingency model of how individuals are affected by the organization, and how the organization is affected by the environment.

In the model which we propose, there are four major topics related to understanding behavior in organization systems:

1. psychological determinants of individual behavior;
2. organizational determinants of individual behavior;
3. characteristics of the organizational system; and
4. environmental determinants of the organization system.

Psychological Determinants of Individual and Group Behavior

The behavior of the individual is the core of the model for two reasons: First, how people act can be better understood when the determinants of behavior are clear. Second,

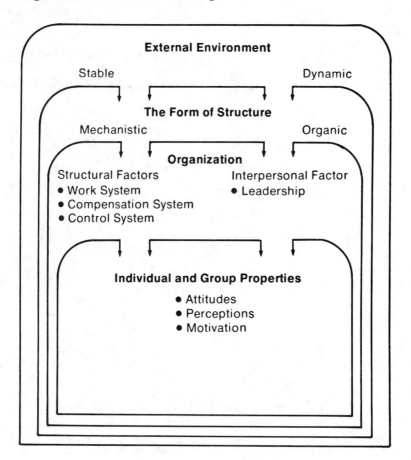

Figure 1. Contingency model of organizational behavior.

the primary level of analysis is the individual; all other subsystems influence groups and individuals to accomplish organizational goals. The individual dimension is represented by the smallest box in figure 1.

Part 2 of this book, "Individual Learning and Socialization," explains how people adapt to their environment. The framework is learning theory, a set of concepts which we use in two ways. First, in part 2, we show how past experiences from childhood are instrumental in determining the orientation of individuals to work organizations. These individual orientations—or personality—affect what a person expects from work and how he will behave. The second use of learning concepts is in part 5, where we suggest ways to use these notions to change behavior patterns through arrangement of the contingencies of reinforcement.

Part 3, "Individual Behavior in the Organization," focuses on attitudes of the person and, in general, how these are affected by the organization setting. Attitudes, perceptions, and motivation are explained as determinants of the individual's behavior in some detail in this section.

In part 4, "Group Behavior and Intergroup Conflict in the Organization," the effects of group pressures on the person are considered, but in terms of how these pressures emanate from the work setting. We examine why people tend to group and the causes and problems that are associated with conflicts between groups.

Organizational Determinants of Individual and Group Behavior

In this model we consider two categories of organizational determinants of individual and group behavior, organization structure and leadership. These two classes of factors have an important effect on how a person behaves and what kind of reactions he has.

Structure

Structure consists of work procedures, rules and policies that affect all individuals in an organization. The effects are discussed in part 5. An individual's task, or job, may range from repetitive to highly varied. In some jobs one may have broad decision-making power, while in another position decision-making discretion is very narrow. Repetitive jobs will induce boredom. Broad decision-making discretion will be associated with high status, resulting in positive feelings.

Compensation practices, and the rationale for compensation increases may condition behavior. For example, a merit increase may not be seen as a reward for "good" performance if given annually, since the "good" performance occurred through the year. So merit increases may not reinforce desired performance. Yet such a compensation system may be used because it is difficult to design it any other way. A piece-rate incentive system, or a sales bonus program, which results in higher pay when higher results are achieved may have a very different result on individual incentive and behavior.

Leadership

Leadership is interpersonal, as distinguished from the impersonal nature of structure. We focus on leader/subordinate relationships in part 6. The power that a manager has to make decisions, allocate rewards and reinforce behavior, and the style used in providing feedback all interplay with the structural factors noted above to affect results.

A manager has several choices of ways to interact with his subordinates. He can give guidance and direction or he can emphasize a less direct approach. The choice of style is not simple, and in part 6 we seek to show how structural and group factors interact to affect the style.

Organization System Characteristics

The form and shape of structural factors and the nature of interpersonal relationships vary in different kinds of organizations. All have policies, but some policies in some organizations are more restrictive than policies in others. The basic postulate of the contingency approach is that there should be differences in the way the structure and management approach of different organizations look. There are two general forms of organizations which we focus on in this book, organic and mechanistic organizations (see figure 1).

Mechanistic Systems

Organizations characterized by relatively routine, repetitive activities at the lowest operating levels are called "mechanistic." There is a high level of task specialization in them, with most of the operating activities broken down into relatively small sets requiring moderate to low levels of skill and ability. The authority/responsibility relationships are fairly well-defined and fairly fixed over time. Authority, or the right to command, is based on position. There are likely to be sharp status distinctions between hierarchical levels.

Jobs are apt to be fairly clearly specified, with limits on discretion, resulting in clear understanding of work relationships and responsibilities. Clear definition of the job, especially if it remains relatively stable over long periods of time, will aid the development of a compensation system in which base levels are defined by job evaluation. Jobs are priced according to their relative worth in an organization.

In mechanistic systems, policies and procedures are in evidence, and there are strong pressures for compliance. Individuals can use procedures and rules as a basis for knowing how to schedule and plan their work. For instance, when a procedure specifies that a report is to be submitted on the first of the month, the individual can plan his work around it. In mechanistic organizations there is likely to be a complex policy and procedural network on which members rely. Therefore, in order to maintain some degree of effectiveness, and for the system to work smoothly, there must be compliance.

Organic Systems

Organic systems are characterized by constantly changing work assignments. The hierarchical authority structure is less rigidly fixed, and authority is usually based on individual competence and skill. The individual, rather than the organizational system, is likely to have major control over what he does and how he does it.

In an organic organization, compensation is based upon the skill level and capability that an individual brings to the organization. In contrast to the mechanistic system, where the base rate is relative to other jobs, salary is usually individually negotiable.

In an organic organization, performance evaluation is less likely to be based on specific output indicators (as would be true in a mechanistic system) and is more probably a function of what, not how much, the individual does. For example, it is difficult to evaluate a research or development scientist on the basis of the results he obtains, especially in the short run. He is typically evaluated on whether or not he conducts his work in generally accepted scientific fashion.

There is more flexibility in an organic organization than in a mechanistic one. Individuals are less constrained by policy and procedures. They are more free to plan their own time and work.

Environmental Determinants of the Organization System

Managers do not have a free choice in determining the form of an organization. External circumstances have an extremely important effect. Because one wants to have either a mechanistic or an organic form of structure has little to do with the level of effectiveness, let alone long-term survival. Organization form is contingent on the outside environment area that the design of an organization must face within the context of the environment.

The external environment is made up of influences, or pressures, which are beyond the boundaries of an organization's interests. Science, cultural values, knowledge, client (or consumer) preferences, availability of resources all are part of this environment. Pressures, or lack thereof, from these sources affect what a manager must do. For instance, technological change which leads to an alteration of the production system may come from outside, but must be dealt with internally. The specific type of environment is different for different kinds of organizations. Steel suppliers, environmental protection agencies, and the automobile-purchasing public are certainly relevant environmental sectors for the automobile industry. Clients, federal and state funding agencies, and local communities may constitute the relevant environment for a welfare agency. The administrator's problem is to define what the relevant environment is, and how to respond within it. The *relevant environment* for an organization is the configuration of environment components which make direct use of output, which provide inputs, and which may otherwise be able to affect directly decision making and policy formulation.

In this book we do not try to categorize the environments for different organizations, but rather to describe the primary environmental characteristic most likely to have an effect, that is, the *rate of environmental change*. The specific environment of an organization may be relatively tranquil, or stable, with changes occurring at a moderately slow and predictable rate. For instance, changes in demand for a product may vary primarily as a function of changes in population; there may be no new markets to tap. Or the technology may be fairly well-established, as is currently characteristic of the automobile industry, which has not had substantial technological changes. There have been no major breakthroughs to change the character of the industry, or the firms in it. Under such conditions of stability, the mechanistic organization is appropriate. In fact, under conditions of extremely high stability, we would argue that the more mechanistic the structure, the more effective the organization.

On the other hand, the elements of the external environment may be relatively dynamic and changing. Change may be extensive and unpredictable. Break-throughs in technology may occur at any time. Markets may be in a state of flux because of changing products, changing demands, or both. Under these conditions the organic form of structure seems to work best since it is more capable of changing than the mechanisitic, whose rigidity restricts adjustment to change. Project management is used extensively in organic organizations so that specialists may be easily shifted from one assignment to another to meet changing needs.

Organizational Change

Changes can take place at all levels of the contingency model, the individual, the group, the organization, and the environment. One basic postulate in this approach is that when a change occurs at one level, say the organizational level, it induces changes at all lower levels, in this case, the individual. There are different approaches to change and they are shown in figure 2.

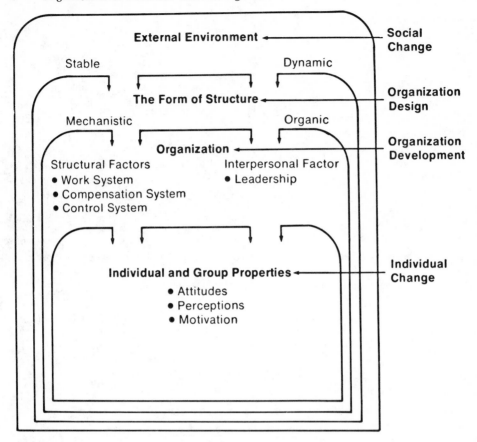

Figure 2. Application of organization change.

Individual Change

Several approaches may be used to change individual and group attitudes, abilities, and knowledge. Lectures, group exercises, and skills training can have an effect upon beliefs, skills, competence, and attitudes. These change efforts are likely to be successful as long as they are consistent with the environmental context. For instance, if a training effort is aimed at increasing one's skill at budgeting and planning, then in order to have the training "take," the person must have the opportunity to use these skills in his job, otherwise the skills will atrophy

Organizational Development

Organizational development includes change activities which focus on both organizational features and individual behavior. Diagnosis of how structural and interpersonal relationships affect performance and satisfaction is aimed at seeking to decide which of a wide range of techniques are likely to be effective in bringing about change. Similar techiques to those used with individuals may be part of the organization development effort, but attention is also directed at changes in policy, procedure, work design, compensation, and evaluation to produce a fine tuning, bringing the human, structural and technical configuration into a more congruent relationship to fit better with environmental constraints.

Organizational Design

Making major changes in structure—moving from organic to mechanistic or vice versa—to cope with the external environment is organization design. Authority/responsibility relationships, the placement of departmental units in relation to each other, and the degree of discretion provided in individual decision making need to be different under different environmental circumstances. When an analyst examines the formal structure of an organization for its congruity with the environment and recommends changes in reporting relationships and discrepancy limits of jobs, he is engaging in organization redesign. This is the quite common consulting activity of "reorganization." Perhaps the primary reason why most reorganization fails is that the designs do not square with the external situation.

Social Change

When the external environment changes in ways that are beyond the control of an organization, this is social change. Changes in social values and consumer preferences fall into this category. Legislation and governmental regulation do also. For example, governmental regulation which increases the required miles per gallon of automobiles dictates sustantial changes for auto manufacturers. To obtain the required miles per gallon, there may have to be drastic changes in production methods, switching to lighter weight components such as aluminum and plastic from the extensive current use of steel. Auto firms are under intense pressure to change and this pressure developed externally. There is little choice but to adapt.

Summary

Individual and group behavior in an organization are determined by factors at different levels. Basic ideas from learning theory provide insights into comprehending how society socializes its members, especially their views about organizations, and how organizations can shape member behavior. Attitudes, perceptions, and motivation are important individual processes. They are regarded as relatively stable characteristics. Group structure and intergroup processes and conflict are a basic unit of analysis in organizational behavior.

All of the above are affected by the setting within which people operate. Organization structure and leadership shape the immediate environment within which the organization member must function. They serve to maintain or change the attitudes, perceptions, and motivation of individuals, singly and in groups. Further, knowing the nature of the external environment can be a basis for understanding the form of the organization system. Finally, to change the performance of the system, alteration can be made at any or all of the four levels above, by way of individual retraining, organization development, organization design, and social change.

In the first reading, Perrow presents an overview of the historical development of the theoretical perspectives whrch have shaped the structure of the approach presented in this book. His article discusses how thinking about organizations has evolved from viewing an organization strictly as a set of relationships among individuals constrained by line and staff authority to an open systems view which attempts to account for internal as well as external forces that shape the organization.

THE SHORT AND GLORIOUS
HISTORY OF ORGANIZATIONAL THEORY

CHARLES PERROW

From the beginning, the forces of light and the forces of darkness have polarized the field of organizational analysis, and the struggle has been protracted and inconclusive. The forces of darkness have been represented by the mechanical school of organizational theory—those who treat the organization as a machine. This school characterizes organizations in terms of such things as:
- centralized authority
- clear lines of authority
- specialization and expertise
- marked division of labor
- rules and regulations
- clear separation of staff and line

The forces of light, which by mid-twentieth century came to be characterized as the human relations school, emphasizes people rather than machines, accommodations rather than machine-like precision, and draws its inspiration from biological systems rather than engineering systems. It has emphasized such things as:
- delegation of authority
- employee autonomy
- trust and openness
- concerns with the "whole person"
- interpersonal dynamics

The Rise and Fall of Scientific Management

The forces of darkness formulated their position first, starting in the early part of this century. They have been characterized as the scientific management or classical management school. This school started by parading simple-minded injunctions to plan ahead, keep records, write down policies, specialize, be decisive, and keep your span of control to about six people. These injunctions were needed as firms

Reprinted by permission of the publisher from *Organizational Dynamics*, Summer 1973 © 1973 by AMACOM, a division of American Management Associations.

grew in size and complexity, since there were few models around beyond the rail-roads, the military, and the Catholic Church to guide organizations. And their injunctions worked. Executives began to delegate, reduce their span of control, keep records, and specialize. Planning ahead still is difficult, it seems, and the modern equivalent is Management by Objectives.

But many things intruded to make these simple-minded injunctions less relevant:

1. Labor became a more critical factor in the firm. As the technology increased in sophistication it took longer to train people, and more varied and specialized skills were needed. Thus, labor turnover cost more and recruitment became more selective. As a consequence, labor's power increased. Unions and strikes appeared. Management adjusted by beginning to speak of a cooperative system of capital, management, and labor. The machine model began to lose its relevancy.

2. The increasing complexity of markets, variability of products, increasing number of branch plants, and changes in technology all required more adaptive organization. The scientific management school was ill-equipped to deal with rapid change. It had presumed that once the proper structure was achieved the firm could run forever without much tampering. By the late 1930s, people began writing about adaptation and change in industry from an organizational point of view and had to abandon some of the principles of scientific management.

3. Political, social, and cultural changes meant new expectations regarding the proper way to treat people. The dark, satanic mills needed at the least a white-washing. Child labor and the brutality of supervision in many enterprises became no longer permissible. Even managers could not be expected to accept the authoritarian patterns of leadership that prevailed in the small firm run by the founding father.

4. As mergers and growth proceeded apace and the firm could no longer be viewed as the shadow of one man (the founding entrepreneur), a search for methods of selecting good leadership became a preoccupation. A good, clear, mechanical structure would no longer suffice. Instead, firms had to search for the qualities of leadership that could fill the large footsteps of the entrepreneur. They tacitly had to admit that something other than either "sound principles" or "dynamic leadership" was needed. The search for leadership traits implied that leaders were made, not just born, that the matter was complex, and that several skills were involved.

Enter Human Relations

From the beginning, individual voices were raised against the implications of the scientific management school. "Bureaucracy" had always been a dirty word, and the job design efforts of Frederick Taylor were even the subject of a congressional investigation. But no effective counterforce developed until 1938, when a business executive with academic talents named Chester Barnard proposed the first new theory of organizations: Organizations are cooperative systems, not the products of mechanical engineering. He stressed natural groups within the organization, upward communication, authority from below rather than from above, and leaders who functioned as a cohesive force. With the spectre of labor unrest and the Great Depression upon him, Barnard's emphasis on the cooperative nature of organizations was well-timed. The year following the publication of his *Functions of the Executive* (1938) saw the publication of F. J. Roethlisberger and William Dickson's *Management and the Worker*, reporting on the first large-scale empirical investigation of productivity and social relations. The research, most of it conducted in the Hawthorne plant of the Western Electric Company during a period in which the workforce was reduced, highlighted the role of informal groups, work restriction norms, the value of decent, humane leadership, and the role of psychological manipulation of employees through the counseling system. World War II intervened, but after the war the human relations movement, building on the insights of Barnard and the Hawthorne studies, came into its own.

The first step was a search for the traits of good leadership. It went on furiously at university centers but at first failed to produce more than a list of Boy Scout maxims: A good leader was kind, courteous, loyal, courageous, etc. We suspected as much. However, the studies did turn up a distinction between "consideration," or employee-centered aspects of leadership, and job-centered, technical aspects labeled "initiating structure." Both were important, but the former received most of the attention and the latter went undeveloped. The former led directly to an examination of group processes, an investigation that has culminated in T-group programs and is moving forward still with encounter groups. Meanwhile, in England, the Tavistock Institute sensed the importance of the influence of the kind of task a group had to perform on the social relations within the group. The first important study, conducted among coal miners, showed that job simplification and specialization did not work under conditions of uncertainty and nonroutine tasks.

As this work flourished and spread, more adventurous theorists began to extend it beyond work groups to organizations as a whole. We now knew that there were a number of things that were bad for the morale and loyalty of groups—routine tasks, submission to authority, specialization of task, segregation of task sequence, ignorance of the goals of the firm, centralized decision making, and so on. If these were bad for groups, they were likely to be bad for groups of groups—i.e., for organizations. So people like Warren Bennis began talking about innovative, rapidly changing organizations that were made up of temporary groups, temporary authority systems, temporary leadership and role assignments, and democratic access to the goals of the firm. If rapidly changing technologies and unstable, turbulent environments were to characterize industry, then the structure of firms should be temporary and decentralized. The forces of light, of freedom, autonomy, change, humanity, creativity, and democracy were winning. Scientific management survived only in outdated text books. If the evangelizing of some of the human relations school theorists was excessive, and if Likert's System 4 or MacGregor's Theory Y or Blake's 9 x 9 evaded us, at least there was a rationale for confusion, disorganization, scrambling, and stress: Systems should be temporary.

Bureaucracy's Comeback

Meanwhile, in another part of the management forest, the mechanistic school was gathering its forces and preparing to outflank the forces of light. First came the numbers men—the linear programmers, the budget experts, and the financial analysts—with their PERT systems and cost-benefit analyses. From another world, unburdened by most of the scientific management ideology and untouched by the human relations school, they began to parcel things out and give some meaning to those truisms, "plan ahead" and "keep records." Armed with emerging systems concepts, they carried the "mechanistic" analogy to its fullest—and it was very productive. Their work still goes on, largely untroubled by organizational theory; the theory, it seems clear, will have to adjust to them, rather than the other way around.

Then the works of Max Weber, first translated from the German in the 1940s—he wrote around 1910, incredibly—began to find their way into social science thought. At first, with his celebration of the efficiency of bureaucracy, he was received with only reluctant respect, and even with hostility. All writers were against bureaucracy. But it turned out, surprisingly, that managers were not. When asked, they acknowledged that they preferred clear lines of communication, clear specifications of authority and responsibility, and clear knowledge of whom they were responsible to. They were as wont to say "there ought to be a rule about this," as to say "there are too many rules around here," as wont to say "next week we've got to get organized," as to say "there is too much red tape." Gradually, studies began to show that bureaucratic organizations could change faster than nonbureaucratic ones, and that morale could be higher where there was clear evidence of bureaucracy.

What was this thing, then? Weber had showed us, for example, that bureaucracy was the most effective way of ridding organizations of favoritism, arbitrary authority, discrimination, payola and kick-backs, and yes, even incompetence. His model stressed expertise, and the favorite or the boss's nephew or the guy who burned up resources to make his performance look good was *not* the one with expertise. Rules could be changed; they could be dropped in exceptional circumstances; job security promoted more innovation. The sins of bureaucracy began to look like the sins of failing to follow its principles.

Enter Power, Conflict, and Decisions

But another discipline began to intrude upon the confident work and increasingly elaborate models of the human relations theorists (largely social psychologists) and the uneasy toying with bureaucracy of the "structionalists" (largely sociologists). Both tended to study economic organizations. A few, like Philip Selznick, were noting conflict and differences in goals (perhaps because he was studying a public agency, the Tennessee Valley Authority), but most ignored conflict or treated it as a pathological manifestation of breakdowns in communication or the ego trips of unreconstructed managers.

But in the world of political parties, pressure groups, and legislative bodies, conflict was not only rampant, but to be expected—it was even functional. This was the domain of the political scientists. They kept talking about power, making it a legitimate concern for analysis. There was an open acknowledgement of "manipulation." These were political scientists who were "behaviorally" inclined—studying and recording behavior rather than constitutions and formal systems of government—and they came to a much more complex view of organized activity. It spilled over into the area of economic organizations, with the help of some economists like R. A. Gordon and some sociologists who were studying conflicting goals of treatment and custody in prisons and mental hospitals.

The presence of legitimately conflicting goals and techniques of preserving and using power did not, of course, sit well with a cooperative systems view of organizations. But it also puzzled the bureaucratic school (and what was left of the old scientific management school), for the impressive Weberian principles were designed to settle questions of power through organizational design and to keep conflict out through reliance on rational-legal authority and systems of careers, expertise, and hierarchy. But power was being overtly contested and exercised in covert ways, and conflict was bursting out all over, and even being creative.

Gradually, in the second half of the 1950s and in the next decade, the political science view infiltrated both schools. Conflict could be healthy, even in a cooperative system, said the human relationists; it was the mode of resolution that counted, rather than prevention. Power became reconceptualized as "influence," and the distribution was less important, said Arnold Tannenbaum, than the total amount. For the bureaucratic school—never a clearly defined group of people, and largely without any clear ideology—it was easier to just absorb the new data and theories as something else to be thrown into the pot. That is to say, they floundered, writing books that went from topic to topic, without a clear view of organizations, or better yet, producing "readers" and leaving students to sort it all out.

Buried in the political science viewpoint was a sleeper that only gradually began to undermine the dominant views. This was the idea, largely found in the work of Herbert Simon and James March, that because man was so limited—in intelligence, reasoning powers, information at his disposal, time available, and means of ordering his preferences clearly—he generally seized on the first acceptable alternative when deciding, rather than looking for the best; that he rarely changed things unless they really got bad, and even then he continued to try what had worked before; that he limited his search for solutions to well-worn paths and traditional sources of information and established ideas; that he was wont to remain preoccupied with routine, thus preventing innovation. They called these characteristics "cognitive limits on rationality" and spoke of "satisficing" rather than maximizing or optimizing. It is now called the "decision making" school, and is concerned with the basic question of how people make decisions.

This view had some rather unusual implications. It suggested that if managers were so limited, then they could be easily controlled. What was necessary was not to give direct orders (on the assumption that subordinates were idiots without expertise) or to leave them to their own devices (on the assumption that they were supermen who would somehow know what was best for the organization, how to coordinate with all the other supermen, how to anticipate market changes, etc.). It was necessary to control only the *premises* of their decisions. Left to themselves, with those premises set, they could be predicted to rely on precedent, keep things stable and smooth, and respond to signals that reinforce the behavior desired of them.

To control the premises of decision making, March and Simon outline a variety of devices, all of which are familiar to you, but some of which you may not have seen before in quite this light. For example, organizations develop vocabularies, and this means that certain kinds of information are highlighted, and others are screened out—just as Eskimos (and skiers) distinguish many varieties of snow, while Londoners see only one. This is a form of attention directing. Another is the reward system. Change the bonus for salesmen and you can shift them from volume selling to steady-account selling, or to selling quality products or new products. If you want to channel good people into a different function (because, for example, sales should no longer be the critical function as the market changes, but engineering applications should), you may have to promote mediocre people in the unrewarded function in order to signal to the good people in the rewarded one that the game has changed. You cannot expect most people to make such decision on their own because of the cognitive limits on their rationality, nor will you succeed by giving direct orders, because you yourself probably do not know whom to order where. You presume that once the signals are clear and the new sets of alternatives are manifest, they have enough ability to make the decision but you have had to change the premises for their decisions about their career lines.

It would take too long to go through the dozen or so devices, covering a range of decision areas (March and Simon are not that clear or systematic about them, themselves, so I have summarized them in my own book), but I think the message is clear.

It was becoming clear to the human relations school, and to the bureaucratic school. The human relationists had begun to speak of changing stimuli rather than changing personality. They had begun to see that the rewards that can change behavior can well be prestige, money, comfort, etc., rather than trust, openness, self-insight, and so on. The alternative to supportive relations need not be punishment, since behavior can best be changed by rewarding approved behavior rather than by punishing disapproved behavior. They were finding that although leadership may be centralized, it can function best through indirect and unobtrusive means such as changing the premises on which decisions are made, thus giving the impression that the subordinate is actually making a decision when he has only been switched to a different set of alternatives. The implications of this work were also beginning to filter into the human relations school through an emphasis on behavioral psychology (the modern version of the much maligned stimulus-response school) that was supplanting personality theory (Freudian in its roots, and drawing heavily, in the human relations school, on Maslow).

For the bureaucratic school, this new line of thought reduced the heavy weight placed upon the bony structure of bureaucracy by highlighting the muscle and flesh that make these bones move. A single chain of command, precise division of labor, and clear lines of communication are simply not enough in themselves. Control can be achieved by using alternative communication channels, depending on the situation; by increasing or decreasing the static or "noise" in the system; by creating organizational myths and organizational vocabularies that allow only selective bits of information to enter the system; and through monitoring performance through indirect means rather than direct surveillance. Weber was all right for a starter, but organizations had changed vastly, and the leaders needed many more means of control and more subtle means of manipulation than they did at the turn of the century.

The Technological Qualification

By now the forces of darkness and forces of light had moved respectively from midnight and noon to about 4 A.M. and 8 A.M. But any convergence or resolution would have to be on yet new terms, for soon after the political science tradition had begun to infiltrate the established schools, another blow struck both of the major positions. Working quite independently of the Tavistock Group, with its emphasis on sociotechnical systems, and before the work of Burns and Stalker on mechanistic and organic firms, Joan Woodward was trying to see whether the classical scientific principles of organization made any sense in her survey of 100 firms in South Essex. She tripped and stumbled over a piece of gold in the process. She picked up the gold, labeled it "technology," and made sense out of her otherwise hopeless data. Job-shop firms, mass-production firms, and continuous-process firms all had quite different structures because the type of tasks, or the "technology," was different. Somewhat later, researchers in America were coming to very similar conclusions based on studies of hospitals, juvenile correctional institutions, and industrial firms. Bureaucracy appeared to be the best form of organization for routine operations; temporary work groups, decentralization, and emphasis on interpersonal processes appeared to work best for nonroutine operations. A raft of studies appeared and are still appearing, all trying to show how the nature of the task affects the structure of the organization.

This severely complicated things for the human relations school, since it suggested that openness and trust, while good things in themselves, did not have much impact, or perhaps were not even possible in some kinds of work situations. The prescriptions that were being handed out would have to be drastically qualified. What might work for nonroutine, high-status, interesting, and challenging jobs performed by highly educated people might not be relevant or even beneficial for the vast majority of jobs and people.

It also forced the upholders of the revised bureaucratic theory to qualify their recommendations, since research and development units should obviously be run differently from mass-production units, and the difference between both of these and highly programmed and highly sophisticated continuous-process firms was obscure in terms of bureaucratic theory. But the bureaucratic school perhaps came out on top, because the forces of evil—authority, structure, division of labor, etc.—no longer looked evil, even if they were not applicable to a minority of industrial units.

The emphasis on technology raised other questions, however. A can company might be quite routine, and a plastics division nonroutine, but there were both routine and nonroutine units within each. How should they be integrated if the prescription were followed that, say, production should be bureaucratized and R&D not? James Thompson began spelling out different forms of interdependence among units in organizations, and Paul Lawrence and Jay Lorsch looked closely at the nature of integrating mechanisms. Lawrence and Lorsch found that firms performed best when the differences between units were *maximized* (in contrast to both the human relations and the bureaucratic school), as long as the integrating mechanisms stood half-way between the two—being neither strongly bureaucratic nor nonroutine. They also noted that attempts at participative management in routine situations were counterproductive, that the environments of some kinds of organizations were far from turbulent and customers did not want innovations and changes, that cost reduction, price, and efficiency were trivial considerations in some firms, and so on. The technological insight was demolishing our comfortable truths right and left. They were also being questioned from another quarter.

Enter Goals, Environments, and Systems

The final seam was being mined by the sociologists while all this went on. This was the concern with organizational goals and the environment. Borrowing from the political scientists to some extent, but pushing ahead on their own, this "institutional school" came to see that goals were not fixed; conflicting goals could be pursued simultaneously, if there were enough slack resources, or sequentially (growth for the next four years, then cost-cutting and profit-taking for the next four); that goals were up for grabs in organizations, and units fought over them. Goals were, of course, not what they seemed to be, the important ones were quite unofficial; history played a big role; and assuming profit as the pre-eminent goal explained almost nothing about a firm's behavior.

They also did case studies that linked the organization to the web of influence of the environment; that showed how unique organizations were in many respects (so that, once again, there was no one best way to do things for all organizations); how organizations were embedded in their own history, making change difficult. Most striking of all, perhaps, the case studies revealed that the stated goals usually were not the real ones; the official leaders usually were not the powerful ones; claims of effectiveness and efficiency were deceptive or even untrue; the public interest was not being served; political influences were pervasive; favoritism, discrimination, and sheer corruption were commonplace. The accumulation of these studies presented quite a pill for either the forces of light or darkness to swallow, since it was hard to see how training sessions or interpersonal skills were relevant to these problems, and it was also clear that the vaunted efficiency of bureaucracy was hardly in evidence. What could they make of this wad of case studies?

We are still sorting it out. In one sense, the Weberian model is upheld because organizations are not, *by nature*, cooperative systems; top managers must exercise a great deal of effort to control them. But if organizations are tools in the hands of leaders, they may be very recalcitrant ones. Like the broom in the story of the sorcerer's apprentice, they occasionally get out of hand. If conflicting goals, bargaining, and unofficial leadership exists, where is the structure of Weberian bones and Simonian muscle? To what extent are organizations tools, and to what extent are they products of the varied interests and group strivings of their members? Does it vary by organization, in terms of some typological alchemy we have not discovered? We don't know. But at any rate, the bureaucratic model suffers again; it simply has not reckoned on the role of the environment. There are enormous sources of variations that the neat, though by now quite complex, neo-Weberian model could not account for.

The human relations model has also been badly shaken by the findings of the institutional school, for it was wont to assume that goals were given and unproblematical, and that anything that promoted harmony and efficiency for an organization also was good for society. Human relationists assumed that the problems created by organizations were largely limited to the psychological consequences of poor interpersonal relations within them, rather than their impact on the environment. Could the organization really promote the psychological health of its members when by necessity it had to define psychological health in terms of the goals of the organization itself? The neo-Weberian model at least called manipulation "manipulation" and was skeptical of claims about autonomy and self-realization.

But on one thing all the varied schools of organizational analysis now seemed to be agreed: organizations are systems—indeed, they are open systems. As the growth of the field has forced ever more variables into our consciousness, flat claims of predictive power are beginning to decrease and research has become bewilderingly complex. Even consulting groups need more than one or two tools in their kit-bag as the software multiplies.

The systems view is intuitively simple. Everything is related to everything else, though in uneven degrees of tension and reciprocity. Every unit, organization, department, or work group takes in resources, transforms them, and sends them out, and thus interacts with the larger system. The psychological, sociological, and cultural aspects of units interact. The systems view was explicit in the institutional work, since they tried to study whole organizations; it became explicit in the human relations school, because they were so concerned with the interactions of people. The political science and technology viewpoints also had to come to this realization, since they dealt with parts affecting each other (sales affecting production; technology affecting structure).

But as intuitively simple as it is, the systems view has been difficult to put into practical use. We still find ourselves ignoring the tenets of the open systems view, possibly because of the cognitive limits on our rationality. General systems theory itself has not lived up to its heady predictions; it remains rather nebulous. But at least there is a model for calling us to account and for stretching our minds, our research tools, and our troubled nostrums.

Some Conclusions

Where does all this leave us? We might summarize the prescriptions and proscriptions for management very roughly as follows:

1. A great deal of the "variance" in a firm's behavior depends on the environment. We have become more realistic about the limited range of change that can be induced through internal efforts. The goals of organizations, including those of profit and efficiency, vary greatly among industries and vary systematically by industries. This suggests that the impact of better management by itself will be limited, since so much will depend on market forces, competition, legislation, nature of the work force, available technologies and innovations, and so on. Another source of variation is, obviously, the history of the firm and its industry and its traditions.

2. A fair amount of variation in both firms and industries is due to the type of work done in the organization—the technology. We are now fairly confident in recommending that if work is predictable and routine, the necessary arrangement for getting the work done can be highly structured, and one can use a good deal

of bureaucratic theory in accomplishing this. If it is not predictable, if it is nonroutine and there is a good deal of uncertainty as to how to do a job, then one had better utilize the theories that emphasize autonomy, temporary groups, multiple lines of authority and communications, and so on. We also know that this distinction is important when organizing different parts of an organization.

We are also getting a grasp on the question of what is the most critical function in different types of organizations. For some organizations it is production; for others, marketing; for still others, development. Furthermore, firms go through phases whereby the initial development of a market or a product or manufacturing process or accounting scheme may require a non-bureaucratic structure, but once it comes on stream, the structure should change to reflect the changed character of the work.

3. In keeping with this, management should be advised that the attempt to produce change in an organization through managerial grids, sensitivity training, and even job enrichment and job enlargement is likely to be fairly ineffective for all but a few organizations. The critical reviews of research in all these fields show that there is no scientific evidence to support the claims of the proponents of these various methods; that research has told us a great deal about social psychology, but little about how to apply the highly complex findings to actual situations. The key word is *selectivity*: We have no broad-spectrum antibiotics for interpersonal relations. Of course, managers should be sensitive, decent, kind, courteous, and courageous, but we have known that for some time now, and beyond a minimal threshold level, the payoff is hard to measure. The various attempts to make work and interpersonal relations more humane and stimulating should be applauded, but we should not confuse this with solving problems of structure, or as the equivalent of decentralization or participatory democracy.

4. The burning cry in all organizations is for "good leadership," but we have learned that beyond a threshold level of adequacy it is extremely difficult to know what good leadership is. The hundreds of scientific studies of this phenomenon come to one general conclusion: Leadership is highly variable or "contingent" upon a large variety of important variables such as nature of task, size of the group, length of time the group has existed, type of personnel within the group and their relationships with each other, and amount of pressure the group is under. It does not seem likely that we'll be able to devise a way to select the best leader for a particular situation. Even if we could, that situation would probably change in a short time and thus would require a somewhat different type of leader.

Furthermore, we are beginning to realize that leadership involves more than smoothing the paths of human interaction. What has rarely been studied in this area is the wisdom or even the technical adequacy of a leader's decision. A leader does more than lead people; he also makes decisions about the allocation of resources, type of technology to be used, the nature of the market, and so on. This aspect of leadership remains very obscure, but it is obviously crucial.

5. If we cannot solve our problems through good human relations or through good leadership, what are we then left with? The literature suggests that changing the structures of organizations might be the most effective and certainly the quickest and cheapest method. However, we are now sophisticated enough to know that changing the formal structure by itself is not likely to produce the desired changes.

In addition, one must be aware of a large range of subtle, unobtrusive, and even covert processes and change devices that exist. If inspection procedures are not working, we are now unlikely to rush in with sensitivity training, nor would we send down authoritative communications telling people to do a better job. We are more likely to find out where the authority really lies, whether the degree of specialization is adequate, what the rules and regulations are, and so on, but even this very likely will not be enough.

According to the neo-Weberian bureaucratic model, as it has been influenced by work on decision making and behavioral psychology, we should find out how to manipulate the reward structure, change the premises of the decision-makers through finer controls on the information received and the expectations generated, search for interdepartmental conflicts that prevent better inspection procedures from being followed, and after manipulating these variables, sit back and wait for two or three months for them to take hold. This is complicated and hardly as dramatic as many of the solutions currently being peddled, but I think the weight of organizational theory is in its favor.

We have probably learned more, over several decades of research and theory, about the things that do *not* work (even though some of them obviously *should* have worked), than we have about things that do work. On balance, this is an important gain and should not discourage us. As you know, organizations are extremely complicated. To have as much knowledge as we do have in a fledgling discipline that has had to borrow from the diverse tools and concepts of psychology, sociology, economics, engineering, biology, history, and even anthropology is not really so bad.

Selected Bibliography

This paper is an adaptation of the discussion to be found in Charles Perrow, *Complex Organizations: A Critical Essay*, Scott, Foresman & Co., Glenview, Illinois, 1972. All the points made in this paper are discussed thoroughly in that volume.

The best overview and discussion of classical management theory, and its changes over time is by Joseph Massie—"Management Theory" in the *Handbook of Organizations* edited by James March, Rand McNally & Co., Chicago, 1965, pp. 387-422.

The best discussion of the changing justifications for managerial rule and worker obedience as they are related to changes in technology, etc., can be found in Reinhard Bendix's *Work and Authority in Industry*, John Wiley & Sons, Inc., New York, 1956. See especially the chapter on the American experience.

Some of the leading lights of the classical view—F. W. Taylor, Col. Urwick, and Henry Fayol—are briefly discussed in *Writers on Organizations* by D. S. Pugh, D. J. Hickson and C. R. Hinings, Penguin, 1971. This brief, readable, and useful book also contains selections from many other schools that I discuss, including Weber, Woodward, Cyert and March, Simon, and Hawthorne Investigations, and the Human Relations Movement as represented by Argyris, Herzberg, Likert, McGregor, and Blake and Mouton.

As good a place as any to start examining the human relations tradition is Rensis Likert, *The Human Organization*, McGraw-Hill, New York, 1967. See also his *New Patterns of Management*, McGraw-Hill Book Company, New York, 1961.

The Buck Rogers school of organizational theory is best represented by Warren Bennis. See his *Changing Organizations*, McGraw-Hill Book Company, New York, 1966, and his book with Philip Slater, *The Temporary Society*, Harper & Row, Inc., New York, 1968. Much of this work is linked into more general studies, e.g., Alvin Toffler's very popular paperback *Future Shock*, Random House, 1970, and Bantam Paperbacks, or Zibigniew Brzezinsky's *Between Two Ages: America's Role in the Technitronic Era*, the Viking Press, New York, 1970. One of the first intimations of the new type of environment and firm and still perhaps the most perceptive is to be found in the volume by Tom Burns and G. Stalker, *The Management of Innovation*, Tavistock, London, 1961, where they distinguished between "organic" and "mechanistic" systems. The introduction, which is not very long, is an excellent and very tight summary of the book.

The political science tradition came in through three important works. First, Herbert Simon's *Administrative Behavior*, The Macmillan Co., New York, 1948, followed by the second half of James March and Herbert Simon's *Organizations*, John Wiley & Sons, Inc., New York, 1958, then Richard M. Cyert and James March's *A Behavioral Theory of the Firm*, Prentice-Hall, Inc., Englewood Cliffs, N.J., 1963. All three of these books are fairly rough going, though chapters 1, 2, 3, and 6 of the last volume are fairly short and accessible. A quite interesting book in this tradition, though somewhat heavy-going, is Michael Crozier's *The Bureaucratic Phenomenon*, University of Chicago, and Tavistock Publications, 1964. This is a striking description of power in organizations, though there is a somewhat dubious attempt to link organization processes in France to the cultural traits of the French people.

The book by Joan Woodward *Industrial Organisation: Theory and Practice*, Oxford University Press, London, 1965, is still very much worth reading. A fairly popular attempt to discuss the implications for this for management can be found in my own book, *Organizational Analysis: A Sociological View*, Tavistock, 1970, Chapters 2 and 3. The impact of technology on structure is still fairly controversial. A number of technical studies have found both support and nonsupport, largely because the concept is defined so differently, but there is general agreement that different structures and leadership techniques are needed for different situations. For studies that support and document this viewpoint see James Thompson, *Organizations in Action*, McGraw-Hill Book Company, New York, 1967, and Paul Lawrence and Jay Lorsch, *Organizations and Environment*, Harvard University Press, Cambridge, Mass., 1967.

The best single work on the relation between the organization and the environment and one of the most readable books in the field is Philip Selznick's short volume *Leadership in Administration*, Row, Peterson, Evanston, Illinois, 1957. But the large number of these studies are scattered about. I have summarized several in my *Complex Organizations: A Critical Essay*.

Lastly, the most elaborate and persuasive argument for a systems view of organizations is found in the first 100 pages of the book by Daniel Katz and Robert Kahn, *The Social Psychology of Organizations*, John Wiley and Co., 1966. It is not easy reading, however.

PART ONE

The Organization
and the Environment

Organizations exist in environments, and each environment takes part in shaping the internal structure of each organization within it. This is basically a systems point of view. An organization can be viewed as a set of subsystems related to one another. A change in one, whether internal or external, is likely to induce changes in the others. These subsystems, operating together as "transformation elements," act upon inputs, transforming them into outputs. In the process, outputs of the organization are exchanged with its external environment for inputs.

In the first article, Jurkovich develops a typology of organization environments. As we have already noted in the Introduction, the organization's environment may be multidimension and multicharacteristic. Organization structure and processes, such as planning and decision making, are conditioned by this environment. This selection places the environment in a perspective, outlining with what type of contingencies an organization must cope.

Burns and Stalker describe in some detail the characteristics of different organizations in different environmental circumstances. The characteristics of the "organic" organization would likely be found in an environment which is extremely dynamic and changing. The "mechanistic" organization is a more appropriate form in a tranquil and stable environment. The most important point made by Burns and Stalker is that "the beginning of administrative wisdom is awareness that there is no one optimum type of management system." The utility of the "notion of mechanistic and organic management systems resides largely in their being related as dependent variables to the rate of organization change."

There is no one appropriate form of organization which cuts across all environmental circumstances. At the two extremes, a relatively rigid authority structure may be effective in adapting to a stable environment, while a flexible structure is likely to be effective in an unstable environment. The appropriate type is a function of the characteristics of the environment.

These characteristics, general in type, describe the various components of the organization's internal subsystems. Katz and Kahn describe five basic internal subsystems that absorb inputs and create and disperse outputs: production or technical, supportive, maintenance, adaptive, and managerial. These "generic" subsystems are useful descriptive categories for various internal organization activities.

These basic subsystems may take different forms, depending upon the characteristics of the external environment. Thompson describes how the technical (production) subsystem may vary under different circumstances. He also provides a useful conceptual basis for determining the manner in which other systemic components may vary. For instance, the long-linked technology, characterized by repetitiveness and standardization, may well be an appropriate structural form under conditions in which the external environment is relatively stable, rather than turbulent. The "intensive" technology may be a more appropriate form in a turbulent, dynamic, or otherwise changing environment. For instance, Thompson suggests that "the development of military combat teams, with the multiplicity of highly skilled capacities to be applied to the requirement of changing circumstances, represents a shift toward the intensive technology in military operations."

Thompson also suggests ways in which the organization can minimize the internal impact of external environmental changes. For example, he notes that, "under norms of rationality, organizations seek to seal off their core technologies from environmental influences." This is done by *buffering, leveling,* or *adaptation.* These concepts as defined in the Thompson article are useful in drawing inferences about how the adaptive and supportive subsystems defined by Katz and Kahn might function in different environmental settings. In a turbulent environment, for example, input and output transactions can be smoothed by supportive subsystems, an important process from a cost standpoint. For instance, where there are substantial cycles in the raw material markets, firms must inventory goods to maintain steady operation.

Lynton, in examining the problem of how innovation may be introduced into an organization, looks at the linkage mechanism which ties the organization to the external sector. The form of the linkage mechanism depends upon whether the need to adapt and change internally is important. Linking an organization to a dynamic or turbulent environment is a difficult, costly, and important function. Thus, the linking mechanism may need a great deal of power and control. Where there is only a minimal need for change, as would be the case in a relatively quiet environment, the authority of the linking subsystem may be less important.

The last selection, by Dodge and Tosi, shows how the concepts developed in other articles in this section can be integrated to understand the relationships and characteristics of the Katz and Kahn subsystems in different types of organizations. The organic and mechanistic forms of Burns and Stalker are clearly delineated, but so are "mixed" organizations. "Mixed organizations," probably more common than either the organic or mechanistic pure types, have major internal systems interacting with different types of environments, leading to intra-organizational differences among internal systems.

The readings in this part, then, show how the internal subsystems of the organization, as defined by Katz and Kahn, take on either mechanistic or organic characteristics. Organizations do so in response to the external environment. Jurkovich describes turbulence as the important characteristic of the external environment. Yet, as Thompson points out, the organization provides a mechanism (buffering, leveling, and adapting) to ease the uncertainties.

Under any circumstances, the organization structure, mechanistic or organic, is the environment within which the individual must operate. In part 2 we present a set of concepts which can be used to understand how this individual adaptation occurs.

A CORE TYPOLOGY OF ORGANIZATIONAL ENVIRONMENTS

RAY JURKOVICH

This article presents a typology of organizational environments and discusses the more relevant relationships. Although environments have been receiving increasing attention, a set of widely accepted, related concepts which effectively describe the subject has not been developed (Organ, 1971). Theorists, in discussing environments, tend to deal in vague terms. A set of established, but more sharply defined terms are presented here in a structured manner, resulting in a core typology. This approach simplifies the subject area, avoiding the case in which the number of possible relationships between phenomena is so large that central issues are obscured by a mass of details.

Designing a typology under these conditions forces one to emphasize the descriptive and deemphasize—or avoid—the predictive features. Thus, a typology becomes an analytic tool that may be applied as an instrument to stimulate thinking on alternate directions in which decision makers can move their organizations. The results might lead them to make adjustments they would otherwise not attempt. Decision makers, of course, do this anyhow, but a good tool can facilitate the process. The next step is to develop predictive statements which, if empirically supported, can make a typology even more powerful.

The main effort here is not to create new concepts. A few new notions are incorporated simply to provide analytical distinctions that are felt to be of importance. In addition, a lengthy review and comparison of the major terms is not undertaken. Some relevant concepts are borrowed from the most important works to date and these are modified for greater clarity. Integration with other concepts is undertaken for the purpose of broadening the current limited scope. Thus, this article is essentially an excursion in broadening and refining the existing parts of a conceptual puzzle and adding a few others to contribute to a better understanding of the whole.

The External Environment

Two frequently cited works provide a basis for a general description. Thompson's (1967: 70-73) simple four-cell typology and Lawrence and Lorsch's (1967: 23-54) dichotomization of diversity and dynamic offer perceptions which appear to be the same:

Thompson
    (1) Homogeneous-stable
    (2) Homogeneous-shifting
    (3) Heterogeneous-stable
    (4) Heterogeneous-shifting

Reprinted by permission of the author and the publisher from *Administrative Science Quarterly*, vol. 19, no. 3 (September 1974), pp. 380-394.

Lawrence and Lorsch
  (1) Low diversity and not dynamic
  (2) Low diversity and highly dynamic
  (3) High diversity and not dynamic
  (4) High diversity and dynamic

Both sets of authors discuss the problems of differentiation between and adaption to directly related organizational components having different kinds of environments. Presumably, the more disparate the environments with which two directly related components are confronted, the more difficult it is to integrate the components.

The typologies above are used here with revisions and additions. Homogeneity and heterogeneity, for instance, are included in the complexity continuum. Emery and Trist's (1965) typology is revised and incorporated in connection with the change rate continuum. The end result is 64 types, a list that can be further expanded by creation of additional categories. The reason for working with the chosen variables is that some of them occur persistently in the literature, but they are presented in a very restricted context. Frequently, attention has been concentrated on two major independent variables when in fact others play an equally important role. The term used can be arranged to form the matrix of figure 1.

Movement		General Characteristics															
		Noncomplex								Complex							
		Routine				Nonroutine				Routine				Nonroutine			
		Organized		Unorganized		Organized		Unorganized		Organized		Unorganized		Organized		Unorganized	
		*D	I	D	I	D	I	D	I	D	I	D	I	D	I	D	I
Low change rate	Stable	1															16
	Unstable																
High change rate	Stable																
	Unstable	49															64

*D = direct I = indirect

Source: Korman, Abraham K., *The Psychology of Motivation*, Prentice-Hall, Inc., 1974, p. 107.

Figure 1. A core typology of organizational environments.

General Characteristics

In designing action alternatives, decision makers or members of scanning units must analyze a variety of environmental factors or questions. Four major ones are (1) complexity, (2) the routineness or nonroutineness of a problem-opportunity state, (3) the presence of organized or unorganized sectors—elements or units of the environmental field, (4) and the issue of whether such sectors are directly or indirectly related to the organization. Sectors refer to those elements or units of behavior—human and nonhuman—in the environment that decision makers perceive as relevant for the organization. Environment is the total set of sectors outside of the organization which, in turn, is a role cluster bound together by a set of rules that prescribes behavior and establishes sanctions when rules are violated.

Complexity

Child (1972: 3) provides a definition of environmental complexity that can be used here: "Environmental complexity refers to the heterogeneity and range of activities which are relevant to an organization's operations." In other words, the more diverse the relevant environmental activities and the more there are, the higher the complexity. His meaning of heterogeneity, however, is not clear. Duncan (1972) deals with environmental simplicity and complexity by considering the variety of locations of decision factors, but just how the various locations differ is assumed rather than explicitly stated. Duncan's finding that heterogeneity has little effect on uncertainty is hardly surprising if one interprets it on the basis of Simon's (1962) definition of complexity. Since in Simon's terms complexity consists of simple pieces added together, the effect of complexity on uncertainty will not be significant. The way in which Buckley defines environment perhaps offers another basis for the present purpose (1967: 62, italics his):

> The environment, however else it may be characterized, can be seen at bottom *as a set* or ensemble of more or less *distinguishable elements*, states, or events, whether these discriminations are made in terms of spatial or temporal relations, or properties. Such distinguishable differences in an ensemble may be most generally referred to as "variety."

Nevertheless, the meaning of variety is not simple. Complexity or noncomplexity is a question of perception and, as Starbuck (1973: 24) stated, "The same environment one organization perceives as unpredictable, complex, and evanescent, another organization might see as static and easily understood." Any inductively derived definition of complexity results in a very abstract statement that is either too vague or too trivial or both. In this article the terms complex and noncomplex refer to whether or not decision makers perceive their environments as complex or noncomplex: the terms do not refer to any universal operational definition that might be applied to a large sample of organizations.

Organizations dealing with noncomplex environments have one advantage: there are fewer critically important information categories necessary for decision making.

When environmental sectors are essentially the same, the range of their expected behavior, strategies and tactics, and formal goals is easier to account for. Complex information systems are not required for environmental monitoring, since the critical information categories are limited even though the range and size of the sectors can be large.

Organizations confronted with a complex environment must come to grips with a memory problem. Since the human brain has a limited capacity for retaining conscious information, special units that can monitor individual or clusters of sectors are required (Thompson, 1967: 70). These units monitor the activities of others and routinely report the behavioral patterns to critical decision-making points that make decisions based on that information and/or feed back requests for further information and advice.

Routine and Nonroutine Problem-Opportunity States

A decision maker can perceive parts of his environment as posing a problem or offering an opportunity. The distinction between problems and opportunities need not be made here, since problems can be perceived as opportunities and opportunities can quickly present their share of problems. Whatever the case, decision makers can look at environmental problem-opportunity states as being approachable as routine or non-routine activity. This idea is borrowed, with revisions, from Perrow (1970: 75-80) and March and Simon (1958). A decision maker can approach an opportunity or problem by asking whether his organization possesses the technologies, people, cash reserves, and other resources to handle or solve a situation without disturbing current activities. It can also be an uncertain or risky adventure he thinks the organization can handle but he is more speculative than realistic in his expectations.

Decision makers' perceptions of their environments depend upon conditions in their own organizations. The process of looking at the environment and comparing it with internal resources can suggest alternatives permitting the organization to take better advantage of opportunities it would otherwise have to pass up.

Problem-opportunity states assume varying degrees of uncertainty. If decision makers approach a situation and find that the analytical strategies resemble computational, judgmental or compromise, or inspirational strategies (Thompson, 1967: 134), they know, at least subjectively, what degree of uncertainty is attached to the problem. Computational strategies assume a high degree of certainty: judgmental and compromise strategies assume a moderate degree of uncertainty, but for different reasons: and an inspirational strategy assumes a high degree of uncertainty. One can ascertain quickly whether the organization can handle the situation as a routine or a nonroutine activity on the basis of the strategies which decision makers design.

The degree of routineness and nonroutineness might also be determined by the state of the information problems. These problems can take three forms: people complain that (a) they cannot gain access to critical information, (b) they cannot trust a significant portion of the information, or (c) the set of information categories they need for decision making is uncertain. The higher the percentage of members with information problems and the more severe those problems, the more nonroutine the problem-opportunity state is.

Where noncomplex routine sectors dominate the environmental field, the basis for decision rests more on deductions and inductions from the information itself. Specialists can exchange opinions and arrive at a consensus much more easily, rapidly, and completely and with greater certainty of having made the right decision. Frequently, nonspecialists can make the decisions, since there is an expected pattern for which standardized or programmed decisions are available.

Faced with complex routine sectors, decision makers primarily devote their attention to the decisions themselves, leaving the information gathering problems—mostly concerning quantity and range—to the decentralized monitoring units. Manageability is a secondary problem.

Organizations with predominantly noncomplex, nonroutine environmental sectors are faced with information problems that cannot always be solved with a data bank. In this situation there is reliance on noncalculable judgments or advice from specialists. Decision-making battles take place over opinions. Information is uncertain or incomplete and reliability and validity cannot be determined.

Faced with complex nonroutine sectors, decision makers concentrate less on the decision and more on the information: they must frequently negotiate, both directly and indirectly, with those at the information source in an attempt to extract better or more useful information than they have access to in order to develop standardized decision program packages. Experience in earlier but similar situations whose abstract pattern resembles the current one is also an important resource here.

In this situation one indicator of managerial and executive frustration could be their turnover rate or expressions of a role occupant's continuous effort to establish alternative information sources in an attempt to reduce ambiguity in order to survive or perform adequately. The interaction frequency of the role occupant's information-monitoring units would be higher and more intense in this case. This would be indicated partly by the longer time involved and partly by a higher number of conflicts. Finally, individuals would work with exceptions more often than performing routine administrative tasks.

March and Simon (1958: 151) and Ashby (1968) have stated that there appear to be limits to the amount of routine and nonroutine activities and variety—complexity—that an individual can comfortably handle. This discussion suggests that complexity and nonroutineness can impose limits on each other. The amount of complexity might be limited by nonprogrammable activities and vice versa.

This notion may be equally valid when applied to the whole organization. In other words, what are the limits of environmental nonroutine complexity an organization can handle before entropy sets in? It could well be that the boundary of entropy is expanded by such techniques as decentralization. Centralization of large multigoal organizations requires much more rule enforcement, and once faced with an uncomfortable environment, it may be cheaper in the long run to allow specific decisions to be made at lower levels. The whole is greater than the sum of its parts. The boundary of entropy can be expanded without changing the fact that the organization as a whole remains.

Organized and Unorganized Sectors

Another important aspect of the problem is whether sectors are organized or unorganized. Evan's (1966) discussion of organizational sets, an extension of Merton's role set, does not include more cumbersome, unorganized situations. Throughout this article the term sector is used to avoid excessive emphasis on interorganizational behavior. While almost everybody has an organizational role, he also plays nonorganizational roles. An important one, for instance, comes under the category of customer. We are not organized members of every organization. Almost everyone has only one central organization in which he earns money to exchange for products and services produced by others. Frequently, we must satisfy certain kinds of criteria to receive services—as patient or student, for instance—but customers and clients generally do not perform any of the essential activities of the supplying organization or strive for its goals, nor do those organizations demand that they do so. An organization's environment consists of more than organizational sets. Here, the term sector is used with a much broader meaning: both organizational sets and categories which represent unorganized individuals and groups are included. Some organizations must concern themselves with the young, old people, or housewives: people in these categories are not in an organizational role network in which interdependencies are present.

An organized sector refers to another organization or cluster of organizations covered by a formal rule set that is legitimate only for the role set intended by those rules. An unorganized sector refers to those actual or potential customers who use the organization's goods and services but are not bound together by formal or informal rules requiring patterned coordinated interaction to reach formally defined goals.

The most important distinction between the two is that organized environments are generally easier to come to grips with than unorganized sectors. For example, Rickson and Simpkins (1972: 286) stated that "Firms are considerably more secure in dealing with a work force represented by a few unions than they would be if power among workers was more dispersed and 'wildcat' strikes were common." Information about the limits of what an organized sector can do and wants to do is more accessible and frequently is explicitly stated in records or by official spokesman. An amount and variety of information is generally available on a routine basis that is not available from unorganized sectors. With the latter, intervening organizations (for example, advertising and market research agencies) or an intervening subsystem of the organization is frequently required to conduct research to assess the attractiveness or legitimacy of goals. Once a goal has been assessed, decision makers can debate whether a decision program should be chosen and, if so, which one, after which they can discuss the necessary alterations or if necessary, design new ones. The question is not whether organized sectors exhibit more certain or uncertain behavior than unorganized sectors: the problem is to locate the sources of certainty or uncertainty in the exchange chain.

Directly and Indirectly Related Sectors

The notion of directly related and indirectly related environments can contribute to the tracing of relevant problems. Direct environments refer to those sectors with which the organization exchanges without the use of intermediaries. Indirect environments refer to those sectors which produce goods and services or provide resources that must be acquired through intermediaries. An example of the latter is found in government agencies, which contract out to an organization which, in turn, contracts out to another to fulfill contractual agreements beyond its own capacity. Such subcontracting firms cannot handle large projects, but specialize in something that others do not. They can therefore get to the resource base indirectly. Wholesalers are intermediaries for retailers' organizations and retailers are often intermediaries between wholesalers and customers.

Indirect sectors can also eventually function as direct sectors. After an intervening market research organization has established which sectors have a need or desire for a particular activity, the organization can work directly with those sectors. This occurs frequently in multinational and intergovernmental relations where two, three, and sometimes even more parties are involved in negotiations. After the negotiations have been successfully completed through indirect contact, formal, direct relationships are often arranged. The fact that organizations can design ways to get to indirect sectors is important since there are all kinds of legal, political, ideological, and ethical problems that can allow or disallow desired exchanges. For instance, Perrow (1970: 126) cited a case showing how important it is to know the environment of a potential customer. A salesman from organization A wanted to sell something to C in a foreign country, but B was already doing so and B was also supplying inputs into A that might have been cut off had A decided to sell to C. Another good example, provided by Sethi (1972: 69-73), demonstrates the web of direct and indirect relationships in which Coca Cola became entangled between the United States and Israel when confronted with the decision to grant Israel a bottling franchise. The notion of direct and indirect relationships might also aid the theorist in defining the kinds of strategies and tactics that organizations use to avoid conflicting spheres of influence.

Finally, the more indirect an exchange sector is, the more difficult it is to exercise control over or act upon that sector. Identification of the interdependence series makes it possible to design methods to alter the interdependencies in a desired way. If the interdependencies cannot be altered or altered only partially, knowledge of them can lead to ideas about how the host organization could change its own structure, policies, and goals to become at least more responsive.

Environmental Change

Little has been said thus far about the movement of environmental sectors. On this point, Thompson (1967), Lawrence and Lorsch (1967), Burns and Stalker (1961), and Emery and Trist (1965) have made major contributions. Although there are undoubtedly many ways in which an organization might change, attention is limited here to formal goals, since information about organizational goals can be obtained from quarterly reports and other sources. This does not mean that a study concerned with organization environments should focus on goal changes. A change in the political situation, law revisions, and even the weather might be more relevant than goals. For example the 1972-1973 winter in the Netherlands was very mild and this just about put a few bootmaking companies out of business. A study of formal goal changes in environmental sectors might be relatively easy to conduct. Unorganized sectors, however—made up of customers, for example—have no such things as formal goals. One might then examine needs, but this could also prove to be extremely difficult to analyze. A more reasonable approach might be to ask decision makers and boundary agents about the kinds of ongoing changes that they perceive as the most relevant.

Environmental change—apart from internal influences—is an important determinant of internal behavior. Organizations are chiefly concerned with diagnosing changes, but they are no less concerned with change rates and their own change rate or timing capacity. One noticeable characteristic of the literature on organizational environments is the vagueness of the discussion on the meaning of the term change rate. This discussion attempts to bring operational clarity to the term. Internal change capacity is not explored here because the body of literature on the planning and the processes of internal change lies mainly outside the scope of this article. The term change rate will be used here in place of the notion of a stable-shifting or dynamic environment. Change rate takes into account the number of major goal alterations during a given period. The higher the number of major goal alterations over the same period, the higher the change rate: the lower the number, the lower the change rate.

Organizations can do one thing or a combination of things in conjunction with their goals: add new ones, drop some, and attempt to revise others. Consequently, change rates should be defined to reflect this behavior. Even a rough estimate of environmental change rates permits comparisons that can facilitate diagnosis. For example, two competitors may have completely different change rates, but the slower organization may actually be doing better. It might be doing the right thing at the right time, whereas the other may be frantically trying to catch up or wildly seeking a better survival base. Change rates are important indicators for the timing of the delivery of new goals and services to the market.

At a more abstract, theoretical level, one can study the expansion and contraction between the types of goals—societal, output, system, product, and derived—suggested by Perrow (1970: 126) and patterns between organizations. Knowing what one's exchange units are doing and how they are shifting can help an organization to keep up with its competitors.

Change rate can be dichotomized into low and high, with these terms being defined relative to one another. Clusters of organizations offering similar products and services may have high change rates in comparison with other clusters, but within clusters, too, there can be lows and highs, some of the lows being closely equivalent to a high in another cluster. Organizations should, however, be able to distinguish which sectors and groups of sectors are moving rapidly, to avoid competing with those whose pace could be difficult to equal.

Hage and Aiken (1970: 33-38) have suggested that internal complexity may lead to a high change rate, which implies that at least two of the variables here are causally related. But they speak of complexity among professional occupations that could cause high change rates. They offer an explanation for a certain type of situation. "However, the effect of this form of complexity," to use Hall's (1972: 151) words, "is minimized when other organizational characteristics are examined." Interest in defining complexity is relatively new in organizational theory. Hall's excellent summary points to the variety of sociological approaches that have produced a variety of results and interpretations, all of which are credible.

Stable and Unstable Change

Both low and high change rates can be dichotomized further into stable and unstable rates. Stable rates occur in a situation where most of the important factors influencing a situation are changing predictably in value and where the set of critical factors remains constant. Unstable rates take place when a situation is loose and erratic. Here, both the value of important variables—independent and intervening—and the kinds of relevant variables in the set are changing unpredictably. Instability can also be represented by an erratic step-function and as Boulding (1971: 20) notes: "Many real systems are governed by step-functions which at certain points display changes in the relation of inputs to outputs, and because you never quite know when steps are going to be taken, step-functions make the future terribly hard to predict." In addition, Ashby (1954: 53) states, "Every stable system has the property that if displaced from a resting state and released, the subsequent movement is so matched to the initial displacement that the system is brought back to the resting state." Thus, in unstable environmental conditions, unpredictability is increasing. While organizations may be rational, the participants can rationalize guesswork or speculate on outcomes that are rationally induced. Participants may also select information sets which, although originally perceived as relevant, become the cause of tension and conflict as the overlap between individual information sets diminishes. The conflict frequently takes the form of debating about the use of certain information units as well as about the outcomes.

The meaning of stability and instability is perhaps more problematic than organizational theorists are willing to admit. At times stability is perceived as the opposite of movement or change. Consider, for example, Thompson's stable-shifting and Duncan's static-dynamic continua. A good example of how theorists fuse the concepts of change rate and stable or unstable environments is found in a recent article by Child (1972: 3) who referred to environmental variability as the "degree of change that . . . in turn may be seen as a function of three variables: (1) the frequency of changes in relevant activities: (2) the degree of difference involved at each change: (3) the degree of irregularity in the overall patterns of change—in a sense the 'variability of change.' "

The first two variables are treated as change rate in the present article. The third involves the stability or instability of an environment. This distinction is made so that the importance of both can be appreciated.

There are four types of environmental movement: low, stable change: high, stable change: low, unstable change: and high, unstable change—all having different effects on an organization.

An organization with predominantly low but stable change rate environmental sectors would be one in which the planning of strategies, operations, and tactics can be expected to be essentially trouble free, since predictability is greater where uncertainty is low and fluctuates in a patterned way. Although the environment changes, it does not change quickly and long-range planning can be conducted without taking into account any major environmental alteration during any planned period.

Organizations with a low but stable change rate environment—the change rate remaining essentially constant but tending to change—will be able to pursue their intentions, but controlling the changing environmental factors becomes more difficult. Internal buffer mechanisms become broader; more roles are assigned to the filtering, coding, and interpreting of information; and current policies and technologies are manipulated so that they can still be used. Older forms are transformed into new versions under the mild threat of unfamiliar behavior. It is easier to rely on reformulated older techniques than to invent new ones, especially when there is a belief that they will work. In the absence of experience with innovations, reformulation is about the only thing an organization can resort to, and this is probably not dangerous.

Thus, with a low but unstable change rate, the planning of strategies, operations, and tactics is not a serious problem. It becomes more complex than dealing with a stable change rate but not uncomfortably problematic. There are more kinds of alternatives, the assumptions underlying each have to be clearly outlined, and assumptions about when to switch to other alternatives have to be more carefully examined. Boundary role activity increases, too, in time and content; the feedback interaction between boundary roles and buffer units increases in number and time and the coordination of feedback loops must be given more attention. Finally, managerial coalitions are farther apart than in an organization with predominantly low but stable changing environmental sectors. Under stable conditions, conflicts can be resolved more quickly and the resulting peace lasts longer. Under unstable conditions, conflict resolution is more difficult and the subsequent period of cooperation is much shorter. The basis of conflict lies in differences in the interpretation of information, the use of different kinds of information, and the assignment of different values, all of which appear appropriate. Political activity increases but can be controlled. Subordinates demand more responsibility in the form of contributing opinions. The status of boundary roles also increases and threatens the higher status role occupants unaccustomed to erratic environmental conditions.

High change rates and stable environments create difficult problems for organizations, too, but for different reasons. Since the change rate is increasing, timing and goal formulation—and reformulation—become crucial. Decisions about what goals and services to add, decrease, or completely drop, and how much of each and when, become frustrating. The design of strategies, operations, and tactics can still be accomplished, but the design itself becomes a goal, that is, it becomes a means of maintaining stability within the organization. Analytical methodologies gain in importance and both routine and nonroutine search behaviors are instituted to find newer or better methodologies offered in the environment: more emphasis is devoted to searching for new ideas within the organization.

Long-range planning is accomplished, but the plans become more general. Incremental planning is adopted to reach the alternative goals which have been generally outlined. The question becomes one of what short-range alternative strategies, operations, and tactics are needed to reach every step to every alternative goal and then when one step is completed, changes in the initially planned strategies, operations, and tactics must be considered. Plans are held open and subject to change, but they are not impossible to construct.

Conflict between coalitions arises not only over what and when but also the methodologies considered and stability within coalitions diminishes. Coalitions are loose and changing: they resemble the intersector change rate and instability in the environment (Cyert and March, 1963: 39).

Because the change rate is high, the frequency of interaction between occupants of boundary roles, decision-making centers, and buffer units is high. Whenever efficiently possible, information is sent directly to decision makers on a continuous basis so that changes in the environmental change rates can be detected with immediacy. Monthly and quarterly reports become old news as the emphasis is on shorter intervals. Decision makers often spend more time in familiarizing themselves directly with the sectors in order to better understand and anticipate changes. To facilitate muddling through, they attempt to assign subjective probabilities to possible changes sometimes by using industrial spies but more often by establishing informal contacts with executives in other organizations and with relevant, indirect information channels within sectors.

Organizations with environmental sectors characterized by instability and high change rates live on the brink of chaos. Rittel and Weber (1973) discussed the problems encountered in planning in this type of environment. Some of the following ideas resemble many of those they developed. Situations change rapidly and unpredictably. No matter how exhaustive and reliable information is, it tends to increase the potential for conflict. Strategies, operations, and tactics in environmental sectors reach such levels of generality and abstraction that counter moves cannot be specifically defined over the long run without allowing for radical, spontaneous revisions. Methodologies are sought which provide a neater, more complete picture. The rise of PPBS—Planning, Programming, Budgeting Systems—in the last 15 years represents an attempt to establish a more precise view of the general situation. Intensive effort to reduce or transform complexity, in unpredictable, rapidly changing organized and unorganized environmental sectors, is intended to yield a more certain view of the situation. Another indicator of the above is the growing interest and application of General Systems Theory, in which the study of wholes is stressed.

Organizations in this state design coping tactics, mainly in the form of decentralization and multidisciplinary research units, in the hope that more specific planning will emerge. Because of increasing interaction, the boundary roles, roles in buffer systems, and executive roles tend to fuse. This is by no means a stable fusion. The structure of the fused roles drifts in unstructured ways. Occasionally, boundaries are temporarily closed to permit analysis of what has taken place and to generate more standardized decision programs, however short lived they may be.

Frequently, when environmental sectors make impossible demands on the organization, the organization does nothing or repeats unsatisfactory, standardized behavior. When the organization does nothing, decision makers fear the risk involved in the disparity between its means and the demands made. A sort of cognitive dissonance develops and the decision makers retreat to safe ground. When organizations repeat standardized behavior, even though it is known to be unsatisfactory to the sectors, they are reflecting trained incapacity. Is it any wonder that organizations are charged with conservativism? In the face of instability and rapid change in the environment—mainly in the unorganized sectors of society—large investments or safe investments are made to stabilize the organization.

Each decision maker uses his own model of the situation, unrelated to the models of his peers, and consequent discussions become tense political debates. Internal and external consultants are often called for analysis and advice in an effort to keep the organization together. In the last few years process consultation (Schein, 1969) has been developed. One important purpose of this method is the cooling off of relations between people. This, of course, does not eliminate the basis of conflict, but it at least contributes to the development of mutual understanding and thus enhances the growth of the members' capacities for mutual tolerance.

When an organization is not afraid of its environment, it can and does plan strategies, operations, and tactics, but frequently on a coping basis. Problem solving is replaced by problem coping. Problems are never completely solved and people are forced to learn to live with the consequences of the unsolved aspects of problems. Some resources are always kept in reserve for investment in initially high-risk goals that start to prove themselves. New Venture Teams (Wileman and Freese, 1972) are set up solely to produce new ideas which keep the organization going.

Organizations generally gravitate towards stability or at least find it preferable. A highly unstable and rapidly changing environment can be perceived as dangerous. Most organizations try to avoid it and if that proves impossible, they either manipulate it to increase its stability or develop methods to maintain or restore internal stability. On the other hand, organizations may temporarily opt for a chaotic situation to loosen crystallized—ultrastable—or boring situations to get a larger share of a market, to create new ones, to extend services to other sectors, and so forth.

This discussion of change and stability resembles in part the notions offered by Emery and Trist (1965), who develop a typology consisting of four types: placid-random, placid-clustered, disturbed-reactive, and turbulent. They stated that the order of the four types constitutes an ascending order of uncertainty. Nevertheless, for the first and fourth types, the uncertainty seems to be about the same for different reasons. A placid-random environment is characterized by discrete sectors. There is no interdependency chain, but if there is, it is temporary and changes randomly. With a turbulent environment, the rapid movement and the complexity of relations are uncertainty sources.

There is a great deal of overlap between strategies and tactics associated with the first type. The fourth type is characterized as an environment in which general rules are substituted for strategies, operations, and tactics. The more general and abstract a discussion becomes, the more overlap there is between categories, thus further supporting the suggestion that the two types are similar. General rules and overlapping strategies and tactics appear to be essentially the same. If this is an ascending order of uncertainty, as the authors have suggested, why have they suggested an ascending order of more certain means to reduce the environmental uncertainty? The ascending order of certain organizational means with increasing environmental uncertainty applies only to the first three types: type 1, intermingling of strategies and tactics: type 2, development of strategies and tactics; and type 3, strategies, operations, and tactics. Organizational means become more complex in the face of environmental uncertainty, but not more certain. If one does not understand the situation with which he is confronted, he can expect to have problems in handling it (March and Simon, 1958: 140). It is reasonable to assume that under conditions of uncertainty, goal setting and means are also more uncertain and complex, since there is an obvious resemblance to the problems of handling increasingly difficult environments.

In spite of these difficulties, some of the terms offered here suggest a revised scheme that makes use of a few of Emery and Trist's (1965) concepts.

TABLE 1. Environmental Effect on Planning

Environmental movement	Design of strategies, operations, and tactics
Low change rate/stable	Easily accomplished
Low change rate/unstable	More complex
High change rate/stable	Very complex—characterized by muddling through
High change rate/unstable	Most difficult—problem coping in the place of problem solving

Summary and Conclusions

The following four propositions will serve to sum up the extreme types of organizational environments discussed. (See fig. 1.)

1 Organizations with type 1 environment have relatively minor information problems: can design long-range strategies, operations, and tactics more easily—more rapidly and in more detail—and implement them without major alterations, have relatively little internal conflict potential: possess a more mechanical structure, have clearly defined and predictable, gradually changing coalitions: and have relatively few problems with their existing decision-making programs when the environment changes.

2 Organizations confronted with a type 49 environment experience the same problems as do those with a type 1 environment, but they experience a higher degree of uncertainty concerning timing in the control of internal problem states.

3 Organizations confronted with a type 64 environment have major information problems, have very abstract, tentative sets of strategies, operations, and tactics and cannot execute them without expecting major alterations: have very vague coalitions that change unpredictably: and are constantly redesigning decision-making programs or constantly making exceptions to existing decision-making programs.

4 Organizations confronted with a type 16 environment have the same problems as are experienced by organizations with a type 64 environment, but they are able to predict and control internal problem states much more easily.

This typology is not a matrix of interdependencies; each cell represents a different situation. It is offered as a core typology, since other dimensions can be added. For example, the direct category might be further subtyped to include friendly competitor, unfriendly competitor, neutral competitor, and the like to obtain an even better idea of how organizations mutually adjust their negotiating styles.[1]

In addition, a typology of environments may be useful in bringing out the fact that certain classes or organizations more rightfully belong to certain kinds of environments. If this is true, a fresh start might be made with organizational typologies, arriving at something considerably more powerful than what is presently available. That is, more useful organizational typologies might be derived by first examining the different environmental situations organizations encounter and then and only then, constructing an organizational typology with types possessing internal organizational characteristics that are reasonably unique to a particular organization environment.

More than a decade ago Dill (1962) noted that typologies of environments were nonexistent. Even though the literature on organization-environment relationships has been growing and has added a great deal of useful information for both theory and practice, a reasonably comprehensible typology has yet to appear. The typology developed above can be seen as an instrument to map the rates and direction of environmental movements, that is, how different kinds of sectors in different locations are moving with respect to each other.

Knowing the environmental map or the direction of its movement may mean switching from one type of strategy and tactic to another. The decision to cooperate, coopt, be coopted, enter a coalition, drop out, or opt for conflict, could be partially dependent upon the environmental state (Thompson and McEwen, 1958). Lammers (1974) has developed a typology of strategies and tactics used by university authorities to counter student opposition. These strategies and tactics are applicable under certain kinds of conditions; mixed forms are also possible under mixed conditions and when the conditions destabilize or change, the mixed forms should congruently change.

General conditions can also influence environmental maps, as Hall (1972: 298-312) has pointed out. This effect is easily observed in cross-cultural studies. For instance, anyone familiar with the management journals knows that business negotiations with the Chinese and Russians are prolonged, detail-ridden exercises that appear to be attempts to keep an agreement stable even if conditions should happen to change. Recessions, inflations, changes in political regimes, and cultural factors can all cause organizations to change relations and alter the change rates. Even the possibility of an unfriendly political personality not yet formally in office can influence the situation. George McGovern's candidacy, for instance, was perceived by many people as one of the principal causes of a drop in the stock market. The launching of new products may be postponed because demand could diminish during a recession. On the other hand, new or revised products may be created to exploit whatever limited resources there are. Foreign investments may be curtailed in countries where a political regime is considering a nationalization program and this may create a partial chain reaction with directly and indirectly related sectors.[2]

Follett (Metcalf and Urwick, 1957) pointed to a dialectical phenomenon in organizational behavior: solved problems create new ones. With the suggested typology, one may be able to locate the source of problems to better study the phenomenon and to design appropriate models of problem states with a complex set of acceptable controls that could prevent the ongoing succession of crisis.

Pushing problems off on other sectors only removes the symptoms from one sector and leaves the agony of treating the causes to someone else which may, in turn, create even larger problems for another sector. A good example of the latter occurs when measures to prevent robberies and stealing are instituted: it is hardly to be expected that criminals with criminal skills will change to honest work just because one kind of resource base has disappeared. Suppression of the symptom does not cure the disease; the suppressed symptoms simply appear elsewhere, compounding already existing problems or forming a new set.

Notes

1. A set of formal operationalized hypotheses has not been developed here, because the purpose was to theoretically establish a descriptive core typology. Informal hypotheses have, however, been used to demonstrate how organizations might react to various kinds of environmental situations. Some of these informal hypotheses were supported by examples, others by reference to other studies, and a few by speculative logic.

2 The exchange currencies—power, status, money—and their combinations are not included, but it would be interesting to see how organizations and their sectors manipulate their resources and those of others within various situations. The ideas of Ilchman and Uphoff (1969), Haas and Drabek (1973: 224-228), and Blau (1966) provide a set of theoretical notions which, unfortunately, are too complex for this article.

References

Ashby, W. Ross, 1954 Design for a Brain, New York: Wiley.

1968 "Principles of the self-organizing system." In Walter Buckley (ed.). Modern Systems Research for the Behavioral Scientist: 108-118. Aldine.

Blau, Peter M., 1966 Exchange and Power in Social Life. New York: Wiley.

Boulding, Kenneth E., 1971 "The dodo didn't make it: survival and betterment." Bulletin of Atomic Scientists: 27: 19-22.

Buckley, Walter, 1967 Sociology and Modern Systems Theory. Englewood Cliffs, N.J.: Prentice-Hall.

Burns, Tom, and G. M. Stalker, 1961 The Management of Innovation, London: Tavistock.

Child, John, 1972 "Organizational structure, environment and performance: the role of strategic choice." Sociology: 6: 2-21.

Cyert, R. M., and J. G. March, 1963 A Behavioral Theory of the Firm. Englewood Cliffs, N.J.: Prentice-hall.

Dill, William R., 1962 "The impact of environment on organizational development." In Sidney Mailick and Edward H. van Ness (eds.), Concepts and Issues in Administrative Behavior: 94-109. Englewood Cliffs, N.J.: Prentice-Hall.

Duncan, Robert B., 1972 "Characteristics of organizational environments and perceived environmental uncertainty." Administrative Science Quarterly. 17: 313-327.

Emery, F. E., and E. L. Trist, 1965 "The causal textgure of organizational environments." Human Relations. 18: 21-32.

Evans, William M., 1966 "The organization set: toward a theory of inter-organizational relations." In J. D. Thompson (ed.), Approaches to organizational design: 174-191. Pittsburgh: University of Pittsburgh.

Haas, J. Eugene, and Thomas E. Brabek, 1973 Complex Organizations: A Sociological Perspective. London: Collier-Macmillan.

Hage, Jerald, and Michael Aiken, 1970 Social Change in Complex Organizations. New York: Random House

Hall, Richard H., 1972 Organizations: Structure and Process. Englewood Cliffs. N.J.: Prentice-Hall.

Ilchman, Warren, and Norman Thomas Uphoff, 1969 The Political Economy of Change. Berkeley, Calif.: The University of California Press.

Lawrence, Paul R., and Jay W. Lorsch, 1967 Organization and Environment. Boston: Harvard Business School.

Lammers, C. J., 1974 "Tactics and strategies adopted by university authorities to counter student opposition." In Donald E. Light, Jr. (ed.). The Dynamics of Protest (forthcoming).

Organ, Dennis, 1971 "Linking pins between organization and environment." Business Horizons, 14: 73-80.

March, James G., and Herbert A. Simon, 1958 Organizations, London: Wiley.

Metcalf, Henry C., and L. Urwick (eds.),1957 Dynamic Administration: The Collected Papers of Mary Parker Follett. London: Pitman.

Rickson, Roy E., and Charles Simpkins, 1972 "Industrial organization and the ecological process: the case of water pollution." In Merlin Brinkerhoff and Phillip R. Kunz (eds.), Complex Organizations and Their Environments: 282-292. Dubuque, Iowa: Brown.

Rittel, Horst W. J., and Merlin M. Weber, 1973 "Dilemmas in a general theory of planning." Policy Sciences, 4: 155-169.

Schein, E. H., 1969 Process Consultation: Its Role in Organizational Development. Reading, Pa.: Addison-Wesley.

Sethi, S. Prakash, 1972 "Coca-Cola and the Middle East crises: international politics and multinational corporations." In Advanced Cases in Multinational Business Operations: 69-73. Pacific Palisades, Calif.: Goodyear.

Simon, H. A., 1965 "The architecture of complexity." General Systems Review, C: 63-76.

Starbuck, William, 1973 Organizations and Their Environments. Berlin: International Institute of Management.

Thompson, James D., 1967 Organizations in Action. London: McGraw-Hill.

Thompson, James D., and William J. McEwen, 1958 "Organizational goals and environment: goal setting as an interaction process." American Sociological Review, 23: 23-31.

Wileman, David, and Howard Freese, 1972 "Problems new-venture teams face." Innovation. 28: 40-47.

THE MANAGEMENT OF INNOVATION

TOM BURNS
G. M. STALKER

The Analysis of Organizations Under Conditions of Relative Stability and Change

The core of all the twenty studies on which [our] book [*The Management of Innovation*] is based is the description and explanation of what happens when new and unfamiliar tasks are put upon industrial concerns organized for relatively stable conditions. When novelty and unfamiliarity in both market situation and technical information become the accepted order of things, a fundamentally different kind of management system becomes appropriate from that which applies to a relatively stable commercial and technical environment. . . . There is very little I would wish to add or to amend in this section, although, so far as I am able to judge from subsequent uses and references, there must be some wrongly placed emphases.

In the first place, the utility of the notions of "mechanistic" and "organic" management systems resides largely in their being related as dependent variables to the rate of "environmental" change. "Environmental", in this connection, refers to the technological basis of production and to the market situation; indeed, as I have argued elsewhere,[1] . . . the increasing rate of technological change characteristic of the last generation could plausibly be regarded as a function of fundamental changes in the relationship of production to consumption.

If the form of management is properly to be seen as dependent on the situation the concern is trying to meet, it follows that there is no single set of principles for "good organization", an ideal type of management system which can serve as a model to which administrative practice should, or could in time, approximate. It follows also that there is an overriding management task in first interpreting correctly the market and technological situation, in terms of its instability or of the rate at which conditions are changing, and then designing the management system

Reprinted by permission of the authors and the publisher, Tavistock Publications Ltd., from *The Management of Innovation*.

appropriate to the conditions, and making it work. "Direction", as I have labelled this activity, is the distinctive task of managers-in-chief, and is discussed in the final chapters in terms of a critical examination of the role of the managing director; but properly speaking the description and explanation of the interpretative, directive functions of top management belong to the earlier section, since it is these functions that largely determine the effectiveness of the organization as a whole. The examination of the role of the chief executive, that is to say, is logically antecedent to the description and analysis of the organizational problems. . . . For it was failure at this level that produced the characteristic forms of management system encountered in most of the concerns—forms which, from the point of view of their overt constitution and purposes, were clearly inefficient and ineffective, although there are, as we shall see, other points of view from which they may be regarded as serving certain ends and performing certain functions in an entirely efficient manner.

For the individual, much of the importance of the difference between mechanistic and organic systems lies in the extent of his commitment to the working organization. Mechanistic systems (sc. "bureaucracies") define his functions, together with the methods, responsibilities, and powers appropriate to them; in other words, however, this means that boundaries are set. That is to say, in being told what he has to attend to, and how, he is also told what he does not have to bother with, what is not his affair, what is not expected of him, what he can post elsewhere as the responsibility of others. In organic systems, the boundaries of feasible demands on the individual disappear. The greatest stress is placed on his regarding himself as fully implicated in the discharge of any task appearing over his horizon, as involved not merely in the exercise of a special competence but in commitment to the success of the concern's undertakings approximating somewhat to that of the doctor or scientist in the discharge of his professional functions. . . .

Mechanistic and Organic Systems

We are now at the point at which we may set down the outline of the two management systems which represent for us the two polar extremities of the forms which such systems can take when they are adapted to a specific rate of technical and commercial change. The case we have tried to establish from the literature . . . is that the different forms assumed by a working organization do exist objectively and are not merely interpretations offered by observers of different schools.

Both types represent a "rational" form of organization, in that they may both, in our experience, be explicitly and deliberately created and maintained to exploit the human resources of a concern in the most efficient manner feasible in the circumstances of the concern. Not surprisingly, however, each exhibits characteristics which have been hitherto associated with different kinds of interpretation. For it is our contention that empirical findings have usually been classified according to sociological ideology rather than according to the functional specificity of the working organization to its task and the conditions confronting it.

We have tried to argue that these are two formally contrasted forms of management system. These we shall call the mechanistic and organic forms.

A *mechanistic* management system is appropriate to stable conditions. It is characterized by:

(*a*) the specialized differentiation of functional tasks into which the problems and tasks facing the concern as a whole are broken down;

(*b*) the abstract nature of each individual task, which is pursued with techniques and purposes more or less distinct from those of the concern as a whole; i.e., the functionaries tend to pursue the technical improvement of means, rather than the accomplishment of the ends of the concern;

(*c*) the reconciliation, for each level in the hierarchy, of these distinct performances by the immediate superiors, who are also, in turn, responsible for seeing that each is relevant in his own special part of the main task.

(*d*) the precise definition of rights and obligations and technical methods attached to each functional role;

(*e*) the translation of rights and obligations and methods into the responsibilities of a functional position;

(*f*) hierarchic structure of control, authority and communication;

(*g*) a reinforcement of the hierarchic structure by the location of knowledge of actualities exclusively at the top of the hierarchy, where the final reconciliation of distinct tasks and assessment of relevance is made.[2]

(*h*) a tendency for interaction between members of the concern to be vertical, i.e., between superior and subordinate;

(*i*) a tendency for operations and working behaviour to be governed by the instructions and decisions issued by superiors;

(*j*) insistence on loyalty to the concern and obedience to superiors as a condition of membership;

(*k*) a greater importance and prestige attaching to internal (local) than to general (cosmopolitan) knowledge, experience, and skill.

The *organic* form is appropriate to changing conditions, which give rise constantly to fresh problems and unforeseen requirements for action which cannot be broken down or distributed automatically arising from the functional roles defined within a hierarchic structure. It is characterized by:

(*a*) the contributive nature of special knowledge and experience to the common task of the concern;

(*b*) the "realistic" nature of the individual task, which is seen as set by the total situation of the concern;

(*c*) the adjustment and continual re-definition of individual tasks through interaction with others;

(*d*) the shedding of "responsibility" as a limited field of rights, obligations and methods. (Problems may not be posted upwards, downwards or sideways as being someone's else's responsibility);

(*e*) the spread of commitment to the concern beyond any technical definition;

(*f*) a network structure of control, authority, and communication. The sanctions which apply to the individual's conduct in his working role derive more from presumed community of interest with the rest of the working organization in the survival and growth of the firm, and less from a contractual relationship between himself and a non-personal corporation, represented for him by an immediate superior;

(*g*) omniscience no longer imputed to the head of the concern; knowledge about the technical or commercial nature of the here and now task may be located anywhere in the network; this location becoming the *ad hoc* centre of control authority and communication;

(*h*) a lateral rather than a vertical direction of communication through the organization, communication between people of different rank, also, resembling consultation rather than command;

(*i*) a content of communication which consists of information and advice rather than instructions and decisions;

(*j*) commitment to the concern's tasks and to the "technological ethos" of material progress and expansion is more highly valued than loyalty and obedience;

(*k*) importance and prestige attach to affiliations and expertise valid in the industrial and technical and commercial milieux external to the firm.

One important corollary to be attached to this account is that while organic systems are not hierarchic in the same sense as are mechanistic, they remain stratified. Positions are differentiated according to seniority—i.e., greater expertise. The lead in joint decisions is frequently taken by seniors, but it is an essential presumption of the organic system that the lead, i.e. "authority", is taken by whoever shows himself most informed and capable, i.e., the "best authority". The location of authority is settled by consensus.

A second observation is that the area of commitment to the concern—the extent to which the individual yields himself as a resource to be used by the working organization—is far more extensive in organic than in mechanistic systems. Commitment, in fact, is expected to approach that of the professional scientist to his work, and frequently does. One further consequence of this is that it becomes far less feasible to distinguish "informal" from "formal" organization.

Thirdly, the emptying out of significance from the hierarchic command system, by which co-operation is ensured and which serves to monitor the working organization under a mechanistic system, is countered by the development of shared beliefs about the values and goals of the concern. The growth and accretion of institutionalized values, beliefs, and conduct, in the form of commitments, ideology, and manners, around an image of the concern in its industrial and commercial setting make good the loss of formal structure.

Finally, the two forms of system represent a polarity, not a dichotomy; there are, as we have tried to show, intermediate stages between the extremities empirically known to us. Also, the relation of one form to the other is elastic, so that a concern oscillating between relative stability and relative change may also oscillate between the two forms. A concern may (and frequently does) operate with a management system which includes both types.

The organic form, by departing from the familiar clarity and fixity of the hierarchic structure, is often experienced by the individual manager as an uneasy, embarrassed, or chronically anxious quest for knowledge about what he should be doing, or what is expected of him, and similar apprehensiveness about what others are doing. Indeed, as we shall see later, this kind of response is necessary if the organic form of organization is to work effectively. Understandably, such anxiety finds expression in resentment when the apparent confusion besetting him is not explained. In these situations, all managers some of the time, and many managers all the time, yearn for more definition and structure.

On the other hand, some managers recognize a rationale of non-definition, a reasoned basis for the practice of those successful firms in which designation of status, function, and line of responsibility and authority has been vague or even avoided.

The desire for more definition is often in effect a wish to have the limits of one's task more neatly defined—to know what and when one doesn't have to bother about as much as to know what one does have to. It follows that the more definition is given, the more omniscient the management must be, so that no functions are left wholly or partly undischarged, no person is overburdened with undelegated responsibility, or left without the authority to do his job properly. To do this, to have all the separate functions attached to individual roles fitting together and comprehensively, to have communication between persons constantly maintained on a level adequate to the needs of each functional role, requires rules or traditions of behaviour proved over a long time and an equally fixed, stable task. The omniscience which may then be credited to the head of the concern is expressed throughout its body through the lines of command, extending in a clear, explicitly titled hierarchy of officers and subordinates.

The whole mechanistic form is instinct with this twofold principle of definition and dependence which acts as the frame within which action is conceived and carried out. It works, unconsciously, almost in the smallest minutiae of daily activity. "How late is late?" The answer to this question is not to be found in the rule book, but in the superior. Late is when the boss thinks it is late. Is he the kind of man who thinks 8:00 is the time, and 8:01 is late? Does he think that 8:15 is all right occasionally if it is not a regular thing? Does he think that everyone should be allowed a 5-minutes grace after 8:00 but after that they are late?

Settling questions about how a person's job is to be done in this way is nevertheless simple, direct, and economical of effort. . . .

One other feature of mechanistic organization needs emphasis. It is a necessary condition of its operation that the individual "works on his own", functionally isolated; he "knows his job", he is "responsible for seeing it's done". He works at a job which is in a sense artificially abstracted from the realities of the situation the concern is dealing with, the accountant "dealing with the costs side", the works manager "pushing production", and so on. As this works out in practice, the rest of the organization becomes part of the problem situation the individual has to deal with in order to perform successfully; i.e., difficulties and problems arising from work or information which has been handed over the "responsibility barrier" between two jobs or departments are regarded as "really" the responsibility of the person from whom they were received. As a design engineer put in, "When you get designers handing over designs completely to production, it's 'their responsibility' now. And you get tennis games played with the responsibility for anything that goes wrong. What happens is that you're constantly getting unsuspected faults arising from characteristics which you didn't think important in the design. If you get to hear of these through a sales person, or a production person, or somebody to whom the design was handed over to in the dim past, then, instead of being a design problem, it's an annoyance caused by that particular person, who can't do his own job—because you'd thought you were finished with that one, and you're on to something else now.''

When the assumptions of the form of organization make for preoccupation with specialized tasks, the chances of career success, or of greater influence, depend rather on the relative importance which may be attached to each special function by the superior whose task it is to reconcile and control a number of them. And, indeed, to press the claims of one's job or department for a bigger share of the firm's resources is in many cases regarded as a mark of initiative, of effectiveness, and even of ''loyalty to the firm's interests''. The state of affairs thus engendered squares with the role of the superior, the man who can see the wood instead of just the trees, and gives it the reinforcement of the aloof detachment belonging to a court of appeal. The ordinary relationship prevailing between individual managers ''in charge of'' different functions is one of rivalry, a rivalry which may be rendered innocuous to the persons involved by personal friendship or the norms of sociability, but which turns discussion about the situations which constitute the real problems of the concern—how to make products more cheaply, how to sell more, how to allocate resources, whether to curtail activity in one sector, whether to risk expansion in another, and so on—into an arena of conflicting interests.

The distinctive feature of the second, organic system is the pervasiveness of the working organization as an institution. In concrete terms, this makes itself felt in a preparedness to combine with others in serving the general aims of the concern. Proportionately to the rate and extent of change, the less can the omniscience appropriate to command organizations be ascribed to the head of the organization; for executives, and even operatives, in a changing firm it is always theirs to reason why. Furthermore, the less definition can be given to status, roles, and modes of communication, the more do the activities of each member of the organization become determined by the real tasks of the firm as he sees them than by instruction and routine. The individual's job ceases to be self-contained; the only way in which ''his'' job can be done is by his participating continually with others in the solution of problems which are real to the firm, and put in a language of requirements and activities meaningful to them all. Such methods of working put much heavier demands on the individual. . . .

We have endeavoured to stress the appropriateness of each system to its own specific set of conditions. Equally, we desire to avoid the suggestion that either system is superior under all circumstances to the other. In particular, nothing in our experience justifies the assumption that mechanistic systems should be superseded by organic in conditions of stability.[3] The beginning of the administrative wisdom is the awareness that there is no one optimum type of management system.

Notes and References

1. T. Burns, ''The Sociology of Industry'', in A. T. Welford (ed.) *Society*, London, Routledge & Kegan Paul, 1962 (p. 191).
2. This functional attribute of the head of a concern often takes on a clearly expressive aspect. It is common enough for concerns to instruct all people with whom they deal to address correspondence to the firm (i.e., to its formal head) and for all outgoing

letters and orders to be signed by the head of the concern. Similarly, the printed letter heading used by Government departments carries instructions for the replies to be addressed to the Secretary, etc. These instructions are not always taken seriously, either by members of the organization or their correspondents, but in one company this practice was insisted upon and was taken to somewhat unusual lengths; *all* correspondence was delivered to the managing director, who would thereafter distribute excerpts to members of the staff, synthesizing their replies into the letter of reply which he eventually sent. Telephone communication was also controlled by limiting the numbers of extensions, and by monitoring incoming and outgoing calls.

3. A recent instance of this assumption is contained in H. A. Shepard's paper addressed to the Symposium on the Direction of Research Establishments, 1956. "There is much evidence to suggest that the optimal use of human resources in industrial organizations requires a different set of conditions, assumptions, and skills from those traditionally present in industry. Over the past twenty-five years, some new orientations have emerged from organizational experiments, observations and inventions. The new orientations depart radically from doctrines associated with 'Scientific Management' and traditional bureaucratic patterns.

"The central emphases in this development are as follows:

1. Wide participation in decision-making, rather than centralized decision-making.

2. The face-to-face group, rather than the individual, as the basic unit of organization.

3. Mutual confidence, rather than authority, as the integrative force in organization.

4. The supervisor as the agent for maintaining intragroup and intergroup communication, rather than as the agent of higher authority.

5. Growth of members of the organization to greater responsibility, rather than external control of the member's performance or their tasks."

GENERIC TYPES OF SUBSYSTEMS

DANIEL KATZ
ROBERT L. KAHN

Social organizations like other systems have a through-put or a transformation of the energic input. Those activities concerned with the through-put have been called *production or technical subsystems* (Parsons, 1960). To insure existence beyond a single cycle of productive activity, there must be new materials to be worked on. *Supportive structures* develop in a surviving system to provide a continuing source of production inputs. They are of two kinds. One is the extension of the production system into the environment by activities which procure raw materials and dispose

Reprinted by permission of John Wiley & Sons, Inc., from *The Social Psychology of Organizations*, by Daniel Katz and Robert L. Kahn, copyright © 1966, John Wiley & Sons, Inc.

of the product. The second type is at the more complex level of maintaining and furthering a favorable environment through relations with other structures in the society—the institutional function, in Parsons' terms.

In addition to the need for production inputs, special attention must be given to the maintenance inputs, i.e., to insuring the availability of the human energy which results in role performance. If the system is to survive, *maintenance substructures* must be elaborated to hold the walls of the social maze in place. Even these would not suffice to insure organizational survival, however. The organization exists in a changing and demanding environment, and it must adapt constantly to the changing environmental demands. *Adaptive structures* develop in organizations to generate appropriate responses to external conditions. Finally, these patterns of behavior need to be coordinated, adjusted, controlled, and directed if the complex substructures are to hold together as a unified system or organization. Hence, *managerial subsystems* are an integral part of permanent elaborated social patterning of behavior.

Thus we can describe the facts of organizational functioning with respect to five basic subsystems: (1) production subsystems concerned with the work that gets done; (2) supportive subsystems of procurement, disposal, and institutional relations; (3) maintenance subsystems for tying people into their functional roles; (4) adaptive subsystems, concerned with organizational change; (5) managerial systems for the direction, adjudication, and control of the many subsystems and activities of the structure.

Production or Technical Subsystems

The production system is concerned with the through-put, the energic or informational transformation whose cycles of activity comprise the major functions of the system. Organizations are commonly classified according to their main productive process, e.g., educational, if concerned with training, political, if concerned with affecting power relations, economic, if concerned with the creation of wealth. . . .

Supportive Subsystems

Supportive subsystems are those which carry on the environmental transactions in procuring the input or disposing of the output or aiding in these processes. They are in part a direct extension of the production activities of the organization in importing the material to be worked on or exporting the finished product. Or they may be indirectly related to the production cycle but supportive of it in maintaining a favorable environment for the operation of the system.

The relating of the system to its larger social environment in establishing its legitimation and support would be an *institutional* function. In general the top echelon of an organization, such as the Board of Trustees, would carry this function and would often have some degree of membership in outside structures. Thus supportive systems concerned with environmental transactions include the specific procurement or disposal structures as well as the more general high level activities of securing favorable relations with larger structures.

Maintenance Subsystems

Maintenance activities are not directed at the material being worked on but at the equipment for getting the work done. In most organizations this equipment consists of patterned human behavior. The arrangement of roles for interrelated performance does not guarantee that people will take or remain in these roles performing their functions. Hence subsystems for recruitment, indoctrination or socialization, rewarding and sanctioning, are found in enduring social structures. These subsystems function to maintain the fabric of interdependent behavior necessary for task accomplishment. They tie people into the system as functioning parts. They are cycles of activity which are tangential to, or criss-cross, the production cycles. Individuals may play both production and maintenance roles, as when members of a college faculty move from their teaching roles to meet as an executive committee to decide on promotions and salary increases for faculty members. In many systems, however, the same individuals do not step from one set of roles to another. The maintenance roles need not be specific to the major differentiating function of the system. The person functioning as an administrator in the maintenance structure is often a generalist who can move from one organization or type of organization to another. Indeed, a director of personnel or training in a given company probably could move more easily and with less strain to a functionally comparable position in another company than to a different subsystem in his own organization.

Whereas the supportive systems of procurement and disposal are concerned with insuring production inputs, i.e., materials and resources for the work of the organization, the maintenance system is concerned with inputs for preserving the system either through appropriate selection of personnel or adequate rewarding of the personnel selected. We have already noted the neglect of the maintenance function in traditional thinking which accepts social structures as objective and fixed in nature as biological relationships. The same neglect characterizes the world of practical action in which attention is centered on the production system and its inputs. Problems of personnel both on the recruitment and morale sides have received belated and inadequate recognition and the position of the director of these operations is generally low in the management hierarchy whether the organization is industrial or governmental.

Reward and sanctioning systems, utilized to maintain role performance, are major maintenance substructures. In social organizations rewards and sanctions are employed with respect to *specific* performances and infractions according to a set of rules. In feudal systems sanctions and rewards tended to be invoked in a more capricious manner. In the small agrarian community punitive actions towards a transgressor were based upon the outraged morality of community members and were not finely attuned to a set of particulars established about the transgressing act.

Social organizations, at least in our culture and era, move toward emphasis upon a reward system rather than a punishment system. To hold members in an organization and to maintain a satisfactory type of role performance means that people's experiences in the system must be rewarding, particularly if they have freedom to move in and out of organizations. Often one set of rewards develops to attract and hold members in a system and another to achieve some optimum level of performance.

In keeping with the relative neglect of maintenance functions is the blindness in most organizational theorizing to a significant characteristic of the reward system, namely its *allocation parameters*, or who gets what and why. The allocation of rewards in most organizations in western nations (and to a greater extent than is realized in communist countries as well) is highly differential between members of various subsystems. The problem is one of keeping people in the organizational system and keeping them motivated to perform when there are conspicuous differences in the amount of return to various subgroups in the organization. Rewards are not only monetary; they also include prestige and status, gratifications from interesting work, identification with group products, and satisfactions from decision making. The distribution of all these types of rewards is a basic dimension for understanding how an organization operates. There is a substantial correlation among the various kinds of reward; the members who are paid the most generally have the highest status, the most interesting jobs, and the opportunity to make decisions. Hence the differentials in rewards to subsystem members are even greater than the differences in monetary return would suggest.

Adaptive Subsystems

Nothing in the production, supportive, and maintenance subsystems would suffice to insure organizational survival in a changing environment. Except for the functions of procurement and disposal, these subsystems face inward; they are concerned with the functioning of the organization as it is rather than with what it might become. The risks of concentrating attention and energies inward are directly proportional to the magnitude and rate of change in the world outside the organization. External changes in taste, in cultural norms and values, in competitive organizations, in economic and political power—all these and many others reach the organization as demands for internal change. To refuse to accede to such demands is to risk the possibility that the transactions of procurement and disposal will be reduced or refused, or that the processes of maintenance will become increasingly difficult. In most formal organizations there arise, therefore, structures which are specifically concerned with sensing relevant changes in the outside world and translating the meaning of those changes for the organization. There may be structures which devote their energies wholly to the anticipation of such changes. All these comprise the adaptive subsystem of the organization and bear such names as product research, market research, long-range planning, research and development, and the like.

Managerial Subsystems

These systems comprise the organized activities for controlling, coordinating, and directing the many subsystems of the structure. They represent another slice of the organizational pattern and are made up of cycles of activities cutting across the structure horizontally to deal with coordination of subsystems and the adjustment of the total system to its environment. The functions of top management require actions affecting large sectors of organizational space, the formulation of rules rather than specific invoking of penalties for the recalcitrant member, or a change in policy to achieve better utilization of the system's resources. The exercise of the management function is observable, however, at all levels of the system. Two major types of managerial subsystems which deserve further description are *regulatory mechanisms* and the *authority structure*.

Our basic model of a social system is a structure which imports energy from the external world, transforms it, and exports a product to the environment which is the source for a reenergizing of the cycle. Substructures may develop which gather and utilize intelligence about the energic transactions. Such devices function to give feedback to the system about its output in relation to its input. Management in modern organizations operates in good part through such *regulatory mechanisms*. When a system operates without a specialized feedback or regulatory mechanism, we shall refer to it as a primitive group rather than a social organization. Voluntary groups, for example, may form from time to time and may carry on some cooperative activity. The degree of accomplishment will be the result of the number of members and their enthusiasm at the moment and will vary greatly from time to time. The group is not guided by any information about its impact upon the world or any intelligence about the contributions of its members. It may not even have a roster of its members and its new chairman may search in vain for the records of what was done under his predecessor, how it was done, and what the outcome was. A voluntary group becomes an organization when it acquires systematic methods for regulating its activities on the basis of information about its functioning. Operationally a voluntary group is identified as an organization when it has a permanent secretariat or some equivalent device for maintaining stability in the offices of secretary and treasurer with respect to membership rolls, finances, and records.

Regulatory mechanisms are highly developed in profit making organizations, and information about the market and the sale of the commodities of the enterprise is constantly used to control the productive activities of the enterprise and its actions with respect to its supply of raw materials. Regulatory mechanisms vary in complexity and sophistication, however, and very primitive mechanisms of regulation may direct the activity of large, complex systems. For example, a medical school may base its admissions upon the number of available microscopes or the size of its laboratories.

The dominant tendency is toward complexity in regulatory mechanisms. Industrial concerns utilize increasingly detailed estimates of economic trends in planning the capture of new markets. A highly significant development in modern industry is the use of electronic computers and automated devices to regulate the activities of the enterprise at two levels. Computers will be used to process all kinds of information about the internal functioning of the organization and about its environment, to guide decisions at the highest echelons about basic policies and procedures—even to help in assigning weights to various factors. Automated devices will be employed within subsystems to provide self-regulation for the performance of certain types of tasks.

The systematic use of information to guide organizational functioning is the sine qua non of an organization. The implications of such regulatory mechanisms are far-reaching. They include the elaboration of the role structure to provide for such a continuing function, and they imply the addition of other structures to coordinate the incoming information with the ongoing activities. The social system of feudalism rested more on status relationships than on highly developed role concepts and relied for stability on a combination of physical force and the mysticism of the masses. Modern role systems, however, need an intelligence function to maintain themselves.

Organizations need not be authoritarian in character, but they must possess an established and definitive form of decision making about organizational matters. The *authority structure* essentially describes the way in which the managerial system is organized with respect to the sources of decision making and its implementation. Decisions are accepted if made in the proper manner, whether by democratic vote or by an edict from duly constituted authority. The essence of authority structure is the acceptance of directives as legitimate, i.e., either the acquiescence or approval by people of rules of the game. The rules may be arrived at through a democratic process or they may be promulgated from above, but in either case they are binding upon the members of the system. They are properties of the system and not of the dominance-submission patterns of individual personalities. We recognize this when we say that a person has exceeded his authority. He has gone beyond the legitimately defined limits of his position. What has obscured this clear theoretical distinction in practice is that authoritarian personalities often select themselves or are selected for positions of power in social systems. Their personality traits may lead them to abuse this legal power in areas where it is difficult to check on their actions. The paradox is that the law enforcement agencies, whether local police, internal revenue agents, immigration authorities, or customs officials, are entrusted with carrying out the rules of the game, but often enjoy a reputation for officiousness or overstepping their authority.

People tend to personalize relationships and often impute personal despotism to the orderly functioning of the social system, confusing the exercise of legal authority with authoritarianism. Since authoritarianism is a bad thing and is the opposite of the desirable qualities of liberty and democracy, there may be rebellion against any rules of the game which the individual does not relish.

Though in some organizations decisions are democratically arrived at, they are abided by until a change is effected through the legitimized channels for change. Or the organization may be authoritarian in character, but again decisions about given types of affairs are made by some appropriate officer. Even in the democratically constructed organization, minor decision making in keeping with lines of policy as determined by majority vote will be entrusted to representatives of the group. Such delegation of power creates a hierarchy of positions within the structure even though the elected official may have to validate his authority from time to time by standing for reelection.

Thus every organization has an *executive system* for carrying out policy or the implementation of administrative decisions. In a democratic structure there is, in addition, a separate *legislative system* with the power vested in the membership to select top executives, to set policy, to choose between alternative policies of the leadership, or to veto policy proposals. In an authoritarian structure a single system may include the *executive* and *legislative* functions, and the top executives do the legislating for the organization. It is also possible for an authoritarian structure to have separate legislative and executive systems, in which an appointed or self-perpetuating board of directors sets policy and a manager and his subordinates execute it. *The essential difference between a democratic and an authoritarian system is not whether executive officers order or consult with those below them but whether the power to legislate on policy is vested in the membership or in the top echelons.*

There is an interpenetration of the authority and reward systems of an organization. The authority structure allocates decision making, and decision making is rewarding in two senses; (1) its exercise is in itself gratifying to the needs of people for participation and autonomy, and (2) it is instrumental in its power potential for achieving other objectives. Hence an authority structure democratically based in a legislative system involving the membership has a built-in reward mechanism not found in an authoritarian system. There are other types of advantages to an authoritarian system but its problems of maintenance differ radically from the democratic system. Organization theorists apart from political scientists have given scant attention to this critical difference between organization forms. In the industrial world the appeal of the unions to workers is often a mystery to industrialists who have failed to grasp the significance of democratic structure and its reward character, even in imperfect manifestation.

Ordinarily the developmental processes by which groups acquire a regulatory mechanism and an authority structure are not independent but interactive. With a regulatory mechanism goes the need for decision making about the uses to which the information will be put. So long as a primitive group can operate in terms of the enthusiasm of its particular adherents at a given time and drop to another level of activity with less motivated followers at another time, it requires only task direction which can be generated within the group itself. But when it moves over to the utilization of information about maintaining some effective ratio of energy input to energy output and some stability in the level of its operations, it needs a more permanent and definitive form of decision making. Thus the authority structure grows in response to the development of a regulatory maintenance mechanism. And conversely, as authority comes to be vested in positions in the group, its exercise is dependent upon information feedback about its functioning. The officers charged with staffing an organization need information about the amount and causes of turnover, and about the kind of people who are lost relative to those who are retained. Some regulatory feedback mechanism is needed to maintain the quantity and quality of personnel which the operations require. The top officers are concerned with the total efficiency of the operations and they will institute cost accounting systems to aid them in the exercise of their authority.

There can be a power structure in primitive groups in terms of the superior personality force of a leader, whether because of physical prowess, mental alertness, or persuasiveness. This is not, however, the same as authority structure in which the order is followed because it comes from the legitimized position in the structure rather than from a certain personality. The soldier salutes the uniform of the superior officer, not the man. The informal group of teenagers on the corner may start as a primitive group with leadership a matter of the interplay of the strongest personalities in the group. After a time a leader may emerge and the group may develop norms about how his legitimate authority should be exercised. It becomes an organization when leaders and followers decide on membership and procedures for admitting novices to membership. This process is one of regulating group functioning through information about its component parts. The gang may, for example, vote to admit Joe Smith because he is a tough fighter, Bill Brown because he has a car, and to restrict other admissions indefinitely in terms of facilities available and activities planned for the future.

The authority structure in feudal and semi-feudal systems is clear and legitimized but is less a matter of role and more a combination of role and status and personality. The noble is obeyed because of his inherited status as a noble which is irretrievably mixed up with him as a person because of the confusion of biological and social inheritance. It is the modern bureaucratic organization, as Max Weber pointed out, which has developed an authority structure of the rational-legal type whereby the rules and prerogatives of authority are quite separated from the person and personality of the wielder of authority. Some structure of authority, some criteria for allocating it, and some rules for its exercise are, however, among the common characteristics of all human organizations.

Reference

Parsons T.. 1960, *Structure and Process in Modern Societies*, New York: Free Press.

ORGANIZATIONS IN ACTION

JAMES D. THOMPSON

Variations In Technologies

Clearly, technology is an important variable in understanding the actions of complex organizations. In modern societies the variety of desired outcomes for which specific technologies areavailable seems infinite. A complete but simple typology of technologies which has found order in this variety would be quite helpful. Typologies are available for industrial production (Woodward, 1965) and for mental therapy (Hawkes, 1962) but are not general enough to deal with the range of technologies found in complex organizations. Lacking such a typology, we will simply identify three varieties which are (1) widespread in modern society and (2) sufficiently different to illustrate the propositions we wish to develop.

The Long-linked Technology
A long-linked technology involves serial interdependence in the sense that act Z can be performed only after successful completion of act Y, which in turn rests

on act X, and so on. The original symbol of technical rationality, the mass production assembly line, is of this long-linked nature. It approaches instrumental perfection when it produces a single kind of standard product, repetitively and at a constant rate. Production of only one kind of product means that a single technology is required, and this in turn permits the use of clear-cut criteria for the selection of machines and tools, construction of work-flow arrangements, acquisition of raw materials, and selection of human operators. Repetition of the productive process provides experience as a means of eliminating imperfections in the technology; experience can lead to the modification of machines and provide the basis for scheduled preventive maintenance. Repetition means that human motions can also be examined, and through training and practice, energy losses and errors minimized. It is in this setting that the scientific-management movement has perhaps made its greatest contribution.

The constant rate of production means that, once adjusted, the proportions of resources involved can be standardized to the point where each contributes to its capacity; none need be underemployed. This of course makes important contributions to the economic aspect of the technology.

The Mediating Technology

Various organizations have, as a primary function, the linking of clients or customers who are or wish to be interdependent. The commercial bank links depositors and borrowers. The insurance firm links those who would pool common risks. The telephone utility links those who would call and those who would be called. The post office provides a possible linkage of virtually every member of the modern society. The employment agency mediates the supply of labor and the demand for it.

Complexity in the mediating technology comes not from the necessity of having each activity geared to the requirements of the next but rather from the fact that the mediating technology requires operating in *standardized ways*, and *extensively*; e.g., with multiple clients or customers distributed in time and space.

The commercial bank must find and aggregate deposits from diverse depositors; but however diverse the depositors, the transaction must conform to standard terms and to uniform bookkeeping and accounting procedures. It must also find borrowers; but no matter how varied their needs or desires, loans must be made according to standardized criteria and on terms uniformly applied to the category appropriate to the particular borrower. Poor risks who receive favored treatment jeopardize bank solvency. Standardization permits the insurance organization to define categories of risk and hence to sort its customers or potential customers into appropriate aggregate categories; the insured who is not a qualified risk but is so defined upsets the probabilities on which insurance rests. The telephone company became viable only when the telephone became regarded as a necessity, and this did not occur until equipment was standardized to the point where it could be incorporated into one network. Standardization enables the employment agency to aggregate job applicants into categories which can be matched against standardized requests for employees.

Standardization makes possible the operation of the mediating technology over time and through space by assuring each segment of the organization that other segments are operating in compatible ways. It is in such situations that the bureaucratic techniques of categorization and impersonal application of rules have been most beneficial (Weber, 1947; Merton, 1957a).

The Intensive Technology

This third variety we label *intensive* to signify that a variety of techniques is drawn upon in order to achieve a change in some specific object; but the selection, combination, and order of application are determined by feedback from the object itself. When the object is human, this intensive technology is regarded as "therapeutic," but the same technical logic is found also in the construction industry (Stinchcombe, 1959) and in research where the objects of concern are nonhuman.

The intensive technology is most dramatically illustrated by the general hospital. At any moment an emergency admission may require some combination of dietary, x-ray, laboratory, and housekeeping or hotel services, together with the various medical specialties, pharmaceutical services, occupational therapies, social work services, and spiritual or religious services. Which of these, and when, can be determined only from evidence about the state of the patient.

In the construction industry, the nature of the crafts required and the order in which they can be applied depend on the nature of the object to be constructed and its setting; including, for example, terrain, climate, weather. Organized or team research may draw from a variety of scientific or technical skills, but the particular combination and the order of application depend on the nature of the problem defined.

The development of military combat teams, with a multiplicity of highly skilled capacities to be applied to the requirements of changing circumstances, represents a shift toward the intensive technology in military operations (Janowitz, 1959).

The intensive technology is a custom technology. Its successful employment rests in part on the availability of all the capacities potentially needed, but equally on the appropriate custom combination of selected capacities as required by the individual case or project.

Boundaries of Technical Rationality

Technical rationality, as a system of cause/effect relationships which lead to a desired result, is an abstraction. It is instrumentally perfect when it becomes a closed system of logic. The closed system of logic contains all relevant variables, and only relevant variables. All other influences, or *exogenous variables*, are excluded; and the variables contained in the system vary only to the extent that the experimenter, the manager, or the computer determines they should.

When a technology is put to use, however, there must be not only desired outcomes and knowledge of relevant cause/effect relationships, but also power to control the empirical resources which correspond to the variables in the logical system. A closed system of action corresponding to a closed system of logic would result in instrumental perfection in reality.

The mass production assembly operation and the continuous processing of chemicals are more nearly perfect, in application, than the other two varieties discussed above because they achieve a high degree of control over relevant variables and are relatively free from disturbing influences. Once started, most of the action involved in the long-linked technology is dictated by the internal logic of the technology itself. With the mediating technology, customers or clients intrude to make difficult the standardized activities required by the technology. And with the intensive technology, the specific case defines the component activities and their combination from the larger array of components contained in the abstract technology.

Since technical perfection seems more nearly approachable when the organization has control over all the elements involved,

Proposition 1: Under norms of rationality, organizations seek to seal off their core technologies from environmental influences.

Organizational Rationality

When organizations seek to translate the abstractions called technologies into action, they immediately face problems for which the core technologies do not provide solutions.

Mass production manufacturing technologies are quite specific, *assuming* that certain inputs are provided and finished products are somehow removed from the premises before the productive process is clogged; but mass production technologies do not include variables which provide solutions to either the input- or output-disposal problems. The present technology of medicine may be rather specific if certain tests indicate an appendectomy is in order, if the condition of the patient meets certain criteria, and if certain medical staff, equipment, and medications are present. But medical technology contains no cause/effect statements about bringing sufferers to the attention of medical practitioners, or about the provision of the specified equipment, skills, and medications. The technology of education rests on abstract systems of belief about relationships among teachers, teaching materials, and pupils; but learning theories assume the presence of these variables and proceed from that point.

One or more technologies constitute the core of all purposive organizations. But this technical core is always an incomplete representation of what the organization must do to accomplish desired results. Technical rationality is a necessary component but never alone sufficient to provide *organizational rationality*, which involves acquiring the inputs which are taken for granted by the technology, and dispensing outputs which again are outside the scope of the core technology.

At a minimum, then, organizational rationality involves three major component activities: (1) input activities, (2) technological activities, and (3) output activities. Since these are interdependent, organizational rationality requires that they be appropriately geared to one another. The inputs acquired must be within the scope of the technology, and it must be within the capacity of the organization to dispose of the technological production.

Not only are these component activities interdependent, but both input and output activities are interdependent with environmental elements. Organizational rationality, therefore, never conforms to closed-system logic but demands the logic of an open system. Moreover, since the technological activities are embedded in and interdependent with activities which are open to the environment, the closed system can never be completely attained for the technological component. Yet we have offered the proposition that organizations subject to rationality norms seek to seal off their core technologies from environmental influences. How do we reconcile these two contentions?

Proposition 2: Under norms of rationality, organizations seek to buffer environmental influences by surrounding their technical cores with input and output components.

To maximize productivity of a manufacturing technology, the technical core must be able to operate as if the market will absorb the single kind of product at a continuous rate, and as if inputs flowed continuously, at a steady rate and with specified quality. Conceivably both sets of conditions could occur; realistically they do not. But organizations reveal a variety of devices for approximating these "as if" assumptions, with input and output components meeting fluctuating environments and converting them into steady conditions for the technological core.

Buffering on the input side is illustrated by the stockpiling of materials and supplies acquired in an irregular market, and their steady insertion into the production process. Preventive maintenance, whereby machines or equipment are repaired on a scheduled basis, thus minimizing surprise, is another example of buffering by the input component. The recruitment of dissimilar personnel and their conversion into reliable performers through training or indoctrination is another; it is most dramatically illustrated by basic training or boot camp in military organizations (Dornbusch, 1955).

Buffering on the output side of long-linked technologies usually takes the form of maintaining warehouse inventories and items in transit or in distributor inventories, which permits the technical core to produce at a constant rate, but distribution to fluctuate with market conditions.

Buffering on the input side is an appropriate and important device available to all types of organizations. Buffering on the output side is especially important for mass-manufacturing organizations, but is less feasible when the product is perishable or when the object is inextricably involved in the technological process, as in the therapeutic case.

Buffering of an unsteady environment obviously brings considerable advantages to the technical core, but it does so with costs to the organization. A classic problem in connection with buffering is how to maintain inventories, input or output, sufficient to meet all needs without incurring obsolescence as needs change. Operations research recently has made important contributions toward this problem of "run out versus obsolescence," both of which are costly.

Thus while a fully buffered technological core would enjoy the conditions for maximum technical rationality, organizational rationality may call for compromises between conditions for maximum technical efficiency and the energy required for buffering operations. In an unsteady environment, then, the organization under rationality norms must seek other devices for protecting its technical core.

Proposition 3: Under norms of rationality, organizations seek to smooth out input and output transactions.

Whereas buffering absorbs environmental fluctuations, smoothing or leveling involves attempts to reduce fluctuations in the environment. Utility firms—electric, gas, water, or telephone—may offer inducements to those who use their services during "trough" periods, or charge premiums to those who contribute to "peaking."

Retailing organizations faced with seasonal or other fluctuations in demand, may offer inducements in the form of special promotions or sales during slow periods. Transportation organizations such as airlines may offer special reduced fare rates on light days or during slow seasons.

Organizations pointed toward emergencies, such as fire departments, attempt to level the need for their services by activities designed to prevent emergencies, and by emphasis on early detection so that demand is not allowed to grow to the point that would overtax the capacity of the organization. Hospitals accomplish some smoothing through the scheduling of nonemergency admissions.

Although action by the organization may thus reduce fluctuations in demand, complete smoothing of demand is seldom possible. But a core technology interrupted by constant fluctuation and change must settle for a low degree of technical rationality. What other devices do organizations employ to protect core technologies?

Proposition 4: Under norms of rationality, organizations seek to anticipate and adapt to environmental changes which cannot be buffered or leveled.

If environmental fluctuations penetrate the organization and require the technical core to alter its activities, then environmental fluctuations are exogenous variables within the logic of technical rationality. To the extent that environmental fluctuations can be anticipated, however, they can be treated as *constraints* on the technical core within which a closed system of logic can be employed.

The manufacturing firm which can correctly forecast demand for a particular time period can thereby plan or schedule operations of its technical core at a steady rate during that period. Any changes in technical operations due to changes in the environment can be made at the end of the period on the basis of forecasts for the next period.

Organizations often learn that some environmental fluctuations are patterned, and in these cases forecasting and adjustment appear almost automatic. The post office knows, for example, that in large commercial centers large volumes of business mail are posted at the end of the business day, when secretaries leave offices. Recently the post office has attempted to buffer that load by promising rapid treatment of mail posted in special locations during morning hours. Its success in buffering is not known at this writing, but meanwhile the post office schedules its technical activities to meet known daily fluctuations. It can also anticipate heavy demand during November and December, thus allowing its input components lead time in acquiring additional resources.

Banks likewise learn that local conditions and customs result in peak loads at predictable times during the day and week, and can schedule their operations to meet these shifts (Argyris, 1954).

In cases such as these, organizations have amassed sufficient experience to know that fluctuations are patterned with a high degree of regularity or probability; but when environmental fluctuations are the result of combinations of more dynamic factors, anticipation may require something more than the simple projection of previous experience. It is in these situations that forecasting emerges as a specialized and elaborate activity, for which some of the emerging management-science or statistical-decision theories seem especially appropriate.

To the extent that environmental fluctuations are unanticipated they interfere with the orderly operation of the core technology and thereby reduce its performance.

When such influences are anticipated and considered as constraints for a particular period of time, the technical core can operate as if it enjoyed a closed system.

Buffering, leveling, and adaptation to anticipated fluctuations are widely used devices for reducing the influence of the environment on the technological cores of organizations. Often they are effective, but there are occasions when these devices are not sufficient to ward off environmental penetration.

Proposition 5: When buffering, leveling, and forecasting do not protect their technical cores from environmental fluctuations, organizations under norms of rationality resort to rationing.

Rationing is most easily seen in organizations pointed toward emergencies, such as hospitals. Even in nonemergency situations hospitals may ration beds to physicians by establishing priority systems for nonemergency admissions. In emergencies, such as community disasters, hospitals may ration pharmaceutical dosages or nursing services by dilution—by assigning a fixed number of nurses to a larger patient population. Mental hospitals, especially state mental hospitals, may ration technical services by employing primarily organic-treatment procedures—electroshock, drugs, insulin—which can be employed more economically than psychoanalytic or *milieu* therapies (Belknap, 1956). Teachers and caseworkers in social welfare organizations may ration effort by accepting only a portion of those seeking service, or if not empowered to exercise such discretion, may concentrate their energies on the more challenging cases or on those which appear most likely to yield satisfactory outcomes (Blau, 1955).

But rationing is not a device reserved for therapeutic organizations. The post office may assign priority to first-class mail, attending to lesser classes only when the priority task is completed. Manufacturers of suddenly popular items may ration allotments to wholesalers or dealers, and if inputs are scarce, may assign priorities to alternative uses of those resources. Libraries may ration book loans, acquisitions, and search efforts (Meier, 1963).

Rationing is an unhappy solution, for its use signifies that the technology is not operating at its maximum. Yet some system of priorities for the allocation of capacity under adverse conditions is essential if a technology is to be instrumentally effective—if action is to be other than random.

The Logic of Organizational Rationality

Core technologies rest on closed systems of logic, but are invariably embedded in a larger organizational rationality which pins the technology to a time and place, and links it with the larger environment through input and output activities. Organizational rationality thus calls for an open-system logic, for when the organization is opened to environmental influences, some of the factors involved in organizational action become *constraints*; for some meaningful period of time they are not variables but fixed conditions to which the organization must adapt. Some of the factors become *contingencies*, which may or may not vary, but are not subject to arbitrary control by the organization.

Organizational rationality therefore is some result of (1) constraints which the organization must face, (2) contingencies which the organization must meet, and (3) variables which the organization can control.

Recapitulation

Perfection in technical rationality requires complete knowledge of cause/effect relations plus control over all of the relevant variables, or closure. Therefore, under norms of rationality (Prop. 1), organizations seek to seal off their core technologies from environmental influences. Since complete closure is impossible (Prop. 2), they seek to buffer environmental influences by surrounding their technical cores with input and output components.

Because buffering does not handle all variations in an unsteady environment, organizations seek to smooth input and output transactions (Prop. 3), and to anticipate and adapt to environmental changes which cannot be buffered or smoothed (Prop. 4), and finally, when buffering, leveling, and forecasting do not protect their technical cores from environmental fluctuations (Prop. 5), organizations resort to rationing.

These are maneuvering devices which provide the organization with some self-control despite interdependence with the environment. But if we are to gain understanding of such maneuvering, we must consider both the direction toward which maneuvering is designed and the nature of the environment in which maneuvering takes place.

References

Argyris, Chris: *Executive Leadership*, New York: Harper & Row, Publishers, Incorporated, 1953.

Belknap, Ivan: *The Human Problems of a State Mental Hospital*, New York: McGraw-Hill Book Company, 1956.

Blau, Peter M.: *The Dynamics of Bureaucracy*, Chicago: The University of Chicago Press, 1955.

Dornbusch, Sanford M.: "The Military Academy as an Assimilating Institution," *Social Forces*, Vol. 33, May, 1955, pp. 316-321.

Hawkes, Robert W.: "Physical Psychiatric Rehabilitation Models Compared", paper presented to the Ohio Valley Sociological Society, 1962.

Janowitz, Morris: "Changing Patterns of Organizational Authority: The Military Establishment," *Administrative Science Quarterly*, Vol. 3, March, 1959, pp. 473-493.

Meir, Richard L.: "Communications Overload," *Administrative Science Quarterly*, Vol 7, March, 1963, pp. 521-544.

Merton, Robert K.: "Bureaucratic Structure and Personality," in Robert K. Merton (Ed.), *Social Theory and Social Structure* (Rev. Ed.), New York: The Free Press of Glencoe, 1957a.

Stinchcombe, Arthur L.: "Bureaucratic and Craft Administration of Production: A Comparative Study," *Administrative Science Quarterly*, Vol. 4, September, 1959, pp. 168-187.

Weber, Max: *The Theory of Social and Economic Organization*, A. M. Henderson and Talcott Parsons (trans.), and Talcott Parsons (Ed.), New York: The Free Press of Glencoe, 1947.

Woodward, Joan: *Industrial Organization: Theory and Practice*, London: Oxford University Press, 1965.

LINKING AN INNOVATIVE SUBSYSTEM INTO THE SYSTEM

ROLF P. LYNTON

> Innovation . . . is not so much the adoption of objects by individuals as it is the acceptance of ideas by (people in) an organization. (Andrews and Greenfield, 1966:81)
>
> Any research process . . . has an inbuilt tendency towards the formation of a relatively closed system, in which self-generated intakes crowd out intakes from the external environment. . . . A major problem is to steer between . . . creative research activities that are irrelevant and . . . relevant research activities that are uncreative. (Miller and Rice, 1967:159-160)

Formal organizational devices for facilitating change in social institutions, particularly institutions in environments characterized by increasing differentiation and complexity, are largely integrative devices. It is on these integrative devices that this paper will concentrate.[1]

Integrative devices provide linkage in two crucial areas: (1) between the institution and its specific publics of consumers and suppliers, as well as its wider public of political and social sanction, which determines the relevance of the institution; and (2) between different parts within the institution, which determines the extent to which the institution operates as a unit.

Both these linkages link subsystems and are commonly themselves subsystems. This paper focuses on systems providing a specified kind of service or material goods which have outgrown the possibility of attaining optimal integration through interpersonal, spontaneous, face-to-face contact, and therefore require formal integrative devices.

In classical organization theory the dominant criterion for this classification was size: a system greater than a given size required formal devices, a smaller system did not. Recent empirical research findings indicate that the degree of differentiation, and therefore the need for integration, correlates much more closely with the degrees of uncertainty in technology and markets than with absolute size (Downs, 1968; Harvey, 1968; Lorsch, 1965). The focus of this paper therefore is on systems (1) that need to cope with high degrees of uncertainty, and (2) that have developed subsystems to develop innovations for the system. In industry, organizations manufacturing electronic apparatus and certain chemicals are examples of such a system; and research and development departments are an example of such a subsystem.

Assessment of Uncertainties

The accuracy with which decision makers in the system assess uncertainties

Reprinted by permission of the author and the publisher from *Administrative Science Quarterly*, vol. 14, no. 3 (Sept. 1969), pp. 398-414.

for the system guides formal differentiation within the system as well as the design of integrating devices. There are two basic models for this assessment. One model treats uncertainties as a succession of discrete stimuli to which the system needs to respond with appropriate innovations. In this model differentiation and integration are functions of the frequency and force of the expected stimuli. It is a model that has affinities with familiar stimulus-response models in learning theory and with the early formulations of an administrator's functions in terms of weight and frequency of decision making. The integrative devices appropriate to this assessment are linkages of minimal complexity and duration. As stimuli for innovative responses increase in frequency, temporary and informal devices may become permanent and formal, but the kinds of devices and their limitations will not change unless the model of assessment changes. The other model treats uncertainties as a continuous general state requiring a continuously varying response from the whole system. This model treats the system and its environment as in continuous interaction in uncertainty and as aiming to achieve and maintain a steady state in and through this interaction. Emery uses the word, "turbulence" to describe the environment in this model (1967:225).

The spontaneous response to a turbulent environment is to reduce the turbulence. The first model aims at reducing the complexity and uncertainty by segmentation or dissociation, which are essentially the defense mechanisms that lead to passive adaptation. The second model aims at establishing hierarchies of goals, which may then serve as guides to behavior, i.e., to allocating attention and other resources to causal strands on the basis of established priorities. Through the development of such codes, the field is no longer perceived as turbulent. Questions about the values themselves, and of the transformation of values into priorities and codes, will not be pursued in this paper, though the later discussion of institutionalized linkages could be analyzed in terms of the values that could emerge from the interactions they encourage (Emery, 1967:225, 229). In the first model, the cost of the responses is a permanent ceiling on the rate of innovation; in the second model, costs occur from the slower rate of innovation due to various rigidities associated with the acceptance and revision of codes.

This paper treats the environment as turbulent and explores the kind of appropriate response by the system, particularly, the design and operation of linkage devices. Figure 1 illustrates the basic two-directional schema for this paper.

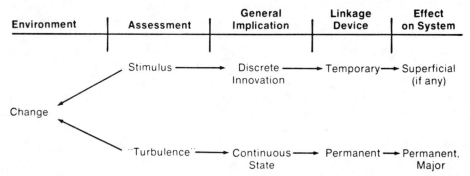

Figure 1. Two models of assessing environmental uncertainties and characteristic linkages.

The empirical data to be introduced and analyzed at some length in later sections of the paper show a heavy incidence of failure for *ad hoc* and temporary linkage devices. They refer to situations in which linkages were designed to perform some specific function(s) and failed to do so. Actually an unrecorded kind of failure may be more serious, namely the system rigidities that the introduction of the inadequate linkages reinforced. The basic weakness of the discrete stimulus-innovation model shows up most sharply when the intended linkage *succeeds*. For there is no evidence that the successful integration of two or three subsystems increases the degree of integration of the system as a whole; on the contrary, commonly, a well-integrated subsystem (or a set of subsystems) may become isolated, and then it and the rest of the system become rigid separately, in defense against one another. Katz and Kahn (1966:390) state that "the major error is to disregard the systemic properties of the organization and to confuse individual change with modifications in organizational variables." Very little of the growing literature on innovation and its diffusion has been attentive to this problem. The prevailing focus of attention is on the individual innovator when he adopts an innovation, why, etc. (Rogers, 1962), not on the organizational setting in which innovation takes place. The early sociological role studies may have unwittingly supported this orientation. In the rural economy the typical adopter was an individual farmer rather than a collectivity, such as an organization. Even in later studies the influence of the larger social setting on the farmer-innovator tended to be underestimated. Studies of innovation in educational systems, like schools of various kinds and school districts, either show a lack of available knowledge about the functioning of organizations and communities or suffer from a kind of great-man orientation (Ross, 1958; Carlson, 1964). In anthropological studies too, the properties of a particular innovation and its diffusion across systems and integration within systems have been overemphasized without corresponding attention to the dynamics and functioning of the receiving organization. Gallagher (1963) discussed the power structure in innovation receiving systems, the actual prestige of advocates of the innovation, and other matters influencing if and how an innovation would be integrated into the local organization. But his primary focus too is on the substance of the particular innovation, taking the local system itself as a kind of unmodifiable ground against which the innovation showed up starkly. The currently widespread emphasis on the importance of "dissemination of research findings" seems to continue the popular view that the content or demonstrated efficacy of a particular innovation as such is crucial in determining whether it will be adopted and used effectively. In short, to use an image from Gestalt psychology, specific planned change attempts have most typically been "in figure," occupying the focus of attention, which the organization itself has remained "the ground." That this model commonly persists in the face of growing experience of its inadequacy indicates its long antecedents in history and also the deep reluctance many decision makers seem to feel about making major system changes that may be required to interact effectively with a turbulent environment. They prefer to assess the uncertainty as small and the response to it as routine, whereas it might be more useful to take as a primary target the improvement of system dynamics, specifically the linkage design. To continue the analogy then, this paper treats linkage design as "figure," and innovative needs as "ground."

In Emery's formulation (1966), turbulent environments require the linkage of dissimilar subsystems whose goals correlate positively, i.e., subsystems which are not in competition, cannot take over the role of the other. Therefore linkages between them will tend to maximize cooperation. As Thompson (1967) has shown, such a matrix can take several shapes, but all provide for two aspects: (1) that which links the system to the environment, through which broad social sanctioning is secured and the system is attuned to the needs of the environment and (2) that linkage which enables subsystems to engage in effective joint search for common ground rules, while retaining the degree of privacy, protection, and autonomy they need to carry out their distinctive functions.

The strategic objective then has to be formulated in terms of institutionalization. As institutionalization becomes a prerequisite for achieving a steady state in a turbulent environment, then subsystem goals have to be found and formulated, which accord with system goals and which offer a maximum convergence between its subsystems.

System Differentiation

Effective linkage presupposes appropriate differentiation, which is in turn required by new task complexities. As these occur, subsystems need to be built to deal with primary tasks. Over time, successive levels of differentiation can be established, each reaching primary production systems. The primary task differentiates one subsystem from other subsystems at the same organizational level, and also from subsystems at higher and lower levels of the hierarchy (Lorsch, 1965:151; Lawrence and Lorsch, 1967:213; Miller and Rice, 1967:157; Thompson, 1967).

Appropriate differentiation has three possible dimensions: technology, territory, and time; and Miller (1959) states: "Task performance is impaired if subsystems . . . are differentiated along any other dimension than these." He indicates that at any one organizational level, these three dimensions can have seven possible combinations.

Types of task dependence have been classified in some detail by Herbst (1958), Emery (1958), and Thompson (1967). It is relevant here to consider how, at a given level of differentiation, the subsystems of a larger system are all dependent on supplies, equipment, and services, and are interdependent for the attainment of the goal of the larger system. Emery's (1958) study classifies interdependence into simultaneous or successional, and classifies successional dependence further into cyclic, convergent, or divergent. He also distinguishes between simple and complex dependence and between reciprocal and nonreciprocal dependence. Thompson (1967) presents a simpler typology of interdependence: "pooled," "sequential," and "reciprocal." Lorsch and Lawrence (1968) used Thompson's typology to distinguish between organizations having different degrees of differentiation and using different linkage devices.

While subsystems have in common "an inherent centrifugal tendency" (Parsons, 1956), Miller (1959) noted some particular tendencies associated with differentiation by technology, territory, or time. Differentiation by technology tended to make the preservation of distinctiveness a primary task of the subsystem (for example, demarcation disputes between skilled craftsmen). Differentiation by territory led subsystems to develop a special climate and culture, a particular proficiency. The most complex tendencies were associated with differentiation by time, e.g., tasks with different time cycles or organized on different shifts (Trist, 1963; Lawrence with Lorsch, 1967).

Three of Litwak's (1961) mechanisms of segregation seem to overlap with Miller's for determining points of development at which a shift from one form of structure to another is to be made. His "transferral occupations" arise in the linkage subsystem which this paper examines.

Research versus Operations

Since linkage devices between research and development subsystem(s) and operating subsystem(s) in industrial systems best illustrate the main issues, most of the data for this paper were drawn from studies in industry. Research scientists and operating personnel differ sharply in all three major dimensions of differentiation. In technology, the researcher deals with nonuniform processes, the man in operations with uniform or nonuniform, but programmed, processes (Perrow, 1967); in territory, the two systems are usually kept physically apart, often to avoid conflict (Litwak, 1961); in time, research scientists have longer-range concerns and expect much later gratification from feedback about the results of their work than operating personnel (Lawrence and Lorsch, 1967:35, 36).

The differences are extreme in organizations in which research scientists have great freedom in their choice of problems and procedures. In these cases, the norms and organization of the research department approximate those of an academic environment (Litwak 1961:183). Burns and Stalker (1961:225, 229) maintain that the "prima donna" scientist is actually a more familiar figure in the electronics industry than in the academic world. The characteristic norms of innovative subsystems include: high energy devoted to "novel, significant, focused, internalized, shared goals"; "esprit de corps," "mutual identification with peers"; high autonomy and spontaneity, with freedom for creative experimentation"; and high involvement and commitment (Miles, 1964:655). The researcher's commitment tends to be to the task or to the discipline, whereas the operating personnel's commitment is to the organization; he therefore responds to the sender's recognized research status, whereas operating personnel responds to the level of administrative authority (Smith, 1966:58). He tends to be a younger person than persons of equivalent rank in operations and to have more years of formal education than they (Dalton, 1950). The differentiation between research and operations is marked further by a series of interlocking signs and differences of conduct, for example, different working hours and differences in dress and leisure pursuits (Burns and Stalker, 1961:186).

The differentiation between research and operating subsystems in industry seems then to be institutionalized at all levels: image and self-image (personal), face-to-face relations (interpersonal), organizational structure (inter-subsystem). Moreover, although differentiated groupings tend to be self-perpetuating, special technological factors reinforce this tendency in the case of research and operating subsystems. For research generates further problems for research, and these tend to crowd out problems on which other subsystems would prefer the researchers to work.

"Research institutions have therefore a natural tendency to become increasingly divorced from their (organizational) environments and their boundaries to become increasingly impermeable" (Miller and Rice, 1967:157). Yet, although researchers prefer to work on their own problems, they may need access to data and certainly do need resources from other subsystems. These needs leave important aspects of control and power in the hands of other kinds of people and other kinds of subsystems. In short, technological factors inherent in the research process exaggerate the centrifugal tendencies of research subsystems (Havelock, 1967:23-24), and feedback loops that tend to develop between individuals in subsystems and restrict communication in self-confirming, stabilizing ways are especially tight in this case (Miles, 1964:644). In such sharply separated subsystems, members have even greater difficulty than usual in understanding the language of the members of other subsystems (Burns and Stalker, 1961:155, 174; Kahn *et al.*, 1964:133; Kast and Rosenzweig, 1962:325-326), for each perceives and internalizes those aspects of any new situation that relate specifically to the activities and goals of his subsystem (Dearborn and Simon, 1958:149-144; Barnes, 1960:3-4). In these circumstances, misunderstandings are a common occurrence and tensions are normal. In an atmosphere of tension, joint decision processes between research and operating subsystems then tend to be characterized by bargaining rather than problem solving (Pondy, 1967:319). Some of the characteristics of this bargaining are "careful rationing of information and its deliberate distortion; rigid, formal, circumscribed relations; (and) suspicion, hostility and disassociation" among the subsystems (Pondy, 1967:319; Burns and Stalker, 1961:192, 194; Kahn *et al.*, 1964:134; Litterer, 1963:405-407; Chandler, 1963:154). Shepard (1956) summarized the differences in outlook between the researcher and the operations man along seven dimensions: Table 1.

TABLE 1. Researcher vs. Operations Man: Differential Perceptions of Seven Items.*

	Researcher	Operations man
Research	Future-oriented, perhaps distant future	Focused on present, or just beyond
Identification of researcher	His profession	The company
Research results	Published achievements	Guarded secrets
Research budget	Based on research requirements	Based on company needs
Authority for research	Shared among scientists	Delegated by management
Organization of research	Project groups	Functional groups
Complexity of research management	Desirable fulfillment of managerial competence	Undesirable regression into poor administrative practice

* After Shepard (1956).

These rigidities and negative attitudes provide the potential for conflict. Joan Woodward found that "hostility between research and production personnel . . . probably exaggerated in turn the differentiation based on task differences. This was a noticeable feature of all the large batch and unit production firms studied" (1965:149-151). Studies in a variety of settings show that conflict and tension add strong impetus to the centrifugal tendencies of differentiation. In this atmosphere the parties each have a set to expect conflict and therefore may perceive conflict even when none exists (Pondy, 1967:319). This separation involves high cost. Miller (1959) found that the higher the degree of tension, the smaller the energy directly invested in the pursuit of the objectives of subsystems or of those of the system as a whole (see also Hermann, 1963).

Hypotheses

It is now possible to focus more systematically on the main thesis of this paper. In a turbulent environment, institutions must innovate to survive. Some institutions have differentiated subsystems with the primary task of working out innovative responses to the turbulent environment for the whole system. This task is inherently different in technology, territory, and time from the tasks of other subsystems. Adoption of the innovative products of the subsystem by other subsystems is essential to the effective response of the system to its environment; therefore, innovative and operational subsystems need to be appropriately linked.

On the assumptions that the decision makers of a system are in control of the system's response and that they act rationally, the degree of innovation and the mechanisms of differentiation and of integration depend on the decision makers' assessment of the changing environment. Down's (1968) study explores some personality factors and develops a concept of "sunk costs" to deal with various patterns of disposing of resources in the system and the tendencies these patterns induce over time. Using assessment for this totality, even without examining its components, may at least indicate that important complexities may be worth studying in this connection and are not to be obscured by the more familiar label "perception."

Assessment, as used in this paper, is a function of the decision makers' joint preference for the goal of the institution after taking into account the costs of innovation. It is therefore both how the decision makers assess the environment and the terms in which they rationally explain the innovation and the mechanisms that they institute for it. In this model the decision makers' dominant assessment of environmental requirements for change is the independent variable, and differentiation and linkage devices are dependent variables.

Four major assessments are possible, each of which can lead to a hypothesis. They are ordered here in their historical sequence which also corresponds to ascending degrees of system change. Relating these situations and hypotheses to the two models shown in Figure 1, Hypotheses 2 and 3 restate the first model, and hypothesis 4 the second.

1. The decision makers see "nothing," "no need to change," therefore any need for change that actually arises will be met by *ad hoc* and informal arrangements, e.g., by individuals adjusting their roles.

Hypothesis 1. If, in a turbulent environment, decision makers assess the need for change as negligible, system differentiation and linkage will then be minimal and unorganized, and the effects on system structure will be negligible.

2. The decision makers assess the need to change as temporary, and will organize to meet it by temporary measures, such as meetings and temporary allocations of resources. In short, they will treat it as a project.

Hypothesis 2. If, in a turbulent environment, decision makers assess the need for change as temporary, they will tend to expect the ratio of benefits and costs to be most favorable if they institute temporary differentiation and linkages; the effects of innovation on system structure will then be small and unpredictable.

3. The decision makers assess the need for change as frequent, but specific, and differentiate a permanent subsystem to deal with these specific changes, while the institution as a whole will proceed as before.

Hypothesis 3. If, in a turbulent environment, decision makers assess the need for change as frequent and specific: (a) they will formally differentiate an innovative subsystem, but limit its linkages to specific purposes and (b) when this kind of device and procedure is found to be ineffective, additional system changes will tend to take the form of further differentiation of innovative subsystems, not of changing the linkage devices and procedures.

4. The decision makers assess turbulence in the environment as a continuous state, which calls for sensitive, multifaceted, often unpredictable, and general innovative responses from the system as a whole. Differentiation and integration are major then foci of attention—for system design and preventive maintenance. Subsystems become sharply differentiated and deliberately linked on a permanent basis, and innovation affects the whole institution to a major extent.

Hypothesis 4. If, in a turbulent environment, decision makers assess the need for change as continuous and major, they will tend to differentiate innovative subsystems clearly and integrate them closely into the rest of the system; the effects on the system as a whole will then be major.

The rest of the paper examines the linkage mechanisms characteristic for these four situations and hypotheses.

Need for Change Assessed as Negligible

Situations in which responses within the normal range of adaptation of the system as currently constituted and of the individuals in it can cope with changes in the environment are outside the scope of this paper. Its proper scope begins only when the integrative needs exceed normal adaptation. This commonly occurs imperceptibly as a system grows. If such a discrepancy occurs and persists unattended, unplanned linkage devices find their way into the system's routine workings. In society at large, these unplanned mechanisms are most widely diffused in the form of new norms through literature, art, folklore, mythology, beliefs, mores, orientations, "small talk," etiquette, and through institutional practices of many kinds (Thayer, 1968:241). This list, certainly from folklore onwards, could be applied to any institution. In industry, "management's attempts toward integration may just happen over time, arise as temporary expedients, or emerge as a solution to a crisis situation" (Jasinsky, 1964:329).

At some stage there is an innovator, perhaps a scientist, or a workman. The initiative for informal attempts on linkage usually lies with this innovator. The point here is that, for application, the innovation requires the involvement of people who are different from the innovative person, and who will perceive him as a stranger or agitator (Inkeles, 1951:38-135; Katz and Lazarsfeld, 1955:162-208). Such informal personal linkage makes it possible to appreciate the roots from which formal differentiation and linkage devices commonly grow. Figure 2 illustrates the position of the informal direct linker in an undifferentiated system.

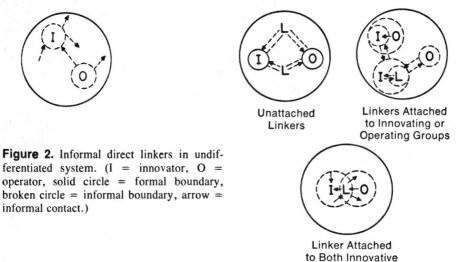

Unattached
Linkers

Linkers Attached
to Innovating or
Operating Groups

Figure 2. Informal direct linkers in undifferentiated system. (I = innovator, O = operator, solid circle = formal boundary, broken circle = informal boundary, arrow = informal contact.)

Linker Attached
to Both Innovative
and Operating Groups

Figure 3. Informal third-party linkers in undifferentiated system. (L = linker, I = innovator, O = operator, solid circle = informal boundary, arrow = informal contact.)

Kahn and his colleagues (1964:125-136) found that innovative activity was associated "significantly and positively with both the degree of role conflict ($p \ll 0.01$) and the amount of tension that the role occupant experienced on the job ($p \ll 0.05$)." The innovator's interpersonal conflicts were "fought out around his proposals for innovation and vary in intensity according to the orientation of decision makers towards innovative functions." His intra-role conflicts arose from his characteristic impatience with uniform and routine procedures and from the lack of trust he felt "in (his) role senders, irrespective of the degree of conflict ($p \ll 0.06$)." He "had significantly less communication than others with their role senders ($p \ll 0.02$)," was also more self-confident in the face of role conflict than persons in uniform work ($p \ll 0.02$), was more highly involved than others in his job ($p \ll 0.05$), and attached more importance to his job relative to other areas of life than people in less innovative roles ($p \ll 0.05$).

The emergence and enthusiasm of such an innovator in the system certainly expands the system's capacity for adaptation, but the cost of informal linkage increases as the expanded limits in turn prove to be too narrow (Burns and Stalker, 1961). Where the main force of innovative activity is concentrated in an energetic scientist-entrepreneur, the linkage problems may overwhelm him.

Linkage may be attempted by an informal third party, most commonly a draughtsman, engineer, sales agent, or purchasing agent. Litwak (1961) calls their role a "transferral occupation." The studies of Burns and Stalker (1961:177) and Woodward (1965:138) are replete with cases in which managers either attach draughtsmen and engineers to development or to production, in the hope that they will "just get along" with their colleagues within the confines of normal bureaucratic rules, or leave them unattached to find their own place in the organization. Figure 3 illustrates the position of the informal third party in such an undifferentiated system.

Kahn and his colleagues conclude that "concentrating the functions of organizational liaison on a very few positions . . . risks much in a few hands, forces a search for champions to fill the crucial positions, and is likely to create inter-organization struggle to insure that their interests will be well represented by the overworked representative" (1964:392-393). The concepts of marginality and tolerated deviance occur again and again in the literature concerning linkage and, along with them, the thought that these marginal men need bases from which to work effectively (Woodward, 1965:142).

Need for Change Assessed as Temporary and Infrequent

The logical response to needs assessed as temporary is to devise correspondingly temporary linkages, a particular type of what Matthew Miles (1964) terms "temporary systems." This paper deals only with situations where this assessment in fact is mistaken, since situations of turbulence are assumed to require permanent linkage devices of a pervasive kind. The situation here differs from that examined in the preceding section, in that (1) the decision makers do see the need for a response beyond the routine capacity of the system; and (2) linkage is made a formal occupation, albeit a temporary one. Formality means more security for the linker at the cost of more constraint. Whereas in the informal situation, the choice of attempting linkage activities, and the manner and timing, were largely the linker's, now the decision makers are likely to play a significant part in initiating, designing and controlling the linkage activities to conform to their assessment. The decision makers' direct interest makes the linker(s) *their* representative. This, in reverse, can give the linker(s) access to possible power and coercion over the people and groups involved in the problem. Figure 4 illustrates formal temporary linkers in a system with no innovative subsystem.

Linkage devices for this situation include temporarily freeing a staff member from his usual activities in order "to deal with the situation," *ad hoc* meetings of people involved in a change, calling in outside consultants, and sending some staff member(s) for training. The first three usually have overtones of "troubleshooting" and of latent coercion by decision makers and their representatives. The question here is whether these overtones promote effective linkage, deter it, or make no difference. The Lawrence and Lorsch (1967) study of within-system linkers found that access to coercive power was not associated with effective linkage. In two high-performing (innovative) companies the linkers were seen as very competent, and the subsystem managers ascribed their influence over decisions to this competence. The linkers in four low-performing (non-innovative) companies on the other hand, were accorded an important voice in decisions "because of the formal

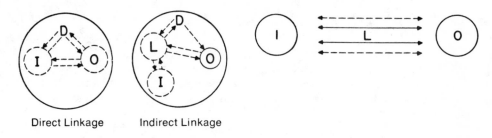

Direct Linkage   Indirect Linkage

Figure 4. Formal temporary linkers in system with no innovation subsystem. (L = linker, D = decision makers, I = innovator, O = operator, solid circle = formal boundary, broken circle = informal boundary, arrow = informal contact.)

Figure 5. Linkages between innovative subsystem and other subsystems.

authority given them by top management and their close reporting relationship to top managers'' (Lawrence and Lorsch, 1967:65-66).

Linkage activities in the lower-performing companies appeared to have many aspects characteristic of bargaining. Some linkers in this situation tried to avoid personal contact and preferred to resolve problems through formal memoranda. Similarly Strauss (1962:182) found that linkers tended to expect that people in affected departments would not change their minds.

Resort to authority and coercion can be very tempting: forcing people to make the specific changes required seems quick and easily controllable, that is, inexpensive. Since the need is specific, it does not seem necessary that people should change their minds or appreciate the change. Many studies report *ad hoc* meetings that are so overshadowed by the latent power of absent decision makers, that joint decisions are avoided on the grounds that top management will make its own decision anyway (Lawrence and Lorsch, 1967:66; Burns and Stalker, 1961; Woodward, 1965). These meetings then serve either ritualistic purposes only or become rather elaborate and ill-constituted mechanisms for exchanging information. The ineffective use of time is itself costly, but the indirect costs of such coercion are likely to be higher still. For in a turbulent environment needs for change recur, and meeting these needs by coercion, open or implied, increases resistance to future changes and decreases initiative by people required to direct the changes.

Many decision makers who assess the need for change as temporary seek to reduce the costs of internal disturbance by contracting for temporary assistance from outside the system. Consultants are seen as offering the advantages, not so much of expertise beyond that of employees in the system, but of the outsider free of the normative and interpersonal constraints of the system, and free also of the need to carry on simultaneously their usual activities. Consultants clearly *are* temporary. In their turn, consultants who conceive of their task as consisting of diagnosis and prescription may thereby support the assessment of the decision makers that the need for change is temporary and specific, and call only for a response equally temporary and specific.

Another means of dealing with linkage in this setting is to change some of the staff members who are important in the linkage process. This may be done by replacing personnel who have been unable to cope with the needs for change by others who are "better at getting on with people." The replacement may be temporary or permanent, depending on the frequency and importance of new linkages and alternative dispositions of staff resources. Changing the staff may also be attempted through training, particularly training in attitudes and interpersonal and organizational skills. The studies of Miles and others of innovation in educational systems indicate that changes of this kind call for *additional* linkage—that between the temporary training system and the parent system. The success of action decisions taken in the temporary system depends not only on the quality of these decisions, but also on the sophistication with which members have been able to anticipate the strategic problems they will encounter upon their return (Miles, 1964:484). Miles (1964:643) reported that in one three-day conference of a management team devoted to the improvement of operations in a chemical plant, the members agreed on a list of 47 action decisions, specified deadlines, and identified the persons responsible for ensuring action. When the consultant pointed to the need for some mechanism to guide implementation and cope with new problems, the top manager declared that implementation could easily be accomplished "through the regular line organization"; yet it was clear that the inability of the line organization to cope with these problems had necessitated the conference.

The probable usefulness of training, as of any other temporary devices for dealing with change, is enhanced if the decision makers of the system themselves take part in the temporary system, for studies show that recommendations are then more likely to be accepted (Miles, 1964). But this participation of decision makers also seems to ensure that any action recommendations will be moderate. This is merely another way of saying that meeting the realistic needs of the system is at variance with the constraints of normal system operations. That is the dilemma with which decision makers in these situations seem unable to cope.

Need for Change Perceived as Frequent, But Specific

When decision makers assess the need for change as frequent but still discrete, then the costs of setting up a formal subsystem with the primary task of designing innovations for the system as a whole are seen as justified. But the change is still conceived as an addition to the system, not as a reshaping of the system as a whole for innovation.

The input for the new subsystem may be proposed by the decision makers, by others in the system, or by members in the new subsystem. The output of the new subsystem is expected to be innovative ideas which the rest of the system will then decide to use or not to use. The task of the subsystem is conceived as terminating with communicating the ideas clearly enough for decision makers to understand and so make their decisions rationally. Linkage mechanisms are then conceived as bridges across the gap that is recognized as existing between the differentiated innovative subsystem and other subsystems. Figure 5 illustrates this concept of linkage as bridging the gap between subsystems.

In their study of Scottish engineering units, Burns and Stalker (1961:194-198) described three situations of this type in different companies. In each, a newcomer was brought in to head a new, innovative subsystem. For each system, successful innovation was "quite essential" for survival as an "independent business with its own capacity to compete with others and to expand." In each case, the innovative subsystem was unable to get innovative ideas accepted, and its manager resigned.

Case 1: A new chief development engineer was brought in on the explicit understanding "that he should take over an increasing share of the general management, i.e., of production as well as of design," and so he himself would be an important linkage of the development subsystem with other subsystems. In fact, he was confined by decision makers to acting as a consultant, supplying technical information at the stage of negotiations for contracts with customers. At a critical point in his endeavors to extend his authority beyond the design department, he proposed a plan for reorganizing the system. He was immediately offered a rise in salary and a new title, but no significant organizational change. He resigned.

Case 2: To render it independent of obsolescent products and methods, an established company brought in an industrial scientist to take charge of the laboratory group. His understanding was that he would "take over the whole technical side and be responsible for technical development." After two years the scientist regarded this venture as "wholly unsuccessful". . . . Everything I've put up has been blocked . . . none accepted. It's been their view that whether or not such and such a development takes place is just not my affair; this is the manufacturer's concern . . . and similarly the question of how something is to be developed and produced." Prior to the scientist's resignation, after three years, interaction between him and the managing director in the adjoining office had ceased altogether.

Case 3: Following the Second World War, the directors of the third company decided to engage an industrial scientist as head of the research and development unit to do exploratory work among recent innovations and possible markets. The new research and technical manager was quickly effective in extending the firm's range of materials and processes along traditional lines, and in increasing technical sales. But these very successes, then, locked him into short-term activities with operating subsystems. When a major opportunity occurred for developing substitute plastic materials, he was not given the resources to explore it. Instead the scientist was appointed manager of a new department in addition to continuing as head of the research and development unit. (Development work then became "virtually impossible," while production in the new department was held back by traditional inappropriate practices.) So he too resigned.

Although the newcomer was placed formally on the same level as the departmental and functional managers immediately below the managing director, the role allowed him in practice added to the existing structure and was external to it: he was not permitted to infringe on the control exercised by established members of management. As a result, he was forced to act in a consultant, advisory role, while members of the established hierarchy retained the decision making and control functions. That is, the innovative subsystem had been appended, and no allowance had been made for altering the fields of control in the system structure. This happens, conclude Burns and Stalker (1961:199), "when a special person or organized group of persons is designated as the agent of change and the existing organization is relegated to the role of spectator or patient."

The issue of significant structural change tends to be evaded in two ways. First, difficulties in effecting changes are ascribed to personal conflicts. Given the view of decision makers that an innovative subsystem is an addition, they then see any conflict as arising from the newcomers' personal interest in acquiring more control than they need. Factors of status and power develop and find expressions in increasingly devious and intractable ways, until system weaknesses are translated wholly into personal terms. Then, since experiences like these, being painful, are likely to be repressed rather than examined, disentangled and shared, this personal focus will tend to perpetuate the structure of the system.

The second way in which the significant system changes are evaded is by faulty system responses to difficulties that the subsystem has in effecting linkage. Although the difficulties really originate in the inadequate design and operation of linkage mechanism, decision makers respond by instituting further changes in the innovative subsystem itself. One change is to assign members of the innovative subsystem additional responsibilities in operating subsystems. Such a combination of roles does not prevent failure (Burns and Stalker, 1961; Havelock, 1964:25; Lawrence and Lorsch, 1967), although Palz and Andrews (1966) consistently reported that scientists and engineers in industrial research and development departments who participated in management and knowledge dissemination were more effective and productive also as scientists, as judged by publications and by peer ratings of their scientific excellence and overall usefulness. There may be a cause-and-effect confusion here which only further empirical study can clarify: does such scientific productivity tend to lead to effective participation in the system? Or, does effective and acknowledged membership in the general system tend to promote scientific productivity? Another possibility is suggested by Sieber's (1966) study of the organization of educational research: that some functions may be combined effectively and profitably, as in the Pelz and Andrews (1966) study, while others, such as research and services, tend to combine badly. Kahn's (1964:393) study suggests that roles may also be effectively occupied in rotation.

A second change following linkage difficulties is to leave scientists alone to get on with their science. This is done by freeing them explicitly from the linking task in which they have failed and by establishing an additional group of a different kind of scientist specifically for the linking task. But without further structural change in the whole system, these different scientists are bound to fail at linkage in their turn; then the same process may be repeated, and yet another group may be entrusted with the linkage task. In time, several additional subsystems may get interposed in this manner between the original innovative subsystem and the operating system. Each of these subsystems has small-step linking tasks to the subsystem on either side of it in a lengthening chain of innovative subsystems. Burns and Stalker (1961:157-158) found that some organizations had separate departments for "pure" and "basic" research, and for "design" and "development," although the subsystems in each pair were "almost indistinguishable." Other studies (Kast and Rosenzweig, 1962; Quinn and Mueller, 1963) point to a similar proliferation of scientists and engineering specialists. This process fails to establish the required linkages to the operating system and at the same time makes the necessary system development more complicated and costly. The tendency to proliferate innovative subsystems in attempting to deal with linkage difficulties can be expected to be reinforced by the personal and professional inclinations of both researchers and operating men described in an earlier section of this paper.

The following hypothesis may be worth examining: In situations of stress between innovative and other subsystems, scientists will seek to safeguard their autonomy of work by proposing that the linkage function be carried out by new subsystems that are oriented more to application and less to science. Operating men support the same tendency when they overestimate the value, and underestimate the cost, of further differentiation in the innovative subsystem, following their erroneous impression that an up-to-date system consists of a multiplicity of subsystems.

All this elaboration of the system leaves the major difficulty untouched and is costly. The direct costs of coordinating go up with every differentiation of subsystems, and indirect costs may be even greater, including the creation of jobs, groups, and even departments of highly paid personnel whose survival in the system depends on the perpetuation of their subsystems. These costs are incurred in the attempt of decision makers to escape the problems of reshaping the system for continuous change.

Need for Change Assessed as Continuous

The data for this section of the paper are drawn predominantly from four major field studies in industry to which frequent reference has already been made (Lorsch, 1965; Lawrence and Lorsch, 1967; Burns and Stalker, 1961; Woodward, 1965). All are published in the 1960's, three since 1965. Two present British data, two American. All contain comparison of linkage mechanisms in similar contexts of technology and uncertain environments. But linkage mechanisms effective in some systems seem to be ineffective in others.

The attempt in this section is to analyze the successes and failures in linkages, so that some common factors can be established. The overall issue is institutionalizing linkage mechanisms so that they function as permanent parts of a system that is continuously and flexibly engaged in change; that is, a system that is functioning effectively in a turbulent environment.

The analysis will be in terms of four dimensions: differentiation of linkage mechanisms, the relation of such a mechanism to the subsystems it links, its norms of operation, and its congruence with system structure.

Differentiation

The studies showed effective linkage mechanisms to be formally organized on a permanent basis; for example, engineering department, product management meeting, research and development committee, goal team. The effective linkage mechanisms consisted of people from the different subsystems to be linked; that is, the linkage mechanisms were cross-functional in composition and represented a particular type of differentiation.

The differentiation of effective mechanisms was clear both *vis à vis* the subsystems to be linked and *vis à vis* the decision makers for the whole system. Regarding the first, Lawrence and Lorsch found differentiation to be effective "to the degree to which managers in all the departments felt that they had influence over decisions" (1967:56). As to the second, they found the influence of effective linkage mechanisms to be "centered at the operating level, neither higher nor lower than where the decisions could be effectively reached and implemented" (1967:56).

Figure 6 illustrates effective and ineffective differentiation in these terms. Lorsch (1965:122) listed the differences between effective differentiation in one company and ineffective differentiation in another as follows:

Effective Differentiation

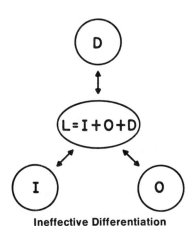

Ineffective Differentiation

Figure 6. Differentiation of linkage mechanism from subsystems and from decision makers. (D = decision makers, L = linker, I = innovator, O = operator, solid circle = formal boundary.)

Effective Mechanism	*Ineffective Mechanism*
Limited attendance to four functional members from the subsystems	Large, included superiors and subordinates
Set out to solve problems and resolve conflict	Set out primarily to exchange information
Did not involve decision makers	Dropped any difficult problems or asked decision makers to solve them

Linkage Mechanism in Relation to Innovative and Operating Subsystems

Effective linkage mechanisms were equidistant between the subsystems they were to link. Lawrence and Lorsch (1967:59) examined this distance in terms of four "orientations": to goals, time, interpersonal relations, and the structure of the linkage mechanism. Linkage mechanisms in high-performance company A were equidistant on all four dimensions, in low-performance company A on only one.

The mechanisms of the other four companies they studied were equidistant on two dimensions.

A second kind of position factor relates the membership of the linkage mechanism with different hierarchical positions in the subsystems. According to Lawrence and Lorsch, a high-level production manager usually has sufficiently specialized knowledge of production processes to consider innovations proposed by scientists and can reach effective decisions about them in a joint meeting. On the other hand, scientific research and development is so specialized that the production manager's peer for linkage is a scientist actually working on the specific problem, or his immediate superior. And the corresponding peer in sales is likely to be a middle manager. The key linkers, whom Lawrence and Lorsch called "integrators," were at different hierarchical levels within their various subsystems and in the system as a whole. Where linkage mechanisms were effective, these hierarchical differences of members outside the linkage subsystem were relinquished upon entry into the linkage subsystem and neither blocked the decision making process nor reduced the acceptability of its results to other subsystems (1967:55-56). The differences in effectiveness related to "the degree to which these key integrators (were) seen by others in his organization as having the most important voice in decisions" (1967:62). In other words, while subsystems may have been formally represented at meetings by their managers, the major activities in and out of formal meetings were those of the various key linkers. Burns and Stalker (1961:88-9) found that the word "committee" captured the essential organizational equality of the members, irrespective of their status outside. In the companies they studied, they found linkage invariably associated with this equality. Effective linkage mechanisms "were indeed devices for abrogating for the length of each meeting the distribution of authority, information, and technical competence pictured in the hierarchic structure of the organization." They saw this abrogation as addressing appropriately the uncertainties in requirements for which the normal management structure was not appropriate (see also Lawrence and Lorsch, 1967:67, ff).

A third position factor is indicated by the reward system. Effective linkage seems to be associated with the extent to which linkers feel evaluated and rewarded according to the overall performance of the subsystems linked. According to Lawrence and Lorsch (1967:67, ff), it was important that linkers "had an incentive for effective integrative activities over and above the supervisory, planning and other functions" they performed within their own subsystems. Similarly, the goal team in Lorsch's (1965:122) study felt responsible for profits in their whole market area, so that each member "should be committed to the decisions we reach as a group."

Operating Norms of Linkage Mechanism

Operating norms relating to two aspects seem to be of particular importance: conflict resolution and flexibility. Lawrence and Lorsch (1967:73-77) list six factors in conflict resolution. According to them, linkage was effective to "the degree of openness with which conflicts were aired and hammered out in departmental meetings." . . .

Flexibility appears to be the second essential norm for the operation of an effective linkage mechanism, with kind and degree of flexibility determined by the functional needs of the mechanisms and the particular situations with which it is dealing at any time. Burns and Stalker (1961:87-89) described the flexible operation of a new research and development committee. It began as "a large, comprehensive affair" but was reduced in size when it became unprofitable to conduct the meetings in a language that shop-floor supervisors could understand readily. Therefore the large meeting was changed. A small professional committee dealt with ongoing projects, and regular foremen's meetings were used to keep the supervisors routinely informed about the committee's work. In short, the hierarchical structure was used as a communication system for this as for other routine matters. However, the committee meetings were expanded to their earlier size whenever a major design change was developed for one of the two main products of the company. Smith mentions a similar flexibility around the question of inviting system decision makers to meetings concerned with linkage (in Bright, 1962:49; see also Thompson, 1966:139-143).

Congruence with System Structure

Lorsch (1965:147) found the locus of formal authority congruent with the norms of conflict resolution: "The level with the authority within each subsystem about scientific transfer was also the level that the norms indicated should resolve differences between subsystems." This congruence existed with both ineffective and effective linkage mechanisms. The effective linkage system had fewer hierarchical levels than the ineffective, as would be expected from other research findings: in a turbulent environment a flatter system structure is associated with higher system performance.

In a turbulent environment, effective linkage mechanisms seem to have structures and operating norms that also characterize the whole system of which they are a part, and the system as a whole reflects more closely the structures and norms characteristic of innovative subsystems than those of traditional operating subsystems.

Discussion and Conclusion

This paper has been concerned with effective linkages in systems relating to turbulent environments. For these systems the problems of effective linkage are particularly difficult and particularly important (Lawrence and Lorsch, 1967:137).

Lawrence and Lorsch (1967) showed a direct relationship between degrees of turbulence, differentiation, and complexity of linkage mechanisms. The mechanisms were least differentiated and complex in the organization belonging to the relatively stable and undifferentiated container industry, more numerous and more complex in the moderately unstable and differentiated food organization, and most clearly differentiated and complex in the highly unstable plastics industry. Each of these high-performing organizations used a different combination of linkage devices (Lawrence and Lorsch, 1967:138, Table IV-1).

For systems in turbulent environments the design, development and operation of linkage mechanisms of appropriate complexity is costly. Decision makers will seek to avoid this investment. Even if they assess the environmental needs correctly, they are inclined to underestimate the response that would be effective and the costs involved in the response. Misjudgment of these costs is frequent among innovators who start their own organizations. As the organization grows, innovators often continue to assume that they can stretch linkage by personal contacts over ever greater numbers of people and finally to a new generation of decision makers and managers. Burns and Stalker (1961:92-94) described this personal pattern of attempted linkage. Characteristically, it results in people left "loose" to find their own way to get done whatever they see as necessary; in continuous definitions and redefinitions of tasks and groups "through a perpetual sequence of encounters" with laboratory chiefs, design engineers, and others "to see the job through"; and in increasing personal costs from "nervous preoccupation with the hazards of social navigation in the structure and with the relative validity of their own claims to authority, information and technical expertise." In one company these disruptive effects were counterbalanced by a general awareness of common purpose and of excitement at the tasks, and by the generally attractive atmosphere in the system. Joan Woodward's study (1965:196) compared the attempts of two other organizations, with similar technology and management structure, to establish a formal linkage mechanism. One organization, less than ten years old, with roles and functions not yet clearly established, persisted and designed an innovative system that fit the formal mechanism closely. The other organization was thirty years old and, the author concluded, too rigid to accept the innovation.

That the development of effective linkage mechanisms is associated with major changes in the system as a whole seems borne out by studies of organizations in a wide variety of settings. From a study of ten cases of organizational development in various settings, Buchanan (1967) established a list of 33 issues arising in each. The one issue that distinguished the seven most successful organizations conspicuously from the three unsuccessful ones was the linkage between the innovative subsystem and the rest of the system. "In two of the three unsuccessful cases, changes were initiated and progress was being made, only to come to a halt because of action by management. . . . Steps taken to accomplish linkage were not effective" (Buchanan 1967:62). In the successful cases, linkage between people at several levels of the system was established either as part of the change-induction plan or by steps taken early in the program. The linkage was in the form of working in small teams on operating problems or in the form of involving members in large numbers and at several levels during the early stages of identifying the linkage task (Buchanan, 1967:62). The successful organizations differed in the model they used for innovating, in the manner in which the model was introduced into the system, the location of the innovative subsystem in the system, and the time at which various levels of decision makers were involved. They were similar, on the other hand, in the following five aspects (Buchanan 1967:64):

1. They differentiated the innovative subsystem sharply and formally.
2. In the models they used they found a basis for establishing goals for improvement.
3. The models focused on problem-solving processes.
4. The models led to changes in the kind, distribution, and amount of power.
5. The models emphasized norms and skills that facilitated collaboration and problem solving rather than negotiation and bargaining.

It seems that as long as the model in its initial conception allows for these five dimensions, the system can develop the appropriate mechanisms for its singular circumstances and needs. In fact, working out its own distinctively appropriate pattern seems to be essential to effectiveness. The freedom to make changes, and the constraint in using this freedom, seem to stem from two sources. One is the shifting technological and informational needs of the system and the ways in which these can be met, given the resources of the system and the particular environment with which it interacts. The other source is the emotions of the people actually involved in the changes, which the linkage mechanisms are to mediate. Uncertainties from both sources have to be reflected in the openness of linkage mechanisms to further change; that is, their flexibility.

The emotional uncertainties seem the more complex. Sofer (1961) analyzed the emotional demands on linkage mechanisms that occurred in three very different organizations. He found that "the organization undertakes an emotional division of labor in attitudes towards innovators in just the same way it distributes any other organizational task" (Sofer, 1961:159). Some members will be for the new venture, others against it. "The relationship (of the innovative subsystem) with colleagues will be uneasy. There occur outbreaks of reciprocal paranoia as well as euphoria." When people in the innovative subsystem get discouraged and uncertain about whether they can perform the innovative task, they tend to withdraw and to create barriers rather than linkages. Sofer noted some of the mechanisms by which innovators tend to drain off internal tension. They called attention to the limitations under which decision makers expected them to succeed, their "rigidity," "shortsightedness," "intolerance" and "conservatism," their unwillingness to collaborate, their wish to see the innovation fail. "All parties will precipitate test cases. These test cases are variously used by all concerned to illustrate those aspects of the total situation that are most favorable to their rationale of the moment" (Sofer 1961:160). Sofer traced the system of defense by which people in the innovative subsystems sought to protect themselves and to explain their reluctance to devise, use and strengthen linkage mechanisms (1961:160-162). The strains in the rest of the system and the ways people express them then tend in turn to isolate the new subsystem further (Burns and Stalker, 1961:171).

In studies of innovation in educational systems, Miles (1964) described how this progressive deterioration of linkage mechanisms made the innovators' fears come true. Support for the innovative subsystem withered, recruitment into it became more difficult, reports of innovative achievements came to lack credibility. Soon the subsystem faced problems of sheer survival (Miles, 1964:654). Under these circumstances intergroup conflict and hostility are very likely to occur, and opposing coalitions develop, with each group magnifying its virtues and the opponents' faults. Such conflict often produced high solidarity *within* the groups. The innovative subsystem, being usually the less powerful, tends to develop substitute satisfactions, like fantasies that some day the others will learn to appreciate them.

Two general conclusions follow. One is that linkage mechanisms need to be flexible and also strong to withstand such strains and such uncertainties. This usually means that they need to be differentiated clearly, be known to have the support of the system's decision makers, and remain highly functional over time. Chin developed the concept of "intersystem" to describe the linkage mechanisms between two subsystems. "The intersystem model exaggerates the virtues of autonomy and the limited nature of interdependence of the interactions between the two connected systems" (Bennis *et al.*, 1964:201-214). The inter-system allows linkage to be rooted in another system, and to offer those "marginal" people who do the linking a base from which to operate and in which to gain and regain perspective and strength.

The second conclusion is simply a forceful reminder that coordination is a heavy cost. This cost may be profitably incurred if, (1) a primary task is clearly differentiated that requires organizational differentiation and, (2) if the new subsystem is maximally autonomous, so that its connections with other subsystems are minimal. In short, the only justification for linkage mechanisms is strict functional interdependence (Kahn *et al.*, 1964:394; Quinn and Mueller, 1963:51). Even if these criteria are rigidly applied, the number of systems that need to design and operate linkage mechanisms will surely increase as more and more decision makers come to recognize the turbulence of the environment.

References

Andrews, John H. M., and T. Barr Greenfield. "Organizational themes relevant to change in schools." Ontario Journal of Educational Research, 8:81-99. 1966.

Barnes, Louis B. Organizational Systems and Engineering Groups: A Comparative Study of Two Technical Groups in Industry. Boston: Graduate School of Business Administration, Harvard University. 1960.

Bennis, Warren G., Kenneth D. Benne, and Robert Chin. The Planning of Change: Readings in the Applied Behavioral Sciences. New York: Holt, Rinehart & Winston. 1964.

Bright, James R. (ed.). Technological Planning on the Corporate Level (Proceedings of a Conference sponsored by The Associates of the Harvard Business School). Boston: Graduate School of Business Administration, Harvard University. 1962.

————. Research, Development and Technological Innovation: An Introduction. Homewood, Illinois: Irwin. 1964.

Buchanan, Paul C. "The concept of organization development, or self-renewal, as a form of social change." In Goodwin Watson (ed.), Concepts for Social Change: 1-9. Washington D. C. National Training Laboratories. 1967.

Burns, Tom, and G. M. Stalker. The Management of Innovation. London: Tavistock. 1961.

Carlson, R. O. "School superintendents and the adoption of modern math: a social structure profile." In Matthew B. Miles (ed.), Innovation in Education: 329-342. New York: Teachers College, Columbia University. 1964.

Chandler, Alfred D., Jr. Strategy and Structure: Chapters in the History of the Industrial Enterprise. Cambridge: M.I.T. Press. 1963.

Churchman, C. W., and A. H. Scheinblatt. "The researcher and the manager: a dialectic of implementation." Management Science, II (February 1965):B-75. 1965.

Dalton, Melville. "Conflicts between staff and line managerial officers." American Sociological Review, XV (June 1950):342-351. 1950.

Dearborn, Dewitt C., and Herbert A. Simon. "Selective perception: a note on the departmental identification of executives." Sociometry, XXI:140-144. 1958.

Downs, Anthony. Inside Bureaucracy. New York: Little, Brown. 1967.

Emery, F. E. "The next thirty years: concepts, methods and anticipations." Human Relations, XX:199-238. 1967.

Gallagher, A. "Characteristics of socio-technical systems." Document 527. London: Tavistock Institute of Human Relations. 1959.

————. The Role of the Advocate and Directed Change. Symposium paper. Lincoln, Nebraska. 1963.

Harvey, Edward. "Technology and the structure of organizations." American Sociological Review, XXXIII (April 1968) 247-259. 1968.

Havelock, Ronald G. Dissemination and Translation Roles in Education and Other Fields. UCEA Career Development Seminar. Eugene, Oregon. 1967.

Havelock, Ronald G., and Kenneth Benne. An Exploratory Study of Knowledge Utilization. Ann Arbor: Institute for Social Research, University of Michigan. 1964.

Herbst, P. G. "Task structure and work relations." Document 528. London: Tavistock Institute of Human Relations. 1959.

Hermann, Charles F. "Some consequences of crisis which limit the viability of organizations." Administrative Science Quarterly, 8 (June 1963):61-82. 1963.

Hirschman, A. O., and C. E. Lindblom. "Economic development, research and development, policymaking: some convergent views." Behavioral Science, 7:211-222. 1962.

Inkeles, Alex. Public Opinion in Soviet Russia. Cambridge, Mass.: Harvard University Press. 1951.

Jasinski, Frank J. "Adapting organization to new technology." In Joseph A. Litterer (ed.), Organizations: Structure and Behavior. New York: Wiley. 1963.

Kahn, Robert L., Donald M. Wofe, Robert P. Quinn, and J. Diedrick Snoek. Organizational Stress: Studies in Role Conflict and Ambiguity. New York: Wiley. 1964.

Kast, Fremont E., and James E. Rosenzweig (eds.). Science, Technology, and Management. New York: McGraw-Hill. 1962.

Katz, Daniel, and Robert L. Kahn. The Social Psychology of Organizations. New York: Wiley. 1966.

Katz, Elihu, and Paul F. Lazarsfeld. Personal Influence. Glencoe, Ill.: Free Press. 1955.

Lawrence, Paul R., and Jay W. Lorsch. Organization and Environment: Managing Differentiation and Integration. Boston: School of Business Administration, Harvard University. 1967.

Litterer, Joseph A. (ed.). Organizations: Structure and Behavior. New York: Wiley. 1963.

Litwak, Eugene. "Models of bureaucracy which permit conflict." The American Journal of Sociology, LXVII (September 1961):177-184. 1961.

Lorsch, Jay W. Product Innovation and Organization. New York: Macmillan. 1965.

Lorsch, Jay W., and Paul R. Lawrence. Environmental Factors and Organizational Integration. Paper prepared for 63rd Annual Meeting of the American Sociological Association, August 27, 1968, Boston, Mass. 1968.

Miles, B. Matthew (ed.). Innovation in Education. New York: Teachers College, Columbia University. 1964.

Miller, Eric J. "Part III: internal differentiation and problems of management." Human Relations, XII: 261-270. 1959.

Miller, E. J., and A. K. Rice. Systems of Organization. London: Tavistock. 1967.

Parsons, Talcott. "Suggestions for a sociological approach to the theory of organizations—I." Administrative Science Quarterly, 1:63-85. 1956.

Pelz, Donald C., and Frank M. Andrews. Scientists in Organizations. New York: Wiley. 1966.

Perrow, Charles. "A framework for the comparative analysis of organizations." American Sociological Review, XXXII (April 1967):194-208. 1967.

Pondy, Louis R. "Organizational conflict: concepts and models." Administrative Science Quarterly, 12 (September 1967):296-320. 1967.

Quinn, James Brian, and James A. Mueller. "Transferring research results to operations." Harvard Business Review, XLI (January 1963):49-66. 1963.

Rice, A. K. Productivity and Social Organization: The Ahmedabad Experiment. London: Tavistock. 1958.

Rodgers, Everett M. Diffusion of Innovations. New York: Free Press. 1962.

Ross, D. H. (ed.) Administration for Adaptability. New York: Metropolitan School Study Council. 1958.

Selznick, P. Leadership in Administration. New York: Row Peterson. 1957.

Shepard, Herbert A. "Nine dilemmas in industrial research." Administrative Science Quarterly, 1 (December):293-309. 1956.

Sieber, Sam D. The Organization of Educational Research in the United States. New York: Columbia University. 1966.

Smith, Alfred G. Communication and Status: The Dynamics of a Research Center. Eugene, Oregon: Center for the Advanced Study of Educational Administration, University of Oregon. 1966.

Sofer, Cyril. The Organization from Within: A Comparative Study of Social Institutions Based on a Sociotherapeutic Approach. London: Tavistock. 1961.

Strauss, George. "Tactics of lateral relationship: the purchasing agent." Administrative Science Quarterly, 7 (September):161-186. 1962.

Thayer, Lee. Communication and Communication Systems: In Organization, Management and Interpersonal Relations. Homewood, Ill.: Irwin. 1968.

Thompson, James D. Organizations in Action. New York: McGraw-Hill. 1967.

Thompson, Victor A. "Bureaucracy and innovation." Administrative Science Quarterly, 10 (June:1-20). 1965.

Trist, E. L., and G. W. Higgin, H. Murray, A. B. Pollock. Organizational Choice. London: Tavistock. 1963.

Watson, Goodwin (ed.). Change in School Systems. Washington, D. C.: NTL, NEA. 1967.

Woodward, Joan. Industrial Organization: Theory and Practice. London: Oxford University Press. 1965.

THE EFFECTS OF ENVIRONMENTS ON ORGANIZATION SYSTEMS

DELF DODGE
HENRY TOSI

The main ideas from the preceding selections lead to this kind of logic: The environment may be characterized as several possible types of external sectors; these external sectors may be simple or complex, static or dynamic (Jurkovich, 1974). When they are simple and certain, a mechanistic organization will be an appropriate form of adaptation and when the external sectors are dynamic, the organization form should be organic (Burns and Stalker, 1961). Both organic and mechanistic organizations are composed of generic types of subsystems (Katz and Kahn, 1966), but the specific form of these subsystems varies. For example, the production subsystem, the technical core, may be highly routine and repetitive or it may be an "intensive" technology (Thompson, 1967). Innovative subsystems also differ (according to Lynton, 1969), depending on whether the environment is placid or turbulent.

In this selection, a model to integrate several of these concepts is shown. Basically, the organization subsystems, as defined by Katz and Kahn (1966), are shown to be different in shape, and relationship to each other when interacting with environmental sectors which have different degrees of turbulence.

Environment and Organization Structure

Levels of certainty in an organization's environment may be thought of as ranging from stability at one extreme to volatility at the other (the analytical structure that follows is more fully developed in Tosi and Carroll, 1976).

This does not mean to imply that no changes ever occur in "stable" environments; it means rather that changes are relatively minor, infrequent and predictable. Conversely, under highly volatile environmental conditions, changes are rapid, of great magnitude, and unpredictable.

Although the complete environment contains a large number of elements of which the organization must be aware, it has been argued that the market a firm serves and the type and source of technology account for a significant difference in organizational structure (Burns and Stalker, 1966). The combination of the environmental sectors (market and technological), and volatility conditions (stability-volatility), when placed on two axes, creates four distinct organizational types (see fig. 1). Keep in mind, however, that the stability-volatility is a continuum. The dichotomy is a matter of theoretical convenience, useful for purposes of analysis but in no way representing the full spectrum of variation to be found between the two categories.

Burns and Stalker (1966) describe, in general terms, the characteristics of firms dealing strictly with volatile environments or stable environments (cells I and IV of fig. 1). Firms in cells II and III, however, operate with organizational subsystems that interact with a combination of stable and volatile elements. The firm in cell II faced with a stable market and a volatile technology, will be most sensitive to changes in the

This article was prepared especially for this book.

technological environment. This type of firm is called "technology-dominated mixed." An organization existing under conditions of a stable technology and a volatile market (cell III) may be called a "market-dominated mixed," since it must be ready to adapt to changes in its market environment, while relevant technological environment would have little impact. (Tosi and Carroll, 1976.)

Technology

	stable				volatile
stable	mechanistic or hierarchic		**I**	**II**	technology-dominated mixed
Market					
volatile	market-dominated mixed		**III**	**IV**	organic or dynamic

These four distinct theoretical organization types, each peculiar to its particular market and technological states, is made up of the same five generic types of subsystems—production, boundary-spanning, adaptive, maintenance, and managerial—within its organizational boundaries (Katz and Kahn, 1966). The general characteristics of these subsystems, however, and the relationships between them will vary greatly from theoretical type to type.

The Mechanistic, Hierarchical Organization

Production Subsystems

The production subsystem of the mechanistic organization is characterized by a high degree of repetitiveness. Methods are well and narrowly defined, standardized, and highly repetitive. Members are often assigned only a few tasks, with a very short work cycle. Operators have little control over the tasks performed, or the method used to complete them. Such extreme division of labor abstracts individuals' tasks to such a degree that workers may feel they are making little contribution to the creation of a complete product. Individual tasks lose their identity in the numerous tasks which combine along an impersonal assembly process to form the stable organization's product.

Work activities, standardized and segmented into very small units, require only very low levels of skill. Since workers are easily replaceable, given an adequate labor force, they will be dependent upon the organization, but not vice versa. This lack of security in the hierarchical firm's production subsystem gives rise to a need for an effective method of protection against potential arbitrary action of managers. Labor unions perform this function.

Boundary-spanning Subsystems

Because the hierarchical organization's market is relatively static, the channels of distribution for their products or services will be fairly well defined and standardized. As methods of distribution become ineffective, new channels will arise, but this will likely be a slow process. The hierarchical organization's distribution subsystem will exercise a great deal of influence over other subsystems in the distribution channel.

Products or services of firms in hierarchical industries will usually be quite similar in function and form. Products of competing firms can thus be substituted for one another. Product differentiation in such industries is created largely through advertising, as each firm attempts to create its own market segment, and price competition may be prevalent in mature product markets.

In the stable environment, sources of raw materials will be well developed and well defined. Captive suppliers are common and, as with the distribution sector, sources of materials input to the firm will probably not change until suppliers prove to be inefficient, or uncompetitive from a cost standpoint. Repetitive production systems function most effectively when they proceed at an even ratio. Maintaining raw materials and finished goods inventories will buffer the production subsystem so that it need not be disrupted as seasonal changes in demand take place.

Adaptive Subsystems

Under stable environmental conditions, adaptive subsystems will have a fairly simple structure. Information is plentiful, and easily gathered. As the organization gains experience, it will usually learn which parts of the environment to monitor, and will probably develop fairly standard methods of adapting to changes. This high degree of environmental stability offers the hierarchical firm the opportunity to make long-range plans and capital commitments. Low risk levels enhance its ability to use external sources of capital. Technological changes in the firm's product (output) may occur from within the organization as researchers and engineers concentrate their efforts on product improvement and on increasing production efficiency.

Maintenance Subsystems

The focus of the hierarchical organization's maintenance subsystem will be on performance measurement and evaluation. The evaluation criteria will probably be developed from past performance records which have achieved organizational credibility. The purpose of the maintenance subsystem is to increase internal effectiveness. Internal effectiveness is critical to the survival of the mechanistic firm, more so than to the other organization types, since increasing returns will be realized internally. Thus, this subsystem will have a great deal of organizational influence.

Managerial Subsystems

There will be centralized control in the hierarchical organization. An individual's organizational power will be based upon position, flowing from the authority and responsibility associated with the position he holds. The hierarchy of authority, responsibility, and communication will be relatively clearly defined by the managerial subsystem, as will be each job's content. There should be a relatively small number of managers (relative to the number of operators) in mechanistic organizations, leading one to expect great homogeneity of attitude among the high-level executives, since promotions will be awarded not only for proven abilities, but also for the "rightness" of one's point of view.

The Organic, Dynamic Organization

Production Subsystems

Production subsystems in organic organizations will be composed primarily of general-purpose equipment, since sequencing of operations will vary from project to project. Routine, repetitive production procedures will not work well here. The intensive technology of the dynamic firm's production subsystem is a custom one; the selection, combination, and ordering of technological application is determined through an evaluation of the particular project at hand. As environments and projects change, so will the technologies used.

Boundary-spanning Subsystems

Dynamic organizations will not have long distribution channels, since the fluctuations of the environment will not allow the routinization of the distribution function and its transfer to outside jobbers. Channels of distribution will be unstructured, changing with environmental demands. Highly skilled individuals will be needed in the marketing areas to read the changing demand structure.

Those involved in procuring raw materials must be skilled in searching out new sources of input, as both the level and type of raw materials needed will be in a state of flux. Keeping in close contact with a variety of suppliers will be essential to the smooth operation of the procurement function.

Adaptive Subsystems

The activities of the adaptive subsystems are vital to an organization's existence and, in the dynamic firm, they take on added significance. The unpredictability of the timing, magnitude, and direction of environmental changes makes personal skill in environmental monitoring and interpretation a necessary attribute for members of the adaptive subsystems. Market research and data interpretation activities will be extensive. Research and development will concentrate on pure, rather than applied research. Although members will be highly trained, they will be required to update their skills, or to leave the organization, as relevant aspects of the environment change. Since the skills required may change as the environments change, the organization may use a strategy of hiring new personnel rather than retraining current members.

Maintenance Subsystems

Historical data will have little utility in volatile environmental conditions, leading to control and evaluation standards which tend to be subjective. Evaluation will focus on *what procedures are followed* to complete a task; in evaluation these will be more important than the actual *results*. It is assumed that a logical sequence of steps can be determined and that if one proceeds according to those steps, satisfactory results will occur.

Personnel in the dynamic firm will probably have only short-range commitments to the organization; their focus will tend to be on their own profession rather than on the organization in which they operate. When the firm no longer needs the abilities an individual has to offer, he will either be relieved or move on voluntarily. Professionals working in dynamic industries are likely willing to exercise their skills in any number of organizations so long as they are able to practice their profession.

Control in the organic firm will reside in the individual with the greatest expertise, or the greatest financial interest. If expertise is the power base, the organization's pattern of influence will change as the nature of the firm's projects change. If influence derives from financial interest, the organization will be an extension of the owner's interests; decisions will reflect the owner's desires.

Managerial Subsystems

Due to extensive environmental fluctuation, managerial subsystems in dynamic organizations will not be characterized by set, well-defined policies. Since guidelines will change frequently to meet new environmental requirements, the managerial subsystems will be relatively less structured than in other organizational types.

As needs for particular skills arise, individuals move from project to project. Over time, an employee may be exposed to several different superiors and authority structures. He may also experience stress from the role ambiguity and uncertainty fostered by this fairly constant change in patterns of authority, communication, and interaction.

To decrease the levels of environmental uncertainty, the managerial subsystems will tend to push the organization toward more stable market or technological sectors of the environment. Such a shift will facilitate planning, control, and the firm's ability to make long-term commitments to its members and creditors, but will diminish its ability to adapt to environmental change. New firms will enter the field to take the place of those dynamic firms making the transition to more stable environments. Because of the flexibility demanded by volatile environments, dynamic firms will tend to be smaller than hierarchical firms.

The Technology-Dominated Firm

In technology-dominated mixed firms, change in the technological sector of environment poses the major threat to effectiveness and survival. The market environment is relatively stable. To gain competitive advantage, skillful monitoring and subsequent adaptation to the technological environment must take place. In the technology-dominated mixed organization, subsystems which interact with the relevant technological environment will be very important, generating requirements for internal change to adapt.

The technology-dominated mixed firm will have a combination of hierarchical and dynamic units. The contrast between the rigidity and formality of the mechanistic portion of the firm, on the one hand, and the less tightly structured dynamic portion, on the other, will pose potential problems in the maintenance of positive working relationships within the total organizational structure.

Production Subsystems

The production subsystems of technology-dominated firms will likely utilize intensive technologies in which the combination and ordering of general-purpose equipment application is determined by the situation at hand. Individuals in this subsystem will be highly skilled and capable or organizing the production processes necessary for the variety of projects handled by the production subsystem. Capital equipment will be general purpose in nature; specialized machinery would have an unpredictable productive life under conditions of environmental uncertainty and would, therefore, not be efficient.

Boundary-spanning Subsystems

Channels of distribution in the technology-dominated mixed firm will not change radically in the short run. Changes in the technology may alter the character of the product, but probably not its form, end use, or the methods by which it is marketed. For example, cameras have undergone tremendous technical improvements since they were first marketed, but they are found in department stores, discount houses and camera shops—just as before.

As the technology of the product changes, those performing the procurement function must find new sources of supply for the new raw materials the product requires. Boundary-spanning units must remain in constant contact with potential new materials sources so that production is not halted while appropriate inputs are sought.

The initial product pricing policy of technology-dominated firms will be market skimming. As competitors begin to enter the market with similar, lower-priced products, however, price competition may begin.

Adaptive Subsystems

The greatest influence on major policy and strategy in a technology-dominated mixed firm will come from the technological segments of the organization. Research and development emphasis will be on the search for new ways to make the product rather than on narrow product/efficiency improvements. Advanced skills and knowledge will be prerequisites of these in this sector.

Since the market environment is relatively stable, market research activities will be standardized and fairly simplistic, relying on easily collectable data which has proved historically to be an adequate indicator of future market events and current conditions.

Maintenance Subsystems

The marketing units of the technology-dominated mixed firm will find it easy to accumulate accurate cost data to judge its efficiency. The stability of the environment makes this possible. The organization's technological activities on the other hand must deal with a volatile environment, which precludes the collection of much relevant historical data for control purposes.

Broad individual discretion is necessary in dealing with changing environments. This may be stifled by the creation and imposition of standard performance and efficiency measures, creating problems for the maintenance subsystems in that standards of performance for the marketing and technological units of the firm must be of separate and distinct types. The evaluation standards appropriate to hierarchical units will not work in dynamic units, and vice versa. The performance appraisal and compensation systems must be carefully managed to fit the varying demands of the different organization substructures, with special care given to seeing that these systems are both internally *and* externally equitable for the organization's members.

Managerial Subsystems

Authority relationships of the technology-dominated mixed firm will be highly structured in the marketing sector, with clearcut lines of authority, communication, and accountability, well-defined responsibilities, and limited amounts of discretion. Rules, policies, and procedures will be standardized.

The technological units of the organization, however, will be much less rigidly structured: their highly-trained individuals will be allowed a greater degree of discretion in their activities. Here, again, there may be some difficulty in maintaining equity and positive working relationships between the different structural extremes within the same organizational boundary.

The Market-Dominated Mixed Firm

The significant policy-influencing group in the market-dominated mixed firm will be the marketing sector, since there is a need to keep in close touch with changes in the market environment. The technological sector of the organization will be structured along hierarchical lines, consistent with the stability of the relevant technological environment.

Production Subsystems

The stable technological environment of the market-dominated mixed firm gives rise to production subsystems similar to those found in the hierarchical organization. Jobs will be precisely and narrowly defined, and will require low skill levels. Workers will be easily replaceable, and are likely to achieve job security through union protection. Objective cost measures will provide performance criteria in the production subsystems, since the production methods themselves will remain relatively stable, even though the design of the product being produced will be altered frequently to meet changes in consumer demand.

Boundary-spanning Subsystems

The procurement function of the market-dominated mixed organization will need to seek new sources of supply only when consumer preferences demand a new type of material to meet their product needs. For instance, men's suits were traditionally made of wool. When the knit and synthetic fabrics came onto the market, demand for wool suits dropped off and demand for synthetic fiber suits increased. Demand for suits, on the whole, remained about the same, and the switch from one fabric to another had little effect on the production system or basic styling of the product.

Channels of product distribution will remain constant until market research determines that some other form of distribution is more effective in reaching the changed market. Product pricing will be placed in the hands of the marketing unit, since it will have the information on the price the consumer is willing to pay for the firm's product.

Adaptive Subsystems

Extensive research will be devoted to uncovering and assessing new markets for the market-dominated mixed firm. Those who are in close touch with the relevant market environment will have most influence on organizational policy and strategy, since it is ability to adapt to the changing market demands which will determine the firm's survival.

The technical engineering functions of the market-dominated mixed firm will focus on application rather than on exploratory research. For instance, engineers may seek to reduce costs rather than develop new product ideas. Since little change occurs in the technological environment, there will be no need for extensive technical research and development activities.

Maintenance Subsystems

It will be difficult for the maintenance subsystems to develop relevant historical cost data to assess the marketing unit's performance. The dynamic nature of the distribution and marketing systems will make stable control measures difficult to establish.

Managerial Subsystems

The market-dominated mixed firm will have hierarchical authority structures in the technical sectors, and flexible authority structures in the marketing and distribution sectors, each of which is the appropriate structural adaptation demanded by the respective environments. The overall organizational control system will be most sensitive to changes occurring in the volatile market environment. Ability to respond effectively to market changes is critical to the organization's survival.

As with the technology-dominated mixed firm, the market-dominated mixed firm may have difficulty establishing, integrating, and maintaining the two sets of different internal structures demanded by its environments. The hierarchical segment's rigid authority and control will create different problems than the dynamic, loosely structured segment of the firm. The integration of these two different organizational forms will be a difficult and critical task.

Discussion

There is, of course, no such thing as a "pure" organizational type. Variations in actual structural characteristics make each organization different in its details from every other organization. The classifications given in this article are intended to order thoughts about organizational structure into coherent patterns.

This interactive model of organization structure assumes that organizational types and methods of subsystems' environmental interaction will vary directly with changes in the relevant market and technological environments. There are, however, other factors which must be taken into consideration. Multidivisional organizations may have a wide variety of substructures within them, some dealing with very stable markets and technologies, others dealing with completely volatile environments. Such firms must take great care to avoid imposing inappropriate organizational structures on any of its subunits. The mechanistic structure appropriate to the production system of a firm, for example, would create havoc if forced upon one of its internal research units. The autonomy a research scientist demands can only be violated at the expense of diminishing his value to the firm. Each segment of a conglomerate must be allowed to respond to the demands of the environments with which it must deal, changing its structure and processes in efforts to remain consistent with and survive in its environmental context. Only through appropriate adaptation will the continued well-being of the firm or subunit be insured in the long run.

References

Burns, T., and G. M. Stalker, *The Management of Innovation*, Tavistock Publications, 1961.

Feidler, F., *A Theory of Leadership Effectiveness*, McGraw-Hill, 1967.

Filley, A. C., R. J. House, and S. Kerr, *Managerial Process and Organizational Behavior*, Scott, Foresman, 1976.

Harvey, E., "Technology and the Structure of Organizations," *Administrative Sociological Review*, 33 (1968): 247-59.

House, R. J., "A Path Goal Theory of Leader Effectiveness," *Administrative Science Quarterly*, 16, 1971.

Jurkovich, R., "A Core Typology of Organizational Environments," *Administrative Science Quarterly*, September, 1974, 380-94.

Katz, D., and R. L. Kahn, *The Social Psychology of Organizations*, John Wiley & Sons, 1966.

Lawrence, P. R., and J. W. Lorsch, *Organization and Environment: Managing Differentiation and Integration*, Graduate School of Business Administration, Harvard, 1967.

Lynton, R. P., "Linking an Innovative Subsystem into the System," *Administrative Science Quarterly*, September, 1969, 398-414.

Thompson, J. D., *Organizations in Action*, McGraw-Hill, 1967.

Tosi, H. L., and S. J. Carroll, *Management: Contingencies, Structure and Process*, St. Clair Press, 1976.

PART TWO

Individual Learning
and Socialization

In the preceding part the emphasis was on the manner in which environmental contingencies affect the structure of an organization. In this part, the focus is on how individuals adapt to the world within which they must function. Organizations learn to survive by developing different patterns of accommodation to the world in which they function. In this part, the focus shifts from the organization to the individual, but the basic idea of environmental adaptation is the same. The readings in this part illustrate how individuals respond to circumstances in their environment and develop different modes of adaptation to both society and the organization in which they work.

The theoretical framework used here is learning theory. Learning theory is a set of concepts which helps us to understand how relatively stable behavior patterns of individuals develop. Organizations are identified not by characteristics such as geographic location, or other demographic factors, but rather by the degree to which individuals engage in some relatively continuous, stable system of interaction. If individuals interact over time, and if this interaction is fairly persistent, then we may attach the label "organization" to that system of behavior. Of interest here is the manner in which these behavior patterns develop, emerge, and stabilize.

In the first selection, Hamner deals with two of the basic learning-theory approaches to understanding behavior. He describes the difference between classical conditioning and operant conditioning. Classical conditioning occurs when an individual relates certain cues to one another so that ultimately several different cues may be capable of eliciting a particular response. In operant conditioning, reinforcement is a critical construct. When behavior is reinforced, the likelihood of it occurring again in response to a particular cue changes. If behavior is positively reinforced, the probability of occurrence of the behavior is increased, but if behavior is negatively reinforced, the likelihood that this response will occur again is decreased.

How and why do these concepts apply to the larger issues with which we are concerned here? It is obvious enough that an individual is constantly exposed to a wide range of stimuli and reinforcement in his life experiences. Over a period of time, the manner in which he responds to these stimuli represents a mode of accommodation or adaptation that may be considered as part of the individual's personality. Socialization is a process by which a society inculcates values, norms, ideals, and beliefs to its members, and may be understood in terms of learning theory. From the time an individual is born, he experiences needs, or tensions, that in one way or another are reinforced. In childhood, one learns over a period of time how to interact with parents who represent authority figures. This is the beginning, Presthus argues, of learning to accommodate to organizations. Interaction with parents represents one's early experience with authority figures. In later life, authority figures are individuals who may be teachers, organizational superiors, or political figures. However, there are different ways in which individuals learn to interact with such authority figures.

Presthus presents some general stereotypes of individuals in organizations, and he defines a behavior pattern that is characterized by each type. The *upward-mobile* may be analogous to the organization man. He is satisfied with his organizational commitment, desires the rewards and status associated with being in the organization, and seeks to satisfy those in higher positions in order to obtain the rewards of the organization. Such an individual may be relatively easy to manage. He is likely to comply with directives simply because compliance is an internalized response for him. The *indifferent* withdraws from the organization. He is there simply because he probably has no alternative. It is difficult, if not impossible, for him to find satisfaction in the organization, but he must work in order to live. The *ambivalent* is likely to be a professional. He is a person highly committed to his own work, rather than to the organization in which he conducts it. In a sense, one can infer from Presthus' types that the ambivalent will be the most difficult to manage and the most difficult person from whom to obtain high levels of organizational commitment. Yet it is possible also that ambivalents may be agents of change or highly competent individuals with whom the organization must come to terms.

If these general modes of accommodation described by Presthus have any usefulness at all, they suggest that organizations are faced with the problem of integrating individuals who come to them with very different points of view about operating within the system. Moreover, different types of organization may be characterized by different proportions of individual types. The bureaucratic organization, it would seem, is more likely to be filled with upward-mobiles and indifferents than with ambivalents. In flexible organizations, which must confront a turbulent environment, it is likely that the ambivalent or highly skilled professional will be found in larger proportions than either the upward-mobile or the indifferent. All this suggests very different managerial problems in dealing with the human resources in the different organizational structures.

Organizations generally face the problem of selecting members from a wide range of backgrounds and experience, a fact which suggests also that members must be selected from a pool of individuals who already have different personality orientations, or patterns of accommodation. As the first reading by Schein in this section notes, socialization continues within an organization. Individuals are subjected to various cues and reinforcements once they become members. People "learn the ropes," which means that they become aware of the values, activities, and behavior required for successful and effective accommodation in the long run. This is the point made by Schein: the organization plays a significant part in shaping the attitudes, values, and beliefs of an individual. Thus, the individual's accommodation pattern prior to joining an organization is affected and perhaps reinforced by the kinds of contingencies that exist within the structure, once he has become a member.

Obviously, the point of view that one brings to an organization will significantly affect the manner in which he reacts to the contingencies in the organizational setting. The upward-mobile may react favorably to a system of rewards which provides high pay-offs, perhaps in increased status, income, or prestige, for loyalty and commitment. The indifferent, on the other hand, may well view the reward system as a manipulative attempt to control his life; thus, his alienation from the organization will only be increased. The ambivalent, viewing the authority system as a nuisance, may interpret the organizational reinforcement mechanism substantially differently than intended, causing problems for upwardly-mobile administrators. In his second reading, Schein defines the interaction between the employee and the organization as the *psychological contract*. Under this contract the employee exchanges work and loyalty for pay, job security, and other reinforcers. But each of the different types of individuals, characterized by Presthus, strike different bargains (psychological contracts).

The point of this part can be summarized easily: Individuals are subject to stimuli and reinforcement in their day-to-day experiences in an organization. These contingencies shape their behavior and cause the development of fairly consistent patterns of performance.

The contention that individuals respond to the reward system has the most significant implications for the manager. It is very possible that some individuals may view rewards differently than the manager does. For example, a manager may feel that he is reinforcing effective work behavior using an existing compensation system. He may, at the appropriate time of the year, give an employee a salary increase, comfortable in the conviction that the raise is an appropriate reward for good performance by the subordinate. Suppose, however, that the salary increase is approximately 6 percent, and the cost of living increase in that particular year is 4 percent. The individual may evaluate the increased effort that he has put forth over the year and decide that the 2 percent salary increase was not worth the 10 percent additional work required to obtain it.

Thus, while the manager believes the situation may be positively reinforcing, the individual for whom the reinforcement is intended does not have the same perception. It is this problem with which managers must deal if they intend to use reinforcement to affect performance. Reinforcements must be perceived as rewards or sanctions in order to be effective.

As we will see in part 5, the linkage between performance and reward may be difficult to establish because of the nature of the system itself; in the case of a highly integrated system such as an assembly line, for example, it may be virtually impossible to segregate the contribution of any one individual. In part 5 we will examine some alternative methods of job design, compensation, and training which can serve to facilitate the performance-reward link. We will examine more closely why the organizational system—the environment in which an individual works—must be supportive of the performance desired.

REINFORCEMENT THEORY

W. CLAY HAMNER

Traditionally management has been defined as the process of getting things done through other people. The succinctness of this definition is misleading in that, while it may be easy to say *what* a manager does, it is difficult to describe the determinants of behavior, i.e. to tell *how* the behavior of the manager influences the behavior of the employee toward accomplishment of a task. Human behavior in organizational settings has always been a phenomenon of interest and concern. However, it has only been in recent years that a concerted effort has been made by social scientists to describe the principles of reinforcement and their implications for describing the determinants of behavior as they relate to the theory and practice of management (e.g. see Nord, 1969; Wiard, 1972; Whyte, 1972; Jablonsky and DeVries, 1972; Hersey and Blanchard, 1972; and Behling, Schriesheim, and Tolliver, in press).[1]

Organizational leaders must resort to environmental changes as a means of influencing behavior. Reinforcement principles are the most useful method for this purpose because they indicate to the leader how he might proceed in designing or modifying the work environment in order to effect specific changes in behavior (Scott and Cummings, 1973). A reinforcement approach to management does not consist of a bag of tricks to be applied indiscriminately for the purpose of coercing unwilling people (Michael & Meyerson, 1962). Unfortunately, many people who think of Skinnerian applications (Skinner, 1969) in the field of management and personnel think of manipulation and adverse control over employees. Increased knowledge available today of the positive aspects of conditioning as applied to worker performance should help to dispel these notions.

The purpose of this paper is to describe the determinants of behavior as seen from a reinforcement theory point of view, and to describe how the management of the contingencies of reinforcement in organizational settings is a key to successful management. Hopefully, this paper will enable the manager to understand how his behavior affects the behavior of his subordinates and to see that in most cases the failure or success of the worker at the performance of a task is a direct function of the manager's own behavior. Since a large portion of the manager's time is spent in the process of modifying behavior patterns and shaping them so that they will be more goal oriented, it is appropriate that this paper begin by describing the processes and principles that govern behavior.

Learning as a Prerequisite for Behavior

Learning is such a common phenomenon that we tend to fail to recognize its occurrence. Nevertheless, one of the major premises of reinforcement theory is that all behavior is learned—a worker's skill, a supervisor's attitude and a secretary's manners. The importance of learning in organizational settings is asserted by Costello and Zalkind when they conclude:

This article was prepared especially for this book.

Every aspect of human behavior is responsive to learning experiences. Knowledge, language, and skills, of course; but also attitudes, value systems, and personality characteristics. All the individual's activities in the organization—his loyalties, awareness of organizational goals, job performance, even his safety record have been learned in the largest sense of that term (1963, p. 205).

There seems to be general agreement among social scientists that learning can be defined as *a relatively permanent change in behavior potentiality that results from reinforced practice or experience*. Note that this definition states that there is change in behavior potentiality and not necessarily in behavior itself. The reason for this distinction rests on the fact that we can observe other people responding to their environments, see the consequences which accrue to them, and be vicariously conditioned. For example, a boy can watch his older sister burn her hand on a hot stove and "learn" that pain is the result of touching a hot stove. This definition therefore allows us to account for "no-trial" learning. Bandura (1969) describes this as imitative learning and says that while behavior can be *acquired* by observing, reading, or other vicarious methods, "*performance* of observationally learned responses will depend to a great extent upon the nature of the reinforcing consequences to the model or to the observer" (p. 128).

Luthans (1973, p. 362) says that we need to consider the following points when we define the learning process:

1. Learning involves a change, though not necessarily an improvement, in behavior. Learning generally has the connotation of improved performance, but under this definition bad habits, prejudices, stereotypes, and work restrictions are learned.

2. The change in behavior must be relatively permanent in order to be considered learning. This qualification rules out behavioral changes resulting from fatigue or temporary adaptations as learning.

3. Some form of practice or experience is necessary for learning to occur.

4. Finally, practice or experience must be reinforced in order for learning to occur. If reinforcement does not accompany the practice or experience, the behavior will eventually disappear.

From this discussion, we can conclude that learning is the acquisition of knowledge, and performance is the translation of knowledge into practice. The primary effect of reinforcement is to strengthen and intensify certain aspects of ensuing behavior. Behavior that has become highly differentiated (shaped) can be understood and accounted for only in terms of the history of reinforcement of that behavior (Morse, 1966). Reinforcement generates a reproducible behavior process in time. A response occurs and is followed by a reinforcer, and further responses occur with a characteristic temporal patterning. When a response is reinforced it subsequently occurs more frequently than before it was reinforced. Reinforcement may be assumed to have a characteristic and reproducible effect on a particular behavior, and usually it will enhance and intensify that behavior (Skinner, 1938; 1953).

Two Basic Learning Processes

Before discussing in any detail exactly how the general laws or principles of reinforcement can be used to predict and influence behavior, we must differentiate between two types of behavior. One kind is known as *voluntary* or *operant* behavior, and the other is known as *reflex* or *respondent* behavior. Respondent behavior takes in all responses of human beings that are *elicited* by special stimulus changes in the environment. An example would be when a person turns a light on in a dark room (stimulus change), his eyes contract (respondent behavior).

Operant behavior includes an even greater amount of human activity. It takes in all the responses of a person that may at some time be said to have an effect upon or do something to the person's outside world (Keller, 1969). Operant behavior *operates* on this world either directly or indirectly. For example, when a person presses the up button at the elevator entrance to "call" the elevator, he is operating on his environment.

The process of learning or acquiring reflex behavior is different from the processes of learning or acquiring voluntary behavior. The two basic and distinct learning processes are known as *classical conditioning* and *operant conditioning*. It is from studying these two learning processes that much of our knowledge of individual behavior has emerged.

Classical Conditioning[2]

Pavlov (1902) noticed, while studying the automatic reflexes associated with digestion, that his laboratory dog salivated (unconditioned response) not only when food (unconditioned stimulus) was placed in the dog's mouth, but also when other stimuli were presented before food was placed in the dog's mouth. In other words, by presenting a neutral stimulus (ringing of a bell) every time food was presented to the dog, Pavlov was able to get the dog to salivate to the bell alone.

A stimulus which is not a part of a reflex relationship (the bell in Pavlov's experiment) becomes a *conditioned stimulus* for the response by repeated, temporal pairing with an *unconditioned* stimulus (food) which already elicits the response. This new relationship is known as a conditioned reflex, and the pairing procedure is known as classical conditioning.

While it is important to understand that reflex behavior is conditioned by a different process than is voluntary behavior, classical conditioning principles are of little use to the practicing manager. Most of the behavior that is of interest to society does not fit in the paradigm of reflex behavior (Michael and Meyerson, 1962). Nevertheless, the ability to generalize from one stimulus setting to another is very important in human learning and problem solving, and for this reason, knowledge of the classical conditioning process is important.

Operant Conditioning[3]

The basic distinction between classical and operant conditioning procedures is in terms of the *consequences* of the conditioned response. In classical conditioning, the sequence of events is independent of the subject's behavior. In operant conditioning, consequences (rewards and punishments) are made to occur as a consequence of the subject's response or failure to respond. The distinction between these two methods is shown in Figure 1.

In Figure 1, we see that classical conditioning involves a three stage process. In the diagram, let S refer to *stimulus* and R to *response*. We see that in stage

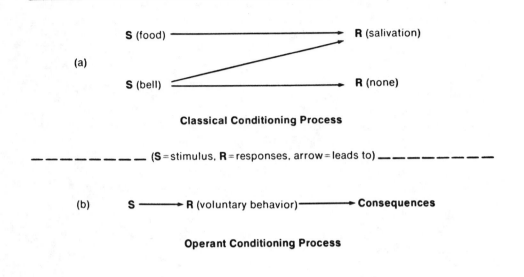

Classical Conditioning Process

— — — — — — — (S = stimulus, R = responses, arrow = leads to) — — — — — — —

(b)   S ⟶ R (voluntary behavior) ⟶ **Consequences**

Operant Conditioning Process

Figure 1. Classical vs. operant conditioning

1, the unconditioned stimulus (food) elicits an unconditioned response (salivation). In stage 2, a neutral stimulus (bell) elicits no known response. However, in stage 3, after the ringing of the bell is repeatedly paired with the presence of food, the bell alone becomes a conditioned stimulus and elicits a conditioned response (salivation). The subject has no control over the unconditioned or conditioned response, but is "at the mercy" of his environment and his past conditioning history.

Note however, that for voluntary behavior, the consequence is dependent on the behavior of the individual in a given stimulus setting. Such behavior can be said to "operate" (Skinner, 1969) on the environment, in contrast to behavior which is "respondent" to prior eliciting stimuli (Michael and Meyerson, 1962). Reinforcement is not given every time the stimulus is presented, but is *only* given when the correct response is made. For example, if an employee taking a work break, puts a penny (R) in the soft drink machine (S), nothing happens (consequence). However, if he puts a quarter (R) in the machine (S), he gets the soft drink (consequence). In other words, the employee's behavior is *instrumental* in determining the consequences which accrue to him.

The interrelationships between the three components of (1) *stimulus* or environment, (2) *response* or performance, and (3) consequences or *reinforcements* are known as the *contingencies* of reinforcement. Skinner (1969) says "The class of responses upon which a reinforcer is *contingent* is called an operant, to suggest the action on the environment followed by reinforcements (p. 7)." Operant conditioning presupposes that human beings explore their environment and act upon it. This behavior, randomly emitted at first, can be constructed as an operant by making a reinforcement contingent on a response. Any stimulus present when an operant is reinforced acquires control in the sense that the rate of response for that individual will be higher when it is present. "Such a stimulus does not act as a *goad*; it does not elicit the response (as was the case in classical conditioning of reflex behavior)[4] in the sense of forcing it to occur. It is simply an essential aspect of the occasion upon which response is made and reinforced (Skinner, 1969; p. 7)."

Therefore, an adequate formulation of the interaction between an individual and his environment must always specify three things: (1) the occasion upon which a response occurs, (2) the response itself and (3) the reinforcing consequences. Skinner holds that the consequences determine the likelihood that a given operant will be performed in the future. Thus to change behavior, the consequences of the behavior must be changed, i.e. the contingencies must be rearranged (the ways in which the consequences are related to the behavior) (Behling, *et al*, in press). For Skinner, this behavior generated by a given set of contingencies can be accounted for without appealing to hypothetical inner states (e.g. awareness or expectancies). "If a conspicuous stimulus does not have an effect, it is not because the organism has not attended to it or because some central gatekeeper has screened it out, but because the stimulus plays no important role in the prevailing contingencies (Skinner 1969, p. 8)."

Arrangement of the Contingencies of Reinforcement

In order to *understand* and *interpret* behavior, we must look at the interrelationship among the components of the contingencies of behavior. If one expects to influence behavior, he must also be able to manipulate the consequences of the behavior (Skinner, 1969). Haire (1964) reports the importance of being able to manipulate the consequences when he says,

> Indeed, whether he is conscious of it or not, the superior is bound to be constantly shaping the behavior of his subordinates by the way in which he utilizes the rewards that are at his disposal, and he will inevitably modify the behavior patterns of his work group thereby. For this reason, it is important to see as clearly as possible what is going on, so that the changes can be planned and chosen in advance, rather than simply accepted after the fact.

After appropriate reinforcers that have sufficient incentive value to maintain stable responsiveness have been chosen, the contingencies between specific performances and reinforcing stimuli must be arranged (Bandura, 1969). Employers intuitively use rewards in their attempt to modify and influence behavior, but their efforts often produce limited results because the methods are used improperly, inconsistently, or inefficiently. In many instances considerable rewards are bestowed upon the workers, but they are not made conditional or contingent on the behavior the manager wishes to promote. Also, "long delays often intervene between the occurrence of the desired behavior and its intended consequences; special privileges, activities, and rewards are generally furnished according to fixed time schedules rather than performance requirements; and in many cases, positive reinforcers are inadvertently made contingent upon the wrong type of behavior (Bandura, 1969, pp. 229-230).''

One of the primary reasons that managers fail to ''motivate'' workers to perform in the desired manner is due to a lack of understanding of the power of the contingencies of reinforcement over the employee and of the manager's role in arranging these contingencies. The laws or principles for arranging the contingencies are not hard to understand, and if students of behavior grasp them firmly, they are powerful managerial tools which can be used to increase supervisory effectiveness.

As we have said, operant conditioning is the process by which behavior is modified by manipulation of the contingencies of the behavior. To understand how this works, we will first look at various *types* (arrangements) of contingencies, and then at various *schedules* of the contingencies available. Rachlin (1970) described the four basic ways available to the manager of arranging the contingencies—*positive reinforcement, avoidance learning, extinction*, and *punishment*. The difference among these types of contingencies depends on the consequence which results from the behavioral act. Positive reinforcement and avoidance learning are methods of strengthening *desired* behavior, and extinction and punishment are methods of weakening *undesired* behavior.

Positive reinforcement. ''A positive reinforcer is a stimulus which, when added to a situation, strengthens the probability of an operant response (Skinner, 1953, p. 73).'' The reason it strengthens the response is explained by Thorndike's (1911) Law of Effect. This law states simply that behavior which appears to lead to a positive consequence tends to be repeated, while behavior which appears to lead to a negative consequence tends not to be repeated. A positive consequence is called a reward.

Reinforcers, either positive or negative, are classified as either; (1) unconditioned or primary reinforcers, or (2) conditioned or secondary reinforcers. Primary reinforcers such as food, water, and sex are of biological importance in that they are innately rewarding and have effects which are independent of past experiences. Secondary reinforcers such as job advancement, praise, recognition, and money derive their effects from a consistent pairing with other reinforcers (i.e., they are conditioned). Secondary reinforcement, therefore, depends on the individual and his past reinforcement history. What is rewarding to one person may not be rewarding to another. Managers should look for a reward system which has maximal reinforcing consequences to the group he is supervising.

Regardless of whether the positive reinforcer is primary or secondary in nature, once it has been determined that the consequence has reward value to the worker, it can be used to increase the worker's performance. So the *first step* in the successful application of reinforcement procedures is to select reinforcers that are sufficiently powerful and durable to ''maintain responsiveness while complex patterns of behavior are being established and strengthened'' (Bandura, 1969, p. 225).

The *second step* is to design the contingencies in such a way that the reinforcing events are made contingent upon the desired behavior. This is the rule of reinforcement which is most often violated. Rewards must result from performance, and the greater the degree of performance by an employee, the greater should be his reward. Money as a reinforcer will be discussed later, but it should be noted that money is not the only reward available. In fact, for unionized employees, the supervisor has virtually no way to tie money to performance. Nevertheless, other forms of rewards, such as recognition, promotion and job assignments, can be made contingent on good performance. Unless a manager is willing to discriminate between employees based on their level of performance, the effectiveness of his power over the employee is nil.

The arrangement of positive reinforcement contingencies can be pictured as follows:

$$\text{Stimulus} \rightarrow \text{Desired Response} \rightarrow \text{Positive Consequences}$$
$$(S \rightarrow R \rightarrow R^+)$$

The stimulus is the work environment which leads to a response (some level of performance). If this response leads to positive consequences, then the probability of that response being emitted again increases (Law of Effect). Now, if the behavior is undesired, then the supervisor is conditioning or teaching the employee that undesired behavior will lead to a desired reward. It is important therefore that the reward administered be equal to the performance input of the employee. Homans (1950) labels this as the rule of distributive justice and stated that this reciprocal norm applies in both formal (work) and informal (friendship) relationships. In other words, the employee *exchanges* his services for the rewards of the organization. In order to maintain desired performance, it is important that the manager design the reward system so that the level of reward administered is proportionately contingent on the level of performance emitted.

The *third step* is to design the contingencies in such a way that a reliable procedure for eliciting or inducing the desired response patterns is established; otherwise, if they never occur there will be few opportunities to influence the desired behavior through contingent management. If the behavior that a manager wishes to strengthen is already present, and occurs with some frequency, then contingent applications of incentives can, from the outset, increase and maintain the desired performance patterns at a high level. However, as Bandura (1969) states, "When the initial level of the desired behavior is extremely low, if the criterion for reinforcement is initially set too high, most, if not all, of the person's responses go unrewarded, so that his efforts are gradually extinguished and his motivation diminished (p. 232)."

The nature of the learning process is such that acquiring the new response patterns can be easily established. The principle of operant conditioning says that an operant followed by a positive reinforcement is more likely to occur under similar conditions in the future. Through the process of *generalization*, the more nearly alike the new situation or stimulus is to the original one, the more the old behavior is likely to be emitted in the new environment. For example, if you contract with an electrician to rewire your house, he is able to bring with him enough old behavioral patterns which he generalized to this unfamiliar, but similar, stimulus setting (the house) in order to accomplish the task. He has learned through his past reinforcement history that, when in a new environment, one way to speed up the correct behavior needed to obtain reward is to generalize from similar settings with which he has had experience. Perhaps one reason an employer wants a person with work experience is because the probability of that person emitting the correct behavior is greater and thus the job of managing that person simplified.

Just as generalization is the ability to react to similarities in the environment, *discrimination* is the ability to react to differences in a new environmental setting. Usually when an employee moves from one environment (a job, a city, an office) to another he finds that only certain dimensions of the stimulus conditions change. While all of the responses of the employee in this new setting will not be correct, by skilled use of the procedures of reinforcement currently being discussed, we can bring about the more precise type of stimulus control called discrimination. When we purchase a new car, we do not have to relearn how to drive a car (generalizable stimulus). Instead we need only to learn the difference in the new car and the old car so that we can respond to these differences in order to get reinforced. This procedure is called *discrimination training*. "If in the presence of a stimulus a response is reinforced, and in the absence of this stimulus it is extinguished, the stimulus will control the probability of the response in high degree. Such a stimulus is called a *discriminative stimulus* (Michael and Meyerson, 1962)."

The development of effective discriminative repertoires is important for dealing with many different people on an interpersonal basis. Effective training techniques will allow the supervisor to develop the necessary discriminative repertoires in his new employees (e.g. see Bass and Vaughan, 1966, *Training in Industry: The Management of Learning*).

Using the principles of generalization and discrimination in a well-designed training program allows the manager to accomplish the third goal of eliciting or inducing the desired response patterns. Training is a method of *shaping* desired behavior so that it can be conditioned to come under the control of the reinforcement stimuli. Shaping behavior is necessary when the response to be learned is not currently in the individual's repertoire and when it is a fairly complex behavior. In shaping, we teach a desired response by reinforcing the series of successive steps which lead to the final response. This method is essentially the one your parents used when they first taught you to drive. You were first taught how to adjust the seat and mirror, fasten the seat belt, turn on the lights and windshield wipers, and then how to start the engine. Each time you successfully completed each stage you were positively reinforced by some comment. You then were allowed to practice driving on back roads and in empty lots. By focusing on one of these aspects at a time and reinforcing proper responses, your parents were able to shape your driving behavior until you reached the final stage of being able to drive. After your behavior was shaped, driving other cars or driving in new territories was accomplished successfully by the process of generalization and discrimination. This same process is used with a management trainee who is rotated from department to department for a period of time until he has "learned the ropes." After his managerial behavior has been minimally shaped, he is transferred to a managerial position where, using the principles of generalization and discrimination, he is able to adjust to the contingencies of the work environment.

Avoidance Learning. The second type of contingency arrangement available to the manager is called escape, or avoidance learning. Just as with positive reinforcement, this is a method of strengthening desired behavior. A contingency arrangement in which an individual's performance can terminate an already noxious stimulus is called *escape* learning. When behavior can prevent the onset of a noxious stimulus the procedure is called *avoidance learning*. In both cases, the results is the development and maintenance of the desired operant behavior (Michael and Meyerson, 1962).

An example of this kind of control can be easily found in a work environment. Punctuality of employees is often maintained by avoidance learning. The noxious stimulus is the criticism by the shop steward or office manager for being late. In order to avoid criticism other employees make a special effort to come to work on time. A supervisor begins criticizing a worker for "goofing off." Other workers may intensify their efforts to escape the criticism of the supervisor.

The arrangement of an escape reinforcement contingency can be diagrammed as follows:

$$\text{Noxious Stimulus} \rightarrow \text{Desired Response} \rightarrow \text{Removal of Noxious Stimulus}$$
$$(S^- \rightarrow R \nrightarrow S^-)$$

The distinction between the process of strengthening behavior by means of positive reinforcement techniques and avoidance learning techniques should be noted carefully. In one case, the individual works hard to gain the consequences from the environment which results from good work, and in the second case, the individual works hard to avoid the noxious aspects of the environment itself. In both cases the same behavior is strengthened.

While Skinner (1953) recognizes that avoidance learning techniques can be used to condition desired behavior, he does not advocate their use. Instead a Skinnerian approach to operant conditioning is primarily based on the principles of positive reinforcement.

Extinction. While positive reinforcement and avoidance learning techniques can be used by managers to strengthen desired behavior, extinction and punishment techniques are methods available to managers for reducing undesired behavior. When positive reinforcement for a learned or previously conditioned response is withheld, individuals will continue to exhibit that behavior for an extended period of time. Under repeated nonreinforcement, the behavior decreases and eventually disappears. This decline in response rate as a result of nonrewarded repetition of a task is defined as *extinction*.

The diagram of the arrangement of the contingency of extinction can be shown as follows:

$$(1) \quad \text{Stimulus} \rightarrow \text{Response} \rightarrow \text{Positive Consequences}$$
$$(S \rightarrow R \rightarrow R^+)$$

$$(2) \quad \text{Stimulus} \rightarrow \text{Response} \rightarrow \text{Withholding of Positive Consequences}$$
$$(S \rightarrow R \nrightarrow R^+)$$

(3) Stimulus → Withholding of Response
(S ⇸ R)

The behavior which was previously reinforced because (a) it was desired or (b) by poor reinforcement practices is no longer desired. To extinguish this behavior in a naturally recurring situation, response patterns substained by positive reinforcement (Stage 1) are frequently eliminated (Stage 3) by discontinuing the rewards (Stage 2) that ordinarily produce the behavior. This method when combined with a positive reinforcement method is the procedure of behavior modification recommended by Skinner (1953). It leads to the least negative side effects and when the two methods are used together, it allows the employee to get the rewards he desires and allows the organization to eliminate the undesired behavior.

Punishment. A second method of reducing the frequency of undesired behavior is through the use of punishment. Punishment is the most controverial method of behavior modification, and most of the ethical questions about operant methods of control center around this technique. "One of the principal objections to aversive control stems from the widespread belief that internal, and often unconscious, forces are the major determinant of behavior. From this perspective, punishment may temporarily suppress certain expressions, but the underlying impulses retain their strength and press continuously for discharge through alternative actions (Bandura, 1969, p. 292)." While Skinner (1953) discounts the internal state hypothesis, he recommends that extinction rather than punishment be used to decrease the probability of the occurrence of a particular behavior.

 Punishment is defined as presenting an aversive or noxious consequence contingent upon a response, or removing a positive consequence contingent upon a response. Based on the Law of Effect, as rewards strengthen behavior, punishment weakens it. This process can be shown as follows:

(1) Stimulus → Undesired Behavior → Noxious Consequence or
    $(S → R → R^-)$ Withholding of Positive
    $(\quad$ or ⇸ $R^+)$ Consequence

(2) Stimulus ⇸ Undesired Behavior
    (S ⇸ R)

Notice carefully the difference in the withholding of rewards in the punishment process and the withholding of rewards in the extinction process. In the extinction process, we withhold rewards for behavior that has previously been administered the rewards because the behavior was desired. In punishment, we withhold a reward because the behavior is undesired, has never been associated with the reward before, and is in fact a noxious consequence. For example, if your young son began imitating an older neighborhood boy's use of profanity and you thought it was "cute," you might reinforce the behavior by laughing or by calling public attention to it. Soon, the son learns one way to get the recognition he craves is to use profanity—even though he may have no concept of its meaning. As the child reaches an accountable age, you decide that his use of profanity is no longer as cute as it once was. To stop the behavior: (1) you can withhold the previous recognition you gave the child by ignoring him (extinction), (2) you can give the child a spanking (punishment by noxious consequence), or (3) you can withhold his allowance or refuse to let him watch television (punishment by withholding of positive consequences not previously connected with the act).

It should be noted that method 2 and perhaps method 3 would be considered cruel because of the parent's own inconsistencies. Punishment should rarely be used to extinguish behavior that has previously been reinforced if the person administering the punishment is the same person who previously reinforced the behavior. However, had the parent failed to extinguish the use of profanity prior to sending the child out in society (e.g. school, church), it is possible that the society may punish the child for behavior that the parent is reinforcing or at least tolerating. It is often argued therefore that the failure to use punishment early in the life of a child for socially unacceptable behavior (e.g., stealing, driving at excessive speeds, poor table manners) is more cruel than the punishment itself, simply because the society will withhold rewards or administer adversive consequences for the behavior which the parents should have extinguished.

The use of aversive control is frequently questioned on the assumption that it produces undesirable by-products. In many cases this concern is warranted. Bandura (1969) states that it depends on the circumstances and on the past reinforcement history of the reinforcement agent and the reinforcement target as to whether punishment or extinction should be used. He says:

Many of the unfavorable effects, however, that are sometimes associated with punishment are not necessarily inherent in the methods themselves but result from the faulty manner in which they are applied. A great deal of human behavior is, in fact, modified and closely regulated by natural aversive contingencies without any ill effects. On the basis of negative consequences people learn to avoid or to protect themselves against hazardous falls, flaming or scalding objects, deafening sounds, and other hurtful stimuli. . . . In instances where certain activities can have injurious effects, aversive contingencies *must* be socially arranged to ensure survival. Punishment is rarely indicted for ineffectiveness or deleterious side effects when used, for example, to teach young children not to insert metal objects into electrical outlets, not to cross busy thoroughfares. . . . Certain types of negative sanctions, if applied considerately, can likewise aid in eliminating self-defeating and socially detrimental behavior without creating any special problems (p. 294).

Schedules of Positive Reinforcement
The previous discussion was primarily concerned with methods of arranging the contingencies of reinforcement in order to modify behavior. Two major points were discussed. First, some type of reinforcement is necessary in order to produce a change in behavior. Second, a combined program of positive reinforcement and extinction are more effective for use in organizations than are programs using punishment and/or avoidance learning techniques. The previous discussion thus tells what causes behavior and why it is important information for the manager, but it does not discuss the several important issues dealing with the scheduling or administering of positive reinforcement.

According to Costello and Zalkind (1963), "The speed with which learning takes place and also how lasting its effects will be is determined by the timing of reinforcement" (p. 193). In other words, the effectiveness of reinforcement varies as a function of the schedule of its administration. A reinforcement schedule is a more-or-less formal specification of the occurrence of a reinforcer in relation to the behavioral sequence to be conditioned, and effectiveness of the reinforcer depends as much upon its scheduling as upon any of its other features (magnitude, quality and degree of association with the behavioral act) (Adam and Scott, 1971).

There are many conceivable arrangements of a positive reinforcement schedule which managers can use to reward their workers (Ferster and Skinner, 1957). Aldis (1961) identifies two basic types of schedules which have the most promise concerning possible worker motivation. These schedules are *continuous* and *partial reinforcement* schedules.

Continuous reinforcement schedule. Under this schedule, every time the correct operant is emitted by the worker, it is followed by a reinforcer. With this schedule, behavior increases very rapidly but when the reinforcer is removed (extinction) performance decreases rapidly. For this reason it is not recommended for use by the manager over a long period of time. It is also difficult or impossible for a manager to reward the employee continuously for emitting desired behavior. Therefore a manager should generally consider using one or more of the partial reinforcement schedules when he administers both financial and nonfinancial rewards.

Partial reinforcement schedules. Partial reinforcement, where reinforcement does not occur after every correct operant, leads to slower learning but stronger retention of a response than total or continuous reinforcement. "In other words, *learning is more permanent when we reward correct behavior only part of the time*" (Bass and Vaughan, 1966, p. 20). This factor is extremely relevant to the observed strong resistance to changes in attitudes, values, norms, and the like.

Ferster and Skinner (1957) have described four basic types of partial reinforcement schedules for operant learning situations. They are:

1. *Fixed interval schedule.* Under this schedule a reinforcer is administered only when the desired response occurs after the passage of a specified period of time since the previous reinforcement. Thus a worker paid on a weekly basis would receive a full pay check every Friday, assuming that the worker was performing minimally acceptable behavior. This method offers the least motivation for hard work among employees (Aldis, 1961). The kind of behavior often observed with fixed-interval schedules is a pause after reinforcement and then an increase in rate of responding until a high rate of performance occurs just as the interval is about to end. Suppose the plant manager visits the shipping department each day at approximately 10:00 A.M. This fixed schedule of supervisory recognition will probably cause performance to be at its highest just prior to the plant manager's visit and then performance will probably steadily decline thereafter and not reach its peak again until the next morning's visit.

2. *Variable interval schedule.* Under this schedule, reinforcement is administered at some variable interval of time around some average. This schedule is not recommended for use with a pay plan (Aldis, 1961), but it is an ideal method to use for administering praise, promotions, and supervisory visits. Since the reinforcers are

dispensed unpredictably, variable schedules generate higher rates of response and more stable and consistent performance (Bandura, 1969). Suppose our plant manager visits the shipping department on an *average* of once a day but at randomly selected time intervals, that is, twice on Monday, once on Tuesday, not on Wednesday, not on Thursday, and twice on Friday, all at different times during the day. Performance will be higher and have less fluctuation than under the fixed interval schedule.

3. *Fixed ratio schedule.* Here a reward is delivered only when a fixed number of desired responses take place. This is essentially the piece-work schedule for pay. The response level here is significantly higher than that obtained under any of the interval (or time-based) schedules.

4. *Variable ratio schedule.* Under this schedule, a reward is delivered only after a number of desired responses with the number of desired responses changing from the occurrence of one reinforcer to the next, around an average. Thus a person working on a 15-to-1 variable ratio schedule might receive reinforcement after 10 responses, then 20 responses, then 15 responses, etc., to an average of 1 reinforcer per 15 responses. Gambling is an example of a variable ratio reward schedule. Research evidence reveals that of all the variations in scheduling procedures available, this is the most powerful in sustaining behavior (Jablonsky and DeVries, 1972). In industry, this plan would be impossible to use as the only plan for scheduling reinforcement. However, Aldis (1961) suggests how this method could be used to supplement other monetary reward schedules:

> Take the annual Christmas bonus as an example. In many instances, this "surprise" gift has become nothing more than a ritualized annual salary supplement which everybody expects. Therefore, its incentive-building value is largely lost. Now suppose that the total bonus were distributed at irregular intervals throughout the year and in small sums dependent upon the amount of work done. Wouldn't the workers find their urge to work increased? (p. 63).

An important point to remember is that to be effective a schedule should always include the specification of a contingency between the behavior desired and the occurrence of a reinforcer. In many cases it may be necessary to use each of the various schedules for administering rewards—for example, base pay on a fixed interval schedule, promotions and raises on a variable interval schedule, recognition of above average performance with a piece-rate plan (fixed ratio) and supplementary bonuses on a variable ratio schedule. The effect of each of the types of reinforcement schedules and the various methods of arranging reinforcement contingencies on worker performance is summarized in Table 1.

The necessity for arranging appropriate reinforcement contingencies is dramatically illustrated by several studies in which rewards were shifted from a response-contingent (ratio) to a time-contingent basis (interval). During the period in which rewards were made conditional upon occurrence of the desired behavior, the appropriate response patterns were exhibited at a consistently high level. When the same rewards were given based on time and independent of the worker's behavior, there was a marked drop in the desired behavior. The reinstatement of the performance-contingent reward schedule promptly restored the high level of responsiveness (Lovaas, Berberich, Perloff, and Schaeffer, 1966; Baer, Peterson, and Sherman, 1967). Similar declines in performance were obtained when workers were provided rewards in advance without performance requirements (Ayllen and Azrin, 1965; Bandura and Perloff, 1967).

TABLE 1. Operant Conditioning Summary

Arrangement of Reinforcement Contingencies	Schedule of Reinforcement Contingencies	Effect on Behavior When Applied to the Individual	Effect on Behavior When Removed from the Individual
	Continuous Reinforcement	Fastest method to establish a new behavior.	Fastest method to extinguish a new behavior.
	Partial Reinforcement	Slowest method to establish a new behavior.	Slowest method to extinguish a new behavior.
	Variable Partial Reinforcement	More consistent response frequencies.	Slower extinction rate.
	Fixed Partial Reinforcement	Less consistent response frequencies.	Faster extinction rate.
Positive Reinforcement ——————— Avoidance Reinforcement		Increased frequency over preconditioning level.	Return to preconditioning level.
Punishment ——————— Extinction		Decreased frequency over preconditioning level.	Return to preconditioning level.

(Adapted from Behling et al., reprinted with permission of the author from "Present Theories and New Directions in Theories of Work Effort," *Journal Supplement and Abstract Service* of the American Psychological Corporation.)

Aldis (1961) encourages businessmen to recognize the importance of a positive reinforcement program. He also says that experimentation with various schedules of positive reinforcement is the key to reducing job boredom and increasing worker satisfaction. He concludes:

Most of us fully realize that a large proportion of all workers hold jobs that are boring and repetitive and that these employees are motivated to work not by positive rewards but by various oblique forms of threat. . . . The challenge is to motivate men by positive rewards rather than by negative punishments or threats of punishments. . . . Businessmen should recognize how much their conventional wage and salary systems essentially rely on negative reinforcement.

Thus the promise of newer methods of wage payments which rely on more immediate rewards, on piece-rate pay, and greater randomization does not lie only in the increase in productivity that might follow. The greater promise is that such experiments may lead to happier workers as well (p. 63).

Management and the Dissemination of Knowledge

Previously we defined *learning* as the acquisition of knowledge (by the process of operant conditioning), and performance as the translation of knowledge into behavior (depending on the consequences). It can be argued therefore that what managers do is disseminate knowledge to those they manage in order to gain the desired level of performance. The question that remains to be answered is "What is knowledge, i.e., what information should one disseminate in order to control behavior?"

There are two types of knowledge according to Skinner (1969). *Private knowledge* (Polanyi, 1960; Bridgeman, 1959) is knowledge established through experience with the contingencies of reinforcement. Skinner says "The world which establishes contingencies of reinforcement of the sort studied in an operant analysis is presumably 'what knowledge is about.' A person comes to know that world and how to behave in it in the sense that he acquires behavior which satisfies the contingencies it maintains" (1969, p. 156). The behavior which results from private knowledge is called *contingency-shaped* behavior. This is the knowledge which one must possess in order to perform correctly in order to get rewarded. This knowledge does not assume any awareness on the part of the person but is based entirely on the person's past reinforcement history. A person can "know how" to play golf, for example, as indicated by a series of low scores—yet it is an entirely different thing to be able to tell others how to play golf. A machine operator may be an excellent employee, but make a poor foreman. One reason may be that, while he possesses private knowledge about his job, he is unable to verbalize the contingencies to other people.

Public knowledge, then, is the ability to derive rules from the contingencies, in the form of injunctions or descriptions which specify occasions, responses, and consequences (Skinner, 1969, p. 160). The behavior which results from public knowledge is called *rule-governed* behavior.

The reason the possession of public knowledge is important to the manager is simple. The employee looks to the manager for information about what behavior is required, how to perform the desired behavior, and what the consequences of the desired behavior will be. Before a manager can give correct answers to these questions, he must understand the true contingencies himself, since his business is not in doing, but in telling others how to do. The point is to be able to analyze the contingencies of reinforcement found in the organization and "to formulate rules or laws which make it unnecessary to be exposed to them in order to behave appropriately" (Skinner, 1969, p. 166).

After living in a large city for a long time, a person is able to go from Point A to Point B with little trouble. The knowledge of how to get around in the city was shaped by the past history with the environment. This behavior is an example of contingency-shaped behavior. If a stranger arrives in the same city and desires to go from Point A to Point B he too will have little trouble. He will look at a map of the city, and follow the path specified by the map. This behavior is an example of rule-governed behavior. Whether or not a person will continue to follow the map (rule) in the future is dependent on the consequences of following the map in the past. If the rule specified the correct contingencies, he probably will continue to use the map, but if a person found the map to be in error, then he will probably look to other sources of information (e.g., asking someone with private knowledge). The same thing happens in industry. If a manager is correct in the specification of the rules—that is, the new worker follows the rules and receives a reward—then the worker will probably follow the other rules specified by the manager. If the manager specifies incorrect rules, then the worker may look to his peers or to other sources for information (e.g., the union steward) and specification of rules which describe behavior that will be rewarded.

There are two kinds of rules the manager can specify to the employee. A command or *mand* is a rule that specifies behavior and consequences of the behavior, where the consequences are arranged by the person giving the command. The specified or implied consequences for failure to act are usually aversive in nature and the judgment of the correctness of the behavior is made by the person giving the command. A foreman who tells the worker to be on time for work is giving the worker a command. The implied consequence is that if the employee fails to report on time, the foreman will take action.

Advice and warnings are called *tacts* and involve rules which specify the reinforcements contingent on prior stimulation from rules, or laws. They specify the same contingencies which would directly shape behavior (private knowledge). The specification of the tact speeds up the conditioning process. If a secretary tells her boss he should take an umbrella when he goes to lunch she is describing a tact. She has no control over the consequences (getting wet) of the behavior (not carrying the umbrella). Instead it is determined by the environment itself (weather). Skinner (1969) says:

> *Go west, young man* is an example of advice (tacting) when the behavior it specifies will be reinforced by certain consequences which do not result from action taken by the advisor. We tend to follow advice because previous behavior in response to similar verbal stimuli has been reinforced. Go west, young man is a command when some consequences of the specified action are arranged by the commander—say, the aversive consequences arranged by an official charged with relocating the inhabitants of a region. When maxims, rules, and laws are advice, the governed behavior is reinforced by consequences which might have shaped the same behavior directly in the absence of the maxims, rules, and laws. When they are commands, they are effective only because special reinforcements have been made contingent upon them. (p. 148).

While a manager must possess public knowledge as well as private knowledge in order to accomplish his task of "getting things done through other people" in keeping with a plea for positive reinforcement and unbiased reward systems, tacting is the method of rule specification recommended. Skinner (1969) recommends that by specifying the contingencies in such a way that the consequences are positive in nature and failure to respond is met with the withholding of a reward rather than by aversive stimuli, "the 'mand' may be replaced by a 'tact' describing conditions under which specific behavior on the part of the listener will be reinforced (p. 158)." Instead of saying "Give me that report" say "I need the report." "The craftsman begins by ordering his apprentice to behave in a given way; but he may later achieve the same effect simply by describing the relation between what the apprentice does and the consequences" (Skinner, 1969, p. 158). Thus, the technique which managers use to direct the employee can make a lot of difference in the acceptance of the rule by the employee. A mand operates from an avoidance learning base while a tact operates from a positive reinforcement base. A tact is more impersonal and gives the employee freedom in that it does not "enjoin anyone to behave in a given way, it simply describes the contingencies under which certain kinds of behavior will have certain kinds of consequences" (Skinner, 1969, p. 158).

Summary

Behavioral scientists generally agree that people fail to perform at a high level because they lack the *ability* to perform correctly or else they lack the *motivation* to perform. This article has discussed, in great detail, the acquisition of knowledge or ability. It was noted that the management of the contingencies of reinforcement in organizational settings is a key to successful management, both in the acquisition stage and in the performing stage of human behavior. The acquisition of knowledge can be discovered by experience (trial-and-error learning) but can be obtained much faster when people are made aware of the relationships between work performance and external rewards. We have noted that both the manner (reward, punishment) and the schedule of reinforcement presentation influences employee performance and satisfaction.

One of the major methods by which organizations mold individuals during the acquisition stage is through a process called socialization. As Presthus and Schein note in the next three readings, socialization includes that part of the learning process by which members learn the value system, the norms, and the required behavior patterns of the organization which he or she is entering. These readings will explain how different personality types and people with differing need states may react differently to the socialization contingencies.

In part 5 of this book, a second article by Hamner discusses basic rules for correctly applying the contingencies in a management setting. In this second article, we will also examine some of the weaknesses of using a reinforcement approach and also examine the important ethical considerations managers must subscribe to when attempting to alter another person's behavior.

Notes

1. The author is indebted to Professor William E. Scott, Jr., Graduate School of Business, Indiana University for sharing with him his Skinnerian philosophy.
2. Classical conditioning is also known as respondent conditioning and Pavlovian conditioning.
3. Operant conditioning is also known as instrumental conditioning and Skinnerian conditioning.
4. Parentheses added.
5. This is true because the criterion variable is some measure of performance, and performance is directly tied to the reinforcement consequences for the current employees used to derive the selection model.

References

Adam, E. E., and Scott, W. E., The application of behavioral conditioning procedures to the problems of quality control. *Academy of Management Journal*, 1971, 14, 175-193.

Adams, J. S., Inequity in social exchange, in L. Berkowitz (ed.), *Advances in Experimental Psychology*, Academic Press, 1965, 157-189.

Aldis, O., Of pigeons and men, *Harvard Business Review*, 1961, 39, 59-63.

Ayllon, T. and Azrin, N. H., The measurement and reinforcement of behavior of psychotics, *Journal of the Experimental Analysis of Behavior*, 1965, 8, 357-383.

Ashby, Sir Eric, Can education be machine made?, *New Scientist*, February 2, 1967.

Baer, D. M., Peterson, R. F., and Sherman, J. A., The development of imitation by reinforcing behavioral similarity to a model. *Journal of the Experimental Analysis of Behavior*, 1967, 10, 405-416.

Bandura, A. and Perloff, B., The efficacy of self-monitoring reinforcement systems, *Journal of Personality and Social Psychology*, 1967, 7, 111-116.

Bandura, A., *Principles of Behavior Modification*, Holt, Rinehart and Winston, Inc., New York, 1969.

Bass, B. M. and Vaughan, J. A., *Training in Industry: The Management of Learning*, Wadsworth Publishing Company, Belmont, Calif., 1966.

Behling, O., Schriesheim, C. and Tolliver, J., Present theories and new directions in theories of work effort, *Journal Supplement Abstract Service* of the American Psychological Corporation, in press.

Bem, D. J., Self-perception: An alternative interpretation of cognitive dissonance phenomena, *Psychological Review*, 1967, 74, 183-200.

Bridgeman, D. W., *The Way Things Are*, Harvard Press, Cambridge, Mass., 1959.

Costello, T. W. and Zalkind, S. S., *Psychology in Administration*, Prentice-Hall, Inc., Englewood Cliffs, N. J., 1963.

Deci, E. L., The effects of contingent and noncontingent rewards and controls on intrinsic motivation, *Organizational Behavior and Human Performance*, 1972, 8, 217-229.

Deci, E. L., The effects of externally mediated rewards on intrinsic motivation, *Journal of Personality and Social Psychology*, 1971, 18, 105-115.

Festinger, L., A theory of social comparison processes, *Human Relations*, 1954, 7, 117-140.

Ferster, C. B., and Skinner, B. F., *Schedules of Reinforcement*, Appleton-Century-Crofts, New York, 1957.

Ferster, C. B., Nurenberger, J. I., and Levitt, E.B., The control of eating, *Journal of Mathematics*, 1962, 1, 87-109.

Fox, L., The use of efficient study habits, In R. Ulrich, T. Stachnik, and J. Mabry (Eds.), *Control of Human Behavior*, Scott, Foresman, Glenview, Ill., 1966, 85-93.

Goffman, E., *The Presentation of Self in Everyday Life*, Doubleday, New York, 1959.

Goodman, Paul, *Compulsory Mis-education*, Horizon Press, New York, 1964.

Haire, Mason, *Psychology in Management*, 2nd ed., McGraw-Hill, New York, 1964.

Harris, M. B., A self-directed program for weight control: a pilot study, *Journal of Abnormal Psychology*, 1969, 74, 263-270.

Henry, Jules, Review of human behavior: An inventory of scientific findings by Bernard Berelson and Gary A. Steiner, *Scientific American*, July, 1964.

Hersey, P. and Blanchard, K. H., The management of change: Part 2, *Training and Development Journal*, February, 1972, 20-24.

Hilgard, E. R., *Theories of Learning*, 2nd ed., Appleton-Century-Crofts, New York, 1956.

Homme, L. E., and Tosti, D. T., Contingency management and motivation, *Journal of the*

National Society for Programmed Instruction, 1965, 4, 14-16.

Jablonsky, S. and DeVries, D., Operant conditioning principles extrapolated to the theory of management, *Organizational Behavior and Human Performance*, 1972, 7, 340-358.

Keller, F. S., *Learning: Reinforcement Theory*, Random House, New York, 1969.

Kelman, H. C., Manipulation of human behavior: An ethical dilemma for the social scientist, *Journal of Social Issues*, 1965, 21, 31-46.

Kolb, D. A., Winter, S. K., and Berlew, D. E., Self-directed change: Two studies, *Journal of Applied Behavioral Science*, 1968, 4, 453-471.

Krasner, L., Behavior control and social responsibility, *American Psychologist*, 1964, 17, 199-204.

Likert, R., *New Patterns of Management*, McGraw-Hill, New York, 1961.

Lovaas, O. I., Berberich, J. P., Perloff, B. F., and Schaeffer, B., Acquisition of imitative speech for schizophrenic children, *Science*, 1966, 151, 705-707.

Luthans, F., *Organizational Behavior*, McGraw-Hill, New York, 1973.

Maslow, A. H., A theory of human motivation, *Psychological Review*, 1943, 50, 370-396.

McGregor, D., *The Human Side of Enterprise*, New York, McGraw-Hill, 1960.

Michael, J. and Meyerson, L., A behavioral approach to counseling and guidance, *Harvard Educational Review*, 1962, 32, 382-402.

Morse, W. H., Intermittent reinforcement, in W. K. Honig, (ed.), *Operant Behavior*, Appleton-Century-Crofts, New York, 1966.

New tool: Reinforcement for good work, *Business Week*, December 18, 1971, 68-69.

Nord, W. R., Beyond the teaching machine: The neglected area of operant conditioning in the theory and practice of management, *Organizational Behavior and Human Performance*, 1969, 375-401.

Pavlov, I. P., *The Work of the Digestive Glands*, (Translated by W. H. Thompson), Charles Griffin, London, 1902.

Polanyi, M., *Personal Knowledge*, Univ. of Chicago Press, 1960.

Rachlin, H., *Modern Behaviorism*, W. H. Freeman and Co., New York, 1970.

Rogers, Carl R., and Skinner, B. F., Some issues concerning the control of human behavior: A symposium, *Science*, 1956, 124, 1057-1066.

Scott, W. E. and Cummings, L. L., *Readings in Organizational Behavior and Human Performance*, Revised Edition, Irwin, Homewood, Ill., 1973.

Scott, W. E., and Hamner, W. Clay, The effects of order and variance in performance on supervisory ratings of workers, Paper presented at the *45th Annual Meeting*, Midwestern Psychological Association, Chicago, 1973.

Scott, W. E. and Hamner, W. Clay, The effect of order and variance in performance on the rewards given workers by supervisory personnel, mimeo, Indiana University, 1973.

Scott, W. E., Activation theory and task design, *Organizational Behavior and Human Performance*, 1966, 1, 3-30.

Skinner, B. F., *The Behavior of Organisms*. New York: Appleton-Century, 1938.

Skinner, B. F., *Walden Two*. New York: The Macmillan Company, 1948.

Skinner, B. F., Are theories of learning necessary? *Psychological Review*, 1950, 57, 193-216.

Skinner, B. F., *Science and Human Behavior*. New York: The Macmillan Company, 1953.

Skinner, B. F., Freedom and the control of men, *American Scholar*, 1956, 25, 47-65.

Skinner, B. F., Some issues concerning the control of human behavior, *Science*, 1956, 124, 1056-1066.

Skinner, B. F., *Verbal Behavior*. New York: Appleton-Century-Crofts, 1957.

Skinner, B. F. Behaviorism at fifty. *Science*, 1963a, 134, 566-602.

Skinner, B. F., Operant behavior. *American Psychologist*, 1963b, 18, 503-515.

Skinner, B. F., *Contingencies of Reinforcement*, Appleton-Century-Crofts, New York, 1969.

Skinner, B. F., *Beyond Freedom and Dignity*, New York: Alfred A. Knopf, 1971.

Thorndike, E. L., *Animal Intelligence*, Macmillan, New York, 1911.

Vroom, V. H., and Deci, E. L., An overview of work motivation, in V. H. Vroom and E. L. Deci (eds.), *Management and Motivation*, Penguin Press, Baltimore, 1970, 9-19.

Wiard, H., Why manage behavior? A case for positive reinforcement, *Human Resource Management*, Summer, 1972, 15-20.

Where Skinner's theories work, *Business Week*, December, 1972, 64-65.

Whyte, W. F., Skinnerian theory in organizations, *Psychology Today*, April, 1972, 67-68, 96, 98, 100.

INDIVIDUAL ADJUSTMENTS TO ORGANIZATIONS

ROBERT PRESTHUS

. . . A basic assumption throughout our analysis is that social values and institutions mold individual personality and behavior. This occurs through a process called socialization. Society, in effect, provides a web of values and expectations that determines the individual's character, his ethical beliefs, and his ideas about progress, success, and failure. "Those drives which make for the differences in men's characters, like love and hatred, the lust for power and the yearning for submission—are all products of the social process."[1] Men may, for example, be born with an impulse to dominate others, but social values such as the democratic ideal of equality determine the manner and extent to which this impulse can be gratified. When men choose, they choose within this context of socially determined values. While our society provides a broad scope for individual choices, organizational influences traced here have significantly changed the conditions under which they are made. . . .

Man's susceptability to socialization is in part explained by the individual's long period of biologic and economic immaturity. While lower animals become self-sufficient shortly after birth, western man is dependent for some two decades before he strikes out alone. During this time he is dependent upon those who provide his emotional and physical sustenance. At the same time, it appears that even as a child he becomes conscious of his power. When toilet training, walking, and speech begin, he learns that he can defy his parents in matters that are obviously important to them. Here again we see that biological impulses are always conditioned by cultural patterns that differ from society to society. Even the Oedipus complex, which Freud believed to be instinctive, is now thought by some anthropologists to be culturally specific, the result of a monogamous, patriarchal family structure.

The family and other authority figures measure the individual's "growth" largely in terms of his adjustment to social norms. Such norms include national traditions and mythology, religious beliefs, economic and political values, in fact, the whole cultural web that sustains us throughout life. These norms include the parents' perception of the kinds of skills and attitudes required by children for success in our organized society. As a result, individual personality tends to reflect the social structure. The dominant values of society become a superego controlling the individual through approval and anxiety. As Fromm observes: "Society must tend to mold the character structure of its members in such a way they will want to do what they have to do under the existing circumstances."[2]

As we have seen, the individual's successive experiences with authority figures result in a "self-system," a way of relating himself to the world. This system becomes a framework for accepting or rejecting the vast number of stimuli that impinge upon him. Millions of sensory fibers transmit such stimuli through his nervous system. Certain reflexes become reinforced and linked together, providing the basis

Reprinted with the permission of the author from Robert Presthus, *The Organizational Society* (New York: Vintage Books, 1965).

for habitual patterns of behavior. *Both an individual's perceptions and his behavior become, so to speak, structured.* He develops a time-tested way of organizing reality, and his reactions become stabilized accordingly. This relatively consistent pattern of behavior is commonly defined as "personality." Moreover, the personality continually reinforces itself by a selective process that tends to accept only approved impressions which are in turn incorporated into the existing value system. Conflicting stimuli are rejected, and when an individual rejects all conflicting stimuli, we say that he has a low tolerance for ambiguity. . . .

Patterns of Accommodation: Upward-Mobiles

We now turn to the discrete types of personal accommodation that seem to occur in organizations. Following interpersonal theory, we assume that men behave according to the perceived expectations of a given social situation. Over a period of time such responses become relatively consistent; they are continually reinforced because they meet compelling individual needs for security, recognition, and group acceptance. While such accommodations are always the result of *interaction* between the bureaucratic situation and personality, social and organizational values mainly determine the character of functional (anxiety-reducing) and dysfunctional (anxiety-producing) behavior in a given culture. Personality is worked out in a social and interpersonal context. As Sullivan observes, man gradually develops through his relations with significant others a self-system, a personal style of behavior that rejects anxiety-producing responses in favor of those that insure approval. The bureaucratic situation seems to evoke three kinds of personal accommodation, each associated with one of our three personality types, the upward-mobiles, the indifferents, and the ambivalents. [Here] we shall consider the most significant of these, the *upward-mobiles*. . . .

If social structure alone were responsible for personality and behavior, our discrete types of accommodation would presumably not exist. The organization would evoke very similar accommodations in all of its members. But as we have seen, not only do different patterns of class socialization and consequent differences in perception and reaction to interpersonal situations characterize individuals, but the same pattern of socialization may evoke different responses among those subject to it. This combining of social and psychological theory is validated by the experience of Durkheim who began his classic study of *Suicide* with the intention of isolating the social roots of self-destruction, but who ended with an essentially psychological and individual cause, *anomie*.

With these qualifications in mind, we now turn to an analysis of the values and behavior of the typical "upward-mobile." Although his behavior may at times appear unappealing, we are concerned with it only as a form of accommodation to the bureaucratic environment. Our interest is analytic rather than clinical.

The upward-mobiles are typically distinguished by high morale; their level of job satisfaction is high. Indeed, the process and criteria by which they are selected insures that they will have an unfailing optimism. The reasons for this are clear. They identify strongly with the organization and derive strength from their involvement. Their dividends also include disproportionate shares of the organization's rewards in power, income, and ego reinforcement. As we have seen, subjective inequality is a built-in feature of big organizations and is rationalized on the basis of equality of opportunity. Power is easily justified by those who have it, since it confirms daily their right (achieved in fair competition) to possess it. The upward-mobiles will not, therefore, seriously question a system that has proved its rationality. The system remains an internalized article of faith until, as in the case of Arthur Miller's hero in *Death of A Salesman*, the disparity between rhetoric and reality becomes irrepressible. But even then, self-punitive mechanisms may be invoked to preserve the myth: *personal failure* rather than the failure of the system provides a rationalization.

This ability to identify strongly with the system is highly productive in personal terms since it qualifies the upward-mobile for the organization's major rewards. (As we saw earlier, group influence and rank are a function of acceptance of the group's values.) The organization qua organization has meaning for him, evoking loyalty, affirmation, and a constant point of reference. Having accepted its legitimacy and rationality, he can act on the basis of its value premises. The capacity for identification has great strategic value today because social power is rather evenly divided among competing groups. This condition sharpens the organization's conflicts with competitors and puts a premium on loyalty and certainty among its members. The organization tends to resemble a church, which needs champions to endorse its values and to increase its survival power. No dissenters need apply. The demand is for conformity. A rational and sustained attention to business is required; and the heterodoxy possible in a less organized, more secure society becomes a luxury, because it impairs unity.

Since he accepts the larger purposes of the organization, the upward-mobile finds involvement easy. His personality enables him to deal in oversimplification and idealization. He can act without an immaculate cause. He can overlook the contradictions in the routine operations of the organization, as distinct from its official myths. He is able to find certainty and consistency in an organization that is imperfect because it is real. In a sense, he must avoid reality by cultivating the illusion that its actions eventuate in perfect justice. This characteristic of perception calls to mind W. I. Thomas' observation: "If men define situations as real, they are real in their consequences."[3] The organization's values are internalized by the upward-mobile, and thus become premises of action. This psychic act provides him with an operational skill: *the capacity for action despite conflicting alternatives and contradictory aims*.

Here a distinction must be made between the upward-mobile's values and his behavior. His low toleration for ambiguity and his deference toward authority might seem to disqualify him for the versatile role playing that big organizations require. In a democratic society, for example, the upward-mobile must pay homage to democratic expectations of equality and impartiality, even though he knows that some are born to lead and others to follow. However, he can usually assume the appropriate roles whether or not he identifies with the underlying ideals. He manipulates the democratic consensus favoring permissive authority relations and recognizes that "getting along with people" has career utility. Such role playing emphasizes the need for mock behavior in which polite fictions, irony, and banter are used to "get a message across" without disrupting the status relations of those concerned. . . .

Since upward-mobiles often get to the top of the organization and must deal with members at every level, the significance of their own values and behavior is clear. If these are marked by a need to ward off anxiety or to dominate others, organizational relations will be complicated. Since such compelling needs and the security operations they encourage are almost impossible to change, they may prove disastrous for the organization. . . .

This suggests that the capacity to rationalize organizational claims is part of the value equipment of the upward-mobile. He may respect individual dissent and error, but the question is one of *priority*, and in the last analysis he will accept the organization's values. His ability to appraise situations objectively and to act appropriately is bound up with his loyalty to collective values and abstractions. Since he identifies himself with the organization, in a measure ranging from casual opportunism to compulsive surrender, he becomes an instrument of such values. He becomes *the organization* and can thus accept its logical imperatives without much regard for competing individual values. The wrongs inflicted in defense of institutionalized ideals are well known. To some extent they can be explained in terms of the total loyalty that organizations demand and some individuals seek.

In the context of Merton's distinction, the upward-mobile is typically a "local."[4] Unlike the "cosmopolitan" who has a broad disciplinary or national perspective, his interests and aspirations are tied to his own organization. Always loyal, he regards its rules and actions as "the one best way" to handle large numbers of people. If the organization's claims occasionally result in injustice, this is inevitable in an imperfect world. Never doubting the supremacy of collective values, the upward-mobile enthrones administrative, keeping-the-organization-going skills and values. This accounts in part for his ambivalence toward the specialist whose professional norms compete with his loyalty to the organization. In all this, he personifies the "routinization of charisma" whereby organizations have tended historically to become ever more rational and monistic. A man without a "calling," he brings little passion to his work. Rather, he is a "quill-bearing mammal," a dealer in means for whom the paraphernalia of organization outweigh claims of "mission," creed, and party. These tend instead to become instrumental, honorific abstractions used to evoke affirmation and loyalty in the rank and file.

Acceptance of the organization's goals commits the upward-mobile to conformity and to impatience with those who qualify and dissent. As a result, he tends to personalize opposition, finding it difficult to accept as a matter of principle or honest divergence, and attributing it instead to a querulous wish on the dissenter's part to be different for difference's sake. His temperamental affinity for clear-cut causes and decisive action is relevant here. He will not understand those who fail to see what to him is so clearly evident. The fact that his personal values are not always shared will escape or puzzle him. His hostility toward heterodoxy may be sharpened by a natural resentment that others should escape the discipline and sacrifice that ambition has required of him.

The upward-mobile's dislike for controversial causes is functional because organizational claims now cover such matters. Political opinions, patterns of consumption, off-work activity, etc., tend to fall into the bureaucratic net. By honoring conventional values the upward-mobile not only reinforces the standards by which he himself is measured, he also increases the probability that conformity will occur throughout the organization. This phenomenon is clearly apparent in countries such as England where a remarkable social control is achieved through each class's imitation of the one above it. In big organizations a similar mechanism is apparent in the elite's personification of majority values and in the internalization of those values by subordinates. The efficiency and discipline insured by the resulting "upward-looking posture" is incalculable. . . .

Another characteristic of the upward-mobile is his status anxiety, often manifested in a compulsive concern with rank and the symbols of prestige. The term "anxiety" is deliberate since his concern with status and with its derivatives of power and prestige goes beyond mere sensitivity to define a general orientation. Like the search for power, status enchantment is a constant element in the upward-mobile equation. The authoritarian-personality research found, significantly, that such an orientation is common among individuals who seem to find the bureaucratic environment congenial. As we have seen, status differentiation plays a critical role in big organizations. It provides a psychological environment that is conducive to efficiency in operational terms, reinforcing authority, minimizing overt conflict, and structuring interpersonal relations.

Status will be defined here as the prestige or deference attached to the role or position one holds in an organizational hierarchy.[5] Although status is not always conferred according to formal hierarchical role, since some members (such as our "ambivalents") will not accept line or hierarchial definitions of relative status, in the main status and prestige are assigned and rewarded by elites in terms of formal organizational values. . . .

Personal status and organizational discipline are also reinforced by structured patterns of communication. Seniors communicate through a secretary who becomes her master's alter ego and who often exaggerates the status factors inherent in the relationship. The senior rarely visits the subordinate, since this would put him at a psychological disadvantage and reduce his control of the interpersonal situation. Normally the subordinate will come to the senior, and the latter will set the tone of the meeting. Displeasure can be nicely weighted. The tone of voice, the form of address, the length of the meeting, the amount of time the subordinate is required to wait, whether interruptions for phone calls will be permitted—all tend to define the relative status of the participants, and all can be manipulated to obtain desired consequences. The upward-mobile must become extremely sensitive in measuring out and receiving such dispensations. Versatile role-playing is therefore a vital career skill.

The upward-mobile's preoccupation with status is functional because he is anxious to rise, and because a disciplined self-promotion is required to impress those above him with his suitability for bigger things. As the objective relationship between status and achievement becomes more difficult to establish, the collection of unearned status increments is encouraged. Here again the displacement of goals mentioned earlier is to be seen. *The acquisition of status and prestige becomes an end in itself rather than a derivative of some significant achievement.* A common manifestation is the discreet cultivation of prestigeful elders by young upward-mobiles in need of a patron. Such behavior is directly related to the co-optative mechanism which now governs bureaucratic succession. Significantly, it is also similar to the individual's early dependence upon authority-figures, e.g., his mother, his father, his teacher, etc. . . .

[The upward-mobile's] values and behavior include the capacity to identify strongly with the organization, permitting a nice synthesis of personal rewards and organizational goals. A typical form of accommodation is adjustment through power and special efforts to control situations and people. His "security operations" stress efficiency, strength, self-control, and dominance. His most functional value is a deep respect for authority. Not only are his interpersonal relations characterized by considerable sensitivity to authority and to status differences, but his superiors are viewed as nonthreatening models for his own conduct. Meanwhile, his subordinates are regarded with a considerable detachment which permits "universalistic" decisions that meet organizational as opposed to individual needs. Finally, we saw that changing social conditions and values have increased the utility of upward-mobile skills and values, as illustrated by the impact of the big foundations upon academic work and changing patterns of mobility in business and industry.

Patterns of Accommodation: Indifferents

Our second ideal type of accommodation in big organizations is one of indifference or withdrawal. Security, prestige, and power are the values that mediate accommodation, and men act in ways that seem to secure them. Such values have been endorsed by society's authority figures, and since we all hope to gain some measure of security and prestige, the behavior of such figures becomes a model for our own. Although anxiety reduction is probably the main impetus for such emulation, the ways of reducing it vary with the individual and with the situation. The same situation impels different reactions from different people. Status anxiety may push some of us into compulsive success striving, while others displace this need upon other values. The upward-mobile regards organizations as excellent instruments for satisfying his claims, but the indifferent defines them as calculated systems of frustration. He refuses to compete for the rewards they promise.

Indifference is the typical pattern of accommodation for the majority of organization men. The indifferents are found among the great mass of waged and salaried employees who work in the bureaucratic situation. . . . The indifferents are those who have come to terms with their *work environment* by withdrawal and by a redirection of their interests toward off-the-job satisfactions. They have also been alienated by the *work itself*, which has often been downgraded by machine processing and by assembly-line methods. This dual basis for alienation must be recognized. In industrial psychology the main effort has been to compensate for the deadening effect of the work itself by providing a happy work place. Less attention has been given to alienation from the job itself.

We are not speaking here of pathological kinds of alienation, but of modes of accommodation that often seem basically healthy. The typical indifferent has rejected majority values of success and power. While the upward-mobile strives for such values, obtainable today mainly through big organizations, the indifferent seeks that security which the organization can also provide for those who merely "go along." Such security seeking varies in accord with the demands of personality. One individual may have been taught to expect more than life can reasonably offer, and anxiety and frustration follow as his unrealistic claims are discounted. Another may have learned to expect less; he may refuse to accept success values or to compete for them. This role is encouraged by such bureaucratic conditions as hierarchy, oligarchy, and specialization.

The indifferent reaction, then, is the product of both social and organizational influences. But organizational factors seem to outweigh class-induced mobility expectations. However strong such expectations, they rarely survive in an unsympathetic institutional environment. Today, many a potential entrepreneur languishes in some cul-de-sac because the organizational context no longer sustains his aspirations. The resulting accommodation may also reflect personal failures of nerve and energy, bad luck, and so on. But, essentially, indifference is manifested in a psychic withdrawal from the work arena and a transfer of interest to off-work activities. The employee "goes through the motions," paying lip-service to organizational values, but he no longer retains any real interest in the organization or in work for its own sake.

This accommodation may occur in two stages: alienation and indifference. The alienated are those who come into the organization with great expectations. They are determined to climb. But when bureaucratic and personal limitations blunt their hopes, they become alienated. Over a period of time, it seems, this reaction works itself into indifference. On another level, we are dealing with indifference as an *initial* orientation. Such individuals, usually of working or lower-middle-class origin, have been taught not to expect very much. Both socialization and work experience reinforce this perception of their life chances. And both alienation and indifference counter the organization's claims for loyalty, predictability, and hard work. . . .

We have analyzed the behavior of the *indifferent* as a modal type of accommodation. Bureaucratic conditions of work have encouraged indifference in white-collar and professional areas as well as in the blue-collar world. The university environment has been used to document this trend because the writer knows it well, and more importantly because it has traditionally been among the least structured of work environments. Nevertheless, with the exception of a few prestige schools, the universities now have a significant proportion of indifferents in their faculties. This is explained in part by the high expectations of academic men for autonomy, as well as by the personal need for independent work which brought them to the university in the first instance. A major cause is bureaucratic conditions of work and evaluation that undercut professional standards and values.

The typical indifferent tends to reject the organizational bargain which promises authority, status, prestige, and income in exchange for loyalty, hard work, and identification with its values. Instead, he separates his work from the "meaningful" aspects of his life, which latter include recreation and leisure activities. Like the Hormel employee who spoke of "accomplishing something for the day," he is referring to what he plans to do *after* work. If the indifferent remains committed to his work, he will sometimes distinguish between it and the organization. If he is a college instructor, he may assume a "cosmopolitan" view in which his interests, loyalty, and future are seen as bound up with his *profession*, rather than with the particular school in which he happens to practice it.[6]

The indifferent posture also mediates preorganizational influences of class and education that failed to honor success and the repression of unprofitable opinions. The tension between such values and the organization's claims encourages withdrawal, the rejection of majority values, and a refusal to compete for them. In so defining the work bargain the worker often reveals a realistic perception of himself and his life chances.

One result of this mode of accommodation seems to be alienation from political and community affairs. The indifferent tends to reject his company, his union, his political party, and other voluntary organizations. The mass character of society, the power and remoteness of its organizations, and one's resulting feelings of helplessness are among the psychological bases for alienation. The structural conditions of big organization often mean, too, that the organization rejects the indifferent. Oligarchy, for example, breeds alienation by excluding the vast majority of employees from real participation. The need for skilled leaders; the difficulty of getting the word to large numbers of people; the leaders' drive for power and continuity in office; the complexity of decisions; the need and the desire for secrecy in negotiations with other power groups—all restrict active participation. . . .

Patterns of Accommodation: Ambivalents

The small disenchanted minority of whom this mode is characteristic will be set against organizational patterns of authority, status, and small groups. In both personal and organizational terms, the ambivalent's self-system is generally dysfunctional. Creative and anxious, his values conflict with bureaucratic claims for loyalty and adaptability. While the upward-mobile finds the organization congenial, and the indifferent refuses to become engaged, the ambivalent can neither reject its promise of success and power, nor can he play the roles required to compete for them. While upward-mobile anxiety is usually adaptive, ambivalent anxiety tends toward the neurotic.[7] In the bureaucratic situation, the ambivalent individual is a marginal man with limited career chances.

One important qualification is required. Despite his inability to meet bureaucratic demands, the ambivalent type plays a critical social role, namely, that of providing the insight, motivation, and the dialectic that inspire change. The upward-mobile honors the status quo and the indifferent accepts it, but the ambivalent is always sensitive to the need for change. His innovating role is often obscured because the authority, leadership, and money needed to institutionalize change remain in the hands of organizational elites. Nevertheless, few ideals or institutions escape his critical scrutiny. In his view custom is no guarantee of either rationality of legitimacy. This perception is sharpened by his inability to accept charismatic and traditional bases of authority; rationality alone provides a compelling standard. Certain personality traits underlie this critical posture.

The ambivalent personality is typically an introvert, with intense intellectual interests and limited interpersonal facility. Unlike the upward-mobiles, who stress action, objectivity, and easy interpersonal relations,[8] ambivalents are often subjective and withdrawn. Introversion has been found to be related to neurosis; anxiety and depression are common ailments.[9] Ambivalents have high aspirations, complicated by habitual under-rating of their own performance. Compared with extroverts, their intellectual interests are narrow and deep, accuracy and persistence are highly developed, and verbal facility and intelligence are markedly superior.[10]

The ambivalent ordinarily plays a *specialist*, "cosmopolitan" role. He honors theory, knowledge, and skill. Socialization as an independent professional often blinds him to legitimate organizational needs for control and co-ordination. Believing explicitly that both motivation and expertise come from within, he resists bureaucratic rules and supervision. Attempts to impose standards from without are seen as presumptuous and denigrating. As a result, there is always a gap between his self-perception as an independent professional and the galling realization, punctuated daily by the organization's authority and status differentiations, that he is really an employee. His skill authority is not always recognized, even though it is perfectly clear that his technical judgments have been decisive. The managerial facade with which he is confronted confirms his belief that hierarchical authority is often specious. This tension between skill and hierarchical authority is aggravated by the organization's subjective criteria of seniority and obedience. In sum, the bureaucratic situation is inapposite to his personal and professional values.

The heart of the ambivalent reaction is a tenacious self-concern. Most events are perceived by the ambivalent in terms of himself; personal goals are usually primary. His own experiences and skills seem unique; and when his career expectations prove unrealistic, as they often do, he may invoke humanistic themes to buttress his claims for preference. In terms of an earlier distinction, we may regard the ambivalent as an idealistic, independent personality. Unable to achieve distinction on the organization's terms, he may adopt idiosyncratic alternatives, a reaction encouraged by the erosion of qualitative standards. . . .

In view of the compelling status needs, the intellectual orientation, and the marked educational achievement often characteristic of the introverted type, we may assume that our ambivalent is typically of middle-class origin. However, his socialization has apparently not included the respect for success which is crucial for bureaucratic success. "Success," probably the dominant value in our society, is usually defined in terms of competitive, personal achievement, with references that are mainly economic, but that also include almost any other value that can nourish self-esteem. . . .

As we have seen, authority is distributed disproportionately in organizations. It clusters around the top and decreases at an increasing rate as one descends the hierarchy. Its gradations are clearly marked. A specialist with idealistic value preferences, the typical ambivalent will find it difficult to accept the legitimacy of this system. He cannot believe that those who have great authority really merit it in terms of talent, wisdom, or morality. In this context, psychological tests and interviews of managerial employees in several companies found "no relationship between intelligence and aptitude and individual success as defined by their ranks or by their salaries."[11] Such evidence suggests that the ambivalent's judgments are not entirely imaginary. . . .

[The ambivalent's] most important dysfunction is a distorted, fearful perception of authority. The resulting anxiety is a constant handicap in dealing with his superiors. As we have seen, perhaps the most significant item in organizational adjustment and mobility is one's attitude toward authority. Is the authority system perceived as threatening, or as the natural result of size, specialization, and task-oriented relationships? Is authority regarded as a necessary evil or a positive good? Here again the ambivalent is disadvantaged. While the upward-mobile has a close bond with his father and accepts authority easily, the ambivalent tends to view authority figures as threatening, probably because of rejection or dominance by his father but also because authority figures personify conventional values which he resists. . . .

As we have seen, the upward-mobile views those above him as friendly models, while the ambivalent regards them as threatening figures having the power to disadvantage him. His interpersonal relations become difficult both for himself and his superiors, who are much less interested in him than he thinks. They will be embarrassed by his rejection of the friendly patina that colors their relationship. Whether his reaction takes the form of passive resistance, resigned acceptance, or eager submission, the ambivalent is bound to disrupt the desired smoothness. If he assumes an air of submission, the senior may resent the fact that the relationship now rests on hierarchy rather than on commonsense, precedent, or his own wisdom. Submissiveness marks again the ambivalent's inability to accept the need for the kind of nimble role playing which insures that such relations *seem* permissive at the same time they nicely accommodate the authority structure of the situation. Although upward-mobiles learn to play such roles facilely, the ambivalent is often disqualified by self-consciousness and by awkward notions about equality, compounded at the same time by inconsistent needs within himself to reduce anxiety by submission. . . .

Bureaucratic structure may . . . reduce anxiety and conflict by objective definitions of authority and status. But the leveling effects of bureaucratic work also induce status anxiety as men try to find ways to recapture their individuality. The routinization of work evokes intense efforts to personalize one's job. Also relevant is the impulse to compensate for any loss of pride in skill attending the mechanization of many jobs.[13] Bureaucratic structure thus aggravates status anxiety by its specialization and anonymity, encouraging a preoccupation with indexes, however trivial, that can validate minute differentiations in prestige and income. If the ambivalent could accept the status system and his position in it, his anxiety would indeed be eased, but both restrict his discretion in favor of organizational goals. Accommodation is viewed as a surrender of his individualistic values. Not only are the organization's rules and rewards the instruments of authority, but they symbolize an ordered system which challenges his preference for complexity and spontaneity. . . .

We have traced the dysfunctional results of the ambivalent's adjustment to the bureaucratic situation. The most critical item is his fear of authority which often distorts his interpersonal relations. His inability to accept the organization's collective goals, which violate his need for personal autonomy, is also at work. His "tender-minded" view of human relations disqualifies him for the "universalistic" decision making required for success on organizational terms. Since his preferences include a desire for creativity and for a work environment that permits spontaneity and experiment, the structured personal relations, stereotyped procedures, and group decision making of big organization prove stifling. He rejects its systems of authority and status which often seem to rest upon subjective bases rather than upon the objective, professional claims that motivate him. Nor can he easily identify with the small group .

in which he works, for here too the conditions of participation are similar to those of the larger system. If his values did not include prestige and influence, a happier accommodation might be possible; but these again emphasize his ambiguity and his inability to assume the roles required to achieve them. In sum, with the exception of his critical function as the agent of change, the ambivalent type is uniquely unsuited to the bureaucratic situation.

Notes and References

1. Erich Fromm: *Man for Himself* (New York: Rinehart & Co., Inc.; 1947), p. 241.
2. Fromm, p. 241.
3. W. I. Thomas: *The Child in America: Behavior Problems and Programs* (New York: Alfred A. Knopf, Inc.; 1932), p. 572.
4. Robert K. Merton: *Social Theory and Social Structure*, rev. ed. (Glencoe, Illinois: The Free Press; 1957), pp. 393-5 and Ch. 10; also, A. W. Gouldner: "Cosmopolitans and Locals: Toward an Analysis of Latent Social Roles," *Administrative Science Quarterly*, Vols. 2, 3, pp. 281-306; 444-80.
5. Sociologists define "status" as the *position* an individual occupies in the social hierarchy, but I use it here in its popular connotation. R. LaPiere: *A Theory of Social Control* (New York: McGraw-Hill Book Co.; 1954); K. Davis: "A Conceptual Analysis of Stratification," *American Sociological Review*, Vol. 7, pp. 309-21.
6. A. W. Gouldner: "Cosmopolitans and Locals: Toward an Analysis of Latent Social Roles," *Admin. Sci. Q.*, Vols. 2, 3, pp. 281-306; 444-80.
7. The distinction between adaptive anxiety and neurotic anxiety is widely accepted in psychology. Among others, see K. Horney: *Neurosis and Human Growth* (New York: W. W. Norton & Co., Inc.; 1950); *The Neurotic Personality of our Time* (New York: W. W. Norton & Co., Inc.; 1937); R. May: *The Meaning of Anxiety* (New York: The Ronald Press Co.; 1950); F. Fromm-Reichmann: *An Outline of Psychoanalysis* (New York: Random House; 1955); R. Grinker: *Psychosomatic Research* (New York: W. W. Norton & Co.; 1953); H. S. Sullivan: *Interpersonal Theory of Psychiatry* and *Conceptions of Modern Psychiatry*; Horney: *New Ways in Psychoanalysis* (New York: W. W. Norton & Co.; 1939); M. R. Stein, *et al.: Identity and Anxiety* (Glencoe, Illinois: The Free Press; 1960).
8. H. J. Eysenck: *The Dimensions of Personality* (London: Routledge, Kegan Paul; 1947), p. 160.
9. In a study of 3,083 factory workers, for example, R. Fraser found that about 30 per cent suffered from minor and disabling neuroses, and that this condition was commonly associated with a "decrease in social contacts," a characteristic behavior of introvert types, *The Incidence of Neuroses Among Factory Workers* (London: H.M.S.O. Report No. 90; 1947).
10. Eysenck: op. cit.
11. F. Herzberg, *et al.: The Motivation to Work* (New York: John Wiley & Sons, Inc.; 1959), p. 129.
12. Adorno, *et al.: The Authoritarian Personality* (New York: Harper & Brothers; 1950); B. K. Ruebush: "Interfering and Facilitating Effects of Test Anxiety," *Journal of Abnormal and Social Psychology*, Vol. 60, pp. 205-12.
13. E. L. Trist and K. W. Bamforth: "Some Social Psychological Consequences of the Long-wall Method of Coal-getting," *Human Relations*, Vol. 4, pp. 3-38.

ORGANIZATIONAL SOCIALIZATION
AND THE PROFESSION OF MANAGEMENT

EDGAR H. SCHEIN

Introduction

Ladies and gentlemen, colleagues and friends. There are few times in one's professional life when one has an opportunity, indeed something of a mandate, to pull together one's thoughts about an area of study and to communicate these to others.[1]

I can define my topic of concern best by reviewing very briefly the kinds of issues upon which I have focused my research over the last several years. In one way or another I have been trying to understand what happens to an individual when he enters and accepts membership in an organization. My interest was originally kindled by studies of the civilian and military prisoners of the Communists during the Korean War. I thought I could discern parallels between the kind of indoctrination to which these prisoners were subjected, and some of the indoctrination which goes on in American corporations when college and business school graduates first go to work for them. My research efforts came to be devoted to learning what sorts of attitudes and values students had when they left school, and what happened to these attitudes and values in the first few years of work. To this end I followed several panels of graduates of the Sloan School into their early career.

When these studies were well under way, it suddenly became quite apparent to me that if I wanted to study the impact of an organization on the attitudes and values of its members, I might as well start closer to home. We have a school through which we put some 200 men per year—undergraduates, regular Master's students, Sloan Fellows, and Senior Executives. Studies of our own students and faculty revealed that not only did the student groups differ from each other in various attitude areas, but that they also differed from the faculty.

For example, if one takes a scale built up of items which deal with the relations of government and business, one finds that the Senior Executives in our program are consistently against any form of government intervention, the Sloans are not as extreme, the Master's students are roughly in the middle, and the faculty are in favor of such intervention. A similar line-up of attitudes can be found with respect to labor-management relations, and with respect to cynicism about how one gets ahead in industry. In case you did not guess, the Senior Executives are least cynical and the faculty are most cynical.

We also found that student attitudes change in many areas during school, and that they change away from business attitudes toward the faculty position. However, a recent study of Sloan Fellows, conducted after their graduation, indicated that most of the changes toward the faculty had reversed themselves to a considerable degree within one year, a finding which is not unfamiliar to us in studies of training programs of all sorts.

The different positions of different groups at different stages of their managerial career and the observed changes during school clearly indicate that attitudes and values change several times during the managerial career. It is the process which brings about these changes which I would like to focus on today—a process which the sociologists would call "occupational socialization," but which I would prefer to call "organizational socialization" in order to keep our focus clearly on the setting in which the process occurs.

Organizational socialization is the process of "learning the ropes," the process of being indoctrinated and trained, the process of being taught what is important in an organization or some subunit thereof. This process occurs in school. It occurs again, and perhaps most dramatically, when the graduate enters an organization on his first job. It occurs again when he switches within the organization from one department to another, or from one rank level to another. It occurs all over again if he leaves one organization and enters another. And it occurs again when he goes back to school, and again when he returns to the organization after school.

Indeed, the process is so ubiquitous and we go though it so often during our total career, that it is all too easy to overlook it. Yet it is a process which can make or break a career, and which can make or break organizational systems of manpower planning. The speed and effectiveness of socialization determine employee loyalty, commitment, productivity, and turnover. The basic stability and effectiveness of organizations therefore depends upon their ability to socialize new members.

Let us see whether we can bring the process of socialization to life by describing how it occurs. I hope to show you the power of this process, particularly as it occurs within industrial organizations. Having done this, I would like to explore a major dilemma which I see at the interface between organizations and graduate management schools. Schools socialize their students toward a concept of a profession, organizations socialize their new members to be effective members. Do the two processes of socialization supplement each other or conflict? If they conflict, what can we do about it in organizations and in the schools?

Some Basic Elements of Organizational Socialization

The term socialization has a fairly clear meaning in sociology, but it has been a difficult one to assimilate in the behavioral sciences and in management. To many of my colleagues it implies unnecessary jargon, and to many of my business acquaintances it implies the teaching of socialism—a kiss of death for the concept right there. Yet the concept is most useful because it focuses clearly on the interaction between a stable social system and the new members who enter it. The concept refers to the process by which a new member learns the value system, the norms, and the required behavior patterns of the society, organization, or group which he is entering. It does not include all learning. It includes only the learning of those values, norms, and behavior patterns which, from the organization's point of view or group's point of view, it is necessary for any new member to learn. This is defined as the price of membership.

What are such values, norms, and behavior patterns all about? Usually they involve:

1. The basic *goals* of the organization.
2. The preferred *means* by which these goals should be attained.
3. The basic *responsibilities* of the member in the role which is being granted to him by the organization.
4. The *behavior patterns* which are required for effective performance in the role.
5. A set of rules or principles which pertain to the *maintenance of the identity and integrity* of the organization.

The new member must learn not to drive Chevrolets if he is working for Ford, not to criticize the organization in public, not to wear the wrong kind of clothes or be seen in the wrong kinds of places. If the organization is a school, beyond learning the content of what is taught, the student must accept the value of education, he must try to learn without cheating, he must accept the authority of the faculty and behave appropriately to the student role. He must not be rude in the classroom or openly disrespectful to the professor.

By what processes does the novice learn the required values and norms? The answer to this question depends in part upon the degree of prior socialization. If the novice has correctly anticipated the norms of the organization he is joining, the socialization process merely involves a reaffirmation of these norms through various communication channels, the personal example of key people in the organization, and direct instructions from supervisors, trainers, and informal coaches.

If, however, the novice comes to the organization with values and behavior patterns which are in varying degrees out of line with those expected by the organization, then the socialization process first involves a destructive or unfreezing phase. This phase serves the function of detaching the person from his former values, of proving to him that his present self is worthless from the point of view of the organization and that he must redefine himself in terms of the new roles which he is to be granted.

The extremes of this process can be seen in initiation rites or novitiates for religious orders. When the novice enters his training period, his old self is symbolically destroyed by loss of clothing, name, often his hair, titles and other self-defining equipment. These are replaced with uniforms, new names and titles, and other self-defining equipment consonant with the new role he is being trained for.

It may be comforting to think of activities like this as being characteristic only of primitive tribes or total institutions like military basic training camps, academies, and religious orders. But even a little examination of areas closer to home will reveal the same processes both in our graduate schools and in the business organizations to which our graduates go.

Perhaps the commonest version of the process in school is the imposition of a tight schedule, of an impossibly heavy reading program, and of the assignment of problems which are likely to be too difficult for the student to solve. Whether these techniques are deliberate or not, they serve effectively to remind the student that he is not as smart or capable as he may have thought he was, and therefore, that there are still things to be learned. As our Sloan Fellows tell us every year, the first summer in the program pretty well destroys many aspects of their self-image.

Homework in statistics appears to enjoy a unique status comparable to having one's head shaved and clothes burned.

Studies of medical schools and our own observations of the Sloan program suggest that the work overload on the students leads to the development of a peer culture, a kind of banding together of the students as a defense against the threatening faculty and as a problem-solving device to develop norms of what and how to study. If the group solutions which are developed support the organizational norms, the peer group becomes an effective instrument of socialization. However, from the school's point of view, there is the risk that peer group norms will set up counter-socializing forces and sow the seeds of sabotage, rebellion, or revolution. The positive gains of a supportive peer group generally make it worthwhile to run the risks of rebellion, however, which usually motivates the organization to encourage or actually to facilitate peer group formation.

Many of our Sloan Fellow alumni tell us that one of the most powerful features of the Sloan program is the fact that a group of some 40 men share the same fate of being put through a very tough educational regimen. The peer group ties formed during the year have proven to be one of the most durable end-results of the educational program and, of course, are one of the key supports to the maintaining of some of the values and attitudes learned in school. The power of this kind of socializing force can be appreciated best by pondering a further statement which many alumni have made. They stated that prior to the program they identified themselves primarily with their company. Following the program they identified themselves primarily with the other Sloan Fellows, and such identification has lasted, as far as we can tell, for the rest of their career.

Let me next illustrate the industrial counterpart of these processes. Many of my panel members, when interviewed about the first six months in their new jobs, told stories of what we finally labeled as "upending experiences." Upending experiences are deliberately planned or accidentally created circumstances which dramatically and unequivocally upset or disconfirm some of the major assumptions which the new man holds about himself, his company, or his job.

One class of such experiences is to receive assignments which are so easy or so trivial that they carry the clear message that the new man is not worthy of being given anything important to do. Another class of such experiences is at the other extreme—assignments which are so difficult that failure is a certainty, thus proving unequivocally to the new man that he may not be as smart as he thought he was. Giving work which is clearly for practice only, asking for reports which are then unread or not acted upon, protracted periods of training during which the person observes others work, all have the same upending effect.

The most vivid example came from an engineering company where a supervisor had a conscious and deliberate strategy for dealing with what he considered to be unwarranted arrogance on the part of engineers whom they hired. He asked each new man to examine and diagnose a particular complex circuit, which happened to violate a number of textbook principles but actually worked very well. The new man would usually announce with confidence, even after an invitation to double-check, that the circuit could not possibly work. At this point the manager would demonstrate the circuit, tell the new man that they had been selling it for several years without customer complaint, and demand that the new man figure out why it did work. None of the men so far tested were able to do it, but all of them were thoroughly chastened and came to the manager anxious to learn where their knowledge was inadequate and needed supplementing. According to this manager, it was much easier from this point on to establish a good give-and-take relationship with his new man.

It should be noted that the success of such socializing techniques depends upon two factors which are not always under the control of the organization. The first factor is the initial motivation of the entrant to join the organization. If his motivation is high, as in the case of a fraternity pledge, he will tolerate all kinds of uncomfortable socialization experiences, even to extremes of hell week. If his motivation for membership is low, he may well decide to leave the organization rather than tolerate uncomfortable initiation rites. If he leaves, the socialization process has obviously failed.

The second factor is the degree to which the organization can hold the new member captive during the period of socialization. His motivation is obviously one element here, but one finds organizations using other forces as well. In the case of basic training there are legal forces to remain. In the case of many schools one must pay one's tuition in advance, in other words, invest one's self materially so that leaving the system becomes expensive. In the case of religious orders one must make strong initial psychological commitments in the form of vows and the severing of relationships outside the religious order. The situation is defined as one in which one will lose face or be humiliated if one leaves the organization.

In the case of business organizations the pressures are more subtle but nevertheless identifiable. New members are encouraged to get financially committed by joining pension plans, stock option plans, and/or house purchasing plans which would mean material loss if the person decided to leave. Even more subtle is the reminder by the boss that it takes a year or so to learn any new business; therefore, if you leave, you will have to start all over again. Why not suffer it out with the hope that things will look more rosy once the initiation period is over.

Several of my panel members told me at the end of one year at work that they were quite dissatisfied, but were not sure they should leave because they had invested a year of learning in that company. Usually their boss encouraged them to think about staying. Whether or not such pressures will work depends, of course, on the labor market and other factors not under the control of the organization.

Let me summarize thus far. Organizations socialize their new members by creating a series of events which serve the function of undoing old values so that the person will be prepared to learn the new values. This process of undoing or unfreezing is often unpleasant and therefore requires either strong motivation to endure it or strong organizational forces to make the person endure it. The formation of a peer group of novices is often a solution to the problem of defense against the powerful organization, and, at the same time, can strongly enhance the socialization process if peer group norms support organizational norms.

Let us look next at the positive side of the socialization process. Given some readiness to learn, how does the novice acquire his new learning? The answer is that he acquires it from multiple sources—the official literature of the organization;

the example set by key models in the organization; the instructions given to him directly by his trainer, coach, or boss; the example of peers who have been in the organization longer and thus serve as big brothers; the rewards and punishments which result from his own efforts at problem solving and experimenting with new values and new behavior.

The instructions and guidelines given by senior members of the organization are probably one of the most potent sources. I can illustrate this point best by recalling several incidents from my own socialization into the Sloan School back in 1956. I came here at the invitation of Doug McGregor from a research job. I had no prior teaching experience or knowledge of organizational or managerial matters. Contrary to my expectations, I was told by Doug that knowledge of organizational psychology and management was not important, but that some interest in learning about these matters was.

The first socializing incident occurred in an initial interview with Elting Morison, who was then on our faculty. He said in a completely blunt manner that if I knew what I wanted to do and could go ahead on my own, the Sloan School would be a great place to be. If I wasn't sure and would look to others for guidance, not to bother to come.

The second incident occurred in a conversation with our then Dean, Penn Brooks, a few weeks before the opening of the semester. We were discussing what and how I might teach. Penn said to me that he basically wanted each of his faculty members to find his own approach to management education. I could do whatever I wanted—so long as I did not imitate our sister school up the river. Case discussion leaders need not apply, was the clear message.

The third incident (you see I was a slow learner) occurred a few days later when I was planning my subject in social psychology for our Master's students. I was quite nervous about it and unsure of how to decide what to include in the subject. I went to Doug and innocently asked him to lend me outlines of previous versions of the subject, which had been taught by Alex Bavelas, or at least to give me some advice on what to include and exclude. Doug was very nice and very patient, but also quite firm in his refusal to give me either outlines or advice. He thought there was really no need to rely on history, and expressed confidence that I could probably make up my own mind. I suffered that term but learned a good deal about the value system of the Sloan School, as well as how to organize a subject. I was, in fact, so well socialized by these early experiences that nowadays no one can get me to coordinate anything with anybody else.

Similar kinds of lessons can be learned during the course of training programs, in orientation sessions, and through company literature. But the more subtle kinds of values which the organization holds, which indeed may not even be well understood by the senior people, are often communicated through peers operating as helpful big brothers. They can communicate the subtleties of how the boss wants things done, how higher management feels about things, the kinds of things which are considered heroic in the organization, the kinds of things which are taboo.

Of course, sometimes the values of the immediate group into which a new person is hired are partially out of line with the value system of the organization as a whole. If this is the case, the new person will learn the immediate group's values much more quickly than those of the total organization, often to the chagrin of the higher levels of management. This is best exemplified at the level of hourly workers where fellow employees will have much more socializing power than the boss.

An interesting managerial example of this conflict was provided by one recent graduate who was hired into a group whose purpose was to develop cost reduction systems for a large manufacturing operation. His colleagues on the job, however, showed him how to pad his expense account whenever they traveled together. The end result of this kind of conflict was to accept neither the cost reduction values of the company nor the cost inflation values of the peer group. The man left the company in disgust to start up some businesses of his own.

One of the important functions of organizational socialization is to build commitment and loyalty to the organization. How is this accomplished? One mechanism is to invest much effort and time in the new member and thereby build up expectations of being repaid by loyalty, hard work, and rapid learning. Another mechanism is to get the new member to make a series of small behavioral commitments which can only be justified by him through the acceptance and incorporation of company values. He then becomes his own agent of socialization. Both mechanisms involve the subtle manipulation of guilt.

To illustrate the first mechanism, one of our graduates went to a public relations firm which made it clear to him that he had sufficient knowledge and skill to advance, but that his values and attitudes would have to be evaluated for a couple of years before he would be fully accepted. During the first several months he was frequently invited to join high ranking members of the organization at their luncheon meetings in order to learn more about how they thought about things. He was so flattered by the amount of time they spent on him, that he worked extra hard to learn their values and became highly committed to the organization. He said that he would have felt guilty at the thought of not learning or of leaving the company. Sending people to expensive training programs, giving them extra perquisites, indeed the whole philosophy of paternalism, is built on the assumption that if you invest in the employee he will repay the company with loyalty and hard work. He would feel guilty if he did not.

The second mechanism, that of getting behavioral commitments, was most beautifully illustrated in Communist techniques of coercive persuasion. The Communists made tremendous efforts to elicit a public confession from a prisoner. One of the key functions of such a public confession, even if the prisoner knew he was making a false confession, was that it committed him publicly. Once he made this commitment, he found himself under strong internal and external pressure to justify why he had confessed. For many people it proved easier to justify the confession by coming to believe in their own crimes than to have to face the fact that they were too weak to withstand the captor's pressure.

In organizations, a similar effect can be achieved by promoting a rebellious person into a position of responsibility. The same values which the new member may have criticized and jeered at from his position at the bottom of the hierarchy suddenly look different when he has subordinates of his own whose commitment he must obtain.

Many of my panel members had very strong moral and ethical standards when they first went to work, and these stood up quite well during their first year at work even in the face of less ethical practices by their peers and superiors. But they reported with considerable shock that some of the practices they had condemned in their bosses were quickly adopted by them once they had themselves been promoted and faced the pressures of the new position. As one man put it very poignantly—"my ethical standards changed so gradually over the first five years of work that I hardly noticed it, but it was a great shock to suddenly realize what my feelings had been five years ago and how much they had changed."

Another version of obtaining commitment is to gain the new member's acceptance of very general ideals like "one must work for the good of the company," or "one must meet the competition." Whenever any counter-organizational behavior occurs one can then point out that the ideal is being violated. The engineer who does not come to work on time is reminded that his behavior indicates lack of concern for the good of the company. The employee who wears the wrong kind of clothes, lives in the wrong neighborhood, or associates with the wrong people can be reminded that he is hurting the company image.

One of my panel members on a product research assignment discovered that an additive which was approved by the Food and Drug Administration might in fact be harmful to consumers. He was strongly encouraged to forget about it. His boss told him that it was the F.D.A.'s problem. If the company worried about things like that it might force prices up and thus make it tough to meet the competition.

Many of the upending experiences which new members of organizations endure are justified to them by the unarguable ideal that they should learn how the company really works before expecting a position of real responsibility. Once the new man accepts this ideal it serves to justify all kinds of training and quantities of menial work which others who have been around longer are unwilling to do themselves. This practice is known as "learning the business from the ground up," or "I had to do it when I first joined the company, now it's someone else's turn." There are clear elements of hazing involved not too different from those associated with fraternity initiations and other rites of passage.

The final mechanism to be noted in a socialization process is the transition to full fledged member. The purpose of such transitional events is to help the new member incorporate his new values, attitudes, and norms into his identity so that they become part of him, not merely something to which he pays lip-service. Initiation rites which involve severe tests of the novice serve to prove to him that he is capable of fulfilling the new role—that he now is a man, no longer merely a boy.

Organizations usually signal this transition by giving the new man some important responsibility or a position of power which, if mishandled or misused, could genuinely hurt the organization. With this transition often come titles, symbols of status, extra rights or prerogatives, sharing of confidential information or other things which in one way or another indicate that the new member has earned the trust of the organization. Although such events may not always be visible to the outside observer, they are felt strongly by the new member. He knows when he has finally "been accepted," and feels it when he becomes "identified with the company."

So much for examples of the process of socialization. Let us now look at some of the dilemmas and conflicts which arise within it.

Failures of Socialization—Non-conformity and Over-conformity

Most organizations attach differing amounts of importance to different norms and values. Some are pivotal. Any member of a business organization who does not believe in the value of getting a job done will not survive long. Other pivotal values in most business organizations might be belief in a reasonable profit, belief in the free enterprise system and competition, belief in a hierarchy of authority as a good way to get things done, and so on.

Other values or norms are what may be called relevant. These are norms which it is not absolutely necessary to accept as the price of membership, but which are considered desirable and good to accept. Many of these norms pertain to standards of dress and decorum, not being publicly disloyal to the company, living in the right neighborhood and belonging to the right political party and clubs. In some organizations some of these norms may be pivotal. Organizations vary in this regard. You all know the stereotype of IBM as a company that requires the wearing of white shirts and hats. In some parts of IBM such values are indeed pivotal; in other parts they are only relevant, and in some parts they are quite peripheral. The point is that not all norms to which the new member is exposed are equally important for the organization.

The socialization process operates across the whole range of norms, but the amount of reward and punishment for compliance or non-compliance will vary with the importance of the norm. This variation allows the new member some degrees of freedom in terms of how far to conform and allows the organization some degrees of freedom in how much conformity to demand. The new man can accept none of the values, he can accept only the pivotal values, but carefully remain independent on all those areas not seen as pivotal, or he can accept the whole range of values and norms. He can tune in so completely on what he sees to be the way others are handling themselves that he becomes a carbon-copy and sometimes a caricature of them.

These basic responses to socialization can be labeled as follows:

Type 1. Rebellion: Rejection of all values and norms

Type 2. Creative individualism: Acceptance only of pivotal values and norms; rejection of all others

Type 3. Conformity: Acceptance of all values and norms

Most analyses of conformity deal only with the type 1 and 3 cases, failing to note that both can be viewed as socialization failures. The rebellious individual either is expelled from the organization or turns his energies toward defeating its goals. The conforming individual curbs his creativity and thereby moves the organization toward a sterile form of bureaucracy. The trick for most organizations is to create the type 2 response—acceptance of pivotal values and norms, but rejection of all others, a response which I would like to call "creative individualism."

To remain creatively individualistic in an organization is particularly difficult because of the constant resocialization pressures which come with promotion or lateral transfer. Every time the employee learns part of the value system of the particular group to which he is assigned, he may be laying the groundwork for conflict when he is transferred. The engineer has difficulty accepting the values of the sales department, the staff man has difficulty accepting the high pressure ways of the production department, and the line manager has difficulties accepting the service and helping ethic of a staff group. With each transfer, the forces are great toward either conforming or rebelling. It is difficult to keep focused on what is pivotal and retain one's basic individualism.

Professional Socialization and Organizational Socialization

The issue of how to maintain individualism in the face of organizational socialization pressures brings us to the final and most problematical area of concern. In the traditional professions like medicine, law, and teaching, individualism is supported by a set of professional attitudes which serve to immunize the person against some of the forces of the organization. The questions now to be considered are (1) Is management a profession? (2) If so, do professional attitudes develop in managers? and (3) If so, do these support or conflict with organizational norms and values?

Professionalism can be defined by a number of characteristics:

1. Professional decisions are made by means of general principles, theories, or propositions which are independent of the particular case under consideration. For management this would mean that there are certain principles of how to handle people, money, information, etc., independent of any particular company. The fact that we can and do teach general subjects in these areas would support management's claim as a profession.

2. Professional decisions imply knowledge in a specific area in which the person is expert, not a generalized body of wisdom. The professional is an expert only in his profession, not an expert at everything. He has no license to be a "wise man." Does management fit by this criterion? I will let you decide.

3. The professional's relations with his clients are objective and independent of particular sentiments about them. The doctor or lawyer makes his decisions independent of his liking or disliking of his patients or clients. On this criterion we have a real difficulty since, in the first place, it is very difficult to specify an appropriate single client for a manager, and, in the second place, it is not at all clear that decisions can or should be made independent of sentiments. What is objectively best for the stockholder may conflict with what is best for the enterprise, which, in turn may conflict with what is best for the customer.

4. A professional achieves his status by accomplishment, not by inherent qualities such as birth order, his relationship to people in power, his race, religion, or color. Industry is increasingly moving toward an acceptance of this principle for managerial selection, but in practice the process of organizational socialization may undermine it by rewarding the conformist and rejecting the individualist whose professional orientation may make him look disloyal to the organization.

5. A professional's decisions are assumed to be on behalf of the client and to be independent of self-interest. Clearly this principle is at best equivocal in manager-customer relations, though again one senses that industry is moving closer to accepting the idea.

6. The professional typically relates to a voluntary association of fellow professionals, and accepts only the authority of these colleagues as a sanction on his own

behavior. The manager is least like the professional in this regard, in that he is expected to accept a principle of hierarchical authority. The dilemma is best illustrated by the previous example which I gave of our Sloan Fellow alumni who, after the program, related themselves more to other Sloans than to their company hierarchy. By this criterion they had become truly professionalized.

7. A professional has sometimes been called someone who knows better what is good for his client than the client. The professional's expertness puts the client into a very vulnerable position. This vulnerability has necessitated the development of strong professional codes and ethics which serve to protect the client. Such codes are enforced through the colleague peer group. One sees relatively few attempts to develop codes of ethics for managers or systems of enforcement.

On several bases, then, management is a profession, but on several others it is clearly not yet a profession.

This long description of what is a profession was motivated by the need to make a very crucial point. I believe that management education, particularly in a graduate school like the Sloan School, is increasingly attempting to train professionals, and in this process is socializing the students to a set of professional values which are, in fact, in severe and direct conflict with typical organizational values.

For example, I see us teaching general principles in the behavioral sciences, economics, and quantitative methods. Our applied subjects like marketing, operations management, and finance are also taught as bodies of knowledge governed by general principles which are applicable to a wide variety of situations. Our students are given very broad concepts which apply to the corporation as a whole, and are taught to see the relationship between the corporation, the community, and the society. They are taught to value the long-range health and survival of economic institutions, not the short-range profit of a particular company. They come to appreciate the necessary interrelationships between government, labor, and management rather than to define these as mutually warring camps. They are taught to look at organizations from the perspective of high ranking management, to solve the basic problems of the enterprise rather than the day-to-day practical problems of staff or line management. Finally, they are taught an ethic of pure rationality and emotional neutrality—analyze the problem and make the decisions independent of feelings about people, the product, the company, or the community. All of these are essentially professional values.

Organizations value many of the same things, in principle. But what is valued in principle by the higher ranking and senior people in the organization often is neither supported by their own behavior, nor even valued lower down in the organization. In fact, the value system which the graduates encounter on their first job is in many respects diametrically opposed to the professional values taught in school. The graduate is immediately expected to develop loyalty and concern for a particular company with all of its particular idiosyncrasies. He is expected to recognize the limitation of his general knowledge and to develop the sort of *ad hoc* wisdom which the school has taught him to avoid. He is expected to look to his boss for evaluation rather than to some group of colleagues outside the company.

Whereas the professional training tells him that knowledge is power, the graduate now must learn that knowledge by itself is nothing. It is the ability to sell knowledge to other people which is power. Only by being able to sell an application of knowledge to a highly specific, local situation, can the graduate obtain respect for what he knows. Where his education has taught the graduate principles of how to manage others and to take the corporate point of view, his organizational socialization tries to teach him how to be a good subordinate, how to be influenced, and how to sell ideas from a position of low power.

On the one hand, the organization via its recruiters and senior people tells the graduate that it is counting on him to bring fresh points of view and new techniques to bear on its problems. On the other hand, the man's first boss and peers try to socialize him into their traditional mold.

A man is hired to introduce linear programming into a production department, but once he is there he is told to lay off because if he succeeds he will make the old supervisors and engineers look bad. Another man is hired for his financial analysis skills but is not permitted access to data worth analyzing because the company does not trust him to keep them confidential. A third man is hired into a large group responsible for developing cost reduction programs in a large defense industry, and is told to ignore the fact that the group is overstaffed, inefficient, and willing to pad its expense accounts. A fourth man, hired for his energy and capability, put it this way as an explanation of why he quit to go into private consulting: "They were quite pleased with work that required only two hours per day; I wasn't."

In my panel of 1962 graduates, 73 percent have already left their first job and many are on their third or fourth. In the class of 1963, the percentage is 67, and in the class of 1964, the percentage is 50. Apparently, most of our graduates are unwilling to be socialized into organizations whose values are incompatible with the ones we teach. Yet these organizations are precisely the ones who may need creative individualists most.

What seems to happen in the early stages of the managerial career is either a kind of postponement of professional socialization while organizational socialization takes precedence, or a rebelling by the graduate against organizational socialization. The young man who submits must first learn to be a good apprentice, a good staff man, a good junior analyst, and perhaps a good low level administrator. He must prove his loyalty to the company by accepting this career path with good graces, before he is trusted enough to be given a position of power. If he has not lost his education by then, he can begin to apply some general principles when he achieves such a position of power.

The businessman wants the school to provide both the professional education and the humility which would make organizational socialization smoother. He is not aware that teaching management concepts of the future precludes justifying the practices of today. Some professional schools clearly do set out to train for the needs of the profession as it is designed today. The Sloan School appears to me to reject this concept. Instead we have a faculty which is looking at the professional manager of five, ten, or twenty years from now, and is training its graduates in management techniques which we believe are coming in the future.

Symptomatic of this approach is the fact that in many of our subjects we are highly critical of the management practices of today, and highly committed to re-educating those managers like Sloan Fellows and Senior Executives who come back to study at M.I.T. We get across in a dozen different ways the belief that most organizations of today are obsolete, conservative, constipated, and ignorant of their own problems. Furthermore, I believe that this point of view is what society and the business community demands of a good professional school.

It would be no solution to abandon our own vision of the manager of the future, and I doubt that those of you in the audience from business and industry would really want us to do this. What you probably want is to have your cake and eat it too—you want us to teach our students the management concepts of tomorrow, and you want us to teach them how to put these concepts into deep freeze while they learn the business of today. Then when they have proven themselves worthy of advancement and have achieved a position of some influence, they should magically resurrect their education and put it to work.

Unfortunately, socialization processes are usually too powerful to permit that solution. If you succeed in socializing your young graduates to your organizations, you will probably also succeed in proving to them that their education was pretty worthless and might as well be put on a permanent rather than temporary shelf. We have research evidence that many well educated graduates do learn to be complacent and to play the organizational game. It is not at all clear whether they later ever resurrect their educational arsenal.

What Is to Be Done about This Situation?

I think we need to accept, at the outset, the reality of organizational socialization phenomena. As my colleague, Leo Moore, so aptly put it, organizations like to put their fingerprints on people, and they have every right to do so. By the same token, graduate schools of business have a right and an obligation to pursue professional socialization to the best of their ability. We must find a way to ameliorate the conflicts at the interface, without, however, concluding that either schools or organizations are to blame and should stop what they are doing.

What the Schools Can Do

The schools, our school in particular, can do several concrete things which would help the situation. First, we can insert into our total curriculum more apprenticeship experience which would bring the realities of organizational life home to the student earlier. But such apprenticeship experiences will not become educational unless we combine them with a second idea, that of providing a practicum on how to change organizations. Such a practicum should draw on each of the course specialties and should be specifically designed to teach a student how to translate his professional knowledge into viable action programs at whatever level of the organization he is working.

Ten years ago we would not have known how to do this. Today there is no excuse for not doing it. Whether the field is operations research, sophisticated quantitative marketing, industrial dynamics, organizational psychology or whatever, we must give our students experience in trying to implement their new ideas, and we must teach them how to make the implementation effective. In effect, we must teach our students to become change-agents, whatever their disciplinary specialty turns out to be. We must teach them how to influence their organizations from low positions of power without sacrificing their professional values in the process. We must teach them how to remain creative individualists in the face of strong organizational socialization pressures.

Combined with these two things, we need to do a third thing. We need to become more involved in the student's efforts at career planning and we need to coordinate our activities more closely with the company recruiters and the university placement officers. At the present I suspect that most of our faculty is quite indifferent to the student's struggles to find the right kind of a job. I suspect that this indifference leaves the door wide open to faulty selection on the part of the student, which can only lead, in the end, to an undermining of the education into which we pour so much effort. We need to work harder to insure that our graduates get jobs in which they can further the values and methods we inculcate.

What the Companies Can Do

Companies can do at least two things. First, they can make a genuine effort to become aware of and understand their own organizational socialization practices. I fear very few higher level executives know what is going on at the bottom of their organization where all the high priced talent they call for is actually employed. At the same time, I suspect that it is their own value system which ultimately determines the socialization activities which occur throughout all segments of the organization. Greater awareness and understanding of these practices should make possible more rational choices as to which practices to encourage and which to de-emphasize. The focus should be on pivotal values only, not on peripheral or irrelevant ones.

Second, companies must come to appreciate the delicate problems which exist both for the graduate and for his first boss in the early years of the career when socialization pressures are at the maximum. If more companies appreciated the nature of this dilemma they would recognize the necessity of giving some training to the men who will be the first bosses of the graduates.

I have argued for such training for many years, but still find that most company effort goes into training the graduate rather than his boss. Yet it is the boss who really has the power to create the climate which will lead to rebellion, conformity, or creative individualism. If the companies care whether their new hires use one or the other of these adaptation strategies, they had better start looking at the behavior of the first boss and training him for what the company wants and hopes for. Too many bosses concentrate on teaching too many peripheral values and thus undermine the possibilities for creative individualism and organization improvement.

Conclusion

The essence of management is to understand the forces acting in a situation and to gain control over them. It is high time that some of our managerial knowledge and skill be focused on those forces in the organizational environment which derive from the fact that organizations are social systems who do socialize their new members. If we do not learn to analyze and control the forces of organizational socialization, we are abdicating one of our primary managerial responsibilities. Let us not shrink away from a little bit of social engineering and management in this most important area of the human side of the enterprise.

References

1. Blau, P.M. and Scott, R.W. *Formal Organizations*. San Francisco: Chandler, 1962.
2. Goffman, E. *Asylums*. Garden City, N.Y.: Doubleday Anchor, 1961.
3. Schein, E. H., Schneier, Inge and Barker, C. H. *Coercive Persuasion*. New York: W. W. Norton, 1961.
4. Schein, E. H. "Management Development as a Process of Influence," *Industrial Management Review*, II (1961), 59-77.
5. Schein, E. H. "Forces Which Undermine Management Development," *California Management Review*, Vol. V, Summer, 1963
6. Schein, E. H. "How to Break in the College Graduate," *Harvard Business Review*, Vol. XLII (1964).
7. Schein, E. H. "Training in Industry: Education or Indoctrination," *Industrial Medicine and Surgery*, Vol. XXXIII (1964).
8. Schein, E. H. *Organizational Psychology*. Englewood Cliffs, N.J.: Prentice-Hall, 1965
9. Schein, E. H. "The Problem of Moral Education for the Business Manager," *Industrial Management Review*, VIII (1966), 3-14
10. Schein, E. H. "Attitude Change During Management Education," *Adminstrative Science Quarterly*, XI (1967), 601-628
11. Schein, E. H. "The Wall of Misunderstanding on the first Job," *Journal of College Placement*, February/March, 1967

THE PSYCHOLOGICAL CONTRACT

EDGAR H. SCHEIN

I would like to underline the importance of the psychological contract as a major variable of analysis. It is my central hypothesis that whether a person is working effectively, whether he generates commitment, loyalty, and enthusiasm for the organization and its goals, and whether he obtains satisfaction from his work, depends to a large measure on two conditions: (1) the degree to which his own expectations of what the organization will provide him and what he owes the organization match what the organization's expectations are of what it will give and get; (2) assuming there is agreement on expectations, what actually is to be exchanged—money in exchange for time at work; social-need satisfaction and security in exchange for work and loyalty; opportunities for self-actualization and challenging work in exchange for high productivity, quality work, and creative effort in the service of organizational goals; or various combinations of these and other things.

Ultimately the relationship between the individual and the organization is interactive, unfolding through mutual influence and mutual bargaining to establish a workable psychological contract. We cannot understand the psychological dynamics if we look only to the individual's motivations or only to organizational conditions and practices. The two interact in a complex fashion, requiring us to develop theories and research approaches which can deal with systems and interdependent phenomena.[1]

Furthermore, we must develop concepts which can deal with the *process* by which the psychological contract is initially negotiated between individual and organization, and the *process* by which it is renegotiated during the employee's organizational career. For example, *organizational socialization* is one such concept, referring to the fact that organizations have goals, norms, values, preferred ways of doing things which are usually taught systematically, though not necessarily overtly, to all new members.[2] Some of the norms can be thought of as *pivotal*, in the sense that adherence to them is a requirement of continued membership in the organization. For a manager it is required that he believe in the validity of the free enterprise system; for a professor, that he accept the canons of research and scholarship. Other organizational norms are *peripheral*, in the sense that it is desirable for members to possess them but not essential. For example, for a manager it may be desirable from the point of view of the organization that he be a man, have certain political views, wear the right kind of clothes, use only the company products, and so on. For a professor, it may be desirable that he like to teach, be willing to help in the administration of the university, spend most of his time on campus rather than on consulting trips, and so on. Violation of these norms does not cause loss of membership, however, if the pivotal norms are adhered to.

In thinking about the adjustment of the individual to the organization, we can identify three types of possible adjustments, based on which sets of norms are adhered to. Acceptance of *neither* the pivotal nor peripheral norms can be thought of as *"active rebellion"* and is likely to lead to voluntary or involuntary loss of membership. Acceptance of *both* pivotal and peripheral norms can be thought of as *"conformity"* and is likely to lead to the loyal but uncreative "organization man" or "bureaucrat." Acceptance of pivotal norms but rejection of peripheral norms can be thought of as *"creative individualism,"* in the sense that the person still works on behalf of those norms of the organization that are pivotal, but retains his sense of identity and exercises creativity in helping the organization to achieve its goals.

Such creativity can be thought of either in terms of new products and new solutions to organizational problems, or in terms of "role innovation," inventing new ways to do a job.[3] Thus, a professor can be creative by finding some new scientific law or he can be "role innovative" by developing new ways of teaching; a manager can invent a new financial control system or he can invent new ways of relating to managers in other departments which improve the overall effectiveness of the organization.

From the point of view of the organization, it is desirable to create conditions which make it possible for members to be creative individualists rather than conformists or rebels. From the point of view of society, it is desirable to have an educational system which predisposes people to want to be creative individualists. If one views schools and colleges as organizations which socialize students as well as educate them, the organizational question becomes, what kind of school organization creates conditions for students to develop a creative individualistic orientation?

Managers of organizations, whether they be of businesses or schools, must become aware not only of the complexities of human motivation, but of the dynamic processes which occur as the person enters into and pursues a career within an organization. Just as the manner in which a person is selected, trained, and assigned influences his image of the organization, so the manner in which he is managed will influence this image. A manager must be aware of the interaction between these various organizational systems and must think integratively about them. For example, if he plans to manage people in a way that will challenge them and provide them with opportunities to use all their potential, he must be careful that the manner in which they are selected, tested, trained, and assigned to their jobs does not undermine the very motivations he wishes to draw on. What this means in practice is that all those members of the organization who are responsible for the various functions should, together, think through carefully the consequences of the various approaches, and coordinate their activities to accomplish whatever shared goals they have.

Notes and References

1. In some experimental studies which attempted to test directly the relationship of feelings of equity in the psychological contract to productivity on a task, Adams showed that subjects who feel they are being overpaid for their level of ability will produce more than subjects who feel they are being fairly paid relative to their level of ability. The interpretation is that if the organization gives more than it gets, in the eyes of the subject, he will work harder to make the relationship more just. J.S.

Adams and W.B. Rosenbaum, "The Relationship of Worker Productivity to Cognitive Dissonance about Wage Inequities," *Journal of Applied Psychology* 46 (1962): 161-64.

2. E.H. Schein, "Organizational Socialization and the Profession of Management," Third Douglas McGregor Address, *Industrial Management Review* 9 (1968): 1-15.

3. E. H. Schein, "Occupational Socialization in the Professions: The Case of Role Innovation," *Technology Review* (October-November 1970): 32-38.

PART THREE

Individual Behavior in the Organization

Previously, we have shown that the contingency model has great importance and usefulness in understanding human performance. In this part we will attempt to build on this model to show how past learning affects work performance. The readings in this part are offered as a starting point for developing a greater understanding of the complexity of human behavior. They are divided into three sections, with each section building upon the previous one.

The first section (A) discusses the effects of attitudes on performance. Because attitudes are learned, we see that the learning process both affects and is affected by attitudes. The second section (B) deals with perception of cues from the environment. A person's ability to perceive and respond to his environment is no better than his ability to generalize and discriminate between cues, and—as we see—a person's needs as well as his attitudes play a major role in determining his perceptual processes. The third section (C), on worker motivation, discusses how attitudes, needs, and perceptions affect motivation. The drive state is often blamed when one fails to perform or is praised when he chooses to perform. It is therefore important that we attempt to understand the components of motivation and try to determine why motivation varies among individuals.

The Effect of Attitudes on Individual Performance

An *attitude* can be defined as an individual's predisposition to evaluate an object in a favorable or unfavorable manner. Attitudes consist of three major components: (1) The cognitive component of an attitude is what a person *believes* about an object. It is determined by the information he possesses about that object. (2) The affective component of an attitude is how a person *feels* about the object. It is his emotional reaction to that object. (3) The *behavioral* component of an attitude is what a person *does* about an object. Further, an individual has a need for internal consistency among the three components of an attitude he holds.

Katz describes the importance of understanding the reasons why people hold the attitudes they do. He says that the *intensity,* the *specificity,* and the *linkage* of an attitude to a related value system are important in determining the resistance of the individual to attitude change. To change a subordinate's attitude, a manager must first know the importance of that attitude for the individual.

Mann, in the second reading, states that the need for consistency of an attitude can exert a powerful force in influencing people to behave in various ways. He discusses a number of theories which deal with the problem of inconsistency among attitude components, and how any disturbance in an individual's attitude system sets in motion active attempts to restore consistency. For example, a male chauvinist confronted with unquestionable competence on the part of subordinate women managers will find himself in a state of attitude inconsistency that must ultimately be resolved. Managers are often faced with the problem of attitudes (beliefs and emotions) interfering with the behavior of employees. One of the key interests of many managers is how such attitudes can be changed.

A study reported by Leiberman says that attitudes follow the reinforcement offered by the organization. Since attitudes are learned, the manager seeking to change the attitude of an employee must change the reinforcement contingencies that shaped the old attitude. Leiberman suggests that it is often helpful to give the individual a new role that leads to adopting the new attitude. One of the fundamental postulates of role theory is that a person's attitude will be influenced by the role that he occupies in a social system.

Specific methods of attitude change are discussed in part 7, "Organizational Change and Development." These methods include (1) a program for changing behavior, with the thought that beliefs and emotional states will follow (behavioral modification), and (2) changing beliefs and emotions, with the thought that behavior will follow (organizational development). Both of these methods are based on consistency theory, and are discussed in part 7.

The Perceptual Process and Human Behavior

The administrator frequently bases decisions and actions on his perceptions of those who work for him. Individual employees perceive the reward structure of the organization, make judgments about it, and then determine what form of behavior is appropriate. Yet different individuals can look at the same object or same person, weigh cues differently based upon their own past history, and come up with unique interpretations. What a person believes to be true about his world is, for him, the "truth." *Facts* are determined by the way people interpret information that they receive, and not by any absolute measure. As Leavitt said, "To ignore differences in perception is to ignore a major determinant of behavior."[1]

Perception involves the selecting, organizing, and interpreting of stimuli from the environment, and can be defined as the process whereby incoming cues from the environment are organized. The organization of such cues through the perceptual process serves a most useful function for the individual. He selectively accepts certain cues from the environment and classifies these cues according to his past history of that stimulus setting. This process enables him to screen out unwanted stimuli, and aids him in organizing his world into a consistent whole. As Mason Haire said, "If we make a separation between the physical world outside of us, on the one hand, and the psychological environment, or the world that we see, on the other, we come to see that the order in organization is not in the physical stimulus, but in the observer."[2] What Haire is saying is that our world is whatever we see it to be. One of the basic assumptions of the individuality of man is that his past history determines the world he sees.

When we meet someone new, we attempt to classify him into a category so that we can predict his behavior. How we classify him will depend upon the situation in which we observe him, his physical and verbal characteristics, our own past history with similar persons, and our own personal and psychological state at the time we perceive him. To aid in perceiving people, we often use certain devices, called perceptual sets, in order to place them into categories for purposes of prediction. Examples of such devices are stereotyping, halo effect, projection, selective perception, and perceptual readiness.

Leavitt points out that the world as it is perceived is the world that is important for determining the behavior of the worker, and he discusses also the importance of managers being able to perceive themselves accurately. The manager must understand his own biases and his own perceptual weaknesses before he can judge other people effectively. Moreover, one of the first steps in changing a person's attitude is getting him to understand how he perceives, or what he feels about, objects or other people.

Zalkind and Costello discuss the importance of understanding the nature of the perceptual process in organizational settings. They describe certain biases which may exist in supervisors and in employees that influence how they judge their fellow workers. They discuss in detail the concepts of stereotyping, halo effect, projection, and perceptual defense mechanisms. They also report on how the characteristics of the perceiver and the perceived affect supervisory ratings given the worker. They conclude their article by saying that managers should be aware of perceptual inaccuracies, and attempt to train supervisors in making accurate perceptual ratings.

Selective perception is discussed by Dearborn and Simon, who report a study showing that a manager perceives only those aspects of a situation that relate specifically to the activities and goals of his department. For the organization as a whole, however, it is important that managers view problems from the organizational rather than departmental standpoint.

Motivation and Individual Performance

Motivation can be defined as an inner state that activates, energizes, or moves behavior toward goals. When we speak of motivation or ask about the motives of a person, we are really asking *why* he acts, or why he acts the way he does. The concept of motivation implies that people choose the paths of action they follow; to explore motivation is to ask what the driving forces are that make a person choose or fail to choose a particular path. If a manager understands the motivation of his workers, he can channel this "inner state" toward common goals, that is, goals shared by both the individual and the organization.

Understanding motivation lies in understanding the meanings of, and relationships among, need states, drives, and goals. (An individual's perception of the world, and his attitudes about objects and people in that world, incidentally, play an important part in determining his needs and his goals.) According to Abraham Maslow, the *needs* underlying human motivation can be organized on five general levels, from lowest to highest.[3] He regards these needs as *prepotent*; that is, as one need is satisfied, the next need level comes into play. The lowest-level need he calls *physiological* need. This is the need for food, shelter, clothing, relief from pain, and the like. The next level is the need for *safety* or security. Examples include the need for protection from crime, and the need for job security. The third need level he calls *social need,* or the need for belonging. It is the need for friendship, for affection, and for identification with a group or an organization. This is probably the need of most individuals when they enter an organization. The fourth level of need is the need for *self-esteem* or autonomy. The person now wants to be accepted for his accomplishments as well. This need is the need to be independent in thinking and to be respected. It involves such things as recognition, status, and appreciation. The highest level of need, according to Maslow, is the need for *self-actualization.* Maslow defines this as the tendency for a person to become everything that he is capable of becoming.

A *drive* is a psychological condition which moves a person toward satisfying a need. The needs for food and water are translated into hunger and thirst drives. A *motive* is a subset of a drive state which has a clearly defined goal toward which it strives; *goals* fulfill or satisfy the relevant need. Thus a goal can be defined as anything that will reduce the need state—for example, eating food, drinking water, joining a group, finishing a project.

We tend to think that thoughts and actions reflect needs, drives, motives, and goals. Since needs can be fulfilled in many ways, different people set different goals to satisfy the same needs. The incentive programs, job procedures, and hiring practices that make up an effective reward system must be able to meet the needs of the group which it is trying to ''motivate to do a good job.''

McClelland suggests that many motives are acquired as a product of past experience. As a result of his research on the need for achievement, he has formulated some ideas of what motive acquisition involves, and how it can be effectively promoted in adults. According to McClelland, the vast majority of successful executives and managers rank high on the personality characteristic he labels *n* achievement, regardless of their nationality or social status. He says that the businessman is not motivated by greed and self-interest, as many people believe, but instead, his success and prestige are a function of his high need for achievement. Characteristics of the high achiever include liking situations in which he is personally responsible for finding solutions to problems, and facing moderately tough goals so that calculated risks can be taken to accomplish them. A high *n* achiever, McClelland says, is always a little overextended, complains of overwork, and has more problems than he can deal with. After research in many countries, McClelland has devised a method for developing high *n* achievers.

When a person in an exchange relationship gets more or less reward than he deserves, we have what Adams defines as *inequity.* Adams offers a detailed discussion of how equitable and inequitable situations can occur, and the effect that they have on the motivation and behavior of individuals within groups.

Basically, this theory suggests that the manager knows that rewards should be contingent on performance and also that the payoff is evaluated in terms of whether or not the recipient feels that it is equitable, compared to what he believes he deserves or to what he feels others have received.

Staw argues that two major types of rewards affect our motivation level. Both intrinsic as well as extrinsic rewards are likely to be energizing motivational factors which may be manipulated to get an individual to perform a task. The question Staw examines in detail deals with whether or not these two sources of motivation can be combined effectively to yield overall positive effects on the individual's task attitudes and behavior.

The last article in this section, by Locke, brings in an additional variable which affects an individual's level of motivation. A person's *goal of performance* will, according to Locke, help a manager predict the person's future performance and satisfaction. Thus he argues that other theories of motivation, such as expectancy theory, are insufficient unless they include a goal-setting dimension.

It may well be that there is no one best way to improve the motivation of the worker, though in all cases worker motivation is directly linked to worker performance and satisfaction. In part 5, "The Effect of the Organizational Environment on Individual and Group Behavior," we give many examples of motivation programs used in various large organizations.

Notes

1. Leavitt, H. J., *Managerial Psychology* (2d ed.), University of Chicago Press, 1972, p. 30.
2. Haire, Mason, *Psychology in Management,* McGraw-Hill, 1956, p. 40.
3. Maslow, Abraham, *Motivation and Personality,* Harper and Row, 1954.

Section A

Attitudes and Performance

THE FUNCTIONAL APPROACH TO THE STUDY OF ATTITUDES

DANIEL KATZ

The study of opinion formation and attitude change is basic to an understanding of the public opinion process even though it should not be equated with this process. The public opinion process is one phase of the influencing of collective decisions, and its investigation involves knowledge of channels of communication, of the power structures of a society, of the character of mass media, of the relation between elites, factions and masses, of the role of formal and informal leaders, of the institutionalized access to officials. But the raw material out of which public opinion develops is to be found in the attitudes of individuals, whether they be followers or leaders and whether these attitudes be at the general level of tendencies to conform to legitimate authority or majority opinion or at the specific level of favoring or opposing the particular aspects of the issue under consideration. The nature of the organization of attitudes within the personality and the processes which account for attitude change are thus critical areas for the understanding of the collective product known as public opinion.

Early Approaches to the Study of Attitude and Opinion

There have been two main streams of thinking with respect to the determination of man's attitudes. The one tradition assumes an irrational model of man: specifically it holds that men have very limited powers of reason and reflection, weak capacity to discriminate, only the most primitive self-insight, and very short memories. Whatever mental capacities people do possess are easily overwhelmed by emotional forces and appeals to self-interest and vanity. The early books on the psychology of advertising, with their emphasis on the doctrine of suggestion, exemplify this

Reprinted from *The Public Opinion Quarterly*, vol. 24, by permission of the publisher.

approach. One expression of this philosophy is in the propagandist's concern with tricks and traps to manipulate the public. A modern form of it appears in *The Hidden Persuaders,* or the use of subliminal and marginal suggestion, or the devices supposedly employed by the "the Madison Avenue boys." Experiments to support this line of thinking started with laboratory demonstrations of the power of hypnotic suggestion and were soon extended to show that people would change their attitudes in an uncritical manner under the influence of the prestige of authority and numbers. For example, individuals would accept or reject the same idea depending upon whether it came from a positive or a negative prestige source.[1]

The second approach is that of the ideologist who invokes a rational model of man. It assumes that the human being has a cerebral cortex, that he seeks understanding, that he consistently attempts to make sense of the world about him, that he possesses discriminating and reasoning powers which will assert themselves over time, and that he is capable of self-criticism and self-insight. It relies heavily upon getting adequate information to people. Our educational system is based upon this rational model. The present emphasis upon the improvement of communication, upon developing more adequate channels of two-way communication, of conferences and institutes, upon bringing people together to interchange ideas, are all indications of the belief in the importance of intelligence and comprehension in the formation and change of men's opinions.

Now either school of thought can point to evidence which supports its assumptions, and can make fairly damaging criticisms of its opponent. Solomon Asch and his colleagues, in attacking the irrational model, have called attention to the biased character of the old experiments on prestige suggestion which gave the subject little opportunity to demonstrate critical thinking.[2] And further exploration of subjects in these stupid situations does indicate that they try to make sense of a nonsensical matter as far as possible. Though the same statement is presented by the experimenter to two groups, the first time as coming from a positive source and the second time as coming from a negative source, it is given a different meaning dependent upon the context in which it appears.[3] Thus the experimental subject does his best to give some rational meaning to the problem. On the other hand, a large body of experimental work indicates that there are many limitations in the rational approach in that people see their world in terms of their own needs, remember what they want to remember, and interpret information on the basis of wishful thinking. H. H. Hyman and P. Sheatsley have demonstrated that these experimental results have direct relevance to information campaigns directed at influencing public opinion.[4] These authors assembled facts about such campaigns and showed conclusively that increasing the flow of information to people does not necessarily increase the knowledge absorbed or produce the attitude changes desired.

The major difficulty with these conflicting approaches is their lack of specification of the conditions under which men do act as the theory would predict. For the facts are that people do act at times as if they had been decorticated and at times with intelligence and comprehension. And people themselves do recognize that on occasion they have behaved blindly, impulsively, and thoughtlessly. A second major difficulty is that the rationality-irrationality dimension is not clearly defined. At the extremes it is easy to point to examples, as in the case of the acceptance of stupid suggestions under emotional stress on the one hand, or brilliant problem solving on the other; but this does not provide adequate guidance for the many cases in the middle of the scale where one attempts to discriminate between rationalization and reason.

Reconciliation of the Conflict in a Functional Approach

The conflict between the rationality and irrationality models was saved from becoming a worthless debate because of the experimentation and research suggested by these models. The findings of this research pointed toward the elements of truth in each approach and gave some indication of the conditions under which each model could make fairly accurate predictions. In general the irrational approach was at its best where the situation imposed heavy restrictions upon search behavior and response alternatives. Where individuals must give quick responses without adequate opportunities to explore the nature of the problem, where there are very few response alternatives available to them, where their own deep emotional needs are aroused, they will in general react much as does the unthinking subject under hypnosis. On the other hand, where the individual can have more adequate commerce with the relevant environmental setting, where he has time to obtain more feedback from his reality testing, and where he has a number of realistic choices, his behavior will reflect the use of his rational faculties.[5] The child will often respond to the directive of the parent not by implicit obedience but by testing out whether or not the parent really meant what he said.

. . . The theory of psychological consonance, or cognitive balance, assumes that man attempts to reduce discrepancies in his beliefs, attitudes, and behavior by appropriate changes in these processes. While the emphasis here is upon consistency or logicality, the theory deals with all dissonances, no matter how produced. Thus they could result from irrational factors of distorted perception and wishful thinking as well as from rational factors of realistic appraisal of a problem and an accurate estimate of its consequences. Moreover, the theory would predict only that the individual will move to reduce dissonance, whether such movement is a good adjustment to the world or leads to the delusional systems of the paranoiac. In a sense, then, this theory would avoid the conflict between the old approaches of the rational and the irrational man by not dealing with the specific antecedent causes of behavior or with the particular ways in which the individual solves his problems.

In addition to the present preoccupation with the development of formal models concerned with cognitive balance and consonance, there is a growing interest in a more comprehensive framework for dealing with the complex variables and for bringing order within the field. . . . Another point of departure is represented by two groups of workers who have organized their theories around the functions which attitudes perform for the personality. Sarnoff, Katz, and McClintock, in taking this functional approach, have given primary attention to the motivational bases of attitudes and the processes of attitude change.[6] The basic assumption of this group is that both attitude formation and attitude change must be understood in terms of the needs they serve and that, as these motivational processes differ, so too will the conditions and techniques for attitude change. Smith, Bruner, and White have also analyzed the different functions which attitudes perform for the personality.[7]

Both groups present essentially the same functions, but Smith, Bruner, and White give more attention to perceptual and cognitive processes and Sarnoff, Katz, and McClintock to the specific conditions of attitude change.

The importance of the functional approach is threefold. (1) Many previous studies of attitude change have dealt with factors which are not genuine psychological variables, for example, the effect on group prejudice of contact between two groups, or the exposure of a group of subjects to a communication in the mass media. Now contact serves different psychological functions for the individual and merely knowing that people have seen a movie or watched a television program tells us nothing about the personal values engaged or not engaged by such a presentation. If, however, we can gear our research to the functions attitudes perform, we can develop some generalizations about human behavior. Dealing with nonfunctional variables makes such generalization difficult, if not impossible.

(2) By concerning ourselves with the different functions attitudes can perform we can avoid the great error of oversimplification—the error of attributing a single cause to given types of attitude. It was once popular to ascribe radicalism in economic and political matters to the psychopathology of the insecure and to attribute conservatism to the rigidity of the mentally aged. At the present time it is common practice to see in attitudes of group prejudice the repressed hostilities stemming from childhood frustrations, though Hyman and Sheatsley have pointed out that prejudiced attitudes can serve a normative function of gaining acceptance in one's own group as readily as releasing unconscious hatred.[8] In short, not only are there a number of motivational forces to take into account in considering attitudes and behavior, but the same attitude can have a different motivational basis in different people.

(3) Finally, recognition of the complex motivational sources of behavior can help to remedy the neglect in general theories which lack specification of conditions under which given types of attitude will change. Gestalt theory tells us, for example, that attitudes will change to give better cognitive organization to the psychological field. This theoretical generalization is suggestive, but to carry out significant research we need some middle-level concepts to bridge the gap between a high level of abstraction and particularistic or phenotypical events. We need concepts that will point toward the types of motive and methods of motive satisfaction which are operative in bringing about cognitive reorganization.

Before we attempt a detailed analysis of the four major functions which attitudes can serve, it is appropriate to consider the nature of attitudes, their dimensions, and their relations to other psychological structures and processes.

Nature of Attitudes: Their Dimensions

Attitude is the predisposition of the individual to evaluate some symbol or object or aspect of his world in a favorable or unfavorable manner. Opinion is the verbal expression of an attitude, but attitudes can also be expressed in nonverbal behavior. Attitudes include both the affective, or feeling core of liking or disliking, and the cognitive, or belief, elements which describe the object of the attitude, its characteristics, and its relations to other objects. All attitudes thus include beliefs, but not all beliefs are attitudes. When specific attitudes are organized into a hierarchical structure, they comprise *value systems*. Thus a person may not only hold specific attitudes against deficit spending and unbalanced budgets but may also have a systematic organization of such beliefs and attitudes in the form of a value system of economic conservatism.

The dimensions of attitudes can be stated more precisely if the above distinctions between beliefs and feelings and attitudes and value systems are kept in mind. The *intensity* of an attitude refers to the strength of the *affective* component. In fact, rating scales and even Thurstone scales deal primarily with the intensity of feeling of the individual for or against some social object. The cognitive, or belief, component suggests two additional dimensions, the *specificity* or *generality* of the attitude and the *degree of differentiation* of the beliefs. Differentiation refers to the number of beliefs or cognitive items contained in the attitude, and the general assumption is that the simpler the attitude in cognitive structure the easier it is to change.[9] For simple structures there is no defense in depth, and once a single item of belief has been changed the attitude will change. A rather different dimension of attitude is the *number and strength of its linkages to a related value system*. If an attitude favoring budget balancing by the Federal government is tied in strongly with a value system of economic conservatism, it will be more difficult to change than if it were a fairly isolated attitude of the person. Finally, the relation of the value system to the personality is a consideration of first importance. If an attitude is tied to a value system which is closely related to, or which consists of, the individual's conception of himself, then the appropriate change procedures become more complex. The *centrality* of an attitude refers to its role as part of a value system which is closely related to the individual's self-concept.

An additional aspect of attitudes is not clearly described in most theories, namely, their relation to action or overt behavior. Though behavior related to the attitude has other determinants than the attitude itself, it is also true that some attitudes in themselves have more of what Cartwright calls an action structure than do others.[10] Brewster Smith refers to this dimension as policy orientation[11] and Katz and Stotland speak of it as the action component.[12] For example, while many people have attitudes of approval toward one or the other of the two political parties, these attitudes will differ in their structure with respect to relevant action. One man may be prepared to vote on election day and will know where and when he should vote and will go to the polls no matter what the weather or how great the inconvenience. Another man will only vote if a party worker calls for him in a car. Himmelstrand's work is concerned with all aspects of the relationship between attitude and behavior, but he deals with the action structure of the attitude itself by distinguishing between attitudes where the affect is tied to verbal expression and attitudes where the affect is tied to behavior concerned with more objective referents of the attitude.[13] In the first case an individual derives satisfaction from talking about a problem; in the second case he derives satisfaction from taking some form of concrete action.

Attempts to change attitudes can be directed primarily at the belief component or at the feeling, or affective, component. Rosenberg theorizes that an effective change in one component will result in changes in the other component and presents experimental evidence to confirm this hypothesis.[14] For example, a political candidate will often attempt to win people by making them like him and dislike his opponent, and thus communicate affect rather than ideas. If he is successful, people will not only like him but entertain favorable beliefs about him. Another candidate may deal primarily with ideas and hope that, if he can change people's beliefs about an issue, their feelings will also change.

Four Functions Which Attitudes Perform for the Individual

The major functions which attitudes perform for the personality can be grouped according to their motivational basis as follows:

1. *The instrumental, adjustive, or utilitarian function* upon which Jeremy Bentham and the utilitarians constructed their model of man. A modern expression of this approach can be found in behavioristic learning theory.

2. *The ego-defensive function* in which the person protects himself from acknowledging the basic truths about himself or the harsh realities in his external world. Freudian psychology and neo-Freudian thinking have been preoccupied with this type of motivation and its outcomes.

3. *The value-expressive function* in which the individual derives satisfactions from expressing attitudes appropriate to his personal values and to his concept of himself. This function is central to doctrines of ego psychology which stress the importance of self-expression, self-development, and self-realization.

4. *The knowledge function* based upon the individual's need to give adequate structure to his universe. The search for meaning, the need to understand, the trend toward better organization of perceptions and beliefs to provide clarity and consistency for the individual, are other descriptions of this function. The development of principles about perceptual and cognitive structure have been the contribution of Gestalt psychology.

Stated simply, the functional approach is the attempt to understand the reasons people hold the attitudes they do. The reasons, however, are at the level of psychological motivations and not of the accidents of external events and circumstances. Unless we know the psychological need which is met by the holding of an attitude we are in a poor position to predict when and how it will change. Moreover, the same attitude expressed toward a political candidate may not perform the same function for all the people who express it. And while many attitudes are predominantly in the service of a single type of motivational process, as described above, other attitudes may serve more than one purpose for the individual. A fuller discussion of how attitudes serve the above four functions is in order.

1. *The adjustment function.* Essentially this function is a recognition of the fact that people strive to maximize the rewards in their external environment and to minimize the penalties. The child develops favorable attitudes toward the objects in his world which are associated with the satisfactions of his needs and unfavorable attitudes toward objects which thwart him or punish him. Attitudes acquired in the service of the adjustment function are either the means for reaching the desired goal or avoiding the undesirable one, or are affective associations based upon experiences in attaining motive satisfactions.[15] The attitudes of the worker favoring a political party which will advance his economic lot are an example of the first type of utilitarian attitude. The pleasant image one has of one's favorite food is an example of the second type of utilitarian attitude.

In general, then, the dynamics of attitude formation with respect to the adjustment function are dependent upon present or past perceptions of the utility of the attitudinal object for the individual. The clarity, consistency, and nearness of rewards and punishments, as they relate to the individual's activities and goals, are important factors in the acquisition of such attitudes. Both attitudes and habits are formed toward specific objects, people, and symbols as they satisfy specific needs. The closer these objects are to actual need satisfaction and the more they are clearly perceived as relevant to need satisfaction, the greater are the probabilities of positive attitude formation. These principles of attitude formation are often observed in the breach rather than the compliance. In industry, management frequently expects to create favorable attitudes toward job performance through programs for making the company more attractive to the worker, such as providing recreational facilities and fringe benefits. Such programs, however, are much more likely to produce favorable attitudes toward the company as a desirable place to work than toward performance on the job. The company benefits and advantages are applied across the board to all employees and are not specifically relevant to increased effort in task performance by the individual worker.

Consistency of reward and punishment also contributes to the clarity of the instrumental object for goal attainment. If a political party bestows recognition and favors on party workers in an unpredictable and inconsistent fashion, it will destroy the favorable evaluation of the importance of working hard for the party among those whose motivation is of the utilitarian sort. But, curiously, while consistency of reward needs to be observed, 100 per cent consistency is not as effective as a pattern which is usually consistent but in which there are some lapses. When animal or human subjects are invariably rewarded for a correct performance, they do not retain their learned responses as well as when the reward is sometimes skipped.[16]

2. The ego-defensive function. People not only seek to make the most of their external world and what if offers, but they also expend a great deal of their energy on living with themselves. The mechanisms by which the individual protects his ego from his own unacceptable impulses and from the knowledge of threatening forces from without, and the methods by which he reduces his anxieties created by such problems, are known as mechanisms of ego defense. . . . They include the devices by which the individual avoids facing either the inner reality of the kind of person he is, or the outer reality of the dangers the world holds for him. They stem basically from internal conflict with its resulting insecurities. In one sense the mechanisms of defense are adaptive in temporarily removing the sharp edges of conflict and in saving the individual from complete disaster. In another sense they are not adaptive in that they handicap the individual in his social adjustments and in obtaining the maximum satisfactions available to him from the world in which he lives. The worker who persistently quarrels with his boss and with his fellow workers, because he is acting out some of his own internal conflicts, may in this manner relieve himself of some of the emotional tensions which beset him. He is not, however, solving his problem of adjusting to his work situation and thus may deprive himself of advancement or even of steady employment.

Defense mechanisms, Miller and Swanson point out, may be classified into two families on the basis of the more or less primitive nature of the devices employed.[17] The first family, more primitive in nature, are more socially handicapping and consist of denial and complete avoidance. The individual in such cases obliterates through withdrawal and denial the realities which confront him. The exaggerated case of such primitive mechanisms is the fantasy world of the paranoiac. The second type of defense is less handicapping and makes for distortion rather than denial. It includes rationalization, projection, and displacement.

Many of our attitudes have the function of defending our self-image. When we cannot admit to ourselves that we have deep feelings of inferiority we may project those feelings onto some convenient minority group and bolster our egos by attitudes of superiority toward this underprivileged group. The formation of such defensive attitudes differs in essential ways from the formation of attitudes which serve the adjustment function. They proceed from within the person, and the objects and situation to which they are attached are merely convenient outlets for their expression. Not all targets are equally satisfactory for a given defense mechanism, but the point is that the attitude is not created by the target but by the individual's emotional conflicts. And when no convenient target exists the individual will create one. Utilitarian attitudes, on the other hand, are formed with specific reference to the nature of the attitudinal object. They are thus appropriate to the nature of the social world to which they are geared. The high school student who values high grades because he wants to be admitted to a good college has a utilitarian attitude appropriate to the situation to which it is related.

All people employ defense mechanisms, but they differ with respect to the extent that they use them and some of their attitudes may be more defensive in function than others. It follows that the techniques and conditions for attitude change will not be the same for ego-defensive as for utilitarian attitudes.

Moreover, though people are ordinarily unaware of their defense mechanisms, especially at the time of employing them, they differ with respect to the amount of insight they may show at some later time about their use of defenses. In some cases they recognize that they have been protecting their egos without knowing the reason why. In other cases they may not even be aware of the devices they have been using to delude themselves.

3. The value-expressive function. While attitudes have the function of preventing the individual from revealing to himself and others his true nature, other attitudes have the function of giving positive expression to his central values and to the type of person he conceives himself to be. A man may consider himself to be an enlightened conservative or an internationalist or a liberal, and will hold attitudes which are the appropriate indication of his central values. Thus we need to take account of the fact that not all behavior has the negative function of reducing the tensions of biological drives or of internal conflicts. Satisfactions also accrue to the person from the expression of attitudes which reflect his cherished beliefs and his self-image. The reward to the person in these instances is not so much a matter of gaining social recognition or monetary rewards as of establishing his self-identity and confirming his notion of the sort of person he sees himself to be. The gratifications obtained from value expression may go beyond the confirmation of self-identity. Just as we find satisfaction in the exercise of our talents and abilities, so we find reward in the expression of any attributes associated with our egos.

Value-expressive attitudes not only give clarity to the self-image but also mold that self-image closer to the heart's desire. The teenager who by dress and speech establishes his identity as similar to his own peer group may appear to the outsider a weakling and a craven conformer. To himself he is asserting his independence of the adult world to which he has rendered childlike subservience and conformity all his life. Very early in the development of the personality the need for clarity of self-image is important—the need to know "who I am." Later it may be even more important to know that in some measure I am the type of person I want to be. Even as adults, however, the clarity and stability of the self-image is of primary significance. Just as the kind, considerate person will cover over his acts of selfishness, so too will the ruthless individualist become confused and embarrassed by his acts of sympathetic compassion. One reason it is difficult to change the character of the adult is that he is not comfortable with the new "me." Group support for such personality change is almost a necessity, as in Alcoholics Anonymous, so that the individual is aware of approval of his new self by people who are like him.

The socialization process during the formative years sets the basic outlines for the individual's self-concept. Parents constantly hold up before the child the model of the good character they want them to be. A good boy eats his spinach, does not hit girls, etc. The candy and the stick are less in evidence in training the child than the constant appeal to his notion of his own character. It is small wonder, then, that children reflect the acceptance of this model by inquiring about the characters of the actors in every drama, whether it be a television play, a political contest, or a war, wanting to know who are the "good guys" and who are the "bad guys." Even as adults we persist in labeling others in the terms of such character images. Joe McCarthy and his cause collapsed in fantastic fashion when the telecast of the Army hearings showed him in the role of the villain attacking the gentle, good man represented by Joseph Welch.

A related but somewhat different process from childhood socialization takes place when individuals enter a new group or organization. The individual will often take over and internalize the values of the group. What accounts, however, for the fact that sometimes this occurs and sometimes it does not? Four factors are probably operative, and some combination of them may be necessary for internalization. (1) The values of the new group may be highly consistent with existing values central to the personality. The girl who enters the nursing profession finds it congenial to consider herself a good nurse because of previous values of the importance of contributing to the welfare of others. (2) The new group may in its ideology have a clear model of what the good group member should be like and may persistently indoctrinate group members in these terms. One of the reasons for the code of conduct for members of the armed forces, devised after the revelations about the conduct of American prisoners in the Korean War, was to attempt to establish a model for what a good soldier does and does not do. (3) The activities of the group in moving toward its goal permit the individual genuine opportunity for participation. To become ego-involved so that he can internalize group values, the new member must find one of two conditions. The group activity open to him must tap his talents and abilities so that his chance to show what he is worth can be tied into the group effort. Or else the activities of the group must give him an active voice in group decisions. His particular talents and abilities may not be tapped but he does have the opportunity to enter into group decisions, and thus his need for self-determination is satisfied. He then identifies with the group in which such opportunities for ego-involvement are available. It is not necessary that opportunities for self-expression and self-determination be of great magnitude in an objective sense, so long as they are important for the psychological economy of the individuals themselves. (4) Finally, the individual may come to see himself as a group member if he can share in the rewards of group activity which includes his own efforts. The worker may not play much of a part in building a ship or make any decisions in the process of building it. Nevertheless, if he and his fellow workers are given a share in every boat they build and a return on the proceeds from the earnings of the ship, they may soon come to identify with the ship-building company and see themselves as builders of ships.

4. *The knowledge function.* Individuals not only acquire beliefs in the interest of satisfying various specific needs, they also seek knowledge to give meaning to what would otherwise be an unorganized chaotic universe. People need standards or frames of reference for understanding their world, and attitudes help to supply such standards. The problem of understanding, as John Dewey made clear years ago, is one "of introducing (1) *definiteness* and *distinction* and (2) *consistency* and *stability* of meaning into what is otherwise vague and wavering."[18] The definiteness and stability are provided in good measure by the norms of our culture, which give the otherwise perplexed individual ready-made attitudes for comprehending his universe. Walter Lippmann's classical contribution to the study of opinions and attitudes was his description of stereotypes and the way they provided order and clarity for a bewildering set of complexities.[19] The most interesting finding in Herzog's familiar study of the gratifications obtained by housewives in listening to daytime serials was the unsuspected role of information and advice.[20] The stories were liked "because they explained things to the inarticulate listener."

The need to know does not of course imply that people are driven by a thirst for universal knowledge. The American public's appalling lack of political information has been documented many times. In 1956, for example, only 13 per cent of the people in Detroit could correctly name the two United States Senators from the state of Michigan and only 18 per cent knew the name of their own Congressman. People are not avid seekers after knowledge as judged by what the educator or social reformer would desire. But they do want to understand the events which impinge directly on their own life. Moreoever, many of the attitudes they have already acquired give them sufficient basis for interpreting much of what they perceive to be important for them. Our already existing stereotypes, in Lippmann's language, "are an ordered, more or less consistent picture of the world, to which our habits, our tastes, our capacities, our comforts, and our hopes have adjusted themselves. They may not be a complete picture of the world, but they are a picture of a possible world to which we are adapted."[21] It follows that new information will not modify old attitudes unless there is some inadequacy or incompleteness or inconsistency in the existing attitudinal structure as it relates to the perceptions of new situations.

Notes and References

1. Muzater Sherif, *The Psychology of Social Norms*, New York, Harper, 1936.
2. Solomon E. Asch, *Social Psychology*, New York, Prentice-Hall, 1952

3. *Ibid.*, pp. 426-427. The following statement was attributed to its rightful author, John Adams, for some subjects and to Karl Marx for others: "those who hold and those who are without property have ever formed distinct interests in society." When the statement was attributed to Marx, this type of comment appeared: "Marx is stressing the need for redistribution of wealth." When it was attributed to Adams, this comment appeared: "The social division is innate in mankind."

4. Herbert H. Hyman and Paul B. Sheatsley, "Some Reasons Why Information Campaigns Fail," *Public Opinion Quarterly*, Vol. II, 1947, pp. 413-423.

5. William A. Scott points out that in the area of international relations the incompleteness and remoteness of the information and the lack of pressures on the individual to defend his views results in inconsistencies. Inconsistent elements with respect to a system of international beliefs may, however, be consistent with the larger system of the personality. "Rationality and Non-rationality of International Attitudes," *Journal of Conflict Resolution*, Vol. 2, 1958 pp. 9-16.

6. Irving Sarnoff and Daniel Katz, "The Motivational Bases of Attitude Change," *Journal of Abnormal and Social Psychology*, Vol. 49, 1954, pp. 115-124.

7. M. Brewster Smith, Jerome S. Bruner, and Robert W. White, *Opinions and Personality*, New York, Wiley, 1956.

8. Herbert H. Hyman and Paul B. Sheatsley, "The Authoritarian Personality: A Methodological Critique," in Richard Christie and Marie Jahoda, editors, *Studies in the Scope and Method of the Authoritarian Personality*, Glencoe, Ill., Free Press, 1954, pp. 50-122.

9. David Krech and Richard S. Crutchfield, *Theory and Problems of Social Psychology*, New York, McGraw-Hill, 1948, pp. 160-163.

10. Dorwin Cartwright, "Some Principles of Mass Persuasion," *Human Relations*, Vol. 2, 1949, pp. 253-267.

11. M. Brewster Smith, "The Personal Setting of Public Opinions: A Study of Attitudes toward Russia," *Public Opinion Quarterly*, Vol. II, 1947, pp. 507-523.

12. Daniel Katz and Ezra Stotland, "A Preliminary Statement to a Theory of Attitude Structure and Change," in Sigmund Koch, Editor, *Psychology: A Study of a Science*, Vol. 3, New York, McGraw-Hill, 1959, pp. 423-475.

13. See pages 224-250 of this issue of the *Quarterly*.

14. See pages 319-340 of this issue of the *Quarterly*.

15. Katz and Stotland, *op.cit.*, pp. 434-443.

16. William O. Jenkins and Julian C. Stanley, "Partial Reinforcement: A Review and Critique," *Psychological Bulletin*, Vol. 47, 1950, pp. 193-234.

17. Daniel R. Miller and Guy E. Swanson, *Inner Conflict and Defense*, New York, Holt, 1960, pp. 194-288.

18. John Dewey, *How We Think*, New York, Macmillan, 1910.

19. Walter Lippmann, *Public Opinion*, New York, Macmillan, 1922.

20. Herta Herzog, "What Do We Really Know about Daytime Serial Listeners?" in Paul F. Lazarsfeld and Frank N. Stanton, editors, *Radio Research 1942-1943*, New York, Duell &Pearce, 1944, pp. 3-33.

21. Lippmann, *op.cit.*, p. 95.

ATTITUDES

LEON MANN

Attitudes and Consistency Theory

In the examination of the relationship between components of attitudes and between attitudes and behaviour, it was noted that although the person strives to maintain consistency between these elements, apparent contradictions often occur. As well as the internal structure of attitudes there is the question of structure of attitude systems, clusters of attitudes about a set of related social objects which fit together in an interconnected, integrated whole. For example, attitudes toward Soviet Russia, the UN, President Nasser, Israel and war belong together in a closely-knit system. Attitudes toward virginity, pre-marital intercourse, birth control and the contraceptive pill also co-exist in one system. Interest lies in the extent to which there is consistency between attitudes in a cognitive system, what happens if attitudes become inconsistent with one another, and how adjustments are made to restore the system to consistency.

In seeking answers to these questions, a number of theories of "cognitive" consistency will be examined. The reference is not to attitudinal consistency but to the more generic cognitive consistency. This is because of concern with cognition in the broadest sense, the image or map of the world held by the person which includes thoughts, values and actions as well as attitudes about some object or set of events. At the core of cognitive consistency is the need to attain harmony and congruity between cognitions of objects and persons in the environment. Here are some examples of inconsistent cognitions relating to the realm of attitudes. Fred is secretary of the League of Animal Lovers and yet I know that Fred savagely beats his dog; I believe that the Nazi Party should be banned yet I support every appeal held by the Nazi Party; I know that smoking causes lung cancer and yet I smoke four packets of cigarettes a day. Each of these three sets of cognitions is disturbing and tension arousing because their elements do not fit together. How can the world be logical, meaningful and stable if animal lovers beat their dogs, if I support my enemies and if my favourite habit is killing me? These examples are overwrought and far-fetched, but they give some flavour of what is meant by cognitive inconsistency.

Consider a miniature system in which all of the cognitive elements are consistent as far as the person is concerned (see Figure 1). Imagine that you are the person in this example. You like Joe very much, and he admires the same things you admire (the church) and dislikes what you dislike (Fred and socialism). You are pleased that the church is also against socialism and it is satisfying to know that Fred is for socialism because it justifies your dislike of him. This system is harmonious and consistent. Now suppose that you receive information that throws the entire system into turmoil. You learn that Joe is secretly an ardent socialist, or you discover that Joe has been inviting Fred over for drinks, or that Fred really despises socialism, or, worse still, that your church is now in favour of socialism. It is clear that these new bits of information represent cognitions that are inconsistent with the cognitions you already hold and a state of tension and discomfort results. However, it is not likely that matters will be left that way for very long. Modifications will occur in your feelings and beliefs that are directed toward the restoration of consistency or equilibrium. For example, you might start to like Fred and dislike Joe, or become attracted to socialism, or antagonistic toward the church. To a great extent the loci of these changes would depend upon the strength and degree of interrelatedness of each of the attitudes and beliefs. In general, the weaker, more isolated attitudes are the first to change in the move to restore consistency, but reverberations occur right through the system and it is possible for all cognitions to be changed.

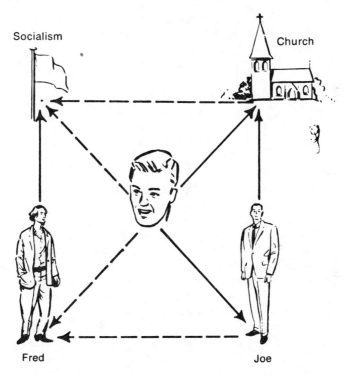

Figure 1. Schematic representation of a miniature cognitive system in which the relationships between each of the elements (socialism, church, Fred, and Joe) are consistent. An unbroken line between two elements represents a positive relationship (support, liking, admiration, etc.). A broken line represents a negative relationship (antagonism, disliking, etc.). Arrows indicate direction of the relationship.

The consistency motive can exert a powerful force in attitude systems influencing the person to make various aspects of his cognitive functioning consistent with one another. There are a number of theories which deal with this problem. All of the theoretical models to be discussed deal with changes toward the restoration of consistency, though they often focus on different modes and specify different theoretical determinants of resolution. All models have as their starting point the consistency principle, though the theorists use different terms, *e.g.*, Heider (1958) talks about "balance", Osgood and Tannenbaum (1955) deal with "symmetry", and Festinger (1957) prefers the term "consonance" to designate much the same state of harmony or equilibrium. Although these models have a good deal in common there are also critical differences among them.

Heider's Balance Principle

The earliest and simplest formulation of the consistency principle is found in Heider's (1958) balance theory. He deals with states of balance and imbalance which exist between three elements: the person (P), another person (O), and some object, idea or issue (X). What are the attitudes of two friends, P and O, toward issue X? A balanced state exists when their attitudes toward the issue are similar, *i.e.*, they both like or both dislike the attitude object. If one of them likes X but the other dislikes it, there will be imbalance, and the resultant feelings of strain will induce pressures toward change in the direction of balance. For example, there may be a falling out between the friends, or they might try to persuade each other to adopt a common harmonious attitude toward the issue. Note that there are three relations in this simple triadic system: P's attitude toward O, P's attitude toward X, and O's attitude toward X. In formal terms, a balanced state would exist if all three relations among P, O, and X were positive, or if two were negative and one positive. An example of the former state: the person admires Churchill and loves cigars; he is delighted that Churchill also loves cigars. An example of the latter: President Nasser (in 1956) despised Jordan and hated Israel; he then assumed that Jordan and Israel liked each other. Feather (1956), an Australian psychologist, has extended and applied Heider's balance principle to the study of communication effects. In his research Feather investigates the relationship between four elements in a communication structure: a *source* presents a *message* about an *issue* to a *receiver*. It was found that when subjects are given hypothetical communication situations, they tend to predict outcomes which represent a state of balance between four elements.

Although it offers a promising start for the analysis of cognitive consistency the balance principle is limited in its scope. Consideration of some novel social contexts and relationships reveal the limitations of the balance principle. If two men were both in love with the same woman would they necessarily have positive attitudes toward each other? If you like chickens and chickens like chicken feed, should you also like chicken feed? Perhaps the balance principle's greatest weakness is its failure to specify the exact location and precise magnitude of attitude change that will occur to restore balance and harmony in a system.

Osgood and Tannenbaum's Congruity Principle

This principle is based on the assumption that it is simpler to hold congruent attitudes toward two related objects, such as President Eisenhower and golf, than to have varying attitudes toward them. The congruity principle goes further than the principle of balance because it makes explicit quantitative predictions about what will happen if the two related objects are not in a state of congruity. For example, a person who has a lukewarm attitude toward Eisenhower and is enthusiastic about golf learns that Eisenhower is a golf fanatic. This person will become more favourable toward Eisenhower and perhaps slightly less enthusiastic about golf, so that the intensities of the two attitudes shift together. Congruity exists when two related objects are evaluated with equal intensity. In the Eisenhower-golf example the person's wishy-washy attitude toward Eisenhower will shift more than his extreme evaluation of golf because highly "polarized" or extreme attitudes change less than moderate ones. Experimental evidence (*e.g.*, Osgood Tannenbaum, 1955) provides support for the congruity principle although, like the balance principle, there are limitations to the scope of its operation.

Festinger's Dissonance Theory

The most provocative of the consistency principles has been put forward by Festinger (1957) in his theory of cognitive dissonance. If the person has cognitions about himself or his environment that are inconsistent with each other, *i.e.*, if one cognition implies the opposite of the other, a state of cognitive dissonance exists. Here are four cases of cognitive dissonance arising from each of the principal sources of inconsistency.

(*a*) Logical inconsistency: I believe there will be a man on the moon by 1970; I think it is impossible to get a device to leave earth's atmosphere.

(*b*) Cultural mores and norms: I believe it is wrong to burp at formal dinners; I burp at formal dinners.

(*c*) Opinion inconsistent with action: I believe that the League to Clothe Animals is a hare-brained outfit; I support every appeal sponsored by the League.

(*d*) Past experience: I always feel pain when I am pricked with a needle; I have just been pricked but I feel no pain.

The state of cognitive dissonance is uncomfortable because it arouses psychological tension and therefore attempts are made to reduce it by changing either or both cognitions or by adding new cognitions. In the examples above I could modify or add cognitions as follows: (*a*) they will no doubt bring the earth closer to the moon; (*b*) I will no longer burp at formal dinners; (*c*) supporting the L.C.A. is good for my income tax deductions; and (*d*) I sometimes feel pain when I am pricked with a needle. The breadth and scope of dissonance theory is best demonstrated by surveying some of the major sources of dissonance that have been studied experimentally.

Unforeseen Negative Consequences

The person who discovers after he has made a choice that it has many negative features is plunged into a state of cognitive dissonance; if he has suffered a great deal for his choice the magnitude of dissonance is very great and attempts are made to reduce it by looking for positive features of the choice. Aronson and Mills (1959) induced dissonance in female students by requiring them to undergo a severe initiation ceremony before they were allowed to join a discussion group on sex. One group of girls underwent a mild initiation ceremony in the form of an "embarrassment" test in which they had to read alone a list of sex-related words such as "prostitute", "virgin", and "petting". The other group, however, was put through a much more severe and demanding test in which they had to read aloud twelve obscene words and two vivid descriptions of sexual activity. All subjects were told that they had passed the test and could join the group. For their first "group" meeting the subjects were allowed to listen to a long and dull tape-recorded discussion about secondary sex behaviour in the lower animals. Finally the subjects were asked to indicate how good they thought the discussion was and how much they liked the members of the group. It was found that those subjects who underwent the severe initiation for the privilege of listening to a dull disappointing discussion reported the group and its discussion to be quite interesting. This suggests that the dissonance aroused by the painful embarrassing test was reduced by seeing the cause for which the individual suffered as worthwhile. Girls who underwent the mild initiation ceremony, and therefore suffered less dissonance, were far more critical and negative in their attitudes to the boring group discussion.

Disconfirmed Expectancies

The person may have prepared himself psychologically for an event that never eventuates, and, worse still, may have even made public his predictions about the event. What happens when an important prophecy fails and dissonance is aroused between what was predicted and what actually occurred is described in the classic field study carried out by Festinger, Riecken and Schachter (1956). In the mid-1950s Mrs. Marion Keech, a suburban housewife, began to receive messages from outer space. Americans and Canadians were intrigued because Mrs. Keech claimed that the message foretold an impending flood that would inundate all of North America on December 21. The publicity given to Mrs. Keech and her messages attracted a small following of believers, as well as Festinger, Riecken and Schachter, who infiltrated the group in order to see how Mrs. Keech would react on December 22. On December 20 Mrs. Keech received a message informing her that the group should be ready to receive a visitor who would arrive at midnight to transport all of them on a flying saucer to the safety of outer space. Midnight came, but no visitor arrived, and the predicted flood was less than seven hours away. Gradually despair and confusion descended upon the group, and Mrs. Keech broke down and began to cry bitterly. The messages were read and reread in case some clue had been overlooked. One explanation after another of the visitor's failure to appear was considered and rejected. Then at 4.45 A.M. Mrs. Keech called the group together and announced she had received a message. In the style of an Old Testament prophet she announced that God had saved the world from destruction because the little group, sitting all night long, had spread so much light that it, and not water, was now flooding the Earth.

Mrs. Keech handled the dissonance existing between the drastic prophecy and the mundane reality by providing a rationalization for the discrepancy between the two. But she also had to deal with the widespread publicity she had received in the mass media. One way of reducing dissonance is to seek the support of others; if others provide social support the individual is better able to convince himself that his belief was correct. Mrs. Keech and the believers, who had been rather shy of publicity before the disconfirmation, now became insatiable publicity seekers and carried out active attempts at proselytization in order to swell the numbers of supporters. In case one is tempted to feel smug about Mrs. Keech's disconfirmed expectancy, it is appropriate to point out that social psychologists also suffer the dissonance of disconfirmed expectations. In 1960, Hardyck and Braden (1962) investigated a group of "faithful" evangelists who prophesied a widespread nuclear disaster on August 15. The disaster did not eventuate but neither did the group seek publicity or social support for their beliefs. Other prophets of doom, completely out of touch with reality, apparently suffer little dissonance when their expectancies are disconfirmed. Thomas Beverly, rector of Lilley, in Hertfordshire, England in the late 17th century was totally immune to cognitive dissonance. In 1695 Beverly wrote a book predicting that the world would end in 1697. In 1698 he wrote a second book complaining that the world had ended in 1697 but that nobody had noticed. It is clear that disconfirmed expectancies may lead to a variety of reactions, not all of them directed toward the reduction of dissonance. It seems that the good people of Hertfordshire have a penchant for prophecy. A religious society placed an advertisement in the local newspaper on Monday, December 9, 1968: "The world is definitely coming to an end on Wednesday December 11, at noon precisely. A full report will appear in this newspaper next Friday . . .".

Forced Compliance and Insufficient Justification

Imagine that you were a subject in an experiment where you spent over an hour performing an extremely boring and tedious task, such as crossing out fives and sevens in columns of digits. Suppose that after this monotonous hour the experimenter offered you one dollar to help him tell a lie about the task to the next subject waiting to take part in the experiment. The lie involved telling the next subject that the task was extremely interesting. If you agreed to do it, would your private attitude toward the boring task be affected by your objectionable behaviour? Festinger and Carlsmith (1959), who carried out such an experiment, assumed that if a person is induced to say or do something opposite to his private attitude (*i.e.*, say that something is interesting when he really believes it is boring), he suffers feelings of dissonance. One way to reduce the dissonance is to bring attitudes toward the task into line with the act, *i.e.*, to start to believe that the task really is quite interesting. But Festinger and Carlsmith were particularly concerned with the effect of the monetary reward offered to induce the dissonant act of lying. They compared attitudes held toward the boring task by two groups of subjects. One group (like youself) was offered one dollar to tell the lie; the other received the fabulous sum of twenty dollars. They argued that if a person received twenty dollars for telling a lie there is very little dissonance between his act and his belief about the task because he can rationalize that twenty dollars is too much to turn down, and he can afford to see the task for what it really was, dull, boring and monotonous; but if he received a mere one dollar for doing something objectionable he can only ease his extreme feelings of dissonance by rationalizing that perhaps the task was quite interesting. Indeed Festinger and Carlsmith found that subjects given twenty dollars to tell the lie showed fewer positive attitudes toward the task than subjects given one dollar.

The dissonance principle leads to the paradoxical postulate that if a person is given only a few inducements for engaging in behaviour that is discrepant with his attitudes, then subsequent dissonance-reducing attitude change will be greater than if a large inducement is offered. This postulate has aroused a considerable amount of controversy and attempts have been made to interpret Festinger and Carlsmith's findings in terms of the suspicion, anxiety, incredulity and resentment that can be aroused when a hard-up college student is offered all of twenty dollars for telling a very small lie.

Unforeseen negative consequences, disconfirmed expectancies and insufficient justification for forced compliance are but three of the sources of inconsistency dealt with by dissonance theory. Exposure to discrepant information and facts that contradict what is already known is another source of inconsistency. . . . It will be seen that, following decisions which involve a choice between two equally prized or despised alternatives, the individual often experiences the discomfort of dissonance. He may attempt to reduce postdecision dissonance by seeking out supportive consonant information about his choice. Alternatively, he may choose to expose himself equally to both dissonant and consonant information if it has utility, but still may be more critical of the dissonant material (Feather, 1963).

Balance, congruity and dissonance are three versions of the consistency principle, sharing the assumption that perceptions, actions and attitudes maintain close and harmonious relationships with one another. Each version emphasizes the structure of attitude elements and how disharmony in the structure leads to a change in the system. Their significance for attitude change is an understanding of how new information which produces a disturbance in the attitude system sets into motion a set of processes, which, in turn, lead to a restoration of consistency and harmony in the system. Balance and congruity are the most limited in their application because they deal with situations in which there is disharmony in cognitions and discrepancies in evaluations of related objects. Dissonance, on the other hand, is much broader in scope; it focuses on discrepancies between elements of knowledge and action as a source of inconsistency, and accordingly has a great deal to say about cognitive processes in general, in addition to attitude change. The consistency principle, although an important factor in attitudinal dynamics, is not universally dominant; high tolerance for ambiguity, immunity to psychological tension and preference for novelty and complexity are factors which sometimes outweigh the need for consistency.

Social Influence: The Attitude Change Process

How is an individual influenced by the attempts of another person or group to change his opinions? Social influence is not a uniform process and does not follow a single principle. Kelman (1961), for example, has distinguished between three traditional approaches to this problem: (a) social influence on judgement and opinion stemming from pressures to conformity, (b) social influence arising from interaction in small primary groups, such as the family and peer group, and (c) social influence stemming from persuasive communications delivered by prestigious sources. The separation of these different origins of influence is important because each has its unique psychological basis and special consequences for attitude change. For Kelman, each of the three approaches corresponds to a unique process of social influence with its own distinct characteristics.

First, in the process labelled *compliance*, the individual accepts influence because he hopes to achieve a favourable reaction from another person or group. In face-to-face situations, where an individual is put under group pressure to adopt an opinion or judgement which is contrary to what he believes, yielding to the influence attempt is based on a desire to conform to the expectations of others in order to receive rewards or avoid punishments. This is an instance of compliance in which the opinion is adopted publicly without actual inner acceptance. As soon as the group releases its pressure on the individual he reverts to his initial opinion. Perhaps the best example of this kind of compliance is the temporary collaboration elicited in POWs of the communist Chinese during the Korean war.

A second influence process is labelled *identification,* and it occurs when an individual adopts the attitudes of a group because his relationship with the person or group is satisfying and forms part of his self-image. The small primary group with which the individual is closely affiliated exerts a special kind of social influence. Many basic attitudes have their source and support in these groups and reflect their norms, values and beliefs. This is normative social influence stemming from reference groups with which the person is closely identified. Family interactions are the source of the earliest and most potent influences on attitudes. Parents transfer to their children their own opinions, prejudices and preferences through the process of identification, the taking on of the attributes of another. Political and religious beliefs, prejudice and voting behaviour are remarkably homogeneous within families. Together with the family, the school stands out as the central and dominant force in the socialization of political and ideological beliefs in the young child. Even during the years at college, group norms influence the development of attitudes toward important public issues, as has been shown in Newcomb's classic Bennington Study (1958). Although such attitudes are the earliest and are often learned with a high degree of emotional involvement, they are maintained only so long as the relationship to parents and peers is rewarding and satisfying. The rewards which come from accepting normative influence, having the "right" attitudes in the group, include status, recognition, support and acceptance. Adhering to group norms also provides reassurance and the satisfaction of knowing that one is not alone in holding an opinion, an important factor in opinions that are deeply rooted in considerations of social definition and reality. The philosopher Santayana (1922) expresses this idea in his pointed aphorism: "Man is a gregarious animal, and much more so in his mind than in his body. He may like to go alone for a walk, but hates to stand alone in his opinions"(p. 174).

The third process of social influence is *internalization*. Attitude-related information is contained in persuasive communications delivered by reliable and trustworthy sources. Influence is accepted because the persuasive inputs fit in with the individual's value system and produce intrinsic satisfaction. The central idea in this approach is that an opinion or attitude becomes accepted because its adoption and expression lead to actual or anticipated feelings of satsifaction and self-approval.

A group of social psychologists at Yale University (Hovland, Janis & Kelley, 1953) has been closely identified with experimental research which investigates the characteristics of an relationships between the communicator, the message transmitted and the audience (recipient) in the attitude-change process. These variables closely parallel the well-known persuasion formula of "who says what to whom and with what effect".

Some of the major findings of the Yale group will be summarized to give an idea of the scope of the work that has been carried out on the persuasion process.

The communicator is more likely to induce attitude change if his credibility (*i.e.*, trustworthiness and expertise) is high; if the communicator advocates a great deal of attitude change he will be more successful up to a point than if he advocates a small amount of change. The way in which a persuasive communication is worded, organized and presented is an important determinant of its reception. If there are two sides to an issue, then a two-sided communication in which both pros and cons are mentioned will be more effective than a one-sided communication for it "innoculates" the audience against later counter-propaganda. If, as in a debate, there are two opposing viewpoints to be communicated, the more effective communication is the first one. If the issues are so complex that the audience is not likely to draw the desired conclusion, the communication will be more effective if a conclusion is drawn for them. Emotional appeals that arouse fear or aggression are more effective with low-intelligence, ignorant people than with well-informed people, but they may boomerang and lead to defensive reactions that prevent acceptance of the message. Finally, among an audience, some people are more susceptible to persuasion than others. In general, women are more persuasible than men; social isolates and people who suffer feelings of low self-esteem are also highly persuasible. Passive listening to, or reading of, the communication is not as effective as role playing, *i.e.*, active participation in rehearsing and improvising arguments in support of the desired attitude. People who experience success or receive approval for their role-playing efforts, or for the position they advocate in the role play, are more likely to adopt the new attitude than those who are not rewarded.

The psychology of persuasive communications has antecedents in the art of rhetoric, essentially the art of persuasion, which flourished during the Roman and Greek Empires. The best account of the development of the art is Aristotle's *Rhetoric*. The political speaker is cautioned to advise what appears to be good. He must understand the audience, knowing what provokes anger, admiration and shame. Clarity is preferred, although a sprinkling of metaphors and figures of speech is permissible. The work of the Yale group on the persuasion process has been regarded as a kind of scientific rhetoric because of its similarity to the ancient art of propagating opinion, and because of its basis in scientifically-established principles.

In this brief discussion of social influence on attitude change a distinction was made between three ways in which social interaction produces modification of opinions and beliefs: compliance following direct pressure to conformity, adherence to group norms because of identification, and internalization stemming from the receipt of persuasive communications in a social relationship. In most social influence situations it is not easy to disentangle the three types since they may function co-jointly. The conceptual distinction, however, has implications for the consequences of any attempt to modify attitudes. One of the most bothersome problems in the area of social influence is the short life of some attitude changes. A seemingly impressive modification of opinion dissipates rapidly soon after the influence attempt and the influence agent becomes bewildered by the apparent display of instability. Recognition that social influence entails different motive patterns helps explain the short-lived nature of some changes in attitude and the relative permanence of others. Pressures to compliance and conformity can rarely be sustained for a long time. For example, in prisoner-of-war camps, as soon as control over the individual lapses he reverts to his own private opinion, an opinion that was never really relinquished. Group norms relevant to attitudes are followed only so long as the individual's relationship to the group remains satisfying or the tension of having a unique opinion cannot be tolerated. If the group outlives its usefulness to the individual, or if a hostile, negative relationship between individual and group develops, the norm-oriented opinion is also discarded. Finally, attitude change produced by a credible persuasive communication persists only as long as the values relevant to the attitude are maintained. In line with the cognitive consistency principle, if the attitude or elements of it become inconsistent with fundamental values regarding the issue, it becomes redundant and is rapidly discarded. An example is found in the large swings and fluctuations in attitudes toward the Vietnam War as information regarding the course and consequences of the war became available to the public.

The mass media of radio, television and newspapers, although they can be "switched off" when something unpalatable to belief is presented, also exert a powerful influence on the public. Often this influence is not direct, but is mediated by opinion leaders, key high-status people in the community who are particularly attentive monitors of the mass media, and who interpret and relay information to their circle of friends and colleagues. In what has been called the "two-step flow of communication", information and ideas flow from the mass media to local community and neighbourhood opinion leaders, and from opinion leaders by word of mouth to rank-and-file members of the community. In the area of intergroup attitudes and relations, direct and enforced contact such as is entailed in working and living together is another medium for modifying attitudes. Contacts between members of various groups, such as Aborigines and whites, are most likely to lead to positive attitude change when the contacts are on a basis of equal social status; when co-operative effort is required to perform a joint task, as in the armed services, a ship or a department store; and when the contact is of sufficient duration to enable mutually satisfying experiences to occur.

Perhaps the most dramatic and least-understood form of attitude change is the sudden conversion which follows some unusual, shocking or painful experience. Stagner (1948) has termed this condition of attitude change "trauma", and illustrates its dynamics with reference to the attraction of some Russian leaders to communism. Such instances of sudden conversion, although unusual, merit closer investigation because of the insights they may yield about the process of belief change. Another illustration of the way in which a brief, dramatic experience is capable of undermining resistance to attitude change is provided in studies of emotional role playing and its use in the modification of smoking habits. In an experiment by Janis and Mann (1965), female college students, all of them heavy smokers, were required to play-act the role of a medical patient suffering from the harmful consequences of cigarette smoking. The experimenter, in the role of "physician", gave each "patient" some "bad news"; a supposed X-ray examination had revealed lung cancer and immediate surgery was necessary. During the spontaneous interchange between "physician" and "patient" additional fear-arousing information was introduced about the pain and risk of surgery, post-operative procedures and the smoking-cancer link. The experience was so realistic and disquieting that almost all of the girls quit or drastically modified their smoking habits after the role-play session, and when followed up 18 months later continued to report a significant decrease in smoking behaviour (Mann & Janis, 1968).

Even within the confines of a laboratory it is possible to develop ego-involving real-life situations which trigger off impressive changes in attitudes and behaviour. . . .

References

Aronson, E., and Mills, J., "The Effect of Severity of Initiation on Liking for a Group," *Journal of Abnormal and Social Psychology*, 1959, 59, 177-181.

Feather, N.T., "Cognitive Dissonance, Sensitivity, and Evaluation," *Journal of Abnormal and Social Psychology*, 1963, 66, 157-163.

Feather, N.T., "A Structural Balance Model of Evaluative Behavior," *Human Relations*, 1965, 18, 171-185.

Festinger, L., and Carlsmith, J.M., "Cognitive Consequences of Forced Compliance," *Journal of Abnormal and Social Psychology*, 1959, 58, 203-210.

Festinger, L., Riecken, H., and Schachter, S. *When Prophecy Fails*. Minneapolis: University of Minnesota Press, 1956.

Hardyck, Jane, and Braden, Marcia, "Prophecy Fails Again: A Report of a Failure to Replicate," *Journal of Abnormal and Social Psychology*, 1962, 65, 136-141.

Heider, F. *The Psychology of Interpersonal Relations*. New York: John Wiley & Sons, Inc. 1958.

Hovland, C., Janis, I.L., and Kelley, H. *Communication and Persuasion*. New Haven: Yale University Press, 1953.

Janis, I.L., and Mann, L., "Effectiveness of Emotional Role-Playing in Modifying Smoking Habits and Attitudes," *Journal of Experimental Research in Personality*, 1965, 1, 84-90.

Kelman, H.C., "Processes of Opinion Change," *Public Opinion Quarterly*, 1961, 25, 57-78.

Mann, L., and Janis, I.L., "A Follow-up Study on the Long-Term Effects of Emotional Role-Playing," *Journal of Personality and Social Psychology*, 1968, 8, 339-342.

Newcomb, T.M., "Attitude Development as a Function of Reference Groups: The Bennington Study," In Eleanor E. Maccoby, T.M. Newcomb, and E.L. Hartley (Eds.), *Readings in Social Psychology*, (3rd edn). New York: Holt, Rinehart & Winston, Inc., 1958. 265-275.

Osgood, C.E., and Tannenbaum, P.H., "The Principle of Congruity in the Prediction of Attitude Change," *Psychological Review*, 1955, 62, 42-55.

Santayana, G., *Soliloquies in England and Later Soliloquies*. New York: Charles Scribner's Sons, 1922.

Stagner, R., *Psychology of Personality*, (2nd edn). New York: McGraw-Hill Book Company, 1948.

THE EFFECTS OF CHANGES IN ROLES
ON THE ATTITUDES OF ROLE OCCUPANTS

SEYMOUR LIEBERMAN

Problem

One of the fundamental postulates of role theory, as expounded by Newcomb (2), Parsons (3), and other role theorists, is that a person's attitudes will be influenced by the role that he occupies in a social system. Although this proposition appears to be a plausible one, surprisingly little evidence is available that bears directly on it. One source of evidence is found in common folklore. "Johnny is a changed boy since he was made a monitor in school." "She is a different woman since she got married." "You would never recognize him since he became foreman." As much as these expressions smack of the truth, they offer little in the way of systematic or scientific support for the proposition that a person's attitudes are influenced by his role.

Somewhat more scientific, but still not definitive, is the common finding, in many social-psychological studies, that relationships exist between attitudes and roles. In other words, different attitudes are held by people who occupy different roles. For example, Stouffer *et al.* (5) found that commissioned officers are more favorable toward the Army than are enlisted men. The problem here is that the mere existence of a relationship between attitudes and roles does not reveal the cause and effect nature of the relationship found. One interpretation of Stouffer's finding might be that being made a commissioned officer tends to result in a person's becoming pro-Army—i.e. the role a person occupies influences his attitudes. But an equally plausible interpretation might be that being pro-Army tends to result in a person's being made a commissioned officer—i.e. a person's attitudes influence the likelihood of his being selected for a given role. In the absence of longitudinal data, the relationship offers no clear evidence that roles were the "cause" and attitudes the "effect".

The present study was designed to examine the effects of roles on attitudes in a particular field situation. The study is based on longitudinal data obtained in a role-differentiated, hierarchical organization. By taking advantage of natural role changes among personnel in the organization, it was possible to examine people's attitudes both before and after they underwent changes in roles. Therefore, the extent to which changes in roles were followed by changes in attitudes could be determined, and the cause and effect nature of any relationships found would be clear.

Method: Phase 1

The study was part of a larger project carried out in a medium-sized Midwestern company engaged in the production of home appliance equipment. Let us call the company the Rockwell Corporation. At the time that the study was done, Rockwell

Reprinted from *Human Relations*, 1956, by permission of the publisher, Plenum Publishing Corporation.

employed about 4,000 people. This total included about 2,500 factory workers and about 150 first-level foremen. The company was unionized and most of the factory workers belonged to the union local, which was an affiliate of the U.A.W., C.I.O. About 150 factory workers served as stewards in the union, or roughly one steward for every foreman.

The study consisted of a "natural field experiment". The experimental variable was a change in roles, and the experimental period was the period of exposure to the experimental variable. The experimental groups were those employees who underwent changes in roles during this period; the control groups were those employees who did not change roles during this period. The design may be described in terms of a three-step process: "before measurement", "experimental period", and "after measurement".

Before Measurement.

In September and October 1951, attitude questionnaries were filled out by virtually all factory personnel at Rockwell—2,354 workers, 145 stewards, and 151 foremen. The questions dealt for the most part with employees' attitudes and perceptions about the company, the union, and various aspects of the job situation. The respondents were told that the questionnaire was part of an overall survey to determine how employees felt about working conditions at Rockwell.

Experimental Period.

Between October 1951 and July 1952, twenty-three workers were made foremen and thirty-five workers became stewards. Most of the workers who became stewards during that period were elected during the annual steward elections held in May 1952. They replaced stewards who did not choose to run again or who were not re-elected by their constituents. In addition, a few workers replaced stewards who left the steward role for one reason or another throughout the year.

The workers who became foremen were not made foreman at any particular time. Promotions occurred as openings arose in supervisory positions. Some workers replaced foremen who retired or who left the company for other reasons; some replaced foremen who were shifted to other supervisory positions; and some filled newly created supervisory positions.

After Measurement

In December 1952, the same forms that had been filled out by the rank-and-file workers in 1951 were readministered to:

1. The workers who became foremen during the experimental period (N=23).
2. A control group of workers who did not become foremen during the experimental period (N=46).
3. The workers who became stewards during the experimental period (N=35).
4. A control group of workers who did not become stewards during the experimental period (N=35).

Each control group was matched with its parallel experimental group on a number of demographic, attitudinal, and motivational variables. Therefore, any changes in attitudes that occurred in the experimental groups but did not occur in the control groups could not be attributed to initial differences between them.

The employees in these groups were told that the purpose of the following questionnaire was to get up-to-date measures of their attitudes in 1952 and to compare how employees felt that year with the way that they felt the previous year. The groups were told that, instead of studying the entire universe of employees as was the case in 1951, only a sample was being studied this time. They were informed that the sample was chosen in such a way as to represent all kinds of employees at Rockwell—men and women, young and old, etc. The groups gave no indication that they understood the real bases on which they were chosen for the "after" measurement or that the effects of changes in roles were the critical factors being examined. . . .[1]

Results: Phase 1.

The major hypothesis tested in this study was that people who are placed in a role will tend to take on or develop attitudes that are congruent with the expectations associated with that role. Since the foreman role entails being a representative of management, it might be expected that workers who are chosen as foremen will tend to become more favorable toward management. Similarly, since the steward role entails being a representative of the union, it might be expected that workers who are elected as stewards will tend to become more favorable toward the union. Moreover, in so far as the values of management and of the union are in conflict with each other, it might also be expected that workers who are made foremen will become less favorable toward the union and workers who are made stewards will become less favorable toward management.

Four attitudinal areas were examined: 1. attitudes toward management and officials of management; 2. attitudes toward the union and officials of the union; 3. attitudes toward the management-sponsored incentive system; and 4. attitudes toward the union-sponsored seniority system. The incentive system (whereby workers are paid according to the number of pieces they turn out) and the seniority system (whereby workers are promoted according to the seniority principle) are two areas in which conflicts between management and the union at Rockwell have been particularly intense. Furthermore, first-level foremen and stewards both play a part in the administration of these systems, and relevant groups hold expectations about foreman and steward behaviors with respect to these systems. Therefore, we examined the experimental and control groups' attitudes toward these two systems as well as their overall attitudes toward management and the union.

The data tend to support the hypothesis that being placed in the foreman and steward roles will have an impact on the attitudes of the role occupants. . . . Both experimental groups undergo systematic changes in attitudes, in the predicted directions, from the "before" situation to the "after" situation. In the control groups, either no attitude changes occur, or less marked changes occur, from the "before" situation to the "after" situation.

Although a number of the differences are not statistically significant, those which are significant are all in the expected directions, and most of the nonsignificant differences are also in the expected directions. New foremen, among other things, come to see Rockwell as a better place to work compared with other com-

·panies, develop more positive perceptions of top management officers, and become more favorably disposed toward the principle and operation of the incentive system. New stewards come to look upon labor unions in general in a more favorable light, develop more positive perceptions of the top union officers at Rockwell, and come to prefer seniority to ability as a criterion of what should count in moving workers to better jobs. In general, the attitudes of workers who become foremen tend to gravitate in a pro-management direction and the attitudes of workers who become stewards tend to move in a pro-union direction.

A second kind of finding has to do with the relative *amount* of attitude change that takes place among new foremen in contrast to the amount that takes place among new stewards. On the whole, more pronounced and more widespread attitude changes occur among those who are made foremen than among those who are made stewards. . . . The workers who are made foremen undergo significant attitude changes, relative to the workers who are not made foremen, on ten of the sixteen attitudinal items. . . . By contrast, the workers who are made stewards undergo significant attitude changes, relative to the workers who are not made stewards, on only three of the sixteen items. However, for the steward role as well as for the foreman role, most of the differences found between the experimental and control groups still tend to be in the expected directions.

The more pronounced and more widespread attitude changes that occur among new foremen than among new stewards can probably be accounted for in large measure by the kinds of differences that exist between the foreman and steward roles. For one thing, the foreman role represents a relatively permanent position, while many stewards take the steward role as a "one-shot" job and even if they want to run again their constituents may not re-elect them. Secondly, the foreman role is a full-time job, while most stewards spend just a few hours a week in the performance of their steward functions and spend the rest of the time carrying out their regular rank-and-file jobs. Thirdly, a worker who is made a foreman must give up his membership in the union and become a surrogate of management, while a worker who is made a steward retains the union as a reference group and simply takes on new functions and responsibilities as a representative of it. All of these differences suggest that the change from worker to foreman is a more fundamental change in roles than the change from worker to steward. This, in turn, might account to a large extent for the finding that, although attitude changes accompany both changes in roles, they occur more sharply among new foremen than among new stewards.

A third finding has to do with the *kinds* of attitude changes which occur among workers who change roles. As expected, new foremen become more pro-management and new stewards become more pro-union. Somewhat less expected is the finding that new foremen become more anti-union but new stewards do not become more anti-management. Among workers who are made foremen, statistically significant shifts in an anti-union direction occur on four of the eight items dealing with the union and the union-sponsored seniority system. Among workers who are made stewards, there are no statistically significant shifts in either direction on any of the eight items having to do with management and the management-sponsored incentive system.

The finding that new foremen become anti-union but that new stewards do not become anti-management may be related to the fact that workers who become foremen must relinquish their membership of the union, while workers who become stewards retain their status as employees of management. New foremen, subject to one main set of loyalties and called on to carry out a markedly new set of functions, tend to develop negative attitudes toward the union as well as positive attitudes toward management. New stewards, subject to overlapping group membership, and still dependent on management for their livelihoods, tend to become more favorable toward the union but they do not turn against management, at least not within the relatively limited time period covered by the present research project. Over time, stewards might come to develop somewhat hostile attitudes toward management, but, under the conditions prevailing at Rockwell, there is apparently no tendency for such attitudes to be developed as soon as workers enter the steward role.

Method: Phase 2

One of the questions that may be raised about the results that have been presented up to this point concerns the extent to which the changed attitudes displayed by new foremen and new stewards are internalized by the role occupants. Are the changed attitudes expressed by new foremen and new stewards relatively stable, or are they ephemeral phenomena to be held only as long as they occupy the foreman and steward roles? An unusual set of circumstances at Rockwell enabled the researchers to glean some data on this question.

A short time after the 1952 re-survey, the nation suffered an economic recession. In order to meet the lessening demand for its products, Rockwell, like many other firms, had to cut its work force. This resulted in many rank-and-file workers being laid off and a number of the foremen being returned to non-supervisory jobs. By June 1954, eight of the twenty-three workers who had been promoted to foreman had returned to the worker role and only twelve were still foremen. (The remaining three respondents had voluntarily left Rockwell by this time.)

Over the same period, a number of role changes had also been experienced by the thirty-five workers who had become stewards. Fourteen had returned to the worker role, either because they had not sought re-election by their work groups or because they had failed to win re-election, and only six were still stewards. (The other fifteen respondents, who composed almost half of this group, had either voluntarily left Rockwell or had been laid off as part of the general reduction in force.)

Once again, in June 1954, the researchers returned to Rockwell to re-administer the questionnaires that the workers had filled out in 1951 and 1952. The instructions to the respondents were substantially the same as those given in 1952—i.e. a sample of employees had been chosen to get up-to-date measures of employees' attitudes toward working conditions at Rockwell and the same groups were selected this time as had been selected last time in order to lend greater stability to the results.

In this phase of the study, the numbers of cases with which we were dealing in the various groups were so small that the data could only be viewed as suggestive, and systematic statistical analysis of the data did not seem to be too meaningful. However, the unusual opportunity to throw some light on an important question suggests that a reporting of these results may be worthwhile.

Results: Phase 2

The principal question examined here was: on those items where a change in roles resulted in a change in attitudes between 1951 and 1952, how are these attitudes influenced by a reverse change in roles between 1952 and 1954?

The most consistent and widespread attitude changes noted between 1951 and 1952 were those that resulted when workers moved into the foreman role. What are the effects of moving out of the foreman role between 1952 and 1954? The data indicate that, in general, most of the "gains" that were observed when workers became foremen are "lost" when they become workers again. . . . The foremen who remain foremen either retain their favorable attitudes toward management or become even more favorable toward management between 1952 and 1954, while the demoted foremen show fairly consistent drops in the direction of re-adopting the attitudes they held when they had been in the worker role. On the whole, the attitudes held by demoted foremen in 1954, after they had left the foreman role, fall roughly to the same levels as they had been in 1951, before they had ever moved into the foreman role.

The results on the effects of moving out of the steward role are less clear-cut. . . . There is no marked tendency for ex-stewards to revert to earlier-held attitudes when they go from the steward role to the worker role. At the same time, it should be recalled that there had not been particularly marked changes in their attitudes when they initially changed from the worker role to the steward role. These findings, then, are consistent with the interpretation offered earlier that the change in roles between worker and steward is less significant than the change in roles between worker and foreman.

A question might be raised about what is represented in the reversal of attitudes found among ex-foremen. Does it represent a positive taking-on of attitudes appropriate for respondents who are re-entering the worker role, or does it constitute a negative, perhaps embittered reaction away from the attitudes they held before being demoted from the foreman role? A definitive answer to this question cannot be arrived at, but it might be suggested that if we were dealing with a situation where a reversion in roles did not constitute such a strong psychological blow to the role occupants (as was probably the case among demoted foremen), then such a marked reversion in attitudes might not have occurred. . . .[2]

Discussion

A role may be defined as a set of behaviors that are expected of people who occupy a certain position in a social system. These expectations consist of shared attitudes or beliefs, held by relevant populations, about what role occupants should and should not do. The theoretical basis for hypothesizing that a role will have effects on role occupants lies in the nature of these expectations. If a role occupant meets these expectations, the "rights" or "rewards" associated with the role will be accorded to him. If he fails to meet these expectations, the "rights" or "rewards" will be withheld from him and "punishments" may be meted out.[3]

A distinction should be made between the effects of roles on people's attitudes and the effects of roles on their actions. How roles affect actions can probably be explained in a fairly direct fashion. Actions are overt and readily enforceable. If a person fails to behave in ways appropriate to his role, this can immediately be seen, and steps may be taken to bring the deviant or non-conformist into line. Role deviants may be evicted from their roles, placed in less rewarding roles, isolated from other members of the group, or banished entirely from the social system.

But attitudes are not as overt as actions. A person may behave in such a way as to reveal his attitudes, but he can—and often does—do much to cover them up. Why, then, should a change in roles lead to a change in actions? A number of explanatory factors might be suggested here. The present discussion will be confined to two factors that are probably generic to a wide variety of situations. One pertains to the influence of reference groups; the other is based on an assumption about people's need to have attitudes internally consistent with their actions.

A change in roles almost invariably involves a change in reference groups. Old reference groups may continue to influence the role occupant, but new ones also come into play. The change in reference groups may involve moving into a completely new group (as when a person gives up membership in one organization and joins another one) or it may simply involve taking on new functions in the same group (as when a person is promoted to a higher position in a hierarchical organization). In both situations, new reference groups will tend to bring about new frames of reference, new self-percepts, and new vested interests, and these in turn will tend to produce new attitudinal orientations.

In addition to a change in reference groups, a change in roles also involves a change in functions and a change in the kinds of behaviors and actions that the role occupant must display if he is to fulfil these functions. A change in actions, let us assume, comes about because these actions are immediately required, clearly visible, and hence socially enforceable. If we further assume a need for people to have attitudes that are internally consistent with their actions, then at least one aspect of the functional significance of a change in attitudes becomes clear. A change in attitudes enables a new role occupant to justify, to make rational, or perhaps simply to rationalize his change in actions. Having attitudes that are consistent with actions helps the role occupant to be "at one" with himself and facilitates his effective performance of the functions he is expected to carry out.

The reference-group principle and the self-consistency principle postulate somewhat different chains of events in accounting for the effects of roles on attitudes and actions. In abbreviated versions, the different chains may be spelled out in the following ways:

1. Reference-group principle: A change in roles involves a change in reference groups . . . which leads to a change in attitudes . . . which leads to a change in actions.

2. Self-consistency principle: A change in roles involves a change in functions . . . which leads to a change in actions . . . which leads to a change in attitudes.

In the former chain, a person's attitudes influence his actions; in the latter chain, a person's actions influence his attitudes. Both chains might plausibly account for the results obtained, but whether either chain, both chains, or other chains is or are valid cannot be determined from the data available. A more direct investigation of the underlying mechanisms responsible for the impact of roles on attitudes would appear to be a fruitful area for further research.

But apart from the question of underlying mechanisms, the results lend support to the proposition that a person's attitudes will be influenced by his role. Relatively consistent changes in attitudes were found both among workers who were made foremen and among workers who were made stewards, although these changes were more clear-cut for foremen than for stewards. The more interesting set of results—as far as role theory in general is concerned—would seem to be the data on the effects of entering and leaving the foreman role. It was pointed out earlier that the foreman role, unlike the steward role, is a full-time, relatively permanent position, and moving into this position entails taking on a very new and different set of functions. When workers are made foremen, their attitudes change in a more pro-management and anti-union direction. When they are demoted and move back into the worker role, their attitudes change once again, this time in a more pro-union and anti-management direction. In both instances, the respondents' attitudes seem to be molded by the roles which they occupy at a given time.

The readiness with which the respondents in this study shed one set of attitudes and took on another set of attitudes might suggest either that 1. the attitudes studied do not tap very basic or deep-rooted facets of the respondents' psyches, or 2. the character structures of the respondents are such as not to include very deeply ingrained sets of value orientations. Riesman (4) deals with this problem in his discussion of "other-directedness" vs. "inner-directedness". How much the rapid shifts in attitudes observed here reflect the particular kinds of respondents who underwent changes in roles in the present situation, and how much these shifts reflect the national character of the American population, can only be speculated on at the present time. . . .

Notes

1. Some of the top officials of management and all of the top officers of the union at Rockwell knew about the nature of the follow-up study and the bases on which the experimental and control groups were selected.
2. There were a number of reactions to demotion among the eight ex-foremen, as obtained from informal interviews with these respondents. Some reached inpunitively (i.e., they blamed uncontrollable situational determinants) and did not seem to be bothered by demotion. Others reacted extrapunitively (i.e., they blamed management) or intrapunitively (i.e., they blamed themselves) and appeared to be more disturbed by demotion. One way of testing the hypothesis that attitude reversion is a function of embitterment would be to see if sharper reversion occurs among extrapunitive and intrapunitive respondents. However, the small number of cases does not permit an analysis of this kind to be carried out in the present situation.
3. An earlier discussion of the role concept, with particular reference to its application to the study complex organizations, is found in Jacobson, Charters, and Lieberman (1).

References

1. Jacobson, E., Charters, W. W., Jr., and Lieberman, S. "The Use of the Role Concept in the Study of Complex Organizations." *J. Soc. Issues,* Vol. 7, No. 3, pp. 18-27, 1951.
2. Newcomb, T.M. *Social Psychology.* New York: The Dryden Press, 1950; London: Tavistock Publications, 1952.
3. Parsons, T. *The Social System.* Glencoe, Ill.: The Free Press, 1951; London: Tavistock Publications Ltd., 1951.
4. Riesman, D. *The Lonely Crowd.* New Haven: Yale Univ. Press, 1950.
5. Stouffer, S.A., Suchman, E.A., DeVinney, L. C., Star, S. A., and Williams, R. M., Jr. *The American Soldier: Adjustment During Army Life* (Vol. 1). Princeton University Press, 1949.
6. Walker, H.M., and Lev, J. *Statistical Inference.* New York: Henry Holt and Co., Inc., 1953.

Section B

The Perceptual Process
and Human Behavior

PERCEPTION FROM THE INSIDE LOOKING OUT

HAROLD J. LEAVITT

The major questions [here] are these: How and why do people see things differently? How objective can people be? Do people see only what they want to see? Or don't want to see? What part do people's personal views of the world play in the supervisory process?

The Perceptual World

Most of us recognize that the world-as-we-see-it is not necessarily the same as the world-as-it-"really"-is. Our answer depends on what we heard, not on what was really said. The housewife buys what she likes best, not what is best. Whether we feel hot or cold depends on us, not on the thermometer. The same job may look like a good job to one of us and a sloppy job to another.

To specify the problem, consider the line drawing in figure 1. This is a picture of a woman. Here are some questions about it: (1) How old is the woman at the time of the picture? (2) Does she have any outstanding physical characteristics? (3) Is she "reasonably attractive" or "downright ugly"?

Show the picture to ten other people. Do they all see the same thing? If some think she looks between twenty and thirty, does anyone think she's over fifty? If

Figure 1. Wife or mother-in-law?

some think she's over fifty, does anyone think she's between twenty and thirty? How does one account for the conflicts? Are the differences simply differences in taste? Or in standards of beauty? Or is each person distorting the "real" world in a different way?

This old psychology-textbook picture is intentionally ambiguous. It can be seen either as an ugly old hag with a long and crooked nose and toothless mouth or as a reasonably attractive young girl with head turned away so that one can barely see one eyelash and part of a nose. More importantly, the picture will be based on the "facts" as they are seen by another viewer.

Incidentally, if the reader still sees only one of the two figures, he is getting a good feeling of what a "need" is. The tension or discomfort that one feels when he thinks he is missing some things others can see or when he feels he hasn't quite closed a gap in his knowledge—that is a need. And it will probably be difficult to concentrate on reading further until he satisfies that unsatisfied need by finding the second face in the picture.

The Influence of Our Needs on Our Perceptions

The hag picture is another demonstration of a commonplace observation, i.e., that people see things differently, that the world is what we make it, that everyone wears his own rose-colored glasses. But consider some additional questions: Whence the rose-colored glasses? Are the glasses always rose-colored? That is, does one always see what he wants to see, or does he see what he is afraid he will see, or both?

These questions are important because the primary issue of "human relations" is to consider ways in which individuals can affect the behavior of other individuals. If it is true that people behave on the basis of the perceived world, then changing behavior in a predetermined direction can be made easier by understanding the individual's present perception of the world. For if there is any common human-relations mistake made by industrial superiors in their relations with subordinates, it is the mistake of assuming that the "real" world is all that counts, that everyone works for the same goals, that the facts speak for themselves.

But if people do act on their perceptions, different people perceive things differently. How, then, is the manager, for example, to know what to expect? What determines how particular people will perceive particular things?

The answer has already been given in the preceding chapters. People's perceptions are determined by their needs. Like the mirrors at amusement parks, we distort the world in relation to our own tensions. Children from poorer homes, when asked to draw a quarter, draw a bigger than actual one. Industrial employees, when asked to describe the people they work with, talk more about their bosses (the people more important to their needs) than about their peers or subordinates, and so on.

But the problem is more complicated than that. People may perceive what is important to their needs, but does this mean people see what they want to see, or what they are afraid to see? Both wishes and fears are important to one's needs. The answer seems to be that we perceive both, but according to certain rules. We magnify a compliment from higher up in the organization but we also magnify a word of disapproval. We dream of blondes, but we also have nightmares. And sometimes we just don't pay attention at all to things that are quite relevant. We forget dentist's appointments; we oversleep when we have examinations coming up; we manage to forget to clean the basement or to call on this particular customer.

Selective Perception

What, then, are the rules of selective perception? The best answer we can give is this one: If one reexamines his memories of the past, he may find that his recall of positive, satisfying things is better than his recall of negative, unpleasant things. He may find it easier to wake early to go fishing than to get to a dentist's appointment. He may look forward, in fact, to doing pleasant, satisfying jobs but may evade mildly disturbing and unpleasant jobs. A senior executive once commented to the author that the biggest problem he encounters with young management people is their tendency to avoid the little unpleasant decisions—like disciplining people or digging through boring and repetitive records or writing unpleasant letters. This executive felt that his younger men would be far more effective if they could learn to deal as promptly with these uncomfortable little decisions as they did with the big ones.

But we can see some sense in this selective remembering if we look for it. There are some advantages to a person in being blind to unpleasantness, even if such blindness cuts down his working effectiveness. Ignoring the unpleasant may represent more than "laziness." It may be a sensible defensive device, psychologically speaking. Thus, most people are able to ignore soft background conversation while working. In effect they are psychologically deaf to a potentially distracting part of the real world. And this defense helps them to concentrate on their work. Similarly, most people manage to ignore the threat of the hydrogen bomb and to go on eating and sleeping as though this dangerous part of the real world were not here. It can even be shown experimentally that words with unpleasant connotations tend to be recognized more slowly when exposed for very brief intervals than words with pleasant connotations.

The strange part of this defensive process, however, is that in order *not* to hear the distracting music or *not* to see the unpleasant words one must first hear and see them. One has to see the word, recognize that it is unpleasant, and reject it almost simultaneously, so that one can say, "No. I didn't see what that word was." Hence the label "defense" attached to this phenomenon—defense against the entry of preselected things mildly disturbing to one's equilibrium. So two of our rules of selective perception become: (1) see what promises to help satisfy needs, and (2) ignore mildly disturbing things.

Suppose, though, that while one is successfully ignoring background talk someone back there starts to shout; or, while one is successfully ignoring the H-bomb, an H-bomb falls on London. At those points, when the unpleasantness becomes intense and dangerous, people stop defending and begin attacking. They stop ignoring the irritation and start directing all their attention to it. This reversal seems to happen suddenly, at some specific threshold. The distant irritation increases to a point at which it becomes so real, so imminent, and so threatening that we reverse our course, discard the blindfold, and preoccupy ourselves completely with the thing previously ignored.

This is the third rule: Pay attention to things that are really dangerous. The whole picture now begins to look like this: *People perceive what they think will help satisfy needs; ignore what is disturbing; and again perceive disturbances that persist and increase. . . .*

This process may not seem entirely logical to an outside observer, but it is quite reasonable psychologically. For this kind of self-imposed psychological blindness helps the person to maintain his equilibrium while moving toward his objectives. An organism lacking this ability to fend off minor threats might well find itself torn apart in its attempt to deal simultaneously with all of them. Or, at least, an individual unable to ignore unpleasant realities might spend so much of his energy dealing with them that he would make little progress toward his major goals. For once a person has learned to perceive a multitude of threats and dangers in his world he needs a system of defense against them. One should add, however, that some individuals may see relatively few things as dangerous and therefore have little need for defense, while for others the world holds dangers at every turn.

. . . [Earlier] we suggested that a person who has encountered a relatively helpful world is likely to perceive more of his environment as potentially helpful. If, however, the world has been mostly frustrating, then more of it, and especially new things in it, will be seen as potentially dangerous. Being dangerous, they must be fended off. But, paradoxically, to be fended off they must first be seen. So to protect himself from more insecurity, the insecure person must first see the things that will provoke insecurity and then manage to deny to himself that he has seen them.

Projections of the Perceived World

The basic point of this [paper], the point that the world as it is perceived is the world that is behaviorally important, underlies the development of the now generally familiar projective tests. Originally projectives were designed for the diagnosis of aberrations in personality, but . . . they are [also] being used industrially. The same idea also underlies what market researchers now call "motivation research" into consumer attitudes, techniques for discovering people's views of the "facts" of advertising and product design. Consumer research in general can be thought of as an attempt to make a diagnosis of the relevant parts of the consumer's view of the world so that products can be designed to be seen as aids rather than obstacles.

For managerial purposes, the importance of the perceptual world is clear. If one's concern as a supervisor or counselor or committee member is to try to effect some change in the behavior of other people, and if in turn people's present behavior is determined largely by their perceptions of their environments, then it is critical that one seek to understand their perceptions if one is to understand the circumstances under which their behavior might change.

For example, managers assume almost universally that subordinates want promotions. And yet more than one subordinate has been driven into panic and disappointment because he felt psychologically forced to accept a promotion that no one (sometimes even himself) bothered to find out he did not want.

Often assumptions about the perceptions of others are wrong because they are incomplete. One may assume correctly that employees want more money, but he may fail to understand that more money is acceptable only within a certain framework of independence. This is the paternalism problem.

Sometimes the problem is simple lack of sensitivity for other people. Thus a foreman once complained to the writer about how odd people seemed. He said one of his employees had gotten terribly upset "for no reason at all." The foreman had said, "Hey, boy, go over there and pick that up!" The employee got angry. He had said, "Don't call me 'boy'; I have a name!" The foreman couldn't understand why the employee, a Negro, should get angry about a "perfectly reasonable" request like that.

Or again many parents argue for the importance of heredity over environment because their own children seem to be so different from one another. "Our second child," they will say, "was just a completely different person from the first, though we treated them both *exactly* alike." Parents may be truthful in feeling that they treated two children alike, but it is unwise to assume that the children were therefore treated alike. The first child's world did not include the second child; but the second's did include the first. Indeed the evidence is now quite good that certain personality variables are related to the birth order of children in families. First-born children tend to be more affiliative and more dependent than later-born, for example, and generally more susceptible to social pressure. Moreover, for the infant whose slate is relatively blank, the minor marks made by parents may be major marks for the child. Thus many parents pass lightly over the differences between feeding an infant now or ten minutes from now. But the child is not likely to pass over the same thing nearly so lightly. The manager is likely to pay little attention to his criticism of a subordinate's work. But for the subordinate it is a week's food for worry.

One more example. Sales managers often complain of the difficulties they encounter in getting salesmen to make cold calls. The salesman says he was too busy, or there were better prospects, or he had to catch up on some reports. Is he lazy? Or just defending himself—perhaps unconsciously—against a perceived threat? If it is a defensive process, there are two general ways in which the manager can try to shake the salesman loose. He can teach him to feel comfortable about cold calls, or he can change the mild threat to a major one so that it can no longer safely be ignored. But if he chooses the latter course he had better consider the by-products.

Perceiving Oneself

So far we have talked about perceptions of things and other people. But one of the people each of us perceives is himself, as he is, and also as he would like other people to see him. Each of us struts his own act before the world, as it were, in an effort to have other people see us as the kind of person we value.

Quite early in life, we begin to learn what kinds of groups we want to join, what kinds of social classes to aspire to, what kinds of status to achieve. Two of us may have equally intense needs for status and prestige, but if we have grown up in different environments, one of us may seek that status by acting masculine and powerful, or by affecting long hair and a beard. Another may seek to fulfill the same needs by costuming himself in high-style fashions or by donning the pin-striped uniform of the executive.

Teenagers are often painfully awkward as they strive to perfect their own private acts. They seem to feel it terribly important to appear to be what they doubt they really are. Later they become more skilful, either because their acts are better or because their acts are not very far from what the actors really are.

Note that our acts are functional for us. They are performed by both teenagers and adults for good reasons. An act is a way of filling a role. It is also a way of protecting the vulnerable parts of ourselves from real or fancied attack. But our act is effective in performing its functions only if other people accept it. And other people usually accept acts when the gap between our acting selves and their estimate of our "real" selves is small. Other people tend to be reasonably accurate judges, too. So acting problems arise as the distance between act and reality increases.

It is also true that acts are often uncomfortable for the actor. The girl friend happily abandons the courting dance as soon as the wedding is over. But until she has the man tied down and delivered, she must play her version of the coquette, no matter how much worry and fret it requires. Similarly the company executive must act decisively, though privately he may yearn for a chance to weep on someone's shoulder.

But though our acts are functional, they contribute to a social world full of distorted signals. You are trying to tell me that you are strong, worldly, and decisive (and you may be—or you may not), and I am just as busily trying to communicate to you that I am the sagacious, understanding, intellectually stimulating character I would like to be (and may actually be—or may not). We have both been practicing our acts for a long time. So we have both developed clever ways of being convincing, ways that the poor inept adolescent has not even dreamed of. But we have also developed clever ways of spotting the other guy's act.

Our relationship becomes even further confounded by the fact that we read one another's cover stories through our own need-distorted glasses. While you stand there trying to radiate strength and decisiveness, I see you as brash and immature. And you, wanting action and recognition, see my efforts at quiet, pipe-smoking wisdom as dullness and lack of imagination. Looked at this way the wonder is not that we find it so difficult to understand one another, but that we are able to understand one another at all.

The first big problem then is the problem of accuracy, of somehow gaining more accurate information about other people—estimating the discrepancy between the actor and the "real" person. The second problem is to estimate how well our act is working. For surely we are in considerable trouble if the self we want to present to the world is presented so badly, so weakly, so transparently that everyone else is discounting it. We are in a bad way if the people around us are saying: "There is a man who is trying to act decisive and sure of himself, while in fact it is as plain as the nose on your face that he is really unsure of himself, indecisive, anxious."

To the best of this writer's knowledge there is only one general mechanism by which such distortions in relationships can be reduced, and that is the mechanism of *feedback*. If somehow we can develop better ways by which we can learn from other people how our act is getting across, then we can either modify it so that it gets across more fully or we can try to reduce the discrepancy between the act and ourselves, so that it is an easier act to play convincingly. The first course leads to a world of intrigue and gamesmanship; the second, to a simpler, less distorted world.

By this reasoning, other people, if we can get them to provide us with appropriate feedback, can do us considerable service in helping us to bring what we wish to be closer to what we are, and to reduce our uncertainty and anxiety in the process. . . .

In Summary

People see things differently. Even "facts" may be seen quite differently by different people. Relevance to one's needs is the most important determinant of one's personal view of the world. Things that seem to be aids to satisfying one's needs are seen quickly. But things that look like obstacles, if they are not critically threatening, may also be seen quickly, only then to be denied so that they appear not to have been seen at all. By denying obstacles, people "protect" themselves temporarily from them. If they really become dangerous, however, people drop the blinders and face the obstacles.

One of the things we perceive is ourselves and other people. To protect and enhance ourselves, we try to manipulate the picture other people have of us by putting up a front that will make them think we are what we want to be. The problem of our act, and getting it across successfully, depends mostly on our ability to pick up audience reactions accurately. And accurate audience reactions are hard to come by because the audience is acting too.

To ignore differences in perception is to ignore a major determinant of behavior. Yet it is easy to assume unwarrantedly that everyone views the world from the same perspective as the viewer. Time spent trying to reach a common view is not wasted time.

PERCEPTION: IMPLICATIONS FOR ADMINISTRATION

SHELDON S. ZALKIND
TIMOTHY W. COSTELLO

Management practice is being increasingly influenced by behavioral science research in the areas of group dynamics, problem solving and decision making, and motivation. One aspect of behavior which has not been fully or consistently emphasized is the process of perception, particularly the recent work on person perception.

In this paper we shall summarize some of the findings on perception as developed through both laboratory and organizational research and point out some of the administrative and managerial implications. We discuss first some basic factors in the nature of the perceptual process including need and set; second, some research on forming impressions; third, the characteristics of the perceiver and the perceived; fourth, situational and organizational influences on perception; and finally, perceptual influences on interpersonal adjustment.

Nature of the Perceptual Process

What are some of the factors influencing perception? In answering the question it is well to begin by putting aside the attitude of naïve realism, which suggests that our perceptions simply register accurately what is "out there." It is necessary rather to consider what influences distort one's perceptions and judgments of the outside world. Some of the considerations identified in the literature up to the time of Johnson's 1944 review of the research on object perception (where distortion may be even less extreme than in person perception) led him to suggest the following about the perceiver:[1]

Reprinted by permission of the authors and the publisher, *Administrative Science Quarterly*, vol. 7, no. 3 (Sept. 1962), pp. 218-35.

1. He may be influenced by considerations that he may not be able to identify, responding to cues that are below the threshold of his awareness. For example, a judgment as to the size of an object may be influenced by its color even though the perceiver may not be attending to color.

2. When required to form difficult perceptual judgments, he may respond to irrelevant cues to arrive at a judgment. For example, in trying to assess honesty, it has been shown that the other person's smiling or not smiling is used as a cue to judge his honesty.

3. In making abstract or intellectual judgments, he may be influenced by emotional factors—what is liked is perceived as correct.

4. He will weigh perceptual evidence coming from respected (or favored) sources more heavily than that coming from other sources.

5. He may not be able to identify all the factors on which his judgments are based. Even if he is aware of these factors he is not likely to realize how much weight he gives to them.

These considerations do not imply that we respond only to the subtle or irrelevant cues or to emotional factors. We often perceive on the basis of the obvious, but we are quite likely to be responding as well to the less obvious or less objective.

In 1958, Bruner, citing a series of researches, described what he called the "New Look" in perception as one in which personal determinants of the perceptual process were being stressed.[2] Bruner summarized earlier work and showed the importance of such subjective influences as needs, values, cultural background, and interests on the perceptual process. In his concept of "perceptual readiness" he described the importance of the framework or category system that the perceiver himself brings to the perceiving process.

Tapping a different vein of research, Cantril described perceiving as a "transaction" between the perceiver and the perceived, a process of negotiation in which the perceptual end product is a result both of influences within the perceiver and of characteristics of the perceived.[3]

One of the most important of the subjective factors that influence the way we perceive, identified by Bruner and others, is *set*. A study by Kelley illustrated the point.[4] He found that those who were previously led to expect to meet a "warm" person, not only made different judgments about him, but also behaved differently toward him, than those who were expecting a "cold" one. The fact was that they simultaneously were observing the same person in the same situation. Similarly, Strickland indicated the influence of set in determining how closely supervisors feel they must supervise their subordinates.[5] Because of prior expectation one person was trusted more than another and was thought to require less supervision than another, even though performance records were identical.

Forming Impressions of Others

The data on forming impressions is of particular importance in administration. An administrator is confronted many times with the task of forming an impression of another person—a new employee at his desk, a visiting member from the home office, a staff member he has not personally met before. His own values, needs, and expectations will play a part in the impression he forms. Are there other factors that typically operate in this area of administrative life? One of the more obvious influences is the physical appearance of the person being perceived. In a study of this point Mason was able to demonstrate that people agree on what a leader should look like and that there is no relationship between the facial characteristics agreed upon and those possessed by actual leaders.[6] In effect, we have ideas about what leaders look like and we can give examples, but we ignore the many exceptions that statistically cancel out the examples.

In the sometimes casual, always transitory situations in which one must form impressions of others it is a most natural tendency to jump to conclusions and form impressions without adequate evidence. Unfortunately, as Dailey showed, unless such impressions are based on important and relevant data, they are not likely to be accurate.[7] Too often in forming impressions the perceiver does not know what is relevant, important, or predictive of later behavior. Dailey's research furthermore supports the cliché that, accurate or not, first impressions are lasting.

Generalizing from other research in the field, Soskin described four limitations on the ability to form accurate impressions of others.[8] First, the impression is likely to be disproportionately affected by the type of situation or surroundings in which the impression is made and influenced too little by the person perceived. Thus the plush luncheon club in which one first meets a man will dominate the impression of the man himself. Secondly, although impressions are frequently based on a limited sample of the perceived person's behavior, the generalization that the perceiver makes will be sweeping. A third limitation is that the situation may not provide an opportunity for the person perceived to show behavior relevant to the traits about which impressions are formed. Casual conversation or questions, for example, provide few opportunities to demonstrate intelligence or work characteristics, yet the perceiver often draws conclusions about these from an interview. Finally, Soskin agrees with Bruner and Cantril that the impression of the person perceived may be distorted by some highly individualized reaction of the perceiver.

But the pitfalls are not yet all spelled out; it is possible to identify some other distorting influences on the process of forming impressions. Research has brought into sharp focus some typical errors, the more important being stereotyping, halo effect, projection, and perceptual defense.

Stereotyping

The word "stereotyping" was first used by Walter Lippmann in 1922 to describe bias in perceiving peoples. He wrote of "pictures in people's heads," called stereotypes, which guided (distorted) their perceptions of others. The term has long been used to describe judgments made about people on the basis of their ethnic group membership. For example, some say "Herman Schmidt [being German] is industrious." Stereotyping also predisposes judgments in many other areas of interpersonal relations. Stereotypes have developed about many types of groups, and they help to prejudice many of our perceptions about their members. Examples of stereotypes of groups other than those based on ethnic identification are bankers, supervisors, union members, poor people, rich people, and administrators. Many unverified qualities are assigned to people principally because of such group memberships.

In a research demonstration of stereotyping, Haire found that labeling a photograph as that of a management representative caused an impression to be formed of the person, different from that formed when it was labeled as that of a union leader.[9] Management and labor formed different impressions, each seeing his opposite as less dependable than his own group. In addition, each side saw his own group as being better able than the opposite group to understand a point of view different from its own. For example, managers felt that other managers were better able to appreciate labor's point of view. Each had similar stereotypes of his opposite and considered the thinking, emotional characteristics, and interpersonal relations of his opposite as inferior to his own. As Stagner pointed out, "It is plain that unionists perceiving company officials in a stereotyped way are less efficient than would be desirable.[10] Similarly, company executives who see all labor unions as identical are not showing good judgment or discrimination."

One of the troublesome aspects of stereotypes is that they are so widespread. Finding the same stereotypes to be widely held should not tempt one to accept their accuracy. It may only mean that many people are making the same mistake. Allport has demonstrated that there need not be a "kernel of truth" in a widely held stereotype.[11] He has shown that while a prevalent stereotype of Armenians labeled them as dishonest, a credit reporting association gave them credit ratings as good as those given other ethnic groups.

Bruner and Perlmutter found that there is an international stereotype for "businessmen" and "teachers."[12] They indicated that the more widespread one's experience with diverse members of a group, the less their group membership will affect the impression formed.

An additional illustration of stereotyping is provided by Luft.[13] His research suggests that perception of personality adjustment may be influenced by stereotypes, associating adjustment with high income and maladjustment with low income.

Halo Effect

The term halo effect was first used in 1920 to describe a process in which a general impression which is favorable or unfavorable is used by judges to evaluate several specific traits. The "halo" in such case serves as a screen keeping the perceiver from actually seeing the trait he is judging. It has received the most attention because of its effect on rating employee performance. In the rating situation, a supervisor may single out one trait, either good or bad, and use this as the basis for his judgment of all other traits. For example, an excellent attendance record causes judgments of productivity, high quality of work, and so forth. One study in the U. S. Army showed that officers who were liked were judged more intelligent than those who were disliked, even though they had the same scores on intelligence tests.

We examine halo effect here because of its general effect on forming impressions. Bruner and Taguiri suggest that it is likely to be most extreme when we are forming impressions of traits that provide minimal cues in the individual's behavior, when the traits have moral overtones, or when the perceiver must judge traits with which he has had little experience.[14] A rather disturbing conclusion is suggested by Symonds that halo effect is more marked the more we know the acquaintance.[15]

A somewhat different aspect of the halo effect is suggested by the research of Grove and Kerr.[16] They found that knowledge that the company was in receivership caused employees to devalue the higher pay and otherwise superior working conditions of their company as compared to those in a financially secure firm.

Psychologists have noted a tendency in perceivers to link certain traits. They assume, for example, that when a person is aggressive he will also have high energy or that when a person is "warm" he will also be generous and have a good sense of humor. This logical error, as it has been called, is a special form of the halo effect and is best illustrated in the research of Asch.[17] In his study the addition of one trait to a list of traits produced a major change in the impression formed. Knowing that a person was intelligent, skillful, industrious, determined, practical, cautious, and warm led a group to judge him to be also wise, humorous, popular, and imaginative. When warm was replaced by cold, a radically different impression (beyond the difference between warm and cold) was formed. Kelley's research illustrated the same type of error.[18] This tendency is not indiscriminate; with the pair "polite-blunt," less change was found than with the more central traits of "warm-cold."

In evaluating the effect of halo on perceptual distortion, we may take comfort from the work of Wishner, which showed that those traits that correlate more highly with each other are more likely to lead to a halo effect than those that are unrelated.[19]

Projection

A defense mechanism available to everyone is projection, in which one relieves one's feelings of guilt by projecting blame onto someone else. Over the years the projection mechanism has been assigned various meanings. The original use of the term was concerned with the mechanism to defend oneself from unacceptable feelings. There has since been a tendency for the term to be used more broadly, meaning to ascribe or attribute any of one's own characteristics to other people. The projection mechanism concerns us here because it influences the perceptual process. An early study by Murray illustrates its effect.[20] After playing a dramatic game, "Murder," his subjects attributed much more maliciousness to people whose photographs were judged than did a control group which had not played the game. The current emotional state of the perceiver tended to influence his perceptions of others; i.e., frightened perceivers judged people to be frightening. More recently, Feshback and Singer revealed further dynamics of the process.[21] In their study, subjects who had been made fearful judged a stimulus person (presented in a moving picture) as both more fearful and more aggressive than did nonfearful perceivers. These authors were able to demonstrate further that the projection mechanism at work here was reduced when their subjects were encouraged to admit and talk about their fears.

Sears provides an illustration of a somewhat different type of projection and its effect on perception.[22] In his study projection is seeing our own undesirable personality characteristics in other people. He demonstrated that people high in such traits as stinginess, obstinacy, and disorderliness, tended to rate others much higher on these traits than did those who were low in these undesirable characteristics. The tendency to project was particularly marked among subjects who had the least insight into their own personalities.

Research thus suggests that our perceptions may characteristically be distorted by emotions we are experiencing or traits that we possess. Placed in the administrative setting, the research would suggest, for example, that a manager frightened by rumored organizational changes might not only judge others to be more frightened than they were, but also assess various policy decisions as more frightening than they were. Or a general foreman lacking insight into his own incapacity to delegate might be oversensitive to this trait in his superiors.

Perceptual Defense
Another distorting influence, which has been called perceptual defense, has also been demonstrated by Haire and Grunes to be a source of error.[23] In their research they ask, in effect, "Do we put blinders on to defend ourselves from seeing those events which might disturb us?" The concept of perceptual defense offers an excellent description of perceptual distortion at work and demonstrates that when confronted with a fact inconsistent with a stereotype already held by a person, the perceiver is able to distort the data in such a way as to eliminate the inconsistency. Thus, by perceiving inaccurately, he defends himself from having to change his stereotypes.

Characteristics of Perceiver and Perceived

We have thus far been talking largely about influences on the perceptual process without specific regard to the perceiver and his characteristics. Much recent research has tried to identify some characteristics of the perceiver and their influence on the perception of other people.

The Perceiver
A thread that would seem to tie together many current findings is the tendency to use oneself as the norm or standard by which one perceives or judges others. If we examine current research, certain conclusions are suggested:

1. *Knowing oneself makes it easier to see others accurately.* Norman showed that when one is aware of what his own personal characteristics are he makes fewer errors in perceiving others.[24] Weingarten has shown that people with insight are less likely to view the world in black-and-white terms and to give extreme judgments about others.[25]

2. *One's own characteristics affect the characteristics he is likely to see in others.* Secure people (compared to insecure) tend to see others as warm rather than cold, as was shown by Bossom and Maslow.[26] The extent of one's own sociability influences the degree of importance one gives to the sociability of other people when one forms impressions of them.[27] The person with "authoritarian" tendencies is more likely to view others in terms of power and is less sensitive to the psychological or personality characteristics of other people than is a nonauthoritarian.[28] The relatively few categories one uses in describing other people tend to be those one uses in describing oneself.[29] Thus traits which are important to the perceiver will be used more when he forms impressions of others. He has certain constant tendencies, both with regard to using certain categories in judging others and to the amount of weight given to these categories.[30]

3. *The person who accepts himself is more likely to be able to see favorable aspects of other people.*[31] This relates in part to the accuracy of his perceptions.

If the perceiver accepts himself as he is, he widens his range of vision in seeing others; he can look at them and be less likely to be very negative or critical. In those areas in which he is more insecure, he sees more problems in other people.[32] We are more likely to like others who have traits we accept in ourselves and reject those who have the traits which we do not like in ourselves.[33]

4. *Accuracy in perceiving others is not a single skill.* While there have been some variations in the findings, as Gage has shown, some consistent results do occur.[34] The perceiver tends to interpret the feelings others have about him in terms of his feelings towards them.[35] One's ability to perceive others accurately may depend on how sensitive one is to differences between people and also to the norms (outside of oneself) for judging them.[36] Thus, as Taft has shown, the ability to judge others does not seem to be a single skill.[37]

Possibly the results in these four aspects of person perception can be viewed most constructively in connection with earlier points on the process of perception. The administrator (or any other individual) who wishes to perceive someone else accurately must look at the other person, not at himself. The things that he looks at in someone else are influenced by his own traits. But if he knows his own traits, he can be aware that they provide a frame of reference for him. His own traits help to furnish the categories that he will use in perceiving others. His characteristics, needs, and values can partly limit his vision and his awareness of the differences between others. The question one could ask when viewing another is: "Am I looking at him, and forming my impression of his behavior in the situation, or am I just comparing him with myself?"

There is the added problem of being set to observe the personality traits in another which the perceiver does not accept in himself, e.g., being somewhat autocratic. At the same time he may make undue allowances in others for those of his own deficiencies which do not disturb him but might concern some people, e.g., not following prescribed procedures.

The Perceived

Lest we leave the impression that it is only the characteristics of the perceiver that stand between him and others in his efforts to know them, we turn now to some characteristics of the person being perceived which raise problems in perception. It is possible to demonstrate, for example, that the status of the person perceived is a variable influencing judgments about his behavior. Thibaut and Riecken have shown that even though two people behave in identical fashion, status differences between them cause a perceiver to assign different motivations for the behavior.[38] Concerning co-operativeness, they found that high status persons are judged as wanting to co-operate and low status persons as having to co-operate. In turn, more liking is shown for the person of high status than for the person of low status. Presumably, more credit is given when the boss says, "Good morning," to us than when a subordinate says the same thing.

Bruner indicated that we use categories to simplify our perceptual activities. In the administrative situation, status is one type of category, and role provides another. Thus the remarks of Mr. Jones in the sales department are perceived differently from those of Smith in the purchasing department, although both may say the same thing. Also, one who knows Jones's role in the organization will perceive his behavior differently from one who does not know Jones's role. The process of categorizing on the basis of roles is similar to, if not identical with, the stereotyping process described earlier.

Visibility of the traits is also an important variable influencing the accuracy of perception.[39] Visibility will depend, for example, on how free the other person feels to express the trait. It has been demonstrated that we are more accurate in judging people who like us than people who dislike us. The explanation suggested is that most people in our society feel constraint in showing their dislike, and therefore the cues are less visible.

Some traits are not visible simply because they provide few external cues for their presence. Loyalty, for example, as opposed to level of energy, provides few early signs for observation. Even honesty cannot be seen in the situations in which most impressions are formed. As obvious as these comments might be, in forming impressions many of us nevertheless continue to judge the presence of traits which are not really visible. Frequently the practical situation demands judgments, but we should recognize the frail reeds upon which we are leaning and be prepared to observe further and revise our judgments with time and closer acquaintance.

Situational Influences on Perception

Some recent research clearly points to the conclusion that the whole process of interpersonal perception is, at least in part, a function of the *group* (or interpersonal) context in which the perception occurs. Much of the research has important theoretical implications for a psychology of interpersonal relations. In addition, there are some suggestions of value for administrators. It is possible to identify several characteristics of the interpersonal climate which have direct effect on perceptual accuracy. As will be noted, these are characteristics which can be known, and in some cases controlled, in administrative settings.

Bieri provides data for the suggestion that when people are given an opportunity to interact in a friendly situation, they tend to see others as similar to themselves.[40] Applying his suggestion to the administrative situation, we can rationalize as follows: Some difficulties of administrative practice grow out of beliefs that different interest groups in the organization are made up of different types of people. Obviously once we believe that people in other groups are different, we will be predisposed to see the differences. We can thus find, from Bieri's and from Rosenbaum's work, an administrative approach for attacking the problem.[41] If we can produce an interacting situation which is co-operative rather than competitive, the likelihood of seeing other people as similar to ourselves is increased.

Exline's study adds some other characteristics of the social context which may influence perception.[42] Paraphrasing his conclusions to adapt them to the administrative scene, we can suggest that when a committee group is made up of congenial members who are willing to continue work in the same group, their perceptions of the goal-directed behavior of fellow committee members will be more accurate, although observations of purely personal behavior (as distinguished from goal-directed behavior) may be less accurate.[43] The implications for setting up committees and presumably other interacting work groups seem clear: Do not place together those with a past history of major personal clashes. If they must be on the same committee, each must be helped to see that the other is working toward the same goal.

An interesting variation in this area of research is the suggestion from Ex's work that perceptions will be more influenced or swayed by relatively unfamiliar people in the group than by those who are intimates.[44] The concept needs further research, but it provides the interesting suggestion that we may give more credit to strangers for having knowledge, since we do not really know, than we do to our intimates, whose backgrounds and limitations we feel we do know.

The *organization*, and one's place in it, may also be viewed as the context in which perceptions take place. A study by Dearborn and Simon illustrates this point.[45] Their data support the hypothesis that the administrator's perceptions will often be limited to those aspects of a situation which relate specifically to his own department, despite an attempt to influence him away from such selectivity.

Perception of self among populations at different levels in the hierarchy also offers an opportunity to judge the influence of organizational context on perceptual activity. Porter's study of the self-descriptions of managers and line workers indicated that both groups saw themselves in different terms, which corresponded to their positions in the organization's hierarchy.[46] He stated that managers used leadership-type traits (e.g., inventive) to describe themselves, while line workers used follower-type terms (e.g., co-operative). The question of which comes first must be asked: Does the manager see himself this way because of his current position in the organization? Or is this self-picture an expression of a more enduring personal characteristic that helped bring the manager to his present position? This study does not answer that question, but it does suggest to an administrator the need to be aware of the possibly critical relationship between one's hierarchical role and self-perception.

Perceptual Influences on Interpersonal Adjustment

Throughout this paper, we have examined a variety of influences on the perceptual process. There has been at least the inference that the operations of such influences on perception would in turn affect behavior that would follow. Common sense judgment suggests that being able to judge other people accurately facilitates smooth and effective interpersonal adjustments. Nevertheless, the relationship between perception and consequent behavior is itself in need of direct analysis. Two aspects may be identified: (1) the effect of accuracy of perception on subsequent behavior and (2) the effect of the duration of the relationship and the opportunity for experiencing additional cues.

First then, from the applied point of view, we can ask a crucial question: Is there a relationship between accuracy of social perception and adjustment to others? While the question might suggest a quick affirmative answer, research findings are inconsistent. Steiner attempted to resolve some of these inconsistencies by stating that accuracy may have an effect on interaction under the following conditions: when the interacting persons are co-operatively motivated, when the behavior which is accurately perceived is relevant to the activities of these persons, and when members are free to alter their behavior on the basis of their perceptions.[47]

Where the relationship provides opportunity only to form an impression, a large number of subjective factors, i.e., set, stereotypes, projections, etc., operate to create an early impression, which is frequently erroneous. In more enduring relationships a more balanced appraisal may result as increased interaction provides additional cues for judgment. In his study of the acquaintance process, Newcomb showed that while early perception of favorable traits caused attraction to the perceived person, over a four-month period the early cues for judging favorable traits became less influential.[48] With time, a much broader basis was used which included comparisons with others with whom one had established relationships. Such findings suggest that the warnings about perceptual inaccuracies implicit in the earlier sections of this paper apply with more force to the short-term process of impression forming than to relatively extended acquaintance-building relationships. One would thus hope that rating an employee after a year of service would be a more objective performance than appraising him in a selection interview—a hope that would be fulfilled only when the rater had provided himself with opportunities for broadening the cues he used in forming his first impressions.

Summary

Two principal suggestions which increase the probability of more effective administrative action emerge from the research data. One suggestion is that the administrator be continuously aware of the intricacies of the perceptual process and thus be warned to avoid arbitrary and categorical judgments and to seek reliable evidence before judgments are made. A second suggestion grows out of the first: increased accuracy in one's self-perception can make possible the flexibility to seek evidence and to shift position as time provides additional evidence.

Nevertheless, not every effort designed to improve perceptual accuracy will bring about such accuracy. The dangers of too complete reliance on formal training for perceptual accuracy are suggested in a study by Crow.[49] He found that a group of senior medical students were somewhat less accurate in their perceptions of others after a period of training in physician-patient relationships than were an untrained control group. The danger is that a little learning encourages the perceiver to respond with increased sensitivity to individual differences without making it possible for him to gauge the real meaning of the differences he has seen.

Without vigilance to perceive accurately and to minimize as far as possible the subjective approach in perceiving others, effective administration is handicapped. On the other hand, research would not support the conclusion that perceptual distortions will not occur simply because the administrator says he will try to be objective. The administrator or manager will have to work hard to avoid seeing only what he wants to see and to guard against fitting everything into what he is set to see.

We are not yet sure of the ways in which training for perceptual accuracy can best be accomplished, but such training cannot be ignored. In fact, one can say that one of the important tasks of administrative science is to design research to test various training procedures for increasing perceptual accuracy.

Notes and References

1. D. M. Johnson, A Systematic Treatment of Judgment, *Psychological Bulletin,* 42 (1945), 193-224.
2. J. S. Bruner, "Social Psychology and Perception," in E. Maccoby, T. Newcomb, and E. Hartley, eds. *Readings in Social Psychology* (3rd ed.: New York, 1958), pp. 85-94.
3. H. Cantril, Perception and Interpersonal Relations, *American Journal of Psychiatry,* 114 (1957), 119-126.
4. H. H. Kelley, The Warm-Cold Variable in First Impressions of Persons, *Journal of Personality,* 18 (1950), 431-439.
5. L. H. Strickland, Surveillance and Trust, *Journal of Personality,* 26 (1958), 200-215.
6. J. Mason, Judgements of Leadership Based upon Physiognomic Cues, *Journal of Abnormal and Social Psychology,* 54 (1957), 273-274.
7. C. A. Dailey, The Effects of Premature Conclusion upon the Acquisition of Understanding of a Person, *Journal of Psychology,* 33 (1952), 133-152.
8. W. E. Soskin, Influence of Information on Bias in Social Perception, *Journal of Personality,* 22, (1953), 118-127.
9. M. Haire, Role Perceptions in Labor-Management Relations: An Experimental Approach, *Indistrial Labor Relations Review,* 8, (1955), 204-216.
10. R. Stagner, *Psychology of Industrial Conflict* (New York, 1956), p. 35.
11. G. Allport, *Nature of Prejudice* (Cambridge, Mass., 1954).
12. S. Bruner and H. V. Perlmutter, Compatriot and Foreigner: A Study of Impression Formation in Three Countries, *Journal of Abnormal and Social Psychology,* 55 (1957), 253-260.
13. J. Luft, Monetary Value and the Perception of Persons, *Journal of Social Psychology,* 46 (1957), 245-251.
14. J. S. Bruner and A. Taguiri, "The Perception of People," ch. xvii in G. Lindzey, ed., *Handbook of Social Psychology* (Cambridge, Mass., 1954).
15. P. M. Symonds, Notes on Rating, *Journal of Applied Psychology,* 7 (1925), 188-195.
16. B. A. Grove and W. A. Kerr, Specific Evidence on Origin of Halo Effect in Measurement of Morale, *Journal of Social Psychology,* 34 (1951), 165-170.
17. S. Asch, Forming Impressions of Persons, *Journal of Abnormal and Social Psychology,* 60 (1946), 258-290.
18. Kelley, *op.cit.*
19. J.Wishner, Reanalysis of "Impressions of Personality," *Psychology Review,* 67 (1960), 96-112.
20. H. A. Murray, The Effect of Fear upon Estimates of the Maliciousness of Other Personalities, *Journal of Social Psychology,* 4, (1933), 310-329.
21. S. Feshback and R. D. Singer, The Effects of Fear Arousal upon Social Perception, *Journal of Abnormal and Social Psychology,* 55, (1957), 283-288.
22. R. R. Sears, Experimental Studies of Perception, I. Attribution of Traits, *Journal of Social Psychology,* 7 (1936), 151-163.
23. M. Haire and W. F. Grunes, Perceptual Defenses: Processes Protecting an Original Perception of Another Personality, *Human Relations,* 3, (1958), 403-412.
24. R. D. Norman, The Interrelationships among Acceptance-Rejection, Self-Other Identity, Insight into Self, and Realistic Perception of others, *Journal of Social Psychology,* 37, (1953), 205-235.
25. E. Weingarten, A Study of Selective Perception in Clinical Judgment, *Journal of Personality,* 17 (1949), 369-400.

26. J. Bossom and A. H. Maslow, Security of Judges as a Factor in Impressions of Warmth in Others, *Journal of Abnormal and Social Psychology,* 55 (1957), 147-148.
27. D. T. Benedetti and J. G. Hill, A Determiner of the Centrality of a Trait in Impression Formation, *Journal of Abnormal and Social Psychology,* 60 (1960), 278-279.
28. E. E. Jones, Authoritarianism as a Determinant of First-Impressions Formation, *Journal of Personality,* 23 (1954), 107-127.
29. A. H. Hastorf, S. A. Richardson, and S. M. Dornbusch, "The Problem of Relevance in the Study of Person Perception," in R. Taguiri and L. Petrullo, *Person Perception and Interpersonal Behavior* (Stanford, Calif. 1958).
30. L. J. Cronbach, Processes Affecting Scores on "Understanding of Others" and "Assumed Similarity," *Psychology Bulletin,* 52 (1955), 177-193.
31. K. T. Omwake, The Relation between Acceptance of Self and Acceptance of Others Shown by Three Personality Inventories, *Journal of Consulting Psychology,* 18 (1954), 443-446.
32. Weingarten, *op. cit.*
33. R. M. Lundy, W. Katovsky, R. L. Cromwell, and D. J. Shoemaker, Self Acceptability and Descriptions of Sociometric Choices, *Journal of Abnormal and Social Psychology,* 51 (1955), 260-262.
34. N. L. Gage, Accuracy of Social Perception and Effectiveness in Interpersonal Relationships, *Journal of Personality,* 22 (1953), 128-141.
35. R. Taguiri, J. S. Bruner, and R. Blake, On the Relation between Feelings and Perceptions of Feelings among Members of Small Groups," in Maccoby *et al., Readings in Social Psychology, op. cit.*
36. U. Bronfenbrenner, J. Harding, and M. Gallway, "The Measurement of Skill in Social Perception," in H. L. McClelland, D.C. Baldwin, U. Bronfenbrenner, and F.L. Strodtbeck, eds., *Talent and Society* (Princeton, N. J., 1958), pp. 29-111.
37. R. Taft, The Ability to Judge People, *Psychological Bulletin,* 52 (1955), 1-21.
38. J. W. Thibaut and H. W. Riecken, Some Determinants and Consequences of the Perception of Social Causality, *Journal of Personality,* 24 (1955), 113-133.
39. Bruner and Taguiri, *op. cit.*
40. J. Bieri, Change in Interpersonal Perception Following Interaction, *Journal of Abnormal and Social Psychology,* 48 (1953), 61-66.
41. J. E. Rosenbaum, Social Perception and the Motivational Structure of Interpersonal Relations, *Journal of Abnormal Psychology,* 59 (1959), 130-133.
42. R. V. Exline, Interrelations among Two Dimensions of Sociometric Status, Group Congeniality and Accuracy of Social Perception, *Sociometry,* 23 (1960), 85-101.
43. R. V. Exline, Group Climate as a Factor in the Relevance and Accuracy of Social Perception, *Journal of Abnormal and Social Psychology,* 55 (1957), 382-388.
44. J. Ex, The Nature of the Relation between Two Persons and the Degree of Their Influence on Each Other, *Acta Psychologica,* 17 (1960), 39-54.
45. D. C. Dearborn and H. A. Simon, Selective Perception. A Note on the Departmental Identifications of Executives, *Sociometry,* 21 (1958), 140-144.
46. L. W. Porter, Differential Self-Perceptions of Management Personnel and Line Workers, *Journal of Applied Psychology,* 42 (1958), 105-109.
47. J. Steiner, Interpersonal Behavior as Influenced by Accuracy of Social Perception, *Psychological Review,* 62 (1955), 168-275.
48. T. M. Newcomb, The Perception of Interpersonal Attraction, *American Psychologist,* 11 (1956), 575-586, and *The Acquaintance Process* (New York, 1961).
49. W. J. Crow, Effect of Training on Interpersonal Perception, *Journal of Abnormal and Social Psychology,* 55 (1957), 355-359.

SELECTIVE PERCEPTION

DEWITT C. DEARBORN
HERBERT A. SIMON

An important proposition in organization theory asserts that each executive will perceive those aspects of the situation that relate specifically to the activities and goals of his department (2, Ch. 5, 10). The proposition is frequently supported by anecdotes of executives and observers in organizations, but little evidence of a systematic kind is available to test it. It is the purpose of this note to supply some such evidence.

The proposition we are considering is not peculiarly organizational. It is simply an application to organizational phenomena of a generalization that is central to any explanation of selective perception: Presented with a complex stimulus, the subject perceives in it what he is "ready" to perceive; the more complex or ambiguous the stimulus, the more the perception is determined by what is already "in" the subject and the less by what is in the stimulus (1, pp. 132-133).

Cognitive and motivational mechanisms mingle in the selective process, and it may be of some use to assess their relative contributions. We might suppose either: (1) selective attention to a part of a stimulus reflects a deliberate ignoring of the remainder as irrelevant to the subject's goals and motives, or (2) selective attention is a learned response stemming from some past history of reinforcement. In the latter case we might still be at some pains to determine the nature of the reinforcement, but by creating a situation from which any immediate motivation for selectivity is removed, we should be able to separate the second mechanism from the first. The situation in which we obtained our data meets this condition, and hence our data provide evidence for internalization of the selective processes.

Method of the Study

A group of 23 executives, all employed by a single large manufacturing concern and enrolled in a company sponsored executive training program, was asked to read a standard case that is widely used in instruction in business policy in business schools. The case, Castengo Steel Company described the organization and activities of a company of moderate size specializing in the manufacture of seamless steel tubes, as of the end of World War II. The case, which is about 10,000 words in length, contains a wealth of descriptive material about the company and its industry and the recent history of both (up to 1945), but little evaluation. It is deliberately written to hold closely to concrete facts and to leave as much as possible of the burden of interpretation to the reader.

When the executives appeared at a class to discuss the case, but before they had discussed it, they were asked by the instructor to write a brief statement of

Reprinted by permission of the authors and the publisher, the American Sociological Association, from *Sociometry*, vol. 21 (1958), pp. 140-43.

what they considered to be the most important problem facing the Castengo Steel Company—the problem a new company president should deal with first. Prior to this session, the group had discussed other cases, being reminded from time to time by the instructor that they were to assume the role of the top executive of the company in considering its problems.

The executives were a relatively homogeneous group in terms of status, being drawn from perhaps three levels of the company organization. They were in the range usually called "middle management," representing such positions as superintendent of a department in a large factory, product manager responsible for profitability of one of the ten product groups manufactured by the company, and works physician for a large factory. In terms of departmental affiliation, they fell in four groups:

Sales (6) Five product managers or assistant product managers, and one field sales supervisor.

Production (5): Three department superintendents, one assistant factory manager, and one construction engineer.

Accounting (4): An assistant chief accountant, and three accounting supervisors —for a budget division and two factory departments.

Miscellaneous (8): Two members of the legal department, two in research and development, and one each from public relations, industrial relations, medical and purchasing.

The Data

. . . We tested our hypothesis by determining whether there was a significant relation between the "most important problem" mentioned and the departmental affiliation of the mentioner. In the cases of executives who mentioned more than one problem, we counted all those they mentioned. We compared (1) the executives who mentioned "sales," "marketing," or "distribution" with those who did not; (2) the executives who mentioned "clarifying the organization" or some equivalent with those who did not; (3) the executives who mentioned "human relations," "employee relations" or "teamwork" with those who did not. The findings are summarized in the Table.

The difference between the percentages of sales executives (83%) and other executives (29%) who mentioned sales as the most important problem is significant at the 5 per cent level. Three of the five nonsales executives, moreover, who mentioned sales were in the accounting department, and all of these were in positions

Department	Total number of executives	Number who mentioned		
		Sales	"Clarify organization"	Human relations
Sales	6	5	1	0
Production	5	1	4	0
Accounting	4	3	0	0
Miscellaneous	8	1	3	3
Totals	23	10	8	3

that involved analysis of product profitability. This accounting activity was, in fact, receiving considerable emphasis in the company at the time of the case discussion and the accounting executives had frequent and close contacts with the product managers in the sales department. If we combine sales and accounting executives, we find that 8 out of 10 of these mentioned sales as the most important problem; while only 2 of the remaining 13 executives did.

Organization problems (other than marketing organization) were mentioned by four out of five production executives, the two executives in research and development, and the factory physician, but by only one sales executive and no accounting executives. The difference between the percentage for production executives (80%) and other executives (22%) is also significant at the 5 per cent level. Examination of the Castengo case shows that the main issue discussed in the case that relates to manufacturing is the problem of poorly defined relations among the factory manager, the metallurgist, and the company president. The presence of the metallurgist in the situation may help to explain the sensitivity of the two research and development executives (both of whom were concerned with metallurgy) to this particular problem area.

It is easy to conjecture why the public relations, industrial relations, and medical executives should all have mentioned some aspect of human relations, and why one of the two legal department executives should have mentioned the board of directors.

Conclusion

We have presented data on the selective perceptions of industrial executives exposed to case material that support the hypothesis that each executive will perceive those aspects of a situation that relate specifically to the activities and goals of his department. Since the situation is one in which the executives were motivated to look at the problem from a company-wide rather than a departmental viewpoint, the data indicate further that the criteria of selection have become internalized. Finally, the method for obtaining that we have used holds considerable promise as a projective device for eliciting the attitudes and perceptions of executives.

References

1. Bruner, J. S., "On Perceptual Readiness," *Psychological Review*, 1957, 64, 123-152
2. Simon, H. A., *Administrative Behavior*, New York: Macmillan, 1947.

Section C

Motivation and Performance

TOWARD A THEORY
OF MOTIVE ACQUISITION

DAVID C. McCLELLAND

Too little is known about the processes of personality change at relatively complex levels. The empirical study of the problem has been hampered by both practical and theoretical difficulties. On the practical side it is very expensive both in time and effort to set up systematically controlled educational programs designed to develop some complex personality characteristic like a motive, and to follow the effects of the education over a number of years. It also presents ethical problems since it is not always clear that it is as proper to teach a person a new motive as it is a new skill like learning to play the piano. For both reasons, most of what we know about personality change has come from studying psychotherapy where both ethical and practical difficulties are overcome by the pressing need to help someone in real trouble. Yet, this source of information leaves much to be desired: It has so far proven difficult to identify and systematically vary the "inputs" in psychotherapy and to measure their specific effects on subsequent behavior, except in very general ways (cf. Rogers & Dymond, 1954).

On the theoretical side, the dominant views of personality formation suggest anyway that acquisition or change of any complex characteristic like a motive in adulthood would be extremely difficult. Both behavior theory and psychoanalysis agree that stable personality characteristics like motives are laid down in childhood. Behavior theory arrives at this conclusion by arguing that social motives are learned by close association with reduction in certain basic biological drives like hunger, thirst, and physical discomfort which loom much larger in childhood than adulthood. Psychoanalysis, for its part, pictures adult motives as stable resolutions of basic con-

From *American Psychologist*, vol. 20 (1965), pp. 321-33. Copyright 1965 by the American Psychological Association. Reprinted by permission.

flicts occurring in early childhood. Neither theory would provide much support for the notion that motives could be developed in adulthood without somehow recreating the childhood conditions under which they were originally formed. Furthermore, psychologists have been hard put to it to find objective evidence that even prolonged, serious, and expensive attempts to introduce personality change through psychotherapy have really proven successful (Eysenck, 1952). What hope is there that a program to introduce personality change would end up producing a big enough effect to study?

Despite these difficulties a program of research has been under way for some time which is attempting to develop the achievement motive in adults. It was undertaken in an attempt to fill some of the gaps in our knowledge about personality change or the acquisition of complex human characteristics. Working with n Achievement has proved to have some important advantages for this type of research: The practical and ethical problems do not loom especially large because previous research (McClelland, 1961) has demonstrated the importance of high n Achievement for entrepreneurial behavior and it is easy to find businessmen, particularly in underdeveloped countries, who are interested in trying any means of improving their entrepreneurial performance. Furthermore, a great deal is known about the origins of n Achievement in childhood and its specific effects on behavior so that educational programs can be systematically planned and their effects evaluated in terms of this knowledge. Pilot attempts to develop n Achievement have gradually led to the formulation of some theoretical notions of what motive acquisition involves and how it can be effectively promoted in adults. These notions have been summarized in the form of 12 propositions which it is the ultimate purpose of the research program to test. The propositions are anchored so far as possible in experiences with pilot courses, in supporting research findings from other studies, and in theory.

Before the propositions are presented, it is necessary to explain more of the theoretical and practical background on which they are based. To begin with, some basis for believing that motives could be acquired in adulthood had to be found in view of the widespread pessimism on the subject among theoretically oriented psychologists. Oddly enough we were encouraged by the successful efforts of two quite different groups of "change agents"—operant conditioners and missionaries. Both groups have been "naive" in the sense of being unimpressed by or ignorant of the state of psychological knowledge in the field. The operant conditioners have not been encumbered by any elaborate theoretical apparatus; they do not believe motives exist anyway, and continue demonstrating vigorously that if you want a person to make a response, all you have to do is elicit it and reward it (cf. Bandura & Walters, 1963, pp. 238 ff.). They retain a simple faith in the infinite plasticity of human behavior in which one response is just like any other and any one can be "shaped up" (strengthened by reward)—presumably even an "achievement" response as produced by a subject in a fantasy test. In fact, it was the naive optimism of one such researcher (Burris, 1958) that had a lot to do with getting the present research under way. He undertook a counseling program in which an attempt to elicit and reinforce achievement-related fantasies proved to be successful in motivating college students to get better grades. Like operant conditioners, the missionaries have gone ahead changing people because they have believed it possible. While the evidence is not scientifically impeccable, common-sense observation yields dozens of cases of adults whose motivational structure has seemed to be quite radically and permanently altered by the educational efforts of Communist Party, Mormon, or other devout missionaries.

A man from Mars might be led to observe that personality change appears to be very difficult for those who think it is very difficult, if not impossible, and much easier for those who think it can be done. He would certainly be oversimplifying the picture, but at the very least his observation suggests that some theoretical revision is desirable in the prevailing views of social motives which link them so decisively to early childhood. Such a revision has been attempted in connection with the research on n Achievement (McClelland, Atkinson, Clark & Lowell, 1953) and while it has not been widely accepted (cf. Berelson & Steiner, 1964), it needs to be briefly summarized here to provide a theoretical underpinning for the attempts at motive change to be described. It starts with the proposition that all motives are learned, that not even biological discomforts (as from hunger) or pleasures (as from sexual stimulation) are "urges" or "drives" until they are linked to cues that can signify their presence or absence. In time clusters of expectancies or associations grow up around affective experiences, not all of which are connected by any means with biological needs (McClelland et al., 1953, Ch. 2), which we label motives. More formally, motives are "affectively toned associative networks" arranged in a hierarchy of strength or importance within a given individual. Obviously, the definition fits closely the operations used to measure a motive: "an affectively toned associative cluster" is exactly what is coded in a subject's fantasies to obtain an n Achievement score. The strength of the motive (its position in the individual's hierarchy of motives) is measured essentially by counting the number of associations belonging to this cluster as compared to others that an individual produces in a given number of opportunities. If one thinks of a motive as an associative network, it is easier to imagine how one might go about changing it: The problem becomes one of moving its position up on the hierarchy by increasing its salience compared to other clusters. It should be possible to accomplish this end by such tactics as: (*a*) setting up the network—discovering what associations, for example, exist in the achievement area and then extending, strengthening, or otherwise "improving" the network they form; (*b*) conceptualizing the network—forming a clear and conscious construct that labels the network; (*c*) tying the network to as many cues as possible in everyday life, especially those preceding and following action, to insure that the network will be regularly rearoused once formed; and (*d*) working out the relation of the network to superordinate associative clusters, like the self-concept, so that these dominant schemata do not block the train of achievement thoughts—for example, through a chain of interfering associations (e.g., "I am not really the achieving type").

This very brief summary is not intended as a full exposition of the theoretical viewpoint underlying the research, but it should suffice to give a rough idea of how the motive was conceived that we set out to change. This concept helped define the goals of the techniques of change, such as reducing the effects of associative interference from superordinate associate clusters. But what about the techniques themselves? What could we do that would produce effective learning of this sort? Broadly speaking, there are four types of empirical information to draw on. From the animal learning experiments, we know that such factors as repetition, optimal time intervals between stimulus, response, and reward, and the schedule of rewards are very important for effective learning. From human learning experiments, we know that such factors as distribution of practice, repetitions, meaningfulness, and recitation are important. From experiences with psychotherapy (cf. Rogers, 1961), we learn that warmth, honesty, non-directiveness, and the ability to recode associations in line with psychoanalytic or other personality theories are important. And, from the attitude-change research literature, we learn that such variables as presenting one side or two, using reason or prestige to support an argument, or affiliating with a new reference group are crucial for developing new attitudes (cf. Hovland, Janis, & Kelley, 1953). Despite the fact that many of these variables seem limited in application to the learning situation in which they were studied, we have tried to make use of information from all these sources in designing our "motive acquisition" program and in finding support for the general propositions that have emerged from our study so far. For our purpose has been above all to produce an effect large enough to be measured. Thus we have tried to profit by all that is known about how to facilitate learning or produce personality or attitude change. For, if we could not obtain a substantial effect with all factors working to produce it, there would be no point to studying the effects of each factor taken one at a time. Such a strategy also has the practical advantage that we are in the position of doing our best to "deliver the goods" to our course participants since they were giving us their time and attention to take part in a largely untried educational experience.[1]

Our overall research strategy, therefore, is "subtractive" rather than "additive." After we have demonstrated a substantial effect with some 10-12 factors working to produce it, our plan is to subtract that part of the program that deals with each of the factors to discover if there is a significant decline in the effect. It should also be possible to omit several factors in various combinations to get at interactional effects. This will obviously require giving a fairly large number of courses in a standard institutional setting for the same kinds of businessmen with follow-up evaluation of their performance extending over a number of years. So obviously it will be some time before each of the factors incorporated into the propositions which follow can be properly evaluated so far as its effect on producing motive change is concerned.

The overall research strategy also determined the way the attempts to develop the achievement motive have been organized. That is to say, in order to process enough subjects to permit testing the effectiveness of various "inputs" in a reasonable number of years, the training had to be both of *short duration* (lasting 1-3 weeks) and *designed for groups* rather than for individuals as in person-to-person counseling. Fortunately these requirements coincide with normal practice in providing short courses for business executives. To conform further with that practice, the training has usually also been *residential* and *voluntary*. The design problems introduced by the last characteristic we have tried to handle in the usual ways by putting half the volunteers on a waiting list or giving them a different, technique-oriented course, etc. So far we have given the course to develop n Achievement in some form or another some eight times to over 140 managers or teachers of management in groups of 9-25 in the United States, Mexico, and India. For the most part the course has been offered by a group of 2-4 consultant psychologists either to executives in a single company as a company training program, or to executives from several different companies as a self-improvement program, or as part of the program of an institute or school devoted to training managers. The theoretical propositions which follow have evolved gradually from these pilot attempts to be effective in developing n Achievement among businessmen of various cultural backgrounds.

The first step in a motive development program is to create confidence that it will work. Our initial efforts in this area were dictated by the simple practical consideration that we had to "sell" our course or nobody would take it. We were not in the position of an animal psychologist who can order a dozen rats, or an academic psychologist who has captive subjects in his classes, or even a psychotherapist who has sick people knocking at his door every day. So we explained to all who would listen that we had every reason to believe from previous research that high n Achievement is related to effective entrepreneurship and that therefore business executives could expect to profit from taking a course designed to understand and develop this important human characteristic. What started as a necessity led to the first proposition dealing with how to bring about motive change.

Proposition 1. The more reasons an individual has in advance to believe that he can, will, or should develop a motive, the more educational attempts designed to develop that motive are likely to succeed. The empirical support for this proposition from other studies is quite impressive. It consists of (a) the prestige-suggestion studies showing that people will believe or do what prestigeful sources suggest (cf. Hovland et al., 1953); (b) the so-called "Hawthorne effect" showing that people who feel they are especially selected to show an effect will tend to show it (Roethlisberger & Dickson, 1947); (c) the "Hello-Goodbye" effect in psychotherapy showing that patients who merely have contact with a prestigeful medical authority improve significantly over waiting list controls and almost as much as those who get prolonged therapy (Frank, 1961); (d) the "experimenter bias" studies which show that subjects will often do what an experimenter wants them to do, even though neither he nor they know he is trying to influence them (Rosenthal, 1963); (e) the goal-setting studies which show that setting goals for a person particularly in the name of prestigeful authorities like "science" or "research" improves performance (Kausler, 1959; Mierke, 1955); (f) the parent-child interaction studies which show that parents who set higher standards of excellence for their sons are more likely to have sons with high n Achievement (Rosen & D'Andrade, 1959). The common factor in all these studies seems to be that goals are being set for the individual by sources he respects—goals which imply that his behavior should change for a variety of reasons and that it *can* change. In common-sense terms, belief in the possibility and desirability of change are tremendously influential in changing a person.

So we have used a variety of means to create this belief: the authority of research findings on the relationship of n Achievement to entrepreneurial success, the suggestive power of membership in an experimental group designed to show an effect, the prestige of a great university, our own genuine enthusiasm for the course and our conviction that it would work, as expressed privately and in public speeches. In short, we were trying to make every use possible of what is sometimes regarded as an "error" in such research—namely, the Hawthorne effect, experimenter bias, etc., because we believe it to be one of the most powerful sources of change.

Why? What is the effect on the person, theoretically speaking, of all this goal setting for him? Its primary function is probably to arouse what exists of an associative network in the achievement area for each person affected. That is, many studies have shown that talk of achievement or affiliation or power tends to increase the frequency with which individuals think about achievement or affiliation or power (cf. Atkinson, 1958). And the stronger the talk, the more the relevant associative networks are aroused (McClelland et al., 1953). Such an arousal has several possible effects which would facilitate learning: (*a*) It elicits what exists in the person of a "response" thus making it easier to strengthen that response in subsequent learning. (*b*) It creates a discrepancy between a goal (a "Soll-lage" in Heckhausen's—1963—theory of motivation) and a present state ("Ist-lage") which represents a cognitive dissonance the person tries to reduce (cf. Festinger, 1957); in common-sense terms he has an image clearly presented to him of something he is not but should be. (*c*) It tends to block out by simple interference other associations which would inhibit change—such as, "I'm too old to learn," "I never learned much from going to school anyway," "What do these academics know about everyday life?" or "I hope they don't get personal about all this."

After the course has been "sold" sufficiently to get a group together for training, the first step in the course itself is to present the research findings in some detail on exactly how n Achievement is related to certain types of successful entrepreneurial performance. That is, the argument of *The Achieving Society* (McClelland, 1961) is presented carefully with tables, charts, and diagrams, usually in lecture form at the outset and with the help of an educational TV film entitled the *Need to Achieve*. This is followed by discussion to clear up any ambiguities that remain in their minds as far as the central argument is concerned. It is especially necessary to stress that not all high achievement is caused by high n Achievement—that we have no evidence that high n Achievement is an essential ingredient in success as a research scientist, professional, accountant, office or personnel manager, etc.; that, on the contrary, it seems rather narrowly related to entrepreneurial, sales, or promotional success, and therefore should be of particular interest to them because they hold jobs which either have or could have an entrepreneurial component. We rationalize this activity in terms of the following proposition.

Proposition 2. The more an individual perceives that developing a motive is consistent with the demands of reality (and reason), the more educational attempts designed to develop that motive are likely to succeed. In a century in which psychologists and social theorists have been impressed by the power of unreason, it is well to remember that research has shown that rational arguments do sway opinions, particularly among the doubtful or the uncommitted (cf. Hovland et al., 1953). Reality in the form of legal, military, or housing rules does modify white prejudice against Negroes (cf. Berelson & Steiner, 1964, p. 512). In being surprised at Asch's discovery that many people will go along with a group in calling a shorter line longer than it is, we sometimes forget that under most conditions their judgments conform with reality. The associative network which organizes "reality"—which places the person correctly in time, place, space, family, job, etc.—is one of the most dominant in the personality. It is the last to go in psychosis. It should be of great assistance to tie any proposed change in an associative network in with this dominant schema in such a way as to make the change consistent with reality demands or *"reasonable"* extensions of them. The word "reasonable" here simply means extensions arrived at by the thought processes of proof, logic, etc., which in adults have achieved a certain dominance of their own.

The next step in the course is to teach the participants the n Achievement coding system. By this time, they are a little confused anyway as to exactly what we mean by the term. So we tell them they can find out for themselves by learning to code stories written by others or by themselves. They take the test for n Achievement before this session and then find out what their own score is by scoring this record. However, we point out that if they think their score is too low, that can be easily remedied, since we teach them how to code and how to write stories saturated with n Achievement; in fact, that is one of the basic purposes of the course: to teach them to think constantly in n Achievement terms. Another aspect of the learning is discriminating achievement thinking from thinking in terms of power or affiliation. So usually the elements of these other two coding schemes are also taught.

Proposition 3. The more thoroughly an individual develops and clearly conceptualizes the associative network defining the motive, the more likely he is to develop the motive. The original empirical support for this proposition came from the radical behaviorist Skinnerian viewpoint: If the associative responses are the motive (by definition), to strengthen them one should elicit them and reinforce them, as one would shape up any response by reinforcement (cf. Skinner, 1953). But, support for this proposition also derives from other sources, particularly the "set" experiments. For decades laboratory psychologists have known that one of the easiest and most effective ways to change behavior is to change the subject's set. If he is responding to stimulus words with the names of animals, tell him to respond with the names of vegetables, or with words meaning the opposite, and he changes his behavior immediately and efficiently without a mistake. At a more complex level Orne (1962) had pointed out how powerful a set like "This is an experiment" can be. He points out that if you were to go up to a stranger and say something like "Lie down!" he would in all probability either laugh or escape as soon as possible. But, if you say "This is an experiment! Lie down!" more often than not, if there are other supporting cues, the person will do so. Orne has demonstrated how subjects will perform nonsensical and fatiguing tasks for very long periods of time under the set that "this is an experiment." At an even more complex level, sociolologists have demonstrated often how quickly a person will change his behavior as he adopts a new role set (as a parent, a teacher, a public official, etc.). In all these cases an associative network exists usually with a label conveniently attached which we call set and which, when it is aroused or becomes salient, proceeds to control behavior very effectively. The purpose of this part of our course is to give the subjects a set or a carefully worked out associative network with appropriate words or labels to describe all its various aspects (the coding labels for parts of the n Achievement scoring system like Ga+, I+, etc.; cf. Atkinson, 1958). The power of words on controlling behavior has also been well documented (cf. Brown, 1958).

It is important to stress that it is not just the label (n Achievement) which is taught. The person must be able to produce easily and often the new associative network itself. It is here that our research comes closest to traditional therapy which could be understood as the prolonged and laborious formation of new associative networks to replace anxiety-laden ones. That is, the person over time comes to form a new associative network covering his relations, for example, to his father and mother, which still later he may label an "unresolved Oedipus complex." When cues arise that formerly would have produced anxiety-laden associations, they now evoke this new complex instead, blocking out the "bad" associations by associative interference. But all therapists, whether Freudian or Rogerian, insist that the person must learn to produce these associations in their new form, that teaching the label is not enough. In fact, this is probably why so-called directive therapy is ineffective: It tries to substitute new constructs ("You should become an achiever") for old neurotic or ineffective ones ("rather than being such a slob") without changing the associative networks which underlie these surface labels. A change in set such as "Respond with names of vegetables" will not work unless the person has a whole associative network which defines the meaning of the set. The relation of this argument is obvious both to Kelly's (1955) insistence on the importance of personal constructs and to the general semanticists' complaints about the neurotic effects of mislabeling or overabstraction (Korzybsky, 1941).

But, theoretically speaking, why should a change in set as an associative network be so influential in controlling thought and action? The explanation lies in part in its symbolic character. Learned acts have limited influence because they often depend on reality supports (as in typewriting), but learned thoughts (symbolic acts) can occur any time, any place, in any connection, and be applied to whatever the person is doing. They are more generalizable. Acts can also be inhibited more easily than thoughts. Isak Dinesen tells the story of the oracle who told the king he would get his wish so long as he never thought of the left eye of a camel. Needless to say, the king did not get his wish, but he could easily have obeyed her prohibition if it had been to avoid *looking* at the left eye of a camel. Thoughts once acquired gain more control over thoughts and actions than acquired acts do because they are harder to inhibit. But why do they gain control over actions? Are not thoughts substitutes for actions? Cannot a man learn to think achievement thoughts and still not act like an achiever in any way? The question is taken up again under the next proposition, but it is well to remember here that thoughts are symbolic acts and that practice of symbolic acts facilitates performing the real acts (cf. Hovland, 1951, p. 644).

The next step in the course is to tie thought to action. Research has shown that individuals high in n Achievement tend to act in certain ways. For example, they prefer work situations where there is a challenge (moderate risk), concrete feedback on how well they are doing, and opportunity to take personal responsibility for achieving the work goals. The participants in the course are therefore introduced to a "work" situation in the form of a business game in which they will have an opportunity to show these characteristics in action or more specifically to develop them through practice and through observing others play it. The game is designed to mimic real life: They must order parts to make certain objects (e.g., a Tinker Toy model bridge) after having estimated how many they think they can construct in the time allotted. They have a real chance to take over, plan the whole game, learn from how well they are doing (use of feedback), and show a paper profit or loss at the end. While they are surprised often that they would have to display their real action characteristics in this way in public, they usually get emotionally involved in observing how they behave under pressure of a more or less "real" work situation.

Proposition 4. The more an individual can link the newly developed network to related actions, the more the change in both thought and action is likely to occur and endure. The evidence for the importance of action for producing change consists of such diverse findings as (*a*) the importance of recitation for human learning, (*b*) the repeated finding that overt commitment and participation in action changes attitudes effectively (cf. Berelson & Steiner, 1964, p. 576), and (*c*) early studies by Carr (cf. McGeoch & Irion, 1952) showing that simply to expose an organism to what is to be learned (e.g., trundling a rat through a maze) is nowhere near as effective as letting him explore it for himself in action.

Theoretically, the action is represented in the associative network by what associations precede, accompany, and follow it. So including the acts in what is learned *enlarges* the associative network or the achievement construct to include action. Thus, the number of cues likely to trip off the n Achievement network is increased. In commonsense terms, whenever he works he now evaluates what he is doing in achievement terms, and whenever he thinks about achievement he tends to think of its action consequences.

So far the course instruction has remained fairly abstract and removed from the everyday experiences of businessmen. So, the next step is to apply what has been learned to everyday business activities through the medium of the well-known case-study method popularized by the Harvard Business School. Actual examples of the development of the careers or firms of business leaders or entrepreneurs are written up in disguised form and assigned for discussion to the participants. Ordinarily, the instructor is not interested in illustrating "good" or "bad" managerial behavior—that is left to participants to discuss—but in our use of the material, we do try to label the various types of behavior as illustrating either n Achievement and various aspects of the achievement sequence (instrumental activity, blocks, etc.), or n Power, n Affiliation, etc. The participants are also encouraged to bring in examples of managerial behavior from their own experience to evaluate in motivational terms.

Proposition 5. The more an individual can link the newly conceptualized association-action complex (or motive) to events in his everyday life, the more likely the motive complex is to influence his thoughts and actions in situations outside the training experience. The transfer-of-training research literature is not very explicit on this point, though it seems self-evident. Certainly, this is the proposition that underlies the practice of most therapy when it involves working through or clarifying, usually in terms of a new, partially formed construct system, old memories, events from the last 24 hours, dreams, and hopes of the future. Again, theoretically, this should serve to enlarge and clarify the associative network and increase the number of cues in everyday life which will rearouse it. The principle of symbolic practice can also be invoked to support its effectiveness in promoting transfer outside the learning experience.

For some time most course participants have been wondering what all this has to do with them personally. That is to say, the material is introduced as something that ought to be of interest to them. But, sooner or later, they must confront the issue as to what meaning n Achievement has in their own personal lives. We do not force this choice on them nor do we think we are brainwashing them to believe in n Achievement. We believe and we tell them we believe in the "obstinate audience" (cf. Bauer, 1964), in the ultimate capacity of people to resist persuasion or to do in the end what they really want to do. In fact, we had one case in an early session of a man who at this point decided he was not an achievement-minded person and did not want to become one. He subsequently retired and became a chicken farmer to the relief of the business in which he had been an ineffective manager. We respected that decision and mention it in the course as a good example of honest self-evaluation. Nevertheless, we do provide them with all kinds of information as to their own achievement-related behavior in the fantasy tests, in the business game, in occasional group dynamics session—and ample opportunity and encouragement to think through what this information implies so far as their self-concept is concerned and their responsibilities to their jobs. Various devices such as the "Who am I?" test, silent group meditation, or individual counseling have been introduced to facilitate this self-confrontation.

Proposition 6. The more an individual can perceive and experience the newly conceptualized motive as an improvement in the self-image, the more the motive is likely to influence his future thoughts and actions. Evidence on the importance of the ego or the self-image on controlling behavior has been summarized by Allport (1943). In recent years, Rogers and his group (Rogers, 1961; Rogers & Dymond, 1954) have measured improvement in psychotherapy largely in terms of improvement of the self-concept in relation to the ideal self. Indirect evidence of the importance of the self-schema comes from the discussion over whether a person can be made to do things under hypnosis that are inconsistent with his self-concept or values. All investigators agree that the hypnotist can be most successful in getting the subject to do what might normally be a disapproved action if he makes the subject perceive the action as consistent with his self-image or values (cf. Berelson & Steiner, 1963, p. 124).

The same logic supports this proposition. It seems unlikely that a newly formed associative network like n Achievement could persist and influence behavior much unless it had somehow "come to terms" with the pervasive superordinate network of associations defining the self. The logic is the same as for Proposition 2 dealing with the reality construct system. The n Achievement associations must come to be experienced as related to or consistent with the ideal self-image; otherwise associations from the self-system will constantly block thoughts of achievement. The person might be thinking, for example: "I am not that kind of person; achievement means judging people in terms of how well they perform and I don't like to hurt people's feelings."

Closely allied to the self-system is a whole series of networks only half conscious (i.e., correctly labeled) summarizing the values by which the person lives which derive from his culture and social milieu. These values can also interfere if they are inconsistent with n Achievement as a newly acquired way of thinking. Therefore, it has been customary at this point in the course to introduce a value analysis of the participants' culture based on an analysis of children's stories, myths, popular religion, comparative attitude surveys, customs, etc., more or less in line with traditional, cultural anthropological practice (cf. Benedict, 1946; McClelland,

1964). For example, in America we have to work through the problem of how being achievement oriented seems to interfere with being popular or liked by others which is highly valued by Americans. In Mexico a central issue is the highly valued "male dominance" pattern reflected in the patriarchal family and in the *macho* complex (being extremely masculine). Since data show that dominant fathers have sons with low n Achievement and authoritarian bosses do not encourage n Achievement in their top executives (Andrews, 1965), there is obviously a problem here to be worked through if n Achievement is to survive among thoughts centered on dominance. The problem is not only rationally discussed. It is acted out in role-playing sessions where Mexicans try, and often to their own surprise fail, to act like the democratic father with high standards in the classic Rosen and D'Andrade (1959) study on parental behavior which develops high n Achievement. Any technique is used which will serve to draw attention to possible conflicts between n Achievement and popular or traditional cultural values. In the end it may come to discussing parts of the *Bhagavad Gita* in India, or the *Koran* in Arab countries, that seem to oppose achievement striving or entrepreneurial behavior.

Proposition 7. The more an individual can perceive and experience the newly conceptualized motive as an improvement on prevailing cultural values, the more the motive is likely to influence his future thoughts and actions. The cultural anthropologists for years have argued how important it is to understand one's own cultural values to overcome prejudices, adopt more flexible attitudes, etc., but there is little hard evidence that doing so changes a person's behavior. What exists comes indirectly from studies that show prejudice can be decreased a little by information about ethnic groups (Berelson & Steiner, 1963, p. 517), or that repeatedly show an unconscious link between attitudes and the reference group (or subculture to which one belongs—a link which presumably can be broken more easily by full information about it, especially when coupled with role-playing new attitudes (cf. Berelson & Steiner, 1963, pp. 566 ff.).

The theoretical explanation of this presumed effect is the same as for Proposition 2 and 6. The newly learned associative complex to influence thought and action effectively must somehow be adjusted to three superordinate networks that may set off regularly interfering associations—namely, the networks associated with reality, the self, and the social reference group or subculture.

The course normally ends with each participant preparing a written document outlining his goals and life plans for the next 2 years. These plans may or may not include references to the achievement motive; they can be very tentative, but they are supposed to be quite specific and realistic; that is to say, they should represent moderate levels of aspiration following the practice established in learning about n Achievement of choosing the moderately risky or challenging alternative. The purpose of this document is in part to formulate for oneself the practical implications of the course before leaving it, but even more to provide a basis for the evaluation of their progress in the months after the course. For it is explained to the participants that they are to regard themselves as "in training" for the next 2 years, that 10-14 days is obviously too short a time to do more than conceive a new way of life: It represents the residential portion of the training only. Our role over the next 2 years will be to remind them every 6 months of the tasks they have set themselves by sending them a questionnaire to fill out which will serve to rearouse many of the issues discussed in the course and to give them information on how far they have progressed toward achieving their goals.

Proposition 8. The more an individual commits himself to achieving concrete goals in life related to the newly formed motive, the more the motive is likely to influence his future thoughts and actions.

Proposition 9. The more an individual keeps a record of his progress toward achieving goals to which he is committed, the more the newly formed motive is likely to influence his future thoughts and actions. These propositions are both related to what was called "pacing" in early studies of the psychology of work. That is, committing oneself to a specific goal and then comparing one's performance to that goal has been found to facilitate learning (cf. Kausler, 1959), though most studies of levels of aspiration have dealt with goal setting as a result rather than as a "cause" of performance. At any rate, the beneficial effect of concrete feedback on learning has been amply demonstrated by psychologists from Thorndike to Skinner. Among humans the feedback on performance is especially effective if they have high n Achievement (French, 1958), a fact which makes the relevance of our request for feedback obvious to the course participants.

The theoretical justification for these propositions is that in this way we are managing to keep the newly acquired associative network salient over the next 2 years. We are providing cues that will regularly rearouse it since he knows he is still part of an experimental training group which is supposed to show a certain type of behavior (Proposition 1 again). If the complex is rearoused sufficiently often back in the real world, we believe it is more likely to influence thought and action than if it is not aroused.

As described so far the course appears to be devoted almost wholly to cognitive learning. Yet this is only part of the story. The "teachers" are all clinically oriented psychologists who also try to practice whatever has been learned about the type of human relationship that most facilitates emotional learning. Both for practical and theoretical reasons this relationship is structured as warm, honest, and nonevaluative, somewhat in the manner described by Rogers (1961) and recommended by distinguished therapists from St. Ignatius[2] to Freud. That is to say, we insist that the only kind of change that can last or mean anything is what the person decides on and works out by himself, that we are there not to criticize his past behavior or direct his future choices, but to provide him with all sorts of information and emotional support that will help him in his self-confrontation. Since we recognize that self-study may be quite difficult and unsettling, we try to create an optimistic relaxed atmosphere in which the person is warmly encouraged in his efforts and given the opportunity for personal counseling if he asks for it.

Proposition 10. Changes in motives are more likely to occur in an interpersonal atmosphere in which the individual feels warmly but honestly supported and respected by others as a person capable of guiding and directing his own future behavior. Despite the widespread belief in this proposition among therapists (except for operant conditioners), one of the few studies that directly supports it has been conducted by Ends and Page (1957) who found that an objective learning-theory approach was less successful in treating chronic alcoholics than a person-oriented, client-centered approach. Rogers (1961) also summarizes other evidence that therapists who are warmer, more empathic, and genuine are more successful in their work. Hovland et al. (1953) report that the less manipulative the intent of a communicator, the greater the tendency to accept his conclusions. There is also the direct evidence that parents of boys with high n Achievement are warmer, more encouraging and less directive (fathers only) than parents of boys with low n Achievement (Rosen & D'Andrade, 1959). We tried to model ourselves after those parents on the theory that what is associated with high n Achievement in children might be most likely to encourage its development in adulthood. This does not mean permissiveness or promiscuous reinforcement of all kinds of behavior; it also means setting high standards as the parents of the boys with high n Achievement did but having the relaxed faith that the participants can achieve them.

The theoretical justification for this proposition can take two lines: Either one argues that this degree of challenge to the self-schema produces anxiety which needs to be reduced by warm support of the person for effective learning to take place, or one interprets the warmth as a form of direct reinforcement for change following the operant-conditioning model. Perhaps both factors are operating. Certainly there is ample evidence to support the view that anxiety interferes with learning (cf. Sarason, 1960) and that reward shapes behavior (cf. Bandura & Walters, 1963, pp. 283 ff.).

One other characteristic of the course leads to two further propositions. Efforts are made so far as possible to define it as an "experience apart," "an opportunity for self-study," or even a "spiritual retreat" (though that term can be used more acceptably in India than in the United States). So far as possible it is held in an isolated resort hotel or a hostel where there will be few distractions from the outside world and few other guests. This permits an atmosphere of total concentration on the objectives of the course including much informal talk outside the sessions about Ga+, Ga−, I+, and other categories in the coding definition. It still comes as a surprise to us to hear these terms suddenly in an informal group of participants talking away in Spanish or Telugu. The effect of this retreat from everyday life into a special and specially labeled experience appears to be twofold: It dramatizes or increases the salience of the new associative network and it tends to create a new reference group.

Proposition 11. Changes in motives are more likely to occur the more the setting dramatizes the importance of self-study and lifts it out of the routine of everyday life. So far as we know there is no scientific evidence to support this proposition, though again if one regards Jesuits as successful examples of personality change, the Order has frequently followed the advice of St. Ignatius to the effect that "the progress made in the Exercizes will be greater, the more the exercitant withdraws from all friends and acquaintances, and from all worldly cares." Theory supports the proposition in two respects: Removing the person from everyday routine (*a*) should decrease interfering associations (to say nothing of interfering appointments and social obligations), and (*b*) should heighten the salience of the experience by contrast with everyday life and make it harder to handle with the usual defenses ("just one more course," etc.). That is to say, the network of achievement-related associations can be more strongly and distinctly aroused in contrast to everyday life, making cognitive dissonance greater and therefore more in need of reduction by new learning. By the same token we have found that the dramatic quality of the experience cannot be sustained very long in a 12-18-hour-a-day schedule without a new routine attitude developing. Thus, we have found that a period somewhere between 6 to 14 days is optimal for this kind of "spiritual retreat." St. Ignatius sets an outside limit of 30 days, but this is when the schedule is less intensive (as ours has sometimes been), consisting of only a few hours a day over a longer period.

Proposition 12. Changes in motives are more likely to occur and persist if the new motive is a sign of membership in a new reference group. No principle of change has stronger empirical or historical support than this one. Endless studies have shown that people's opinions, attitudes, and beliefs are a function of their reference group and that different attitudes are likely to arise and be sustained primarily when the person moves into or affiliates with a new reference group (cf. Berelson & Steiner, 1963, pp. 580 ff.). Many theorists argue that the success of groups like Alcoholics Anonymous depends on the effectiveness with which the group is organized so that each person demonstrates his membership in it by "saving" another alcoholic. Political experience has demonstrated that membership in small groups like Communist or Nazi Party cells is one of the most effective ways to sustain changed attitudes and behavior.

Our course attempts to achieve this result (*a*) by the group experience in isolation—creating the feeling of alumni who all went through it together; (*b*) by certain signs of identification with the group, particularly the language of the coding system, but also including a certificate of membership; and (*c*) by arranging where possible to have participants come from the same community so that they can form a "cell" when they return that will serve as an immediate reference group to prevent gradual undermining of the new network by other pressures.

In theoretical terms a reference group should be effective because its members constantly provide cues to each other to rearouse the associative network, because they will also reward each other for achievement-related thoughts and acts, and because this constant mutual stimulation, and reinforcement, plus the labeling of the group, will prevent assimilation of the network to bigger, older, and stronger networks (such as those associated with traditional cultural values).

In summary, we have described an influence process which may be conceived in terms of "input," "intervening," and "output" variables as in Table 1. The propositions relate variables in Column A via their effect on the intervening variables in Column B to as yet loosely specified behavior in Column C, which may be taken as evidence that "development" of n Achievement has "really" taken place. The problems involved in evaluation of effects are as great and as complicated as those involved in designing the treatment, but they cannot be spelled out here, partly for lack of space, partly because we are in an even earlier stage of examining and classifying the effects of our training 1 and 2 years later preparatory to conceptualizing more clearly what happens. It will have to suffice to point out that we plan extensive comparisons over a 2-year period of the behaviors of our trained subjects compared with matched controls along the lines suggested in Column C.

What the table does is to give a brief overall view of how we conceptualize the educational or treatment process. What is particularly important is that the propositions refer to *operationally defined* and *separable* treatment variables. Thus, after having demonstrated hopefully a large effect of the total program, we can subtract a variable and see how much that decreases the impact of the course. That is to say, the course is designed so that it could go ahead perfectly reasonably with very

TABLE 1. Variables Conceived as Entering into the Motivation Change Process

A. Input or independent variables	B. Intervening variables	C. Output or dependent variables
1. Goal setting for the person (P1, P11)	Arousal of associative network (salience)	Duration and/or extensiveness of changes in:
2. Acquisition of n Achievement associative network (P2, P3, P4, P5)	Experiencing and labeling the associative network	1. n Achievement associative network
3. Relating new network to superordinate networks	Variety of cues to which network is linked	2. Related actions: use of feedback, moderate risk taking, etc.
reality (P2)	Interfering associations assimilated or bypassed by reproductive interference	3. Innovations (job improvements)
the self (P6)		4. Use of time and money
cultural values (P7)		5. Entrepreneurial success as defined by nature of job held and its rewards
4. Personal goal setting (P8)		
5. Knowledge of progress (P3, P4, P9)		
6. Personal warmth and support (P10)	Positive affect associated with network	
7. Support of reference group (P11, P12)		

Note.—P1, P11, etc. refer to the numbered propositions in the text.

little advanced goal setting (P1), with an objective rather than a warm personal atmosphere (P11), without the business game tying thought to action (P9), without learning to code n Achievement and write achievement-related stories (P3), without cultural value analysis (P7), or an isolated residential setting (P1, P11, P12). The study units are designed in a way that they can be omitted without destroying the viability of the treatment which has never been true of other studies of the psychotherapeutic process (cf. Rogers & Dymond, 1954).

But is there any basis for thinking the program works in practice? As yet, not enough time has elapsed to enable us to collect much data on long-term changes in personality and business activity. However, we do know that businessmen can learn to write stories scoring high in n Achievement, that they retain this skill over 1 year or 2, and that they like the course—but the same kinds of things can be said about many unevaluated management training courses. In two instances we have more objective data. Three courses were given to some 34 men from the Bombay area in early 1963. It proved possible to develop a crude but objective and reliable coding system to record whether each one had shown *unusual* entrepreneurial activity in the 2 years prior to the course or in the 2 years after course. "Unusual" here means essentially an unusual promotion or salary raise or starting a new business venture of some kind. Of the 30 on whom information was available in 1965, 27% had been unusually active before the course, 67% after the course ($x^2 = 11.2$, $p \ll .01$). In a control group chosen at random from those who applied for the course in 1963, out of 11 on whom information has so far been obtained, 18% were active before 1963, 27% since 1963.

In a second case, four courses were given throughout 1964 to a total of 52 small businessmen from the small city of Kakinada in Andhra Pradesh, India. Of these men, 25% had been unusually active in the 2-year period before the course, and 65% were unusually active immediately afterwards ($x^2 = 17.1$, $p \ll .01$). More control data and more refined measures are needed, but it looks very much as if, in India at least, we will be dealing with a spontaneous "activation" rate of only 25%—35% among entrepreneurs. Thus we have a distinct advantage over psychotherapists who are trying to demonstrate an improvement over a two-thirds spontaneous recovery rate. Our own data suggest that we will be unlikely to get an improvement or "activation" rate much above the two-thirds level commonly reported in therapy studies. That is, about one-third of the people in our courses have remained relatively unaffected. Nevertheless the two-thirds activated after the course represent a doubling of the normal rate of unusual entrepreneurial activity—no mean achievement in the light of the current pessimism among psychologists as to their ability to induce lasting personality change among adults.

One case will illustrate how the course seems to affect people in practice. A short time after participating in one of our courses in India, a 47-year-old businessman rather suddenly and dramatically decided to quit his excellent job and go into the construction business on his own in a big way. A man with some means of his own, he had had a very successful career as employee-relations manager for a large oil firm. His job involved adjusting management-employee difficulties, negotiating union contracts, etc. He was well-to-do, well thought of in his company, and admired in the community, but he was restless because he found his job increasingly boring. At the time of the course his original n Achievement score was not very high and he was thinking of retiring and living in England where his son was studying. In an interview, 8 months later, he said the course had served not so much to "motivate" him but to "crystallize" a lot of ideas he had vaguely or half consciously picked up about work and achievement all through his life. It provided him with a new language (he still talked in terms of standards of excellence, blocks, moderate risk, goal anticipation, etc.), a new construct which served to organize those ideas and explain to him why he was bored with his job, despite his obvious success. He decided he wanted to be an n-Achievement-oriented person, that he would be unhappy in retirement, and that he should take a risk, quit his job, and start in business on his own. He acted on his decision and in 6 months had drawn plans and raised over $1,000,000 to build the tallest building in his large city to be called the "Everest Apartments." He is extremely happy in his new activity because it means selling, promoting, trying to wangle scarce materials, etc. His first building is partway up and he is planning two more.

Even a case as dramatic as this one does not prove that the course produced the effect, despite his repeated use of the constructs he had learned, but what is especially interesting about it is that he described what had happened to him in exactly the terms the theory requires. He spoke not about a new motive force but about how existing ideas had been crystallized into a new associative network, and it is this new network which *is* the new "motivating" force according to the theory.

How generalizable are the propositions? They have purposely been stated generally so that some term like "attitude" or "personality characteristic" could be substituted for the term "motive" throughout, because we believe the propositions will hold for other personality variables. In fact, most of the supporting experimental evidence cited comes from attempts to change other characteristics. Nevertheless, the propositions should hold best more narrowly for motives and especially the achievement motive. One of the biggest difficulties in the way of testing them more generally is that not nearly as much is known about other human characteristics or their specific relevance for success in a certain type of work. For example, next to nothing is known about the need for power, its relation to success, let us say, in politics or bargaining situations, and its origins and course of development in the life history of individuals. It is precisely the knowledge we have about such matters for the achievement motive that puts us in a position to shape it for limited, socially and individually desirable ends. In the future, it seems to us, research in psychotherapy ought to follow a similar course. That is to say, rather than developing "all purpose" treatments, good for any person and any purpose, it should aim to develop specific treatments or educational programs built on laboriously accumulated detailed knowledge of the characteristic to be changed. It is in the spirit that the present research program in motive acquisition has been designed and is being tested out.

Notes

1. Parenthetically, we have found several times that our stated desire to evaluate the effectiveness of our course created doubts in the minds of our sponsors that they did not feel about many popular courses for managers that no one has ever evaluated or plans to evaluate. An attitude of inquiry is not always an asset in education. It suggests one is not sure of his ground.
2. In his famous spiritual exercises which have played a key role in producing and sustaining personality change in the Jesuit Order, St. Ignatius states: "The director of the Exercizes ought not to urge the exercitant more to poverty or any promise than to the contrary, nor to one state of life or way of living more than another . . . [while it is proper to urge people outside the Exercizes] the director of the Exercizes . . . without leaning to one side or the other, should permit the Creator to deal directly with the creature, and the creature directly with his Creator and Lord."

References

Allport, G. W. The ego in contemporary psychology. *Psychological Review*, 1943, 50, 451-478.

Andrews, J. D. W. The achievement motive in two types of organizations. *Journal of Personality and Social Psychology*, 1965, in press.

Atkinson, J. W. (Ed.) *Motives in fantasy, action and society.* Princeton, N. J.: Van Nostrand, 1958.

Bandura, A., & Walters, R. H. *Social learning and personality development.* New York: Holt, Rinehart & Winston, 1963.

Bauer, R. A. The obstinate audience: The influence process from the point of view of social communication. *American Psychologist*, 1964, 19, 310-329.

Benedict, Ruth. *The chrysanthemum and the sword.* Boston: Houghton Mifflin, 1946.

Berelson, B., & Steiner, G. A. *Human Behavior: An inventory of scientific findings.* New York: Harcourt, Brace, 1964.

Brown, R. W. *Words and things.* Glencoe, Ill.: Free Press, 1958.

Burris, R. W. The effect of counseling on achievement motivation. Unpublished doctoral dissertation, University of Indiana, 1958.

Ends, E. J., & Page, C. W. A study of three types of group psychotherapy with hospitalized male inebriates *Quarterly Journal on Alcohol*, 1957, 18, 263-277.

Eysenck, H. J. The effects of psychotherapy: An evaluation. *Journal of Consulting Psychology*, 1952, 16, 319-324.

Festinger, L. *A theory of cognitive dissonance.* New York: Harper & Row, 1957.

Frank, J. *Persuasion and healing.* Baltimore: Johns Hopkins Press, 1961.

French, E. G. Effects of the interaction of motivation and feedback on task performance. In J. W. Atkinson (Ed.), *Motives in fantasy, action and society.* Princeton, N. J.: Van Nostrand, 1958. Pp. 400-408.

Heckhausen, H. Eine Rahmentheorie der Motivation in zehn Thesen. *Zeitschrift für experimentelle und angewandte Psychologie*, 1963, X/4, 604-626.

Hovland, C. I. Human learning and retention. In S. S. Stevens (Ed.), *Handbook of experimental psychology.* New York: Wiley, 1951.

Hovland, C. I., Janis, I. L., & Kelley, H. H. *Communication and persuasion: Psychological studies of opinion change.* New Haven: Yale Univer. Press, 1953.

Kausler, D. H. Aspiration level as a determinant of performance. *Journal of Personality*, 1959, 27, 346-351.

Kelley, G. A. *The psychology of personal constructs.* New York: Norton, 1955.

Korzybski, A. *Science and sanity.* Lancaster, Pa.: Science Press, 1941.

McClelland, D. C. *The achieving society.* Princeton, N. J.: Van Nostrand, 1961.

McClelland, D. C. *The roots of consciousness.* Princeton, N. J.: Van Nostrand, 1964.

McClelland, D. C., Atkinson, J. W., Clark, R. A., & Lowell, E. L. *The achievement motive.* New York: Appleton-Century, 1953.

McGeoch, J. A., & Irion, A. L. *The psychology of human learning.* (2nd ed.) New York: Longmans, Green, 1952.

Mierke, K. *Wille und Leistung.* Göttingan: Verlag für Psychologie, 1955.

Orne, M. On the social psychology of the psychological experiment: With particular reference, to demand characteristics and their implications. *American Psychologist*, 1962, 17, 776-783.

Roethlisberger, F. J., & Dickson, W. J. *Management and the worker.* Cambridge: Harvard Univer. Press, 1947.

Rogers, C. R. *On becoming a person.* Boston: Houghton Mifflin, 1961.

Rogers, C.R., & Dymond, R. F. (Eds.) *Psychotherapy and personality change.* Chicago: Univer. Press, 1954.

Rosen, B. C., & D'Andrade, R. G. The psychosocial origins of achievement motivation. *Sociometry*, 1959, 22, 185-218.

Rosenthal, R. On the social psychology of the psychological experiment: The experimenter's hypothesis as unintended determinant of experimental results. *American Scientist*, 1963, 51, 268-283.

Sarason, I. Empirical findings and theoretical problems. 1960, 57, 403-416.

INEQUITY IN SOCIAL EXCHANGE

J. STACY ADAMS

Introduction

Philosophers, political scientists, politicians, jurists, and economists traditionally have been the ones concerned with the just distribution of wealth, power, goods, and services in society. Social psychologists and their brethren, with the notable exceptions of Blau (1964), Homans (1961), and Thibaut and Kelley (1959), have displayed remarkably little professional interest in this, despite the fact that the process of exchange is almost continual in human interactions. They have, of course, studied social behavior involving reciprocal, as distinguished from unilateral, transactions, but their sights have been focused on the amount and content of communications; attitudinal, affective, motivational, perceptual, and behavioral changes; changes in group structure, leadership, and so on, rather than on exchange proper. Yet, the process of exchange appears to have characteristics peculiar to itself and to generate affect, motivation, and behavior that cannot be predicted unless exchange processes are understood.

A distinguishing characteristic of exchange processes is that their resultants have the potentiality of being perceived as just or unjust. But what are the consequences of outcomes being perceived as meeting or not meeting the norms of justice? Nearly all the attention given to this question has been to establish a relationship between perceived injustice and dissatisfaction (Homans, 1950, 1953, 1961; Jaques, 1956, 1961a; Patchen, 1959, 1961; Stouffer *et al.*, 1949; Vroom, 1964; Zaleznik *et al.*, 1958). Not surprisingly, this has been accomplished with success. Does a man treated unfairly simply express dissatisfaction? Are there not other consequences of unfair exchanges? What behavior is predictable? These questions and related ones are a principal concern of this paper.

Rather than simply present a theory from which the behavior of persons engaged in a social exchange may be deduced, the plan of this chapter is to present first in chronological order two major concepts relating to the perception of justice and injustice. First is the concept of relative deprivation and the complementary concept of relative gratification, developed by Stouffer and his associates (1949). Homans' highly elaborated concept of distributive justice (1961) will be discussed next. These will then be integrated into a theory of inequity from which it will be possible to specify the antecedents and consequences of injustice in human exchanges.

Relative Deprivation

Following World War II, the publication of the first *American Soldier* volume by Stouffer and his colleagues (1949) excited interest among sociologists and social

Reprinted by permission of the author and the publisher, Academic Press, Inc., from *Advances in Experimental Psychology*, L. Berkowitz, ed. (1965).

psychologists. The effect was at least in part due to the introduction of a new concept, relative deprivation, used by the authors to explain what were seemingly paradoxical findings. According to Merton and Kitt (1950), the formal status of the concept was that of an intervening variable which explained the observed relationship between an independent variable, such as education level or rate of promotion, and a dependent variable, such as satisfaction with some aspect of Army life.

Relative deprivation was not formally defined by the authors, however, nor by Merton and Kitt (1950), who analyzed in great detail the implication of the concept for sociological theory in general and for reference group theory in particular. The essential meaning of the concept may be inferred from two illustrations of its use by the authors of *The American Soldier*. Despite the objective fact that soldiers with a high school education had better opportunities for advancement in the Army, high school graduates were not as satisfied with their status and jobs as were less educated men. This apparent paradox is explained by assuming that the better-educated men had higher levels of aspiration, partly based on what would be realistic status expectations in civilian life, and that they were, therefore, relatively deprived of status and less satisfied with the status they achieved. It may be noted that the validity of this explanation depends upon showing that level of aspiration is greater than status achieved among high school graduates as contrasted to soldiers with less education. While this is not demonstrated by the authors, it appears to be a credible assumption. It is the relative deprivation, then, that accounts for less satisfaction among better-educated men.

A second illustrative use of relative deprivation is made by the authors of *The American Soldier* in accounting for the puzzling fact that Army Air Corps men were less satisfied with promotion opportunities than were men in the Military Police, even though objective opportunities for mobility were vastly greater in the Air Corps. Relative deprivation is invoked to explain the anomaly as follows: The high promotion rate in the Air Corps induces high expectations of mobility; lower-ranking and low-mobile men, compared to high-ranking and high-mobile men, feel deprived in the face of their expectations and express dissatisfaction. Among military policemen, on the other hand, expectations of promotion are low, and the fate of most policemen is quite similar: namely, low rank. In sum, there is a discrepancy between expectation and achievement among Air Corps enlisted men and little or no discrepancy between expectation and achievement among men in the Military Police. The discrepancy results in dissatisfaction with mobility. Or more precisely, the assumed existence of a discrepancy between expectation and achievement is held to account for the empirical observation that men were less satisfied in one branch than in the other.

Spector (1956), in an experiment directly related to these findings by Stouffer *et al.*, varied perceived probability of promotion and fulfillment and tested the hypothesis that "*on failing to achieve* an attractive goal, an individual's morale will be higher if the probability of achieving the goal had been perceived to be low than if it had been perceived to be high" (p. 52). He found that the high expectations-nonpromotion group had lower morale and was less satisfied with the promotion system than was the low expectations-nonpromotion group, thus corroborating experimentally the military survey findings. Comparable findings have been made by Gebhard (1949).

The effects of relative deprivation (the unfair violation of expectations) upon sociometric choices are clearly shown in an experiment designed by Thibaut (1950) to learn about the conditions that affect group cohesiveness. Underprivileged boys from camps and settlement houses in the Boston area participated in the experiment in groups of 10 to 12 boys, all of whom had known, played, and lived with one another for some time. After filling out a questionnaire in which they were asked to rank the four boys they would most like to have on their team to play games if their groups were to be divided, the boys in each group were split into two teams of five or six. Thibaut formed each team so that each boy would have about an equal number of preferred and of nonpreferred partners and so that each team would be composed of approximately the same number of popular, or *central,* and less popular, or *peripheral,* boys in terms of sociometric choices received. Although there were several experimental conditions in his study, only one of them concerns us here. This is the condition in which each set of two teams played four games and one of the pairs was given consistently an inferior, menial, uninteresting, or unpleasant role during the series of games. These were the *low-status* teams (called "unsuccessful low-status" by Thibaut).

Following the last game, each boy answered a questionnaire in which he was again asked to order his preferences for teammates. A general finding was that a boy tended to shift his sociometric choices after the games to boys who had actually been teammates. Of greater interest here is the fact that low-status *central* boys were more likely to display such shifts than were low-status *peripheral* boys. The former were popular boys, presumably aware of their status among their fellows, who were forced to assume low-status roles in violation of the roles they would customarily play. The role of the low-status peripheral boys, on the other hand, were more or less a confirmation of their relatively low popularity among their friends. Compared to the peripheral boys, then, the central boys were relatively deprived, and they manifested their greater dissatisfaction with their fate by shifting to a greater extent their sociometric choices from central boys on the opposing team to boys on their own team. Thibaut also reports evidence that the low-status central boys displayed exceptional hostility to members of the opposing (high-status) teams and that all low-status boys keenly felt the injustice of their fate.

These findings are of especial interest because they cannot be accounted for simply on the hypothesis that abuse or minority group membership will result in withdrawal and increased cohesiveness. Such a hypothesis would have required that low-status peripheral and central boys show the same behavior. But, as noted, central boys were more likely to shift their sociometric choices and to display overt hostility to opponents. They were the ones who suffered the greater relative deprivation.

The studies that have been described form an interesting set. In the data from the surveys by Stouffer *et al.* (1949), there is no empirical evidence of relative deprivation. None of the soldiers or airmen were asked, for example, if specific expectations were violated or, more directly, if they felt relatively deprived with respect to status. Relative deprivation was used, ex post facto, to explain anomalous findings. The concept had no existential character; it was a hypothetical construct—rather than an intervening variable, as Merton and Kitt classified it (1950). The Spector (1956) experiment, by manipulating expectations of promotions and achievement, created a condition of relative deprivation. Thus, operationally, relative deprivation took on the status of a variable, an independent variable, variations in which were related to variations in "morale." In another laboratory experiment, Thibaut (1950) created conditions of relative deprivation, which were not any the less real for having been created unintentionally by his manipulations of group status and group success. In this respect his experiment is analogous to Spector's. But the nature of his experimental task allowed a very broad range of behavior to be displayed spontaneously. As a result there was direct evidence of feelings of injustice in reaction to the manipulation of relative deprivation, as well as of dissatisfactiòn, hostility, withdrawal, and changes in sociometric choices. Thus, proceeding from the military surveys to the Thibaut experiment, a useful construct emerges, receives experimental support, and its meaning becomes elaborated.

Bearing this and the survey and experimental data described earlier in mind, there emerge certain conclusions. First, it seems that manifest dissatisfaction and other behavior are responses to acutely felt injustice, rather than directly to relative deprivation. Relative deprivation is a condition occurring naturalistically or an experimental manipulation which elicits feelings of injustice. In turn, feelings of injustice trigger expressions of dissatisfaction and, in addition, the kind of behavior exhibited by Thibaut's juvenile subjects. Injustice, then, may be said to mediate the effects of relative deprivation. A second conclusion is that what is just is based upon relatively strong expectations, such as that educational achievement will be correlated with job status achievement and that one will be promoted at about the same rate as one's fellows, or that the role one plays in one situation—in laboratory games—will be in line and with the role one usually assumes—in the settlement house or camp.

Thirdly, it is clear that a comparative process is inherent in the development of expectations and the perception of injustice, as implied by the term *relative* deprivation. Well-educated men felt unfairly treated in comparison to the treatment they would have received in civilian life or in comparison to the treatment civilians did receive. Injustice was suffered by unpromoted or less-mobile airmen in relation to the general mobility of men in the Air Corps, whereas there was no such felt injustice among low-mobile military policemen when they compared their rate of promotion to the low promotion rate prevalent in the Military Police.

A particularly felicitous additional example of the process of comparison and its importance is provided by Sayles (1958). He notes that ". . . foundries are often hot spots, highly aggressive in seeking fulfillment of their demands where they are part of larger manufacturing organizations. However, when the plant is entirely devoted to the foundry operation, they are relatively weak and inactive" (p. 104). Foundry workers are highly paid to compensate for the unpleasant work conditions and the high physical exertion required and because of a short labor supply in this skill area. Other workers, however, rank foundry operators quite low and look down on them, according to Sayles. Thus, when foundry employees are present for purposes of comparison, other workers feel relatively deprived as regards earnings, and the resulting dissatisfaction may take hostile forms. Conversely, the foundry workers, being the butt of the despisement of others, may react by being unusually assertive and demanding.

Finally, it may be noted, if it is not obvious, that felt injustice is a response to a *discrepancy* between what is perceived to be and what is perceived should be.

In the illustrative cases taken from *The American Soldier* and from the Spector and Thibaut experiments, it is a response to a discrepancy between an achievement and an expectation of achievement.

Distributive Justice

The existence of relative deprivation necessarily raises the question of distributive justice, or of the fair share-out of rewards; for, as noted earlier, deprivation is perceived relationally. The concept is not new, having been explored by political philosophers and others from the time of Aristotle. In the hands of Homans (1950, 1953, 1961) and of his colleagues (Zaleznik *et al.*, 1958), the concept of distributive justice has taken on the articulated character of what may be more properly called a theory. As fully developed by Homans (1961), it is a theory employing quasi-economic terms. According to him, distributive justice among men who are in an exchange relationship with one another obtains when the profits of each are proportional to their investments. Profit consists of that which is received up in the exchange, such as foregoing the rewards obtainable in another exchange, or a burden assumed as a specific function of the exchange, such as a risk, which would include not only potential real loss but the psychological discomfort of uncertainty as well. Investments in an exchange are the relevant attributes that are brought by a party to the exchange. They include, for example, skill, effort, education, training, experience, age, sex and ethnic background.

Schematically, for a dyad consisting of A and B, distributive justice between them is realized when :

$$\frac{\text{A's rewards less A's costs}}{\text{A's investments}} = \frac{\text{B's rewards less B's costs}}{\text{B's investments}}$$

When an inequality between the proportions exists, the participants to the exchange will experience a feeling of injustice and one or the other party will experience deprivation. The party specifically experiencing relative deprivation is the one for whom the ratio of profits to investments is the smaller.

Making explicit that it is the relation between *ratios* of profits to investments that results in felt justice or injustice is a distinct contribution that takes us beyond the concept of relative deprivation. To be sure, an individual may feel deprived, but he feels deprived not merely because his rewards or profits are less than he expected or felt was fair. Many men, when comparing their rewards to those of another, will perceive that their rewards are smaller, and yet they will not feel that this state of affairs is unjust. The reason is that persons obtaining the higher rewards are perceived as deserving them. That is, their rewards are greater because their investments are greater. Thus, for example, if being of the male sex is perceived as a higher investment than being of the female sex, a woman operator earning less than a man doing the same work will not feel unjustly treated. The proportionality of profits to investments is comparable for the woman and for the man. Similarly, a young instructor usually does not feel that his rewards, low as they may be, compare unfairly with those of an associate professor in his department. As Homans notes, "Justice is a curious mixture of equality within inequality" (1961, p. 244).

The theory of distributive justice also addresses itself to the case of two or more persons, each of whom receives his rewards from a third party: an employer, for example. In such an instance, each of the persons is in an exchange with the employer, as in the simple dyadic situation discussed; but, in addition, each man will expect that the employer will maintain a fair ratio of rewards to investments between himself and other men. This, of course, is the perennial dilemma of employers, and it almost defies a perfect solution, though it is capable of better solutions than are often developed. One difficulty with finding neat solutions is that A's perception of his rewards, costs, and investments are not necessarily identical with B's perception of A's situation. To complicate matters, two persons, though they might agree as to what their investments are, may disagree as to the weight each investment should be given. Should age count more than sex? Should education be given as much weight as job experience? The psychometrics of this have not yet received much attention.

The relationship of distributive justice to satisfaction is treated only briefly by Homans, but it is nevertheless the subject of a formal theoretical proposition. If a state of injustice exists and it is to a man's disadvantage—that is, the man experiences deprivation—he will "display the emotional behavior we call anger" (Homans, 1961, p. 75). Here Homans is overly influenced by Skinnerian rhetoric. He means, plainly, that dissatisfaction will be felt or expressed. If, on the other hand, distributive justice fails of realization and is, to an observer at least, to a man's advantage, he will feel guilty. This aspect of the proposition is more novel and is substantiated by observations by Jaques (1956, 1961a) and by laboratory experiments by Adams (1963a) that will be discussed later. Homans also implies that the thresholds for displaying dissatisfaction and guilt are different when he remarks that ". . . he (the guilty man) is less apt to make a prominent display of his guilt than of his anger" (1961, p. 76). This suggestion, also made by Adams (1963a) and deducible from observations made by Jaques (1956), implies that distributive justice must fail of realization to a greater extent when it is favorable to an individual before he reacts than when it is to his disadvantage.

Others have stated formal propositions that obviously refer to the same phenomena as encompassed by the theory of distributive justice. The propositions listed by two writers are especially noteworthy because they were expressed in terms similar to those of Homans. Sayles (1958, p. 98), discussing the manifestation of dissatisfaction in industrial work groups, surmised that factory workers "compute" the fairness of their wages as follows:

$$\frac{\text{Our importance in the plant}}{\text{Any other group's importance}} = \frac{\text{Our earnings}}{\text{Their earnings}}$$

When the equality obtains, satisfaction is experienced. An inequality between the ratios causes pressures for redress, accompanied by dissatisfaction. "Importance in the plant" may be taken as equivalent to the perceived investments of group members, including skills and type of work performed, length of service, and such. This is made explicit in his model of the "economic world of the worker in his work group.'' According to this analysis, men are portrayed as comparing their jobs to other jobs and asking the questions, "Are these higher paying jobs actually more skilled than our own?" and "Do we earn *enough more* than the lower rated jobs to compensate for the skill difference?" (Sayles, 1958, p. 105). The term "earnings" is, of course, comparable to Homans' rewards but is a less comprehensive term, excluding other outcomes such as intrinsic job rewards. It also subsumes less than the concept of profit or net reward, since it makes no provision for negative outcomes or costs, such as unfavorable work conditions or tyrannical supervision. Nevertheless, it is clear that Sayles conceives of justice as being a function of the perceived equality of ratios of investments and of rewards.

Using the terms of Festinger's theory of cognitive dissonance (1957), Patchen postulates that workers making wage comparisons make a cognitive relation of the following type (1961, p. 9):

$$\frac{\text{My pay}}{\text{His (their) pay}} \quad \text{compared to} \quad \frac{\text{My position on dimensions related to pay}}{\text{His (their) position on dimensions related to pay}}$$

This formulation is similar to Sayles' but more explicit, for dimensions related to pay are specified as being attributes such as skill, education, and seniority. These are clearly the same as Homans' investments. Patchen differs somewhat from Homans in his conceptualization, however, in that he also includes job interest among his "dimensions" related to pay. This is not so much an investment as it is a reward, either with positive or negative valence. When, according to Patchen, an inequality results from the comparison of the two proportions, cognitive dissonance is experienced. In turn, dissatisfaction is manifested. However, dissonance and the attendant dissatisfaction are not necessarily a bad state of affairs from the point of view of the individual. Patchen points this out in an interesting departure from dissonance theory. Although consonant comparisons may be satisfying, they provide no basis for mobility aspirations, whereas dissonant comparisons unfavorable to the person permit a man to think that he is more deserving, that he merits higher pay or status. In effect, then, Patchen suggests that the motivation to attain consonance may be dominated by achievement motivation, and that under these circumstances dissatisfaction resulting from dissonant comparisons may be tolerated. Parenthetically, it may be pointed out that the pitting of these two motivations may partially explain why researchers have been unable to replicate some experiments that offered support for dissonance predictions (see Conlon, 1965, for example).

Relative deprivation and distributive justice, as theoretical concepts, specify some of the conditions that arouse perceptions of injustice and, complementarily, the conditions that lead men to feel that their relations with others are just. But they fail to specify theoretically what are the consequences of felt injustice, other than dissatisfaction. To be sure, Sayles (1958) mentions the use of grievance procedures and strikes to force redress, Homans (1961) cites a study by Clark (1958) in which a female employee reported slowing her pace of work as a means of establishing a more just relation with a co-worker, and Patchen (1961) gives evidence of dissonance reduction when wage comparisons are dissonant. However, these are more or less anecdotal and are not an articulated part of a theory. Men do not simply become dissatisfied with conditions they perceive to be unjust. They usually do something about them. In what follows, then, a theory will be developed that will specify both the antecedents of perceived injustice and its consequences. It is not a new theory. There are already too many "little" theories in social psychology. Rather, it builds upon the work previously described, and, in addition, derives a number of major propositions from Festinger's theory of cognitive dissonance (1957).

Inequity

In what follows it is hoped that a fairly comprehensive theory of inequity will be elaborated. The term *inequity* is used instead of *injustice* first, because the author has used this term before (Adams and Rosenbaum, 1962; Adams, 1963a,b, 1965; Adams and Jacobsen, 1964), second, to avoid the confusion of the many connotative meanings associated with the term *justice,* and third, to emphasize that the primary concern is with the causes and consequences of the absence of equity in human exchange relationships. In developing the theory, major variables affecting perceptions of inequity in an exchange will be described. A formal definition of inequity will then be proposed. From this point the effects of inequity upon behavior and cognitive processes will be discussed and research giving evidence of the effects will be presented. For heuristic purposes employee-employer exchanges will be a focus because such relations are within the experience of almost everyone and constitute a significant aspect of human intercourse. Moreover, much empirical research relating to inequity has been undertaken in business and industrial spheres or in simulated employment situations. It should be evident, however, that the theoretical notions offered are quite as relevant to any social situation in which an exchange takes place, explicitly or implicitly, whether between teammates, teacher and student, lovers, child and parent, patient and therapist, or opponents or even enemies, for between all there are expectations of what is fair exchange.

Antecedents of Inequity

Whenever two individuals exchange anything, there is the possibility that one or both of them will feel that the exchange was inequitable. Such is frequently the case when a man exchanges his services for pay. On the man's side of the exchange are his education, intelligence, experience, training, skill, seniority, age, sex, ethnic background, social status, and, of course, the effort he expends on the job. Under special circumstances other attributes will be relevant. These may be personal appearance or attractiveness, health, possession of certain tools, the characteristics of one's spouse, and so on. They are what a man perceives as his contributions to the exchange, for which he expects a just return. As noted earlier, these are the same as Homans' (1961) investments. A man brings them into an exchange, and henceforth they will be referred to as his *inputs*. These inputs, let us emphasize, are *as perceived by their contributor* and are not necessarily isomorphic with those perceived by the other party to the exchange. This suggests two conceptually distinct characteristics of inputs, *recognition* and *relevance*.

The possessor of an attribute, or the other party to the exchange, or both, may recognize the existence of the attribute in the possessor. If either the possessor or both members of the exchange recognize its existence, the attribute has the potentiality of being an input. If only the nonpossessor recognizes its existence, it cannot be considered psychologically an input so far as the possessor is concerned. Whether or not an attribute having the potential of being an input is in fact an input is contingent upon the possessor's perception of its relevance to the exchange. If he perceives it to be relevant, if he expects a just return for it, it is an input. Problems of inequity arise if only the possessor of the attribute considers it relevant to the exchange, or if the other party to the exchange considers it irrelevant and acts accordingly. Thus, unless prohibited from doing so by contract terms, an employer may consider seniority irrelevant in granting promotions, thinking it wiser to consider merit alone, whereas the employee may believe that seniority is highly relevant. In consequence, the employee may feel that injustice has been done. Conversely, the employer who is compelled to use seniority rather than merit as a promotion criterion may well feel that he has been forced into an inequitable exchange. In a personal communication Crozier (1960) made a relevant observation. Paris-born bank clerks worked side by side with clerks who did identical work and earned identical wages but who were born in the provinces. The Parisians were dissatisfied with their wages, for they considered that a Parisian upbringing was an input deserving recognition. The bank management, although recognizing that place of birth distinguished the two groups, did not, of course, consider birthplace relevant in the exchange of services for pay.

The principal inputs that have been listed vary in type and in their degree of relationship to one another. Some variables such as age are clearly continuous; others, such as sex and ethnicity, are not. Some are intercorrelated: seniority and age, for example. Sex, on the other hand, is largely independent of the other variables, with the possible exception of education and some kinds of effort. Although these intercorrelations, or the lack of them, exist in a state of nature, it is probable that the individual cognitively treats all input variables as independent. Thus, for example, if he were assessing the sum of his inputs, he might well "score" age and seniority separately. It is as if he thought, "I am older and have been with Acme longer than Joe," without taking account of the fact that the two attributes are correlated. This excursion into the "black box" should not imply, as Homans (1961) seems to imply, that men assess various components of an exchange on an ordinal scale. If the work of Jaques on equitable payment (1956, 1961a) is taken at face value, there is reason to believe in this respect that men employ interval and ratio scales, or that, at the very least, they are capable of making quite fine ordinal discriminations.

On the other side of an exchange are an individual's receipts. These *outcomes*, as they will be termed, include in an employee-employer exchange pay, rewards intrinsic to the job, satisfying supervision, seniority benefits, fringe benefits, job status and status symbols, and a variety of formally and informally sanctioned perquisites, such as the right of a higher-status person to park his car in a privileged location. These are examples of positively valent outcomes. But outcomes may have negative valence. Poor working conditions, monotony, fate uncertainty, and the many "dissatisfiers" listed by Herzberg *et al.* (1959) are no less "received" than, say, wages and are negatively valent. They would be avoided, rather than approached, if it were possible. As in the case of job inputs, job outcomes are often intercorrelated. For example, greater pay and higher job status are likely to go hand-in-hand.

In other than employee-employer exchanges, though they are not precluded from these exchanges, relevant positive outcomes for one or both parties may consist of affection, love, formal courtesies, expressions of friendship, fair value (as in merchandise), and reliability (as part of the purchase of a service). Insult, rudeness, and rejection are the other side of the coin. It may be noted that in a vast array of social relations reciprocity is a functional element of the relation. What is in fact referred to by reciprocity is equality of exchange. The infinitive "to reciprocate" is commonly used to denote an obligation to give someone equal, positively valent outcomes in return for outcomes received. When a housewife says, "John, we must have the Browns over, to reciprocate," she means to maintain a social relationship by reestablishing a parity in the outcomes of the two families. In this connection, it can be observed that reciprocation is usually "in kind." That is, there is a deliberate effort to match outcomes, to give equal value for value received. People who undershoot or overshoot the mark are called "cheapskates" or "uppish" and pretentious, respectively.

In a manner analogous to inputs, outcomes are *as perceived,* and, again, they should be characterized in terms of recognition and relevance. If the recipient or both the recipient and giver of an outcome in an exchange recognize its existence, it has the potentiality of being an outcome psychologically. If the recipient considers it relevant to the exchange and it has some marginal utility for him, it *is* an outcome. Not infrequently the giver may give or yield something which, though of some cost to him, is either irrelevant or of no marginal utility to the recipient. An employer may give an employee a carpet for his office in lieu, say, of a salary increment and find that the employee is dissatisfied, perhaps because in the subculture of that office a rug has no meaning, no psychological utility. Conversely, a salary increment may be inadequate, if formalized status recognition was what was wanted and what had greater utility. Or, in another context, the gift of a toy to a child may be effectively irrelevant as reciprocation for a demonstration of affection on his part is he seeks affection. Fortunately, in the process of socialization, through the reinforcing behavior of others and of the "verbal community" (Skinner, 1957), the human organism learns not only what is appropriate reciprocation, but he learns also to assess the marginal utility of a variety of outcomes to others. In the absence of this ability, interpersonal relations would be chaotic, if not impossible. An idea of the problems that would exist may be had by observing travelers in a foreign culture. Appropriate or relevant reciprocation of outcomes is difficult, even in such mundane exchanges as tipping for services.

In classifying some variables as inputs and others as outcomes, it is not implied that they are independent, except conceptually. Inputs and outcomes are, in fact, intercorrelated, but imperfectly so. Indeed, it is because they are imperfectly correlated that there need be concern with inequity. There exist normative expectations of what constitute "fair" correlations between inputs and outcomes. The expectations are formed—learned—during the process of socialization, at home, at school, at work. They are based by observation of the correlations obtaining for a reference person or group—a co-worker or a colleague, a relative or neighbor, a group of co-workers, a craft group, an industry-wide pattern. A bank clerk, for example, may determine whether her outcomes and inputs are fairly correlated, in balance so to speak, by comparing them with the ratio of the outcomes to the inputs of other female clerks in her section. The sole punch-press operator in a manufacturing plant may base his judgment on what he believes are the inputs and outcomes of other operators in the community or region. For a particular professor the relevant reference group may be professors in the same discipline and of the same academic "vintage." While it is clearly important to be able to specify theoretically the appropriate reference person or group, this will not be done here, as the task is beyond the scope of the paper and is discussed by others (e.g., Festinger, 1954; Hyman, 1942; Merton and Kitt, 1950; Patchen, 1961). For present purposes, it will be assumed that the reference person or group will be one comparable to the comparer on one or more attributes. This is usually a co-worker in industrial situations, according to Livernash (1953), but, as Sayles (1958) points out, this generalization requires verification, as plausible as it may appear.

When the normative expectations of the person making social comparisons are violated, when he finds that his outcomes and inputs are not in balance in relation to those of others, feelings of inequity result. But before a formal definition of inequity is offered, two terms of reference will be introduced to facilitate later discussion, *Person* and *Other*. *Person* is any individual for whom equity or inequity exists. *Other* is any individual with whom Person is in an exchange relationship, or with whom Person compares himself when both he and Other are in an exchange relationship with a third party, such as an employer, or with third parties who are considered by Person as being comparable, such as employers in a particular industry or geographic location. Other is usually a different individual, but may be Person in another job or in another social role. Thus, Other might be Person in a job he held previously, in which case he might compare his present and past outcomes and inputs and determine whether or not the exchange with his employer, present or past, was equitable. The terms Person and Other may also refer to groups rather than to individuals, as when a class of jobs (e.g., toolmakers) is out of line with another class (e.g., lathe operators), or when the circumstances of one ethnic group are incongruous with those of another. In such cases, it is convenient to deal with the class as a whole rather than with individual members of the class.

Definition of Inequity

Inequity exists for Person whenever he perceives that the ratio of his outcomes to inputs and the ratio of Other's outcomes to Other's inputs are unequal. This may happen either (a) when he and Other are in a direct exchange relationship or (b) when both are in an exchange relationship with a third party and Person compares himself to Other. The values of outcomes and inputs are, of course, as perceived by Person. Schematically, inequality is experienced when either

$$\frac{O_p}{I_p} < \frac{O_a}{I_a} \quad \text{or} \quad \frac{O_p}{I_p} > \frac{O_a}{I_a},$$

Where $O = \Sigma_{oi}$, $I = \Sigma_{oi}$ and p and a are subscripts denoting Person and Other, respectively. A condition of equity exists when

$$\frac{O_p}{I_p} = \frac{O_a}{I_a}.$$

The outcomes and inputs in each of the ratios are conceived as being the sum of such outcomes and inputs as are perceived to be relevant to a particular exchange. Furthermore, each sum is conceived of as a weighted sum, on the assumption that individuals probably do not weight elemental outcomes or inputs equally. The work of Herzberg *et al.* (1959) on job "satisfiers" and "dissatisfiers" implies strongly that different outcomes, as they are labeled here, have widely varying utilities, negative as well as positive. It also appears reasonable to assume that inputs as diverse as seniority, skill, effort, and sex are not weighted equally. Zaleznik *et al.* (1958), in attempting to test some predictions from distributive justice theory in an industrial corporation, gave equal weight to five factors which correspond to inputs as defined here—age, seniority, education, ethnicity, and sex—but were unable to sustain their hypotheses. In retrospect, they believe (Zaleznik *et al.*, 1958) that weighting these inputs equally may have represented an inadequate assumption of the manner in which their respondents summed their inputs.

From the definition of inequity it follows that inequity results for Person not only when he is, so to speak, relatively underpaid, but also when he is relatively overpaid. Person, will, for example, feel inequity exists not only when his effort is high and his pay low, while Other's effort and pay are high, but also when his effort is low and his pay high, while Other's effort and pay are low. This proposition receives direct support from experiments by Adams and Rosenbaum (1962), Adams (1963a), and Adams and Jacobsen (1964) in which subjects were inequitably overpaid. It receives some support also from an observation by Thibaut (1950) that subjects in whose favor the experimenter discriminated displayed "guilty smirks" and "sheepishness." The magnitude of the inequity experienced will be a monotomically increasing function of the size of the discrepancy between the ratios of outcomes to inputs. The discrepancy will be zero, and equity will exist, under two circumstances: first, when Person's and Other's outcomes are equal and their inputs are equal. This would be the case, for example, when Person perceived that Other's wages, job, and working conditions were the same as his and that Other was equal to him on such relevant dimensions as sex, skill, seniority, education, age, effort expended, physical fitness, and risk incurred (risk of personal injury, of being fired for errors committed, for instance). Secondly, the ratios will be equal when Person perceives that Other's outcomes are higher (or lower) than his and that Other's inputs are correspondingly higher (or lower). A subordinate who compares himself to his supervisor or work group leader typically does not feel that he is unjustly treated by the company that employs them both, because the supervisor's greater monetary compensation, better working conditions, and more interesting, more varied job are matched on the input side of the ratio by more education, wider range of skills, greater responsibility and personal risk, more maturity and experience, and longer service.

Although there is no direct, reliable evidence on this point, it is probable, as Homans (1961) conjectured, that the thresholds for inequity are different (in absolute terms from a base of equity) in cases of under- and overreward. The threshold would be higher presumably in cases of overreward, for a certain amount of incongruity in these cases can be acceptably rationalized as "good fortune" without attendant discomfort. In his work on pay differentials, Jaques (1961b) notes that in instances of undercompensation, British workers paid 10% less than the equitable level show "an active sense of grievance, complaints or the desire to complain, and, if no redress is given, an active desire to change jobs, or to take action . . ." (p. 26). In cases of overcompensation, he observes that at the 10 to 15% level above equity "there is a strong sense of receiving preferential treatment, which may harden into bravado, with underlying feelings of unease . . ." (p. 26). He states further, "The results suggest that it is not necessarily the case that each one is simply out to get as much as he can for his work. There appear to be equally strong desires that each one should earn the right amount—a fair and reasonable amount relative to others" (p. 26).

In the preceding discussion, Person has been the focus of attention. It should be clear, however, that when Person and Other are in an exchange interaction, Other will suffer inequity if Person does, but the nature of his experience will be opposite to Person, it will be favorable to Other, and vice versa. This will hold provided Person's and Other's perceptions of outcomes and inputs are equivalent and provided that the outcome-input ratio discrepancy attains threshold level. When Person and Other are not engaged in an exchange with one another but stand in an exchange relationship with a third party, Other may or may not experience inequity when Person does. Given the prerequisites mentioned above, he will experience inequity if he compares himself to Person with respect to the same question as induces Person to use Other as a referent (e.g., "Am I being paid fairly?").

Consequences of Inequity

Although there can be little doubt that inequity results in dissatisfaction, in an unpleasant emotional state, be it anger or guilt, there will be other effects. A major purpose of this paper is to specify these in terms that permit specific predictions to be made. Before turning to this task, two general postulates are presented, closely following propositions from cognitive dissonance theory (Festinger, 1957). First, the presence of inequity in Person creates tension in him. The tension is proportional to the magnitude of inequity present. Second, the tension created in Person will motivate him to eliminate or reduce it. The strength of the motivation is proportional to the tension created. In short, the presence of inequity will motivate Person to achieve equity or to reduce inequity, and the strength of motivation to do so will vary directly with the magnitude of inequity experienced. From these postulates and from the theory of cognitive dissonance (Festinger, 1957; Brehm and Cohen, 1962), means of reducing inequity will be derived and presented. As each method of reduction is discussed, evidence demonstrating usage of the method will be presented. Some of the evidence is experimental; some of it is the result of field studies, either of a survey or observational character.

1. Person Altering His Inputs. Person may vary his inputs, either increasing them or decreasing them, depending on whether the inequity is advantageous or disadvantageous. Increasing inputs will reduce felt inequity, if

$$\frac{O_p}{I_p} > \frac{O_a}{I_a}$$

conversely, decreasing inputs will be effective, if

$$\frac{O_p}{I_p} < \frac{O_a}{I_a} \ .$$

In the former instance, Person might increase either his productivity or the quality of his work, provided that it is possible, which is not always the case. In the second instance, Person might engage in "production restriction," for example. Whether Person does, or can, reduce inequity by altering his inputs is partially contingent upon whether relevant inputs are susceptible to change. Sex, age, seniority, and ethnicity are not modifiable. Education and skill are more easily altered, but changing these requires time. Varying inputs will also be a function of Person's perception of the principal "cause" of the inequity. If the discrepancy between outcome-input ratios is primarily a function of his inputs being at variance with those of Other, Person is more likely to alter them than if the discrepancy is largely a result of differences in outcomes. Additionally, it is postulated that given equal opportunity to alter inputs and outcomes, Person will be more likely to lower his inputs when

$$\frac{O_p}{I_p} < \frac{O_a}{I_a}$$

than he is to increase his inputs when

$$\frac{O_p}{I_p} > \frac{O_a}{I_a} \ .$$

This is derived from two assumptions: first, the assumption stated earlier that the threshold for the perception of inequity is higher when Person is overrewarded than when he is underrewarded; secondly, the assumption that Person is motivated to minimize his costs and to maximize his gains. By the second assumption, Person will reduce inequity, insofar as possible, in a manner that will yield him the largest outcomes.

Altering certain inputs has the corollary effect of altering the outcomes of Other. A change in the quality and amount of work performed, for instance, will usually affect the outcomes of Other. When this is the case, the effect of both changes will operate in the same direction in the service of inequity reduction. It follows, therefore, that *less* a change in inputs is required to eliminate inequity than if the change had no effect on Other's outcomes. Inputs, a change in which would have no or very little impact on Other's outcomes, are attributes such as education, age,

and seniority—at least to the extent that they are uncorrelated with performance. . . .

Person Altering His Outcomes. Person may vary his outcomes, either decreasing
or increasing them, depending on whether the inequity is advantageous or disadvantageous to him. Increasing outcomes will reduce inequity, if

$$\frac{O_p}{I_p} < \frac{O_a}{I_a}$$

conversely, decreasing outcomes will serve the same function, if

$$\frac{O_p}{I_p} > \frac{O_a}{I_a}.$$

Of these two possibilities, the second is far less likely, and there is no good evidence
of the use of this means of reducing inequity, though some may be available in
the clinical literature. There are, however, data bearing on attempts to increase outcomes, data other than those related to wage increase demands in union-management
negotiations, probably only a part of which are directly traceable to wage inequities. . . .

Person Distorting His Inputs and Outcomes Cognitively. Person may cognitively distort his inputs and outcomes, the direction of the distortion being the same as if
he had actually altered his inputs and outcomes, as discussed above. Since most
individuals are heavily influenced by reality, substantial distortion is generally difficult. It is pretty difficult to distort to oneself, to change one's cognitions about
the fact, for example, that one has a BA degree, that one has been an accountant
for seven years, and that one's salary is $700 per month. However, it is possible,
within limits, to alter the utility of these. For example, State College is a small
backwoods school with no reputation, or, alternatively, State College has one of
the best business schools in the state and the dean is an adviser to the Bureau of
the Budget. Or, one can consider the fact that $700 per month will buy all of the
essential things of life and a few luxuries, or, conversely, that it will never permit
one to purchase a Wyeth oil painting or an Aston Martin DB5. There is ample evidence in the psychological literature, especially that related to cognitive dissonance
theory, that individuals do modify or rearrange their cognitions in an effort to reduce
perceived incongruities (for a review, see Brehm and Cohen, 1962). Since it has
been postulated that the experience of inequity is equivalent to the experience of
dissonance, it is reasonable to believe that cognitive distortion may be adopted as
a means of reducing inequity. In a variety of work situations, for example in paced
production line jobs, actually altering one's inputs and outcomes may be difficult;
as a consequence these may be cognitively changed in relatively subtle ways.
    Although not a cognitive change in inputs and outcomes per se, related methods

of reducing inequity are for Person to alter the *importance* and the *relevance* of his inputs and outcomes. If, for example, age were a relevant input, its relative importance could be changed to bring about less perceived inequity. Person could convince himself that age was either more or less important than he thought originally. In terms of the statement made earlier that net inputs (and outcomes) were a weighted sum of inputs, changing the importance of inputs would be equivalent to changing the weights associated with them. Altering the relevance of inputs and outcomes is conceived of as more of an all-or-none process: Present ones are made irrelevant or new ones are made relevant. For instance, if Person perceived that the discrepancy between his and Other's outcome-input ratios were principally a result of his outcomes being too low, he might become "aware" of one or more outcomes he had not recognized as being relevant before, perhaps that his job had variety absent from Other's job. Obviously, importance and relevance of inputs and outcomes are not completely independent. An outcome suddenly perceived as being relevant automatically assumes some importance; conversely, one that is made irrelevant in the service of inequity reduction assumes an importance of zero. Nevertheless, the psychological processes appear to be different and it is useful, therefore, to keep them conceptually distinct. . . .

Person Leaving the Field. Leaving the field may take any of several ways of severing social relationships. Quitting a job, obtaining a transfer, and absenteeism are common forms of leaving the field in an employment situation. These are fairly radical means of coping with inequity. The probability of using them is assumed to increase with magnitude of inequity and to decrease with the availability of other means. . . .

Person Acting on Other. In the face of injustice, Person may attempt to alter or cognitively distort Other's inputs and outcomes, or try to force Other to leave the field. These means of reducing inequity vary in the ease of their use. Getting Other to accept greater outcomes, which was a possible interpretation of some of the findings by Leventhal *et al.* (1964), would obviously be easier than the opposite. Similarly, inducing Other to lower his inputs may be easier than the reverse. For example, all other things being equal, such as work group cohesiveness and the needs and ability of an individual worker, it is probably easier to induce a "rate buster" to lower his inputs than to get a laggard to increase them. The direction of the change attempted in the inputs and outcomes of Other is the reverse of the change that Person would make in his own inputs and outcomes, whether the change be actual or cognitive. By way of illustration, if Person experienced feelings of inequity because he lacked job experience compared to Other, he could try to induce Other to decrease a relevant input instead of increasing his own inputs. . . .

Person Changing the Object of His Comparison. Person may change Other with whom he compares himself when he experiences inequity and he and Other stand in an exchange relationship with a third party. This mode is limited to the relationship specified; it is not applicable when Person and Other are in a direct exchange. Changing the object of comparison in the latter situation would reduce to severing the relationship.

The resolution of inequity by changing comparison object is undoubtedly difficult of accomplishment, particularly if Person has been comparing himself to Other for some time. Person would need to be able to make himself noncomparable to Other on one or more dimensions. For instance, if Other, whose outcome-input ratio was previously equal to Person's received a salary increase without any apparent increment in inputs, Person could try to reduce the resulting feeling of inequity by conceiving of Other as belonging now to a different organizational level. But this would likely meet with little success, at least in this culture. A cognitive change of this sort would be extremely unstable, unless it were accompanied by changes in the perception of Other's inputs: for instance, that Other had assumed greater responsibility when his salary was increased. But this involves a process of inequity reduction already referred to. . . .

Choice among Modes of Inequity Reduction. Although reference has been made previously to conditions that may affect the use of one or another method of reducing inequity, there is need for a general statement of conditions that will govern the adoption of one method over another. Given the existence of inequity, any of the means of reduction described earlier are potentially available to Person. He may alter or attempt to alter any of the four terms in the inequality formula or change his cognitions about any of them, or he may leave the field and change his comparison Other, but it is improbable that each of the methods are equally available to him *psychologically* (no reference is made to environmental constraints that may affect the availability of methods), as the work of Steiner and his colleagues on alternative methods of dissonance reduction suggests (Steiner, 1960; Steiner and Johnson, 1964; Steiner and Peters, 1958; Steiner and Rogers, 1963).

Set forth below are some propositions about conditions determining the choice of modes by person. As will be noted, the propositions are not all independent of one another, and each should be prefaced by the condition, *ceteris paribus*.

(*a*) Person will maximize positively valent outcomes and the valence of outcomes.

(*b*) He will minimize increasing inputs that are effortful and costly to change.

(*c*) He will resist real and cognitive changes in inputs that are central to his self-concept and to his self-esteem. To the extent that any of Person's outcomes are related to his self-concept and to his self-esteem, this proposition is extended to cover his outcomes.

(*d*) He will be more resistant to changing cognitions about his own outcomes and inputs than to changing his cognitions about Other's outcomes and inputs.

(*e*) Leaving the field will be resorted to only when the magnitude of inequity experienced is high and other means of reducing it are unavailable. Partial withdrawal, such as absenteeism, will occur more frequently and under conditions of lower inequity.

(*f*) Person will be highly resistant to changing the object of his comparisons, Other, once it has stabilized over time and, in effect, has become an anchor.

These propositions are, admittedly, fairly crude, but they permit, nevertheless, a degree of prediction not available otherwise. In the resolution of a particular injustice, two or more of the processes proposed may be pitted one against the other. To propose which would be dominant is not possible at this stage of the development of the theory. One might propose that protection of self-esteem would dominate maximization of outcomes, but it would be conjecture in the absence of evidence.

Conclusion

Dissatisfaction is both so commonplace and such an irritant, particularly in industrial and other large organizations, that it has been the subject of widespread research (see Vroom, 1964, for a . . . thorough review). Despite prima facie evidence that feelings of injustice underlay a significant proportion of cases of dissatisfaction, thorough behavioral analyses of injustice were not made until recently. In the classic Hawthorne studies (Roethlisberger and Dickson, 1939), there was ample evidence that much of the dissatisfaction observed among Western Electric Company employees was precipitated by felt injustice. Describing complaints, the authors referred frequently to reports by workers that wages were not in keeping with seniority, that rates were too low, that ability was not rewarded, and the like, as distinguished from reports that, for example, equipment was not working and that the workshop was hot. They stated that "no physical or logical operations exist which can be agreed upon as defining them" (p. 259), and they sought "personal or social situations" (p. 269) that would explain the complaints parsimoniously. Yet, the notion of injustice was not advanced as an explanatory concept.

It is not contended here, of course, that all dissatisfaction and low morale are related to a person's suffering injustice in social exchanges. But it should be clear from the research described that a significant portion of cases can be usefully explained by invoking injustice as an explanatory concept. More importantly, much more than dissatisfaction may be predicted once the concept of injustice is analyzed theoretically. . . .

The need for much additional research notwithstanding, the theoretical analyses that have been made of injustice in social exchanges should result not only in a better general understanding of the phenomenon, but should lead to a degree of social control not previously possible. The experience of injustice need not be an accepted fact of life.

References

Adams, J. S. (1961). Wage inequities in a clerical task. Unpublished study. General Electric Company, New York.

Adams J. S. (1963a). Toward an understanding of inequity. *J. abnorm. soc. Psychol.* 67, 422-436.

Adams, J. S. (1936b). Wage inequities, productivity, and work quality. *Industr. Relat.* 3, 9-16.

Adams, J. S. (1965). Etudes expérimentales en matière d'inégalités de salaires, de productivité et de qualité du travail. *Synopsis* 7, 25-34.

Adams, J. S., and Jacobsen, Patricia R. (1964). Effects of wage inequities on work quality. *J. abnorm. soc. Psychol.* 69, 19-25.

Adams, J. S., and Rosenbaum, W. B. (1962). The relationship of worker productivity to cognitive dissonance about wage inequities. *J. appl. Psychol.* 46, 161-164.

Arrowood, A. J. (1961). Some effects on productivity of justified and unjustified levels of reward under public and private conditions. Unpublished doctoral disseration (Dep. Psychol.), Univer. of Minnesota.

Blau, P. (1964). *Exchange and power in social life.* New York: Wiley.

Bramel, D. (1962). A dissonance theory approach to defensive projection. *J. abnorm. soc. Psychol.* 64, 121-129.

Brehm, J. W., and Cohen, A. R. (1962). *Explorations in cognitive dissonance.* New York: Wiley.

Clark, J. V. (1958). A preliminary investigation of some unconscious assumptions affecting labor efficiency in eight supermarkets. Unpublished doctoral dissertation (Grad. Sch. Business Admin.), Harvard Univer.

Conlon, Elizabeth T. (1965). Performance as determined by expectation of success and failure. Unpublished doctoral dissertation (Dep. Social Psychol.), Columbia Univer.

Crozier, M. (1960). Personal communication to the author.

Festinger, L. (1954). A theory of social comparison processes. *Hum. Relat.* 7, 117-140.

Festinger, L. (1957). *A theory of cognitive dissonance.* Evanston, Ill.: Row, Peterson.

Gebhard, Mildred E. (1949). Changes in the attractiveness of activities: the effect of expectation preceding performance. *J. exp. Psychol.* 39, 404-413.

Herzberg, F., Mausner, B., and Snyderman, Barbara B. (1959). *The motivation to work.* New York: Wiley.

Homans, G. C. (1950). *The human group.* New York: Harcourt, Brace.

Homans, G. C. (1963). Status among clerical workers. *Hum. Organiz.* 12, 5-10.

Homans, G. C. (1961). *Social behavior: its elementary forms.* New York: Harcourt, Brace.

Hyman, H. (1942). The psychology on status. *Arch. Psychol.* 38, No. 269.

Jaques, E. (1956). *Measurement of responsibility.* London: Tavistock.

Jaques, E. (1961a). *Equitable payment.* New York: Wiley.

Jaques, E. (1961b). An objective approach to pay differentials. *Time Motion Study* 10, 25-28.

Leventhal, G., Reilly, Ellen, and Lehrer, P. (1964). Change in reward as a determinant of satisfaction and reward expectancy. Paper read at West. Psychol. Assoc. Portland, Ore.

Livernash, E. R. (1953). Job evaluation. In W. S. Woytinsky *et al.* (Eds.), *Employment and wages in the United States.* New York: Twentieth Century Fund, pp. 427-435.

Merton, R. K., and Kitt, Alice S. (1950). Contributions to the theory of reference group behavior. In *Continuities in social research.* R. K. Merton and P. F. Lazarsfeld (Eds.), Glencoe, Ill.: Free Press, pp. 40-105.

Newcomb, T. M. (1943). *Personality and social change: attitude formation in a student community.* New York: Dryden.

Patchen, M. (1959). Study of work and life satisfaction, Report No. II: Absences and attitudes toward work experience. Inst. for Social Res., Ann Arbor, Mich.

Patchen, M. (1961). *The choice of wage comparison.* Englewood Cliffs, N.J.: Prentice-Hall.

Pilisuk, M. (1962). Cognitive balance and self-relevant attitudes. *J. abnorm. soc. Psychol.* 65, 95-103.

Roethlisberger, F. J., and Dickson, W. J. (1939). *Management and the worker.* Cambridge, Mass.: Harvard Univer. Press.

Sayles, L. R. (1958). *Behavior of industrial work groups: prediction and control.* New York: Wiley.

Skinner, B. F. (1957). *Verbal behavior.* New York: Appleton.

Spector, A. J. (1956). Expectations, fulfillment, and morale. *J. abnorm. soc. Psychol.* 52, 51-56.

Steiner, I. D. (1960). Sex differences in the resolution of A-B-X conflicts. *J. Pers.* 28, 118-128.

Steiner, I. D. and Johnson, H. H. (1964). Relationships among dissonance reducing responses. *J. abnorm. soc. Psychol.* 68, 38-44.

Steiner, I. D., and Peters, S. C. (1958). Conformity and the A-B-X model. *J. Pers.* 26, 229-242.

Steiner, I. D., and Rogers, E. D. (1963). Alternative responses to dissonance. *J. abnorm. soc. Psychol.* 66, 128-136.

Stouffer, S. A., Suchman, E. A., DeVinney, L. C.,Starr, Shirley A., and Williams R. M., Jr. (1949). *The American soldier: adjustment during army life.* Vol. 1. Princeton, N. J.: Princeton Univer. Press.

Thibaut, J. (1950). An experimental study of the cohesiveness of underprivileged groups. *Hum. Relat.* 3, 251-278.

Thibaut, J. W., and Kelley, H. H. (1959). *The social psychology of groups.* New York: Wiley.

Vroom, V. H. (1964). *Work and motivation.* New York: Wiley.

Weick, K. E. (1964). Reduction of cognitive dissonance through task enhancement and effort expenditure. *J. abnorm. soc. Psychol.* 66, 533-539.

Zaleznik, A., Christensen, C. R., and Roethlisberger, F. J. (1958). The motivation, productivity, and satisfaction of workers. A prediction study (Grad. Sch. Business Admin.) Harvard Univer.

INTRINSIC AND EXTRINSIC MOTIVATION

BARRY M. STAW

The study of motivation is not only a specialized research area within the field of psychology, but also an important pursuit for nearly everyone. People engage widely in the art of untangling the causes of human behavior and stand ready to predict the future actions of others. The scientific study of motivation is an organized effort to go beyond these native skills or common sense in explaining, predicting, and possibly controlling, individual behavior.

Typically, explanations of motivational phenomena attempt to answer such questions as, "Why does this worker spend so much time at his job?" or "Why did that student write a fifty page term paper when everyone else stopped at ten?" To the layman these questions are often answered, or the behavior is "explained," by verbally linking a given action with a recognized goal or desirable outcome [Koch 1956; Lawler 1973]. For example, if Person X performs a given act y, his behavior can be made intelligible to the

Staw, Barry M., *Intrinsic and Extrinsic Motivation*, (General Learning Press, Morristown, N.J.). © 1976 Silver Burdett Company. Reprinted by permission.

lay person by completing the sentence, "X did y in order to. . . ." Thus, acceptable commonsense explanations of a worker's behavior would include such reasons as "in order to increase his salary" or "to be promoted to a better job," while a student's high level of performance could be explained by such goals as "to receive the highest grade" or "to please others."

Commonsense theorizing, however, rarely constitutes a scientific explanation of behavior. It does not specify why a particular goal or end state was valued by an individual or why particular behaviors were chosen to reach the goal. As noted by Vroom [1964], the study of motivation by psychologists has been in large part directed toward filling in this missing empirical content of commonsense reasoning. The scientific effort basically has been one of specifying which objects or outcomes have value to the individual (e.g., those which reduce primary, biologically based drives or accomplish ends ultimately related to these basic needs), how attraction to various end states undergoes change (e.g., via deprivation, satiation, stimulus generalization), and how behavior directed toward particular outcomes is acquired, refined, and persists over time.

In this module we would like to emphasize, as Koch [1956] has done earlier, that there is an important similarity between commonsense reasoning and scientific theories of motivation. Both are based on an assumption of instrumentalism such that individuals are considered to be doing things for specifiable ends. For example, two of the most dominant approaches to the study of motivation—drive theory [Hull 1943; Spence 1956] and expectancy x value theory [Lewin 1938; Tolman 1932]—include the notion of a reward or desired outcome and posit a learned connection within the organism. For drive theory this learned connection is an S-R habit strength; for expectancy x value theory it is a behavior-outcome expectancy which is perceived by the individual [Campbell et al. 1970]. In sum, the instrumentalism present in scientific theories of motivation is not far removed from the layman's "in order to . . ." explanation.

The instrumental view of human behavior is most readily apparent in several formulations of the expectancy x value theory of motivation. As shown in table 1, the formal statements of expectancy x value theory specify that motivation is a product of the utility or valence of a particular goal and the probability of achieving the desired outcome. For each theoretical formulation, the individual is assumed to take the shortest or most direct path toward a valued goal. However, it is important to recognize that in each case the valued goal is also considered to be *external* to the process of "doing." That is, in analyzing behavior, an individual will probably be considered to be performing an act for some goal independent of the activity itself (e.g., higher pay, promotion to a better job). Unfortunately, these expectancy x value formulations (like many others in motivational psychology) do not easily allow for the fact that a worker may be highly productive simply because he enjoys working hard or is satisfied by good work. Likewise, the theories do not readily lead one to an explanation that a student's work is due to a sheer love of writing or a desire to get something fully explained regardless of the grade or praise to be received from others.

Viewed as a whole, the expectancy x value theories outlined in table 1 can be classified as theories of extrinsic motivation, since each assumes a specific goal that provides satisfaction independent of the activity itself.[1] But, actions may sometimes be valued for their own sake, and they may be self-sustained without any external induce-

Table 1. *Summary of Expectancy × Value Theories.*

Theorist	Major Motivational Constructs			Resultant
Lewin et al. (1944)	Subjective probability of achieving desired outcome	× (Valence) value of desired outcome		→ Force
Tolman (1955)	Expectation of achieving desired outcome	× Demand level for given outcome	× Level of given outcome	→ Performance vector
Edwards (1955)	Subjective probability of achieving desired outcome	× Utility of desired outcome		→ Behavior choice
Rotter (1954)	Expectancy of achieving desired reinforcement	× Value of reinforcement		→ Behavior potential
Atkinson (1966)	Probability of achieving desired outcome	× Motive level for achieving desired outcome	× Incentive level of desired outcome	→ Resultant motivation
Vroom (1964)	Expectancy of achieving desired outcome	× (Valence) value of desired outcome		→ Force

SOURCE: Abraham K. Korman. *The Psychology of Motivation.* © 1974. Reprinted by permission of Prentice-Hall. Inc. Englewood Cliffs. N.J.

ment. In these situations, behavior can be said to be intrinsically motivated. Thus whereas extrinsic motivation emphasizes the value an individual places on the ends of an action and the probability of reaching these ends, intrinsic motivation refers to the pleasure or value associated with the activity itself. Let us examine more closely the theoretical and empirical basis of intrinsic motivation so that we may explicitly build this factor into a revised theory of motivation that takes both factors into account.

The Basis of Intrinsic Motivation

Value Inherent in Behavior

There is strong evidence that many activities such as manipulation, exploration, and information processing provide satisfaction in and of themselves. For example, in some early studies on animal behavior, Harlow and his associates [Harlow, Harlow, & Meyer 1950; Harlow & McClearn 1954] demonstrated that monkeys will learn to disassemble puzzles for no reward other than the opportunity to manipulate things. Similarly, Montgomery [1954] showed that rats will systematically select the path in a maze which leads to an opportunity to explore additional mazes. Also, in studies using human subjects it has been shown that the absence of stimulation and environmental change can lead to extreme discomfort. In one of the most vivid demonstrations of the need for stimulation, Bexton, Heron, and Scott [1954] employed college students to lie on a cot for 24 hours a day in a sound-deadened room (with time out for meals and toilet needs). In this study visual and tactile stimulation was also minimized since subjects were required to wear translucent goggles and special gloves. Although the participants were paid extremely well for their time ($20 in 1954 currency), few could tolerate the experiment for as long as two or three days.

In general, research has shown that in the absence of either external pleasureful-painful stimulation or basic homeostatic needs, an individual is not quiescent. In fact, there is some evidence that it is precisely when external pressures (e.g., hunger, thirst, sex) are minimized that play, exploration, manipulation, and curiosity behaviors are most likely to be manifested [Hunt 1965]. As a result of these findings, several psychologists have gone so far as to posit new human needs for manipulation [Harlow & McClearn 1954], exploration [Montgomery 1954], and curiosity [Berlyne 1960]. Tasks engaging these needs can be considered instrinsically motivating, since the activity provides value to the individual independent of any external sources of satisfaction.

Value Inherent in Accomplishment

In addition to the value an individual may derive from the physical or mental activities involved in a task, he may also gain satisfaction from knowing that his efforts have led to a completed product or accomplishment. McClelland [1951, 1961] has conceptualized this source of satisfaction as the fulfillment of a need for achievement. Using a projective test (the TAT) to assess the strength of achievement motivation, it has been shown that situations involving competition or the testing of individual abilities produce the greatest motive arousal [McClelland 1971]. A learned drive to achieve is thought to be activated when performance can be readily evaluated as a success or failure, and the affect potentially associated with a task (the incentive value of success) is hypothesized to be a function of both the strength of this achievement need and the probability of success. The greatest satisfaction or pride in accomplishment would therefore be derived by persons with high need for achievement who are successful in performing a difficult task (see Litwin [1961] and Cook [1970] for empirical tests of this hypothesis).

Also consistent with the notion that many people seek out or value accomplishment are the theoretical statements of White [1959] and Maslow [1954, 1970]. White posits that individuals are motivated toward competence or mastery over their environments— that they not only manipulate and explore their surroundings but strive to master them through higher levels of motor and mental coordination. In a similar vein, Maslow states that many individuals possess active higher-order needs for esteem and self-actualization. Esteem needs include a need for personal feelings of achievement or success, while a self-actualization need is considered to be a striving for personal growth and development through one's *own* actions. Thus like McClelland's formulation of achievement motivation, both White's and Maslow's theoretical statements suggest that individuals may be motivated to perform certain tasks without an apparent need for external reward. If a task involves the opportunity for one to use new skills or is challenging to one's ability, it may therefore provide satisfaction in and of itself.

A Revised Expectancy x Value Theory of Motivation

Although expectancy x value theories were originally conceived as models of extrinsic motivation, they can be amended to include intrinsic factors. As we have seen, it is important to recognize two sources of individual satisfaction that are not generally included in an expectancy x value model. First, a person may work on a task merely for the activity and stimulation involved regardless of whether his actions lead to a specific accomplishment or tangible rewards provided by others. Second, individual accomplishments may provide satisfaction regardless of whether they lead to external rewards such as money, praise, or increased status. We may thus, think of task performance as involving three distinct sources of value to an individual: (1) value associated with a behavior itself, (2) value associated with accomplishment, and (3) value associated with rewards presented by others. The first two sources of value are mediated by the individual and can be considered intrinsic to his performance, while the third comprises an extrinsic source of satisfaction.

Several recent formulations of task motivation within organizational settings have incorporated intrinsic as well as extrinsic factors into the expectancy x value framework. Galbraith and Cummings [1967], Porter and Lawler [1967], and Lawler [1971, 1973] have each noted that task accomplishment can be rewarding to an individual independent of any externally mediated rewards. However, their models of motivation have each defined intrinsic rewards as those derived only from achievement, and they have not specifically considered the intrinsic rewards associated with behavior irrespective of task accomplishment. A recent expectancy model put forth by House and his associates [House 1971; House, Shapiro, & Wahba 1974] is most inclusive in that it specifies both these potential sources of intrinsic motivation. A slightly amended version of the model is presented below.

$$M = IV_a + (P_1)(IV_b) + \left[\sum_{i=1}^{n}(P_{2i})(EV_i)\right]$$

where:

M = task motivation

IV_a = intrinsic valence associated with task behavior

IV_b = intrinsic valence associated with task accomplishment

EV_i = extrinsic valences associated with task accomplishment

P_1 = perceived probability that one's behavior will lead to accomplishment of the task

P_{2i} = perceived probabilities that one's task accomplishment will lead to extrinsic valences

House's theory of task motivation posits that the individual estimates the instrumentality of his behavior, P_1, for accomplishing a task goal and also the likelihood, P_{2i}, that a task accomplishment will lead to valued extrinsic rewards. In assessing P_1 the individual may take into consideration such factors as the level of his abilities relevant to the task, barriers to work goal accomplishment in the environment (e.g., not getting sufficient materials to finish a job correctly), and the help or support he will receive from others in the work setting. In assessing P_2 the individual may consider the likelihood that his supervisor will recognize good performance through praise, favoritism, a salary raise, or promotion to a better job. In addition, the individual is assumed to place some subjective value upon the behaviors involved in task performance, task accomplishment, and the extrinsic rewards potentially available through work performance. Thus a worker who is bored at home may possess a high IV_a, a worker who has a high need for achievement will be high on IV_b, while the person in dire need of a bigger paycheck should have a high EV_i. We will make use of this revised version of expectancy x value theory in predicting individual task motivation and formulating specific strategies for changing motivation.[2]

Methods of Increasing Task Motivation: Extrinsic Factors

Probably the most common action individuals take to change another's task behavior is to alter extrinsic motivation. From the expectancy x value model presented above, we can see that extrinsic motivation can be increased by changing either the extrinsic valences associated with task accomplishment (EV_i) or the perceived probabilities linking accomplishment to rewards (P_{2i}).

One procedure by which the valence of extrinsic rewards can be altered is through deprivation. Numerous laboratory studies have shown that by depriving a subject of a valued commodity (e.g., food, water, sex), motivation can be increased for any task which leads to its attainment. The same principle no doubt holds in everyday life, but the use of deprivation to motivate someone to perform a task is considered an ethically undesirable way to change behavior. Fortunately, few allocators of rewards have the amount of control over the lives of others necessary to use it successfully. At present, for example, if an industrial firm chose to restrict workers' pay, it would, in addition to increasing the perceived value of money, cause workers to transfer quickly to another job. Only when the workers' options are extremely limited (e.g., during periods of high unemployment or a government-controlled labor market) would deprivation be an effective motivational tool.

A preferable way to increase extrinsic motivation is to assess the desires or needs of the individuals performing a task and to make available those extrinsic rewards with the greatest utility. For instance, one purpose of periodic meetings between supervisors and subordinates within small task groups and attitude surveys within large organizations could be to assess regularly the changing needs of employees. Ideally, extrinsic rewards could be tailored to groups of individuals with similar needs (e.g., for security, money, verbal praise) or provided on an individual basis. By simply restructuring the mix of rewards to achieve the greatest extrinsic valences, motivation to perform a task could thus be increased (see Lawler [1971] for a discussion of "cafeteria style" pay schemes as applied to industry).

In addition to the valences associated with extrinsic rewards, considerable attention should also be given to the perceived probability that task accomplishment will lead to rewards. The most effective procedure in terms of increasing motivation is to make rewards contingent upon performance. As shown in figure 1, dramatic changes in behavior can result from tying extrinsic rewards to behavior. Depicted in the figure is the level of desired behavior emitted by patients of a mental hospital when rewards are both contingent and noncontingent on behavior. The extrinsic rewards used in the study were tokens which could be exchanged for food, cigarettes, or other valued commodities.

In practice, there are many ways of designing a contingent reward system. When task accomplishments are easily defined and measureable, it is often feasible to institute some sort of piece-rate incentive system. In these cases, the level of extrinsic rewards is based upon the quantity and/or quality of performance. Often, however, task accomplishments are neither clearly defined nor easily measured. In these cases, a judgment of the individual's performance is required by a supervisor or allocator of rewards. Obviously, any error in evaluation or sudden change in the criteria of performance will sharply reduce the individual's perception that task accomplishment leads to rewards. As a consequence, the perceived objectivity or fairness of the appraisal system can be as important a determinant of the individual's task motivation as the actual contingency between rewards and performance.

Making valued extrinsic rewards contingent upon performance is generally an effective motivational strategy. However, it is not without some problems. First, it requires that a supervisor possess a sufficient quantity of extrinsic rewards to motivate workers to complete a task. Although most formal organizations (e.g., industry, government) can afford literally to purchase a worker's services, a lack of valued extrinsic rewards can present a motivational problem in many informal work settings (e.g., social clubs, volunteer organizations, home environment). Also, as discussed, an effective strategy of extrinsic motivation requires that performance be accurately assessed by

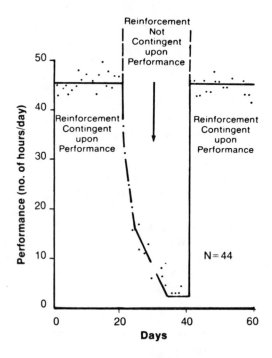

Source: Ayllon, T., and Azrin, N.H., "The Measurement and Reinforcement of Behavior of Psychotics," *Journal of the Experimental Analysis of Behavior*, 1965, 8: 357-383. Copyright 1965 by the Society for the Experimental Analysis of Behavior, Inc. (Additional information and related research can be found in *The Token Economy: A Motivational System for Therapy and Rehabilitation*, by T. Ayllon and N. Azrin, published by Appleton-Century-Crofts, 1968.)

Figure 1. The total number of hours of onward performance by a group of 44 patients under contingent and non-contingent reinforcement schemes.

supervisors so that rewards can be dispensed on a contingent basis. Although this is no problem on a routine task for which the supervisor can clearly set the criteria of performance and measure it, frequently (on tasks involving a great deal of skill and creativity) the supervisor may actually know less about the job than the worker and be in a very poor position to evaluate his performance.

Methods of Increasing Task Motivation: Intrinsic Factors

From the revised expectancy x value model we can see that intrinsic motivation results from the perception of rewards inherent in either task behavior (IV_a) or accomplishment (IV_b). Several factors can be expected to account for the intrinsic valences associated with both behavior and accomplishment, but not all of them are easily alterable. For example, it would be most difficult to change individual needs for activity, manipulation, or exploration, except on a temporary basis. McClelland and his associates have had some success in increasing an individual's achievement needs and motivating entrepreneurial behavior through intensive training sessions [McClelland & Winter 1969]. However, it is doubtful that achievement motivation can, by itself, affect the performance of persons on routine organizational tasks or other activities which are not highly achievement oriented [McClelland 1973a, 1973b].

Perhaps the most practical method of increasing a person's intrinsic motivation to perform a task is to purposely alter the characteristics of his work activities. Assuming that individuals possess at least a moderate need for activity and achievement, many tasks can be changed so that individuals derive greater satisfaction from either task behavior or accomplishment. Many industrial firms have, in effect, followed these principles in programs of job enlargement and job enrichment. For example, the intrinsic rewards associated with task behavior are often improved by increasing the variety of skills necessary to perform a task or by rotating workers among several different tasks. Similarly, the intrinsic rewards associated with task accomplishment can be improved by increasing the responsibility of workers or the importance of the tasks they perform.

Increasing intrinsic motivation has several advantages as a motivational strategy. When individuals can derive satisfaction from task behaviors or accomplishment, there may, for example, be a reduced need for extrinsic rewards to motivate behavior. This may be especially important in cases where supervisors have a limited supply of extrinsic inducements or where individuals do not value those that are readily available. A second advantage of intrinsic motivation is that the need to monitor another's task behavior is reduced. With intrinsic motivation, it may not be necessary to rely totally upon piece-rate incentive systems or periodic performance appraisals to induce a high level of task performance. Instead, a task can be designed so that the quantity and/or quality of performance fulfills the individual's needs for achievement. When this is done, the worker who values achievement can monitor his own task accomplishment and reward himself on a completely contingent basis.

There are a number of ways a task can be changed to increase intrinsic motivation and some of the most important ones are listed in figure 2. The job characteristics shown in the figure are based heavily upon the recent research and theory of Hackman and Oldham [1975; in press]; but are framed within the expectancy x value model of motivation discussed earlier. It should be noted that the research underlying the model presented here has been conducted largely within industrial organizations. However, the characteristics of tasks are stated in rather general terms and may be applicable to many other settings (e.g., educational organizations). A brief consideration of each of these task characteristics and how they might be altered is given [below].

Task variety. In order to increase the intrinsic valence associated with task behavior (IV_a), greater variety can often be introduced into a job. A greater assortment of tasks can be performed by the individual on a single job or, if this is impossible, he can be rotated periodically from job to job. Many industrial firms have followed this procedure to reduce boredom, and increases in task satisfaction commonly result from such changes. Within educational organizations, a similar increase in the variety of learning tasks can often be used to maintain student interest.

Task uncertainty. Very mechanistic tasks, even if they comprise a varied set of activities, may not be totally satisfying to most individuals. Because of our needs for exploration and cognitive stimulation, a task that involves information processing and/or the resolution of uncertainty may be of greater intrinsic interest (e.g., Hunt [1971],

Lanzetta [1971]). Obviously, there may be some upper limit to the degree of uncertainty satisfying to an individual. Both the individual's level of task-relevant skills needed to resolve uncertainty and his personal tolerance for ambiguity may therefore determine the optimal task design.

Social interaction inherent to the job. The fact that individuals generally derive satisfaction from interacting with others can be an important inducement for working. For most persons, the intrinsic valence associated with task behavior is greater when social interaction is an integral part of the job. The formation of task groups and exchange of information are techniques used by schools for increasing the intrinsic interests of students. Also, within industry, there are now experiments in which previously isolated workers can increase their contact with the ultimate users of their services as well as with their co-workers [Hackman et al. in press].

Task identity. Another way to improve the intrinsic valence associated with task accomplishment might be to increase the "wholeness" or identity of a person's work output. At present, within industry, many jobs are so specialized that the worker cannot see the relationship between his small task and the final finished product. In order to increase task identity, jobs can often be redesigned. The individual can be allowed to produce a larger module of work, or a small team of workers can be formed to complete an entire assembly process.

Task significance. The intrinsic valence associated with task accomplishment (IV_b) can often be improved by increasing the perceived significance of a person's work output. This can be done either by changing the individual to a more important job or by increasing the salience of his present work output. An example of the latter course of action would be to emphasize the usefulness of the person's work or to place the person in direct contact with the ultimate users of his product. Within the educational setting, an increase of task significance may translate itself into a stress for "relevance" in learning activities.

Responsibility for results. If an individual does not feel responsible for his work output, it is doubtful that he will place a high value on task accomplishment. Only when the person can experience success or failure on a task is he likely to value the intrinsic rewards associated with accomplishment. Therefore, to increase intrinsic motivation, the person might be given a larger amount of discretion over his task activities and held more accountable for his results. In industry, the autonomy of workers is often increased by allowing them to schedule their own work activities, decide on work methods, and check the quality of their own output. Quite similar procedures could be devised within a school environment in order to increase the felt responsibility of students for their own learning.

Barriers to task accomplishment. Within any task setting (e.g., industrial, educational, etc.) the perceived probability that behavior leads to accomplishment (P_2) may depend on the extent to which there are barriers to task accomplishment. Some of these barriers may be internal to the individual, such as his ability or training to perform a task; others may be related to his immediate task environment (e.g., not getting the necessary material or social support to complete the job). Restructuring a job (or educational task) to remove external barriers to accomplishment and providing requisite training and supervision may thus serve to increase an individual's intrinsic motivation.

Knowledge of results. Knowledge of results can also be expected to affect a person's intrinsic motivation to perform a task. Clearly, if the individual receives no feedback on the quality of his performance, it will be difficult for him to derive satisfaction from accomplishment. Thus it is important for supervisors to relate to workers exactly how they are doing. This feedback should be on a continuous basis so that the individual can quickly change his behavior, and not merely on a periodic review basis. Ideally, a feedback system should be built into the work itself. At present many industrial tasks do contain their own quality checks which can be performed by the worker, and within the educational context, computerized instruction provides a good example of learning tasks in which immediate feedback is provided so that changes in behavior can be effected by the individual.

Effects of Intrinsic Motivation.

Figure 2 shows that intrinsic motivation can influence both an individual's task attitudes and his behavior. If the individual values the behaviors associated with a task actively (IV_a), he can be expected to participate in the task, be satisfied with it, and perhaps even to volunteer for additional tasks of a similar nature. If the individual values task accomplishment and perceives a strong link between his behavior and accomplishment $[(IV_b) (P_1)]$, he can also be expected to produce high-quality work. Empirical support for these hypotheses is derived from research on both task design and work effectiveness within organizational settings [see Hackman & Lawler 1971; Hackman and Oldham 1975; in press; House 1971; Oldham 1974].

Combining Intrinsic and Extrinsic Motivation

It is apparent from our discussion that both intrinsic and extrinsic motivation can be effective methods of energizing behavior. Either of these motivational strategies can be used to get an individual to perform a task, and both intrinsic and extrinsic rewards can bring satisfaction to the individual. The question remains, however, whether these two sources of motivation can be combined effectively to yield overall positive effects on the individual's task attitudes and behavior.

In the expectancy x value model presented above, intrinsic and extrinsic factors are added to form an overall measure of motivation. This model, like those of Galbraith and Cummings [1967], Porter and Lawler [1967], and Lawler [1971, 1973], *assumes* that the perception of intrinsic rewards and the perception of extrinsic rewards are additive in their effect on anticipated work satisfaction. It assumes that intrinsic motivation $[(IV_a) + (P_1)(IV_b)]$ and extrinsic motivation $\left[\sum_{i=1}^{n}(P_{2i})(EV_i)\right]$, summate to produce overall task motivation and that intrinsic and extrinsic motivation are separate, independent factors.

Whether or not intrinsic and extrinsic sources of motivation are independent or do in fact have an effect upon each other is a question of considerable practical as well as theoretical significance. For example, if they are positively interrelated, we might expect extrinsic rewards to increase a person's intrinsic interest in a task, whereas if they are negatively interrelated, the administration of an extrinsic reward could drive out intrinsic motivation. This issue is of importance to any setting (e.g., industrial organization, schools, or voluntary work situations) in which extrinsic rewards are administered and the allocator of the rewards is interested in the individual's resultant task attitudes and behavior.

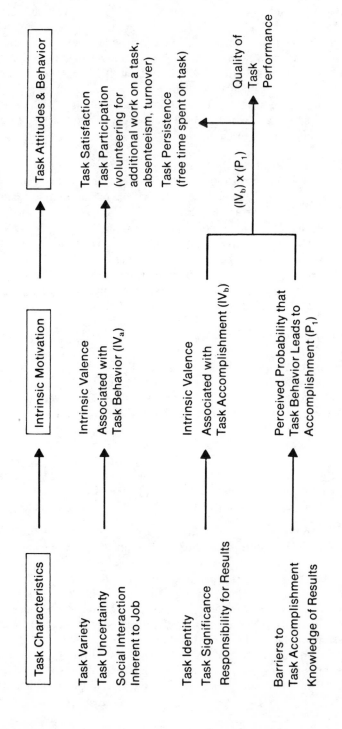

Figure 2. Task determinants of intrinsic motivation.

The Interrelationship of Intrinsic and Extrinsic Motivation

Historically, the interrelationship of intrinsic and extrinsic motivation has been the subject of considerable controversy. In fact, it can be said that there exist psychological theories which will predict either a positive relationship between intrinsic and extrinsic motivation, a negative relationship, or no relationship at all. As a consequence, we will examine each of these theoretical positions in some detail and, in the light of recent empirical research, attempt to formulate a unified view of the interrelationship between intrinsic and extrinsic factors.

Long ago, Woodworth [1918] suggested that in the process of acquiring a set of skills toward some end, the skills themselves could develop their own motivating force that might endure even after the end is no longer sought. He made the point in the following context:

> . . . while a man may enter a certain line of business from a purely external economic motive, he develops an interest in the business for its own sake . . . and the motive force that drives him in the daily task, provided of course this does not degenerate into mere automatic routine, is precisely an interest in the problems confronting him and in the processes by which he is able to deal with those problems. The end furnishes the motive force for the search for means but once the means are found, they are apt to become interesting on their own account [p. 104].

Allport [1973] has argued in a similar vein that certain behaviors develop their own motive power or "functional autonomy." He noted that while many activities, such as making money and solving problems, orginally may have served some other motive, their persistence in the absence of external force necessitates their having developed a value on their own.

The notion that an activity or task behavior can become valued by an individual through its continued association with an external reward can be explained by the process of *secondary reinforcement.* Secondary reinforcement refers to a process by which an originally neutral stimulus acquires reinforcing properties through its pairing with a primary reinforcer [Ferster & Skinner 1957; Uhl & Young 1967]. Thus in these terms it is possible to assert that an intrinsically motivating activity is simply one in which the reinforcement value of an extrinsic goal has associatively rubbed off on the behavior. Irrespective of temporal considerations (i.e., how long it might take for an activity to acquire reinforcing properties on its own), we can therefore predict, through secondary reinforcement, that there will be a positive relationship between intrinsic and extrinsic motivation. In short, no matter what a person's original reaction to a task, secondary reinforcement predicts that it may improve over time if it leads to valued extrinsic rewards.

Other psychologists, as we have seen, might disagree with the notion that all activities currently valued by individuals are merely those which have previously led to positive external outcomes. As noted by Harlow [1950], Montgomery [1954], and Berlyne [1970], an intrinsically motivated activity may stem from an innate human need for stimulation, information, or knowledge and is not necessarily dependent upon external reinforcement. Since certain activities may be valued independently of homeostatic needs or acquired drives based upon them, we might therefore posit that there is no clear relationship between intrinsic and extrinsic motivation.

A New Approach to the Problem

Recently, investigations have been undertaken into the relationship between intrinsic and extrinsic motivation from an entirely different perspective. Instead of asking how intrinsic motivation might be derived from extrinsic reward contingencies or independent human motives, several researchers have concluded that both intrinsic and extrinsic motivation may be more usefully studied as perceptions on the part of individuals. From a perceptual approach it is not necessary to know how specific behaviors originally acquired reinforcing properties, but only that an individual at a given point in time may perceive a task to be rewarding in and of itself. That is, if individuals *think* they are intrinsically motivated, this self-perception alone may be enough to influence future behavior and attitudes. This new approach is consistent with our expectancy x value formulation of motivation, since in that model individuals are assumed to hold perceptions of rewards to be derived from their actions, and behavior is assumed to be based on the direction and magnitude of these perceptual states.

Within the area of interpersonal perception, it has been noted [Heider 1958] that an individual may infer the causes of another's actions to be a function of personal and environmental force:

Action = f(personal force + environmental force)

This is quite close to saying that individuals attempt to determine whether another person is intrinsically motivated to perform an activity (action due to personal force), or extrinsically motivated (action due to environmental force), or both. The extent to which an individual will infer intrinsic motivation on the part of another is predicted to be affected by the clarity and strength of external forces within the situation [Kelley 1967; Jones & Davis 1965; Jones & Nisbett 1971]. When there are strong forces bearing on the individual to perform an activity, there is little reason to assume that a behavior is self-determined, whereas a high level of intrinsic motivation might be inferred if environmental force is minimal. Several studies dealing with interpersonal perception have supported this general conclusion [Jones, Davis, & Gergen 1961; Thibaut & Riecken 1955; Jones & Harris 1967; Strickland 1958].

Bem [1967a, 1967b] extrapolated this interpersonal theory of causal attribution to the study of self-perception or how one views his *own* behavior within a social context. Bem hypothesized that the extent to which external pressures are sufficiently strong to account for one's behavior will determine the likelihood that a person will attribute his own actions to internal causes. Thus if a person acts under strong external rewards or punishments, he is likely to assume that his behavior is under external control. However, if extrinsic contingencies are not strong or salient, the individual is likely to assume that his behavior is due to his own interest in the activity or that his behavior is intrinsically motivated. De Charms has made a similar point in his discussion of individuals' perception of personal causation [1968, p. 328]:

As a first approximation, we propose that whenever a person experiences himself to be the locus of causality for his own behavior (to be an Origin), he will consider himself to be intrinsically motivated. Conversely, when a person perceives the locus of causality for his behavior to be external to himself (that he is a Pawn), he will consider himself to be extrinsically motivated.

De Charms emphasized that the individual may attempt psychologically to label his actions on the basis of whether or not he has been instrumental in affecting his own behavior; that is, whether his behavior has been intrinsically or extrinsically motivated.

The Case for a Negative Relationship Between Intrinsic and Extrinsic Motivation

The self-perception approach to intrinsic and extrinsic motivation leads to the conclusion that there may be a negative interrelationship between these two motivational factors. The basis for this prediction stems from the assumption that individuals may work backward from their own actions in inferring sources of causation [Bem 1967a; 1967b; 1972]. For example, if external pressures on an individual are so high that they would ordinarily cause him to perform a given task regardless of the internal characteristics of the activity, then the individual might logically infer that he is extrinsically motivated. In contrast, if external reward contingencies are extremely low or nonsalient, the individual might logically infer that he is extrinsically motivated. In contrast, if external reward contingencies are extremely low or nonsalient, the individual might then infer that his behavior is intrinsically motivated. What is important is the fact that a person, in performing an activity, may *seek out* the probable cause of his own actions. Since behavior has no doubt been caused by something, it makes pragmatic, if not scientific, sense for the person to conclude that the cause is personal (intrinsic) rather than extrinsic if he can find no external reasons for his actions.

Two particular situations provide robust tests of the self-perception prediction. One is a situation in which there is insufficient justification for a person's actions, a situation in which the intrinsic rewards for an activity are very low (e.g., a dull task) and there are no compensating extrinsic rewards (e.g., monetary payment, verbal praise). Although rationally, one ordinarily tries to avoid these situations; there are occasions when one is faced with the difficult question of "Why did I do that?" The self-perception theory predicts that in situations of insufficient justification, the individual may cognitively reevaluate the intrinsic characteristics of an activity in order to justify or explain his own behavior. For example, if the individual performed a dull task for no external reward, he may "explain" his behavior by thinking that the task was not really so bad after all.

Sometimes a person may also be fortunate enough to be in a situation in which his behavior is over sufficiently justified. For example, a person may be asked to perform an interesting task and at the same time be lavishly paid for his efforts. In such situations, the self-perception theory predicts that the individual may actually reevaluate the activity in a downward direction. Since the external reward would be sufficient to motivate behavior by itself, the individual may mistakenly infer that he was extrinsically motivated to perform the activity. He may conclude that since he was forced to perform the task by an external reward, the task probably was not terribly satisfying in and of itself.

Figure 3 graphically depicts the situations of insufficient and overly sufficient justification. From the figure, we can see that the conceptual framework supporting

LEVEL OF EXTRINSIC REWARDS

	LOW	HIGH
LOW	Insufficient Justification (unstable perception)	Perception of Extrinsically Motivated Behavior
HIGH	Perception of Intrinsically Motivated Behavior	Overly Sufficient Justification (unstable perception)

LEVEL OF INTRINSIC REWARDS

Figure 3. A conceptual framework of self-perception theory.

self-perception theory raises several interesting issues. First, it appears from this analysis that there are only two fully stable attributions of behavior: (1) the perception of extrinsically motivated behavior in which the internal rewards associated with perform- ing an activity are low while external rewards are high; and (2) the perception of intrinsically motivated behavior in which the task is inherently rewarding but external rewards are low. Furthermore, it appears that situations of insufficient justification (where intrinsic and extrinsic rewards are both low) and oversufficient justification (where intrinsic and extrinsic rewards are both high) involve unstable attribution states. As shown in figure 4, individuals apparently resolve this attributional instability by altering their perceptions of intrinsic rewards associated with the task.

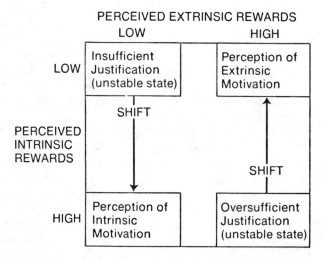

PERCEIVED EXTRINSIC REWARDS

	LOW	HIGH
LOW	Insufficient Justification (unstable state)	Perception of Extrinsic Motivation
HIGH	Perception of Intrinsic Motivation	Oversufficient Justification (unstable state)

PERCEIVED INTRINSIC REWARDS

SHIFT · SHIFT

Figure 4. A schematic analysis of the self-perception of intrinsic and extrinsic motivation.

An interesting question posed by the self-perception analysis is why individuals are predicted to resolve an unstable attribution state by cognitively reevaluating a task in terms of its intrinsic rewards rather than changing their perceptions of extrinsic factors. The answer to this question may lie in the relative clarity of extrinsic as compared with intrinsic rewards, and the individual's relative ability to distort the two aspects of the situation. Within many settings (and especially within laboratory experiments) extrinsic rewards are generally quite salient and specific, whereas an individual must judge the intrinsic nature of a task for himself. Any shifts in the perception of intrinsic and extrinsic rewards may therefore by more likely to occur in the intrinsic factor. As shown in figure 4, it is these predicted shifts in perceived intrinsic rewards that may theoretically underlie a negative relationship between intrinsic and extrinsic motivation.

Empirical Evidence: Insufficient Justification

Several studies have shown that when an individual is induced to commit an unpleasant act for little or no external justification, he may subsequently conclude that the act was not so unpleasant after all. Actually, the first scientific attempt to account for this phenomenon was the theory of cognitive dissonance [Festinger 1957]. It was predicted by dissonance theorists [Festinger 1957; Aronson 1966] that, since performing an unpleasant act for little or no reward would be an inconsistent (and seemingly irrational) thing to do, an individual might subsequently change his attitude toward the act in order to reduce the inconsistency or to appear rational. Bem's self-perception theory yields the same predictions but does not require one to posit that there is a motivating state such as dissonance reduction or self-rationalization. To Bem, since the individual examines his own behavior in light of the forces around him, he is simply more likely to come to the conclusion that his actions were intrinsically satisfying if they were performed under minimal external force.

In general, two types of experiments have been designed to assess the consequences of insufficient justification. One type of design has involved the performance of a dull task with varied levels of reward [Brehm & Cohen 1962; Weick 1964; Freedman 1963; Weick & Penner 1965]. A second and more popular design has involved some form of counterattitudinal advocacy, either in terms of lying to a fellow subject about the nature of an experiment or writing an essay against one's position on an important issue [Festinger & Carlsmith 1959; Carlsmith, Collins, & Helmreich 1966; Linder, Cooper, & Jones 1967]. Fundamentally, the two types of designs are not vastly different. Both require subjects to perform an intrinsically dissatisfying act under varied levels of external inducement, and both predict that, in the low payment condition, the subject will change his attitude toward the activity (i.e., think more favorably of the task or begin to believe the position advocated).

The most well-known experiment designed to test the insufficient justification paradigm was conducted by Festinger and Carlsmith [1959]. Subjects participated in a repetitive and dull task (putting spools on trays and turning pegs) and were asked to tell other waiting subjects that the experiment was enjoyable, interesting, and exciting. Half the experimental subjects were paid $1 and half were paid $20 for the counterattitudinal advocacy (and to be "on call" in the future), while control subjects were not paid and did not perform the counterattitudinal act. As predicted, the smaller the reward used to induce subjects to perform the counterattitudinal act, the greater the positive change in their attitudes toward the task. Although the interpretation of the results of this study have been actively debated (e.g., between dissonance and self-perception theorists) the basic findings have been replicated by a number of different researchers. It should be noted, however, that several mediating variables have also been isolated as being necessary for the attainment of this dissonance or self-perception effect: free choice [Linder, Cooper, & Jones 1967], commitment or irrevocability of behavior [Brehm & Cohen 1962], and substantial adverse consequences [Calder, Ross, & Insko 1973; Collins & Hoyt 1972].

Recently, a strong test of the insufficient justification paradigm was also conducted outside the laboratory [Staw 1974a]. A natural field experiment was made possible by the fact that many young men had joined an organization (Army ROTC) in order to avoid being drafted, *and* these same young men subsequently received information (a draft lottery number) that changed the value of this organizational reward. Of particular relevance was the fact that those who joined ROTC did so not because of their intrinsic interest in the activities involved, (e.g., drills, classes, and summer camp), but because they anticipated a substantial extrinsic reward (draft avoidance). As a result, those who received draft numbers that exempted them from military service subsequently faced a situation of low extrinsic as well as intrinsic rewards, a situation of insufficient justification. In contrast, persons who received draft numbers that made them vulnerable to military call-up found their participation in ROTC perfectly justified—they were still successfully avoiding the draft by remaining in the organization. To test the insufficient justification effect, both the attitudes and the performance of ROTC cadets were analyzed by draft number before and after the national draft lottery. The results showed that those in the insufficient justification situation enhanced their perception of ROTC and even performed somewhat better in ROTC courses after the lottery. It should be recognized, however, that this task enhancement occurred only under circumstances very similar to those previously found necessary for the dissonance or self-perception effect (i.e., high commitment, free choice, and adverse consequences).

Empirical Evidence: Overly Sufficient Justification

There have been several empirical studies designed to test the self-perception prediction within the context of overly sufficient justification. Generally, a situation in which an extrinsic reward is added to an intrinsically rewarding task has been experimentally contrived for this purpose. Following self-perception theory, it is predicted that an increase in external justification will cause individuals to lose confidence in their intrinsic interest in the experimental task. Since dissonance theory cannot make this prediction (it is neither irrational nor inconsistent to perform an activity for too many rewards), the literature on overly sufficient justification provides the most important data on the self-perception prediction. For this reason, we will examine the experimental evidence in some detail.

In an experiment specifically designed to test the effect of overly sufficient justification on intrinsic motivation, Deci [1971] enlisted a number of college students to participate in a problem-solving study. All the students were asked to work on a series of intrinsically interesting puzzles for three experimental sessions. After the first session, however, half of the students (the experimental group) were told that they would also be given an extrinsic reward (money) for correctly solving the second set of puzzles, while the other students (the control group) were not told anything about the reward. In the third session, neither the experimental nor the control subjects were rewarded. This design is schematically outlined below:

Basic Design of Deci [1971] Study

	Time 1	Time 2	Time 3
Experimental group	No payment	Payment	No payment
Control group	No payment	No payment	No payment

Deci had hypothesized that the payment of money in the second experimental session might decrease subjects' intrinsic motivation to perform the task. That is, the introduction of an external force (money) might cause participants to alter their self-perception about why they were working on the puzzles. Instead of being intrinsically motivated to solve the interesting puzzles, they might find themselves working primarily to get the money provided by the experimenter. Thus Deci's goal in conducting the study was to compare the changes in subjects' intrinsic motivation from the first to third sessions for both the experimental and control groups. If the self-perception hypothesis was correct, the intrinsic motivation of the previously paid experimental subjects would decrease in the third session, whereas the intrinsic motivation of the unpaid controls should remain unchanged.

As a measure of intrinsic motivation, Deci used the amount of free time participants spent on the puzzle task. To obtain this measure, the experimenter left the room during each session, supposedly to feed some data into the computer. As the expermenter left the room, he told the subjects they could do anything they wanted with their free time. In addition to the puzzles, current issues of *Time, The New Yorker,* and *Playboy* were placed near the subjects. However, while the first experimenter was out of the laboratory, a second experimenter, unknown to the subjects, observed their behavior through a one-way mirror. It was reasoned that if the subject worked on the puzzles during this free time period, he must be intrinsically motivated to perform the task. As show in table 2, the amount of free time spent on the task decreased for those who were previously paid to perform the activity, while there was a slight increase for the unpaid controls. Although the difference between the experimental and control groups was only marginally significant, the results are suggestive of the fact that an overly sufficient extrinsic reward may decrease one's intrinsic motivation to perform a task.

Table 2.
Mean Number of Seconds Spent Working on Puzzles during Free Time Periods.

Group	Time 1	Time 2	Time 3	Time 3 − Time 1
Experimental (n = 12)	248.2	313.9	198.5	−49.7
Control (n = 12)	213.9	202.7	241.8	27.9

Source: Deci, E. L., "The Effects of Externally Mediated Rewards on Intrinsic Motivation." *Journal of Personality and Social Psychology,* 1971, 18:105-115. Copyright 1971 by the American Psychological Association. Reprinted by permission.

Lepper, Greene, and Nisbett [1973] also conducted a study that tested the self-perception prediction in a situation of overly sufficient justification. Their study involved having nursery school children perform an interesting activity (playing with Magic Markers) with and without the expectation of an additional extrinsic reward. Some children were induced to draw pictures with the markers by promising them a Good Player Award consisting of a big gold star, a bright red ribbon, and a place to print their name. Other children either performed the activity without any reward or were told about the reward only after completing the activity. Children who participated in these three experimental conditions (expected reward, no reward, unexpected reward) were then covertly observed during the following week in a free-play period. As in the Deci [1971] study, the amount of time children spent on the activity when they could do other interesting things (i.e., playing with other toys) was taken to be an indicator of intrinsic motivation.

The findings of the Lepper, Greene, and Nisbett study showed that the introduction of an extrinsic reward for performing an already interesting activity caused a significant decrease in intrinsic motivation. Children who played with Magic Markers with the expectation of receiving the external reward did not spend as much subsequent free time on the activity as did children who were not given a reward or those who were unexpectedly offered the reward. Moreover, the rated quality of drawings made by children with the markers was significantly poorer in the expected reward group than either the no-reward or unexpected reward groups.

The results of the Lepper et al. study help to increase our confidence in the findings of the earlier Deci experiment. Not only are the earlier findings replicated with a different task and subject population, but an important methodological problem is minimized. By reexamining table 2, we can see that the second time period in the Deci experiment was the period in which payment was expected by subjects for solving the puzzles. However, we can also see that in time 2 there was a whopping increase in the free time subjects spent on the puzzles. Deci explained this increase as an attempt by subjects to practice puzzle solving to increase their chances of earning money. However, what Deci did not discuss is the possibility that the subsequent decrease in time 3 was due not to the prior administration of rewards but to the effect of satiation or fatigue. One contribution of the Lepper et al. study is that its results are not easily explained by this alternative. In the Lepper et al. experiment, there was over one week's time between the session in which an extrinsic reward was administered and the final observation period.

Although both the Deci and Lepper et al. studies support the notion that the expectation of an extrinsic reward may decrease intrinsic interest in an activity, there is still one important source of ambiguity in both these studies. You may have noticed that the decrease in intrinsic motivation follows not only the prior administration of an extrinsic reward, but also the withdrawal of this reward. For example, in the Deci study, subjects were not paid in the third experimental session in which the decrease in intrinsic motivation was reported. Likewise, subjects were not rewarded when the final observation of intrinsic motivation was taken by Lepper, Greene, and Nisbett. It is therefore difficult to determine whether the decrease in intrinsic interest is due to a change in the self-perception of motivation following the application of an extrinsic reward or merely to frustration following the removal of the reward. An experiment by Kruglanski, Freedman, and Zeevi [1971] helps to resolve this ambiguity.

Kruglanski et al. induced a number of teenagers to volunteer for some creativity and

memory tasks. To manipulate extrinsic rewards, the experimenters told half the participants that because they had volunteered for the study, they would be taken on an
interesting tour of the psychology laboratory; the other participants were not offered this
extrinsic reward. The results showed that teenagers offered the reward were less satisfied
with the experimental tasks and were less likely to volunteer for future experiments of a
similar nature than were teenagers who were not offered the extrinsic reward. In
addition, the extrinsically rewarded group did not perform as well on the experimental
task (in terms of recall, creativity, and the Zeigarnik effect) as the nonrewarded group.
These findings are similar to those of Deci [1971] and Lepper et al. [1973], but they
cannot be as easily explained by a frustration effect. Since in the Kruglanski et al. study
the reward was never withdrawn for the experimental group, the differences between the
experimental (reward) and control (no reward) conditions are better explained by a
change in self-perception than by a frustration effect.

The designs of the three overly sufficient justification studies described above have
varying strengths and weakness [Calder & Staw 1975a], but taken together, their results
can be interpreted as supporting the notion that extrinsic rewards added to an already
interesting task can decrease intrinsic motivation. This effect, if true, has important
ramifications for educational, industrial, and other work settings. There are many
situations in which people are offered extrinsic rewards (grades, money, special privileges) for accomplishing a task which may already be intrinsically interesting. The
self-perception effect means that, by offering external rewards, we may sometimes be
sacrificing an important source of task motivation and not necessarily increasing either
the satisfaction or the performance of the participant. Obviously, because the practical
implications of the self-perception effect are large, we should proceed with caution.
Thus, in addition to scrutinizing the validity of the findings themselves (as we have done
above), we should also attempt to determine the exact conditions under which they might
be expected to hold.

Earlier, Deci [1971, 1972] had hypothesized that only rewards contingent on a high
level of task performance are likely to have an adverse effect on intrinsic motivation. He
had reasoned that a reward contingent upon specific behavioral demands is most likely to
cause an individual to infer that his behavior is extrinsically rather than intrinsically
motivated and that a decrease in intrinsic motivation may result from this change in
self-perception. Although this assumption seems reasonable, there is not a great deal of
empirical support for it. Certainly in the Kruglanski et al. and Lepper et al. studies all that
was necessary to cause a decrease in intrinsic motivation was for rewards to be
contingent upon the completion of an activity. In each of these studies what seemed to be
important was the cognition that one was performing an activity *in order to get an
extrinsic reward* rather than a prescribed goal for a particular level of output. Thus as
long as it is salient, a reward contingency based upon the completion of an activity may
decrease intrinsic motivation just like a reward contingency based on the quality or
quantity of performance.

Ross [1975] recently conducted two experiments that dealt specifically with the
effect of the salience of rewards on changes in intrinsic motivation. In one study,
children were asked to play a musical instrument (drums) for either no reward, a
nonsalient reward, or a salient reward. The results showed that intrinsic motivation, as
measured by the amount of time spent on the drums versus other activities in a free play
situation, was lowest for the salient reward condition. Similar results were found in a

second study in which some children were asked to think either of the reward (marshmal-lows) while playing a musical instrument, think of an extraneous object (snow), or not think of anything in particular. The data for this second study showed that intrinsic motivation was lowest when children consciously thought about the reward while performing the task.

In addition to the salience of an external reward, there has been empirical research on one other factor mediating the self-perception effect, the existing norms of the task situation. In examining the prior research using situations of overly sufficient justifica-tion, Staw, Calder, and Hess [1975] reasoned that there is one common element which stands out. Always, the extrinsic reward appears to be administered in a situation in which persons are not normally paid or otherwise reimbursed for their actions. For example, students are not normally paid for laboratory participation, but the Deci [1971] and Kruglanski et al. [1971] subjects were. Likewise, nursery school children are not normally enticed by special recognition or rewards to play with an interesting new toy, but both the Lepper et al. [1973] and Ross [1975] subjects were. Thus Staw, Calder, and Hess [1975] manipulated norms for payment as well as the actual payment of money for performing an interesting task. They found an interaction of norms and payment such that the introduction of an extrinsic reward decreased intrinsic interest in a task only when there existed a situational norm for no payment. From these data and the findings of the Ross study, it thus appears that an extrinsic reward must be both salient and situationally inappropriate for there to be a reduction in intrinsic interest.

Reassessing the Self-perception Effect

At present there is growing empirical support for the notion that intrinsic and extrinsic motivation *can* be negatively interrelated. The effect of extrinsic rewards on intrinsic motivation has been replicated by several researchers using different classes of subjects (males, females, children, college students) and different activities (puzzles, toys), and the basic results appear to be internally valid. As we have seen, however, the effect of extrinsic rewards is predicated on certain necessary conditions (e.g., situational norms and reward salience), as is often the case with psychological findings subjected to close examination.

To date, the primary data supporting the self-perception prediction have come from situations of insufficient and overly sufficient justification. Empirical findings have shown that individuals may cognitively reevaluate intrinsic rewards in an upward direction when their behavior is insufficiently justified and in a downward direction when there is overly sufficient justification. In general, it can be said that the data of these two situations are consistent with the self-perception hypothesis. Still, theoretical-ly, it is not immediately clear why previous research has been restricted to these two particular contexts. No doubt it is easier to show an increase in intrinsic motivation when intrinsic interest is initially low (as under insufficient justification) or a decrease when intrinsic interest is initially high (as under overly sufficient justification). Nevertheless, the theory should support a negative interrelationship of intrinsic and extrinsic factors at *all levels*, since it makes the rather general prediction that the greater the extrinsic rewards, the less likely is the individual to infer that he is intrinsically motivated.

One recent empirical study has tested the self-perception hypothesis by manipula-ting *both* intrinsic and extrinsic motivation. Calder and Staw [1975b] experimentally manipulated both the intrinsic characteristics of a task as well as extrinsic rewards in an attempt to examine the interrelationship of these two factors at more than one level. In the study male college students were asked to solve one of two sets of puzzles identical in all respects except the potential for intrinsic interest. One set of puzzles contained an assortment of pictures highly rated by students (chiefly from *Life* magazine but including several *Playboy* centerfolds); another set of puzzles was blank and rated more neutrally. To manipulate extrinsic rewards, half the subjects were promised $1 for their 20 minutes of labor (and the dollar was placed prominently in view), while for half of the subjects, money was neither mentioned nor displayed. After completing the task, subjects were asked to fill out a questionnaire on their reactions to the puzzle-solving activity. The two primary dependent variables included in the questionnaire were a measure of task satisfaction and a measure of subjects' willingness to volunteer for additional puzzle-solving exercises. The latter consisted of a sign-up sheet on which subjects could indicate the amount of time they would be willing to spend (without pay or additional course credit) in future experiments of a similar nature.

The results of the Calder and Staw experiment showed a significant interaction between task and payment on subjects' satisfaction with the activity and a marginally significant interaction on subjects' willingness to volunteer for additional work without extrinsic reward. These data provided empirical support for the self-perception effect in a situation of overly sufficient justification, but not under other conditions. Specifically, when the task was initially interesting (i.e., using the picture puzzle activity), the introduction of money caused a reduction of task satisfaction and volunteering. However, when the task was initially more neutral (i.e., using the blank puzzle activity), the introduction of money increased satisfaction and subjects' intentions to volunteer for additional work. Thus if we consider Calder and Staw's dependent measures as indicators of intrinsic interest, the first finding is in accord with the self-perception hypothesis, while the latter result is similar to what one might predict from a reinforcement theory. The implications of these data, together with previous findings, are graphically depicted in figure 5.

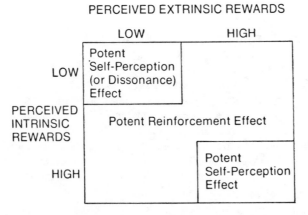

PERCEIVED EXTRINSIC REWARDS

Figure 5. The relative potency of self-perception and reinforcement mechanisms.

As shown in the figure, self-perception effects have been found *only* at the extremes of insufficient and overly sufficient justification. Thus it may be prudent to withhold judgment on the general hypothesis that there is a uniformly negative relationship between intrinsic and extrinsic motivation. Perhaps we should no longer broadly posit that the greater external rewards and pressures, the weaker the perception of intrinsic interest in an activity; and the lower external pressures, the stronger intrinsic interest. Certainly, under conditions other than insufficient and overly sufficient justification, reinforcement effects of extrinsic rewards on intrinsic task satisfaction have readily been found [Cherrington, Reitz, & Scott 1971; Cherrington 1973; Greene 1974].

At present it appears that only in situations of insufficient or overly sufficient reward will there be attributional instability of such magnitude that shifts will occur in the perception of intrinsic rewards. We might therefore speculate that either no attributional instability is evoked in other situations or it is just not strong enough to overcome a countervailing force. This writer would place his confidence in the latter theoretical position. It seems likely that both self-perception *and* reinforcement mechanisms hold true, but that their relative influence over an individual's task attitudes and behavior varies according to the situational context. For example, only in situations with insufficient or overly sufficient justification will the need to resolve attributional instability probably be strong enough for external rewards to produce a decrease in intrinsic motivation. In other situations we might reasonably expect a more positive relationship between intrinsic and extrinsic factors, as predicted by reinforcement theory.

Although this new view of the interrelationship between intrinsic and extrinsic motivation remains speculative, it does seem reasonable in light of recent theoretical and empirical work. Figure 6 graphically elaborates this model and shows how the level of intrinsic and extrinsic motivation may depend on the characteristics of the situation. In the figure, secondary reinforcement is depicted to be a general force for producing a positive relationship between intrinsic and extrinsic motivation. However, under situations of insufficient and oversufficient justification, self-perception (and dissonance) effects are shown to provide a second but still potentially effective determinant of a negative interrelationship between intrinsic and extrinsic motivation. Figure 6 shows the joint operation of these two theoretical mechanisms and illustrates their ultimate effect on individuals' satisfaction, persistence, and performance on a task.

Implications of Intrinsic and Extrinsic Motivation

In this discussion we have noted that the administration of both intrinsic and extrinsic rewards can have important effects on a person's task attitudes and behavior. Individually, extrinsic rewards may direct and control a person's activity on a task and provide an important source of satisfaction. By themselves, intrinsic rewards can also motivate task-related behavior and bring gratification to the individual. As we have seen, however, the joint effect of intrinsic and extrinsic rewards may be quite complex. Not only may intrinsic and extrinsic factors not be additive in their overall effect on motivation and satisfaction, but the interaction of intrinsic and extrinsic factors may under some conditions be positive and under other conditions negative. As illustrated in figures 5 and 6, a potent reinforcement effect will often cause intrinsic and extrinsic

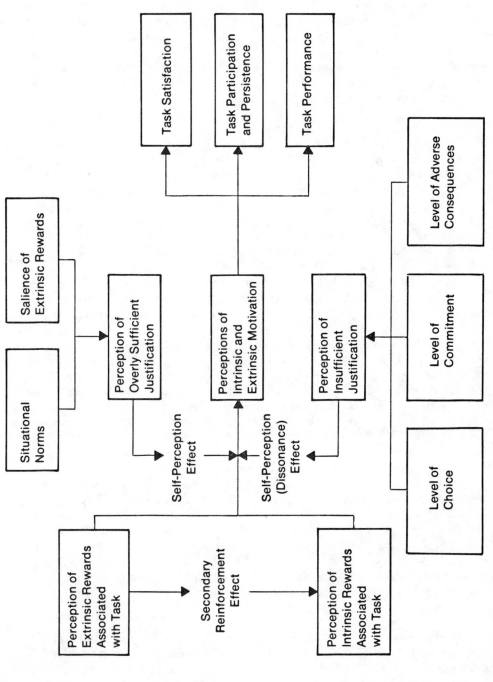

Figure 6. The interrelationship of intrinsic and extrinsic motivation as a function of situational characteristics.

motivation to be positively interrelated, although on occasion a self-perception mechanism may be so powerful as to create a negative relationship between these two factors.

The reinforcement predictions of figures 5 and 6 are consistent with our common sense. In practice, extrinsic rewards are relied upon heavily to induce desired behaviors, and most allocators of rewards (administrators, teachers, parents) operate on the theory that extrinsic rewards will positively affect an individual's intrinsic interest in a task. We should therefore concentrate on those situations in which our common sense may be in error—those situations in which there may in fact be a negative relationship between intrinsic and extrinsic motivation.

Motivation in Educational Organizations

One of the situations in which intrinsic and extrinsic motivation may be negatively interrelated is our schools. As Lepper and Greene [in press] have noted, many educational tasks are inherently interesting to students and would probably be performed without any external force. However, when grades and other extrinsic inducements are added to the activity, we may, via overly sufficient justification, be converting an interesting activity into work. That is, by inducing students to perform educational tasks with strong extrinsic rewards or by applying external force, we may be converting learning activities into behaviors that will not be performed in the future without some additional outside pressure or extrinsic force.

Within the educational context, a negative relationship between intrinsic and extrinsic motivation poses a serious dilemma for teachers who allocate external rewards. For example, there is no doubt that grades, gold stars, and other such incentives can alter the direction and vigor of specific "in school" behaviors (e.g., getting students to complete assigned exercises by a particular date). But because of their effect on intrinsic motivation, extrinsic rewards may also weaken a student's general interest in learning tasks and decrease voluntary learning behavior that extends beyond the school setting. In essence, then, the extrinsic forces that work so well at motivating and controlling specific task behaviors may actually cause the extinction of these same behaviors within situations devoid of external reinforcers. This is an important consideration for educational organizations, since most of an individual's learning activity will no doubt occur outside the highly regulated and reinforced setting of the classroom.[3]

In order to maintain students' intrinsic motivation in learning activities it is recommended that the use of extrinsic rewards be carefully controlled. As a practical measure, it is recommended that when a learning task is inherently interesting (and would probably be performed without any external force) all external pressures on the individual be minimized. Only when a task is so uninteresting that individuals would not ordinarily perform it should extrinsic rewards be applied. In addition, it is suggested that the student role be both enlarged and enriched to increase rather directly the level of intrinsic motivation. The significance of learning tasks, responsibility for results, feedback, and variety in student activities are all areas of possible improvement.

Motivation in Work Organizations

Voluntary work organizations are very much like educational organizations; their members are often intrinsically motivated to perform certain tasks and extrinsic rewards are generally not necessary to induce the performance of many desired behaviors. Moreover, if for some reason extrinsic rewards were to be offered to voluntary workers for performing their services, we would expect to find, as in the educational setting, a decrease in intrinsic motivation. As in the educational context, we would expect an external reward to decrease self-motivated (or voluntary) behavior in settings free from external reinforcement, although the specific behaviors which are reinforced might be increased. As a concrete example, let us imagine a political candidate who decides to "motivate" his volunteer campaign workers by paying them for distributing flyers to prospective voters. In this situation, we might expect that the administration of an extrinsic reward will increase the number of flyers distributed. However, the political workers' subsequent interest in performing other campaign activities *without pay* may subsequently be diminished. Similarly, the volunteer hospital worker who becomes salaried may no longer have the same intrinsic interest in his work. Although the newly professionalized worker may exert a good deal of effort on the job and be relatively satisfied with it, his satisfaction may stem from extrinsic rather than intrinsic sources of reward.

Let us now turn to the implications of intrinsic and extrinsic motivation for nonvoluntary work organizations. Deci [1972], in reviewing his research on intrinsic motivation, cautioned strongly against the use of contingent monetary rewards within industrial organizations. He maintained that paying people contingently upon the performance of specific tasks may reduce intrinsic motivation for these activities, and he recommended noncontingent reinforcers in their stead. As we have seen, however, a decrease in intrinsic motivation does not always occur following the administration of extrinsic rewards; certain necessary conditions must be present before there is a negative relationship between intrinsic and extrinsic motivation. Generally, industrial work settings do not meet these necessary conditions.

First, within industrial organizations, a large number of jobs are not inherently interesting enough to foster high intrinsic motivation. Persons would not ordinarily perform many of the tasks of the industrial world (e.g., assembly-line work) without extrinsic inducements, and this initial lack of intrinsic interest will probably preclude the effect of overly sufficient justification. Second, even when an industrial job is inherently interesting, there exists a powerful norm for extrinsic payment. Not only do workers specifically join and contribute their labor in exchange for particular inducements, but the instrumental relationship between task behavior and extrinsic rewards is supported by both social and legal standards. Thus the industrial work situation is quite unlike that of either a voluntary organization or an educational system. In the former cases, participants may be initially interested in performing certain tasks without external force, and the addition of overly sufficient rewards may convey information that the task is not intrinsically interesting. Within industrial organizations, on the other hand, extrinsic reinforcement *is* the norm, and tasks may often be perceived to be even more interesting when they lead to greater extrinsic rewards.

The very basic distinction between nonvoluntary work situations and other task settings (e.g., schools and voluntary organizations) is that, without extrinsic rewards, nonvoluntary organizations would be largely without participants. The important question for industrial work settings is therefore not one of payment versus nonpayment, but of the recommended degree of contingency between reward and performance. On the basis of current evidence, it would seem prudent to suggest that, within industrial organizations, rewards continue to be made contingent upon behavior. This could be accomplished through performance evaluation, profit sharing, or piece-rate incentive schemes. In addition, intrinsic motivation should be increased directly via the planned alteration of specific job characteristics (e.g., by increasing task variety, complexity, social interaction, task identity, significance, responsibility for results, and knowledge of results).

A Final Comment

Although the study of the interaction of intrinsic and extrinsic motivation is a relatively young area within psychology, it has been the intent of this paper to outline a theoretical model and provide some practical suggestions based upon the research evidence available to date. As we have seen, the effects of intrinsic and extrinsic motivation are not always simple, and several mediating variables must often be taken into account before specific predictions can be made. Thus in addition to providing "answers" to theoretical and practical problems, this paper may illustrate the complexities involved in drawing conclusions from a limited body of research data. The main caution for the reader is to regard these theoretical propositions and practical recommendations as working statements subject to the influence of future empirical evidence.

Notes

The author wishes to express his gratitude to Bobby J. Calder and Greg R. Oldham for their critical reading of the manuscript, and to the Center for Advanced Study at the University of Illinois for the resources and facilities necessary to complete this work.

1. Although Lewin's construct of "resultant force" emphasized the goal-directed nature of motivation, its formulation did actually include the intrinsic valence associated with a behavioral path as well as the extrinsic ends of an action.

2. Clearly, any effort to change the motivation or behavior of another individual implies certain ethical considerations. For example, as a change agent, one must assess the likely consequences of a change intervention; the results of not intervening; and the rights, both legal and
ethical, of the "target" individual. In the sections that follow, several motivational strategies
are described in terms of increasing another person's intrinsic and/or extrinsic motivation to perform a task. The examples that illustrate these strategies consider the change agent to be someone in control of resources or other sources of social power such as a task supervisor, educational instructor, or group leader. Obviously, there may be alternative initiators of change interventions (workers, students, outside consultants), and some of the strategies illustrated here may be (justifiably) rejected by a change agent on the basis of local values and
social norms.

3. It is interesting to note that Kazdin and Bootzin [1972] have made a quite similar point in their recent review of research on token economies. They noted that while operant conditioning procedures have been quite effective in altering focal behaviors within a controlled setting, seldom have changes been found to generalize to natural, nonreinforcing environments.

References

G. W. Allport, *Personality, A Psychological Interpretation.* Holt, 1937.

E. Aronson, "The Psychology of Insufficient Justification: An Analysis of Some Conflicting Data." In S. Feldman, ed., *Cognitive Consistency: Motivational Antecedents and Behavior Consequences.* Academic Press, 1966.

J. W. Atkinson, *An Introduction to Motivation.* Van Nostrand, 1964.

T. Ayllon and N. H. Azrin, "The Measurement and Reinforcement of Behavior of Psychotics." *Journal of Experimental Analysis of Behavior,* 1965, 8:357-383.

D. J. Bem, "Self-perception: An Alternative Interpretation of Cognitive Dissonance Phenomena." *Psychological Review,* 1967a, 74:183-200.

D. J. Bem, "Self-perception: The Dependent Variable of Human Performance." *Organizational Behavior and Human Performance,* 1967b, 2:105-121.

D. J. Bem, "Self-perception Theory." In L. Berkowitz, ed., *Advances in Experimental Social Psychology,* Vol. 6. Academic Press, 1972.

D. E. Berlyne, *Conflicts, Arousal, and Curiosity.* McGraw-Hill, 1960.

W. H. Bexton, W. Heron, and T. H. Scott, "Effects of Decreased Variation in the Sensory Environment." *Candian Journal of Psychology*, 1954, 8:70-76.

J. W. Brehm and A. R. Cohen, *Explorations in Cognitive Dissonance.* Wiley, 1962.

B. J. Calder and B. M. Staw, "The Interaction of Intrinsic and Extrinsic Motivation: Some Methodological Notes." *Journal of Personality and Social Psychology,* 1975a, 31:76-80.

B. J. Calder and B. M. Staw, "Self-perception of Intrinsic and Extrinsic Motivation." *Journal of Personality and Social Psychology*, 1975b, 31: 599-605.

B. J. Calder, M. Ross, and C. A. Insko, "Attitude Change and Attitude Attribution: Effects of Incentive, Choice, and Consequences." *Journal of Personality and Social Psychology*, 1973, 25:84-100.

J. P. Campbell, M. D. Dunnette, E. E. Lawler, and K. E. Weick, *Managerial Behavior, Performance, and Effectiveness.* McGraw-Hill, 1970.

J. M. Carlsmith, B. E. Collins, and R. L. Helmreich, "Studies in Forced Compliance: The Effect of Pressure for Compliance on Attitude Change Produced by Face-to-Face Role Playing and Anonymous Essay Writing." *Journal of Personality and Social Psychology,* 1966. 4:1-13.

D. J. Cherrington, "The Effects of a Central Incentive-Motivational State on Measures of Job Satisfaction." *Organizational Behavior and Human Performance,* 1973, 10:271-289.

D. J. Cherrington, H. J. Reitz, and W. E. Scott, "Effects of Reward and Contingent Reinforcement on Satisfaction and Task Performance." *Journal of Applied Psychology,* 1971, 55:531—536.

B. E. Collins and M. F. Hoyt, "Personal Responsibility. For-Consequences: An Integration and Extension of the Forced Compliance Literature." *Journal of Experimental Social Psychology,* 1972, 8:558-594.

R. E. Cook, "Relation of Achievement Motivation and Attribution to Self-reinforcement." Ph.D. dissertation. University of California, 1970.

R. de Charms, *Personal Causation: The Internal Affective Determinants of Behavior.* Academic Press, 1968.

E. L. Deci, "The Effects of Externally Mediated Rewards on Intrinsic Motivation." *Journal of Personality and Social Psychology,* 1971, 18:105-115.

E. L. Deci, "The Effects of Contingent and Noncontingent Rewards and Controls on Intrinsic Motivation." *Organizational Behavior and Human Performance,* 1972, 8:217-229.

W. Edwards, "The Prediction of Decision Among Bets." *Journal of Experimental Psychology,* 1955, 50:201-214.

C. B. Ferster and B. F. Skinner, *Schedules of Reinforcement.* Appleton-Century-Crofts, 1957.

L. Festinger, *A Theory of Cognitive Dissonance.* Stanford University Press, 1957.

L. Festinger and J. M. Carlsmith, "Dognitive Consequences of Forced Compliance." *Journal of Abnormal and Social Psychology,* 1959, 58:203-210.

J. L. Freedman, "Attritudinal Effects of Inadequate Justification," *Journal of Personality,* 1963, 31:371-385.

J. Galbraith and L. L. Cummings, "An Empirical Investigation of the Motivational Determinants of Task Performance: Interactive Effects Between Instrumentality-Valence and Motivation-Ability." *Organizational Behavior and Human Performance,* 1967, 2:237-257.

C. N. Green, "Casual Connections Among Managers' Merit Pay, Job Satisfaction, and Performance." *Journal of Applied Psychology,* 1974, 58:95-100.

J. R. Hackman and E. E. Lawler, "Employee Reactions to Job Characteristics." *Journal of Applied Psychology,* 1971, 55:259-286.

J. R. Hackman and G. R. Oldham, "Development of the Job Diagnostic Survey." *Journal of Applied Psychology,* 1975 , 60:159-170.

J. R. Hackman and G. R. Oldham, "Motivation Through the Design of Work." *Organizational Behavior and Human Performance,* in press.

J. R. Hackman, G. R. Oldham, R. Janson, and K. Purdy, "A New Strategy for Job Enrichment." *California Management Review,* in press, 1975.

H. F. Harlow, "Learning and Satiation of Response in Intrinsically Motivated Complex Puzzle Performance by Monkeys." *Journal of Comparative and Physiological Psychology,* 1950, 43:289-294.

H. F. Harlow, M. K. Harlow, and D. R. Meyer, "Learning Motivated by a Manipulation Drive." *Journal of Experimental Psychology,* 1950, 40:228-234.

H. F. Harlow and G. E. McClearn, "Object Discrimination Learned by Monkeys on the Basis of Manipulation Motives." *Journal of Comparative and Physiological Psychology,* 1954, 47:73-76.

F. Heider, *The Psychology of Interpersonal Relations.* Wiley, 1958.

R. J. House, "A Path-Goal Theory of Leader Effectiveness." *Administrative Science Quarterly,* 1971, 16:321-338.

R. J. House, H. J. Shapiro, and M. A. Wahba, "Expectancy Theory as a Predictor of Work Behavior and Attitude: A Reevaluation of Empirical Evidence." *Decision Sciences,* 1974, 5:481-506.

C. L. Hull, *Principles of Behavior.* Appleton-Century-Crofts, 1943.

J. McV. Hunt, "Toward a History of Intrinsic Motivation." In H. I. Day, D. E. Berlyne, and D. E. Hunt, eds., *Intrinsic Motivation: A New Direction in Education.* Holt, Rinehart, and Winston of Canada, 1971.

E. E. Jones and K. E. Davis, "From Acts to Dispositions: The Attribution Process in Person Perception." In L. Berkowitz, ed., *Advances in Experimental Psychology,* Vol. 2. Academic Press, 1965.

E. E. Jones, K. E. Davis, and K. E. Gergen, "Role Playing Variations and Their Informational Value for Person Perception." *Journal of Abnormal and Social Psychology,* 1961, 63:302-310.

E. E. Jones and V. A. Harris, "The Attribution of Attitudes." *Journal of Experimental Social Psychology,* 1967, 3:1-24.

E. E. Jones and R. E. Nisbett, *The Actor and the Observer: Divergent Perceptions of the Causes of Behavior.* General Learning Press, 1971.

A. E. Kazdin and R. R. Bootzen, "The Token Economy: An Evaluative Review." *Journal of Applied Behavior Analysis,* 1972, 5:343-372.

F. S. Keller, *Learning: Reinforcement Theory,* 2nd ed. Random House, 1969.

H. H. Kelley, "Attribution Theory in Social Psychology." In D. Levine, ed., *Nebraska Symposium on Motivation,* Vol. 15. University of Nebraska Press, 1967.

H. H. Kelly, *Attribution in Social Interaction.* General Learning Press, 1971.

S. Koch, "Behavior as 'Intrinsically' Regulated: Work Notes Towards a Pretheory of Phenomena Called Motivational." In M. R. Jones, ed., *Nebraska Symposium on Motivation.* University of Nebraska Press, 1956.

A. K. Korman, *The Psychology of Motivation.* Prentice-Hall, 1974.

A. W. Kruglanski, I. Freedman, and G. Zeevi, "The Effects of Extrinsic Incentives on

Some Qualitative Aspects of Task Performance." *Journal of Personality*, 1971, 39:606-617.

J. T. Lanzetta, "The Motivational Properties of Uncertainty." In H. I. Day, D. E. Berlyne, and D. E. Hunt, eds., *Intrinsic Motivation: A New Direction in Education*. Holt, Rinehart, and Winston of Canada, 1971.

E. E. Lawler, *Pay and Organizational Effectiveness: A Psychological View*. McGraw-Hill, 1971.

E. E. Lawler, *Motivation in Work Organizations*. Brooks/Cole, 1973.

M. R. Lepper and D. Greene, "Turning Play into Work: Effects of Adult Surveillance and Extrinsic Rewards on Children's Intrinsic Motivation." *Journal of Personality and Social Psychology*, in press.

M. R. Lepper, D. Greene, and R. E. Nisbett, "Undermining Children's Intrinsic Interest with Extrinsic Rewards: A Test of the 'Overjustification' Hypothesis." *Journal of Personality and Social Psychology*, 1973, 28:129-137.

K. Lewin, *The Conceptual Representation and the Measurement of Psychological Forces*. Duke University Press, 1938.

K. Lewin, T. Dembo, L. Festinger, and P. W. Sears, "Level of Aspiration." In J. McV. Hunt, ed., *Personality and the Behavior Disorders*, Vol. 1. Ronald Press, 1944.

D. E. Linder, J. Cooper, and E. E. Jones, "Decision Freedom as a Determinant of the Role of Incentive Magnitude in Attitude Change." *Journal of Personality and Social Psychology*, 1967, 6:245-254.

G. H. Litwin, "Motives and Expectancies as Determinants of Preference for Degrees of Risk." In J. W. Atkinson and N. T. Feather, eds., *A Theory of Achievement Motivation*. Wiley, 1966.

A. H. Maslow, *Motivatio and Personality*. Harper and Row, 1954.

A. H. Maslow, *Motivation and Personality*, 2nd ed. Harper and Row, 1970.

D. C. McClelland, "Measuring Motivation in Phantasy: The Achievement Motive." In H. Guetzkow, ed., *Groups, Leadership, and Man*. Carnegie Press, 1951.

D. C. McClelland, *The Achieving Society*. Van Nostrand, 1961.

D. C. McClelland, *Assessing Human Motivation*. General Learning Press, 1971.

D. C. McClelland, "The Role of Educational Technology in Developing Achievement Motivation." In D. C. McClelland and R. W. Steele, eds., *Human Motivation: A Book of Readings*. General Learning Press, 1973a.

D. C. McClelland, "What Is the Effect of Achievement Motivation Training in the Schools?" In D. C. McClelland and R. S. Steele, eds., *Human Motivation: A Book of Readings*. General Learning Press, 1973b.

D. C. McClelland and D. G. Winter, *Motivating Economic Achievement*. Free Press, 1969.

K. C. Montgomery, "The Role of the Exploratory Drive in Learning." *Journal of Comparative Physiological Psychology*, 1954, 47:60-64.

G. R. Oldham, "Intrinsic Motivation: Relationship to Job Characteristics and Performance." Paper presented at Eastern Psychological Association, 1974.

L. W. Porter and E. E. Lawler, *Managerial Attitudes and Performance*. Irwin Dorsey Press, 1974.

M. Ross, "Salience of Reward and Intrinsic Motivation." *Journal of Personality and Social Psychology*, 1975, 32:245-54.

J. B. Rotter, "Generalized Expectancies for Internal Versus External Control of Reinforcement." *Psychological Monographs*, 1966, 80:(1),1-28.

K. W. Spence, *Behavior Theory and Conditioning*. Yale University Press, 1956.

B. M. Staw, "Attitudinal and Behavioral Consequences of Changing a Major Organizational Reward: A Natural Field Experiment." *Journal of Personality and Social Psychology*, 1974a, 6:742-751.

B. M. Staw, "Notes Toward a Theory of Intrinsic and Extrinsic Motivation." Paper presented at Eastern Psychological Association, 1974b.

B. M. Staw, "Attribution of the 'Causes' of Performance: A New Alternative Interpretation of

Cross-sectional Research on Organizations." *Organizational Behavior and Human Performance,* 1975, 13:414-432.

B. M. Staw, B. J. Calder, and R. Hess, "Intrinsic Motivation and Norms about Payment." Working paper, Northwestern University, 1976.

L. H. Strickland, "Surveillance and Trust." *Journal of Personality,* 1958, 26:200-215.

J. W. Thibaut and H. W. Riecken, "Some Determinants and Consequences of the Perception of Social Causality." *Journal of Personality,* 1955, 24:113-133.

E. C. Tolman, *Purposive Behavior in Animals and Men.* Appleton-Century-Crofts, 1932.

E. C. Tolman, "Principles of Performance." *Psychological Review,* 1955, 62:315-326.

C. N. Uhl and A. G. Young, "Resistance to Extinction as a Function of Incentive, Percentage of Reinforcement, and Number of Nonreinforced Trials," *Journal of Experimental Psychology,* 1967, 73:556-564.

V. H. Vroom, *Work and Motivation.* Wiley, 1964.

K. E. Weick, "Reduction of Cognitive Dissonance Through Task Enhancement and Effort Expenditure." *Journal of Abnormal and Social Psychology,* 1964, 68:533-539.

K. E. Weick and D. D. Penner, "Justification and Productivity." Unpublished manuscript, University of Minnesota, 1965.

R. W. White, "Motivation Reconsidered: The Concept of Competence." *Psychological Review,* 1959, 66:297-333.

R. S. Woodworth, *Dynamic Psychology.* Columbia University Press, 1918.

TOWARD A THEORY OF
TASK MOTIVATION AND INCENTIVES

EDWIN A. LOCKE

In 1929, Bills and Brown introduced a report concerned with the effects of mental set as follows:

> One of the most important factors determining the level of efficiency which an individual may attain in . . . work is the attitude or set with which he enters upon the task. . . . But more effort has been directed toward controlling attitude as a disturbing variable than toward studying it for its own sake. As a result little is known regarding the . . . influence of set in . . . work (p. 301).

In 1963, Ryan[1] made the following observation about recent work in human motivation:

> It is impossible to perform a psychological experiment upon a human subject without manipulating and controlling his intention or task. In spite of this fact, the experimental study of tasks has been relatively neglected in modern psychology (Ch. V. p. 1).

These two statements, made nearly 35 years apart, indicate a persistent neglect in experimental psychology of the study of conscious factors in task performance. The cause of this neglect is a doctrine which has dominated experimental psychology for the last several decades: the doctrine of behaviorism. Its fundamental thesis is that psychology is the study of observable behavior and that (human) behavior can be understood without the use of explanatory concepts referring to states or actions of consciousness.

In recent years, however, some psychologists have become dissatisfied with the limitations placed upon research and theory by the behaviorist dogma. A growing number of investigators have begun to study the effects of conscious goals, intentions, desires, and purposes on task performance. The basic (implicit or explicit) premise of this research is that man's conscious ideas affect what he does, i.e., that one of the (biological) functions of consciousness is the regulation of action (see Branden, 1966; Rand, 1964, for a fuller discussion of the nature and functions of consciousness).[2]

It is argued here, in agreement with Ryan (1958), that:

> Tasks [intentions, goals, etc.] . . . are to be treated as casual factors in behavior. By this I mean that a task is a necessary condition for most kinds of behavior. (To find and account for the exceptions is an empirical problem). . . . I shall assert that a very large proportion of behavior is initiated by tasks, and that a very large proportion of tasks lead to the behavior specified by the tasks (p. 79).

Locke, E. A., "Toward a Theory of Task Motivation and Incentives," from *Organizational Behavior and Human Performance*, vol. 3 (1968), pp. 157-159. © 1968 by Academic Press, Inc. Used by permission of the author and the publisher.

It is the purpose of this paper to draw together and integrate the existing literature on the relationship between conscious goals or intentions and task performance. For our purposes the terms goal and intention will be used in their vernacular meaning as "what the individual is consciously trying to do." (Some distinctions between these two terms will be made later in the paper.)

It should be stressed that in the last analysis the content of a particular individual's goals and intentions must be inferred from his verbal report (based on his introspection). However, there are still a number of different procedures that may be used to study the relationship between conscious goals or intentions and task performance: (1) goals can be assigned by the experimenter before performance and the subject's acceptance of these goals (i.e., his decision to actually try for them) checked later by questioning; (2) subjects can be given a limited choice of goals before task performance and asked to choose one of them; (3) subjects can be allowed to set any goals they wish on the task and then asked to indicate what their goal was after performance. In addition, these methods can be used in various combinations; for example, results obtained using method (3) can be checked using method (1), i.e., by assigning the same goals to a new group of subjects that a previous group had set themselves. In the studies to be reported here, all three methods were used and all yielded substantial relationships between goals or intentions and task performance. Thus for our purposes, the advantages and disadvantages of the different procedures are not important (though in other contexts, it might be of interest to study them).

No attempt is made in the studies reported to specify the ultimate roots or causes of the particular goals or intentions an individual develops on a task. Our interest here is only in the relationship between these goals and intentions, once established, and subsequent behavior. Thus, we are not presenting a complete theory of task performance but only some foundations for a theory.

Turning briefly to the issue of nonintentional behavior, it is obvious that no individual is aware of or consciously intends every single action or movement he makes. But it remains to be seen just how much behavior can be explained with reference to conscious intent. For instance, Ryan (1958) argues: "The concept of *determining tendency* would suggest that the effect of a task [intention] may operate over such a timespan that it may produce an effect at a time when the individual is no longer aware of the task as such" (p. 82).

It may be instructive in this context to discuss four types of "unintentional" behavior that occur frequently in everyday life in order to see to what degree these might be explained in terms of conscious intent: 1) *One category is behavior whose end is foreseen but in which each movement in the sequence that is the means to the end is not consciously initiated.* For example, in returning an opponent's shot in tennis, an experienced player is not consciously aware of his footwork, backswing, or grip, but only of the intent to approach and return the shot. In such cases as this, the action leading to the goal has become automated through extended practice; each response automatically sets off the next response in the sequence. However, it should be recognized that the behavior sequence as a whole must still be *triggered* by a conscious intent (e.g., as "to return the shot" or "win the point" in the example above). Once the initial intent is abandoned, action ceases, e.g., if the tennis player suddenly decides not to try to return a shot, the usual action sequence will not occur.

Furthermore, automated behavior of this type is *initially learned* consciously and intentionally. This is true of any series of skilled goal-directed movements or actions taken by man (though such actions will involve physiological activities of which he may never be aware introspectively; see type 4 below).

2) A second category involves *behavior in which a different end occurs than is intended due to error or lack of ability*. For instance, one could try to return a tennis shot but hit the net instead. The behavior would be consciously initiated but the outcome would be imperfectly correlated with the intended outcome due to lack of knowledge or ability. Such behavior is usually described as "accidental." Clearly concepts other than conscious intent are required to explain accidents, but it should be recognized that accidents often involve very small deviations from the intended outcome (e.g., as when a tennis shot goes out of bounds by an inch). Thus conscious intent would be *one* factor in the explanation of the action sequence as a whole.

3) A third type of nonintentional behavior is *behavior in which the end that is foreseen logically entails another end that is not foreseen as such*. For example, in a verbal "conditioning" or a free-association experiment, one might intentionally give only the names of "jewels" (rubies, emeralds, diamonds, etc.). In doing so one would also be giving "plural nouns," Plural nouns would not be consciously intended as such but would be logically entailed by the intention to list jewels. Dulany (1961, 1962) uses the term "correlated hypotheses" to describe subjects' hypotheses in verbal-conditioning experiments which are correlated with the "correct" hypothesis. One could similarly use the term "correlated behavior" to describe behavior which was not intended as such but which was logically correlated with intended behavior.

4) Finally, there is *behavior which is not and never was under direct conscious control, but may be indirectly controlled*. For instance, in the course of carrying out a voluntary act, many automatic, nonconscious physiological actions will occur (e.g., muscle contractions, neural activity, glandular secretions, etc.)—actions which one could not become aware of using the unaided senses. But by initiating certain molar actions one may indirectly control some of these molecular actions.

The key point to recognize in the above four cases is that all the actions in question were or could be *initiated* by a mental act, that they were or could be originally *set in motion* by a conscious goal or intention. In addition, the results or outcomes of the behaviors are ordinarily either the ones intended or are correlated with those intended (the size of the correlation depending upon the individual's capacity, knowledge, ability, and the situation).

The research to be reported here involves predominantly simple tasks in which learning complex new skills and making long-term plans and strategies is not necessary to achieve goals—tasks of the type in which effort and concentration are likely to have a relatively direct effect on output or choice.

The paper is divided into two parts. Part 1 reports research dealing with direct relationships between goals or intentions and task performance. Part II is an extension of the theory to attempt to account for the motivational effects of external incentives on task performance. *An external incentive is defined as an event or object external to the individual which can incite action.* It is argued that if goals or intentions are a necessary condition for most kinds of behavior, then incentives will affect behavior only through their effects on goals and intentions and will have no effect independent of their effects on goals and intentions. Part II reports research relevant to this deduction.

I. Goals, Intentions, and Task Performance

Goal Difficulty and Level of Performance

The studies in this section are concerned with the relationship between the level or difficulty of the goal the subject is trying for and the quantitative level of his performance (amount of output, speed of reaction time, school grades, etc.). If goals regulate performance, then hard goals should produce a higher level of performance than easy goals, other things (such as ability) being equal.

Figure 1 shows the combined results of 12 studies on this topic by the present investigator and colleagues. In some of these studies goals were assigned to subjects by the experimenter and goal acceptance was checked by interviews. In other studies subjects set their own goals. In all cases goals were expressed in terms of some specific quantitative score that the subject was trying to achieve on each trial or on the task as a whole. Goal difficulty is expressed in Fig. 1 in terms of the percentage trials on which the subjects trying for a particular goal actually beat that goal. Performance level is expressed in terms of the within-study z-score for performance for the particular goal group in question. Thus each point represents a particular group (a particular goal) in a particular study; it indicates the probability of the subjects in that group reaching their goal and their mean output in relation to the other goal groups in that study.

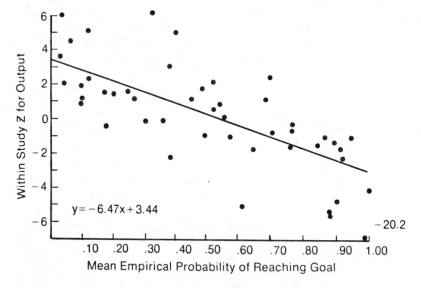

Figure 1. Output as a function of goal difficulty for 12 studies combined.

The results are unequivocal: the harder the goal the higher the level of performance. (This was also true within each study.[3]) Although subjects with very hard goals reached their goals far less often than subjects with very easy goals, the former consistently performed at a higher level than the latter. The rank-order correlation between goal difficulty and performance for all the points shown in Fig. 1 is .78 ($p<.01$). (The one extreme point, circled in Fig. 1, was not used, however, in calculating the slope of the function, as this would have given a misleading picture of the general relationship between the two variables.)

The nature of the experiments from which the above data were obtained utilized a variety of different tasks: brainstorming, complex computation, addition, perceptual speed, toy construction, reaction time, grade achievement in college—thus indicating the generality of the results across tasks. . . .

Relationship of Qualitatively Different
Goals to Level of Performance

The studies in this section are concerned with the relationship of qualitatively different goals to level of performance. Most of them deal with a comparison of the assigned goal of "do your best" with specific hard goals. The former was chosen for research by the present writer because it is used, explicitly or implicitly, in virtually all psychological experiments. Yet, just what it means is not exactly clear. It was believed that such a goal did not necessarily lead to the highest performance possible. Thus it was decided to compare the output induced by a "do-best" goal with that which could be produced by specific quantitative hard goals of the type used in the studies described in the previous section.

Eight studies were conducted by the present writer and Bryan in which these two types of goals were compared.[4] In six of the eight studies the subjects trying for specific hard goals performed at a significantly higher level than subjects trying to "do their best." Thus, a "do best" goal does not tend to produce (under the conditions of these studies) the highest possible level of performance. . . .

Behavioral Intentions and Choice

The designs of the studies reported in the preceding sections required all subjects to work at the same task (do the same thing) and the focus of interest was on how well they did it (i.e., output). The experiments to be reported in this section were designed so that subjects had a *choice* either as to the difficulty of the *task* they would work on or the particular kinds of *responses* they would give. The intention to make a certain task choice or to respond in a certain way will henceforth be called a *behavioral intention* (after Dulany, 1962).

Three studies conducted by the present writer and colleagues (Locke, Bryan, and Kendall, 1968) examined the relationship between hehavioral intentions and task choice. The task in all cases was word unscrambling and subjects were allowed to choose, on each trial, the length of the word (e.g., four letters, five letters, six letters, etc.) they would try to unscramble. Subjects had 45 seconds to try to solve each word chosen. Word-length choice was the dependent variable.

In the first study there were three blocks of ten trials each and subjects filled out a 5-point behavioral-intention scale before each trial and before each block of trials. The scale asked the subject to indicate whether she intended to choose a "very hard word," a "hard word," a "moderately hard word," etc., on the next trial or block of trials. The intention ratings were quantified on a 5-point scale: 1 for the "very easy words" alternative, to 5 for the "very hard words" alternative. The mean within-subject correlation between word length choice and intentions across the 30 trials was .81 (median=.80). The mean within-block, between-individual correlation between block intention and mean word choice on that block was .60 ($p<01$).

In the second study, the first block consisted of ten choices. Before trial 1, one third of the subjects were told to try to ''succeed'' as much as possible; one third were told to ''get as great a sense of personal achievement as possible,'' and one third were told to try to ''overcome the greatest possible challenges.'' Behavioral intentions were measured on a 5-point scale completed before the block began and were quantified on a 5-point scale as in the previous study (see above). The relationship between instructions, intentions and mean word choice is shown in Fig. 2. Clearly the ''challenge'' group developed the ''hardest'' intentions and chose the hardest (longest) words while the ''success'' group developed the easiest intentions and chose the easiest (shortest) words. The ''achievement'' group was intermediate on both variables. The correlation between instructions (quantified 5, 3, and 1 for the challenge, achievement and success groups, respectively) and mean word-length choice on the ten trials was .67 ($p<.01$), while that between intentions and mean word-length was .88 ($p<.01$).

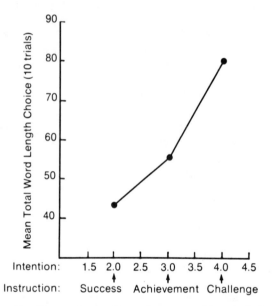

Figure 2. The relationship of instructions and intentions to word-length choice.

On block 11, there were ten more trials but no specific instructions. The correlation between intentions and word-length choice was .81 ($p<01$).

In the third study, subjects had five blocks of five choices each and they filled out an intention rating before each block. The within-block correlations between mean word-length choice and intentions were .78, .83, .79, .85, and .79 for the five blocks, respectively (all p's$<.01$).

Let us turn now to studies in which all subjects had to work on the same task but had a choice of *responses*. These studies have all been in the ''verbal-conditioning'' area. Subjects are asked to free associate or to make up sentences and are ''reinforced'' (by the experimenter saying ''good'' etc.) for listing certain types of words or certain kinds of sentences. Dulany (1962) gave his subjects postexperimental interviews asking them to report their behavioral intentions and found highly significant correlations in three different studies between the subjects' behavioral intentions and the actual number of responses given in the intended category. For instance, subjects who intentionally tried to make up only sentences beginning with "I" or "We" actually made more such sentences than those who did not try to do this.

A study of a similar nature was conducted by Holmes (1966). Subjects who tried intentionally to give "I" or "We" sentences gave significantly more of them than those who did not try to do this, even when both groups were aware that "I," "We" sentences were the kind the experimenter was "reinforcing" them for giving.

Two later studies by Dulany (1968) reported correlations of .94 and .90, respectively, between behavioral intentions and responses on a task where the subject was to select, on each trial, one of two sentences presented to him.

Finally, a field study by Leventhal and Niles (1964) showed subjects films which demonstrated the danger of smoking and its relationship to lung cancer. Afterwards, they asked each subject to indicate how much *desire* he had to get a chest X-ray. The stronger the desire to get an X-ray the more likely the subject was to actually have one taken.

II. Goals and Intentions as Mediators of the Effects of External Incentives

A General Note on Instructions

In a number of the experiments reported in Part 1, goals were manipulated by instructions. However, in most of the studies conducted by the author subjects' *acceptance* of their assigned goals was corroborated by interviews. Thus these studies were legitimately described as dealing with the relationship between goals and performance rather than the relationship between instructions and performance.

As every experimenter and shop foreman knows, one of the most efficient ways to get somebody to do something is to ask him, i.e., to *assign* him a goal or task. But it is important to recognize that instructions do not inevitably nor automatically affect an individual's goals or behavior. For example, in some of the studies reported in Part 1, post-experimental interviews revealed that subjects did *not* accept their assigned goals. For these subjects there was no relationship between assigned goals and performance. Only when these subjects were re-classified according to the goals they actually reported working for did a relationship between goals and performance emerge (e.g., see Locke and Bryan, 1966b, 1967a).

Our theory suggests that instructions will affect behavior only if they are consciously accepted by the individual and translated into specific goals or intentions. This applies equally well to the instruction by an experimenter to "try for quality in your answers" to the instruction by a shop foreman to "produce 400 portzeebies an hour." It is not enough to know that an order or request was made: one has to know whether or not the individual heard it and understood it, how he appraised it, and what he decided to do about it before its effects on his behavior can be predicted and explained. . . .

Goals as Mediators of the Effects of Incentives on Level of Performance

Money. In a study reported by Locke *et al.* (1968) subjects worked on a brainstorming task (giving uses for objects) for three blocks of seven trials each. Goal-setting instructions and amount of incentive offered for output were systematically manipulated. It was found that subjects who set their goals high on block III relative to block II improved their performance on block III more than those whose block III goals were not substantially higher than their block II goals. On the other hand, there was no main effect of incentive independent of goal level. Subjects who had the same output goals produced the same amount whether they were paid a bonus for reaching the goal or not. Using groups means as the units of analysis, the rank order correlation between output and toal level was .85 ($p<.01$).

In a second study reported by Locke *et al.*, 30 subjects worked for 50 minutes at a toy construction task. The subjects set output goals at the beginning and at the halfway point of the work period. Half the subjects were paid on a piece-rate system and half were paid only for participation. It was found that the mean output of the two groups did not differ significantly in either half of the work period. This finding was congruent with the fact that mean goal level of the two groups did not differ significantly in either period. On the other hand, when all subjects were combined, there was a significant relationship between second-half performance and second-half goal level.

Numerous industrial studies of the effects of monetary incentives on performance have found that the effectiveness of piece-rate incentive systems depends on the particular production quotas that workers have (e.g., Mathewson, 1931; Roethlisberger and Dickson, 1939; Whyte, 1955). If the workers feel that their long-term self-interest (either in terms of interpersonal relations, effort, or job tenure) will be threatened by trying to go "all out" for piece-rate earnings, they will restrict production to what they consider to be a "safe" level (a level that will protect their jobs and/or keep the time study man from retiming the job and setting new rates, etc.).

One effect of a well-run incentive system is that (providing the workers value money) it will encourage workers to accept tasks and set goals that they would not accept or set on their own (i.e., for the intrinsic enjoyment of the work itself). Thus, money can serve to *commit* subjects to tasks which they would not otherwise undertake. The use of incentives to insure goal acceptance was a key element in Taylor's (1911) "scientific management" system.

Knowledge of score. The studies to be reported in this section are concerned only with the effects of overall scores (KS) on a task or knowledge of score on a task where there are no right or wrong answers (e.g., reaction time). Thus, we are concerned with "motivational" knowledge as opposed to epistemic knowledge of the type that can be used to correct errors (e.g., visual feedback on a dart-throwing task).

An initial study by Locke and Bryan (1966b) compared the effect of KS vs. NoKS on a complex computation task. Some subjects were allowed to compute their scores after each trial and some were not. The subjects had six trials of 10 minutes each. No difference was found between the KS and NoKS groups in performance. However, when the subjects were reclassified according to their postexperimental goal descriptions, a significant relationship of goals to performance was found.

Two subsequent studies manipulated goal-setting and KS independently, using a 2×2 design (Locke, 1967b; Locke and Bryan, 1967c). In both studies subjects worked on five trials of irregular duration (mean = 12 minutes) at an addition task. Periodically half the subjects (KS group) were given their scores and half (NoKS group) were not. In the first study, half the subjects were given specific hard goals to aim for on each trial, while the other half were told to "do their best." In the second study, half the subjects were given easy goals to aim for and half were given hard goals. In both studies, the subjects with hard goals performed significantly better than those with easy or do-best goals, but no difference in performance was found between the KS and NoKS groups. The results for the Locke (1967b) study are shown in Figs. 3a and b. The hard-goal group is clearly superior to the do-best group in performance, whereas the KS and NoKS groups have very similar performance curves.

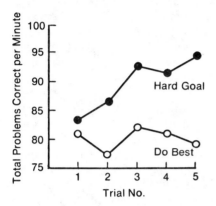 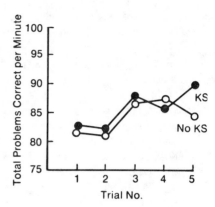

Figure 3. The relationship of goals and knowledge of score to performance.

Another study (Locke and Bryan, 1967b) found that when KS does facilitate performance, it does so only *through* its effects on goal-setting. Subjects were given 16 5-minute trials on a complex computation task. One group of subjects was allowed to compute their scores after each trial and another was not. Subjects filled out goal description questionnaires before, during, and after performance. It was found that the KS subjects performed significantly better than the NoKS subjects on the last eight trials, and it was only on these trials that the KS subjects set harder goals than the NoKS subjects. When differential goal-setting was controlled by partialing, the relationship of KS condition to performance was vitiated.

The important thing about KS, then, is not merely whether it is given or not given but how a subject interprets and evaluates it, and what goals he sets in response to it. The *form* in which KS is given, of course, can influence its effectiveness. For instance, if KS is given in such a form that it cannot be used to set goals or to judge one's progress in relation to a standard (as in Locke, 1967b; Locke and Bryan, 1967c) it will not affect motivation.

If, on the other hand, KS is given in relation to standards, the level of the standard can influence goal level. Locke (1967c) gave subjects feedback on a reaction-time task in relation to different standards; some subjects were told on each trial whether or not they had beaten their *best* previous score and others whether or not they had beaten their *worst* previous score. Positive feedback was given by means of a green light which signalled that subject successfully beat the standard. In this study, subjects with the harder ("best") standards showed faster reaction times than those with easier ("worst") standards. To get greenlight feedback, they had to try harder in the former case than in the latter. Thus giving knowledge in relation to the different standards in effect influenced the difficulty of the goals subjects tried for.

Time limits. Two studies by Bryan and Locke (1967b) gave subjects different amounts of time to complete an addition task. One group of individuals was given just enough time to complete the problems (the number being geared to the subject's level of ability) while another group was given twice this amount of time. It was found that the subjects given an excess amount of time took longer to complete the task than those given a minimum amount of time. The subjects given an excess amount of time also set easier goals on the task than did those given a minimum amount of time. When time limits were removed and subjects were free to work at their own pace, both experimental groups set their goals at the same level and worked at the same pace. Thus, the effect of the different time limits appeared to be a function of the differing performance subgoals which they induced. Their effects did not extend to a situation where the work was self-paced.

The foregoing studies of time limits can be viewed as belonging to a wider class of studies concerned with the effect of task difficulty on performance. The difference between these studies and those discussed above is that in the present case no goals (other than completing the problems in the time allowed) were assigned as such; the subject was simply given a task and told how much time he had to complete it. The effect of the imposed time limits was a function of the goals the subjects set in response to them.

The above studies virtually exhaust the literature on the topic of goals as mediators of the effect of incentives on performance level. Our treatment of the next three incentives: participation, competition, and praise and reproof, is therefore confined mainly to a discussion of experiments in which goal-setting was mentioned only incidentally, or to discussion at the theoretical level.

Participation. A number of investigators have argued that employee participation in the decisions that affect them motivates better job performance (e.g., Maier, 1955; Likert, 1961; Viteles 1953; Vroom, 1964), and there is research evidence that would appear to support this claim. However, the question that concerns us here is *how* participation serves to motivate job performance when it does so. In the typical field experiment on participation, many aspects of the job are likely to be changed: e.g., job method (method of performing the task), method of payment, rate of pay, quality and quantity of training, type of supervision, commitment of the worker to his assigned quota, the level of the quota, etc. Any one of these factors could affect subsequent production, but experimental research has not systematically tested the relative importance of each.

It will suffice for our purposes to point out that goal-setting, specifically a change in the production quota, has been an explicit element in many participation studies. For example, see the following description of Bavelas' study by Viteles (1953, p. 167):

> . . . in the course of . . . [participation] meetings, the experimenter . . . talked about the greater ease of working together as a team; discussed individual production levels with the group; questioned its members as to the level of production which might be obtained if they worked as a team, and *asked if they would like to set a team goal for higher production* (italics mine).

In another study of participation by Lawrence and Smith (1955), the authors write:

Members of these groups were encouraged to use their own judgement in setting goals, but were reminded that *unless they set the goal a little above their present accomplishment they would be unable to determine the effectiveness of the group when working as a team* (p. 334, italics mine).

Similarly in a study of participation at General Electric reported by Sorcher (1967): "The employees were asked . . . to set quality goals for themselves, and to discuss how they might improve their performance so as to improve the quality of their output" (p. 16). In this study substantial improvements in work quality were obtained as a result of the group meetings.

Most revealing of all is a recent field study conducted by Meyer *et al*. (1965) where the effects of participation and goal-setting were more clearly separated. The authors found that: "While subordinate participation in the goal-setting process had some effect on improved performance, *a much more powerful influence was whether goals were set at all*" (p. 126, italics mine). In other words the content of the participation sessions was more important than the fact of participation itself. (The results of goal-setting in this study were given previously in Part I.)

The above quotes should not be taken to imply that participation has no motivational effect in and of itself. For example, Macoby (quoted in Viteles, 1953) suggests that participation may help to internalize motivation—to increase a subject's *commitment* to performance standards. The point is that goal-setting has been an integral part of previous studies of participation. Considering the amount of evidence there is (see Part I) that goals regulate performance, it must be concluded that the results of at least some of these studies can be attributed largely, if not entirely, to the goal-setting which was associated with or induced by the experimental design.

Competition. It is well known, both from experimental studies and from everyday experience, that competition can serve as an incentive to increase one's effort on a task. This phenomenon is an intrinsic part of athletics and business and is not unknown in academia. In the paradigm case of competition *another person's or groups' performance is the standard by which goals are set and success and failure judged.* One reason competition in athletics is so effective is that winning requires that one surpass the performance of the *best* existing competitor. This typically results in the standard of success becoming progressively more difficult with time. Each time a record is broken, the level of performance required to win (against the record holder) is raised. Each competitor must then readjust his goal and his level of effort to the difficulty of the task. The result is progressively better performance. (Of course cognitive factors can facilitate performance improvement, i.e., discovering better methods of performing the task. But it is the individual's *goal* to win or improve that generally motivates the search for such innovations.)

The case is similar though not identical in business. (Unlike athletics, business is not a "zero-sum game," where one man's gain necessarily means another man's loss. In business, wealth is *created* and therefore everyone benefits in the long run.) Competition will encourage the development of better and better products as long as there are firms who wish to increase their share of the market. Competition may also spur firms to increase their quality or lower prices in order not to lose business.

The effect or competition, both between individuals and between groups, depends upon the particular person or persons one is competing with and one's own values. In athletics, the goal is typically to beat the best other competitor. In business this is not always the case; typically, business firms are satisfied to surpass their own best previous performances. Students, if they are competing, will ordinarily pick other students with grades or abilities similar to their own to compete with, or else will try to surpass their own best previous grade-point average.

The case of an individual trying to improve over his own previous performance on a task can be considered a special case of competition: *self-competition*.

As with participation, competition may have other effects besides inducing goal-setting. Above all, competition probably encourages individuals to remain *committed* to goals that they might otherwise abandon in the face of fatigue and difficulty. For instance, if mile runners only ran against themselves or against a stop watch, the 4-minute mile might never have been broken.

In addition, competition encourages the setting of goals that might not have been set at all in the absence of the other party. For example, if the Ford Motor Company had not developed a mass-produced low-priced automobile, General Motors might not have thought of developing a similar (competing) model (at that particular time).

Praise and reproof. A recent review of the literature on praise and reproof (Kennedy and Willcutt, 1964) concluded that the effects of both incentives were highly variable, though praise was generally more effective in improving performance. Most studies have found complex interactions between praise and reproof and such variables as: age, social class, race, sex, task, and intelligence.

As with all the other incentives discussed heretofore, the present theory suggests that the effects of praise and reproof will be a function of what goals the individual sets in response to them. It is clear from introspection and from everyday experience that sometimes the reaction to criticism is to clench one's teeth and try harder; at other times, the reaction is to give up (and "sulk") or to deliberately do badly (to "get even" with the critic). Similarly, praise sometimes leads to the setting of new and higher goals and at other times it is taken as a signal to "goof-off."

A theory explaining the precise circumstances in which praise and reproof will lead to the setting of higher and/or lower goals is beyond the scope of this paper. The important point is, however, that the effects of these incentives on performance should be a function of the goals the individuals set in response to them. The highly inconsistent results obtained by previous investigators may be attributed to their failure to control for differential goal-setting by subjects in the different experimental conditions.

The importance of goal-setting was implicitly recognized in one study, whose authors Kennedy and Willcutt (1964) paraphrase as follows:

> The authors concluded that when the examiner's statements led subjects to assume that a particular level of performance is expected or that his performance is less satisfactory than that of other subjects, failure increases motivation; but when the examiner's statements only comment upon the subject's performance, failure lowers motivation (p. 329).

This implies that reproof will have a facilitative effect on performance when it is given *in relation to a standard*. Our previous discussion of knowledge of score suggested the same thing; giving scores in relation to a standard is one means of implicitly manipulating or encouraging goal-setting by a subject.

Another factor that has not always been controlled in studies of praise and reproof is that of success and failure. In some studies (e.g., Anderson, White, and Wash, 1966) subjects were given fictitious test scores in relation to some (fictitious) norm and then praised (for high scores) or reproved (for low scores). Without two control groups given success and failure feedback alone, the relative contribution of praise and reproof as compared with task success and failure cannot be determined.

Let us turn now to the effects of incentives on choice.

Behavioral Intentions and Desires as Mediators of the Effects of Incentives on Choice

Money. Each of the three studies of word unscrambling described above (and reported in Locke *et al.*, 1968) involved monetary incentives. In the first study, subjects were offered: 0 cents for successfully unscrambling their chosen word on the first block of ten trials; 2 cents for each word solved correctly (regardless of length) on the second block; and 10 cents for each word solved correctly (regardless of length) on the third block. It was found that subjects tended to choose easier words as the payment for success became greater. There was a correlation across blocks between amount of incentive and mean word length choice of $-.51$ ($p<.05$). However, the correlation was vitiated ($r = .22$, ns) when the effects of intentions were partialed out, indicating that the money did not affect word choice independent of its effects on the subjects' intentions.

In the second study discussed above, subjects were given "success," "achievement," or "challenge" instructions on the first block of ten trials, but were offered no money for correct solutions. On the second block, subjects were given no instructions but were offered 4 cents for each word correctly solved regardless of length. The point biserial correlation, for all subjects combined, between mean word-length choice and incentive (coded 0 and 1 for blocks I and II, respectively) across blocks was $-.48$ ($p<.01$). However, when intentions were partialed out this r was reduced to a nonsignificant $-.10$. In contrast, intentions correlated .86 ($p<.01$) with word choice across blocks after incentive was partialed out.

In the third study in this series described above, subjects had five blocks of five trials each; on each block the subject was offered either 1, 2, 3, 4, or 5 cents for each word solved correctly on that block regardless of length. (The order was counterbalanced across subjects.) Again subjects tended to choose easier words when offered the higher incentive. The relationship of intentions and incentive to mean word choice is shown in Fig. 4, where word choice is plotted as a function of incentive for each of three levels of intention. (Intention level 1.0 corresponds to the "very easy words" alternative on the intention scale; 2.0 corresponds to the "fairly easy words" alternative; 3.0 corresponds to the "neither too easy nor too hard" alternative; the few subjects who checked intentions harder than this are also included in this group.) It is clear that the effect of intention on word choice was considerable but there was no effect of incentive within any given intention level. As in the previous two studies, incentive had no effect on word choice independent of the subjects' behavioral intentions. (There was also a no-incentive comparison group in this study. The results were the same whether or not this group was included. For the complete report, see Locke *et al.*, 1968, Study 5.) The overall correlation across blocks between intentions and word choice was .83 ($p<.01$); this correlation remained unchanged after partialing incentive. In contrast, the correlation across blocks of incentive with word choice after partialing intentions was .04 (ns).

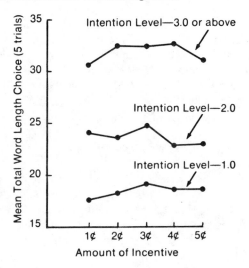

Figure 4. Word-length choice as a function of incentive for three levels of intention.

Verbal "reinforcement." The previously discussed findings of Dulany (1962, 1968) and Holmes (1966) regarding behavioral intentions and verbal responses were obtained in studies of "verbal conditioning." The subjects in these studies were instructed to free associate or to make up sentences beginning with one of a number of pronouns, and the experimenter reinforced some arbitrarily designated class of words (e.g., plural nouns) or pronouns (e.g., I, or We) by saying "good" or "Mmm-hmm" after each response in that class. In the above three studies it was found that such "reinforcement" had no effect on responses independent of subjects' intention to give the "correct" response.

Another series of studies in this same area examined the effects of the subjects' conscious *desires* on behavior. In these studies subjects were asked to indicate the strength of their desire to get the reinforcement ("good," etc.) which the experimenter provided (e.g., DeNike, 1965; Spielberger, Berger, and Howard, 1963; Spielberger, Bernstein, and Ratliff, 1966; Spielberger, Levin, and Shepard, 1962). It was found that the frequency of emission of the "correct" response class was a direct function of the strength of the subjects' desire to get the reinforcement (provided he knew what the "correct" response class was).

III. Discussion

There is considerable evidence to support the view that goals and intentions are important determinants of task performance. It is argued that these long-neglected concepts are important enough so that any tenable theory of human motivation must take account of them. This conclusion is based both on the fact that consciousness is man's means of survival (Rand, 1964) and on the strong empirical relationships that have been obtained between goals and behavior.

The experimental findings also indicate that goals and intentions mediate the effects of incentives on behavior. It appears that a necessary condition for incentives to affect behavior is that the individual recognize and evaluate the incentive and develop goals, and/or intentions in response to this evaluation. A careful examination of the subjects' goals and intentions in research on incentives should produce more clear-cut results as well as providing a theoretical rationale for explaining how incentives affect action.

A highly simplified schematic showing the hypothesized sequence of events leading from events in the environment to action is given below:

Environmental			Goal-setting	
Event $\longrightarrow$ Cognition $\longrightarrow$		Evaluation $\longrightarrow$	Intention $\longrightarrow$	Performance
(e.g., incentive)				
(1)	(2)	(3)	(4)	(5)

The present research examined only the relationships between stages 4 and 5, and between 1, 4, and 5. Cognition and evaluation were assumed to occur, but their contents were not specified. The focus of interest was on the *results* of these processes (the goals or intentions established) and subsequent action. A complete theory of task motivation would, of course, have to deal with the processes of cognition and evaluation (and their determinants) as well as their outcomes.

It may be useful theoretically to classify the various incentives that were discussed in Part II. For our purposes the dimension of interest is the degree to which the different types of incentives suggest *specific* goals or intentions to subjects.

Instructions, of course, are the most direct means of manipulating goals and intentions. Instructions will influence behavior providing: (1) the individual accepts them, i.e., accepts the assignment as his own goal or intention, and (2) he is able to do what is asked (this will depend upon his knowledge, ability and the situation).

Giving an individual specific *time limits* is another fairly direct means of manipulating goals, given the same qualifications as for instructions. It was shown previously that individuals who accept different time limits will set different subgoals as well, but these were a result of their accepting the different time limit initially.

Two less direct means of manipulating goals are giving *knowledge of score* and providing *competition*. These incentives do not tell the subject directly what goal to try for, but if given in the right form, they may *suggest* specific standards to him. For instance, giving a subject his raw scores after each trial may suggest the goal of improvement (providing the trials are all the same length so that the trial scores are comparable). Similarly, giving KS in relation to some external standard is certain to imply a goal to the subject. Giving scores in relation to those of another person is a common way of combining KS and competition. Again the effects of both incentives will be dependent upon the subject choosing to use the KS to set goals or to try to beat the other individual. These two incentives are usually quite effective in experimental situations where the subject is actively looking for cues as to what he is supposed to do and is anxious to cooperate (Orne, 1962).

Money, praise and *reproof*, and *participation*, in contrast to the above incentives, are quite indirect means of manipulating goals. None of them directly suggests or implies that the subject should try for a *particular* goal as such. Offering an individual money for output may motivate him to set his goals higher than he would otherwise but this will depend entirely upon how much money he wishes to make and how much effort he wishes to expend to make it. It is useful in this context to recall the well-known sociologist Max Weber's observation that the introduction of high incentive pay may reduce output if the worker's income aspirations remain the same as before the incentive was introduced. Some workers would prefer to make the same money in less time than to make more money in the same amount of time. The most important role played by money is probably to get a subject to accept an assigned task or goal or to insure his commitment to a job.

Similarly participation as such will not necessarily suggest a higher output goal; this will depend on the particular *content* of the participation process (the particular nature of the decisions reached). The most direct effect of participation is probably to commit a subject to the decision reached (as with money), whatever that might be.

The effects of praise and reproof on goal-setting are also indirect. Praise and reproof per se represent only evaluations of the subject's past performance and do not imply what *he should do* in the future. A subject's reaction to these incentives will depend on such factors as whether he considers the comments just or unjust, the particular work context in which the comments were made, his liking and respect for the person making the comments, his own personality, etc.

In most real life work situations a combination of all of these incentives are employed. A worker is hired and *instructed* on what to do and *how fast* to do it; he is given or gets *knowledge of performance* either from others or from the task itself; he may *compete* with others for promotion; he is *paid* for working, he is *evaluated* by his supervisor, and sometimes he *participates* in decision making. All of these factors can be considered ways of (1) getting the subject to set or accept work goals, and (2) retaining his commitment to them and insuring persistence over time.

The issue of goal commitment has not been dealt with in any of the research discussed above, but it is no doubt an important factor in performance. The subject's degree of commitment to his goal may play an important role in determining how easily he will give up in the face of difficulty, how likely he will be to "goof-off" when not being pressured from the outside, how likely he will be to abandon hard goals, and how prone he will be to "leave the field" (i.e., job) in the face of stress.

Finally, a word is in order about the possible industrial applications of the finding that goal setting is a major determinant of task performance. There are two recent trends in industry, which, although they were not inspired by this research, are quite congruent with its implications. One is a motivational program called *Zero Defects* (American Management Association, 1965). The purpose of a zero-defects program is basically to reduce errors in workmanship (i.e., increase the quality of work) by persuading workers to adopt higher goals with regard to quality. Carrying out the program often involves the gathering of more precise quality data (knowledge of results of the epistemic type) and changing of work methods, and some programs are supplemented by the introduction of group competition and prizes for accomplishment. Huse (1966) has argued that another important aspect of zero-defects programs is the opening up of channels of communication between the workers and management.

Without carefully controlled studies, of course, it cannot be determined just what particular aspects of the zero-defects programs are most responsible for the success that they have apparently enjoyed. But changing the quality goals of individual workers and managers does seem to be the key element; not only does it affect work directly but it apparently stimulates employees to try to *discover* better methods of doing the work.

While zero-defects programs are usually focused on work at the blue collar level, the focus of a second major trend is on work at the white collar level. It is called *Management by Objectives* (see Hughes, 1965; Valentine, 1966, for details). The key element in this system is the setting of specific performance goals by executives and managers. Goals are usually set jointly by the manager and his supervisor, thus participation is involved. Goals can involve sales, growth, output, income, costs or some combination of these, depending upon the particular type of job. The process involves: the delineation of company goals and the translation of these into goals relevant to the individual's own job, setting up hierarchies of objectives, planning out the means by which each goal is to be reached, and agreeing upon the criteria to be used in evaluation. (Zero defects could be interpreted as the application of this general approach to the particular problem of work quality.) Again, many different factors are involved in management by objectives programs but the setting of specific goals is the cardinal element.

Notes

The research on which many of the studies cited in this paper were based, was supported by Nour contract 4792(00) from the Office of Naval Research. Other studies were supported by grant No. MH 12103-01 from the National Institutes of Mental Health. The author would like to thank Miss Judith F. Bryan of the American Institutes for Research for her help in all phases of the research.
1. The following mimeographed chapters by Ryan are available from the Department of Psychology, Cornell University, Ithaca, New York: Chapter 1: Explaining behavior: Chapter II: Explanatory concepts: Chapter V: Experiments on intention, task and set; Chapter VI: Intentional learning; and Chapter VII: Unintentional learning.
2. There are important philosophical issues involved in the decision to use or not to use concepts referring to states of consciousness as explanatory terms. These issues are both epistemological, e.g., the problem of the privacy of conscious states, and metaphysical, e.g., the mind-body problem. Due to space limitations, however, the present paper is confined exclusively to a discussion of experimental findings.
3. The studies are marked with an asterisk in the References.
4. These are marked with a dagger (†) in the References.

References

American Management Association, *Zero Defects: doing it right the first time*, Management Bulletin, 71, 1965.

Anderson, H. E., White, W. F., and Wash, J. A. Generalized effects of praise and reproof. *Journal of Educational Psychology*, 1966, 57, 169-173.

Atkinson, J. W. Towards experimental analysis of human motivation in terms of motives, expectancies, and incentives. *In* J. W. Atkinson (Ed.), *Motives in fantasy, action and society*. New York: Van Nostrand, 1958, pp. 288-305.

Atkinson, J. W., and Feather, N. T. *A theory of achievement motivation*. New York: Wiley, 1966.

Battle, Esther S. Motivational determinants of academic competence. *Journal of Personality and Social Psychology*, 1966, 4, 634-642.

Bills, A. G., and Brown, C. The quantitative set. *Journal of Experimental Psychology*, 1929, 12, 301-323.

Branden, N. The Objectivist theory of volition. *The Objectivist*, 1966, 5, No. 1, 7-12.

†Bryan, J. F., and Locke, E. A. Goal-setting as a means of increasing motivation. *Journal of Applied Psychology*, 1967, 51, 274-277, (a).

Bryan, J. F., and Locke, E. A. Parkinson's law as a goal-setting phenomenon. *Organizational Behavior and Human Performance*, 1967, 2, 258-275, (b).

DeNike, L. D. Recall of reinforcement and conative activity in verbal conditioning. *Psychological Reports*, 1965, 16, 345-346.

Dey, M. K., and Kaur, G. Facilitation of performance, by experimentally induced ego motivation. *Journal of General Psychology*, 1965, 73, 237-247.

Dulaney, D. E., Jr. Hypothesis and habits in verbal "operant conditioning" *Journal of Abnormal and Social Psychology*, 1961, 63, 251-263.

Dulany, D. E., Jr. The place of hypotheses and intentions: an analysis of verbal control in verbal conditioning. *In* C. W. Eriksen (Ed.), *Behavior and awareness*. Durham, North Carolina: Duke Univ. Press, 1962, pp. 102-129.

Dulany, D. E. Jr., Awareness, rules and propositional control: a confrontation with S-R behavior theory. *In* D. Horton and T. Dixon (Eds.), *Verbal behavior and general behavior theory*. Englewood Cliffs, New Jersey: Prentice-Hall, 1968, pp. 340-387.

Eagle, M. N. The effect of learning strategies upon free recall. *American Journal of Psychology*, 1967, 80, 421-425.

Eason, R. G., and White, C. T. Muscular tension, effort, and tracking of difficulty; studies of parameters which affect tension level and performance efficiency. *Perceptual and Motor Skills*, 1961, 12, 331-372.

Henderson, E. H. A study of individually formulated purposes for reading in relation to reading achievement comprehension and purpose attainment. Unpublished Ph.D. dissertation, Univ. of Delaware, 1963.

Holmes, D. S. Verbal conditioning or problem solving and cooperation? Midwestern Psychological Association, 1966.

Hughes, C. L. *Goal-setting*. New York: American Management Association, 1965.

Huse, E. F. Do zero defects programs really motivate workers? *Personnel*, 1966, 43, 14-21.

Kennedy, W. A., and Willcutt, H. C. Praise and blame as incentives. *Psychological Bulletin*, 1964, 62, 323-332.

Lawrence, L. C., and Smith, P. C. Group decision and employee participation. *Journal of Applied Psychology*, 1955, 39, 334-337.

Leventhal, H., and Niles, P. A. A field experiment on fear arousal with data on the validity of questionnaire measures. *Journal of Personality*, 1964, 32, 459-479.

Likert, R. *New patterns of management*. New York: McGraw-Hill, 1961.

Locke, E. A. The relationship of intentions to level of performance. *Journal of Applied Psychology*, 1966, 50, 60-66. (a)

*Locke, E. A. A closer look at level of aspiration as a training procedure: A reanalysis of Fryer's data. *Journal of Applied Psychology*, 1966, 50, 417-420. (b)

Locke, E. A. Relationship of goal level to performance level. *Psychological Reports*, 1967, 20, 1068. (a)

†Locke, E. A. The motivational effects of knowledge of results: Knowledge or goal-setting? *Journal of Applied Psychology*, 1967, 51, 324-329. (b)

*Locke, E. A. The effects of knowledge results and knowledge in relation to standards on reaction time performance. American Institutes for Research (unpublished results), 1967. (c)

†Locke, E. A., and Bryan, J. F. Cognitive aspects of psychomotor performance: The effects of performance goals on level of performance. *Journal of Applied Psychology*, 1966, 50, 286-291. (a)

†*Locke, E. A., and Bryan, J. F. The effects of goal-setting, rule-learning and knowledge of score on performance. *American Journal of Psychology*, 1966, 79, 451-457. (b)

‡*Locke, E. A., and Bryan, J. F. Performance goals as determinants of level of performance and boredom. *Journal of Applied Psychology*, 1967, 51, 120-130. (a)

Locke, E. A., and Bryan, J. F. Goal-setting as a determinant of the effect of knowledge of score on performance. American Institutes for Research (unpublished results), 1967. (b)

*Locke, E. A., and Bryan, J. F. Knowledge of score and goal difficulty as determinants of work rate. American Institutes for Research (unpublished results), 1967. (c)

*Locke, E. A., and Bryan, J. F. Grade goals as determinants of academic performance. *Journal of General Psychology*, 1968 (in press).

*Locke, E. A., Bryan, J. F., and Kendall, L. M. Goals and intentions as mediators of the effects of monetary incentives on behavior. *Journal of Applied Psychology*, 1968 (in press).

McClelland, D. C. *The achieving society*. Princeton, New Jersey: Van Nostrand, 1961.

Mace, C. A. Incentives: Some experimental studies. Industrial Health Research Board (Great Britain), 1935, Report No. 72.

Maier, N. F. *Psychology in industry*. New York: Houghton, 1955, pp. 137-180.

Mathewson, S. B. *Restriction of output among unorganized workers*. New York: Viking Press, 1931.

Meyer, H. H., Kaye, E., and French, J. R. P., Jr. Split roles in performance appraisal. *Harvard Business Review*, 1965, 43, 123-129.

Orne, M. T. On the social psychology of the psychological experiment with particular reference to demand characteristics. *American Psychologist*, 1962, 17, 776-783.

Rand, Ayn. The Objectivist ethics. *In* Ayn Rand (Ed.), *The virtue of selfishness*. New York: Signet, 1964, pp. 13-35.

Roethlisberger, F. J., and Dickson, W. J. *Management and the worker*. Cambridge, Massachusetts: Harvard Univ. Press, 1939.

Ryan, T. A. Drives, tasks, and the initiation of behavior. *American Journal of Psychology*, 1958, 71, 74-93.

Siegal, S., and Fouraker, L. E. *Bargaining and group decision making*. New York: McGraw-Hill, 1960, pp. 61-70.

Smith, P. C. The curve of output as a criterion of boredom. *Journal of Applied Psychology*, 1935, 37, 69-74.

Sorcher, M. Motivating the hourly employee. General Electric. Behavioral Research Services, 1967.

Spielberger, C. D., Berger, A., and Howard, K. Conditioning of verbal behavior as a function of awareness, need for social approval, and motivation to receive reinforcement. *Journal of Abnormal and Social Psychology*, 1963, 67, 241-246.

Speilberger, C. D., Bernstein, I. H., and Ratliff, R. G. Information and incentive value of the reinforcing stimulus in verbal conditioning. *Journal of Experimental Psychology*, 1966, 71, 26-31.

Spielberger, C. D., Levin, S. M., and Shepard, M. The effects of awareness and attitude toward the reinforcement on the operant conditioning of verbal behavior. *Journal of Personality*, 1962, 30, 106-121.

Stedry, A. C. *Budget control and cost behavior*. Englewood Cliffs, New Jersey: Prentice-Hall, 1960.

Taylor, F. W. *The principles of scientific-management*. New York: Harper, 1911.

Uhlinger, C. A., and Stephens, M. W. Relations of achievement motivation to academic achievement in students of superior ability. *Journal of Educational Psychology*, 1960, 51, 259-266.

Valentine, R. F. *Performance objectives for managers*. New York: American Management Association, 1966.

Viteles, M. S. *Motivation and morale in industry*. New York: Norton, 1953.

Vroom, V. H. *Work and motivation*. New York: John Wiley, 1964.

Whyte, W. F. *Money and motivation*. New York: John Wiley, 1955.
Zander, A., and Newcomb, T. Group levels of aspiration in United Fund campaigns. *Journal of Personality and Social Psychology*, 1967, 6, 157-162.

PART FOUR

Group Behavior
and Intergroup Conflict
in the Organization

We now examine how group behavior, both within and between groups or departments, plays a major part in determining the effectiveness of the organization itself. As
we discuss the group as a unit of behavior, it will become apparent that individual goals,
group goals, and organizational goals are often not compatible. We then examine how
conflict arises, causing many forms of dysfunctional behavior to emerge. Again, just as
with the individual, the contingencies of the group and the organization must be
examined in order to determine why this conflict has taken place, and how a manager can
go about resolving or managing it.

Determinants of Group Behavior

A *group* can be defined as two or more people who (1) interact with one another, (2)
are psychologically aware of one another, (3) perceive themselves to be a member of the
group, and (4) work toward a common goal. The key words here are *interaction,
awareness,* and *goal.* In other words, some degree of inter-dependence determines
group membership. Much like the individuals discussed by Schein in his article,
"Organizational Socialization and the Profession of Management" (part 2), groups
develop *norms, interaction patterns* and *role expectations* for the behavior of individual
members. Groups enable individuals to have an outlet for their affiliation needs. They
also enable members to develop a sense of identity or self-esteem and help them gain
status. Primarily, however, groups are established to accomplish a task. Modern technology is such that individuals alone cannot accomplish as much as groups of individuals
working together.

In every organization there are *formal* groups—that is, groups to which a member is
assigned as a part of his work role—and *informal* groups, or friendship groups, which
develop on the basis of mutual attraction. In both types of groups the individual's
attitudes, perceptions, judgments, and goals are important in determining the groups'
effectiveness. For this reason a great deal of group effort is spent socializing the new
member when he enters.

There are basically six properties of groups which determine their structure and
which can be used to measure group effectiveness in reaching goals. The first property is

status, defined as social ranking. Within a group, the status of each individual is based on his importance to the group and his influence on group members. As group members gravitate toward one another in striving for common goals, the interaction becomes stabilized in a pattern of reciprocities manifested in a hierarchical status ranking of individual members.

Just as individuals have status within the group, various groups have status within the organization. For example, staff departments often have higher status in the organization than do line departments, even though line-department members may feel they are doing the real work.

The second group property is *cohesiveness,* defined as the positive mutual attraction of the group and its members. The more cohesive the group, the more likely the group's goals will be accepted by the members of the group, and therefore the more likely the group will reach its goals.

The third group property is *size.* Research has found that performance quality and productivity are positively correlated with the group size, under most circumstances. The exception is decision-making, where a decision is reached faster in a smaller group.

The fourth group property is *goal*, defined as a successful level of performance—in the group's terms. A group's goal can be either pro- or anti-organizational. For example, a work group can decide to meet organizational goals, or it can decide to restrict output to maintain group identity and power base.

The fifth group property is *communication pattern.* Communication channels among individuals in a group influence their interaction and the functioning of the group as a whole. Research presented in several of the readings in this part shows that this property has a great deal to do with the satisfaction of group members and their willingness to accept group goals.

The sixth and perhaps most important property is *leadership style*, defined as interpersonal *influence* directed through the communication process toward a specific goal or goals. Contingencies of reinforcement are a primary tool available to the group leader for influencing group members.

The selections in this part explore the first five properties of group structure that determine group effectiveness. Because leadership is perhaps the most important property, it is treated in a separate part (part 6). Here, we consider the formation of groups, the structural characteristics of groups, and the social relationships in groups as they affect goal attainment within the organization.

McGinnies discusses various group terms and distinguishes between various types of groups. He then reports on the effect that various properties of the group have on task performance. From this reading, managers can gain knowledge which will aid them in structuring groups so that they can increase their potential effectiveness. McGinnies concludes that the primary tool available to the manager for influencing group task performance is the incentive arrangement, or the contingencies of reinforcement.

Shaw says that people join groups in order to fulfill a need state. He examines the question: If a person wants to join a particular group, what attraction does the specific group have for him and what is it about him that attracts the group? Shaw concludes by saying, "it appears that interpersonal attraction is a function of the degree to which the person expects affiliation with the others to be rewarding. The difficult task is to identify the many sources of reinforcement in interpersonal relationships."

Kolasa notes several ways in which a group can influence its members. He then goes on to discuss several of the properties of groups which are significant for determining the output of the group and the satisfaction of its members with the group itself.

Katz explains how informal work groups form in complex organizations, and the various positive and negative effects that they can have on organizational structure and goal accomplishment.

For instance, the Hawthorne studies demonstrate how group pressures to produce at certain levels can be more influential than production quotas. Katz points out that workers in groups have "status," which is accorded to them by others. An individual may react to a manager's directive in terms of whether or not it will increase or decrease his status position in the group.

Intergroup Conflict in the Organization

Conflict arises primarily because of different goals, or because of disagreement about the best or correct solution to a problem. There are many kinds of conflict. Some types of conflict are constructive; others are dysfunctional. There are four basic types of conflict in an organization. The first type is *issue* conflict, which generally results from disagreement between two groups on the basis of differences in organizational viewpoint. For example, a sales department may want to ease credit restrictions because of pressure from the marketing vice president to increase sales. The credit department, however, feels pressure from the comptroller to keep credit losses to a minimum. Interdepartmental conflict will result.

The second type of conflict is *interpersonal.* This is conflict between two people based on personal differences. It may have originally started as an issue conflict and then, over a period of time, developed into a personality conflict.

A third type of conflict is called *role* conflict. This occurs when an individual has incompatible or overloading pressure from two or more sources. If a manufacturing vice president asks a plant manager to increase output of product X, for example, and the sales force is asking for more of product Y, the plant manager is in a state of role conflict; that is, incompatible demands are being made upon him.

The fourth type of conflict is *intrapersonal,* wherein a person's values and beliefs are incompatible with his behavior. For example, an employee whose religious faith forbids him to work on Sunday learns that he must work on Sunday or lose his job. He is in a state of intrapersonal conflict in that his behavior (working on Sunday) will be in direct conflict with his belief that working on Sunday is wrong.

In the past, all conflict within organizations has been viewed as dysfunctional. Conflict can, however, be a first step in making organizational changes that may lead to more effective organizational functioning.

Pondy discusses conflict within and between organizations. He reviews three conceptual models of major classes of conflict, discussing the dysfunctional and functional aspects of conflict. Pondy shows how equilibrium, or stability, can be established in a conflict situation. He says the main way a manager can reduce conflict is to rearrange the contingencies of reinforcement so that efforts in the direction of conflict reduction and equilibrium are positively rewarded.

Another method of dealing effectively with conflict is the exercise of control and authority over the individuals in conflict. Frequently, questions of organizational control focus on the relations among units, departments, or groups within an organization, rather than upon individuals. For example, when two units conflict over how scarce resources are allocated, an effective managerial tactic may be to introduce some sort of participative mechanism, by which both units can influence the final decision. Some organization development strategies (see part 7) are aimed primarily at conflict reduction. Groups, confrontation strategies, or simple organization redesign may be intended to create a situation in which one can live with problems intrinsic to the character of the "system."

One type of conflict which occurs within a group is a conflict of "silence." Some group leaders have such a high need for group consensus and cohesiveness that dissent and disagreement is rarely expressed and when expressed is quickly extinguished. Soon the group members learn, through the reinforcement practices of the group leader and other members of the group, that agreement is the highest group goal. Janis calls this the phenomenon of "groupthink" and credits this phenomenon with many downfalls resulting from group decision making.

Hickson et al. argue that differential power among organizational units is the basis of organizational control. Drawing upon the work of such organization theorists as March, Thompson, Lawrence, Lorsch, and Perrow, the Hickson group argues that all organizations, just as all individuals and all groups, are limited in their power to determine what they do, and are interdependent with other units. One of the results of such limits and interdependencies is conflict, growing out of unequal power and dependencies among various departments in the organization. Hickson et al. discuss how different individual units gain power within the organization, and the functional and dysfunctional results.

This jockeying for power, with resultant interpersonal and interunit conflict, can often create structural arrangements that are difficult to change. The Hickson et al. article not only gives insight into potential causes of conflict between organizations, but also offers an understanding of the bases of power needed by leaders to direct and control.

Section A

The Structure
and Process of Groups

BEHAVIOR IN SMALL GROUPS

ELLIOTT McGINNIES

In considering the manner in which perceptions and judgments are influenced by social variables, particularly in a group setting, we focused our attention on the individual. But the group itself is also a legitimate object of study, and there is evidence that the products of group interaction cannot necessarily be predicted from the performance of the individuals outside the group situation. Experiments on group behavior frequently are designed to permit observation of the effects of social interaction on all of the members, not just the effects on one person selected for study. Both the composition and the behavior history of a group are determinants of its effective stimuli for the individual members. The group also determines the nature and pattern of the reinforcements the members receive in the course of their interactions with one another. Group composition and other salient features of the situation can be manipulated in the social-psychological laboratory, and we shall examine some of the studies of small groups in which this has been done.

Primary and Secondary Groups

Group influences are most apparent in face-to-face situations where communication between individuals is immediate and direct. But everyone reveals his past history of interaction in groups, even when he is alone. The behaviors that have been acquired in group situations become habitual, so that in a real sense each of us is the product of a number of social groups. To be sure, the behavior of some persons seems to reflect group influence more than the behavior of others; that is, they

From *Social Behavior: A Functional Analysis*, by Elliott McGinnies. Houghton Mifflin Company, 1970. Reprinted by permission of the publishers.

behave more in accordance with the prevailing norms of their society. The striking differences that can be observed among individuals in matters of opinion and attitude can be traced to affiliation with different groups and consequent differences in histories of social reinforcement.

Individuals seek different kinds of group memberships depending upon their particular habits and attitudes. These behavioral dispositions, in turn, have derived from earlier social interactions, the most important of which involved the family. Parents are not only the most important stimulus figures for the child, they also provide the reinforcements that shape his behavior. Behavior acquired at this early stage, with minor changes, frequently characterizes the individual for the rest of his life. Certainly most of our important attitudes dealing with such matters as religion, morals, and political philosophy are learned in the family. A group such as the family, where the members have intimate and immediate access to one another, is called a *primary group*. A group in which the members, due to geographical or other circumstances, may only occasionally engage in face-to-face interaction, is called a *secondary group*. This is a classic distinction derived from German sociology, in which the terms *Gemeinschaft* and *Gesellschaft* are used to distinguish between a smaller community and a larger society.

The distinction between a primary and a secondary group is sometimes tenuous and arbitrary. As the children in a family grow older, they increasingly interact with individuals outside this primary group. They join with their peers to form new primary groups, in which the members share interests relating to politics, education, religion, work, or recreation, to mention just a few possibilities. These primary groups may, in turn, be parts of a larger, secondary group, such as a political party or a church organization. The resources of secondary groups generally exceed those of primary groups, and membership in a secondary group frequently enables the individual to extend his behavior repertoire in ways that cannot be supported by a smaller, primary group. Joining a political party, for example, provides one with a greater opportunity to effect social change than he would have when acting either entirely by himself or in concert with others in a small group. The members of a political group are held together not just by certain commonalities of interest and intent but also by long-term expectancies of reward for their efforts.

Reference Groups

The term reference group is sometimes used to denote that primary or secondary group from which an individual has acquired certain attitudes or certain behavior patterns. Because most persons belong to a number of different groups, both primary and secondary, i.e., the family, church, labor union, fraternal or civic organization, their behavior often can be understood in terms of those groups in which it was acquired. What happens when different groups reinforce incompatible behaviors? Consider a college freshman who comes from a family where drinking alcoholic beverages is disapproved but who joins a fraternity in which a certain amount of alcohol consumption is not only tolerated but encouraged. He may behave discriminatively by drinking when with his companions and abstaining when at home. In this manner, he is positively reinforced for his behavior in both groups. Or he may attempt to demonstrate his newfound independence and striving for maturity by drinking both in college and at home. Inasmuch as he will experience aversive consequences in the home situation, we must assume that his behavior is controlled more by the immediate consequences of drinking than by his family's reactions. What he does when not in the presence of either his family or his fraternity brothers will depend upon which of these two reference groups has more effectively reinforced his behavior of drinking or not drinking.

An illustration of the role of reference groups in social behavior is provided by some observations made at Bennington College in the 1930's by Theodore Newcomb. Questionnaires measuring political-economic progressivism were given to members of the student body each year to determine how these attitudes might change over four years of college experience. A steady decrease in conservatism, with a concomitant increase in progressivism, was found in students as they advanced from the freshman through the senior years. For example, significant differences existed among these four groups in support for the conservative Republican presidential candidate of 1936, Alfred Landon. Sixty-two per cent of the freshmen, 43 per cent of the sophomores, 15 per cent of the juniors, and 15 per cent of the seniors favored Landon. Interestingly, 66 per cent of the parents of the students favored Landon, a figure most closely approximating that of the freshmen. It was apparent that political-economic attitudes became increasingly divorced from parental attitudes as the students proceeded from freshman class to senior class. An additional finding was that the more popular students scored more often as progressives than as conservatives on the attitude measure (Newcomb, 1943).

Charters and Newcomb (1958) asked students from a large psychology class who had identified themselves as members of the Roman Catholic Church to participate in an experiment ostensibly designed to construct an attitude scale. The students were divided into two groups. Members of a control group were given no special instructions other than to respond to the items on the scale. The members of the experimental group, however, were reminded of their membership in the Catholic Church, after which they discussed certain basic assumptions of the Church. Follwing this procedure, which was designed to emphasize their religious affiliation, they responded to the items on the attitude scale. Certain items were worded so that they could be answered not only from a Catholic point of view but from other points of view as well. It was found that the students in the experimental group, for whom membership in the Catholic Church had been made salient, responded to the critical items in a more orthodox Catholic fashion than did the students in the control group.

Both of the experiments just cited demonstrate that behavior often can be predicted from information about a person's history of affiliation with different social groups. An individual can be said to behave in accordance with his identification with certain reference groups which are important and significant to him. Or he can be said to have adopted a typical performance, or *role*, that is appropriate to the group situation in which he finds himself. Although the concepts of role and reference group are useful as descriptive devices, it will suit our purposes better to view the behavior as reflecting an acquired capacity of the individual to make discriminations that maximize his chances of being positively reinforced in a particular social situation. Consider the Bennington students studied by Newcomb. Many of the freshmen undoubtedly found themselves in a conflict situation. Certain verbal responses (attitudes) that had been positively reinforced within the family failed to evoke similar approval from those they recognized as campus leaders. As they progressed from freshman class to senior class standing, these students must occasionally have made utterances on political and economic issues that were not in accord with the attitudes they had acquired in their families. These utterances, we may assume, were promptly reinforced, and the probability that they would be repeated was thus increased. Because the sources of reinforcement were fellow students, including upperclassmen with more liberal attitudes, the attitudes of the freshmen were gradually modified in the direction of conformity to those prevailing in the college community.

The results obtained by Charters and Newcomb may be explained in a similar manner if we are willing to make several additional assumptions. The verbal habits in this situation were probably acquired in large part through prior education in Catholic ideology. Why did those subjects for whom membership in the Catholic Church was made salient respond in a more typically Catholic fashion than those who were not reminded of this particular group affiliation? The simplest explanation of this is that the instructions altered the stimulus characteristics of the situation so as to make the s^Ds similar to those associated with previously reinforced, pro-Catholic verbalizations. In other words, if I am reminded of the fact that I am a Catholic in a group of fellow Catholics and then am asked to respond to questions that allow for doctrinal interpretation, I will tend to make those responses that have been reinforced in similar situations in the past. In short, my behavior will generalize to this new situation. If, on the other hand, I am not made aware of the special nature of the group, then my behavior is controlled by a different set of stimuli, and I will not necessarily emit characteristically Catholic responses. Identifying a group as having certain properties relevant to an individual's attitudes gives a unique structure to the situation and highlights the discriminative stimuli to which he will respond. The *behavior most likely to occur in a new situation is that which has a history of positive reinforcement in similar prior situations.*

Even the selectivity of perception may in some instances be attributed to the influence of reference groups. As Shibutani (1961) points out, a prostitute and a social worker walking through a slum area probably notice different things. Differences in taste concerning art, music, and decor reflect the influence of the social groups to which one has belonged. These groups provided the occasions on which certain behaviors were learned and from which responses will generalize to new situations that contain some of the same stimulus elements.

Audience Effects on Task Performance

Floyd Allport (1920) has taken the position that an individual's motivational state is altered in the context of a group. The effect on behavior is generally one of enhancement, or *social facilitation*. Allport studied groups composed of three to five students at Harvard and Radcliffe colleges. The task of all the subjects in the groups was to write associations to stimulus words such as "building" and "laboratory." Their responses were compared with those of other subjects who formed associations working alone instead of in a group. The results, according to Allport, showed that the presence of a coworking group had the effect of speeding up the process of free association. To be sure, individual differences were manifested; some subjects were distracted in the group situation and were less productive of verbal associations. In general, however, Allport's experiment revealed the operation of a subtle social influence on behavior that had traditionally been studied only with single individuals. In work groups, this facilitation effect is sometimes manifested as greater quantity but poorer quality of output.

Social Facilitation

We may consider it an established principle, then, that being in a group has unique stimulus value for the individual. Can the group situation be shown to influence behavior more complex than that involving simple discriminations or judgments? For example, do individuals perform skilled tasks better alone or in a group? An early attempt to answer this question was made by Travis (1925), who trained twenty-two college undergraduates to perform fairly skillfully on a pursuit rotor. This device resembles a phonograph turntable near the edge of which is mounted a small metal disc about the size of a nickel. The subject's task is to keep a flexible pointer in contact with this target while the turntable revolves at 60 R.P.M. After the students had practiced on this task until their performances had reached a stable level, they were asked to do the same thing in front of a small "audience" consisting of other students. The average time on target for the subjects when performing before their peers was somewhat longer than when they had performed alone, indicating an apparent group influence on accuracy in a simple task involving motor skill. Other early demonstrations of this sort included the discovery that individuals solved simple multiplication problems more rapidly and produced more associations to words when in the presence of passive spectators than when working alone (Dashiell, 1930).

Taylor and Faust (1952) also obtained evidence that the performance of individuals in a group may be superior in some respects to their individual efforts. They recorded the number of questions asked as well as the time required by individuals alone and in groups to guess the correct answer in a game of Twenty Questions. The groups, composed of either two or four individuals, required on the average fewer questions and less time to solve the problems than did individuals. Size of the group, within these limits, was not an important variable. The authors point out, however, that in terms of man-minutes required for solution, the performance of individuals was superior to that of groups and the performance of groups of two was superior to that of groups of four. Two persons, however, did not solve a given problem in less than half the time required by one person, as would be necessary to demonstrate group superiority. These experimental results suggest that the performance of individuals in a group is indeed likely to be different from their performance alone, but not necessarily more efficient.

A vigilance problem. More recently, Bergum and Lehr (1963) recorded the performances of twenty National Guard trainees who were required to sit in isolated booths and observe a panel on which twenty red lights were mounted in a circle. The lights were lit up in sequence, and this circular pattern was repeated every five seconds. During an hour, however, there were twenty-four instances of a light failing to go on in its proper sequence. It was the task of the subjects to monitor the display and press a button whenever such an interruption in the sequence occurred. After twenty minutes of training, followed by a ten-minute rest, the subjects performed alone on this vigilance task for two hours and fifteen minutes. Twenty additional subjects, similarly trained, were told that from time to time during the test period their booths would be visited by a Lieutenant Colonel or a Master Sergeant. Four such visits were actually made to each subject. The mean performance of these "supervised" subjects was then compared with that of the "unsupervised" subjects over five successive twenty-seven minute intervals.

As a result of fatigue, the performance of both the groups deteriorated with time. But the subjects who were subjected to unannounced visits by their superiors maintained a distinctly higher level of performance than those who monitored the light panel unsupervised. The occasional visits by a military superior placed these subjects on a variable interval schedule of reinforcement, and their performances—aside from fatigue decrement—were typical of those found with this type of schedule.

Decision-making. A different type of task, devised by Banta and Nelson (1964), required college students to judge the reactions of a hypothetical individual to a list of attitude statements after first being told the person's reaction to five similar statements. Dyads (two-person groups) were formed to work on this task, and the partners were told that they must agree on a decision, then record their action by pressing a signal button. A light was flashed by the experimenter whenever the decision favored by a previously designated member of each pair was adopted. Control groups performed the same task under noncontingent reinforcement. The probability that the reinforced partner would have his opinions reported out of the dyad rose with successive trials. The nonreinforced subjects, on the other hand, made fewer and fewer proposals for a solution, and their partners began to dominate the decision-making process. This experimental result has its counterpart in committee processes, where those members whose proposals are consistently adopted are often seen to play an increasingly dominant role in the group's deliberations. Nonreinforcement, through repeated failure to have their suggestions acted on by the group, causes some individuals to virtually withdraw from debate in favor of those whose contributions are rewarded. As we shall see later in this chapter, it is possible by selective manipulation of the reinforcement contingencies to encourage the performance of the more reticent members of a group and to depress that of the more aggressive individuals.

Social Inhibition

Social interaction may also have an inhibiting rather than a facilitating effect. Allport (1920) reported, for example, that individuals who free associated to words in the presence of others gave more common and fewer uncommon responses. Idiosyncratic associations, in other words, seem to be inhibited, or suppressed, in a group situation. This observation is consistent with the findings of Sherif (1966) and Asch (1952). These investigators, as you will recall, observed a trend toward development of a group norm in situations where individuals reported their perceptions of either the movement of a point of light or the length of a line. The giving of more "common" associations to stimulus words in a group situation reveals the operation of a similar movement toward established norms. The general principle that seems to emerge from these experiments is that individual behavior in a group situation is modified in accordance with the particular stimulus features that characterize the group. Differences in the prior experiences of the individual group members determine whether task performance will be facilitated or inhibited in any single case.

Zajonc (1966) has argued that a distinction should be made between situations where individuals are performing tasks in the mere *presence of others* and those where several persons are *simultaneously engaged in* the same activity. We might add a third category, where a task can be solved only through the *joint or combined efforts* of several individuals. This last situation involves a special sort of social interaction, called cooperation, and may be deferred for later discussion. Consider for a moment just those situations where a person performs in the company of others or where several persons perform simultaneously but independently. Although we have focused our attention on results that indicated a *facilitation effect* in both of these instances, several investigators have reported just the opposite. Pessin (1933) found that subjects who memorized lists of nonsense syllables in the presence of spectators required more repetitions and made more errors than when they learned equivalent materials alone. Previously, Husband (1931) had reported that finger-maze learning was slower in the presence of an observer. As we have already noted, there is evidence that both the quality and orginality of performance may suffer in a group situation. Apparently, a social context for individual task performance does not provide unalloyed advantages.

Learning vs. performance. Zajonc (1966), after reviewing this general problem, suggests that "learning is impaired and performance facilitated by the presence of an audience" (p. 14). *Learning,* Zajonc points out, refers to the acquisition of new responses, while *performance* refers to the emission of previously learned responses. He argues that in any learning situation the subject tends at first to make a great many incorrect responses. When performing a previously learned task, however, an individual emits more correct than incorrect responses. An audience has the effect of enhancing the emission of *dominant responses,* and these are predominantly incorrect during learning and predominantly correct during performance.

Although Zajonc offers an explanation of this effect in terms of increased motivation and arousal in the presence of an audience, let us suggest an alternative interpretation. First, as pointed out, individuals tend to make a great many errors during learning. As a consequence of previous experiences in performing before a group, the individual comes to anticipate reactions of disparagement when he commits blunders. He is likely to generalize this expectancy to a learning situation in which other persons are present. In other words, his behavior is controlled not only by stimuli representing the task but also by stimuli provided by the audience; and the latter have been the occasions for ridicule contingent upon the commission of blunders. Consequently, every error he makes during learning serves as a conditioned stimulus for the anxiety occasioned by public disparagement, whether or not such a reaction is actually forthcoming from the present audience. Because he makes more incorrect than correct responses during the early phases of learning, the emotional reactions that have been conditioned to public ineptness interfere with both his attention and his coordination. The individual, therefore, does not acquire new response patterns as readily when he is in a situation that has the potentiality of becoming aversive whenever he makes a mistake.

Consider, on the other hand, the behavior of a person who is engaged before an audience in a previously learned, well-practiced task. If he has any degree of competence in the task, he will make more correct than incorrect responses. Previous experience has taught him that a competent performance will earn the plaudits of onlookers. Insofar as the correct responses are already within his repertoire, he will be reinforced by the sheer presence of an audience whenever they occur. Incorrect responses, although they will be more aversive in the presence of a group, will occur less frequently, and the attendant emotional reactions will not be as disruptive of the total performance as those that would occur during learning under similar circumstances. Whether or not the presence of others facilitates or inhibits performance, then, is seen to depend upon the overall level of task competence that the individual has attained. His operant level of correct responses must exceed that of incorrect responses in order for reinforcing consequences to occur more frequently than aversive consequences. We need not look far in everyday experience to find examples of this principle. The amateur performer in any field—entertainment, sports, public speaking—finds his behavior progressively deteriorating as soon as he commences to fumble and blunder before an audience. The task that was incompletely mastered when practiced alone becomes a nightmare in the presence of a group, the very existence of which is aversive when one performs inadequately. To the skilled professional, on the other hand, an audience serves as an additional source of reinforcement, adding to the satisfaction that the performer experiences when he practices competently alone.

Reasoning from everyday observation, however, is not an adequate substitute for experimental data. Fortunately, several studies have been reported that bear upon the adequacy of this analysis. Cottrell, Rittle, and Wack (1967) examined both the difficulty of the task and the degree of competence of their subjects in relation to speed of learning either alone or in the presence of an audience. Their subjects were 102 male undergraduates confronted with the task of learning lists of paired associates. This is a situation in which the subject views pairs of words, presented one pair at a time on a memory drum. On successive trials, he must try to name correctly the *second* word of each pair upon presentation of the first word. Items typical of such pairs would be *barren-fruitless, avid-grouchy,* and *desert-leading.* These particular pairs, in fact, were part of a difficult list used by these investigators. The difficulty lies in the fact that there are few within-pair associations and many strong associations between members of different pairs, for example, *barren, arid,* and *desert.* This means that a subject is apt to respond to the first word of a pair with its associate from another pair. In an easier task, the words in each pair had strong associations, and there were few associations between members of different pairs. Thus, the correct responses in the case of pairs such as *adept-skillful* and *barren-fruitless* would be learned more readily than those in the pairs previously mentioned.

The subjects were divided into slow, medium, and fast learners on the basis of the number of trials required for them to learn a practice list. The numbers of errors they made in learning the test lists were then computed as a function of the presence and the absence of a two-person audience watching the subject attentively while he learned. When the subjects learned the easy lists, it apparently made little difference whether the two observers were present or not. Nor did differences in learning skill of the subjects appear to affect their reactions markedly in the presence of an audience. In the case of the difficult list, however, the presence of an audience had the effect of causing the less able learners to commit more errors. The fast learners made slightly fewer errors when their performance was being observed.

Attentive vs. inattentive audiences. Zajonc's view that the mere presence of other persons increases the subject's "motivation" to perform suggests that it should make little difference whether or not the audience members are attending to what the subject is doing. If, as we have suggested, the potential of other individuals as agents of reinforcement is critical in their effect upon a performer, then it should matter whether they are merely physically present or are present as spectators. Cottrell and his colleagues (1968) examined the possibility that subjects engaged in a recognition task would perform differently in the presence of an audience and in the presence of others who did not constitute an audience. Forty-five male college sutdents first practiced pronouncing ten nonsense words like *afworbu* and *biwonji*. Two words were assigned to each of five training frequencies: 1, 2, 5, 10, and 25. Thus, the subjects read and repeated some of the words twenty-five times and others only once. This procedure established certain of these new verbal habits as more dominant than others. Dominant responses, remember, have been found to occur more readily than weaker responses in the presence of an audience.

The subjects were then assigned to one of three test conditions. They attempted to recognize the words they had just practiced when the words were projected at very short durations on a screen seven feet away. Some of the subjects did this alone, others were observed by two spectators, and still others performed in the presence of two *blindfolded* individuals, who were ostensibly becoming dark-adapted for another experiment. Out of 160 flashes on the screen, 120 constituted pseudo-recognition trials; that is, the stimulus was one of the training words but presented in a reversed position and thereby rendered unreadable. Inasmuch as the subjects were instructed to guess on every trial, the experimenters could determine the extent to which they would emit responses that had been made more or less dominant during training. And they could relate these differences to the particular conditions in which the subjects found themselves.

The data revealed that the presence of an audience enhances the emission of dominant responses in preference to subordinate responses. The mere presence of other persons, however, produces no such effect upon performance; that is, the subjects guessed as many of the high frequency training words when alone as they did in the presence of two blindfolded students. In reconsidering these and related findings, Cottrell (1968) suggests what amounts to a reinforcement interpretation. He observes that if performance before an audience usually results in positive or negative outcomes for the individual, he will come to anticipate such outcomes when placed in an audience situation. Although Cottrell goes further and speaks of a learned source of drive, it is not necessary to do so. The nonsense words that were practiced less frequently by the subjects may be viewed as having the status of potentially "incorrect" responses during the guessing phase, while those that were frequently practiced are analogous to "correct" responses. As we have previously suggested, an audience provides cues for the emission of performances having the greatest likelihood of being positively reinforced. Responses that are most likely to be correct ordinarily are those that have been practiced most frequently. Individuals who are present but are not able to observe what one is doing do not provide the same cues to potential consequences as an audience does. Performance in these circumstances is not likely to differ from performance when alone. This analysis proceeds from a consideration of the individual's history of reinforcement in situations similar to the one in which he now finds himself. No inferences about drive states are needed, and none are made. We can make fairly accurate predictions about how an individual will perform if we know something about his level of skill, his past experience in similar situations, and the nature of the occasion on which he is currently being required to demonstrate his proficiency.

The Role of Incentives

One way of facilitating task performance is to offer incentives for increased competence. The most generally effective incentive seems to be money, but money will serve this function only in situations where its potential as a reinforcer will not be offset by other, aversive consequences. An experiment conducted in the late 1920's (Roethlisberger and Dickson, 1947) illustrates this point. As one of a series of studies done at Western Electric's Hawthorne plant in Chicago, the experiment involved workers who attached and soldered banks of wires to a telephone switchboard component. Fourteen workers and one observer were placed in a special room, and various wage incentives were introduced in an attempt by the management to discover which ones would most facilitate production.

Taken at face value, this experiment would seem to represent a straightforward manipulation of amount of anticipated monetary reinforcement to discover the effect on productivity. The results, however, were disappointing. Level of productivity remained relatively constant despite variations in the wage incentives that were offered. The apparent explanation for this failure to increase production through wage incentives is one of those that seems obvious after the fact. Each worker feared that if output were increased, management would maintain its current level of expenses by decreasing the payment for each unit produced. Management did not, of course, threaten any such readjustment of incentives in the event of an increase in output, but the workers apparently assumed that this might happen. Olmstead (1959) summarizes the situation in the vernacular of the participants: "A good guy won't be a chiseler: he'll do his share and not expect others to 'carry' him (except in certain circumstances). Thirdly, he won't be a squealer; he will protect the group code against outside interference. Finally, he won't put on airs or be a snob, that is, he will manifest in his non-work behavior his 'democratic' submission to group ideals" (p. 29).

This classic study illustrates the danger of attempting to define a reinforcer independent of its effects upon behavior. Money, in this instance, was rendered ineffective as an incentive because of the way in which the workers interpreted the situation. This interpretation was reinforced by the group, and deviant behavior by an individual member in the form of increased productivity would probably have had aversive consequences to that individual. In fact, Coch and French (1948) observed a clothespresser who was "scapegoated" by her coworkers because her efficiency rating had climbed above the average for the group.

References

Aiken, E. G. Interaction process analysis changes accompanying operant conditioning of verbal frequency in small groups. *Perceptual and Motor Skills,* 1965a, 21, 52-54.

Aiken, E. G. Changes in interpersonal descriptions accompanying the operant conditioning of verbal frequency in groups. *Journal of Verbal Learning and Verbal Behavior,* 1965b, 4, 243-247.

Allport, F. H. The influence of the group upon association and thought. *Journal of Experimental Psychology,* 1920, 3, 159-182.

Allport, F. H. *Social psychology.* Boston: Houghton Mifflin, 1924.

Altman, I., and Haythorn, W. W. The ecology of isolated groups. *Behavioral Science,* 1967, 12, 169-182.

Altman, I., and McGinnies, E. Interpersonal perception and communication in discussion groups of varied attitudinal composition. *Journal of Abnormal and Social Psychology,* 1960, 60, 390-395.

Asch, S. E. Effects of group pressure upon the modification and distortion of judgments. In G. E. Swanson, T. M. Newcomb, and E. L. Hartley (Eds.), *Readings in social psychology* (rev. ed.). New York: Holt, Rinehart and Winston, 1952.

Azrin, N. H., and Lindsley, O. R. The reinforcement of cooperation between children. *Journal of Abnormal and Social Psychology,* 1956, 52, 100-102. Copyright 1956 by the American Psychological Association. Data in Table 6.1 of this book reprinted by permission.

Bales, R. F. *Interaction process analysis.* Reading, Mass.: Addison-Wesley, 1950.

Banta, T. J., and Nelson, C. Experimental analysis of resource location in problem solving groups. *Sociometry,* 1964, 27, 488-501.

Bavelas, A. Communication patterns in task oriented groups. *Journal of the Acoustical Society of America,* 1950, 22, 725-730.

Bavelas, A., Hastorf, R. H., Gross, A. E., and Kite, W. R. Experiments on the alteration of group structure. *Journal of Experimental Social Psychology,* 1965, 1, 55-70.

Bergum, B.O., and Lehr, D. J. Effects of authoritarianism on vigilance performance. *Journal of Applied Psychology,* 1963, 47, 75-77.

Brown, J. F. *Psychology and the social order.* New York: McGraw-Hill, 1936.

Burgess, R. L. Communication networks: An experimental reevaluation. *Journal of Experimental Social Psychology,* 1968, 4, 324-337.

Butler, D. C., and Miller, N. "Power to reinforce" as a determinant of communication. *Psychological Reports,* 1965a, 16, 705-709.

Butler, D. C., and Miller, N. Power to reward and punish in social interaction. *Journal of Experimental Social Psychology,* 1965b, 1, 311-322.

Charters, W. W., and Newcomb, T. M. Some attitudinal effects of experimentally increased salience of a membership group. In E. E. Maccoby, T. M. Newcomb, and E. L. Hartley (Eds.), *Readings in social psychology* (3rd ed.). New York: Holt, Rinehart and Winston, 1958, pp. 276-280.

Cieutat, J. J. Surreptitious modification of verbal behavior during class discussion, *Psychological Reports,* 1959, 5, 648.

Coch, L., and French, J. R. P., Jr. Overcoming resistance to change. *Human Relations*, 1948, 1, 512-532.

Cohen, D. J. Justin and his peers: An experimental analysis of a child's social world. *Child Development*, 1962, 23, 697-717.

Collins, B. E., Davis, H. L., Myers, J. G., and Silk, A. J. An experimental study of reinforcement and participant satisfaction. *Journal of Abnormal and Social Psychology*, 1964, 68, 463-467.

Cottrell, N. B. Performance in the presence of other human beings: Mere presence, audience, and affiliation effects. In E.C. Simmel, R. A. Hoppe, and G. A. Milton (Eds.), *Social facilitation and imitative behavior*. Boston: Allyn and Bacon, 1968.

Cottrell, N. B., Rittle, R. H., and Wack, D. L. Presence of an audience and list type (competitional or noncompetitional) as joint determinants of performance in paired associates learning. *Journal of Personality*, 1967, 35, 425-434.

Cottrell, N. B., Sekerak, G. J., Wack, D. L., and Rittle, R. H. Social facilitation of dominant responses by the presence of an audience and the mere presence of others. *Journal of Personality and Social Psychology*, 1968, 9, 245-250.

Dashiell, J. F. An experimental analysis of some group effects. *Journal of Abnormal and Social Psychology*, 1930, 25, 190-199.

Deutsch, M. An experimental study of the effects of cooperation and competition upon group process. *Human Relations*, 1949, 2, 129-152, 199-231.

Deutsch, M. Field theory in social psychology. In G. Lindzey and E. Aronson (Eds.), *Handbook of social psychology* 2nd ed.). Reading, Mass.: Addison-Wesley, 1968

Gerwirtz, J. L., and Baer, D. M. The effect of brief social deprivation on behaviors for a social reinforcer. *Journal of Abnormal and Social Psychology*, 1958, 56, 49-56.

Hare, A. P., and Bales, R. F. Seating position and small group interaction. *Sociometry*, 1963, 25, 480-486.

Haythorn, W. W. Project Argus: A program of isolation and confinement research. *Naval Research Reviews*, December 1967, 1-8.

Haythorn, W. W., and Altman, I. Together in isolation. *Trans-Action*, January/February 1967.

Heise, G. A., and Miller, G. A. Problem solving by small groups using various communication nets. *Journal of Abnormal and Social Psychology*, 1951, 46, 327-336.

Heyns, R. W., and Lippitt, R. Systematic observational techniques. In G. Lindzey (Ed.), *Handbook of social psychology* 2nd ed.). Reading, Mass.: Addison-Wesley, 1968.

Husband, R. W. Analysis of methods in human maze learning. *Journal of Genetic Psychology*, 1931, 39, 258-277.

Kelley, H. H., and Thibaut, J. W. Experimental studies of group problem solving and process. In G. Lindzey (Ed.), *Handbook of social psychology*. Vol. 2. Reading, Mass.: Addison-Wesley, 1954.

Kelley, H. H., Thibaut, J. W., Radloff, R., and Mundy, D. The development of cooperation in a "minimal social situation." *Psychological Monographs*, 1962, 76, No. 19.

Krech, D., and Crutchfield, R. S. *Theory and problems of social psychology*. New York: McGraw-Hill, 1948.

Leavitt, H. J. Some effects of certain communication patterns on group performance. *Journal of Abnormal and Social Psychology*, 1951, 46, 38-50.

Levin, G., and Shapiro, D. The operant conditioning of conversation. *Journal of the Experimental Analysis of Behavior*, 1962, 5, 309-316.

Lewin, K. *Field theory in social science*. New York: Harper and Row, 1951.

McGinnies, E., and Altman, I. Discussion as a function of attitudes and content of a persuasive communication. *Journal of Applied Psychology*, 1959, 43, 53-59.

McGrath, J. E., and Altman, I. *Small Group research*. New York: Holt, Rinehart and Winston, 1966.

McNair, D. M. Reinforcement of verbal behavior. *Journal of Experimental Psychology*, 1957, 53, 40-46.

Newcomb, T. M. *Personality and social change*. New York: Dryden Press, 1943.

Oakes, W. F. Reinforcement of Bales' categories in group discussion. *Psychological Reports*, 1962a, 11, 427-435.

Oakes, W. F. Effectivness of signal light reinforcers given various meanings on participation in group discussion. *Psychological Reports*, 1962b, 11, 469-470.

Oakes, W. F., Droge, A. E., and August, B. Reinforcement effects on participation in group discussion. *Psychological Reports*, 1960, 7, 503-514.

Oakes, W. F., Droge, A. E., and August, B. Reinforcement effects on conclusions reached in group discussions. *Psychological Reports*, 1961, 9, 27-34.

Olmstead, M. S. *The small group*. New York: Random House, 1959.

Pessin, J. The comparative effects of social and mechanical stimulation on memorizing. *American Journal of Psychology*, 1933, 45, 263-270.

Rabinowitz, L., Kelley, H. H., and Rosenblatt, R. M. Effects of different types of interdependence and response conditions in the minimal social situation. *Journal of Experimental Social Psychology*, 1966, 2, 169-197.

Roethlisberger, F. J., and Dickson, W. J. *Management and the worker*. Cambridge, Mass.: Harvard University Press, 1947.

Rosenberg, S. The maintenance of a learned response in controlled interpersonal conditions. *Sociometry*, 1959, 22, 124-138.

Rosenberg, S. Cooperative behavior in dyads as a function of reinforcement parameters. *Journal of Abnormal and Social Psychology*, 1960, 60, 318-333.

Rosenberg, S. Influence and reward in structured two-person interactions. *Journal of Abnormal and Social Psychology*, 1963, 67, 379-387.

Rosenberg, S., and Hall, R. L. The effects of different social feedback conditions upon performance in dyadic teams. *Journal of Abnormal and Social Psychology*, 1958, 57, 271-277.

Shapiro, D. The reinforcement of disagreement in a small group. *Behavior Research and Therapy*, 1963, 1, 267-272.

Shaw, M. E. Communication networks. In L. Berkowitz (Ed.), *Advances in experimental psychology*. Vol. I. New York: Academic Press, 1964.

Shepherd, C. R. *Small groups: Some sociological perspectives*. San Francisco: Chandler, 1964.

Sherif, M. *The psychology of social norms*. New York: Harper and Row Torchbooks, 1966. Originally published in the *Archives of Psychology*, 1935, No. 187, under the title "A study of some social factors in perception."

Shibutani, S. *Society and personality*. Englewood Cliffs, N. J.: Prentice-Hall, 1961.

Sidowski, J. B. Reward and punishment in a minimal social situation. *Journal of Experimental Psychology*, 1957, 54, 318-326.

Sidowski, J. B., Wyckoff, L. B., and Tabory, L. The influence of reinforcement and punishment in a minimal social situation. *Journal of Abnormal and Social Psychology*, 1956, 52, 115-119.

Steinzor, B. The spatial factor in face-to-face discussion groups. *Journal of Abnormal and Social Psychology*, 1950, 45, 552-555.

Taylor, D. W., and Faust, W. L. Twenty questions: Efficiency in problem solving as a function of size of group. *Journal of Experimental Psychology*, 1952, 44, 360-368.

Travis, L. E. The effect of a small audience upon eye-hand coordination. *Journal of Abnormal and Social Psychology*, 1925, 20, 142-146.

Tsai, L. T. Cited in O. Koehler, Team arbeit bei ratten. *Orion*, 1953, 8, 5.

Ward, C. D. Seating arrangement and leadership emergence in small discussion groups. *Journal of Social Psychology*, 1968, 74, 83-90.

Zajonc, R. B. *Social psychology: An experimental approach*. Belmont, Calif.: Wadsworth, 1966.

WHY PEOPLE JOIN GROUPS

MARVIN E. SHAW

If we assume that people join groups voluntarily, the first question that must be asked then is, Why do people join groups? The question can, of course, be answered at many levels. At the most general level, we may say that people join groups because the group meets some individual need. There are some tasks that can be accomplished only by groups, there may exist a personal need for affiliation, etc. In fact, a number of theorists have proposed theories of interpersonal attraction based upon the notion of reinforcement. Thibaut and Kelley (1959) formulated the concepts of *comparison level* (CL) and *comparison levels for alternatives* (CLalt). According to this theory, the comparison level is the standard which an individual uses to evaluate an interpersonal relationship. If the rewards and costs which accrue from the relationship are above the CL, the relationship is evaluated favorably; if they are below the CL, the relationship is evaluated unfavorably. The CLalt is the standard the individual uses to determine whether to enter into a new relationship or to remain in an already existing one. If the net reward-cost outcome is above that expected from other available relationships, the individual will enter into or continue the relationship; if below available alternatives, he will not enter (or continue) the relationship. Clearly, this theory assumes that the individual establishes and maintains an interpersonal relationship because of the rewards that accrue from it.

A similar theory was proposed by Newcomb (1956), who equated attraction and repulsion to another person with positive or negative attitudes toward that person. These attitudes are established according to reinforcement principles, and hence the individual is attracted or repulsed, depending upon the rewards or punishments that derive from his relationship with another. We will have more to say about these theories after we have discussed some of the relevant research findings.

General explanations have a certain appeal because they seem intuitively correct. But it is not enough to offer general explanations. One may well ask, What are the needs that are satisfied by group membership? What constitute rewards and punishments? The next level of explanation is represented by Cartwright and Zander's (1960) statement that the group itself may be the object of need or the group may simply be the means for satisfying some need that lies outside the group. When these two general classes are examined more closely, it becomes evident that each of them can be analyzed into several smaller classes, which in turn can be subdivided even further. Sources of need satisfaction residing in the group include at least (1) attraction to the members of the group (interpersonal attraction), (2) attraction to the activities of the group, (3) attraction to the goals of the group (i.e., the goals of the group are valued by the individual), and (4) group membership per se. Needs outside the group that may be satisfied through group membership include at least (1) attraction to others outside the group and (2) attraction to goals outside the group. Let us examine these factors in greater detail.

Interpersonal Attraction

The variables influencing the attraction of one person to another have probably been studied more extensively than any other determinant of group formation. The early studies tended to consider secondary determinants, such as propinquity (Festinger, 1953a) and interaction (Bovard, 1956; Palmore, 1955). However, these variables merely provide the opportunity for the operation of primary variables, such as attitude similarity, value congruence, personality characteristics, and the like. Nevertheless, it is instructive to consider some of the environmental factors that make it possible for other variables to exert their effects on interpersonal attraction.

Proximity, Contact, and Interaction

Investigations of environmental and group process variables as determinants of group formation and interpersonal attraction are usually discussed under one of three headings: proximity, contact, or interaction. These factors are closely related and represent varying degrees of association rather than unique variables. In general, *proximity* has been used to refer to the physical distance between individuals, *contact* to situations in which individuals are likely to be in each other's presence frequently, and *interaction* to situations in which the behavior of each person influences the other.

In a number of field studies the physical distance between individuals has been found to be related to affiliation. The classical study of the formation of friendships in a student housing complex (Festinger, Schachter, & Back, 1950) clearly revealed the role of proximity in the establishment of interpersonal relationships. Married couples were assigned to housing by the university housing office in order of application, without regard to college major, classification, or other variables that might influence the formation of friendships. Festinger et al. found that such relationships were determined largely by proximity. Persons living next door to each other most frequently became friends. Couples who occupied corner units or end units which faced the street frequently became social isolates. The results of other investigations agree in showing a positive relationship between attraction and proximity; e.g., Maissonneuve, Palmade, and Fourment (1952) observed that propinquity and liking choices were related in boarding school classes; Byrne and Buehler (1955) found that seat neighbors in college classes were more likely to become acquainted; and Sommer (1959) noted that persons who sat near each other in the cafeteria of a large mental hospital interacted more than persons in more distant positions. It is clear, then, that proximity contributes to group formation.

There has been considerable interest in the degree to which contact between minority groups affects the relationships between such groups. Many investigations reveal that contact results in more favorable attitudes toward members of minority groups and an increased willingness to affiliate with them. During World War II, Stouffer, Suchman, DeVinney, Star, and Williams (1949) observed that the degree to which white soldiers thought it was a good idea to have Negroes in the company varied directly with the amount of contact they had had with Negroes. Results consistent with this finding have been obtained in a variety of settings. Deutsch and Collins (1951) compared black-white relations in a housing project in which black and white families were assigned to buildings in segregated areas with those in an integrated apartment house. They found there were more frequent and more intimate interpersonal relations among blacks and whites in the integrated project than in the segregated one. Furthermore, they were able to demonstrate that this difference did not exist prior to residence in the housing projects. Similarly, Jahoda (1961) found a considerable reduction in preferences for residential segregation following black-white contact as neighbors or on the job, and Harding and Hogrefe (1952) found that white persons who had worked with Negroes on an equal basis were more willing to do so again than those who had not.

It has already been suggested that proximity, contact, and interaction probably are not primary determinants of attraction; i.e., proximity makes it possible for individuals to come into contact and interact with each other, and such interaction makes it possible for them to learn about characteristics of others that make them attractive (e.g., their physical attractiveness, their attitudes, etc.). This interpretation is supported by evidence that proximity and interaction do not always lead to increased attraction. Festinger (1953a) described a housing project in which few group memberships existed among residents. In this project, the residents felt they were forced to live in the project because of a housing shortage, and their attitudes toward fellow residents were quite negative. Gundlach (1956) reported similar negative attitudes on the part of white women workers who had been assigned to work with Negroes with similar educations and backgrounds. Experimental studies in which interaction provided no evidence concerning the characteristics of others also yielded generally negative results, i.e., no relationship between amount of interaction and liking (Stotland & Cottrell, 1962; Stotland, Cottrell, & Laing, 1960).

If we are correct in believing that proximity and interaction merely provide the opportunity for individuals to learn about the characteristics of others that make them attractive, it is important to know what these other characteristics are and to explore just how they function to determine attractiveness.

Physical Attractiveness

Probably the most obvious source of attraction between two persons is sheer physical attractiveness. When a person exemplifies the physical characteristics which contribute to the perception of beauty or handsomeness (in a given culture), others are prone to be attracted to him and to want to associate with him. The importance of physical attractiveness in dating behavior, for example, has been demonstrated by Walster, Aronson, Abrahams, and Rottman (1966). They conducted a field study in which subjects were randomly paired at a "computer dance." They found that, regardless of a subject's own attractiveness, how much he liked his partner, how much he wanted to date her again, and how often he actually asked her out again were a function of her physical attractiveness. Scores on the Minnesota Multiphasic Personality Inventory, the Minnesota Counseling Inventory, Berger's (1952) Scale of Self-acceptance, the Minnesota Scholastic Aptitude test, and high school percentile rank—all were found to be unrelated to how much the partner wanted to continue the interaction. A recent study by Schlosser (1969) also demonstrated that physical attractiveness is a determinant of interpersonal attraction, even when the physically attractive other behaves in a way which interferes with attainment of a common goal.

Similarity

It has been proposed by a number of writers that individuals are attracted to those who are similar to themselves. For example, Newcomb (1956) suggested that it is more likely that an interaction will be rewarding when the two interactors are similar, since one of the rewards deriving from interaction is social support for one's attitudes, beliefs, and opinions. Heider (1958) also theorized that similarity should produce interpersonal attraction. It is important to remember, however, that similarity is not a general quality. It is appropriate to consider similarity only with respect to specified characteristics (see Cronbach & Gleser, 1953). Hence, it is reasonable to expect that interpersonal attraction is related to similarity with respect to those characteristics which are judged important by the persons involved in the interaction. The variable most widely investigated within this general category of significant characteristics is probably *attitude similarity*. For instance, Newcomb (1961) invited students to live in a house rent-free in exchange for serving as research subjects. Seventeen men were selected for each of two years. At the time they moved into the house, no one knew any other member of the group. The men completed a series of attitude and value inventories and also estimated the attitudes of others in the group. Initially, proximity of room assignments was the primary determinant of attraction. Later, attraction was found to be a function of perceived similarity of attitudes.

The effects of attitude similarity on interpersonal attraction have been studied extensively by Byrne and his associates. In an initial study, Byrne (1961) followed Newcomb in assuming that reciprocal rewards and punishments are important determinants of attraction and that perceived similarity-dissimilarity is rewarding-punishing. Byrne devised the following technique for examining the similarity-attraction hypothesis, using twenty-six issues ranging from such relatively important things as integration, God, and premarital sexual relations to such relatively unimportant things as western movies and television programs. Subjects were asked to express their attitudes on these issues on a 7-point rating scale and to indicate how important each item was to them. Two weeks later subjects were falsely informed that the scale had been given as part of a study of interpersonal prediction, that students in another class had taken the same test, and that they were now to be given each other's test with the name removed in the hope that they could learn about one another from this information. Actually, fake scales were made up to represent four conditions: the other's attitudes were (1) the same as those expressed by the subject, (2) exactly opposite to those expressed by the subject, (3) the same on important issues but opposite on unimportant issues, and (4) the same on unimportant but opposite on important issues. The subjects then indicated how well they liked the other person and how much they would enjoy working with him. Attraction was significantly higher when the other person's attitudes were similar than when they were dissimilar according to both measures. Importance of issues had a significant effect only for the liking ratings. Using essentially the same technique, Byrne and Nelson (1964, 1965b) systematically varied both attitude similarity and topic importance, and found only similarity to be related to attraction. However, in a subsequent study, Byrne, London, and Griffitt (1968) demonstrated that importance significantly influenced attraction when topics heterogeneous in importance are associated with one other person.

Several subsequent studies by Byrne and his coworkers have consistently found attitude similarity to be a determinant of attraction (Byrne & Griffitt, 1966; Byrne & Nelson, 1965a; Byrne, Nelson, & Reeves, 1966; Byrne & Rhamey, 1965). The study by Byrne and Rhamey probably illustrates the relationship between attraction and attitude similarity most clearly. They required 180 subjects to read questionnaires purportedly filled out by an anonymous stranger and to evaluate him on a number of variables, including attraction. The stranger's responses agreed with those of the subject on 100 percent, 67 percent, 33 percent, or none of the items. Subjects were also given information about the stranger's evaluation of them, which was positive, neutral, or negative. [From the] attraction scores . . . [it was] quite evident that attraction is a positive, increasing function of the proportion of attitudes that are similar to those expressed by the subject. The effects are most strongly operative in the neutral evaluation condition, which suggests that evaluation by the other person also influences one's attraction to him.

That attitude similarity may not always be positively related to attraction has been shown by Novak and Lerner (1968). Forty-eight males and forty-eight females evaluated a "partner" who held either similar or dissimilar attitudes and who was described as either normal or emotionally disturbed. Subjects were less willing to interact with an emotionally disturbed person when he held similar attitudes than when he held dissimilar attitudes.

Similarity with respect to other characteristics has also been shown to be a determinant of attraction. *Similarity of personality* as a determinant of attraction was studied by Griffitt (1966), using the Byrne technique of evaluation of a stranger on the basis of his responses to a self-concept inventory. When the self-descriptions of the subject and those of the stranger agreed on 33 percent of the tiems, the mean attraction score was 8.76 as compared with a mean score of 11.61 when there was 100 percent agreement. Byrne, Griffitt, and Stefanik (1967) had 151 subjects examine the responses of strangers to a repression-sensitization scale. The stranger had responded as the subject did on 25 percent, 50 percent, or 80 percent of the items. The subjects then rated the stranger's attractiveness; mean attraction scores were 6.17, 8.29, and 9.70 for the three degrees of response agreement, respectively. The evidence therefore indicates that similarity of personality characteristics is also positively related to interpersonal attraction. This conclusion is supported by Izard

(1960a, 1960b), who found that friends were more alike on personality profiles than were random pairs.

There is evidence to suggest, however, that mere similarity may not always be a determinant of attractiveness. Rychlak (1965) examined the effects of similarity and compatibility of needs upon preferences for interpersonal role relationships. Similarity was based upon two persons having the same need (e.g., both have a need for dominance), compatibility upon two persons having complementary needs (e.g., one has a need for nurturance and the other a need for succorance), and incompatibility upon one person's having a need that is inconsistent with that of the other (e.g., one has a need for order and the other a need for change). After participation in two small group problems, subjects selected most and least preferred coworkers for the roles of boss, employee, and neighbor. Rychlak's findings supported the hypothesis that need compatibility is a determinant of attraction, whereas need similarity and need incompatibility are not related to attraction. A study by Jellison and Zeisset (1969) indicated that the degree to which trait similarity is related to attractiveness depends upon the desirability of the trait and also upon the degree to which the trait is common in the general population. When a desirable trait is shared by another, the other is more attractive when the shared trait is uncommon in the general population than when it is common; however, when the shared trait is undesirable, the other person is more attractive when the trait is common than when it is uncommon. A. R. Cohen (1956) found similarity of ego defenses to be related to attraction, whereas similarity based on projection preferences had the opposite effect.

These studies demonstrate that similarity of certain personality characteristics is related to interpersonal attraction, at least under some conditions. However, it should be evident that the similarity of personality traits must be perceived by the individual in order for it to influence his attraction to the other person. The relation between perceived or assumed similarity and interpersonal attraction was investigated many years ago by Fiedler, Warrington, and Blaisdell (1952). Members and pledges of a college fraternity sorted seventy-six statements descriptive of personality traits four times: (1) describing self, (2) describing how one would ideally like to be, (3) predicting how one's best-liked fellow group member would describe himself, and (4) predicting how one's least-liked fellow group member would describe himself. There was no correlation between real similarity (descriptions of self) and choices of best-liked or least-liked group member. However, subjects perceived persons whom they liked best as more similar to their ideal self and as more similar to themselves than others whom they liked least. A later study by Fiedler, Hutchings, and Dodge (1959) yielded similar findings.

Economic similarity has been shown to be a determinant of attractiveness by Byrne, Clore, and Worchel (1966). High and low economic status subjects evaluated strangers on the basis of responses to economic items dealing with spending money. Ratings of attractiveness were higher when the stranger's responses indicated an economic status similar to that of the subject.

Similarity of race and similarity of sex as determinants of attraction were investigated by Smith, Williams, and Willis (1967). White and black subjects rated a stimulus person on acceptability as a friend. The stimulus person was described as to race, sex, and belief congruence relative to the subject. Race and sex were found to be related to attractiveness, but neither was as strong as belief congruence. Since the investigators' manipulation of belief congruence was essentially the same as the variations used in the studies of attitude similarity-dissimilarity, their findings support earlier studies concerning the importance of attitude similarity as a determinant of attraction.

The *perceived ability* of others also appears to be a determinant of the degree to which an individual desires to affiliate with another. Gilchrist (1952) demonstrated that subjects in a problem-solving situation prefer to work with individuals who have been successful previously in solving problems. This effect was verified in a subsequent study by Shaw and Gilchrist (1955). These studies also showed that although successful persons were initially chosen by both previously successful and previously unsuccessful persons, there was an increasing tendency (over time) for unsuccessful persons to shift to choices of other unsuccessful persons for affiliation. There is some suggestion, then, that similarity of perceived ability may also be a determinant of attraction. Zander and Havelin (1960) reported results consistent with this interpretation; subjects preferred to associate with others having similar ability.

In summary, the degree to which one person is attracted to another has been shown to be due to physical attractiveness of the other person, the degree to which the two persons are similar with respect to a variety of characteristics, and the perceived ability of the other person. Similarity has been studied far more extensively than other determinants of attractiveness and the evidence is highly consistent: Attraction is a function of attitude similarity, belief congruence, personality similarity, race similarity, sex similarity, and economic similarity. It is also evident that under some circumstances similarity of characteristics may lead to reduced attraction, e.g., when the other person is seen as emotionally disturbed or when needs are the characteristics under consideration. In the latter case, need compatibility appears to be the important factor. The implicit assumption in the foregoing discussion is, of course, that attraction between two persons will influence the formation of groups with these persons as members. Undoubtedly, there are many other determinants of interpersonal attraction that we have not considered here.

Group Activities

An individual may be attracted to a group because he enjoys the things the group members do. A person may join a bridge club, not because he enjoys playing bridge (although he might enjoy it), but because he finds the social activities pleasant. A person may join the Kiwanis Club merely because he enjoys meetings and civic activities, although, of course, he may be in agreement with the goals of the club. One could cite many examples of this kind of attraction to the activities of a group, but data from controlled studies are scarce.

Perhaps the most convincing evidence was provided by Sherif and Sherif (1953), who studied group formation in summer camps for boys. They were able to demonstrate, among other things, that boys who were interested in the same activities tended to form groups. Related evidence has also been provided by Thibaut (1950). He found that the attractiveness of the activities in a group affected the attractiveness of group membership. Thus, although the empirical evidence is not extensive, it generally supports the proposition that group activities constitute one source of attraction to the group.

Group Goals

In many ways it is difficult to separate the activities of a group from its goals, and an individual may be attracted to a group because he both enjoys its activities and values its goals or purposes. For example, a person may join a group formed for the purpose of raising funds to support the local church because he enjoys fund-raising activities and because he believes it is good to support the church. On the other hand, a person who very much disliked soliciting funds might join this group if he valued highly the goal of church support. It is improbable, however, that a person who enjoyed the activities in a particular group would join it if he negatively valued the group's goals and purposes.

The role of group goals in group formation has been demonstrated most clearly in the investigations of group relations by Sherif and Sherif (1953). After initially establishing intergroup hostility and tension through a series of ingenious manipulations, they attempted to reestablish harmony and integration. In the initial stages of the study, members of a boys' summer camp were formed into two groups on the basis of selected activities. For approximately five days, situations were arranged in which it seemed that one group interfered with or frustrated the other group. For example, following an athletic victory by one group (the Bull Dogs) over the other (the Red Devils), both were invited to attend a party in the mess hall with the stated purpose of reducing intergroup conflict. However, it was arranged so that the Red Devils got to the mess hall first and found ice cream and cake on a table. Half of the refreshments were battered and broken whereas the other half were in good condition. The Red Devils were told to serve themselves and leave the Bull Dogs their share. Without comment, they chose the good half and carried it to their table. The reaction of the Bull Dogs to this treatment was predictable: They called the Red Devils "pigs," "bums," etc., and generally derogated them. When the intergroup conflict created by procedures of this sort had been firmly established, Sherif and Sherif attempted to reduce the conflict and to rearrange group boundaries by introducing common "supraordinate" goals. The most effective of these was a campwide softball game in which a team of best players from both groups were elected by the boys from the entire camp to compete with a team coming from a neighboring camp. Although the supraordinate goal approach did not completely eliminate the hostilities produced by the earlier manipulations, there was a significant reduction in the amount of hostility and tension and some realignment of group boundaries.

The results of this extensive series of studies demonstrate two ways in which attraction to group goals can contribute to group formation. In the early stages of group development, the conflict between groups led to increased group cohesiveness. One element of this cohesiveness was the "common enemy." Or to say it another way, one of the goals of the Bull Dogs was to get even with the Red Devils. More significant, perhaps, is the demonstration that a common group goal can produce new group memberships.

The effects that being in a common predicament has on group attraction are also demonstrated by a study of the consequences of shared stress on interpersonal liking (Latane, Eckman, & Joy, 1966). The investigators proposed that people who are undergoing stress together do something for one another that serves to reduce the stress, thus positively reinforcing each other. Female subjects were assigned to either an experimental condition in which they shared an electric shock or a condition in which each received the same shock but not together. It was found that ratings of liking for the other person were significantly greater in the shared condition, but only when subjects were firstborns. The treatment in such a study is certainly rather weak, and perhaps it is surprising that it had any effect at all. To the extent that it did, however, the results support the hypothesis that attraction to goals constitutes one basis for group attraction.

Group Membership

It has also been proposed that membership in a group per se may be rewarding to an individual, quite apart from the particular individuals who are members of the group, the group activities, or the pruposes of the group. The results reported by Latane et al. and discussed above might be interpreted as supporting this proposition. It was suggested many years ago that there exists an "affiliation want" (Trotter, 1920), which is one of four instincts that govern man's life. Later theorists have denied the instinctual nature of the need for affiliation, but nevertheless posit such a need as playing an important role in social groupings (McClelland, Atkinson, Clark, & Lowell, 1953; Schachter, 1959). Schachter proposed that one of the functions of affiliation is to reduce anxiety, and his research generally supported this view. Research by others also agrees with this hypothesis. Pepitone and Kleiner (1957) varied the amount of threat experienced by group members and found that high threat yielded greater increases in attraction to the group than low threat. In a second study (Kleiner, 1960) it was found that reduction of threat increased the attractiveness of a confederate who played the role of group member.

Another reason for need affiliation was suggested by Singer and Schockley (1965), namely, that people affiliate in order to compare abilities (cf. Festinger, 1954). Thirty-nine female students were randomly assigned to either a condition in which they had knowledge concerning their performance on an experimental task or one in which they did not have this information. All subjects were then given a choice of waiting for the next part of the study alone or with others. Those who had no knowledge of their performance chose to affiliate significantly more than did those who had such information (6 of 8 versus 2 of 22).

The strongest support for the existence of a need for affiliation is provided by a series of investigations which attempted to show that the need for affiliation can be manipulated through deprivation in the same manner as a physiological need such as hunger.

Gewirtz and Baer (1958b) invited children, aged from three years ten months to five years three months, to play a game using toys. In a deprivation condition, the subject was deprived of social contact for twenty minutes before playing the game. When the child arrived at the laboratory, a familiar adult appeared and announced that the toy was broken but was being repaired. He was given plausible assurance that the toy would be repaired in a few minutes and, since the experimenter did not want the child to miss his turn, he was to wait. The adult then left him alone in a relatively barren room for the twenty-minute period. In the control (non-deprivation) condition, the child began the game immediately upon arrival at the laboratory. Each child played a game which required him to drop marbles into holes in the toy. After a four-minute period to establish a base-line rate, the experimenter dispensed social reinforcements according to a predetermined schedule immediately after the subject had dropped a marble into the least preferred hole (as determined during the base-line period). Reinforcements were verbal expressions of approval such as "good," "fine," "good one," etc. The reinforcements increased the rate of dropping marbles in the nonpreferred hole significantly more in the deprivation condition than in the nondeprivation condition, but only when the experimenter was a member of the opposite sex. In a follow-up study (Gewirtz & Baer, 1958a), a satiation condition was added in which the experimenter maintained a steady stream of conversation with the subject for twenty minutes before the game was started. The effects of reinforcement were significantly greater in the deprivation than in the nondeprivation condition, and greater in the nondeprivation than in the satiation condition. Both boys and girls served as subjects, but only a female experimenter was used. The opposite-sex effect observed in the first study was not found.

Gewirtz and Baer concluded that social deprivation enhances the effectiveness of a social reinforcer, thus supporting the hypothesis that there exists a need for affiliation. However, Walters and Karal (1960) were unable to replicate these findings with college students. Obviously, there is some question whether a twenty-minute period of deprivation is sufficient to arouse the need for affiliation in adults. In a second study (Walters & Ray, 1960), it was found that anxious isolated subjects differed in their response to deprivation whereas nonanxious subjects did not. These investigators concluded that the results reported by Gewirtz and Baer were due to anxiety aroused in the isolated subjects. On the other hand, Stevenson and Cruse (1961) found that social reinforcements were effective in changing behavior, and Stevenson and Odom (1962) demonstrated that the enhanced effects of social reinforcements after social deprivation could not be accounted for in terms of general deprivation. Thus, although there are some conflicting findings, the bulk of the evidence supports the hypothesis that need for affiliation can be manipulated in a manner similar to the manipulation of physiological needs, and that such manipulation has similar effects on responses to reinforcers.

Instrumental Effects of Group Membership

It is perhaps unnecessary to note that an individual may join a group in order to achieve some goal outside the group. A young man may join a college fraternity as a means of meeting young ladies who are members of college sororities. In this case, the source of attraction to the group resides in the person(s) of others who are not members of the group; that is, the joiner is attracted to persons outside the group whom he believes he can affiliate with more readily if he becomes a member of the group in question. It is also obvious that a person may join a group because he believes this will be instrumental in the achievement of goals outside the group. For example, a businessman may join a civic club because he believes that such membership will "be good for business." It is not always easy to separate attraction to others outside the group and attraction to goals outside the group. Therefore, we will examine the general proposition that the sources of reinforcement attainable from group membership may reside outside the group itself.

A number of studies have shown that a group may be perceived as a means to an end outside the group. In a study of labor unions Rose (1952) found that members of local unions report that the major benefits from membership are higher wages and greater job security. However, since attainment of such benefits is a major goal of labor union, this finding could just as easily be interpreted in terms of attraction to group goals. A more direct bit of evidence was provided by Willerman and Swanson (1953) in their study of college sororities. They found that one important reason for joining a sorority was the increased prestige in the college community that can be achieved through sorority membership. A similar study of reasons for belonging to a business organization demonstrated that goals outside the group, such as need for recognition and autonomy, were important factors in the desire to remain in the organization (Ross & Zander, 1957). Although not extensive, the empirical data thus support the hypothesis that individuals sometimes join groups to achieve goals that lie outside the group. Group membership is seen as instrumental in achieving these outside goals.

So, why do people join groups? After reviewing the multitude of factors related to group formation and membership, we find that the answer still seems to be: because the group is perceived as a means of satisfying some individual need or needs. But we have identified and examined some of the things about group membership that are perceived as sources of need satisfaction. For example, Newcomb (1956) has shown how similarity may affect attraction via generalization. It is more likely that an individual will receive reward from another person if that other person is similar to persons who have been rewarding in the past. The effects of need complementarity also may be interpreted in terms of reinforcements. If one person has a need to be dominant and the other a need to be submissive, affiliation will lead to need satisfaction for both. The effects of perceived success of the other person, group activities, group goals, and group instrumentality also may be seen as due to the fact that they satisfy individual needs. Thibaut and Kelley's (1959) analysis of attraction in terms of rewards and costs relative to comparison levels also shows how need satisfaction may be related to such factors as personal success of the other and attitude similarity. For example, the successful person is undoubtedly seen as possessing abilities that will help the group achieve its goals or that may be useful in helping the individual achieve individual goals. In either case, the successful person is seen as contributing to the satisfaction of personal needs, if one affiliates with him. In like manner, the effects of attitude similarity can be shown to be due to the expectation of need satisfaction. One of the rewards or benefits deriving from association with others is the validation of beliefs and attitudes; one may certainly expect validation if the other person holds similar attitudes. Therefore, it appears that interpersonal attraction is a function of the degree to which the person expects affiliation with the other to be rewarding. The difficult task is to identify the many sources of reinforcement in interpersonal relationships.

References

Berger, E. The relation between expressed acceptance of self and expressed acceptance of others. *Journal of Abnormal and Social Psychology*, 1952, 47, 778-782.

Bovard, E. W. Conformity to social norms and attraction to the group. *Science*, 1953, 118, 598-599.

Byrne, D., & Buehler, J. A. A note on the influence of propinquity upon acquaintanceships. *Journal of Abnormal and Social Psychology*, 1955, 51, 147-148.

Byrne, D., Clore, J. L., Jr. & Worchel, P. Effect of economic similarity-dissimilarity on interpersonal attraction. *Journal of Personality and Social Psychology*, 1966, 4, 220-224.

Byrne, D., & Griffitt, W. A developmental investigation of the law of attraction. *Journal of Personality and Social Psychology*, 1966, 4, 699-702.

Byrne, D., Griffitt, W., & Stefaniak, D. Attraction and similarity of personality characterisitcs. *Journal of Personality and Social Psychology*, 1967, 5, 82-90.

Byrne, D., London, O., & Griffitt, W. The effect of topic importance and attitude similiarity-dissimilarity on attraction in an intrastranger design. *Psychonomic Science*, 1968, II, 303-304.

Byrne, D., & Nelson, D. Attraction as a function of attitude similarity-dissimilarity: The effect of topic importance. *Psychonomic Science*, 1964, I, 93-94.

Byrne, D., & Nelson, D. Attraction as a linear function of proportion of positive reinforcements. *Journal of Personality and Social Psychology*, 1965a, 1, 659-663.

Byrne, D., & Nelson, D. The effect of topic importance and attitude similarity-dissimilarity on attraction in a multi-stranger design. *Psychonomic Science*, 1965b, 3, 449-450.

Byrne, D., Nelson, D., & Reeves, K. Effects of consensual validation and invalidation on attraction as a function of verifiability. *Journal of Experimental Social Psychology*, 1966, 2, 98-107.

Byrne, D., & Rhamey, R. Magnitude of positive and negative reinforcements as a determinant of attraction. *Journal of Personality and Social Psychology*, 1965, 2, 885-889.

Cartwright, D., & Zander, A. (Eds.) *Group dynamics: Research and theory.* (3d ed.) Evanston, Ill.: Row, Peterson, 1960.

Cohen, A. R. Experimental effects of ego-defense preference on interpersonal relations. *Journal of Abnormal and Social Psychology*, 1956, 52, 19-27.

Cronbach, L. J., & Cleser, G. C. Assessing similarity between profiles. *Psychological Bulletin*, 1953, 50, 456-473.

Deutsch, M., & Collins, M. E. *Interracial housing: A psychological evaluation of a social experiment.* Minneapolis: University of Minnesota Press, 1951.

Festinger, L. A theory of social comparison processes. *Human Relations*, 1954, 7, 117-140.

Festinger, L. Group attraction and membership. In D. Cartwright and A. Zander (Eds.), *Group dynamics: Research and theory.* Evanston, Ill.: Row, Peterson, 1953. Pp. 92-101.

Festinger, L. Schachter, S., & Back, K. W. *Social pressure in informal groups.* New York: Harper, 1950.

Fiedler, F. E., Hutchings, E. B., & Dodge, J. S. Quasi-therapeutic relations in small college and military groups. *Psychological Monographs*, 1959, 73, no. 473.

Fiedler, F. E., Warrington, W. G., & Blaisdell, F. J. Unconscious attitudes as correlates of sociometric choice in a social group. *Journal of Abnormal and Social Psychology*, 1952, 47, 790-796.

Gewirtz, J. L., & Baer, D. M. Deprivation and satiation of social reinforcers as drive conditions. *Journal of Abnormal and Social Psychology*, 1958a, 57, 165-172

Gewirtz, J. L., & Baer, D. M. The effect of brief social deprivation on behaviors for a social reinforcer. *Journal of Abnormal and Social Psychology,* 1958b, 56, 49-56.

Gilchrist, J. C. The formation of social groups under conditions of success and failure. *Journal of Abnormal and Social Psychology,* 1952, 47, 194-187.

Griffitt, W. Interpersonal attraction as a function of self concept and personality similarity-dissimilarity. *Journal of Personality and Social Psychology,* 1966, 4, 581-584.

Gundlach, R. H. Effects of on-the-job experiences with Negroes upon racial attitudes of white workers in union shops. *Psychological Reports,* 1956, 2, 67-77.

Harding, J., & Hogrefe, R. Attitudes of white department store employees toward Negro coworkers. *Journal of Social Issues,* 1952, 8, 18-28.

Heider, F. *The psychology of interpersonal relations.* New York: Wiley, 1958.

Izard, C. E. Personality similarity and friendship. *Journal of Abnormal and Social Psychology,* 1950a, 61, 47-51.

Izard, C. E. Personality similarity, positive affect, and interpersonal attraction. *Journal of Abnormal and Social Psychology,* 1960b, 61, 484-485.

Jahoda, M. Race relations and mental health. In UNESCO, *Race and sicence.* New York: Columbia, 1961.

Jellison, J. M., & Zeisset, P. J. Attraction as a function of the commonality and desirability of a trait shared with another. *Journal of Personality and Social Psychology,* 1969, II, 115-120.

Kleiner, R. J. The effect of threat reduction upon interpersonal attractiveness. *Journal of Personality,* 1960, 28, 145-155.

Latane, B., Eckman, J., & Joy, V. Shared stress and interpersonal attraction. *Journal of Experimental Social Psychology,* 1966, I, 80-94.

McClelland, D. C., Atkinson, J. W., Clark, R. A., & Lowell, E. L. *The achievement motive.* New York: Appleton-Century-Crofts, 1953.

Maissonneuve, J., Palmade, G., & Fourment, C. Selective choices and propinquity. *Sociometry,* 1952, 15, 1350140.

Newcomb, T. M. The prediction of interpersonal attraction. *American Psychologist,* 1956, II, 575-586.

Newcomb, T. M. *The acquaintance process.* New York: Holt, 1961.

Novak, D. W., & Lerner, M. J. Rejection as a consequence of perceived similarity. *Journal of Personality and Social Psychology,* 1968, 9, 147-152.

Palmore, E. B. The introduction of Negroes into white departments. *Human Organization,* 1955, 14, 27-28.

Pepitone, A., & Kleiner, R. J. The effects of threat and frustration on group cohesiveness. *Journal of Abnormal and Social Psychology,* 1957, 54, 192-199.

Rose, A. *Union solidarity.* Minneapolis: University of Minnesota Press, 1952.

Ross, I., & Zander, A. Need satisfaction and employee turnover. *Personnel Psychology,* 1957, 10, 327-338.

Rychlak, J. F. The similarity, compatibility, or incompatibility of needs in interpersonal selection. *Journal of Personality and Social Psychology,* 1965, 2, 334-340.

Schachter, S. *The psychology of affiliation.* Stanford, Calif.: Stanford University Press, 1959.

Schlosser, M. Liking as a function of physical attractiveness and task performance. Unpublished master's thesis, University of Florida, Gainesville, 1969.

Shaw, M. E., & Gilchrist, J. C. Repetitive task failure and sociometric choice. *Journal of Abnormal and Social Psychology,* 1955, 50, 29-32.

Sherif, M., & Sherif, C. W. *Groups in harmony and tension.* New York: Harper & Row, 1953.

Singer, J. E., & Schockley, V. L. Ability and affiliation. *Journal of Personality and Social Psychology,* 1965, 1, 95-100.

Smith, C. R., Williams, L., & Willis, R. H. Race, sex, and belief as determinants of friendship acceptance. *Journal of Personality and Social Psychology,* 1967, 5, 127-137.

Sommer, R. Studies in personal space. *Sociometry,* 1959, 22, 247-260.

Stevenson, H. W., & Cruse, D. B. The effectiveness of social reinforcement with normal and feebleminded children. *Journal of Personality,* 1961, 29, 124-135.

Stevenson, H. W., & Odom, R. D. The effectiveness of social reinforcement following two conditions of social deprivation. *Journal of Abnormal and Social Psychology,* 1962, 65, 429-431.

Stotland, E., & Cottrell, N. B. Similarity of performance as influenced by interaction, self-esteem, and birth order. *Journal of Abnormal and Social Psychology,* 1962, 64, 183-191.

Stotland, E., Cottrell, N. B., & Laing, G. Group interaction and perceived similarity of members. *Journal of Abnormal and Social Psychology,* 1960, 61, 335-340.

Stouffer, S. A., Suchman, E. A., DeVinney, L. C., Star, S. A. & Williams, R. M., Jr. *The American soldier: Adjustment during army life.* Vol. 1. Princeton, N. J.: Princeton, 1949.

Thibaut, J. W. An experimental study of the cohesiveness of underprivileged groups. *Human Relations,* 1950, 3, 251-278.

Thibaut, J. W., & Kelley, H. H. *The social psychology of groups.* New York: Wiley, 1959.

Trotter, W. *Instincts of the herd in peace and war.* (rev. ed.) London: Allen, 1920.

Walster, E., Aronson, V., Abrahams, D., & Rottman, L. Importance of physical attractiveness in dating behavior. *Journal of Personality and Social Psychology,* 1966, 4, 508-516.

Walters, R. H., & Karal, P. Social deprivation and verbal behavior. *Journal of Personality,* 1960, 28, 89-107.

Walters, R. H., & Ray, E. Anxiety, social isolation, and reinforcer effectiveness. *Journal of Personality,* 1960, 28, 358-367.

Willerman, B., & Swanson, L. Group prestige in voluntary organizations. *Human Relations,* 1953, 6, 57-77.

Zander, A., & Havelin, A. Social comparison and interpersonal attraction. *Human Relations,* 1960, 13, 21-32.

SOCIAL INFLUENCE OF GROUPS

BLAIR J. KOLASA

Social Influence

The influence of the group on its members can take place in many ways. Often there are well-known and accepted norms to follow, but where the standards are not very clear the actions of the individual members are affected still more by their view of the patterns of behavior exhibited by others in the group. Even definite criteria are followed, however, because of the real or implied pressures of the social group. What is of greater importance, however, is that the mere presence of other people affects the performance of a person.

In an early and well-known experiment, Sherif (1936) asked subjects in a darkened room to estimate the extent and direction of movement of a tiny pinpoint of light. (The light really did not move although people ordinarily perceived movement—a phenomenon known as the *autokinetic effect*). Individual estimates were very close together when made in a group and did not diverge significantly when the subjects were later asked to make estimates while alone. When Sherif started with subjects making estimates when no other members were present, the estimates were quite divergent. When later gathered into a group, the estimates of individuals began to converge and, while they were very close, these were not as close as the nearly identical estimates given by members of the group that started out together as a group. The earlier individual experiences clearly played a role even though the group influences were more significant.

A closer look at the influence processes in a group setting reveals the role of already familiar social concepts such as norms in the specific context of interaction in groups.

Group Norms

Norms [are of course] very important in human affairs; this is no less true when we look more closely into the functioning of groups. The rules of behavior that are important for the functioning of the group become even more important when the group or the task becomes larger. Some guidelines are necessary to help the group reach a goal, although, as Thibaut and Kelley (1959) point out, the norm structure can become so complex that it interferes with the effective functioning of the group. In this situation it is likely that more attention is paid to the following of the rules to the letter than to the fulfillment of the functions those rules were intended to serve originally. Norms may be described in various ways, depending on the focus of attention. There may be a concentration on the processes at work in the social situation or on the effects of the functioning of norms. Looking at norms as sanctions emphasizes their role as a process; common behavior of group members is an immediate effect, and the support of group activity may be regarded as an only slightly more distant effect.

Real or imagined pressures to conform to the norms of the group often have been described by casual observers of the social scene. There is some general opinion that the very notion of conformity is antagonistic to individual fulfillment and, eventually, the attainment of societal well-being. Indeed it might, but such superficial pronouncements overlook the positive and sometimes necessary aspects of conformity to group norms. Cartwright and Zander (1960, p. 159) point out that pressures for conformity can help the group accomplish its goals by providing information on "reality" to its members so that the group can maintain itself. These social pressures can provide stability and information for both individual members and the total group in the common pursuit of functional goals.

The influence of the group toward conformity can be demonstrated in many ways. An early experiment by Asch (1952) indicated that even simple tasks could be altered by group pressures. Asch had members of a small group make judgments in the presence of each other. The subjects were to match a criterion line with one of three lines presented along with it; this was a task so simple that a large number of subjects given the choices earlier made virtually no mistakes. The experimental group itself was composed of individuals who were unaware of the fact that some of the other members were instructed by the experimenter to give incorrect answers occasionally. The naive subjects, when faced with unanimous choices by the other members, often gave the same incorrect choices. This did not occur with some subjects and even those who did conform did not always do so; the number of incorrect choices, however, was quite high. Asch varied the experiment by changing the number in the group and in the majority. A majority of three was found to be as influential as any larger ones (up to 16 were tried). If one other person was present who supported the naive subject, this was enough to reduce the influence of the majority or even eliminate it entirely.

The Asch experiment called for very simple judgments—ones where there should have been little doubt as to outcome. If the group influence was strong with respect to easy judgments of lengths of lines, it should not be too surprising to find strong group influences in more common social situations where the "correct" choices are less easy to find than are the group guidelines.

Other experimenters have confirmed the basic results of Asch's study (Rosenberg, 1961). Milgram (1964) also found that naive subjects administered more pain to other subjects under the social pressure of a group (accomplices of the experimenter) than they would on their own initiative.

Some individuals find it easier to conform than do others; the differences between the independent and the submissive undoubtedly are based in personality factors. Steiner and Johnson (1963) confirm the generally accepted guess that authoritarians are more conforming than are nonauthoritarians. The authors found an easy acceptance of the decisions of a respected group of peers. When strong needs for social approval are considered in addition to the authoritarian pattern, subjects who are highly motivated with respect to this factor are more likely to agree with expressed opinions of their peers (Stickland and Crowne, 1962).

Other variables play a role too, however. Older subjects are less likely to conform (DiVesta and Cox, 1960). The same authors found also that females and those with less intellectual ability showed more conformity. Milgram (1964) supported the latter point in finding that college graduates conformed less than those in lower educational brackets.

There is substantial evidence to support a statement that when an individual takes a stand publicly, he is more likely to be influenced by group norms than when he arrives at a conclusion in private. Raven (1959) found greater pressure to conform to the group norm when the individual either had to communicate his opinion or where possibility of rejection for nonconformity existed. Kelley and Volkart (1952) found similar results when they presented a critical speech to a group of boy scouts. Half the group was told that the results of a later questionnaire about the speech would be made public while the other half was assured that their responses would not be disclosed. Those boy scouts who were told their questionnaires would be made public tended to agree more with the speaker.

Cohesiveness

The perceptions of the bonds between individuals are important aspects of group functioning. There is even some doubt as to whether there will be any unifying adherence to group norms without cohesiveness, the condition defined as "that group property which is inferred from the number and strength of mutual positive attitudes among the members of a group" (Lott, 1961 p. 279).

It might be expected that the influence a group will exert upon its members will be related to the cohesiveness of the group, that is, the greater the cohesiveness the greater the influence. Festinger et al. (1950) found this to be the case. The same authors described the basis for the influence as being in the attractiveness of the group for its members. Individuals may want to belong to the group for several reasons—the group may be the mediator for certain goals that are important for members, being a member of the group may have certain attractions in itself, or people may want to belong to the group simply because they like the other members.

Since norms involve criteria for behavior, they tend to reduce any anxiety about what is "right" or proper. The more homogeneous the group, the more consistent the criteria are likely to be; this, in turn, makes the group more cohesive, and so on, in a reinforcing cycle. The more the values of the group are shared, the more cohesive the group is likely to be. The "tightly knit group" means a greater sharing of values and more identification with group perspectives.

Cohesiveness of the group will be greater if changes in the membership of the group occur less or not at all (Lasswell and Kaplan, 1950). A few new members may not be resisted or may even be welcomed by the existing membership; when there is a chance of the intrusion of a large number of new participants, there is less likely to be acceptance of the new members. The newcomers, on the other hand, may come into the new situation with trepidation or feelings of inferiority (Shils, 1950). Cohesiveness may be enhanced in many different ways or through the use of many different techniques. It has been characteristic of many "in" groups that their existence has been furthered by the use of secret symbols, passwords, or any mystical arrangements that unify them and set them apart from others.

Cohesiveness of a group influences communications within it and, at the same time, communications have some effect on cohesiveness. Festinger and Thibaut

(1951) found that where there was a wide range of opinion in decision-making groups, there was a tendency for communications to be directed to those members who were at the extremes of the range of opinions. There are more communications to the deviate from group norms, since these are attempts to bring him "back into the fold." The attempts are made partly because the deviate may represent a threat to the existence and stability of the group. Because of this threat, there is, in addition, hostility often expressed toward the nonconformist, the rejection being particularly strong in high-cohesiveness groups (Schachter, 1951).

Lott (1961) suggests that a more cohesive group has a higher level of communication between the members. There is also some suggestion that cohesiveness will increase if communication among members of a group increases, particularly if there are visible rewards in this procedure for the various members. This may be similar to the point that Homans (1950) has indicated, that interaction between members of a group and attractiveness were directly related. This would mean that interaction and communication would bring increased liking of other members and vice versa.

As might be expected, a cohesive group is more likely to arise in a situation calling for cooperative activity and is likely to be more effective in performance than is one where competition occurs internally. Klein (1956) has indicated that compatibility of members and similarity in characteristics of individuals lead to more effective collaboration and performance. He indicates that the badly organized group is no better than one that is composed of members in competition with one another where individuals hinder others in attainment of a goal. There is also more likelihood of communication of hostile feelings, criticism, withholding of information, and less communication in a poorly organized group. What communication does occur may be largely irrelevant or unrelated to the task.

Group discussions of problems to be faced and procedures to be followed is probably more effective in carrying out group performance than is any individual educational effort.

Competition

A competitive atmosphere involving groups may play an important role in their functioning in many practical situations. It may be commonly believed, especially in industrial concerns, that competition between individuals and groups within the company is of value in stimulating higher performance. Whether this is so or not is important to determine.

Some contribution to an understanding of the effects of competition and cooperation on individual and group performance is gained through a reading of results of a basic experiment by Mintz (1951). Mintz arranged metal cones in a bottle with an opening just large enough for the cones to be withdrawn one at a time. Water was introduced into the jar from below in the experiment while the subjects were instructed to withdraw the cones without getting them wet. There were two experimental conditions; in one a reward was promised to the person who retrieved his cone without getting it wet; a fine was paid if the cone was dampened by the rising water. The second experimental variation indicated that a similar group of students succeeded in cooperating and getting their cones out within a short period of time. There were no "traffic jams" under the cooperative pattern of behavior while the reward-and-fine conditions produced blockage and nonadaptive behavior over half the time. The experimenter obtained this result with no more than the threat of a mild fear of failure or the payment of a 10 cent fine.

Another of the earlier experimental studies of competition versus cooperation was done by Deutsch (1949). His subjects performed tasks ranging from simple puzzles to more complex problems of human relations. On most tasks the cooperative groups produced at a higher level than did the competitive groups, perhaps because of greater coordination in the cooperative teams. An added feature was a friendlier spirit among the cooperators. A later attempt by Jones and Vroom (1964) to isolate key factors in a similar situation led to the conclusion that the more effective performance of cooperative groups was the result of an effective division of labor. Performance was likely to be adversely affected when members had strong preferences for a particular task. This was true in cooperative as well as competitive groups.

These results and those of other researchers give some indication of the influence of group norms and the resulting cohesiveness on the performance of the members' conformity to norms. Hammond and Goldman (1961, p. 60) phrase it in terms of "noncompetition (being) more favorable to the group process."

Participation

In one way or another, various group studies have buttressed the view that a significant factor contributing to the effectiveness of the group is that of participation by the members in its functioning. Several research studies, particularly in industry, have indicated the importance of this factor.

The "Hawthorne studies" represent one of the most significant conceptual influences in the area of organizational behavior, particularly in an industrial setting. While the experiments focused on the influence of the group on productivity of workers, the deeper implications for a general theory of human behavior and the applications of it in an administrative framework have had great impact on organizational theorists and practitioners. These studies, begun in the 1920's in the Hawthorne plant of the Western Electric Company, have been discussed by many, including Roethlisberger and Dickson (1947) and Homans (1950).

The original interest of the experimenters in this series of studies was in the effects of environmental factors on work performance. They varied the level of illumination, for instance, and related this to measures of output, using small groups of workers selected from the general work force as subjects placed in specially prepared test facilities. During the course of the experiments, the investigators recognized that variables other than those with which they were concerned were playing a very important role in the final output. It was the recognition of the social factors contribution to performance for which these studies became justly famous. The girls who were selected for the test room experience participated in the planning of the experiment, and their views were taken into account throughout. The girls felt "it was fun" and, even though the number of observers was greater and their attention higher in the test situation than in the ordinary work environment, the girls felt no sense of anxiety because of tight control. The group developed leadership and common purpose; the work situation became a very cohesive one, where, when individuals may not have felt up to par, the other members of the group "carried" them. In short, there emerged an effectively functioning social group in a warm relationship with its supervisors. What about the original dependent variable—work output? There need not be any concern on this score by those who concentrated only on production. Output progressed to consistently higher levels without stress on the individuals and, of course, while this could not continue indefinitely, the workers were highly motivated to show increasing improvement.

This was in distinct contrast to the situation the workers said existed in their original work stations. It was also distinctly different from the situation existing in another work group that was observed without any of the preliminary discussion or participation by the workers in the new investigation. Even though there was a wage incentive system in this group, which should have provided some increase in output and wages, production figures remained remarkably constant over a period of time. Work procedures and the resulting output were influenced by the shared attitudes and values of the group; the work group set norms which maintained a ceiling on output. Those workers who exceeded the ceiling were given evidence of social disapproval, verbally or physically. Output was not exceedingly low, however, since the group norms included a floor for production, below which employees could not fall without being called a "chiseler" or something similar.

This work unit proved to be less cohesive than the original experimental one. While there was a common set of values and sentiments, the main group was characterized by a set of cliques, each with limited interests. Relationships with supervisors were less friendly and more formal than in the cohesive participating group. Workers felt more closely supervised when, in reality, there was less overall supervision in the regular work situation than in the test group. Both groups seemed to be organized; the difference arose from the fact that the test group was organized in cooperation with management for a common purpose while the second informal work group was organized in opposition to management. In both cases, however, an analysis of the informal group clearly indicated the strong influence of social factors on individual and group performance.

Another well-known study of the importance of participation in the functioning of groups was done at the Harwood Manufacturing Corporation by Coch and French (1948). While the study focused on the change process and the specific techniques possible in the overcoming of resistance to change, the techniques used and the results illustrate several aspects of group dynamics. The experiment was conducted at a time when the factory was involved in a style change that necessitated a revision of work roles and procedures. The investigators arranged to have matched groups of employees exposed to three degrees of participation in determining the new work assignments. One group had virtually no participation in the process; they were assigned tasks from the very beginning. The second group participated indirectly through a group of representatives selected from the original group. The final variation involved complete participation in the determining of programs and assignments in the changeover. After the changeover, the no-participation group showed little or no improvement in their performance. Resistance was notable among the members of the production crew, and many examples of hostility and aggression between workers and supervisors were common. The group that participated through representatives worked well with the supervisor or staff man and showed a substantial increase in performance, particularly in the second week after the change. The total participation group adapted to the change very rapidly and progressed to levels that were significantly higher than their earlier performance. The emotional tone of the group was very good; there was excellent cooperation between individuals in the group and the supervisor, and no aggression was evident.

At the end of the month, the no-participation group had made no progress and were assigned to new jobs somewhere else in the factory. When they were reassembled after a few months and permitted to participate in still another change, this group operated at the same high levels that earlier participation groups achieved, a level that, again, was significantly higher than the positions reached where they were not permitted to participate. The experimenters felt that such participation leads to higher morale or better labor-management relations in addition to higher production. The entire management of the company felt that the practical results were very valuable, over and above any of the theoretical additions this study has made to concepts of group processes and intergroup relations generally.

It may be, however, that, while there is a strong motivational basis for individual participation, the strength of this factor may not be uniform for all individuals. Vroom (1959) related personality with group participation and performance. He found the highest satisfaction in the job and the best performance in those individuals who had a high need for independence. Individuals who are highly dependent and were authoritarian-oriented were affected less by the opportunity to participate and showed no relationship between felt participation and job performance. This study indicates that, while participation is related to performance and is important in group functioning, we should also look to variations in individuals in terms of the need for participation.

Broader situational and demographic variables are not, of course, without their influence on the interaction within the small group. A series of studies on an important small group in the legal area, the jury, has indicated several avenues of influence from outside the immediate group situation. Strodtbeck, James, and Hawkins (1958) determined the influence of socioeconomic status and occupation on the interaction in the mock jury. It was found that those individuals who participated more were most often chosen as foreman. Men participated in jury deliberations much more frequently than did women, and there was much more activity from those individuals in higher socioeconomic brackets.

Group Problem Solving

One of the aspects of group functioning that has attracted considerable interest down through the years is that of group problem solving. The basic question has been whether the product of the intellectual functioning of a group is superior to that of a group of individuals functioning separately.

In one of the earliest studies on the question of group versus individual problem solving, Allport (1920) found a difference in favor of the group because a greater variety of ideas arose in that social setting. Lorge and Solomon (1960) replicated an earlier study by Shaw (1932) and found (as Shaw did) that, generally, groups were superior to individuals. Level of aspiration was a significant factor; no individual without aspiration was able to solve the problem, while groups were not affected as strongly. Argyle (1957) agreed in terms of superiority of the group. He isolated two factors in the process, namely, the improvement of judgment through prior judgment and the superiority achieved through a combination of individual judgments. Group problem solving increased the number of alternatives available and stimulated activity toward a typical solution to identify blind alleys that individuals might find themselves in if they pursue the task alone.

It is safe to say that most of the studies in this area report a superiority of group over individual approaches although at least one (Moore and Anderson, 1954) does not. It may be that the source of disagreement lies mainly in the conditions surrounding the task and in the individuals who are subjects. The preponderance of expert opinion, however, is in favor of superiority of the group in problem-solving performance.

There has been further interest in a specific variant of group problem solving known popularly as "brainstorming" where the focus is on unrestricted and uninhibited associative responses by members of an assembled group. The group is under instructions to be unconcerned about the logic or validity of an idea and to respond with as many as possible.

Results of experiments in this area have been somewhat controversial. Osborn (1957), among others, has noted evidence for a greater variety and creativity in group solutions under the brainstorming instructions to provide ideas without concern for their value or logic. Taylor et al. (1958) indicate that this has not been true in their experience. The latter findings may represent, however, an inability of the individuals in the group to rid themselves of limiting attitudes; other situational and relational factors also may be playing an inhibiting role.

Structural Factors

Simple physical factors affect social relationships of individuals. In a small group situation they may play an even greater role than in broad social interaction, since the more immediate psychological factors have a tendency to be highlighted in the more proximate influences of the small group.

Size

The number of individuals in a group can, at least at a casual initial impression, determine much of the activity of the group. It would seem logical that the greater the number of individuals interacting, the less intimate their relationships would be. The sheer volume of interactions then necessary would tend to make any concerted action much more difficult. The role of the leader would, however, be much more significant in a group of larger size.

What the "proper" number of individuals in the group may be could depend upon the circumstances in which the group operates, particularly the purpose or function. Sargent and Williamson (1958) indicate, after a survey of the field, that a fact-finding group is probably most effective when it is composed of about 14 members. An executive or action-taking group functions best at a size of approximately seven members. The validity of these figures is reinforced by information from many legislative bodies that indicates memberships in the two different types of functioning groups as hovering close to the figures given.

An experimental study (Bales and Borgatta, 1955) of the effect of size on the interaction within the group provides some empirical results. The experimenters varied group size from two up to seven and recorded observations in the 12 categories of the Bales Interaction Analysis procedure. The overall results indicate, not surprisingly, that each member is faced with the greater number of individuals with whom to interact as size increases and the amount of time available to talk to others then is reduced per capita. When specific types of interaction are considered in the increase in size, the following actions also increase: showing solidarity, releasing tension, and giving suggestion. The following activities show a decrease with size: showing agreement, asking for opinion, and showing tension. These patterns of initiated behavior probably show the increased pressure on the individuals for activities that will further the functioning of the group despite the increase in size.

Berelson and Steiner (1964) conclude that even-numbered groups show more disagreement than odd-numbered groups because of the possibility for subgroups of equal size to be pitted against each other. They further state that the "perfect" group size is five, where, if subgroups develop, a minority group of two permits participation and individual development in support of a position while a majority of three is not completely overwhelming yet strong enough to prevail.

Simmel was one of the first researchers to point out the characteristics of two-person and three-person groups and to discuss the differences between them. Three-person groups quickly break down into two subgroups, that is, two persons team up as a majority against the remaining member. This division may not be an active or aggressive one, however, since the minority of one may simply be a less interested or even apathetic member of the group. It is more stable than a two-man group in the sense of accomplishment of purpose by the majority but unstable in that it breaks down very quickly into subgroups of two and one. The group of two is less stable because there is a great deal of tension in the evenly balanced person-to-person situation. There is, however, a recognition of the need for understanding, tolerance, and the avoidance of disagreement. The husband-wife group is a good example, and many of the characteristics of their situation can apply generally to all groups of two.

These findings have given rise to the statements of small group researchers that the dyad (two-person group) is more stable than the triad (three-person group). This may be only a newer and more precise way of stating the old maxim "two is company and three is a crowd."

Placement

Interaction between individuals and groups often is affected by their location with respect to each other. It might be expected that individuals who do not interact do not get to know each other. The converse, however, is not so readily guessed, that is, that those who do interact are more likely to be attracted to each other (Homans, 1950).

Festinger et al. (1950) compared sociometric choices with the physical distance between individuals and found a high relationship. Individuals living closest were chosen more often and, as the distances between persons increased, choices between them became less frequent. This study was conducted in a housing project where even minor distances such as a few feet were significant; people whose front doors face each other directly are more likely to interact with greater frequency than when they are located in other ways.

Further evidence of the impact of physical placement on primary relationships is presented by Whyte (1956) in *The Organization Man*. No demographic variables such as occupation, background, religion, or education could explain the "web of friendship" that existed in the example of suburbia studied. The basis for primary social relationships turned out to be propinquity—groups at social events were composed of those who lived in the same geographic area. Whyte also noted, among other factors, the link between centrality of location and popularity. The more introverted could remain so by locating in peripheral areas.

There is much more to the patterning of groups than physical placement, of course. Similarities of interest, status, and life style are apt to be just as important as location, and perhaps even more so. The author recalls, from several years as a "participant observer" in a planned and cohesive community, that friendship groups were frequently structured along occupational lines. Just as important seemed to be the memberships of the wives in social or charitable organizations. Despite the overlapping that inevitably occurs in any complex social relationship, the common thread between individuals was most often a shared set of values and status.

Communication in Groups

Communication is a basic aspect of the interaction in groups of individuals. Whether on a person-to-person basis or on a level involving a greater number in the network, communication serves to provide information and is a prime vehicle for influencing others. Of all aspects of communication that might be of special interest in a group setting, those relating to the direction of transmission and the arrangements of networks are probably of greatest pertinence for discussion.

Direction of Communication
Communication may proceed only one-way or the information may be transmitted back and forth; that is, two-way communication may take place. A speaker may simply lecture to an audience or a boss may not permit any questioning of his position by subordinates. In those situations, the communication is pretty much limited to one-way. Certainly, subtle cues may be transmitted by the audience back to the speaker but, for all practical purposes, the direction is unilateral. In two-way communication the channels are utilized in both directions. Statements and questions are made back and forth.

Each type of communication has its own characteristics which may determine the usefulness of procedure. Leavitt (1964, p. 143), long an active researcher in this area, has summarized the findings of experiments on direction of communication. Two-way may be slower than one-way communication, but it is more accurate. Senders in the two-way process may have more anxiety or feel under attack because receivers communicate their feelings. At the same time, the receivers feel more sure of themselves since they get a better idea of whether they are correct in their judgments. Two-way communication appears more disorderly and less efficient to an outside observer, but it works better.

The implications for a communicator in any type of organization are striking. An administrator in business or a teacher in an educational setting may feel that a one-way communication system is mandatory to preserve order and promote efficiency in the organization. While "giving orders" has been a traditional pattern of behavior in many business or school situations, there is some doubt that, apart from reducing the anxiety of "boss" or "teacher," it is an effective means of promoting organizational welfare.

Communication Networks

The structuring of communication channels between individuals in a group influences the interaction of its members and the functioning of the group as a whole. Research on communication networks was stimulated by some original work by Bavelas (1948) but was expanded upon by others, notably Leavitt (1951) and Guetzkow and Simon (1955). The experiments on the effects of communication networks, while very basic and spartan as precise experiments must be, can provide valuable information for an understanding of the functioning of communications in groups placed in various institutional settings. Small group communication networks can be structured in the patterns shown in Figure 1. All are patterns of communication involving individuals in groups of five and, while still other patterns of communication are possible (a "chain" of individuals, for example), the patterns in Figure 1 are sufficient for describing salient features of experiments in small group communication nets.

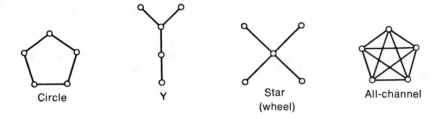

Circle   Y   Star   All-channel
                          (wheel)

Figure 1. Some communication networks in groups (Leavitt, H. 1951).

Those who would wish to transfer behavioral information to an applied setting would undoubtedly have greatest interest in the relationships between communication networks and performance of the group. Questions such as "which network is most efficient?" might be asked. The difficulty in answering comes in the further specification of effectiveness; speed or accuracy may be the prime consideration. In addition, the nature of the task, the order of presentation, or other conditions play a role, and there are other factors that have an additional influence on performance, if only indirectly. Motivation and morale can show some relationships with type of communication network and, as has been pointed out repeatedly, these factors can influence the performance of a group or individual.

Leavitt (1964) summarized his work and that of others in a comparison of networks operating under various conditions. The "star" network will be faster than the "circle," at least in the initial stages of organization if not throughout the entire handling of the task. The star will provide a great deal of satisfaction for the member in the central position; the others in the network are likely to be considerably less satisfied in the outcome of the task. Of possible greater importance is the difference between the star and the circle in terms of having to cope with new tasks once the networks have been organized and the earlier tasks completed. With new tasks that call for a change in approach or method of problem solving, the circle shows that it can cope much better with the changed conditions. Undoubtedly the superiority in problem solving in new situations is a result of the opportunity for greater participation by circle members in the problem-solving task. The centrality of the star network seems to be the basis for the continuing errors made in new problems.

Satisfaction in the outcome is higher in the circle networks where everyone participates in all aspects of the decision making. Morale in a group where the members are allowed to participate is much higher than in one in which few get the opportunity to play a role. Satisfaction is high, of course, for the member who occupies the central position in the star, but the peripheral members' morale is usually much lower than that of those in the circle.

With some reservations, based on the fact of limited applications to "real" situations, Leavitt (1964, pp. 236-237) suggests that "good" networks are those that are equalitarian in nature, that is, where individuals have many neighbors or equal access to at least two direct channels in the group. The reader is reminded to consider these findings in connection with the earlier considerations of one-way and two-way communications.

References

Allport, F. (1920). The influence of the group upon association and thought. *Journal of Experimental Psychology,* 3, 159-182.

Argyle, M. (1957). Social pressure in public and private situations. *Journal of Abnormal and Social Psychology,* 54, 172-175.

Asch, S. (1952). *Social psychology.* Englewood Cliffs, N.J.: Prentice-Hall.

Bales, R. (1951). *Interaction process analysis: a method for the study of small groups.* Cambridge, Mass.: Addison-Wesley.

Bales, R., and Borgatta, E. (1955). Size of group as a factor in the interaction profile. In Hare, A. et al. (eds.) *Small groups: studies in social interaction.* New York: Knopf, 395-413.

Bavelas, A. (1948). A mathematical model for group structures. *Applied Anthropology,* 7, 16-30.

Bennett, E. (1955). Discussion, decision, commitment, and consensus in "group decisions." *Human Relations,* 8, 251-274.

Berelson, B. and Steiner, G. (1964). *Human behavior.* New York: Harcourt, Brace and World.

Browne, C. (1951). Study of executive leadership in business; sociometric pattern. *Journal of Applied Psychology,* 35, 34-37.

Burgess, E. (1926). The family a unity of interacting personalities. *Family* 7, 3-9.

Cartwright, D. and Zander, A. eds. (1960). *Group dynamics: research and theory* (2nd ed.). New York: Harper & Row.

Chapple, E. (1940). Measuring human relations: an introduction to the study of the interaction of individuals. *Genetic Psychology Monograph,* 22, 1-147.

Coch, L. and French, J. (1948). Overcoming resistance to change. *Human Relations,* 1, 512-534.

Cooley, C. (1909). *Social organization.* New York: Scribner's.

Dalton, M. (1959). *Men who manage.* New York: Wiley.

Deutsch, M. (1949). An experimental study of the effects of cooperation and competition upon group processes. *Human Relations,* 2, 199-231.

DiVesta, F. and Cox, L. (1960). Some dispositional correlates of conformity behavior. *The Journal of Social Psychology,* 52, 259-268.

Festinger, L. (1950). Laboratory experiments: the role of group belongingness. In Miller, J. (ed.). *Experiments in social process.* New York: McGraw-Hill, 31-46.

Festinger, L., Schachter, S., and Back, K. (1950). *Social pressures in informal groups: a study of a housing project.* New York: Harper.

Festinger, L. and Thibaut, J. (1951). Interpersonal communication in small groups. *Journal of Abnormal and Social Psychology,* 46, 92-99.

Gouldner, A. and Gouldner, H. (1963). *Modern sociology.* New York: Harcourt, Brace and World.

Guetzkow, H. and Simon, H. (1955). The impact of certain communication nets upon organization and performance in task-oriented groups. *Management Science,* 1, 233-250.

Hammond, L. and Goldman, M. (1961). Competition and non-competition and its relationship to individual and group productivity. *Sociometry,* 24, 46-60.

Heyns, R. and Lippitt, R. (1954). Systematic observational techniques. In Lindzey, G. (ed.). *Handbook of Social Psychology,* Chap. 10. Reading, Mass.: Addison-Wesley.

Hollander, E. and Webb, W. (1955). Leadership, followership and friendship: an analysis of peer nominations. *Journal of Abnormal and Social Psychology,* 50, 163-167.

Homans, G. (1950). *The human group.* New York: Harcourt, Brace and World.

Horsfall, A. and Arensberg, C. (1949). Teamwork and productivity in a shoe factory. *Human Organization,* 8, 13-25.

Jacobs, J. (1945). The application of sociometry to industry. *Sociometry,* 8, 181-198.

Jennings, H. (1937). Structure of leadership-development and sphere of influence. *Sociometry,* 1, 99-143.

Jones, S. and Vroom, V. (1964). Division of labor and performance under cooperative and competitive conditions. *Journal of Abnormal and Social Psychology,* 68, 313-320.

Kelley, H. and Volkhart, E. (1952). The resistance to change of group-anchored attitudes. *American Sociological Review,* 17, 453-465.

Kerstetter, L. and Sargent, J. (1940). Re-assignment therapy in the classroom. *Sociometry,* 3, 292-306.

Klein, J. (1956). *The study of groups.* London: Routledge.

Krech, D., Crutchfield, R., and Ballachey, E. (1962). *Individual in society.* New York: McGraw-Hill.

Lasswell, H. and Kaplan, A. (1950). *Power and society: a framework for political inquiry.* New Haven, Conn.: Yale University Press.

Leavitt, H. (1951). Some effects of certain communication patterns on group performance. *The Journal of Abnormal and Social Psychology,* 46, 38-50.

Leavitt, H. (1964). *Managerial psychology.* Chicago: University of Chicago Press.

Lorge, I. and Solomon, H. (1960). Group and individual performance in problem solving related to previous exposure to problem, level of aspiration, and group size. *Behavioral Science,* 5, 28-38.

Lott, B. (1961). Group cohesiveness: a learning phenomenon. *The Journal of Social Psychology,* 55, 275-286.

McGregor, D. (1960). *The human side of enterprise.* New York: McGraw-Hill.

Menzel, A. and Katz, E. (1956). Social relations and innovation in the medical profession: the epidemiology of a new drug. *Public Opinion Quarterly,* 19, 337-352.

Milgram, S. (1964). Group pressure and action against a person. *Journal of Abnormal and Social Psychology,* 69, 137-143.

Mintz, A (1951). Nonadaptive group behavior. *The Journal of Abnormal and Social Psychology,* 46, 150-159.

Moore, O. and Anderson, S. (1954). Search behavior in individual and group problem solving. *American Sociological Review,* 19, 702-714.

Moreno, J. L. (1934). *Who shall survive?* Washington: Nervous and Mental Disease Publishing Co.

Osborn, A. (1957). *Applied imagination.* New York: Scribner's.

Raven, B. (1959). Social influence on opinions and the communication of related content. *Journal of Abnormal and Social Psychology,* 58, 119-128.

Roethlisberger, F. and Dickson, W. (1939). *Management and the worker.* Cambridge, Mass.: Harvard University Press.

Rosenberg, L. (1961). Group size, prior experience, and conformity. *Journal of Abnormal and Social Psychology,* 63, 436-437.

Sargent, S. and Williamson, R. (1958). *Social psychology.* New York: Ronald.

Schachter, S. (1951). Deviation, rejection, and communication. *Journal of Abnormal and Social Psychology,* 46, 190-207.

Schein, E. (1965). *Organizational psychology.* Englewood Cliffs, N.J.: Prentice-Hall.

Shaw, M. (1932). A comparison of individuals and small groups in the rational solution of complex problems. *American Journal of Psychology,* 44, 491-504.

Sherif, M. (1936). *The psychology of social norms.* New York: Harper.

Sherif, M. and Sherif, C. (1956). *An outline of social psychology* (rev. ed.). New York: Harper.

Shils, E. (1950). Primary groups in the American army. In Merton, R. and Lazarsfeld, P. (eds). *Continuities in social research: studies in the scope and method of "the American soldier."* New York: Free Press.

Speroff, B. and Kerr, W. (1952). Steel mill "hot strip" accidents and interpersonal desirability values. *Journal of Clinical Psychology,* 8, 89-91.

Steiner, I. and Johnson, H. (1963). Authoritarianism and conformity. *Sociometry,* 26, 21-34.

Strickland, B. and Crowne, D. (1962). Conformity under conditions of simulated group pressure as a function of the need for social approval. *The Journal of Social Psychology,* 58, 171-181.

Strodtbeck, F., James, R. and Hawkins, C. (1958). Social status in jury deliberations. In Maccoby, E., Newcomb, T., and Hartley, E. (eds). *Readings in social psychology,* (3rd ed.). New York: Holt.

Taylor, D., Berry, P., and Block, C. (1958). Does group participation when using brainstorming facilitate or inhibit creative thinking? *Administrative Science Quarterly,* 3, 23-47.

Thelen, H. (1963). *Dynamics of groups at work.* Chicago: University of Chicago Press.

Thibaut, J. and Kelley, H. (1959). *The social psychology of groups.* New York: Wiley.

Tönnies, F. (1st ed., 1887). *Gemeinshaft and gesellschaft* (Loomis, C., trans.) (1940). *Fundamental concepts of sociology.* New York: American Book Co.

Van Zelst, R. (1952). Validation of a sociometric regrouping procedure. *Journal of Abnormal and Social Psychology,* 47, 299-301.

Vroom, V. (1959). Some personality determinants of the effects of participation. *Journal of Abnormal and Social Psychology,* 59, 322-327.

Whyte, W. (1956). *The organization man.* New York: Simon & Schuster.

Williams, S. and Leavitt, H. (1947). Group opinion as a prediction of military leadership. *Journal of Consulting Psychology,* 11, 283-291.

Zeleny, L. (1941). Status: its measurements and control in education. *Sociometry,* 4, 193-204.

EXPLAINING INFORMAL WORK GROUPS IN COMPLEX ORGANIZATIONS: THE CASE FOR AUTONOMY IN STRUCTURE

FRED E. KATZ

A generation after the Hawthorne studies, no one questions the existence of informal groups in complex organizations. Numerous studies have documented their existence, especially among employees in the lowest ranks. But the task remains of developing an adequate *conceptual* explanation of how persons in the lowest ranks, with their limited career prospects in their work and slight opportunity for advancement, are incorporated into work organizations on a relatively permanent basis. Stated differently, how can one account for the integration of organizations that include a large number of persons who are largely disenfranchised from the organization's reward system? How can one account for the apparent collaboration, if not loyalty, of persons who, since the time of Marx, have been described as being alienated from their work?[1] A brief, though oversimplified answer is that workers need work and factories need workers. One can hardly argue with this statement. Yet, the economic interdependence of workers and factories does not clarify the nature of the structural arrangement under which the interdependence is worked out.

The proposed answer to the question of how workers are incorporated into complex organizations has two aspects: (1) Workers have considerable autonomy within the confines of the organization. Even when their work is prescribed in exact detail, the work role tends to be defined narrowly. This leaves a considerable portion of the worker's life within the work organization *undefined.* (2) Workers tend to use this autonomy to bring their working-class culture into the organization, even though this is alien to the bureaucratic ethos of the higher echelons of the organization. This produces continuity between the workman's outside life and his participation in the work setting—a setting to which he has very limited allegiance.[2] This continuity in turn, promotes worker's integration into work organizations. After a general presentation of this perspective, it is illustrated through a detailed review of one of Donald Roy's case studies of factory workers. No attempt will be made to assess the degree of fit of this perspective to particular types of industries.

Reprinted by permission of the author and the publisher from *Administrative Science Quarterly,* vol. 10, no. 2 (Sept. 1965), pp. 204-21.

The guiding perspective is that the culture of informal work groups is a manifestation of autonomy within the confines of the organization, and that autonomy is an aspect of organizational structure that needs systematic study. Autonomy is defined as independence from external control. Here, it means that the activities of workers within the organization are not fully controlled by the organization. This leaves room for development of informal patterns of various sorts—those that lessen boredom of workers, those that help get work done, as well as those that are alienative to the organization. I shall attempt to view autonomy as an aspect of the very structure of organizations, as spheres of independence which are delegated by the organization. Direct and indirect delegation of autonomy suggest themselves. The first refers to specific rules that delimit an area of autonomy. For example, a rule specifying that the foreman can decide who will work the night shift indicates a sphere in which the foreman has autonomy, one in which he exercises discretion. By contrast indirect delegation of autonomy results from the absence of rules; in a sphere where no clear rules exist, autonomy exists by default. Both direct and indirect delegation of autonomy promotes spheres of activity that are not closely controlled by the organization. The present thesis is that the resulting autonomous behavior needs to be considered as an aspect of organizational structure, not merely as deviance. This paper will mainly examine autonomy based on indirect delegation, since this seems to characterize informal patterns among workers.

Worker autonomy can be regarded as part of the barter arrangement between workers and the organization, where limited affiliation with the organization is exchanged for a degree of autonomy. The arrangement has important adaptive functions for both parties. For the organization it is a way of promoting the affiliation of some of its employees with the organization, while at the same time excluding them from certain vital spheres of organizational activity. For workers it permits continuation of the working-class style of life and provides ties of sociability in a context that in many ways is alien to the workman's culture. In short, the autonomy appears to have adaptive and pattern-maintenance functions for the workers, and adaptive and goal-attainment functions for the organization. It must be noted that worker autonomy, although enacted *in* the work organization is essentially *external* to his work role. This contrasts with the autonomy pattern for white collar workers, that is, all those who—from the lowliest clerk to the president—make up the administrative hierarchy. They have greater autonomy *within* their work role, but their role is more broadly defined than that of the worker.[3] In a sense the white-collar worker takes his work role *outside* the organization; the blue-collar worker brings his non-work role *into* the organization.

This use of the term "autonomy" covers part of the same ground that is now covered by the term "informal organization"; but I hope it will eliminate some of the difficulties that exist in the way informal organization is now distinguished from formal organization. Simon and his colleagues summarize the existing distinction.[4] Formal organization is defined as "a planned system of cooperative effort in which each participant has a recognized role to play and duties or tasks to perform."[5] Informal organization is defined as "the whole pattern of actual behavior—the way members of the organization really do behave—insofar as these actual behaviors do not coincide with the formal plan."[6] One reason for questioning this distinction is that it has led to research strategies that appear to have produced a self-fulfilling prophecy by inadvertently reiterating the contention that informal patterns deviate from the planned system, without subjecting this contention to critical analysis. It comes about somewhat as follows: The official rules do not prescribe informal behavior patterns; therefore, informal behavior must be discovered through direct, detailed investigation—usually by direct observation of ongoing behavior. Direct observation is very likely to emphasize actual behavior rather than abstract rules, collaboration on the local level rather than collaboration with the total organization, innovation and departure from rules rather than compliance. All these artifacts of the research process are conducive to perpetuating the initial contention that informal patterns deviate from the planned system. As a result, despite evidence that informal patterns may be very firmly established within an organization,[7] the view persists that informal patterns lack legitimacy and permanence. If the behavior patterns that are relevant to formal structure were subjected to detailed observational scrutiny, one might well discover a picture far closer to so-called informal patterns than we now have.[8]

The definition of formal organization focuses on a planned system, and the definition of informal organization on actual behavior. This is a weak distinction, theoretically. Actual behavior is undoubtedly relevant to planned systems; and system characteristics, even planned ones, are relevant to actual behavior. The distinction seems to need refocusing to enable orderly analysis of structure and ongoing behavior. I would suggest the following perspective: Organizational structure includes relatively controlled and relatively autonomous spheres. The controlled sphere is based on direct specification of behavior; the autonomous sphere is based on both direct and indirect specification of behavior. Direct specification of behavior approximates the formal organization concept; but it allows spheres of autonomy as well as spheres of controlled activity. The indirect specification of behavior approximates the traditional informal organization, but under comparable conceptual footing with the planned formal system.

The writings of Chester Barnard illustrate that autonomous and controlled behavior coexist within organizations and that the executive must fuse them together.[9] He notes that autonomy among personnel is not necessarily a disaster to executive control but may, in fact, be an asset to administrative processes. He suggests that the executive must rely on the "willingness to serve"[10] of those under his command; he must recognize that there is a "zone of indifference"[11] in which persons are prepared to accept orders, and beyond which they are prone to oppose orders. Informal patterns, in Barnard's view of the executive, are not divisive forces, but instead, are "expansion of the means of communication with reduction in the necessity for formal decisions, the minimizing of undesirable influences, and the promotion of desirable influences concordant with the scheme of formal responsibilities."[12] From Barnard's perspective both formal and informal patterns can be harnessed in the service of a "co-operating system." But it seems that the real point is not the blending of formally and informally organized behavior, but the blending of controlled and autonomous behaviors that exist within organizations. Barnard's model of the organization is suffused with autonomy patterns that can serve the whole organization; some of these patterns proceed from direct official specification of behavior and some come from indirect specification.

The Worker's Place in the Organization

Workers are here viewed as being permitted to develop relatively autonomous subcultures and subsystems of social interaction in their day-to-day routines. The autonomous patterns diverge from the officially prescribed patterns, but are very much in line with the workman's style of life and culture outside the organization. The culture of the working-class man is in many ways alien to the decorum and demeanor expected of white-collar members of the organization. In the routinized work of the white-collar worker there is no room for the sudden display of anger of the working-class male; in the face-the-public white-collar worker there is little scope for the pervasive sexual allusions of the working-class male. Yet within the working clique inside the organization the workman can enact the culture patterns of his life outside the organization. He can, for example, indulge freely in what is perhaps the workman's major form of creative mental activity: verbal play, imaginative exploits, and the romanticism on the theme of sex.[13] Indeed, the workman has a large sphere of verbal freedom, since much of what he says "doesn't count," so far as his work is concerned. Unlike the white-collar worker, whose work consists of a world of words, written and spoken, the worker is basically measured by the contributions of his hands. Therefore, his verbal jostlings, such as the razzing of the lowest person on the prestige totem pole, are not considered part of his job. There is every indication (as is shown in the review of the study by Donald Roy), that the content of the verbal banter contains reference to the workman's niche in the social order and the conditions of his social existence.[14] These are also reflected in patterns of practical jokes and prankish physical contact, which are characteristic of the workman's culture, but taboo in the culture of the white-collar worker.[15]

By contrast, the white-collar workers, whether senior executive or junior administrators, have a broad affinity for the organizational style of behavior. They are likely to be members of the middle or upper class, where they have learned the demeanor and proprieties of manner they will be expected to exercise in their position in the organization.[16] There is little abrupt discontinuity, for instance, between the style of dress and speech of their social class and that associated with the bureaucratic style of behavior. Stated differently, they can carry over elements of their external life into the organization and apply them to their job without having to make fundamental adjustments in their general style of behavior; although this does not mean that they have nothing to learn in their work. The organization-man thesis makes the same point in converse terms: The work habits and interests of the white-collar worker spill over into his family and community life. For the white-collar worker, the organization is less clearly differentiated from the culture of his private world than it is from the private world of the worker; the organization is not the enemy camp. The blue-collar worker, on the other hand, is eager to leave his work behind him as he leaves the gates of the factory.[17]

How does autonomy in the role of white-collar worker differ from that of the worker? Briefly stated, white-collar workers have greater autonomy *in their task-related activities* than does the blue-collar worker: the time clock; the regimentation involved in feeding a machine and gearing one's work to the pace of a machine, of doing one's work exclusively at the location of a particular machine—these apply to the blue-collar worker to a far larger extent than to the white-collar worker. For the latter, work is defined more broadly than it is for the blue-collar worker, requiring a more diffuse commitment. This means that for the white-collar worker a broad range of activities and personal attributes are defined as relevant to work, from personal grooming to getting along with others. Organizing a Little League baseball team, the fate of the local community chest drive, and participation in college alumni affairs—a good organization man's allegiance to the organization and his style of work include taking part in these activities after working hours and communicating these interests to his work peers. It is difficult to assess which activities are regarded as clearly *external* to his work role. On the other hand, the worker's tasks are defined more narrowly, leaving scope for activity that is defined as *external* to his work, but enacted while he is at his place of work.

The limited bases for the worker's *allegiance* to the work organization are given tacit recognition not only in the worker being excluded from administrative decision making, but also in his being allowed to bring into the work setting working-class culture patterns and to fashion them into relatively autonomous subcultures. In short, the worker's external affiliations; i.e., with the working-class style of life, are permitted to intrude into the organization that employs him. This can be viewed as part of the exchange (in addition to monetary pay) for limited forms of reward and participation that the worker is allowed by the employing organization. In view of the differentiation between worker subculture and bureaucratic culture, the worker's immersion in working-class patterns may serve to perpetuate his disenfranchisement from the administrative sphere, resulting in a vicious cycle.

The pattern pictured thus far of workers in relation to factory is chiefly characteristic of the modern western world. A contrasting example exists in the Japanese pattern, where the worker is expected to make a lifetime commitment to one firm.[18] The worker does not expect to leave his initial place of employment—the idea of moving to a better job seems highly incongruous. The firm does not intend to dismiss employees, no matter how uneconomical this may prove to be. In this arrangement the worker's affiliation with the firm is a relatively complete one, and there appears to be little external autonomy.

Enactment of Worker Autonomy: An Example

The empirical study of workers in factories has been a favorite of sociologists and social psychologists. The focus of many of these studies is on what actually goes on in work settings. Among the most eloquently descriptive studies of the culture and interaction patterns of workers are those by Donald F. Roy. One of his studies, his "Banana Time," will therefore be examined at some length.[19] Roy describes a small work group of men engaged in exceedingly simple manual work operating a punch press—it took about fifteen minutes to learn the job. Roy himself participated, and his description bears the mark of intimate immersion in the field situation while, at the same time, bringing to it keen observational skills. He describes how he attempted, during the early days of work, to meet the problems of great boredom by inventing little games. He partly succeeded. After a while he noticed that the banterings and "kidding" by the workers around him were not purely haphazard, but actually served a similar function as his games; they, too, reduced boredom. Following this insight he made systematic studies and discovered *patterns* among the bantering and joking.

> What I saw at first, before I began to observe, was occasional flurries of horse play so simple and unvarying in pattern and so childish in quality that they made no strong bid for attention. For example, Ike would regularly switch off the power at Sammy's machine whenever Sammy made a trip to the lavatory or the drinking fountain. Correlatively, Sammy invariably fell victim to the plot by making an attempt to operate his clicking hammer after returning to the shop. And, as the simple pattern went, this blind stumbling into the trap was always followed by indignation and reproach from Sammy, smirking satisfaction from Ike, and mild paternal scolding from George. My interest in this procedure was at first confined to wondering when Ike would weary of his tedious joke or when Sammy would learn to check his power switch before trying the hammer.
>
>   But, as I began to pay closer attention, as I began to develop familiarity with the communication system, the disconnected became connected, the non-sense made sense, the obscure became clear, and the silly actually funny. And, as the content of the interaction took on more and more meaning, the interaction began to reveal structure.[20]

Roy discovered that the day's routine was broken by activities other than those formally instituted (by the company) or "idiosyncratically developed disjunctions," but were an "ordered series of informal interactions." He describes many forms of interruption that took place and the patterning involved in them. One of these was "peach time," when one worker, Sammy, provided a peach and shared it. His beneficiaries greeted his contribution with disgruntlement and complaints about the quality of the peach. "Banana time" followed.

> Banana time followed peach time by approximately an hour. Sammy again provided the refreshments, namely, one banana. There was, however, no four-way sharing of Sammy's banana. Ike would gulp it down by himself after surreptitiously extracting it from Sammy's lunch box, kept on a shelf behind Sammy's work station. Each morning, after making the snatch, Ike would call out, "Banana time!" and proceed to down his prize, while Sammy made futile protests and denunciations. George would join in with mild remonstrances, sometimes scolding Sammy for making so much fuss. The banana was one which Sammy brought for his own consumption at lunch time; he never did get to eat his banana, but kept bringing one for his lunch. At first this daily theft startled and amazed me. Then I grew to look forward to the daily seizure and the verbal interaction that followed.[21]

In addition to peach time and banana time there was coffee time, fish time, coke time, lunch time, and window-opening time. Each of them was marked by a distinctive pattern of interaction. In addition to these patterned times, Roy notes themes in verbal interplay.

The themes had become standardized in their repetition . . . topics of conversation ranged in quality from an extreme of nonsensical chatter to another extreme of serious discourse. Unlike the times, these themes flowed one into the other in no particular sequence of predictability. Serious conversation could suddenly melt into horse play, and vice versa. In the middle of a serious discussion on the high cost of living, Ike might drop a weight behind the easily startled Sammy, or hit him over the head with a dusty paper sack. Interaction would immediately drop to a low comedy exchange of slaps, threats, guffaws, and disapprobations. . . .[22]

In this verbal interplay exaggeration was a common feature. For instance, one of the men had received one hundred dollars from his son; from that day he was seen as a man with a sizable, steady income—a man ready to retire. Roy, after having admitted that he owned two acres of land, became a large landowner, and his farm became populated with horses, cows, pigs, and chickens. Sexuality also came in for a large share of regular and inventive verbal play.

Roy's article is perhaps a culmination in a series of research findings that, since the days of the Hawthorne studies, have pointed to the demise of the economic man without, however, completing the task of making social organization the focus of analysis. The early studies, in their opposition to the economic-man thesis, pointed out that the individual was not guided only by his own monetary self-interest. Indeed, he could be guided against his own self-interest by his worker peer group; the individual worker might actually lose income by following the output control patterns of his peers. It was emphasized that there was a "group factor" in work situations; but an individualistic, social psychological focus was retained for this group factor. In the Hawthorne studies there was much concern with changes in attitude toward work; the meaning of work was considered a basic factor in individuals' performance; and work groups were considered in molding the meaning and attitudes for members of the group.[23] Roy's interpretation of his findings is similarly social psychological. It is that the informal patterns serve primarily to provide job satisfaction by relieving *boredom*. Along with many students of industrial relations in the last thirty years, he notes the existence of relatively distinct subgroups that have relatively distinct culture and interaction patterns, and that are separate from the formal structure in the factory. Yet, the basic interpretation is in individualistic, psychological terminology: it relieves boredom. Even if one accepts the psychological perspective, one must question whether routine, repetitive work is necessarily conducive to boredom. For example, Chinoy's study of automobile assembly-line workers suggests that workers' response to routine, repetitive work is perhaps better characterized by irritation over lack of control over one's work than by boredom.[24] To realize that routine, repetitive activity does not necessarily lead to boredom, one should allow for the influence of culture. The researcher may be exaggerating the activistic theme of Western societies. The Jicarilla Apache, for example, "have an infinite capacity for not being bored. They can sit for hours on end and apparently do nothing; they certainly don't intellectualize about doing nothing."[25]

The focus of the present paper suggests attention to what seems to be a basic feature in the social organization of the work situation, the autonomy enjoyed by the work group.[26] It does this on Roy's evidence that *considerable structuring of the work situation is done by the workers themselves*. What, then, is the content of the autonomous group culture? As Roy describes it, the work situation includes a great variety of behaviors that are not directly connected with *work*. Many of these fit Simmel's description of play forms of social reality.[27] Subjects that are of serious concern, such as economic security, sexual virility, health and death, submission to the authority of other men, family loyalty, and status aspirations, are examined in a context where they are stripped of their serious content. But the manner in which attention is paid to these subjects is particularly important. Flitting from one topic to another—from the deeply serious to the comic, from the immediately practical to the remotely romantic—indicates the decided irrelevance of the practical, concrete reality in which each of the subjects is embedded. Perhaps it is because members are simultaneously engaged in serious work that they feel free to treat other concerns so detachedly. Roy's group appears to be a veritable haven for the enactment of play forms. Elements of life that are largely beyond the control of the individual are exposed and, in a fashion, are dealt with. All this is most clearly evident in the verbal themes. In addition to play forms, it may well be that the various social interaction patterns—the "razzing" of Sammy, the paternalism of George—are reiterations of serious realities in the larger social context in which the men find themselves. It is noteworthy that it is Sammy, the newest immigrant (all three men are immigrants) who is the scapegoat; it is George, the only Gentile, who quietly occupies the superior status; it is the Negro handyman who is the object of sterotypical banter about uncontrolled sexuality.

These elements, whether they are fairly explicit reiterations or play forms of the workman's life outside the factory, are continuities between life outside the factory and life inside the factory and therefore are important for understanding the nature of the bond between the worker and the organization in which he is employed. Work peers participate in a common culture, which relies heavily on their common fate both within and *outside* the organization. In their commonality they retain a fundamental alienation from the white-collar ranks in the organization. This appears to be demonstrated in Chinoy's findings of workers' widespread lack of interest in becoming foremen or white-collar workers.[28] It is also supported by Walker and Guest's study of assembly-line workers. They found largely favorable reaction by workers to their immediate job, but intense dissatisfaction with the factory as a whole.[29] Although there is a lack of affiliation with the white-collar ranks of the organization, the worker *does* form bonds within the organization—with his own work peers.[30] For the organization, this dual relationship provides an uneasy truce without lessening the fundamental internal antithesis, and manifests itself in problems of morale and communications. At the same time the structure of the situation—the existence of two cultures—assures the continuity of the basic antithesis.

Roy points out that the group had developed a "full-blown socio-cultural system." The group was to a considerable extent a separate and distinct system, one in which the members had active, at times even creative, participation—in sharp contrast to their minimal participation in the larger organization. But it does not seem that *work* was at all a major focus of this sociocultural system! If one accepts this point, one gains a tool for reconciling the dilemma as to whether factory workers are strongly alienated from their work.[31] It appears that work is *one of a variety* of topics around which Roy's group had developed behavioral patterns, but work was by no means the central point of attention of this "full-blown sociocultural system."

The contention that work is not a central feature of Roy's work group differs considerably from traditional explanations of informal groups. Although no claim is made about the representativeness of the Roy group, it must be understood that the sort of data he presented has traditionally been interpreted largely in terms of its relevance to *work*. Statements to the effect that informal activities give meaning to dull, routine factory work[32] and that "work output is a function of the degree of work satisfaction, which in turn depends upon the informal social patterns of the work group"[33] are typical examples. These statements provide a social-psychological explanation of the group's mediating effect between the individual and his work, but they are hardly adequate in providing a structural explanation of the place of informal groups in a complex organization.

In addition to the social-psychological interpretations, there are well-documented studies—by Roy and others—which show production control and worker collusion against management by informal groups of workers.[34] Here there can be no doubt that informal patterns are relevant to work. But it is not certain, even here, that informal groups exist primarily for the worker's control over work or whether the explanation should not be reversed: that control over work exists because of the presence of informal groups which, in turn, exist because of the worker's relative autonomy.

In summary, it is suggested that Roy's work group exhibits a rich sociocultural system that is made possible by substantial worker autonomy. The autonomy exists by default; worker's roles are narrowly defined, leaving a considerable sphere of undefined action within the confines of the organization. The content of worker's sociocultural system is made up of a variety of elements from the culture and social context of workers outside the factory. These elements manifest themselves as direct reiterations as well as play forms of the reality. They provide continuity between the workman's life outside the factory and his participation within the factory.

In using the Roy study to illustrate autonomy patterns among informal groups, certain cautionary statements must be made. The group Roy studied may be atypical in the small amount of managerial supervision and in the degree of isolation from the rest of the factory, which might allow a disproportionately high degree of autonomy, as compared with other work groups. One can only answer that this requires investigation; it has not been demonstrated at this time. Also, worker autonomy structure is evident in other studies, as implied, for example, in Gouldner's conception of the managerial "indulgency pattern" toward workers,[35] and Bensman and Gerver's study of "deviancy in maintaining the social system" in a factory.[36] In addition, autonomy patterns among employees who are operating on higher echelons than laborers have been explored by Chester Barnard[37] and in the various writings of Peter Blau;[38] but these are outside the scope of the present paper.[39]

Note on the Theory of Integration of Complex Organizations

Complex organizations must have ways of procuring and integrating the services of a variety of participants. On a common-sense level one can see the process of procurement and integration accomplished most readily in organizations that have coercive means at their disposal. Prisons can force inmates to peel potatoes. But organizations that do not have coercion at their disposal provide a problem for the analyst. There can be little doubt that most complex organizations do, in fact, solve the problem. How is it accomplished?

The concern of this paper has been the integration of a particular segment of the membership of complex organizations, namely blue-collar workers in factories. The particular issue, here, is how these persons are recruited and integrated into the organization, which offers them few of the rewards that it can bestow. The answer is that a federalistic type of solution exists: Workers are permitted ample separation from the total organization and, to a considerable extent, their integration into the larger system is left to them. Informal work group cultures are the concrete structures that make up the solution.

The separation of workers from the employing organization provides workers with flexibility and options as to the degree of alienation from the whole organization. At the same time, the separation gives the organization freedom to adopt means and goals that are disparate, if not alien, to those of the workers. The federalistic balance of autonomy for the blue-collar workers as against the white-collar staff allows flexibility to both sides; but it is also a potential source of divergence and conflict, which finds nurture in the separate subcultures.

In contrast to the form of integration suggested here, other writings have shown much concern with models of organization that dwell on lessening internal differentiation. Workers and the white-collar staff are seen as diverging in interest and this divergence can *and needs to be* lessened if the organization is to operate effectively.[40] These writings differ from the present essay both in theoretical and practical focus. On the theoretical side, the present exposition is based strongly on the view that autonomy can be viewed as a structural principle of organizations, which can have positive or negative consequences for the operation of organizations. Structured autonomy manifests itself in internal divergencies, but these are not necessarily disruptive and maladaptive for the whole organization or any part of it. As to practical goals, many writers, notably Whyte and Argyris,[41] are concerned with the problem of improving human relations in industrial concerns. The practical focus here is not on improving social relationships in complex organizations; it is on the problem of improving the analytic theory of complex organizations. I do not claim that this is a more worthy or pressing problem than that of improving human relationships in complex organizations, merely that it *is* a problem. . . .

Notes and References

1. For a survey and research application of the the theme of worker alienation, see Robert Blauner, *Alienation and Freedom: The Factory Worker and His Industry* (Chicago: University of Chicago, 1964).

2. For a summary of the literature on the limited commitment of workers to the complex organizations in which they work, as well to work itself, see Chris Argyris, *Integrating the individual and the Organization* (New York: John Wiley, 1964). In Pt. IV the author provides a summary of the debate as to whether the worker is alienated. Argyris' book is addressed to the same general issue as the present paper, but his approach differs in that it focuses on the issue—a very important one—of developing organizational patterns so that there is congruence between the psychological needs of members and the administrative requirements of the organization. The present paper, in contrast, attempts to remain entirely on the level of social structure. See, also, R. Dubin, ''Industrial Workers' World: A Study of the 'Central Life Interests' of Industrial Workers,'' in Erwin O. Smigel (ed.), *Work and Leisure* (New Haven: College and University Press, 1963), pp. 53-72.

3. This viewpoint is more fully developed in Fred E. Katz, ''The School As a Complex Organization,'' *Harvard Educational Review,* 34 (Summer, 1964).

4. Herbert A. Simon, Donald W. Smithburg, and Victor Thompson, *Public Administration* (New York: Alfred Knopf, 1962).

5. *Ibid.,* p. 5.

6. *Ibid.,* p. 87.

7. Fritz J. Roethlisberger and William J. Dickson, *Management and the Worker* (Cambridge: Harvard University, 1939). This classic report is still one of the most complete studies of informal groups. See also Peter M. Blau. ''Structural Effects,'' *American Sociological Review,* 25 (1960), 178-193; also his *The Dynamics of Bureaucracy* (Chicago: University of Chicago, 1955).

8. Indeed, Blau's work comes close to providing just such a picture; see Blau, *The Dynamics of Bureaucracy, op. cit.*

9. Chester I. Barnard, *The Functions of the Executive* (Cambridge: Harvard University, 1938).

10. *Ibid.,* 83 ff.

11. *Ibid.,* 167 ff.

12. *Ibid.,* p. 227.

13. I am not suggesting that middle and upper class males do not engage in this form of mental sport, but I do suggest that for the working-class male it is a *major* creative outlet, and much less so for the middle and upper classes.

14. S. M. Miller and Frank Riessman suggest that the ''factory 'horseplay,' the ritualistic kidding'' are partly an expression of the working-class theme of person centeredness; see their ''The Working-Class Subculture,'' in A. B. Shostak and W. Gomberg (eds.), *Blue Collar World* (Englewood Cliffs, N. J.: Prentice-Hall, 1964), pp. 24-35.

15. Participating in physical contact—be it fighting, prankish shoving, or contact sports—are chiefly characteristic of male preadult culture. Presumably it is only at the low socioeconomic levels that this pattern continues into adulthood. It is not clear whether similar continuities exist in *preadult* and adult female culture among working-class women.

16. It makes little difference whether they are members of the middle or upper class or use these classes as a reference group to guide their behavior.

17. Robert Blauner ''Occupational Differences in Work Satisfaction,'' in R. L. Simpson and I. H. Simpson (eds.) *Social Organization and Behavior* (New York: John Wiley, 1964), pp. 287-292.

18. James C. Abegglen, *The Japanese Factory: Aspects of Its Social Organization* (New York: Free Press, 1960). Opinion differs as to whether Abegglen's formulation about

life-long commitment applies to blue-collar workers in large factories. (I am indebted to the editors for this insight.)

19. Donald F. Roy, " 'Banana Time,' Job Satisfaction and Informal Interaction," *Human Organization,* 18 (1960), 158-168.

20. *Ibid.,* p. 161.

21. *Ibid.,* p. 162.

22. *Ibid.,* p. 163.

23. Fritz J. Roethlisberger and William J. Dickson, *op. cit.,* and Edward Gross, *Work and Society* (New York: Thomas Crowell, 1958), ch. xiv.

24. Ely Chinoy, *Automobile Workers and the American Dream* (Garden City, N. Y.: Doubleday, 1955).

25. Personal communication from H. Clyde Wilson.

26. Focus on autonomy structure does not altogether avoid the pitfall of potentially over-emphasizing one set of structures and one set of functions, just as social-psychological studies have done. But it should serve to broaden the existing basis of analysis.

27. K. H. Wolff (ed. and transl.), *The Sociology of George Simmel* (New York: Free Press, 1950).

28. Ely Chinoy, *op. cit.*; see especially, ch. v. See also, E. W. Bakke, *The Unemployed Worker* (New Haven: Yale University, 1940); and poll conducted by *Fortune* (May, 1947), both cited by Chinoy. Chinoy's explanation of the lack of desire for promotion is that workers have become so discouraged in the course of their work careers that they have given up. He notes that workers are reacting to "the limited opportunities available, to the uncertainties stemming from the informal procedures by which foremen were chosen, and to the nature of the foreman's job itself . . ." (p. 49). This explanation is not irreconcilable with the one offered here. The young factory worker, who does have visions of advancement, is presumably not sufficiently knowledgeable about the culture wall between himself and the administrative bureaucrat.

29. Charles R. Walker and Robert H. Guest, *The Man on the Assembly Line* (Cambridge, Mass.: Harvard University, 1952); see, for example, pp. 139-140

30. Dubin's studies suggest, however, that workers' friendship bonds with work peers are less important than bonds with peers outside the work setting; see Robert Dubin, *op. cit.*

31. Argyris, *op. cit.,* believes that workers are strongly alienated; Walker and Guest, *op. cit.,* note that workers they studied were relatively contented doing simple, repetitive work.

32. Edward Gross, *op. cit.,* p. 526.

33. Reinhard Bendix and Lloyd H. Fisher, "The Perspectives of Elton Mayo," in Amitai Etzioni, (ed.), *Complex Organizations: A Sociological Reader* (New York: Holt, Rinehart, and Winston, 1961), p. 119.

34. See, Donald Roy "Efficiency and 'The Fix': Informal Intergroup Relations in a Piecework Machine Shop," in S. M. Lipset and N. J. Smelser (ed.), *Sociology: The Progress of a Decade* (Englewood Cliffs, N. J.: Prentice-Hall, 1961), pp. 378-390; also his "Quota Restriction and Goldbricking in a Machine Shop," *American Journal of Sociology,* 57 (March, 1952), 427-442.

35. Alvin W. Gouldner, *Wildcat Strike* (Yellow Springs, Ohio: Antioch Press, 1954).

36. Joseph Bensman and Israel Gerver, "Crime and Punishment in the Factory: The Function of Deviancy in Maintaining the Social System," *American Sociological Review,* 28 (August, 1963), 588-598.

37. Chester Barnard, *op. cit.*

38. Peter M. Blau, "Structural Effects," *op. cit.*, and *The Dynamics of Bureaucracy, op. cit.*

39. A broader formulation of autonomy structure has been attempted in Fred E. Katz, *op. cit.*

40. Argyris, *op. cit.*, and other writings by the same author. See also the writings of W. F. Whyte; for example, *Patterns of Industrial Peace* (New York: Harper and Row, 1951) and *Money and Motivation* (New York: Harper and Row, 1955).

41. *Ibid.*

Section B

Conflict Between Groups

ORGANIZATIONAL CONFLICT: CONCEPTS AND MODELS

LOUIS R. PONDY

There is a large and growing body of literature on the subject of organizational conflict. The concept of conflict has been treated as a general social phenomenon, with implications for the understanding of conflict within and between organizations.[1] It has also assumed various roles of some importance in attempts at general theories of management and organizational behavior.[2] Finally, conflict has recently been the focus of numerous empirical studies of organization.[3]

Slowly crystallizing out of this research are three conceptual models designed to deal with the major classes of conflict phenomena in organizations.[4]

1. *Bargaining model*. This is designed to deal with conflict among interest groups in competition for scarce resources. This model is particularly appropriate for the analysis of labor-management relations, budgeting processes, and staff-line conflicts.

2. *Bureaucratic model*. This is applicable to the analysis of superior-subordinate conflicts or, in general, conflicts along the vertical dimension of a hierarchy. This model is primarily concerned with the problems caused by institutional attempts to control behavior and the organization's reaction to such control.

3. *Systems model*. This is directed at lateral conflict, or conflict among the parties to a functional relationship. Analysis of the problems of coordination is the special province of this model.

Running as common threads through each of these models are several implicit orientations. The most important of these orientations follow:

1. Each conflict relationship is made up of a sequence of interlocking conflict episodes; each episode exhibits a sequence or pattern of development, and the conflict relationship can be characterized by stable patterns that appear across the se-

Reprinted by permission of the author and the publisher from *Administrative Science Quarterly*, vol. 12, no. 2 (Sept. 1967), pp. 296-320.

quence of episodes. This orientation forms the basis for a working definition of conflict.

2. Conflict may be functional as well as dysfunctional for the individual and the organization; it may have its roots either within the individual or in the organizational context; therefore, the desirability of conflict resolution needs to be approached with caution.

3. Conflict is intimately tied up with the stability of the organization, not merely in the usual sense that conflict is a threat to stability, but in a much more complex fashion; that is, conflict is a key variable in the feedback loops that characterize organizational behavior. These orientations are discussed before the conceptual models are elaborated.

A Working Definition of Conflict

The term "conflict" has been used at one time or another in the literature to describe: (*1*) *antecedent conditions* (for example, scarcity of resources, policy differences) of conflictful behavior, (*2*) *affective states* (e.g., stress, tension, hostility, anxiety, etc.) of the individuals involved, (*3*) cognitive states of individuals, i.e., their perception or awareness of conflictful situations, and (*4*) conflictful behavior, ranging from passive resistance to overt aggression. Attempts to decide which of these classes—conditions, attitude, cognition, or behavior—is really conflict is likely to result in an empty controversy. The problem is not to choose among these alternative conceptual definitions, since each may be a relevant stage in the development of a conflict episode, but to try to clarify their relationships.

Conflict can be more readily understood if it is considered a dynamic process. A conflict relationship between two or more individuals in an organization can be analyzed as a sequence of conflict episodes. Each conflict episode begins with conditions characterized by certain conflict potentials. The parties to the relationship may not become aware of any basis of conflict, and they may not develop hostile affections for one another. Depending on a number of factors, their behavior may show a variety of conflictful traits. Each episode or encounter leaves an aftermath that affects the course of succeeding episodes. The entire relationship can then be characterized by certain stable aspects of conditions, affect, perception, and behavior. It can also be characterized by trends in any of these characteristics.

This is roughly analogous to defining a "decision" to include activities preliminary to and following choice, as well as the choice itself. In the same sense that a decision can be thought of as a process of gradual commitment to a course of action, a conflict episode can be thought of as a gradual escalation to a state of disorder. If choice is the climax of a decision, then by analogy, open war or aggression is the climax of a conflict episode.

This does not mean that every conflict episode necessarily passes through every stage to open aggression. A potential conflict may never be perceived by the parties to the conflict, or if perceived, the conflict may be resolved before hostilities break out. Several other alternative courses of development are possible. Both Coleman and Aubert make these points clearly in their treatments of the dynamics of conflict.[5]

Just as some decisions become programmed or routinized, conflict management in an organization also becomes programmed or institutionalized sometimes. In fact, the institutionalization of means for dealing with recurrent conflict is one of the important aspects in any treatment of the topic. An organization's success hinges to a great extent on its ability to set up and operate appropriate mechanisms for dealing with a variety of conflict phenomena.

Five stages of a conflict episode are identified: (*1*) latent conflict (conditions), (*2*) perceived conflict (cognition), (*3*) felt conflict (affect), (*4*) manifest conflict (behavior), and (*5*) conflict aftermath (conditions). The elaboration of each of these stages of a conflict episode will provide the substance for a working definition. Which specific reactions take place at each state of a conflict episode, and why, are the central questions to be answered in a theory of conflict. Only the framework within which those questions can be systematically investigated is developed here.

Latent Conflict

A search of the literature has produced a long list of underlying sources of organizational conflict. These are condensed into three basic types of latent conflict: (*1*) competition for scarce resources, (*2*) drives for autonomy, and (*3*) divergence of subunit goals. Later in the paper each of these fundamental types of latent conflict is paired with one of the three conceptual models. Briefly, competition forms the basis for conflict when the aggregated demands of participants for resources exceed the resources available to the organization; autonomy needs form the basis of conflict when one party either seeks to exercise control over some activity that another party regards as his own province or seeks to insulate itself from such control; goal divergence is the source of conflict when two parties who must cooperate on some joint activity are unable to reach a consensus on concerted action. Two or more types of latent conflict may, of course, be present simultaneously.

An important form of latent conflict, which appears to be omitted from this list, is role conflict. The role conflict model treats the organization as a collection of role sets, each composed of the focal person and his role senders. Conflict is said to occur when the focal person receives incompatible role demands or expectations from the persons in his role set.[6] This model has the drawback that it treats the focal person as merely a passive receiver rather than as an active participant in the relationship. It is argued here, that the role conflict model does not postulate a distinct type of latent conflict. Instead, it defines a conceptual relationship, the role set, which may be useful for the analysis of all three forms of latent conflict described.

Perceived Conflict

Conflict may sometimes be perceived when no conditions of latent conflict exist, and latent conflict conditions may be present in a relationship without any of the participants perceiving the conflict.

The case in which conflict is perceived when no latent conflict exists can be handled by the so-called "semantic model" of conflict.[7] According to this explanation, conflict is said to result from the parties' misunderstanding of each others' true position. It is argued that such conflict can be resolved by improving communications between the parties. This model has been the basis of a wide variety of management techniques aimed at improving interpersonal relations. Of course, if the parties' true positions *are* in opposition, then more open communication may only exacerbate the conflict.

The more important case, that some latent conflicts fail to reach the level of awareness also requires explanation. Two important mechanisms that limit perception of conflict are the suppression mechanism and the attention-focus mechanism.[8] Individuals tend to block conflicts that are only mildly threatening out of awareness.[9] Conflicts become strong threats, and therefore must be acknowledged, when the conflicts relate to values central to the individual's personality. The suppression mechanism is applicable more to conflicts related to personal than to organizational values. The attention-focus mechanism, however, is related more to organizational behavior than to personal values. Organizations are characteristically faced with more conflicts than can be dealt with given available time and capacities. The normal reaction is to focus attention on only a few of these, and these tend to be the conflicts for which short-run, routine solutions are available. For organizations successfully to confront the less programmed conflicts, it is frequently necessary to set up separate subunits specifically to deal with such conflicts.

Felt Conflict

There is an important distinction between perceiving conflict and feeling conflict. *A* may be aware that *B* and *A* are in serious disagreement over some policy, but it may not make *A* tense or anxious, and it may have no effect whatsoever on *A*'s affection towards *B*. The personalization of conflict is the mechanism which causes most students of organization to be concerned with the dysfunctions of conflict. There are two common explanations for the personalization of conflict.

One explanation is that the inconsistent demands of efficient organization and individual growth create anxieties within the individual.[10] Anxieties may also result from identity crises or from extra-organizational pressures. Individuals need to vent these anxieties in order to maintain internal equilibrium. Organizational conflicts of the three latent types described earlier provide defensible excuses for displacing these anxieties against suitable targets. This is essentially the so-called "tension-model."[11]

A second explanation is that conflict becomes personalized when the whole personality of the individual is involved in the relationship. Hostile feelings are most common in the intimate relations that characterize total institutions, such as monasteries, residential colleges, and families.[12] In order to dissipate accumulated hostilities, total institutions require certain safety-valve institutions such as athletic activities or norms that legitimize solitude and withdrawal, such as the noncommunication norms prevalent in religious orders.

Thus, felt conflict may arise from sources independent of the three types of latent conflict, but latent conflicts may provide appropriate targets (perhaps symbolic ones) for undirected tensions.

Manifest Conflict

By manifest conflict is meant any of several varieties of conflictful behavior. The most obvious of these is open aggression, but such physical and verbal violence is usually strongly proscribed by organizational norms. Except for prison riots, political revolutions, and extreme labor unrest, violence as a form of manifest conflict in organizations is rare. The motivations toward violence may remain, but they tend to be expressed in less violent form. Dalton has documented the covert attempts to sabotage or block an opponent's plans through aggressive and defensive coalitions.[13] Mechanic has described the tactics of conflict used by lower-level participants, such as apathy or rigid adherence to the rules, to resist mistreatment by the upper levels of the hierarchy.[14]

How can one decide when a certain behavior or pattern of behavior is conflictful? One important factor is that the behavior must be interpreted in the context in which it takes place. If A does not interact with B, it may be either because A and B are not related in any organizational sense, or because A has withdrawn from a too stressful relationship, or because A is deliberately frustrating B by withdrawing support, or simply because A is drawn away from the relationship by other competing demands upon his time. In other words, knowledge of the organizational requirements and of the expectations and motives of the participants appears to be necessary to characterize the behavior as conflictful. This suggests that behavior should be defined to be conflictful if, and only if, some or all of the participants perceive it to be conflictful.

Should the term manifest conflict be reserved for behavior which, in the eyes of the actor, is deliberately and consciously designed to frustrate another in the pursuit of his (the other's) overt or covert goals? But what of behavior which is not *intended* to frustrate, but does? Should not that behavior also be called conflictful? The most useful definition of manifest conflict seems to be that behavior which, in the mind of the actor, frustrates the goals of at least some of the other participants. In other words, a member of the organization is said to engage in conflictful behavior if he consciously, but not necessarily deliberately, blocks another member's goal achievement. He may engage in such behavior *deliberately* to frustrate another, or he may do so in spite of the fact that he frustrates another. To define manifest conflict in this way is to say that the following question is important: "Under what conditions will a party to a relationship *knowingly* frustrate another party to the relationship? Suppose A unknowingly blocks B's goals. This is not conflictful behavior. But suppose B informs A that he perceives A's behavior to be conflictful; if then A acknowledges the message and *persists* in the behavior, it is an instance of manifest conflict.

The interface between perceived conflict and manifest conflict and the interface between felt conflict and manifest conflict are the pressure points where most conflict resolution programs are applied. The object of such programs is to prevent conflicts which have reached the level of awareness or the level of affect from erupting into noncooperative behavior. The availability of appropriate and effective administrative devices is a major factor in determining whether conflict becomes manifest. The collective bargaining apparatus of labor-management disputes and budgeting systems for internal resource allocation are administrative devices for the resolution of interest-group conflicts. Evan and Scott have described due process or appeal systems for resolving superior-subordinate conflicts.[5] Mechanisms for resolving lateral conflicts among the parties to a functional relationship are relatively undeveloped. Transfer-pricing systems constitute one of the few exceptions. Much more common are organizational arrangements designed to *prevent* lateral conflicts, e.g., plans, schedules, and job descriptions, which define and delimit subunit responsibilities. Another alternative is to reduce the interdependence between conflicting subunits by introducing buffers, such as inventories, which reduce the need for sales and production departments in a business firm to act in perfect accord.

The mere availability of such administrative devices is not sufficient to prevent conflict from becoming manifest. If the parties to a relationship do not value the relationship, or if conflict is strategic in the pursuit goals, then conflictful behavior is likely. Furthermore, once conflict breaks out on some specific issue, then the conflict frequently widens and the initial specific conflict precipitates more general and more personal conflicts which had been suppressed in the interest of preserving the stability of the relationship.[16]

Conflict Aftermath

Each conflict episode is but one of a sequence of such episodes that constitute the relationships among organization participants.[17] If the conflict is genuinely resolved to the satisfaction of all participants, the basis for a more cooperative relationship may be laid; or the participants, in their drive for a more ordered relationship may focus on latent conflicts not previously perceived and dealt with. On the other hand, if the conflict is merely suppressed but not resolved, the latent conditions of conflict may be aggravated and explode in more serious form until they are rectified or until the relationship dissolves. This legacy of a conflict episode is here called "conflict aftermath."[18]

However, the organization is not a closed system. The environment in which it is imbedded may become more benevolent and alleviate the conditions of latent conflict, for example, by making more resources available to the organization. But a more malevolent environment may precipitate new crises. The development of each conflict episode is determined by a complex combination of the effects of preceding episodes and the environmental milieu. The main ideas of this view of the dynamics of conflict are summarized in Figure 1.

Functions and Dysfunctions of Conflict

Few students of social and organizational behavior have treated conflict as a neutral phenomenon to be studied primarily because of scientific curiosity about its nature and form, its causes, and its effects. Most frequently the study of conflict has been motivated by a desire to resolve it and to minimize its deleterious effects on the psychological health of organizational participants and the efficiency of organization performance. Although Kahn and others pay lip service to the opinion that, "one might well make a case for interpreting some conflict as essential for the continued development of mature and competent human beings," the overriding bias of their report is with the "personal costs of excessive emotional strain," and, they state, "the fact that common reactions to conflict and its associated tensions are often dysfunctional for the organization as an on-going social system and self-defeating for the person in the long run."[19] Boulding recognizes that some optimum level of conflict and associated personal stress and tension are necessary for progress and productivity, but he portrays conflict primarily as a personal and social cost.[20] Baritz argues that Elton Mayo has treated conflict as "an evil, a symptom of the lack of social skills," and its alleged opposite, cooperation, as "symptomatic of

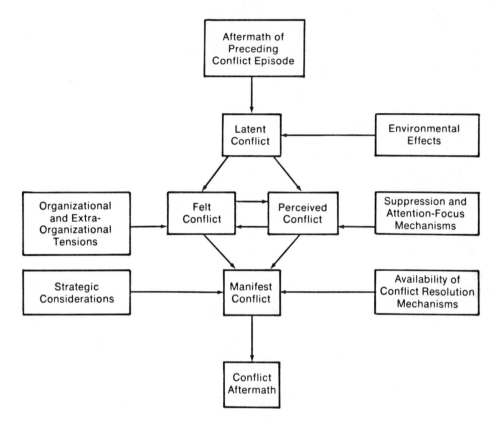

Figure 1. The dynamics of a conflict episode.

health.''[21] Even as dispassionate a theory of organization as that of March and Simon defines conflict conceptually as a *''breakdown* in the standard mechanisms of decision making''; i.e., as a malfunction of the system.[22]

It has become fashionable to say that conflict may be either functional or dysfunctional and is not necessarily either one. What this palliative leaves implicit is that the effects of conflict must be evaluated relative to some set of values. The argument with those who seek uniformly to abolish conflict is not so much with their *a priori* assertion that conflict is undesirable, as it is with their failure to make explicit the value system on which their assertion rests.

For the purposes of this research, the effects of organizational conflict on individual welfare are not of concern. Conflict may threaten the emotional well-being of individual persons; it may also be a positive factor in personal character development; but this research is not addressed to these questions. Intra-individual conflict is of concern only in so far as it has implications for organizational performance. With respect to organizational values, *productivity,* measured in both quantitative and qualitative terms, is valued; other things being equal, an organization is ''better'' if it produces more, if it is more innovative, and if its output meets higher standards of quality than other organizations. *Stability* is also valued. An organization improves if it can increase its cohesiveness and solvency, other things being equal. Finally *adaptability* is valued. Other things being equal, organizations that can learn and improve performance and that can adapt to changing internal and environmental pressures are preferred to those that cannot. In this view, therefore, to say that conflict is functional or dysfunctional is to say that it facilitates or inhibits the organization's productivity, stability, or adaptability.

Clearly, these values are not entirely compatible. An organization may have to sacrifice quality of output for quantity of output; if it pursues policies and actions that guarantee stability, it may inhibit its adaptive abilities. It is argued here that a given conflict episode or relationship may have beneficial or deleterious effects on productivity, stability, and adaptability. Since these values are incompatible, conflict may be simultaneously functional and dysfunctional for the organization. . . .

Conflict and Equilibrium

One way of viewing an organization is to think of each participant as making contributions, such as work, capital, and raw materials, in return for certain inducements, such as salary, interest, and finished goods. The organization is said to be in "equilibrium" if inducements exceed contributions (subjectively valued) for every participant, and in "disequilibrium" if contributions exceed inducements for some or all of the participants. Participants will be motivated to restore equilibrium either by leaving the organization for greener pastures, when the disequilibrium is said to be "unstable," or by attempting to achieve a favorable balance between inducements and contributions within the organization, when it is considered "stable." Since changing organizational affiliation frequently involves sizable costs, disequilibria tend to be stable.

If we assume conflict to be a cost of participation, this inducements-contributions balance theory may help in understanding organizational reactions to conflict. It suggests that the perception of conflict by the participants will motivate them to reduce conflict either by withdrawing from the relationship, or by resolving the conflict within the context of the relationship, or by securing increased inducements to compensate for the conflict.

The assumption that conflict creates a disequilibrium is implicit in nearly all studies of organizational conflict. For example, March and Simon assume that "where conflict is perceived, motivation to reduce conflict is generated," and conscious efforts to resolve conflict are made.[23] Not all treatments of the subject make this assumption, however. Harrison White attacks the March-Simon assumption of the disequilibrium of conflict as "naive."[24] He bases his assertion on his observation of chronic, continuous, high-level conflict in administrative settings. This, of course, raises the question, "Under what conditions *does* conflict represent a disequilibrium?"

To say that (perceived) conflict represents a state of disequilibrium and generates pressures for conflict resolution, is to say three things: *(1)* that perceived conflict is a cost of participation; *(2)* that the conflict disturbs the inducements-contributions balance; and *(3)* that organization members react to perceptions of conflict by attempting to resolve the conflict, *in preference to* (although this is not made explicit in the March-

Simon treatment) other reactions such as withdrawing from the relationship or attempting to gain added inducements to compensate for the conflict.

1. *Conflict as a cost.* Conflict is not necessarily a cost for the individual. Some participants may actually enjoy the ''heat of battle.'' As Hans Hoffman argues, ''The unique function of man is to live in close creative touch with chaos and thereby experience the birth of order.''[25]

Conflict may also be instrumental in the achievement of other goals. One of the tactics of successful executives in the modern business enterprise is to create confusion as a cover for the expansion of their particular empire.[26] or, as Sorensen observes, deliberately to create dissent and competition among one's subordinates in order to ensure that he will be brought into the relationship as an arbiter at critical times, as Franklin D. Roosevelt did.[27] Or, conflict with an out-group may be desirable to maintain stability within the in-group.

In general, however, conflict can be expected to be negatively valued; particularly if conflict becomes manifest, and subunit goals and actions are blocked and frustrated. Latency or perception of conflict should be treated as a cost, only if harmony and uniformity are highly valued. Tolerance of divergence is not generally a value widely shared in contemporary organizations, and under these conditions latent and perceived conflict are also likely to be treated as costly.

2. *Conflict as a source of disequilibrium.* White's observation of *chronic* conflict creates doubt as to whether conflict represents a disequilibrium.[28] He argues that if conflict *were* an unstable state for the system, then only transient conflict or conflict over shifting foci would be observable. Even if organizational participants treat conflict as a cost, they may still endure intense, chronic conflict, if there are compensating inducements from the organization in the form of high salary, opportunities for advancement, and others. To say that a participant will endure chronic conflict is not to deny that he will be motivated to reduce it; it is merely to say that if the organization member is unsuccessful in reducing conflict, he may still continue to participate if the inducements offered to him exceed the contributions he makes in return. Although conflict may be one of several sources of disequilibrium, it is neither a necessary nor a sufficient condition of disequilibrium. But, as will be shown, equilibrium nevertheless plays an important role in organizational reactions to conflict.[29]

3. *Resolution pressures a necessary consequence of conflict.* If conflicts are relatively small, and the inducements and contributions remain in equilibrium, then the participants are likely to try to resolve the conflict within the context of the existing relationship.[30] On the other hand, when contributions exceed inducements, or when conflict is intense enough to destroy the inducements-contributions balance and there is no prospect for the re-establishment of equilibrium, then conflict is likely to be reduced by dissolving the relationship. Temporary imbalances, of course, may be tolerated; i.e., the relationship will not dissolve if the participants perceive the conflicts to be resolvable in the near future.

What is the effect of conflict on the interaction rate among participants? It depends on the stability of the relationship. If the participants receive inducements in sufficient amounts to balance contributions, then perception of conflict is likely to generate pressures for *increased* interaction, and the content of the interaction is likely to deal with resolution procedures. On the other hand, if conflict represents a cost to the participant and this cost is not compensated by added inducements, then conflict is likely to lead to *decreased* interaction or withdrawal from the relationship.

To summarize, conflict is frequently, but not always, negatively valued by organization members. To the extent that conflict *is* valued negatively, minor conflicts generate pressures towards resolution without altering the relationship; and major conflicts generate pressures to alter the form of the relationship or to dissolve it altogether. If inducements for participation are sufficiently high, there is the possibility of chronic conflict in the context of a stable relationship. . . .

Summary

It has been argued that conflict within an organization can be best understood as a dynamic process underlying a wide variety of organizational behaviors. The term conflict refers neither to its antecedent conditions, nor individual awareness of it, nor certain affective states, nor its overt manifestations, nor its residues of feeling, precedent, or structure, but to all of these taken together as the history of a conflict episode.

Conflict is not necessarily bad or good, but must be evaluated in terms of its individual and organizational functions and dysfunctions. In general, conflict generates pressures to reduce conflict, but chronic conflict persists and is endured under certain conditions, and consciously created and managed by the politically astute administrator.

Conflict resolution techniques may be applied at any of several pressure points. Their effectiveness and appropriateness depends on the nature of the conflict and on the administrator's philosophy of management. The tension model leads to creation of safety-valve institutions and the semantic model to the promotion of open communication. Although these may be perfectly appropriate for certain forms of imagined conflict, their application to real conflict may only exacerbate the conflict. . . .

Notes and References

1. Jessie Bernard, T. H. Pear, Raymond Aron, and Robert C. Angell, *The Nature of Conflict* (Paris: UNESCO, 1957); Kenneth Boulding, *Conflict and Defense* (New York: Harper, 1962); Lewis Coser, *The Functions of Social Conflict* (Glencoe, Ill.: Free Press, 1956); Kurt Lewin, *Resolving Social Conflict* (New York: Harper, 1948); Anatol Rapaport, *Fights, Games, and Debates* (Ann Arbor: University of Michigan, 1960); Thomas C. Schelling, *The Strategy of Conflict* (Cambridge, Mass.: Harvard Univ., 1961); Muzafer Sherif and Carolyn Sherif, *Groups in Harmony and Tension* (Norman, Okla.: University of Oklahoma, 1953): Georg Simmel, *Conflict*, trans. Kurt H. Wolff (Glencoe, Ill.: Free Press, 1955).
2. Bernard M. Bass, *Organizational Psychology* (Boston, Mass.: Allyn and Bacon, 1965); Theodore Caplow, *Principles of Organization* (New York: Harcourt, Brace, and World, 1964); Eliot D. Chapple and Leonard F. Sayles, *The Measure of Management* (New York: Macmillan, 1961); Michel Crozier, *The Bureaucratic Phenomenon* (Glencoe, Ill.: Free Press, 1964); Richard M. Cyert and James G. March, *A Behavioral Theory of the Firm* (Englewood Cliffs, N. J.: Prentice-Hall, 1963); Alvin W. Gouldner, *Patterns of Industrial Bureaucracy* (Glencoe, Ill.: Free Press, 1954); Harold J. Leavitt, *Managerial Psychology* (Chicago: University of Chicago, 1964); James G. March and

Herbert A. Simon, *Organizations* (New York: Wiley, 1958); Philip Selznick, *TVA and the Grass Roots* (Berkeley: University of California, 1949); Victor Thompson, *Modern Organization* (New York: Knopf, 1961).

3. Joseph L. Bower, The Role of Conflict in Economic Decision-making Groups, *Quarterly Journal of Economics*, 79 (May 1965), 253-257; Melville Dalton, *Men Who Manage* (New York: Wiley, 1959); J. M. Dutton and R. E. Walton, "Interdepartmental Conflict and Cooperation: A Study of Two Contrasting Cases," dittoed, Purdue University, October 1964; William Evan, Superior-Subordinate Conflict in Research Organizations, *Administrative Science Quarterly*, 10 (June 1965), 52-64; Robert L. Kahn, *et al.*, *Studies in Organizational Stress* (New York: Wiley, 1964); L. R. Pondy, Budgeting and Inter-Group Conflict in Organizations, *Pittsburgh Business Review*, 34 (April 1964), 1-3; R. E. Walton, J. M. Dutton, and H. G. Fitch, *A Study of Conflict in the Process, Structure, and Attitudes of Lateral Relationships* (Institute Paper No. 93; Lafayette, Ind.: Purdue University, November 1964); Harrison White, Management Conflict and Sociometric Structure, *American Journal of Sociology*, 67 (September 1961), 185-199; Mayer N. Zald, Power Balance and Staff Conflict in Correctional Institutions, *Administrative Science Quarterly*, 7 (June 1962), 22-49.

4. The following conceptualization draws heavily on a paper by Lawrence R. Ephron, Group Conflict in Organizations: A critical Appraisal of Recent Theories, *Berkeley Journal of Sociology*, 6 (Spring 1961), 53-72.

5. James S. Coleman, *Community Conflict* (Glencoe, Ill.: Free Press, 1957); Vilhelm Aubert, Competition and Dissensus: Two Types of Conflict and Conflict Resolution, *Journal of Conflict Resolution*, 7 (March 1963), 26-42.

6. Kahn, *et al.*, *op. cit.*, pp. 11-35.

7. Bernard, Pear, Aron, and Angell, *op. cit.*

8. These two mechanisms are instances of what Cyert and March, *op. cit.*, pp. 117-118, call the "quasi-resolution" of conflict.

9. Leavitt, *op. cit.*, pp. 53-72.

10. Chris Argyris, *Personality and Organization: The Conflict Between the System and the Individual* (New York: Harper, 1957).

11. Bernard, Pear, Aron, and Angell, *op. cit.*

12. It should be emphasized that members of total institutions characteristically experience both strong positive *and* negative feelings for one another and toward the institution. It may be argued that this ambivalence of feeling is a primary cause of anxiety. See Coser, *op. cit.*, pp. 61-65; and Amitai Etzioni and W. R. Taber, Scope, Pervasiveness, and Tension Management in Complex Organizations, *Social Research*, 30 (Summer 1963) 220-238.

13. Dalton, *op. cit.*

14. David Mechanic, "Sources of Power of Lower Participants in Complex Organizations," in W. W. Cooper, H. J. Leavitt, and M. W. Shelly (eds.), *New Perspectives in Organization Research* (New York: Wiley, 1964), pp. 136-149.

15. Evan, *op. cit.*; William G. Scott, *The Management of Conflict: Appeals Systems in Organizations* (Homewood, Ill.: Irwin, 1965). It is useful to interpret recent developments in leadership and supervision (e.g., participative management, Theory Y, linking-pin functions) as devices for preventing superior-subordinate conflicts from arising, thus, hopefully, avoiding the problem of developing appeals systems in the first place.

16. See Coleman, *op. cit.*, pp. 9-11, for an excellent analysis of this mechanism. A chemical analogue of this situation is the supersaturated solution, from which a large amount of chemical salts can be precipitated by the introduction of a single crystal.

17. The sequential dependence of conflict episodes also plays a major role in the analysis of role conflicts by Kahn, *et al., op. cit.,* pp. 11-35. Pondy, *op. cit.* has used the concept of "budget residues" to explain how precedents set in budgetary bargains guide and constrain succeeding budget proceedings.
18. Aubert, *op. cit.*
19. Kahn, *et al., op. cit.,* p. 65.
20. Boulding, *op. cit.,* pp. 305-307.
21. Loren Baritz, *The Servants of Power* (Middletown, Conn.: Wesleyan University, 1960). p. 203.
22. March and Simon, *op. cit.,* p. 112, italics mine. At least one author, however, argues that a "harmony bias" permeates the entire March-Simon volume. It is argued that what March and Simon call conflicts are mere "frictions" and "differences that are not within a community of interests are ignored." See Sherman Krupp, *Pattern in Organization Analysis* (New York: Holt, Rinehart and Winston, 1961), pp. 140-167.
23. March and Simon, *op. cit.,* pp. 115, 129.
24. Harrison White, *op. cit.*
25. Quoted in H. J. Leavitt and L. R. Pondy. *Readings in Managerial Psychology* (Chicago: University of Chicago, 1964), p. 58.
26. Dalton, *op. cit.*
27. Theodore Sorensen, *Decision Making in the White House* (New York: Columbia University, 1963), p. 15. This latter tactic, of course, is predicated and the fact that, *for the subordinates,* conflict is indeed a ccst!
28. Harrison White, *op. cit.*
29. Conflict may actually be a source of equilibrium and stability, as Coser, *op. cit.,* p. 159, points out. A multiplicity of conflicts internal to a group, Coser argues, may breed solidarity, provided that the conflicts do not divide the group along the same axis, because the multiplicity of coalitions and associations provide a web of affiliation for the exchange of dissenting viewpoints. The essence of his argument is that some conflict is inevitable, and that it is better to foster frequent minor conflicts of interest, and thereby gradually adjust the system, and so forestall the accumulation of latent antagonisms which might eventually disrupt the organization. Frequent minor conflicts also serve to keep the antagonists accurately informed of each other's relative strength, thereby preventing a serious miscalculation of the chances of a successful major conflagration and promoting the continual and gradual readjustment of structure to coincide with true relative power.
30. For example, labor unions, while they wish to win the economic conflict with management, have no interest in seeing the relationship destroyed altogether. They may, however, choose to threaten such disruptive conflict as a matter of strategy.

GROUPTHINK

IRVING L. JANIS

"How could we have been so stupid?" President John F. Kennedy asked after he and a close group of advisers had blundered into the Bay of Pigs invasion. For the past two years I have been studying that question, as it applies not only to the Bay of Pigs decision-makers but also to those who led the United States into such other major fiascos as the failure to be prepared for the attack on Pearl Harbor, the Korean War stalemate and the escalation of the Vietnam War.

Stupidity certainly is not the explanation. The men who participated in making the Bay of Pigs decision, for instance, comprised one of the greatest arrays of intellectual talent in the history of American Government—Dean Rusk, Robert McNamara, Douglas Dillon, Robert Kennedy, McGeorge Bundy, Arthur Schlesinger Jr., Allen Dulles and others.

It also seemed to me that explanations were incomplete if they concentrated only on disturbances in the behavior of each individual within a decision-making body: temporary emotional states of elation, fear, or anger that reduce a man's mental efficiency, for example, or chronic blind spots arising from a man's social prejudices or idiosyncratic biases.

I preferred to broaden the picture by looking at the fiascos from the standpoint of group dynamics as it has been explored over the past three decades, first by the great social psychologist Kurt Lewin and later in many experimental situations by myself and other behavioral scientists. My conclusion after poring over hundreds of relevant documents—historical reports about formal group meetings and informal conversations among the members—is that the groups that committed the fiascos were victims of what I call "groupthink."

"Groupy"

In each case study, I was surprised to discover the extent to which each group displayed the typical phenomena of social conformity that are regularly encountered in studies of group dynamics among ordinary citizens. For example, some of the phenomena appear to be completely in line with findings from social-psychological experiments showing that powerful social pressures are brought to bear by the members of a cohesive group whenever a dissident begins to voice his objections to a group consensus. Other phenomena are reminiscent of the shared illusions observed in encounter groups and friendship cliques when the members simultaneously reach a peak of "groupy" feelings.

Above all, there are numerous indications pointing to the development of group norms that bolster morale at the expense of critical thinking. One of the most common norms appears to be that of remaining loyal to the group by sticking with the policies to which the group has already committed itself, even when those policies are obviously working out badly and have unintended consequences that disturb the conscience of each member. This is one of the key characteristics of groupthink.

1984

I use the term groupthink as a quick and easy way to refer to the mode of thinking that persons engage in when *concurrence-seeking* becomes so dominant in a cohesive ingroup that it tends to override realistic appraisal of alternative courses of action. Groupthink is a term of the same order as the words in the newspeak vocabulary George Orwell used in his dismaying world of *1984*. In that context, groupthink takes on an invidious connotation. Exactly such a connotation is intended, since the term refers to a deterioration in mental efficiency, reality testing and moral judgments as a result of group pressures.

The symptoms of groupthink arise when the members of decision-making groups become motivated to avoid being too harsh in their judgments of their leaders' or their colleagues' ideas. They adopt a soft line of criticism, even in their own thinking. At their meetings, all the members are amiable and seek complete concurrence on every important issue, with no bickering or conflict to spoil the cozy, "we-feeling" atmosphere.

Kill

Paradoxically, soft-headed groups are often hard-hearted when it comes to dealing with outgroups or enemies. They find it relatively easy to resort to dehumanizing solutions—they will readily authorize bombing attacks that kill large numbers of civilians in the name of the noble cause of persuading an unfriendly government to negotiate at the peace table. They are unlikely to pursue the more difficult and controversial issues that arise when alternatives to a harsh military solution come up for discussion. Nor are they inclined to raise ethical issues that carry the implication that *this fine group of ours, with its humanitarianism and its high-minded principles, might be capable of adopting a course of action that is inhumane and immoral.*

Norms

There is evidence from a number of social-psychological studies that as the members of a group feel more accepted by the others, which is a central feature of increased group cohesiveness, they display less overt conformity to group norms. Thus we would expect that the more cohesive a group becomes, the less the members will feel constrained to censor what they say out of fear of being socially punished for antagonizing the leader or any of their fellow members.

In contrast, the groupthink type of conformity tends to increase as group cohesiveness increases. Groupthink involves nondeliberate suppression of critical thoughts as a result of internalization of the group's norms, which is quite different from deliberate suppression on the basis of external threats of social punishment. The more cohesive the group, the greater the inner compulsion on the part of each member to avoid creating disunity, which inclines him to believe in the soundness of whatever proposals are promoted by the leader or by a majority of the group's members.

In a cohesive group, the danger is not so much that each individual will fail to reveal his objections to what the others propose but that he will think the proposal is a good one, without attempting to carry out a careful, critical scrutiny of the pros and cons of the alternatives. When groupthink becomes dominant, there also is considerable suppression of deviant thoughts, but it takes the form of each person's deciding that his misgivings are not relevant and should be set aside, that the benefit of the doubt regarding any lingering uncertainties should be given to the group consensus.

Stress

I do not mean to imply that all cohesive groups necessarily suffer from groupthink. All ingroups may have a mild tendency toward groupthink, displaying one or another of the symptoms from time to time, but it need not be so dominant as to influence the quality of the group's final decision. Neither do I mean to imply that there is anything necessarily inefficient or harmful about group decisions in general. On the contrary, a group whose members have properly defined roles, with traditions concerning the procedures to follow in pursuing a critical inquiry, probably is capable of making better decisions than any individual group member working alone.

The problem is that the advantages of having decisions made by groups are often lost because of powerful psychological pressures that arise when the members work closely together, share the same set of values and, above all, face a crisis situation that puts everyone under intense stress.

The main principle of groupthink, which I offer in the spirit of Parkinson's Law, is this: *The more amiability and esprit de corps there is among the members of a policy-making ingroup, the greater the danger that independent critical thinking will be replaced by groupthink, which is likely to result in irrational and dehumanizing actions directed against outgroups*

Symptoms

In my studies of high-level governmental decision-makers, both civilian and military, I have found eight main symptoms of groupthink.

1. Invulnerability

Most or all of the members of the ingroup share an *illusion* of invulnerability that provides for them some degree of reassurance about obvious dangers and leads them to become over-optimistic and willing to take extraordinary risks. It also causes them to fail to respond to clear warnings of danger.

The Kennedy ingroup, which uncritically accepted the Central Intelligence Agency's disastrous Bay of Pigs plan, operated on the false assumption that they could keep secret the fact that the United States was responsible for the invasion of Cuba. Even after news of the plan began to leak out, their belief remained unshaken. They failed even to consider the danger that awaited them: a worldwide revulsion against the U.S.

A similar attitude appeared among the members of President Lyndon B. Johnson's ingroup, the "Tuesday Cabinet," which kept escalating the Vietnam War despite repeated setbacks and failures. "There was a belief," Bill Moyers commented after he resigned, "that if we indicated a willingness to use our power, they [the North Vietnamese] would get the message and back away from an all-out confrontation. . . . There was a confidence—it was never bragged about, it was just there—that when the chips were really down, the other people would fold."

A most poignant example of an illusion of invulnerability involves the ingroup around Admiral H. E. Kimmel, which failed to prepare for the possibility of a Japanese attack on Pearl Harbor despite repeated warnings. Informed by his intelligence chief that radio contact with Japanese aircraft carriers had been lost, Kimmel joked about it: "What, you don't know where the carriers are? Do you mean to say that they could be rounding Diamond Head (at Honolulu) and you wouldn't know it?" The carriers were in fact moving full-steam toward Kimmel's command post at the time. Laughing together about a danger signal, which labels it as a purely laughing matter, is a characteristic manifestation of groupthink.

2. Rationale

As we see, victims of groupthink ignore warnings; they also collectively construct rationalizations in order to discount warnings and other forms of negative feedback that, taken seriously, might lead the group members to reconsider their assumptions each time they recommit themselves to past decisions. Why did the Johnson ingroup avoid reconsidering its escalation policy when time and again the expectations on which they based their decisions turned out to be wrong? James C. Thompson Jr., a Harvard historian who spent five years as an observing participant in both the State Department and the White House, tells us that the policymakers avoided critical discussion of their prior decisions and continually invented new rationalizations so that they could sincerely recommit themselves to defeating the North Vietnamese.

In the fall of 1961, before the bombing of North Vietnam began, some of the policymakers predicted that six weeks of air strikes would induce the North Vietnamese to seek peace talks. When someone asked, "What if they don't?" the answer was that another four weeks certainly would do the trick.

Later, after each setback, the ingroup agreed that by investing just a bit more effort (by stepping up the bomb tonnage a bit, for instance), their course of action would prove to be right. *The Pentagon Papers* bear out these observations.

In *The Limits of Intervention,* Townsend Hoopes, who was acting Secretary of the Air Force under Johnson, says that Walt W. Rostow in particular showed a remarkable capacity for what has been called "instant rationalization." According to Hoopes, Rostow buttressed the group's optimism about being on the road to victory by culling selected scraps of evidence from news reports or, if necessary, by inventing "plausible" forecasts that had no basis in evidence at all.

Admiral Kimmel's group rationalized away their warnings, too. Right up to December 7, 1941, they convinced themselves that the Japanese would never dare attempt a full-scale surprise assault against Hawaii because Japan's leaders would realize that it would precipitate an all-out war which the United States would surely win. They made no attempt to look at the situation through the eyes of the Japanese leaders—another manifestation of groupthink.

3. Morality

Victims of groupthink believe unquestioningly in the inherent morality of their ingroup; this belief inclines the members to ignore the ethical or moral consequences of their decisions.

Evidence that this symptom is at work usually is of a negative kind—the things that are left unsaid in group meetings. At least two influential persons had doubts about the morality of the Bay of Pigs adventure. One of them, Arthus Schlesinger Jr., presented his strong objections in a memorandum to President Kennedy and Secretary of State Rusk but suppressed them when he attended meetings of the Kennedy team. The other, Senator J. William Fulbright, was not a member of the group, but the President invited him to express his misgivings in a speech to the policymakers. However, when Fulbright finished speaking the President moved on to other agenda items without asking for reactions of the group.

David Kraslow and Stuart H. Loory, in *The Secret Search for Peace in Vietnam*, report that during 1966 President Johnson's ingroup was concerned primarily with selecting bomb targets in North Vietnam. They based their selections on four factors—the military advantage, the risk to American aircraft and pilots, the danger of forcing other countries into the fighting, and the danger of heavy civilian casualties. At their regular Tuesday luncheons, they weighed these factors the way school teachers grade examination papers, averaging them out. Though evidence on this point is scant, I suspect that the group's ritualistic adherence to a standardized procedure induced the members to feel morally justified in their destructive way of dealing with the Vietnamese people—after all, the danger of heavy civilian casualties from U. S. air strikes was taken into account on their checklists.

4. Stereotypes

Victims of groupthink hold stereotyped views of the leaders of enemy groups: they are so evil that genuine attempts at negotiating differences with them are unwarranted, or they are too weak or too stupid to deal effectively with whatever attempts the ingroup makes to defeat their purposes, no matter how risky the attempts are.

Kennedy's groupthinkers believed that Premier Fidel Castro's air force was so ineffectual that obsolete B-26s could knock it out completely in a surprise attack before the invasion began. They also believed that Castro's army was so weak that a small Cuban-exile brigade could establish a well-protected beachhead at the Bay of Pigs. In addition, they believed that Castro was not smart enough to put down any possible internal uprisings in support of the exiles. They were wrong on all three assumptions. Though much of the blame was attributable to faulty intelligence, the point is that none of Kennedy's advisers even questioned the CIA planners about these assumptions.

The Johnson advisers' sloganistic thinking about "the Communist apparatus" that was "working all around the world" (as Dean Rusk put it) led them to overlook the powerful nationalistic strivings of the North Vietnamese government and its efforts to ward off Chinese domination. The crudest of all stereotypes used by Johnson's inner circle to justify their policies was the domino theory ("If we don't stop the Reds in South Vietnam, tomorrow they will be in Hawaii and next week they will be in San Francisco,"

Johnson once said). The group so firmly accepted this stereotype that it became almost impossible for any adviser to introduce a more sophisticated viewpoint.

In the documents on Pearl Harbor, it is clear to see that the Navy commanders stationed in Hawaii had a naive image of Japan as a midget that would not dare to strike a blow against a powerful giant.

5. Pressure

Victims of groupthink apply direct pressure to any individual who momentarily expresses doubts about any of the group's shared illusions or who questions the validity of the arguments supporting a policy alternative favored by the majority. This gambit reinforces the concurrence-seeking norm that loyal members are expected to maintain.

President Kennedy probably was more active than anyone else in raising skeptical questions during the Bay of Pigs meetings, and yet he seems to have encouraged the group's docile, uncritical acceptance of defective arguments in favor of the CIA's plan. At every meeting, he allowed the CIA representatives to dominate the discussion. He permitted them to give their immediate refutations in response to each tentative doubt that one of the others expressed, instead of asking whether anyone shared the doubt or wanted to pursue the implications of the new worrisome issue that had just been raised. And at the most crucial meeting, when he was calling on each member to give his vote for or against the plan, he did not call on Arthur Schlesinger, the one man there who was known by the President to have serious misgivings.

Historian Thomson informs us that whenever a member of Johnson's ingroup began to express doubts, the group used subtle social pressures to "domesticate" him. To start with, the dissenter was made to feel at home, provided that he lived up to two restrictions: (1) that he did not voice his doubts to outsiders, which would play into the hands of the opposition; and (2) that he kept his criticisms within the bounds of acceptable deviation, which meant not challenging any of the fundamental assumptions that went into the group's prior commitments. One such "domesticated dissenter" was Bill Moyers. When Moyers arrived at a meeting, Thomson tells us, the President greeted him with. "Well, here comes Mr. Stop-the-Bombing."

6. Self-censorship

Victims of groupthink avoid deviating from what appears to be group consensus: they keep silent about their misgivings and even minimize to themselves the importance of their doubts.

As we have seen, Schlesinger was not at all hesitant about presenting his strong objections to the Bay of Pigs plan in a memorandum to the President and the Secretary of State. But he became keenly aware of his tendency to suppress objections at the White House meetings. "In the months after the Bay of Pigs I bitterly reproached myself for having kept so silent during those crucial discussions in the cabinet room," Schlesinger writes in *A Thousand Days*. "I can only explain my failure to do more than raise a few timid questions by reporting that one's impulse to blow the whistle on this nonsense was simply undone by the circumstances of the discussion."

7. Unanimity

Victims of groupthink share an *illusion* of unanimity within the group concerning almost all judgments expressed by members who speak in favor of the majority view.

This symptom results partly from the preceding one, whose effects are augmented by the false assumption that any individual who remains silent during any part of the discussion is in full accord with what the others are saying.

When a group of persons who respect each other's opinions arrives at a unanimous view, each member is likely to feel that the belief must be true. This reliance on consensual validation within the group tends to replace individual critical thinking and reality testing, unless there are clear-cut disagreements among the members. In contemplating a course of action such as the invasion of Cuba, it is painful for the members to confront disagreements within their group, particularly if it becomes apparent that there are widely divergent views about whether the preferred course of action is too risky to undertake at all. Such disagreements are likely to arouse anxieties about making a serious error. Once the sense of unanimity is shattered, the members no longer can feel complacently confident about the decision they are inclined to make. Each man must then face the annoying realization that there are troublesome uncertainties and he must diligently seek out the best information he can get in order to decide for himself exactly how serious the risks might be. This is one of the unpleasant consequences of being in a group of hardheaded, critical thinkers.

To avoid such an unpleasant state, the members often become inclined, without quite realizing it, to prevent latent disagreements from surfacing when they are about to initiate a risky course of action. The group leader and the members support each other in playing up the areas of convergence in their thinking, at the expense of fully exploring divergencies that might reveal unsettled issues.

"Our meetings took place in a curious atmosphere of assumed consensus," Schlesinger writes. His additional comments clearly show that, curiously, the consensus was an illusion—an illusion that could be maintained only because the major participants did not reveal their own reasoning or discuss their idiosyneratic assumptions and vague reservations. Evidence from several sources makes it clear that even the three principals—President Kennedy, Rusk and McNamara—had widely differing assumptions about the invasion plan.

8. Mindguards

Victims of groupthink sometimes appoint themselves as mindguards to protect the leader and fellow members from adverse information that might break the complacency they shared about the effectiveness and morality of past decisions. At a large birthday party for his wife, Attorney General Robert F. Kennedy, who had been constantly informed about the Cuban invasion plan, took Schlesinger aside and asked him why he was opposed. Kennedy listened coldly and said, "You may be right or you may be wrong, but the President has made his mind up. Don't push it any further. Now is the time for everyone to help him all they can."

Rusk also functioned as a highly effective mindguard by failing to transmit to the group the strong objections of three "outsiders" who had learned of the invasion plan—Undersecretary of State Chester Bowles, USIA Director Edward R. Murrow, and Rusk's intelligence chief, Roger Hilsman. Had Rusk done so, their warnings might have reinforced Schlesinger's memorandum and jolted some of Kennedy's ingroup, if not the President himself, into reconsidering the decision.

Products

When a group of executives frequently displays most or all of these interrelated symptoms, a detailed study of their deliberations is likely to reveal a number of immediate consequences. These consequences are, in effect, products of poor decision-making practices because they lead to inadequate solutions to the problems under discussion.

First, the group limits its discussions to a few alternative courses of action (often only two) without an initial survey of all the alternatives that might be worthy of consideration.

Second, the group fails to reexamine the course of action initially preferred by the majority after they learn of risks and drawbacks they had not considered originally.

Third, the members spend little or no time discussing whether there are nonobvious gains they may have overlooked or ways of reducing the seemingly prohibitive costs that made rejected alternatives appear undesirable to them.

Fourth, members make little or no attempt to obtain information from experts within their own organizations who might be able to supply more precise estimates of potential losses and gains.

Fifth, members show positive interest in facts and opinions that support their preferred policy; they tend to ignore facts and opinions that do not.

Sixth, members spend little time deliberating about how the chosen policy might be hindered by bureaucratic inertia, sabotaged by political opponents, or temporarily derailed by common accidents. Consequently, they fail to work out contingency plans to cope with foreseeable setbacks that could endanger the overall success of their chosen course.

Support

The search for an explanation of why groupthink occurs has led me through a quagmire of complicated theoretical issues in the murky area of human motivation. My belief, based on recent social psychological research, is that we can best understand the various symptoms of groupthink as a mutual effort among the group members to maintain self-esteem and emotional equanimity by providing social support to each other, especially at times when they share responsibility for making vital decisions.

Even when no important decision is pending, the typical administrator will begin to doubt the wisdom and morality of his past decisions each time he receives information about setbacks, particularly if the information is accompanied by negative feedback from prominent men who originally had been his supporters. It should not be suprising, therefore, to find that individual members strive to develop unanimity and esprit de corps that will help bolster each other's morale to create an optimistic outlook about the success of pending decisions, and to reaffirm the positive value of past policies to which all of them are committed.

Pride

Shared illusions of invulnerability, for example, can reduce anxiety about taking risks. Rationalizations help members believe that the risks are really not so bad after all.

The assumption of inherent morality helps the members to avoid feelings of shame or guilt. Negative stereotypes function as stress-reducing devices to enhance a sense of moral righteousness as well as pride in a lofty mission.

The mutual enhancement of self-esteem and morale may have functional value in enabling the members to maintain their capacity to take action, but it has maladaptive consequences insofar as concurrence-seeking tendencies interfere with critical, rational capacities and lead to serious errors of judgment.

While I have limited my study to decision-making bodies in Government, group-think symptoms appear in business, industry and any other field where small, cohesive groups make the decisions. It is vital, then, for all sorts of people—and especially group leaders—to know what steps they can take to prevent groupthink.

Remedies

To counterpoint my case studies of the major fiascos, I have also investigated two highly successful group enterprises, the formulation of the Marshall Plan in the Truman Administration and the handling of the Cuban missile crisis by President Kennedy and his advisers. I have found it instrinctive to examine the steps Kennedy took to change his group's decision-making processes. These changes ensured that the mistakes made by his Bay of Pigs ingroup were not repeated by the missile-crisis ingroup, even though the membership of both groups was essentially the same.

The following recommendations for preventing groupthink incorporate many of the good practices I discovered to be characteristic of the Marshall Plan and missile-crisis groups:

1. The leader of a policy-forming group should assign the role of critical evaluator to each member, encouraging the group to give high priority to open airing of objections and doubts. This practice needs to be reinforced by the leader's acceptance of criticism of his own judgments in order to discourage members from soft-pedaling their disagreements and from allowing their striving for concurrence to inhibit critical thinking.

2. When the key members of a hierarchy assign a policy-planning mission to any group within their organization, they should adopt an impartial stance instead of stating preferences and expectations at the beginning. This will encourage open inquiry and impartial probing of a wide range of policy alternatives.

3. The organization routinely should set up several outside policy-planning and evaluation groups to work on the same policy question, each deliberating under a different leader. This can prevent the insulation of an ingroup.

4. At intervals before the group reaches a final consensus, the leader should require each member to discuss the group's deliberations with associates in his own unit of the organization, assuming that those associates can be trusted to adhere to the same security regulations that govern the policy-makers—and then to report back their reactions to the groups.

5. The group should invite one or more outside experts to each meeting on a staggered basis and encourage the experts to challenge the views of the core members.

6. At every general meeting of the group, whenever the agenda calls for an evaluation of policy alternatives, at least one member should play devil's advocate, functioning as a good lawyer in challenging the testimony of those who advocate the majority position.

7. Whenever the policy issue involves relations with a rival nation or organization, the group should devote a sizable block of time, perhaps an entire session, to a survey of all warning signals from the rivals and should write alternative scenarios on the rivals' intentions.

8. When the group is surveying policy alternatives for feasibility and effectiveness, it should from time to time divide into two or more subgroups to meet separately, under different chairmen, and then come back together to hammer out differences.

9. After reaching a preliminary consensus about what seems to be the best policy, the group should hold a "second-chance" meeting at which every member expresses as vividly as he can all his residual doubts, and rethinks the entire issue before making a definitive choice.

How

These recommendations have their disadvantages. To encourage the open airing of objections, for instance, might lead to prolonged and costly debates when a rapidly growing crisis requires immediate solution. It also could cause rejection, depression and anger. A leader's failure to set a norm might create cleavage between leader and members that could develop into a disruptive power struggle if the leader looks on the emerging consensus as anathema. Setting up outside evaluation groups might increase the risk of security leakage. Still, inventive executives who know their way around the organizational maze probably can figure out how to apply one or another of the prescriptions successfully, without harmful side effects.

They also could benefit from the advice of outside experts in the administrative and behavioral sciences. Though these experts have much to offer, they have had few chances to work on policy-making machinery within large organizations. As matters now stand, executives innovate only when they need new procedures to avoid repeating serious errors that have deflated their self-images.

In this era of atomic warheads, urban disorganization and ecocatastrophes it seems to me that policymakers should collaborate with behavioral scientists and give top priority to preventing groupthink and its attendant fiascos.

A STRATEGIC CONTINGENCIES' THEORY
OF INTRAORGANIZATIONAL POWER

D. J. HICKSON
C. R. HININGS
C. A. LEE
R. E. SCHNECK
J. M. PENNINGS

Typically, research designs have treated power as the independent variable. Power has been used in community studies to explain decisions on community programs, on resource allocation, and on voting behavior: in small groups it has been used to explain decision making; and it has been used in studies of work organizations to explain morale and alienation. But within work organizations, power itself has not been explained. This paper sets forth a theoretical explanation of power as the dependent variable with the aim of developing empirically testable hypotheses that will explain differential power among subunits in complex work organizations.

The problems of studying power are well known from the cogent reviews by March (1955, 1966) and Wrong (1968). These problems led March (1966: 70) to ask if power was just a term used to mask our ignorance, and to conclude pessimistically that the power of the concept of power "depends on the kind of system we are confronting."

Part of March's (1966) pessimism can be attributed to the problems inherent in community studies. When the unit of analysis is the community, the governmental, political, economic, recreational, and other units which make up the community do not necessarily interact and may even be oriented outside the supposed boundaries of the community. However, the subunits of a work organization are mutually related in the interdependent activities of a single identifiable social system. The perspective of the present paper is due in particular to the encouraging studies of subunits by Lawrence and Lorsch (1967a, 1967b) and begins with their (1967a: 3) definition of an organization as "a system of interrelated behaviors of people who are performing a task that has been differentiated into several distinct subsystems."

Previous studies of power in work organizations have tended to focus on the individual and to neglect subunit or departmental power. This neglect led Perrow (1970: 84) to state: "Part of the problem, I suspect, stems from the persistent attempt to define power in terms of individuals and as a social-psychological phenomenon. . . . Even sociological studies tend to measure power by asking about an individual. . . . I am not at all clear about the matter, but I think the term takes on different meanings when the unit, or power-holder, is a *formal group* in an *open system* with *multiple goals*, and the system is assumed to reflect a political-domination model of organization, rather than only a cooperative model. . . . The fact that after a cursory search I can find only a single study that asks survey questions regarding

Reprinted by permission of the author and the publisher from *Administrative Science Quarterly*, vol. 16, no. 2 (June 1971), pp. 216-27.

the power of functional *groups* strikes me as odd. Have we conceptualized power in such a way as to exclude this well-known phenomenon?''

The concept of power used here follows Emerson (1962) and takes power as a property of the social relationship, not of the actor. Since the context of the relationship is a formal organization, this approach moves away from an overpersonalized conceptualization and operationalization of power toward structural sources. Such an approach has been taken only briefly by Dubin (1963) in his discussion of power, and incidentally by Lawrence and Lorsch (1967b) when reporting power data. Most research has focused on the vertical superior-subordinate relationship, as in a multitude of leadership studies. This approach is exemplified by the extensive work of Tannenbaum (1968) and his colleagues, in which the distribution of perceived power was displayed on control graphs. The focus was on the vertical differentiation of perceived power, that is, the exercise of power by managers who by changing their behavior could vary the distribution and the total amount of perceived power.

By contrast, when organizations are conceived as interdepartmental systems, the division of labor becomes the ultimate source of intraorganizational power, and power is explained by variables that are elements of each subunit's task, its functioning, and its links with the activities of other subunits. Insofar as this approach differs from previous studies by treating power as the dependent variable, by taking subunits of work organizations as the subjects of analysis, and by attempting a multivariate explanation, it may avoid some of the previous pitfalls.

Elements of a Theory

Thompson (1967: 13) took from Cyert and March (1963) a viewpoint which he hailed as a newer tradition: "A newer tradition enables us to conceive of the organization as an open system, indeterminate and faced with uncertainty, but subject to criteria of rationality and hence needing certainty . . . we suggest that organizations cope with uncertainty by creating certain parts specifically to deal with it, specializing other parts in operating under conditions of certainty, or near certainty.''

Thus organizations are conceived of as interdepartmental systems in which a major task element is coping with uncertainty. The task is divided and allotted to the sub-systems, the division of labor creating an interdependency among them. Imbalance of this reciprocal interdependence (Thompson, 1967) among the parts gives rise to power relations. The essence of an organization is limitation of the autonomy of all its members or parts, since all are subject to power from the others; for subunits, unlike individuals, are not free to make a decision to participate, as March and Simon (1958) put it, nor to decide whether or not to come together in political relationships. They must. They exist to do so. Crozier (1964: 47) stressed in his discussion of power "the necessity for the members of the different groups to live together; the fact that each group's privileges depend to quite a large extent on the existence of other group's privileges." The groups use differential power to function within the system rather than to destroy it.

If dependency in a social relation is the reverse of power (Emerson, 1962), then the crucial unanswered question in organizations is: what factors function to vary dependency, and so to vary power? Emerson (1962: 32) proposed that "the dependence of actor A upon actor B is (*1*) directly proportional to A's motivational investment in goals mediated by B, and (*2*) inversely proportional to the availability of those goals to A outside of the A—B relation." In organizations, subunit B will have more power than other subunits to the extent that (*1*) B has the capacity to fulfill the requirements of the other subunits and (*2*) B monopolizes this ability. If a central problem facing modern organizations is uncertainty, then B's power in the organization will be partially determined by the extent to which B copes with uncertainties for other subunits, and by the extent to which B's coping activities are available elsewhere.

Thus, intraorganizational dependency can be associated with two contributing variables: (*1*) the degree to which a subunit copes with uncertainty for other subunits, and (*2*) the extent to which a subunit's coping activities are substitutable. But if coping with uncertainty, and substitutability, are to be in some way related to power, there is a necessary assumption of some degree of task interconnection among subunits. By definition, organization requires a minimum link. Therefore, a third variable, centrality, refers to the varying degree above such a minimum with which the activities of a subunit are linked with those of other subunits.

Before these three variables can be combined in a theory of power, it is necessary to examine their definition and possible operationalization, and to define power in this context.

Power

Hinings *et al.* (1967: 62) compared power to concepts such as bureaucracy or alienation or social class, which are difficult to understand because they tend to be treated as "large-scale unitary concepts." Their many meanings need disentangling. With the concept of power, this has not yet been accomplished (Cartwright, 1965), but two conceptualizations are commonly employed: (*1*) power as coercion, and (*2*) power as determination of behavior.

Power as coercive force was a comparatively early conceptualization among sociologists (Weber, 1947; Bierstedt, 1950). Later, Blau (1964) emphasized the imposition of will despite resistance.

However, coercion is only one among the several bases of power listed by French and Raven (1959) and applied across organizations by Etzioni (1961); that is, coercion is a means of power, but is not an adequate definition of power. If the direction of dependence in a relationship is determined by an imbalance of power bases, power itself has to be defined separately from these bases. Adopting Dahl's (1957) concept of power, as many others have done (March, 1955); Bennis *et al.*, 1958; Emerson, 1962; Harsanyi, 1962; Van Doorn, 1962; Dahlstrom, 1966; Wrong, 1968; Tannenbaum, 1968; Luhmann, 1969), power is defined as the determination of the behavior of one social unit by another.

If power is the determination of A's behavior by B, irrespective of whether one, any, or all the types of bases are involved, then authority will here be regarded as that part of power which is legitimate or normatively expected by some selection of role definers. Authority may be either more or less than power. For subunits it might be represented by the formally specified range of activities they are officially required to undertake and, therefore, to decide upon.

Discrepancies between authority and power may reflect time lag. Perrow (1970) explored the discrepancy between respondent's perceptions of power and of what power should be. Perhaps views on a preferred power distribution precede changes in the exercise of power, which in turn precede changes in expectations of power, that is in its legitimate authority content. Perhaps today's authority hierarchy is partly a fossilized impression of yesterday's power ranking. However this may be, it is certainly desirable to include in any research not only data on perceived power and on preferred power, but also on positional power, or authority, and on participation, or exercised power (Clark [ed.], 1968).

Kaplan (1964) succinctly described three dimensions of power. The weight of power is defined in terms of the degree to which B affects the probability of A behaving in a certain way, that is, determination of behavior in the sense adopted here. The other dimensions are domain and scope. Domain is the number of A's, persons or collectivities, whose behavior is determined; scope is the range of behaviors of each A that are determined. For subunit power within an organization, domain might be the number of other subunits affected by the issues, scope the range of decision issues affected, and weight the degree to which a given subunit affects the decision process on the issues. In published research such distinctions are rarely made. Power consists of the sweeping undifferentiated perceptions of respondents when asked to rank individuals or classes of persons, such as supervisors, on influence. Yet at the same time the complexity of power in organizations is recognized. If it is taken for granted that, say, marketing has most to do with sales matters, that accounting has most to do with finance matters, supervisors with supervisory matters, and so on, then the validity of forcing respondents to generalize single opinions across an unstated range of possibilities is questionable.

To avoid these generalized opinions, data collected over a range of decision topics or issues are desirable. Such issues should in principle include all recognized problem areas in the organization, in each of which more than one subunit is involved. Examples might be marketing strategies, obtaining equipment, personnel training, and capital budgeting.

Some suggested subvariables and indicators of power and of the independent variables are summarized in Table 1. These are intended to include both individual perceptions of power in the form of questionnaire responses and data of a somewhat less subjective kind on participation in decision processes and on formal position in the organization.

It is now possible to examine coping with uncertainty, substitutability and centrality.

Uncertainty and Coping with Uncertainty

Uncertainty may be defined as a lack of information about future events, so that alternatives and their outcomes are unpredictable. Organizations deal with environmentally derived uncertainties in the sources and composition of inputs, with uncertainties in the processing of throughputs, and again with environmental uncertainties in the disposal of outputs. They must have means to deal with these uncertainties for adequate task performance. Such ability is here called coping.

In his study of the French tobacco manufacturing industry, Crozier (1964: 164) suggested that power is related to "the kind of uncertainty upon which depends

TABLE 1.   Variables and Operationalizable Subvariables

Power (weight, domain, scope)	*Coping with uncertainty*, classified as:
Positional power (authority)	By prevention (forestalling uncertainty)
Participation power	By information (forecasting)
Perceived power	By absorption (action after the event)
Preferred power	
Uncertainty	*Substitutability*
Variability of organizational inputs	Availability of alternatives
Feedback on subunit performance;	Replaceability of personnel
Speed	
Specificity	*Centrality*
Structuring of subunit activities	Pervasiveness of workflows
	Immediacy of workflows

the life of the organization.'' March and Simon (1958) had earlier made the same point, and Perrow (1961) had discussed the shifting domination of different groups in organizations following the shifting uncertainties of resources and the routinization of skills. From studies of industrial firms, Perrow (1970) tentatively thought that power might be due to uncertainty absorption, as March and Simon (1958) call it. Lawrence and Lorsch (1967b) found that marketing had more influence than production in both container-manufacturing and food-processing firms, apparently because of its involvement in (uncertain) innovation and with customers.

Crozier (1964) proposed a strategic model of organizations as systems in which groups strive for power, but his discussion did not clarify how uncertainty could relate positively to power. Uncertainty itself does not give power: coping gives power. If organizations allocate to their various subunits task areas that vary in uncertainty, then those subunits that cope most effectively with the most uncertainty should have most power within the organization, since coping by a subunit reduces the impact of uncertainty on other activities in the organization, a shock absorber function. Coping may be by prevention, for example, a subunit prevents sales fluctuations by securing firm orders; or by information, for example, a subunit forecasts sales fluctuations; or by absorption, for example, a drop in sales is swiftly countered by novel selling methods (Table 1). By coping, the subunit provides pseudo certainty for the other subunits by controlling what are otherwise contingencies for other activities. This coping confers power through the dependencies created.

Thus organizations do not necessarily aim to avoid uncertainty nor to reduce its absolute level, as Cyert and March (1963) appear to have assumed, but to cope with it. If a subunit can cope, the level of uncertainty encountered can be increased by moving into fresh sectors of the environment, attempting fresh outputs, or utilizing fresh technologies.

Operationally, raw uncertainty and coping will be difficult to disentangle, though theoretically the distinctions are clear. For all units, uncertainty is in the raw situation which would exist without the activities of the other relevant subunits, for example, the uncertainty that would face production units if the sales subunit were not there to forecast and/or to obtain a smooth flow of orders. Uncertainty

374 *Organizational Behavior and Management*

might be indicated by the variability of those inputs to the organization which are taken by the subunit. For instance, a production subunit may face variability in raw materials and engineering may face variability in equipment performance. Lawrence and Lorsch (1967a) attempted categorizations of this kind. In addition, they (1967a: 14) gave a lead with "the time span of definitive feedback from the environment." This time span might be treated as a secondary indicator of uncertainty, making the assumption that the less the feedback to a subunit on the results of what it is doing, and the less specific the feedback, the more likely the subunit is to be working in a vague, unknown, unpredictable task area. Both speed and specificity of feedback are suggested variables in Table 1.

Furthermore, the copious literature on bureaucratic or mechanistic structures versus more organic and less defined structures could be taken to imply that routinized or highly structured subunits, for example, as conceptualized and measured by Pugh *et al.* (1968), will have stable homogeneous activities and be less likely to face uncertainty. This assumption would require empirical testing before structuring of activities could be used as an indicator of uncertainty, but it is tentatively included in Table 1.

In principle, coping with uncertainty might be directly measured by the difference between the uncertainty of those inputs taken by a subunit and the certainty with which it performs its activities nonetheless. This would indicate the degree of shock absorption.

The relation of coping with uncertainty to power can be expressed by the following hypothesis:

Hypothesis 1. The more a subunit copes with uncertainty, the greater its power within the organization.

The hypothesis is in a form which ignores any effects of centrality and substitutability.

Substitutability

Concepts relating to the availability of alternatives pervade the literature on power. In economics theory the degree of competition is taken as a measure of the extent to which alternatives are available from other organizations, it being implied that the power of an organization over other organizations and customers is a function of the amount of competition present. The same point was the second part of Emerson's (1962) power-dependency scheme in social relations, and the second requirement or determinant in Blau's (1964) model of a power relationship.

Yet only Mechanic (1962) and Dubin (1957, 1963) have discussed such concepts as explanations of organizational power. Mechanic's (1962: 358) hypothesis 4 stated: "Other factors remaining constant, a person difficult to replace will have greater power than a person easily replaceable." Dubin (1957) stressed the very similar notion of exclusiveness, which as developed later (Dubin, 1963: 21), means that: "For any given level of functional importance in an organization, the power residing in a functionary is inversely proportional to the number of other functionaries in the organization capable of performing the function." Supporting this empirically, Lipset *et al.* (1956) suggested that oligarchy may occur in trade unions because of the official's monopoly of political and negotiating skills.

The concept being used is represented here by the term substitutability, which can, for subunits, be defined as the ability of the organization to obtain alternative performance for the activities of a subunit, and can be stated as a hypothesis for predicting the power of a subunit as follows:

Hypothesis 2. The lower the substitutability of the activities of a subunit, the greater its power within the organization.

Thus a purchasing department would have its power reduced if all of its activities could be done by hired materials agents, as would a personnel department if it were partially substituted by selection consultants or by line managers finding their staff themselves. Similarly, a department may hold on to power by retaining information the release of which would enable others to do what it does.

The obvious problem in operationalization is establishing that alternative means of performing activities exist, and if they do, whether they could feasibly be used. Even if agents or consultants exist locally, or if corporation headquarters could provide services, would it really be practicable for the organization to dispense with its own subunit? Much easier to obtain are data on replaceability of subunit personnel such as length of training required for new recruits and ease of hiring, which can be regarded as secondary indicators of the substitutability of a subunit, as indicated in Table 1.

Centrality

Given a view of organizations as systems of interdependent roles and activities, then the centrality of a subunit is the degree to which its activities are interlinked into the system. By definition, no subunit of an organization can score zero centrality. Without a minimum of centrality, coping with uncertainty and substitutability cannot affect power; above the minimum, additional increments of centrality further differentiate subunit power. It is the degree to which the subunit is an interdependent component, as Thompson (1967: 54) put it, distinguishing between pooled, sequential, and reciprocal interdependence patterns. Blau and Scott (1962) made an analogous distinction between parallel and interdependent specialization. Woodward (1965: 126) also introduced a concept of this kind into her discussion of the critical function in each of unit, large batch and mass, and process production: "there seemed to be one function that was central and critical in that it had the greatest effect on success and survival."

Within the overall concept of centrality, there are inconsistencies which indicate that more than one constitutive concept is being used. At the present stage of conceptualization their identification must be very tentative. First, there is the idea that the activities of a subunit are central if they are connected with many other activities in the organization. This workflow pervasiveness may be defined as the degree to which the workflows of a subunit connect with the workflows of other subunits. It describes the extent of task interactions between subunits, and for all subunits in an organization it would be operationalized as the flowchart of a complete systems analysis. For example, the integrative subsystems studied by Lawrence and Lorsch (1967a: 30), "whose members had the function of integrating the sales-research and the production-research subsystems" and which had structural and cultural characteristics intermediate between them, were presumably high on workflow pervasiveness because everything they did connected with the workflows of these several other subsystems. Research subsystems, however, may have been low on this variable if they fed work only to a single integrative, or production, subsystem.

Secondly, the activities of a subunit are central if they are essential in the sense that their cessation would quickly and substantially impede the primary workflow of the organization. This workflow immediacy is defined as the speed and severity with which the workflows of a subunit affect the final outputs of the organization. Zald (1962) and Clark (1956) used a similar idea when they explained differential power among institution staff and education faculty by the close relation of their activities to organization goals.

The pervasiveness and immediacy of the workflows of a subunit are not necessarily closely related, and may empirically show a low correlation. A finance department may well have pervasive connections with all other subunits through the budgeting system, but if its activities ceased it would be some time before the effects were felt in, say, the production output of a factory; a production department controlling a stage midway in the sequence of an automated process, however, could have high workflow immediacy though not high pervasiveness.

The two main centrality hypotheses can therefore be stated as follows:

Hypothesis 3a. The higher the pervasiveness of the workflows of a subunit, the greater its power within the organization.

Hypothesis 3b. The higher the immediacy of the workflows of a subunit, the greater its power within the organization.

Control of Contingencies

Hypotheses relating power to coping with uncertainty, substitutability, and the subvariables of centrality have been stated in a simple single-variable form. Yet it follows from the view of subunits as interdependent parts of organizational systems that the hypotheses in this form are misleading. While each hypothesis may be empirically upheld, it is also hypothesized that this cannot be so without some values of both the other main independent variables. For example, when a marketing department copes with a volatile market by forecasting and by switching sales staff around to ensure stable orders, it acquires power only because the forecast and the orders are linked to the workflow of production, which depends on them. But even then power would be limited by the availability of a successful local marketing agency which could be hired by the organization, and the fact that salesmen were low skilled and easily replaceable.

To explain this interrelationship, the concept of control of contingencies is introduced. It represents organizational interdependence; subunits control contingencies for one another's activities and draw power from the dependencies thereby created. As a hypothesis:

Hypothesis 4. The more contingencies are controlled by a subunit, the greater its power within the organization.

A contingency is a requirement of the activities of one subunit which is affected by the activities of another subunit. What makes such a contingency strategic, in the sense that it is related to power, can be deduced from the preceding hypotheses.

The independent variables are each necessary but not sufficient conditions for control of strategic contingencies, but together they determine the variation in interdependence between subunits. Thus contingencies controlled by a subunit as a consequence of its coping with uncertainty do not become strategic, that is, affect power, in the organization without some (unknown) values of substitutability and centrality. A strategic contingencies theory of power is therefore proposed and is illustrated by the diagram in Figure 1.

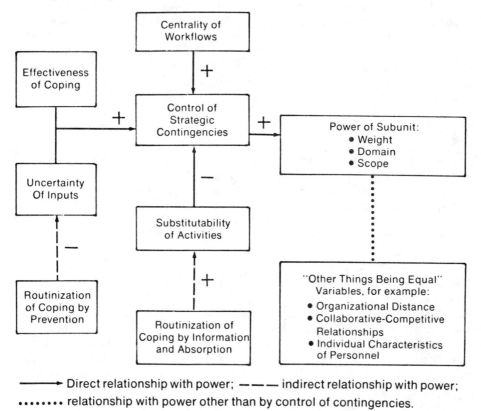

———► Direct relationship with power; — — — indirect relationship with power;
•••••••• relationship with power other than by control of contingencies.

Figure 1. The strategic contingencies theory and routinization.

In terms of exchange theory, as developed by Blau (1964), subunits can be seen to be exchanging control of strategic contingencies one for the other under the normative regulation of an encompassing social system, and acquiring power in the system through the exchange. The research task is to elucidate what combinations of values of the independent variables summarized in hypotheses 1-3 allow hypothesis 4 to hold. Ultimately and ideally the aim would be to discover not merely the weightings of each in the total effect upon power, but how these variables should be operationally interrelated to obtain the best predictions. More of one and less of another may leave the resulting power unchanged. Suppose an engineering subunit has power because it quickly absorbs uncertainty by repairing breakdowns which interfere with the different workflows for each of several organization outputs. It is moderately central and nonsubstitutable. A change in organization policy bringing in a new technology with a single workflow leading to a single output would raise engineering's centrality, since a single breakdown would immediately stop everything, but simultaneously the uncertainty might be reduced by a maintenance program which all but eliminates the possibility of such an occurrence.

Though three main factors are hypothesized, which must change if power is to change, it is not assumed that all subunits will act in accord with the theory to increase their power. This has to be demonstrated. There is the obvious possibility of a cumulative reaction in which a subunit's power is used to preserve or increase the uncertainty it can cope with, or its centrality, or to prevent substitution, thereby increasing its power, and so on. Nor is it argued that power or authority are intentionally allocated in terms of the theory, although the theory is open to such an inference.

Routinization

Most studies that refer to uncertainty contrast it with routinization, the prior prescription of recurrent task activities. Crozier (1964) held that the power of the maintenance personnel in the tobacco plants was due to all other tasks being routinized. A relative decline in the power of general medical personnel in hospitals during this century is thought to be due to the routinization of some tasks, which previously presented uncertainties which could be coped with only by a physician, and the transfer of these tasks to relatively routinized subunits, such as inoculation programs, mass X-ray facilities, and so on (Perrow, 1965; Gordon and Becker, 1964). Crozier (1964: 165) crystallized the presumed effects of routinization; ''But the expert's success is constantly self-defeating. The rationalization process gives him power, but the end results of rationalization curtail his power. As soon as a field is well covered, as soon as the first intuitions and innovations can be translated into rules and programs, the expert's power disappears.''

The strategic contingencies' theory as developed in Figure 1 clarifies this. It suggests that research has been hampered by a confusion of two kinds of routinization, both of which are negatively related to power but in different ways. Routinization may be (*a*) of coping by prevention, which prevents the occurrence of uncertainty; and (*b*) of coping by information or absorption which define how the uncertainty which does occur shall be coped with.

Preventive routinization reduces or removes the uncertainty itself, for example, planned maintenance, which maintenance in Crozier's (1964) tobacco factories would have resisted; inoculation or X-ray programs; and long-term supply contracts, so that the sales staff no longer have to contend with unstable demand. Such routinization removes the opportunity for power, and it is this which is self-defeating (Crozier, 1964: 165) if the expert takes his techniques to a point when they begin not only to cope but to routinely diminish the uncertainty coped with. Thus reducing the uncertainty is not the same as reducing the impact of uncertainty. According to the hypothesis, a sales department which transmits steady orders despite a volatile market has high power; a sales department which reduces the uncertainty itself by long-term tied contracts has low power.

Routinization of coping by information and absorption is embodied in job descriptions and task instructions prescribing how to obtain information and to respond to uncertainty. For maintenance personnel, it lays down how to repair the machine; for physicians, it lays down a standard procedure for examining patients and sequences of remedies for each diagnosis. How does this affect power, since it does not eliminate the uncertainty itself, as preventive routinization does? What it does is increase substitutability. The means of coping become more visible and possible substitutes more obvious, even if those substitutes are unskilled personnel from another subunit who can follow a standard procedure but could not have acquired the previously unexpressed skills.

There is probably some link between the two kinds of routinization. Once preventive routinization is accomplished, other coping routinization more easily follows, as indeed it follows any reduction of uncertainty.

Studies of Subunit Power

Testing of Hypotheses on Earlier Work

The utility of the strategic contingencies theory should be tested on published work, but it is difficult to do this adequately, since most studies stress only one possibility. For example, Crozier (1964) and Thompson (1967) stressed uncertainty, Dubin (1963) stressed exclusiveness of function, and Woodward (1965) spoke of the critical function.

The difficulty is also due to the lack of data. For example, among several studies in which inferences about environmental uncertainty are drawn, only Lawrence and Lorsch (1967b) presented data. They combine executive's questionnaire responses on departmental clarity of job requirements, time span of definitive feedback on departmental success in performance, and uncertainty of cause and effect in the department's functional area.

Lawrence and Lorsch (1967b: 127) found that in two food-processing organizations, research was most influential, then marketing, excluding the field selling unit, and then production. However, influence, or perceived power as it is called here, was rated on the single issue of product innovation and not across a range of issues as suggested earlier in this paper; validity therefore rests on the assumption of equal potential involvement of each function in this one issue. Would research still be most influential if the issues included equipment purchase, or capital budgeting, or personnel training? Even so, on influence over product innovation, an uncertainty hypothesis could be said to fit neatly, since the subunits were ordered on perceived uncertainty of subenvironment exactly as they were on influence.

But uncertainty alone would not explain power in the other firms studied. Although in six plastics firms, coordinating sections or integrating units were perceived as having more influence than functional subunits because "integration itself was the most problematic job" (Lawrence and Lorsch 1967b: 62), it was also a central job in terms of workflow pervasiveness.

Furthermore, in two container manufacturing organizations, although the market subenvironment was seen as the least uncertain, the sales subunit was perceived as the most influential (Lawrence and Lorsch 1967b: 111). An explanation must be sought in the contingencies that the sales subunit controls for production and for research. In this industry, outputs must fit varying customer requirements for containers. Scheduling for production departments and design problems for research departments are therefore completely subject to the contingencies of orders brought in by the sales department. Sales has not only the opportunity to cope with such uncertainty as may exist over customer requirements, it is highly central; for its activities connect it directly to both the other departments—workflow pervasiveness—and if it ceased work production of containers would stop—workflow immediacy. The effects of centrality are probably bolstered by nonsubstitutability, since the sales subunit develops a necessary particularized knowledge of customer requirements. Production and research are, therefore, comparatively powerless in face of the strategic contingencies controlled by the sales subunit.

In short, only a sensitive balancing of all three factors can explain the patterns of contingencies from which power strategically flows.

This is plain also in Crozier's (1964) insightful study of small French tobacco-manufacturing plants. Crozier (1964: 109) had the impression that the maintenance engineers were powerful because "machine stoppages are the only major happenings that cannot be predicted"; therefore the engineers had (Crozier, 1964: 154) "control over the last source of uncertainty remaining in a completely routinized organizational system." But this is not enough for power. Had it been possible to contract maintenance work to consulting engineers, for example, then programs of preventive maintenance might have been introduced, and preventive routinization would have removed much of the uncertainty. However, it is likely that union agreements ensured that the plant engineers were nonsubstitutable. In addition, in these small organizations without specialist control and service departments, the maintenance section's work linked it to all production subunits, that is, to almost every other subunit in the plant. So workflow pervasiveness was high, as was workflow immediacy, since cessation of maintenance activities would quickly have stopped tobacco outputs. The control of strategic contingencies which gave power to the engineers has to be explained on all counts and not by uncertainty alone.

Crozier's (1964) study is a warning against the facile inference that a power distribution fitting the strategic contingencies theory is necessarily efficient, or rational, or functional for an organization; for the power of the engineers to thwart the introduction of programmed maintenance was presumably neither efficient, rational, nor functional.

A challenge to the analysis made is presented by Goldner's (1970) description of a case where there was programmed maintenance and yet the maintenance section held power over production. Goldner (1970) attributed the power of the maintenance subunit to knowing how to install and operate such programs, to coping with breakdowns as in the Crozier (1964) cases, and to knowing how to cope with a critical problem of parts supplies. The strategic contingencies theory accords with his interpretation so long as knowing how to install a program takes effect as coping with uncertainty and not yet as preventive routinization which stops breakdowns. This is where an unknown time element enters to allow for changes in the variables specified and in any associated variables not yet defined. For a time, knowing the answer to an uncertainty does confer power, but the analyses of routinization derived from the theory, as shown in Figure 1, suggests that if this becomes successful preventive routinization, it takes a negative effect upon power. The net result for power in Goldner's (1970) case would then be from the interplay of the opposed effects of activities some of which are preventively routinized, thus decreasing power, and some of which continue to be nonroutine, thus increasing power.

On the other hand, Goldner's (1970) description of the powerful industrial relations subunit in the same plant clearly supports the strategic contingencies theory by showing that coping with uncertainty, centrality, and substitutability had the effect predicted here. The industrial relations subunit exploited uncertainty over the supply and cost of personnel, which arose from possible strikes and pay increases, by (Goldner, 1970: 104) "use of the union as an outside threat." It coped effectively by its nonroutinized knowledge of union officials and of contract interpretation; and its activities were centrally linked to those of other subunits by the necessity for uniform practice on wages and employment. Industrial relations staff developed nonsubstitutable interpersonal and bargaining skills.

There are no means of assessing whether the univariate stress on uncertainty in the handful of other relevant studies is justified. Perrow (1970) explained the greater perceived power of sales as against production, finance, and research, in most of 12 industrial firms, by the concept of uncertainty absorption (March and Simon, 1958). Sales was strategic with respect to the environment. Is the one case where it came second to production the only case where it was also substitutable? Or not central?

White (1961) and Landsberger (1961) both suggested that power shifts over periods of time to follow the locus of uncertainty. Both studied engineering factories. From the histories of three firms, Landsberger (1961) deduced that when money was scarce and uncertain, accounting was powerful; when raw materials were short, purchasing was powerful; and, conversely, when demand was insatiable sales were weakened. In the Tennessee Valley Authority, a nonmanufacturing organization, Selznick (1949) attributed the eventual power of the agricultural relations department to its ability to cope with the uncertain environmental threat represented by the Farm Bureau.

Yet while these earlier studies emphasized uncertainty in one way or another, others called attention to substitutability and probably also to centrality. Again the implication is that contingencies are not strategically controlled without some combination of all three basic variables. For example, the engineers described by Strauss (1962, 1964) appeared to have more power than purchasing agents because the latter were substitutable, that is, the engineers can set specifications for what was to be bought even though the purchasing agents considered this their own responsibility. Thompson (1956: 300) attributed variations in perceived power within and between two U.S. Air Force wings to the changing "technical requirements of operations," which may have indicated changing centralities and substitutabilities.

In the absence of data, consideration of further different kinds of organization must remain pure speculation, for example, the power of surgical units in hospitals, the power of buyers in stores, the power of science faculties in universities.

Other Variables Affecting Power

In order that it can be testable, the strategic contingencies theory errs on the side of simplicity. Any theory must start with a finite number of variables and presume continual development by their alteration or deletion, or by the addition of new variables. As stated, the theory uses only those variables hypothesized to affect power by their contribution to the control of contingencies exercised by a subunit. Other possible explanations of power are not considered. This in itself is an assumption of the greater explanatory force of the theory. Blalock :1961: 8) put the problem clearly: "The dilemma of the scientist is to select models that are at the same time simple enough to permit him to think with the aid of the model but also sufficiently realistic that the simplifications required do not lead to predictions that are highly inaccurate."

In recognition of this, Figure 1 includes several "other things being equal" variables as they are called, that may affect power, but are assumed to do so in other ways than by control of contingencies. One such range of possible relevant variables is qualities of interdepartmental relationships, such as competitiveness versus collaborativeness (Dutton and Walton, 1966). Does the power exercised relate to the style of the relationship through which the power runs? Another possibility is pinpointed by Stymne (1968: 88): "A unit's influence has its roots partly in its strategical importance to the company and partly in nonfunctional circumstances such as tradition, or control over someone in top management through, for example, family relationship." The tradition is the status which may accrue to a particular function because chief executives have typically reached the top through it. Many case studies highlight the personal links of subunits with top personnel (Dalton, 1959; Gouldner, 1955). The notion might be entitled the organizational distance of the subunit, a variant of social distance.

Finally, but perhaps most important, individual differences must be accepted, that is, differences in the intelligence, skills, ages, sexes, or personality factors such as dominance, assertiveness, and risk-taking propensity, of personnel in the various subunits.

Conclusion

The concept of work organizations as interdepartmental systems leads to a strategic contingencies theory explaining differential subunit power by dependence on contingencies ensuing from varying combinations of coping with uncertainty, substitutability, and centrality. It should be stressed that the theory is not in any sense static. As the goals, outputs, technologies, and markets of organizations change so, for each subunit, the values of the independent variables change, and patterns of power change.

Many problems are unresolved. For example, does the theory implicitly assume perfect knowledge by each subunit of the contingencies inherent for it in the activities of the others? Does a workflow of information affect power differently to a workflow of things? But with the encouragement of the improved analysis given of the few existing studies, data can be collected and analyzed, hopefully in ways which will afford a direct test.

References

Bennis, Warren G., N. Berkowitz, M. Affinito, and M. Malone. "Authority, power and the ability to influence." Human Relations, 11: 143-156. 1958.

Bierstedt, Robert. "An analysis of social power." American Sociological Review, 15: 730-736. 1950.

Blalock, Hubert M. Causal Inferences in Nonexperimental Research. Chapel Hill: University of North Carolina Press. 1961.

Blau, Peter. Exchange and Power in Social Life. New York: Wiley. 1964.

Blau, Peter, and W. Richard Scott. Formal Organizations: A Comparative Approach. London: Routledge and Kegan Paul. 1962.

Cartwright, Darwin. "Influence, leadership, control." In James G. March (ed.), Handbook of Organizations: 1-47. Chicago: Rand McNally. 1965.

Clark, Burton R. "Organizational adaptation and precarious values: a case study." American Sociological Review, 21: 327-336. 1956.

Clark, Terry N. (ed.) Community Structure Analyses. San Francisco: Chandler. 1968.

Crozier, Michel. The Bureaucratic Phenomenon. London: Tavistock. 1964.

Cyert, Richard M., and James G. March. A Behavioral Theory of the Firm. Englewood Cliffs, N. J.: Prentice-Hall. 1963.

Dahl, Robert A. "The concept of power." Behavioral Science, 2: 201-215. 1957.

Dahlstrom, E. "Exchange, influence, and power." Acta Sociologica, 9: 237-284. 1966.

Dalton, Melville. Men Who Manage. New York: Wiley. 1959.

Dubin, Robert. "Power and union-management relations." Administrative Science Quarterly, 2: 60-81. 1957.

———."Power, function, and organization." Pacific Sociological Review, 6: 16-24. 1963.

Dutton, John M., and Richard E. Walton. "Interdepartmental conflict and cooperation: two contrasting studies." Human Organization, 25: 207-220. 1966.

Emerson, R. E. "Power-dependence relations." American Sociological Review, 27: 31-41. 1967.

Etzioni, Amitai. A Comparative Analysis of Complex Organizations. New York: Free Press. 1961.

French, John R. P., and Bertram Raven. "The bases of social power." In D. Cartwright (ed.); Studies in Social Power: 150-167. Ann Arbor: University of Michigan. 1959.

Goldner, Fred H. "The division of labor: process and power." In Mayer N. Zald (ed.), Power in Organizations: 97-143. Nashville: Vanderbilt University Press. 1970.

Gordon, Gerald, and Selwyn Becker. "Changes in medical practice bring shifts in the patterns of power." The Modern Hospital (February): 89-91, 154-156. 1964.

Gouldner, Alvin W. Wildcat Strike. London: Routledge. 1955.

Harsanyi, John C. "Measurement of social power, opportunity costs, and the theory of two-person bargaining games." Behavioral Science, 7: 67-80. 1962.

Hinings, Christopher R., Derek S. Pugh, David J. Hickson, and Christopher Turner. "An approach to the study of bureaucracy." Sociology, 1: 61-72. 1967.

Kaplan, Abraham. "Power in perspective." In Robert L. Kahn and Elise Boulding (eds.), Power and Conflict in Organizations: 11-32. London: Tavistock. 1964.

Landsberger, Henry A. "The horizontal dimension in bureaucracy." Administrative Science Quarterly, 6: 299-332. 1961.

Lawrence, Paul R., and Jay W. Lorsch. "Differentiation and integration in complex organizations." Administrative Science Quarterly, 12: 1-47. 1967a.

———. Organization and Environment. Cambridge: Division of Research, Graduate School of Business Administration, Harvard University. 1967.

Lipset, Seymour M., Martin A. Trow, and James A. Coleman. Union Democracy. Glencoe, Ill.: Free Press. 1956.

Luhmann, Niklaus. "Klassische theorie der macht." Zeitschrift fur Politik, 16: 149-170.

March, James G. "An introduction to the theory and measurement of influence." American Political Science Review, 49: 431-450. 1955.

——. "The power of power." In David Easton (ed.), Varieties of Political Theory: 39-70. Englewood Cliffs. N. J.: Prentice-Hall. 1966.

March, James G., and Herbert A. Simon. Organizations. New York: Wiley. 1958.

Mechanic, David. "Sources of power of lower participants in complex organizations." Administrative Science Quarterly, 7: 349-364. 1962.

Perrow, Charles. "The analysis of goals in complex organizations." American Sociological Review, 26: 854-866. 1961.

——. "Hospitals: technology, structure, and goals." In James G. March (ed.), Handbook of Organizations: 910-971. Chicago: Rand McNally. 1965.

——. "Departmental power and perspectives in industrial firms." In Mayer N. Zald (ed.), Power in Organizations: 59-89. Nashville: Vanderbilt University Press. 1970.

Pugh, Derek S., David J. Hickson, Christopher R. Hinings, and Christopher Turner, "Dimensions of organization structure." Administrative Science Quarterly, 13: 65-105. 1968.

Selznick, Philip. T.V.A. and the Grass Roots. Berkeley: University of California Press. 1949.

Strauss, George. "Tactics of lateral relationship: the purchasing agent." Administrative Science Quarterly, 7: 161-186. 1962.

——. "Work-flow frictions, interfunctional rivalry, and professionalism." Human Organization, 23: 137-150. 1964.

Stymne, Bengt. "Interdepartmental communication and intraorganizational strain." Acta Sociologica, 11: 82-100. 1968.

Tannenbaum, Arnold S. Control in Organizations. New York: McGraw-Hill. 1968.

Thompson, James D. "Authority and power in 'identical' organizations." American Journal of Sociology, 62: 290-301. 1956.

——. Organizations in Action. New York: McGraw-Hill. 1967.

Van Doorn, Jaques A. A. "Sociology and the problem of power." Sociologica Neerlandica, 1: 3-47. 1962.

Weber, Max. The Theory of Social and Economic Organization. Glencoe, Ill.: Free Press. 1947.

White, Harrison. "Management conflict and sociometric structure." American Journal of Sociology, 67: 185-199. 1961.

Woodward, Joan. Industrial Organization: Theory and Practice. London: Oxford University Press. 1965.

Wrong, Dennis H. "Some problems in defining social power." American Journal of Sociology, 73, 673-681. 1968.

Zald, Mayer, N. "Organizational control structures in five correctional institutions." American Journal of Sociology, 68: 335-345. 1962.

PART FIVE

The Effects of the Organizational Environment on Individual and Group Behavior

In part 2 we showed that behavior patterns can be understood in terms of reinforcement associated with behavior, but one cannot assume that in every case reinforcements are knowingly and explicitly administered by other people. Behavior is also patterned by reinforcements implicit in the organizational setting in which it occurs.

The activity of a person is limited, for example, by the physical space and conditions in which he functions; his decisions are limited by the amount of authority he has. Assigning a person to a job, in effect, designates both a work space and a level of decision-making authority. Behavior within these limits is acceptable; deviation may be sanctioned.

The organizational setting may influence and reinforce behavior in many ways, and it may often be precisely the undesirable behavior which is system-reinforced. Redesigning the system or the task may prove much more effective than pleading with an individual to change his behavior.

Among the factors which may influence and shape the behavior of individuals in organizations are the nature of the work, the physical location of the job, rules and policies, performance evaluation systems, compensation practices. The readings in this part are chosen to give the reader some understanding of how structural factors affect attitudes and performance, and—it is hoped—some insight into effective structuring for effective performance.

The *nature of an individual's work assignment* can affect his attitudes and performance. Sayles and Strauss treat this point extensively. Assembly lines, for instance, are relatively repetitive and routine, with a controlled work pace. The work of various individuals is highly interdependent and any one person has little or no control over what he does or when he does it. Boredom, fatigue, and high levels of dissatisfaction are often present because harder work is unlikely to lead to greater productivity. At best, the worker may be able to minimize scrap losses. While this certainly may represent cost saving, significant increases in performance levels are unlikely. If more output is needed, the whole line must speed up.

In nonroutine work assignments, an individual has greater control over the work pace. This greater freedom is usually associated with high levels of satisfaction because increases in effort are likely to lead to improved performance. The individual may also

385

have some discretion over the kind of work he is doing. In essence, the job controls the person less, and he controls the job more.

The *physical location* of the work assignment determines, in part, the nature and intensity of interaction patterns. *Where* an individual works is a determinant of *whom* he works with. People located close to each other will interact more frequently, increasing group cohesiveness. A work group located at a site far removed from the home office, for example, may well feel left out, or individuals in a geographically dispersed organization may feel less organizational commitment than individuals in close geographic proximity. Frequent geographical moves on behalf of an organization may prevent an employee from developing long-term social contacts in a community. This limits his social interaction mostly to others in the same organization. Such limitations could contribute to a closer identification with the organization than with external groups.

Rules and policies specify action to be taken. They define what to do, when to do it, and the general range of discretion in decision-making. In general, rules and policies are applicable to all who hold a particular job, or work within a particular group. Rules and policies are highly impersonal but are important for work planning and scheduling, since individuals in various parts of the organization base their expectations of others upon them. Rules and policies of course describe contingency relationships; they attempt to specify behavior which will be punished or rewarded.

Formal *authority structure* defines status and rights of decision. Formal role definition, specifying authority and responsibility, is associated with a position, rather than an individual, and is vested in who holds the position. These rights transfer to new incumbents. Thus, the authority structure is a stable characteristic of the organization over time. When a formal job description allows an individual the right to allocate resources and make decisions about their use, it gives him an important base of power. He may use it to extract compliance within the bounds of the psychological contract. Thus, formal role definition is an important systemic property.

The behavior of individuals is strongly influenced by the *performance evaluation system*, which is intended as a formal means of monitoring performance. In general, quantitative measures, often derived from budgets and plans, are meant to be performance *indicators,* judged and assessed in light of many other factors. It is often true, however, that a manager relies primarily on these measures in the evaluation of individual performance. Once an organization unit has determined that certain assessment factors are to be used as a basis for rewards and sanctions, and ultimately in personnel decisions, individuals in the organization learn to work toward the achievement of the measure, sometimes disregarding the manner in which the level of achievement is obtained.

For example, if cost savings are used as an assessment factor, a department head may forego needed maintenance to keep his operating costs at a minimum. While this decision may result in a better performance measure for him, he may incur excessive costs for the organization in the long run; that is, the equipment on which the maintenance should have been performed may need replacement sooner than otherwise necessary. By this time, however, the manager may have been promoted. Just as a student learns to be grade-conscious in taking exams, perhaps at the expense of true learning, so organization members may learn to meet their performance measures rather than focus on the intended purpose of the measures. If performance evauation is to be effective, reward must be associated with behavior patterns which result in desirable outcomes.

Budgets, from which performance measures are derived, are a systemic organizational factor which can induce a wide range of useful as well as negative organization effects. As Tosi notes, "the seductive nature of the budget is objective . . . but the manager must go beyond it."

Finally, the *compensation system,* and the manner in which it is used, must be considered a structural factor affecting performance. It is often mistakenly assumed that the compensation system itself can positively or negatively reinforce behavior. Compensation often does *not* have a positive reinforcing effect, simply because there is relatively little relationship between increased performance and increased compensation. In many instances, compensation increases are viewed as systems rewards; that is discussed by Katz and Kahn. Payments of this type may help acquire and keep good people, but they are not likely to affect level of achievement.

To make compensation an *instrumental* reward, as defined by Katz and Kahn, is extremely difficult. Compensation is paid at fixed intervals. Yet work activities go on continuously, so specific behavior which a manager might wish to reinforce may occur at other intervals than when payments are made. It seems impossible to develop a compensation system which can be flexible enough for a manager to use to reinforce behavior when it occurs. In addition, the amount of compensation associated with performance increases may be relatively small. An employee may well find the increased effort not worth the money. Compensation *does* have a reinforcing effect when its level or amount of increase is an indicator of status or rank in an organization. High value may be placed on relatively small, modest increments in pay—if they are larger than those given to others. Thus, even small pay increases may be reinforcing if they are perceived as general social reinforcements, or status indicators.

The selection by Hamner brings together some of the themes developed in part 2 with those in this part. He provides the manager with some things a manager can do to affect performance patterns of subordinates. These approaches focus on both the effects of structure as well as some of the interpersonal aspects of control, while Schwab and Cummings in their article present a model linking task scope to motivation and performance, with emphasis on objective, environmental (as opposed to psychological) conceptualizations of task scope.

In summary, this part focuses on the effects of the procedural and structural system on the members of an organization. These systemic factors, recognized or not, are likely to be significant conditions of behavior, imposing constraints, providing guidelines, and otherwise setting conditions which influence behavior patterns.

Alteration of structural factors may be difficult, costly, and difficult to perceive as a need, but the system must be congruent with effective performance for the latter to occur. This problem of organization change is the subject of part 7.

USING REINFORCEMENT THEORY
IN ORGANIZATIONAL SETTINGS

W. CLAY HAMNER

In my article in part 2 on reinforcement theory, I discussed the principles of reinforcement and how the management of these principles is necessary for achieving organizational effectiveness. In that article I noted that managers need to understand how the principles of reinforcement and the schedules of reinforcement influence individual performance.

This article continues the discussion begun in part 2, focusing on how verbal rules expressed by a manager can reduce the time it takes employees to learn and to become socialized. This article gives six rules managers can make use of to help them implement reinforcement principles. But because extreme reinforcements are so powerful, the limitations and ethical implications of using these principles are also discussed.

Rules for Using Operant Conditioning Techniques

While these rules have common sense appeal, the research findings indicate that they are often violated by managers when they design control systems.

Rule 1. Don't Reward All People the Same.

In other words, differentiate the rewards based on performance as compared to some defined objective or standard. We know that people compare their own performance to that of their peers to determine how well they are doing ("Social Comparison Theory," Festinger, 1954) and they compare their rewards to the rewards of their peers ("Equity Theory," Adams, 1965) in order to determine how to evaluate their rewards. While some managers seem to think that the fairest system of compensation is one where everyone in the same job classification gets the same pay, employees want differentiation so that they know their importance to the organization. Based on social comparison and equity theory assumptions, it can be argued that managers who reward all people the same are encouraging, at best, only average performance. Behavior of high-performance workers is being extinguished (ignored) while the behavior of average performance and poor performance workers is being strengthened by positive reinforcement.

Rule 2. Failure to Respond Has Reinforcing Consequences.

Managers who find the job of differentiating between workers so unpleasant that they fail to respond must recognize that failure to respond modifies behavior. "Indeed, whether he is conscious of it or not, the superior is bound to be constantly shaping the behavior of his subordinates by the way in which he utilizes the rewards that are at his disposal, and he will inevitably modify the behavior of his work group (Haire, 1964)."

This article was prepared especially for this book.

Managers must be careful that they examine the performance consequence of their non-action as well as their action.

Rule 3. Be Sure to Tell a Person What He Can Do to Get Reinforced.

By making clear the contingencies of reinforcement to the worker, a manager may be actually increasing the individual freedom of the worker. The employee who has a standard against which to measure his job will have a built-in feedback system which allows him to judge his own work. The awarding of the reinforcement in an organization where the worker's goal is specified will be associated with the performance of the worker and not based on the biases of the supervisor. The assumption is that the supervisor rates the employee accurately (see Scott and Hamner, 1973a) and that he then reinforces the employee based on his ratings (see Scott and Hamner, 1973b). If the supervisor fails to rate accurately or administer rewards based on performance, then the stated goals for the worker will lose stimulus control, and the worker will be forced to search for the "true" contingencies; that is, what behavior should he perform in order to get rewarded (e.g., ingratiation? loyalty? positive attitude?).

Rule 4. Be Sure to Tell a Person What He Is Doing Wrong.

As a general rule, very few people find the act of failing rewarding. One assumption of behavior therefore is that a worker wants to be rewarded in a positive manner. A supervisor should never use extinction or punishment as a sole method for modifying behavior, but if used judiciously in conjunction with other techniques designed to promote more effective response options (Rule 3), such combined procedures can hasten the change process. If the supervisor fails to specify why a reward is being withheld, the employee may associate it with past desired behavior instead of the undesired behavior that the supervisor is trying to extinguish. The supervisor then extinguishes good performance while having no affect on the undesired behavior.

Rules 3 and 4, when used in combination, should allow the manager to control behavior in the best interest of reaching organizational goals. At the same time they should give the employee the clarity he needs to see that his own behavior and not the behavior of the supervisor controls his outcomes.

Rule 5. Don't Punish in Front of Others.

The reason for this rule is quite simple. The punishment (e.g., reprimand) should be enough to extinguish the undesired behavior. By administering the punishment in front of the work group, the worker is doubly punished in the sense that he also loses face (Goffman, 1959). This additional punishment may lead to negative side-effects in three ways. First, the worker whose self-image is damaged may feel that he must retaliate in order to protect himself. Therefore, the supervisor has actually increased undesired responses. Second, the work group may misunderstand the reason for the punishment and through "avoidance learning" may modify their own behavior in ways not intended by the supervisor. Third, the work group is also being punished in the sense that observing a member of their team being reprimanded has noxious or aversive properties for most people. This may result in a decrease in the performance of the total work group.

Rule 6. Make the Consequences Equal to the Behavior.

In other words be fair. Don't cheat the worker out of his just rewards. If he is a good worker, tell him. Many supervisors find it very difficult to praise an employee. Others find it very difficult to counsel an employee about what he is doing wrong. When a manager fails to use these reinforcement tools, he is actually reducing his effectiveness. When a worker is overrewarded he may feel guilty (Adams, 1965) and based on the principles of reinforcement, the worker's current level of performance is being conditioned. If his performance level is less than others who get the same reward, he has no reason to increase his output. When a worker is underrewarded, he becomes angry with the system (Adams, 1965). His behavior is being extinguished and the company may be forcing the good employee (underrewarded) to seek employment elsewhere while encouraging the poor employee (overrewarded) to stay.

Controversies Surrounding an Operant Approach to Management

The reinforcement approach to the study and control of human behavior has met with resistance and criticism, primarily through a lack of understanding of its recommended uses and limitations. Goodman (1964) wrote, "To be candid, I think operant-conditioning is vastly overrated." Henry (1964) said, "Learning theory has two simple points to make and does so with talmudic ingenuity, variability, intricacy, and insistence. They are reinforcement and extinction. What has to be left out. . . . is thought."

While the criticisms would be too numerous to mention here, an attempt will be made to examine three of the major controversies surrounding an operant approach to the management of people in organizational settings.

1. *The application of operant conditioning techniques ignores the individuality of man.* Ashby (1967) said "now the chief weakness of programmed instruction is that it rewards rote learning, and worse than that—it rewards only those responses which are in agreement with the programme." Proponents of an operant approach to contingency management recognize that a poorly designed program can lead to rigidity in behavior. This is one of the major reasons that they recommend a program of reinforcement which best fits the group or individuals being supervised. It is untrue, however, that behaviorists ignore the individuality of man. Each man is unique based on his past reinforcement history. When personnel psychologists build sophisticated selection models to predict future performance, they are actually trying to identify those applicants who will perform well under the contingencies of that particular organization. That does not mean that a person rejected cannot be motivated, but only that the current reward system of that organization is better suited for another applicant. (This is true because the criterion variable is some measure of performance, and performance is directly tied to the reinforcement consequences for the current employees used to derive the selection model.)

In other words, the problem a manager faces is not to design contingencies that will be liked by all men, "but a way of life which will be liked by those who live it" (Skinner, 1969, p. 41). As Hersey and Blanchard (1972) point out, "Positive reinforcement is anything that is rewarding to the individual being reinforced. Reinforcement, therefore, depends on the individual (p. 22)." What is reinforcing to one may not be reinforcing to someone else based on the person's past history of satiation, deprivation and conditioning operations. A manager can do two things to insure that the contingencies of reinforcement are designed to support the individuality of the worker. First, as noted earlier he can strive to hire the worker who desires the rewards offered by the firm; that is, can the person be happy or satisfied with this firm? Second, if it seems that the contingencies are ineffective, the manager can change the contingencies by using a democratic process—letting the employees design their own reward structure, within the limits set by the organization. "Democracy is an effort to solve the problem by letting the people design the contingencies under which they are to live or—to put it another way—by insisting that the designer himself live under the contingencies he designs" (Skinner, 1969, p. 43).

In summary, therefore, it can be concluded that in a voluntary society, where man has freedom to move from one organization to another, operant methods of control should not ignore the individuality of man. Instead, man should seek work where his individuality can best be appreciated and industries should select employees who can best be motivated by the contingencies available to them. It should be noted, however, that through the unethical application of conditioning principles, some employers may exploit workers. The overall evidence would seem to indicate that this is not due to the weakness in behavioral theory, but due to the weakness of man himself.

2. *The application of operant conditioning techniques restricts freedom of choice.*

Discussions of the moral implications of behavioral control almost always emphasize the Machiavellian role of change agents and the self-protective maneuvers of controllers. . . . The tendency to exaggerate the powers of behavioral control by psychological methods alone, irrespective of willing cooperation by the client, and the failure to recognize the reciprocal nature of interpersonal control obscure both the ethical issues and the nature of the social influence processes (Bandura, 1969, p. 85).

Kelman (1965) noted that the primary criterion that one might apply in judging the ethical implications of social influence approaches is the degree to which they promote freedom of choice. If individualism is to be guaranteed, it must be tempered by a sense of social obligation by the individual and by the organization.

Bandura (1969) noted that a person is considered free insofar as he can partly influence future events by managing his own behavior. A person in a voluntary society can within limits exert some control over the variables that govern his own choices. Skinner (1969) noted that "Men are happy in an environment in which active, productive, and creative behavior is reinforced in effective ways" (p. 64). One method of effectively reinforcing behavior is by allowing the employee some determination in the design of the reinforcement contingencies. Another method is to design self-control reinforcement systems in which individuals regulate their own activities (Ferster, Nurnberger and Levitt, 1962; Harris, 1969).

While it cannot be denied that reinforcers, which are "all too abundant and powerful" (Skinner, 1966), can restrict freedom of choice, it is not true that a behavioral or Skinnerian approach is against freedom of choice; the opposite is true. As Bandura noted, "Contrary to common belief, behavioral approaches not only support a humanistic morality, but because of their relative effectiveness in establishing self-determination these methods hold much greater promise than traditional procedures for enhancement of behavioral freedom and fulfillment of human capabilities" (p. 88).

3. *Operant theory, through its advocacy of an external reward system, ignores the fact that individuals can be motivated by the job itself.* Deci (1971, 1972) among others (Likert, 1967; Vroom and Deci, 1970) criticizes behaviorists for advocating a system of employee motivation that only utilizes externally mediated rewards; that is, rewards such as money and praise administered by someone other than the employee himself. In so doing, according to Deci, management is attempting to control the employee's behavior so he will do what he is told. The limitations of this method of worker motivation, for Deci, is that it only satisfies man's "higher-order" needs for self-esteem and self-actualization. Deci states, "It follows that there are many important motivators of human behavior which are not under the direct control of managers and, therefore, cannot be contingently administered in a system of piece-rate payments" (1972, p. 218).

Deci recommends that we should move away from a method of external control, and toward a system where individuals can be motivated by the job itself. He says that this approach will allow managers to focus on higher-order needs where the rewards are mediated by the person himself (intrinsically motivated). To motivate employees intrinsically, tasks should be designed which are interesting, creative and resourceful, and workers should have some say in decisions which concern them "so they will feel like causal agents in the activities which they engage in" (Deci, 1972, p. 219). Deci concludes his argument against a contingency approach to management by saying:

> It is possible to pay workers and still have them intrinsically motivated. Hence the writer favors the prescription that we concentrate on structuring situations and jobs to arouse intrinsic motivation, rather than trying to structure piece-rate and other contingency payment schemes. Workers would be intrinsically motivated and would seek to satisfy their higher-order needs through effective performance. The noncontingent payments (or salaries) would help to satisfy the workers and keep them on the job, especially if the pay were equitable (Adams, 1965; Pritchard, 1969), (1972, p. 227).

Deci levels criticism at a positive reinforcement contingency approach on the basis of four issues: (1) advocating that external rewards be administered by someone else, (2) ignoring the importance of the task environment, (3) ignoring the importance of internal rewards, and (4) advocating of a contingent payment plan. Deci makes two errors, from a reinforcement theory point of view, when he advocates noncontingent equitable pay plans. First, equity theory (Adams, 1965) assumes that rewards are based on performance. If they weren't, then the pay would be equal, not equitable. Second, and more crucial, is Deci's assumption that a pay plan can be noncontingent. Bandura notes that "all behavior is inevitably controlled, and the operation of psychological laws cannot be suspended by romantic conceptions of human behavior, any more than indignant rejection of the law of gravity as antihumanistic can stop people from falling" (1969, p. 85). Homme and Tosti (1965) made the point that, "either one manages the contingencies or they get managed by accident. Either way there will be contingencies, and they will have their effect" (p. 16): In other words, if managers instituted a pay plan that was "noncontingent," they would in fact be rewarding poor performance and extinguishing good performance (see Rules 1, 2, and 6).

The assertion that a contingency approach advocates that the rewards always be administered by someone else is false. Skinner specifically (1969, p. 158) recommends that manding behavior be replaced by tacting methods for achieving the same effect. Skinner suggested that one safeguard against exploitation is to make sure that the designer of the contingencies never controls. In addition to recommending that the contingencies be so designed that they are controlled by the environment (tacting), operant theorists have advocated self-control processes in which individuals regulate their own behavior by arranging appropriate contingencies for themselves (Ferster, Nurnberger and Leavitt, 1962). Bandura (1969) concluded that:

> The selection of well-defined objectives, both intermediate and ultimate, is an essential aspect of any self-directed program of change. The goals that individuals choose for themselves must be specified in sufficiently detailed behavioral terms to provide adequate guidance for the actions that must be taken daily to attain desired outcomes. . . . Individuals can, therefore, utilize objective records of behavioral changes as an additional source of reinforcement for their self-controlling behavior (p. 255).

Studies which have explored the effect of self-reinforcement on performance have shown that systems which allowed workers to keep a record of their own output to use as a continuous feedback system and for reinforcement purposes helped the workers to increase their performance (Kolb, Winter and Berlew, 1968; Fox, 1966). Michigan Bell Telephone Company and the Emery Air Freight Corporation are two of several firms which are currently using self-reinforcement programs in order to increase worker motivation and performance. Both programs have been immensely successful (see *Business Week,* December 18, 1971; and December 2, 1972).

It should be noted that even though the individual is determining his own reward in the self-feedback program, the reinforcers are both externally (money, recognition, praise) and internally (self-feedback) mediated. According to Skinner (1957) and Bem (1967) the self-report feedback is a "tact" or description of an internal feeling state. In both cases, the rewards must be contingent on performance for effective control of the behavior to take place.

Deci's recommendation that jobs should be designed so that they are interesting, creative, and resourceful is wholeheartedly supported by proponents of a positive reinforcement program. Skinner (1969) warns managers that too much dependency on force and a poorly designed monetary reward system may actually reduce performance, while designing the task so that it is automatically reinforcing can have positive effects on performance. Skinner says:

> The behavior of an employee is important to the employer, who gains when the employee works industriously and carefully. How is he to be induced to do so? The standard answer was once physical force: men worked to avoid punishment or death. The by-products were troublesome, however, and economics is perhaps the first field in which an explicit change was made to positive reinforcement. Most men now work, as we say, 'for money'.
>
> Money is not a natural reinforcer; it must be conditioned as such. Delayed reinforcement, as in a weekly wage, raises a special problem. No one works on Monday morning because he is reinforced by a paycheck on Friday afternoon. The employee who is paid by the week works during the week to avoid losing the

standard of living which depends on a weekly system. Rate of work is determined by the supervisor (with or without the pacing stimuli of a production line), and special aversive contingencies maintain quality. The pattern is therefore still aversive. It has often been pointed out that the attitude of the production-line worker toward his work differs conspicuously from that of the craftsman, who is envied by workers and industrial managers alike. One explanation is that the craftsman is reinforced by more than monetary consequences, but another important difference is that when a craftsman spends a week completing a given set object, each of the parts produced during the week is likely to be automatically reinforcing because of its place in the completed object (p. 18).

Skinner (1969) also agrees with Deci that the piece-rate may actually reduce performance in that it is so powerful it is most often misused, and "it is generally opposed by those concerned with the welfare of the worker (and by workers themselves when, for example, they set daily quotas)" (p. 19).

It appears therefore, that critics of operant conditioning methods misunderstand the recommendations of behaviorists in the area of worker motivation. Operant theory does advocate interesting job design and self-reinforcement feedback systems, where possible. It does not advocate force or try to control the employee's behavior by making the employee "do what he is told." It is not against humanistic morality; rather it advocates that workers be rewarded on their performance and not on their needs alone.

While other controversies about operant conditioning could be reviewed, the examination of these three issues should give the reader a flavor of the criticisms which surround the use of a contingency approach to behavioral control.

An Argument for Positive Reinforcement

Most workers enter the work place willingly if not eagerly. They have a sense of right and wrong and have been thoroughly conditioned by their parents and by society. By the time they reach adulthood, it can be assumed that they are mature. For these reasons, it is argued here, as well as by others (Skinner, 1953; Wiard, 1972), that the only tool needed for worker motivation is the presence or absence of positive reinforcement. In other words, managers do not, as a general rule, need to use avoidance learning or punishment techniques in order to control behavior.

Whyte (1972) says "positive reinforcers generally are more effective than negative reinforcers in the production and maintenance of behavior" (p. 67). Wiard (1972) points out, "There may be cases where the use of punishment has resulted in improved performance, but they are few and far between. The pitfalls of punishment can be encountered with any indirect approach" (p. 16). However, a positive reinforcement program is geared toward the desired results. It emphasizes what needs to be done, rather than what should not be done. A positive reinforcement program is result-oriented, rather than process-oriented. A well-designed program encourages individual growth and freedom, whereas a negative approach (avoidance learning and punishment) encourages immaturity in the individual and therefore eventually in the organization itself.

The reason organizations are ineffective according to Skinner (1969) is because they insist on using avoidance learning or punishment techniques, and because they fail to use a positive reinforcement program in an effective manner. He says:

The contingencies of positive reinforcement arranged by governmental and religious agencies are primitive, and the agencies continue to lean heavily on the puritanical solution. Economic reinforcement might seem to represent an environmental solution, but it is badly programmed and the results are unsatisfactory for both the employer (since not much is done) and the employee (since work is still work). Education and the management of retardates and psychotics are still largely aversive. In short, as we have seen, the most powerful forces bearing on human behavior are not being effectively used. . . . Men are happy in an environment in which active, productive, and creative behavior is reinforced in effective ways (pp. 63-64).

Ethical Implications for Worker Control

The deliberate use of positive and negative reinforcers often gives rise to ethical concern about harmful effects which may result from such practices. Poorly designed reward structures can interfere with the development of spontaneity and creativity. Reinforcement systems which are deceptive and manipulative are an insult to the integrity of man. The employee should be a willing party to the influence attempt, with both parties benefiting from the relationship.

The question of whether man should try to control human behavior is covered in a classic paper by Rogers and Skinner (1956). The central issue discussed was one of personal values. Rogers contends that "values" emerge from the individual's "freedom of choice," a realm unavailable to science. Skinner, in rebuttal, points out that the scientific view of man does not allow for such exceptions, and that choice and the resulting values are, like all behavior, a function of man's biology and his environment. Since biology and environment lie within the realm of science, "choice" and "value" must be accessible to scientific inquiry. Skinner and Rogers are both concerned with abuse of the power held by scientists, but Skinner is optimistic that good judgment will continue to prevail. Krasner (1964) agrees with Skinner that we should apply scientific means to control behavior, but warns that behavioral control can be horribly misused unless we are constantly alert to what is taking place in society.

Probably few managers deliberately misuse their power to control behavior. Managers should realize that the mismanagement of the contingencies of reinforcement is actually self-defeating. Workers will no longer allow themselves to be pushed around, but instead will insist that the work environment be designed in such a way that they have a chance at a better life. The effective use of a positive reinforcing program is one of the most critical challenges facing modern management.

The first step in the ethical use of behavioral control in organizations is the understanding by managers of the determinants of behavior. Since reinforcement is the single most important concept in the learning process, managers must learn how to design reinforcement programs that will encourage creative, productive, satisfied employees.

References

See *References* for the article "Reinforcement Theory" in part 2 of this book.

A THEORETICAL ANALYSIS OF THE IMPACT OF TASK SCOPE ON EMPLOYEE PERFORMANCE

DONALD P. SCHWAB
L. L. CUMMINGS

The motivational benefits of designing tasks with broad scopes have been extolled by numerous commentators (14, 16, 24, 38).[1] Despite the well publicized successes, Hackman (19) recently suggested that job enrichment may become a victim of the "too quick to accept—too quick to reject" theme that has been the fate of many earlier behavioral science intervention strategies. He suggests that one possible cause for this outcome is the lack of a systematic, diagnostic strategy to use in deciding when, where, and how to use expanded task scopes. While Hackman and Oldham (21) have suggested such a strategy, it is anchored in the perceptions, psychological characteristics, and affective reactions of the performer. It does not deal directly with diagnosing and assessing the objective task environment.

In a critical review of the literature, Hulin and Blood suggest that much of the evidence is not as supportive of the benefits of job enrichment as has been assumed. They observe:

> The studies reviewed appear to be of two types. Those which have used acceptable methodology, control groups, appropriate analysis, and multivariate designs have generally not yielded evidence which could be considered as supporting the job enlargement thesis (i.e., increased satisfaction and productivity; lower turnover and absenteeism). Those studies which do appear to support such a thesis frequently contain a number of deviations from normally acceptable research practice (27, p. 50).

They also suggest that "the case for job enlargement has been drastically overstated and overgeneralized."

Thus, the evidence regarding the consequences of job enrichment is not clear. Besides the methodological problems noted by Hulin and Blood, there has been little theoretical work attempting to specify the conditions that must prevail for variations in task scope to have a predictable impact on attitudes or behavior. The benefits of increased task scope are presumed to apply to a variety of potential variables including motivation, alienation, satisfaction, turnover, and absenteeism. The focus here is on employee performance because of its importance to the organization and because it tends not to be highly related to these other variables. The purpose of this article is to provide a theoretical framework and to set forth a set of hypotheses about probable relationships between task scope and employee performance.

It is first necessary to delineate the construct "task scope." While many terminologies have been employed, the next section will show that most current formulations have serious deficiencies. As a consequence, an alternative conceptualization of task scope is proposed. Following the definitional section, expectancy theory is used as a

Reprinted from *The Academy of Management Review*, vol. 1 (April) 1976, with permission.

framework for predicting the impact of variation in task scope on employee performance. A series of hypotheses is formulated predicting how task scope is likely to influence each of the components in the expectancy model. Finally, the constraints and boundaries which condition the applicability of the model as well as additional issues suggested by the definition of task scope are discussed. This discussion points to the complex nature of the impacts of changes in task scope and to the likely importance of individual differences in reactions to such changes. It also suggests the need for caution in accepting and generalizing many current prescriptions for work humanization as a route toward enhanced human performance.

Task Scope

Current Formulations

Recent efforts to measure task scope have tended to assess the affective and/or cognitive reactions of the employee as measured through the employee's perceptions. For example, perceptions of variability in autonomy, task identity, variety, feedback, and opportunities for self-development are typically used in operational definitions of task scope (3, 20, 21, 44). These formulations do not anchor their definitions with environmental, objectively observable characteristics of the task. They are essentially *psychological* (as contrasted to objective) definitions of task scope (18).

There are at least three problems with psychological definitions of task scope. First, psychologically based measures confound personal needs and preferences of the performer with the objective characteristics of the task.

The second limitation partially derives from the first. Measures based on performers' perceptions provide few clues about how task scope can be manipulated for either research or applied purposes. The environmental manipulations required to vary such things as task identity, autonomy, or meaningfulness are not clear. Psychological reactions to jobs may deserve study, but they are likely to tell us relatively little about how to create actual variations in objective task dimensions.

Finally, a significant measurement problem is raised when psychological definitions are used. For example, when task scope is defined in terms of the performer's perception of the degree of autonomy or variety in the job and these perceptions are related to other perceptual and cognitive variables (e.g., job satisfaction, involvement, commitment, motivational potential), these results probably will indicate more about method variance than real task effects. Other areas of organizational behavior share the same general difficulties noted with psychological measures of task scope. For example, when leadership behavior is measured through subordinates' perceptions, as it is in most leadership studies, the behavior of the leader is confounded with the idiosyncratic characteristics of the subordinate.

Objective Formulations

Deficiencies inherent in psychologically based measures suggest that alternative formulations should attempt to measure task characteristics objectively (or at least in a manner which is verifiable from a source other than the task performer). Such measures would permit examination of psychological consequences of variation in task scope free of confounding effects and the other limitations noted above.

An objective conceptualization of task scope implies that the psychological reactions of performers should be conceived of as dependent variables to be explained in terms of variations on the objective measure, individual characteristics, and their likely interactions. These psychological reactions can be thought of as intervening between the task and performance or other behavior outcomes. The potential advantages of this approach will be discussed later.

Investigators interested in affective and behavioral consequences of task scope have tended not to think in terms of objective definitions (29). Nevertheless, there is a body of literature stemming from the traditional personnel areas of job placement and evaluation that can serve as a fruitful starting point for such an approach. For example, the definitions of jobs in the Dictionary of Occupational Titles (45) and implied by time span of discretion (28) represent efforts to measure jobs in objective and quantitative terms. The work of McCormick and his colleagues in developing and testing the Position Analysis Questionnaire (PAQ) looks particularly promising. The PAQ attempts to quantitatively measure tasks in terms of activities required of workers to perform the task. Ratings of tasks on the PAQ by job analysts, supervisors, and incumbents have shown the instrument to have acceptable reliability and cultural generality (15, 34).

Task scope is viewed here in terms of its impact on five sense modalities (visual, auditory, olfactory, gustatory, and tactile). It may be viewed in terms of task based stimulation (TBS) consisting of three dimensions: (a) magnitude of stimulation provided by the task (M), (b) variation of stimulation (V), and (c) number of sensory modalities impacted by the task (N). TBS is thus defined as a positive function of M, V, and N where:

$$M = + f_1 (M_1 + M_2 \ldots + M_i + \ldots M_n)$$
M_i = Magnitude of stimulation of the ith sensory modality
    (1 ... n)
$$V = + f_2 (V_1 + V_2 + \ldots + V_i + \ldots V_n)$$
V_i = Variation of stimulation on the ith sensory modality
    (1 ... n)
$$N = n$$
$$\sum K_i$$
$$i = 1$$
K_i = the *ith* sensory modality and n = the number of modalities
    effected by the task.

Each dimension is conceived of as measurable by directly observable indexes with ratio or at least interval properties. Examples might include number of sound decibels as one indicant of M, and variability in decibels across some time period as an indicant of V.

At least two problems concerning this formulation of task scope need to be emphasized. First, the three dimensions of TBS probably are correlated. For example, N and M will be positively related in most tasks. Second, the dimensions may interact in their influences on affective, cognitive, and behavioral outcomes. For example, the effects of variation in stimulation on any one sense modality may depend on the number of sense modalities activated by the task environment. In an extreme case of all modalities being activated, the stimulus overload may mask the effects of variation in stimuli on any single modality.

Both of these problems are researchable and amenable to empirical verification. The framework proposed above will doubtless require revision as these issues are studied and as evidence becomes available. Moreover, the acceptance of TBS is not critical to the arguments developed next. What is critical is that task scope be viewed in objective rather than psychological terms and that the processes through which scope impacts affect and behavior be identified (43).

The Proposed Model

Our basic conceptualization comes from Vroom (46) who proposed that employee performance be viewed as a function of individual ability and motivation. Ability, in Vroom's scheme and in this one, is defined broadly to include all relatively stable cognitive and motor characteristics determining current capability for performing a set of tasks. Motivation, as derived from expectancy theory, (see also 7, 32, 39 for similar theoretical formulations; and 23, 26, 33, 36, 37 for reviews of the empirical literature) is hypothesized to be dependent on an employee's perceptions regarding: (a) one's capability for performing, given that one exerts performance related effort (expectancy), (b) the likelihood that second-level outcomes (e.g., pay increase) will result if one performs at some performance level (instrumentalities), and (c) the attractiveness of these outcomes (valences of second-level outcomes).

Given the model, the impact of task scope (or any other organizational variable) on performance will operate through or in combination with the individual's ability and/or

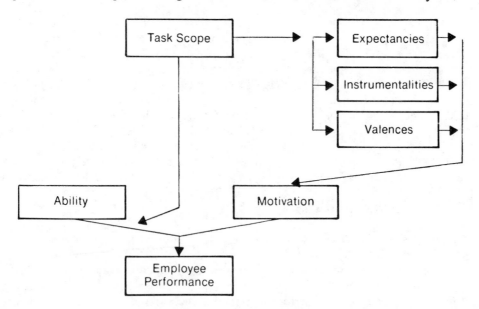

Figure 1. Hypothesized relationship between task scope and employee performance.

motivation. (Evans (13) and House (25) have developed a similar model for the prediction of the effects of leader behavior.) That is, task scope can influence performance only as it influences or interacts with ability and motivation. In general, the hypothesis is that task scope will influence performance in conjunction with ability and motivation (see Figure 1). Specifically, task scope is hypothesized to interact with ability and to serve an independent variable in regard to motivation. Figure 1 includes only those linkages that are of direct importance to the proposed model. The following discussion introduces a number of issues that make the model more complex.

Task Scope and Ability

A potentially valuable but little known approach for understanding the probable linkages between task scope and ability has been postulated by Dawis, England, and Lofquist (8) in their theory of work adjustment. They suggest that employee satisfactoriness (performance) is determined primarily by two variables. The first pertains to broadly defined abilities that the individual brings to the task. The second refers to job characteristics (task scope) that require abilities of the job incumbent. Dawis, et al. view performance primarily as a function of the correspondence or degree of agreement between an individual's abilities and the ability demands of the job, holding motivation constant.

Their model suggests that the ability of the individual interacts with the ability requirements of the job. The individual's *relative ability* to perform is highest when the ability demands of the task match the abilities of the individual. Undermatching (when the individual does not possess adequate capabilities to perform the task) obviously results in lower relative ability to perform. Some evidence suggests that overmatching (when the individual is overqualified) also results in lower relative ability to perform (17).

The implications of this line of reasoning for the probable relation between task scope and performance considering only the individual's relative ability are shown in Figure 2. At a given time, the individual's relative ability is highest at task scope X. Tasks of greater scope require more abilities than the individual possesses, while tasks of less scope call for less. Both conditions are dysfunctional for performance although it is anticipated that the former condition is more so, as shown by the greater relative ability decrement to the right of X. In undermatching, the individual literally does not possess sufficient abilities to perform the task. The individual who is overqualified is obviously capable of performing if he or she so desires. While the performance decrements observed in these overqualification situations have not been adequately explained empirically, they are probably due to the individual allocating effort to nonperformance behaviors.

Thus, it is hypothesized that:

Hypothesis 1a: Each individual has an optimal task scope which maximizes his or her relative ability to perform.

Hypothesis 1b: As task scope increases, relative ability to perform first increases to an optimal level and then decreases.

Hypothesis 1c: The negative performance consequences (through decreasing relative ability, holding motivation constant) are greater for excessive task scope than for deficient task scope.

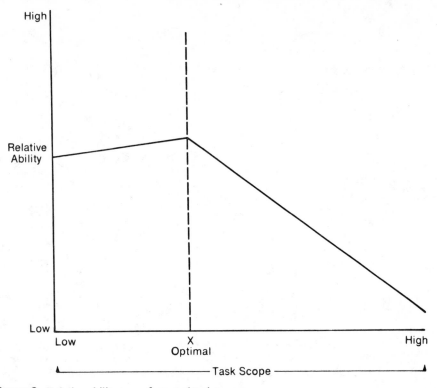

Figure 2. Relative ability to perform and task scope.

Two other considerations apply directly to the form of the hypothesized relationship. First, the curve drawn for any individual need not be highly stable through time. Training and experience, for example, may shift the maximum point of the curve to the right towards greater scope. Second, there is no reason to expect that relative ability curves for different individuals will be similar. Indeed, the evidence from differential psychology should lead us to expect wide individual differences in relative ability to perform a given job (1).

Task Scope and Motivation
   Variations in task scope may be related to each of the motivational components discussed in the model: expectancy, instrumentality and valence.
   Expectancy perceptions—Although employee perceptions about expectancy have not received much research attention, they may be positively correlated with ability to perform. Indeed, expectancy perceptions may provide an estimate by the individual of his or her ability to perform a given task. It is hypothesized that:

Hypothesis 2a: Increases in task scope beyond the individual's current task level (Y in Figure 3) will result in a reduction, at least in the short run, in expectancy perceptions (as shown by the broken line in Figure 3).

   A major exception to this hypothesis would be the case where increased job scope allowed effort to be more efficiently directed toward performance—for example, where

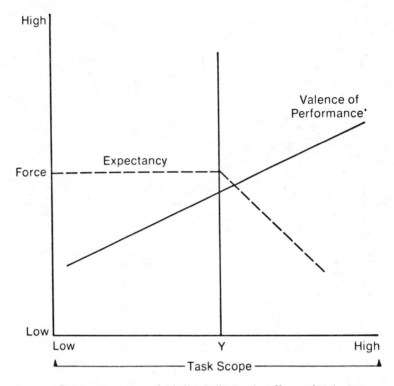

*The positive slope of this line is due to the effects of task scope
on instrumentality perceptions (not on valence of outcomes) which,
in turn, is one of the determinants of the valence of performance.

Figure 3. Force to perform and task scope.

the employee is ritualistically following "red tape" which he or she knows to be
inefficient or incorrect but which is specified and controlled by others.

On the other hand, if the employee has mastered the present task, there is little
reason to expect that a decrease in task scope would increase the perceived probability of
successful task performance. Thus:

Hypotheses 2b: Decreases in task scope beyond the experienced individual's current
task level will not result in increased expectancy perceptions (as shown by the
horizontal line to the left of Y in Figure 3).

Major additional determinants of expectancy perceptions are probably the specificity with which task performance can be defined and the extent to which the individual can
control his/her own performance. For example, Schwab (40) found that expectancy
perceptions of individual piece-rate workers (representing high control over performance) were significantly higher than those of group incentive workers (whose perfor-

mance depends in part on the efforts of others). Thus, any manipulation in scope (either lower or higher) which decreased the clarity of the definition of performance or decreased control would likely decrease expectancy perceptions.

Instrumentality perceptions—A distinction must be made between two types of second-level outcomes before discussing the probable impact of task scope on instrumentality perceptions. One type of outcome is an integral part of the interaction between the individual and the behavior or accomplishment. These outcomes will be referred to as *task-administered*, rather than as intrinsic to the job, to avoid the implication that they reside exclusively in the task (as generally suggested in discussions of intrinsic outcomes). Instead of implying that all individuals performing on a task would experience these outcomes, it is more useful to view these outcomes as resulting from the interaction between the task and the person. Frequently cited as illustrative of such outcomes are the feeling of enjoying the activities inherent in one's task or the feeling of achievement following the successful completion of one's task.

A second type of outcome may be thought of as being administered or managed by elements outside of the task itself. These outcomes, frequently referred to as extrinsic to the job, will here be designated as *externally-administered.* The relation of such outcomes to performance is primarily a function of the organization's ability to measure performance and its ability to link reinforcements to performance (6).

Some empirical evidence supports the argument that task and externally administered outcomes are at least conceptually independent constructs. Lawler and Suttle (33) found that task-administered (internally mediated in their terms) and externally-administered (externally mediated) outcomes loaded on, and essentially defined, separate factors in a sample of retail store department managers. The nature of the interaction of these two types of outcomes as they impact on attitudes and behavior is not entirely clear. Deci (9, 11) and Calder and Staw (4, 5) report that task and externally administered outcomes do exert interaction effects on several dependent variables. Similar findings have been reported by Kruglanski, Riter, Arazi, Agassi, Montegion, Peri and Peretz (31) using an attributional framework and by Kruglanski, Riter, Amitai, Margolin, Shabtai and Zaksh (30) within the context of attribution of causation to either task content or consequences. Contrary evidence has been offered by Hamner and Foster (22). While the two types of outcomes are conceptually, and perhaps empirically, distinct, their impacts upon behavioral and attitudinal dependent variables may not be additive.

Because task-administered outcomes are intimately bound up with doing the job, successful performance is likely to lead to their attainment (i.e., have high instrumentality for intrinsic outcomes) only if the task itself is psychologically meaningful to the performer. Deci (10) hypothesized that instrinsic motivation requires interesting tasks that involve employee participation in job decisions. Lawler (32) postulated that three conditions must be present for a job to provide high instrumentality for the attainment of task-administered outcomes. First, the job must allow the incumbent to receive meaningful feedback so he or she knows how well he or she is performing. Second, the job must require the incumbent to use valued abilities so that successful performance leads to feelings of achievement and accomplishment. Finally, the incumbent must feel that he or she has some responsibility in defining the task goals so that he or she can feel successful if he or she performs well. These comments by Deci and Lawler generally describe jobs with high scope as opposed to low scope tasks. Thus:

Hypothesis 3a: Increases in task scope will increase instrumentality perceptions pertaining to task-administered outcomes.

Frequently, organizations couple task scope change programs with other personnel policy changes such as implementation of management by objectives. These accompanying changes may influence instrumentality perceptions for externally-administered outcomes. There appears little reason to expect that changes in externally administered instrumentality perceptions will result from manipulation of task scope, per se. As a consequence:

Hypothesis 3b: Changes in task scope will not influence instrumentality perceptions regarding externally-administered outcomes.

Increasing task scope may result in greater ambiguity about what constitutes successful performance. Such would be likely, for example, if the increase involved adding activities to the worker's task which, in turn, decreased task closure (e.g., being responsible for the entire product). Greater ambiguity about performance would lower the employee's task-administered instrumentalities if he or she could no longer be as certain about success in performing the job. Greater ambiguity about performance also would probably reduce perceptions of externally-administered instrumentalities since the organization would likely have more difficulty measuring performance and thus more difficulty linking rewards to performance. Thus:

Hypothesis 3c: Hypotheses 3a and 3b will hold only if changes in task scope do not lead to an increase in ambiguity regarding the meaning and measurement of performance.

Valence perceptions—Although increased task scope is likely to be instrumental for obtaining task administered outcomes, there is little reason to believe that variation in task scope will have a direct impact on the perceived attractiveness of these outcomes. Task scope may indirectly influence valence to the extent that it influences the actual reinforcement patterns experienced on the job (e.g., results in the worker earning more pay). However, the evidence is not clear on whether the attainment reinforcements leads to higher or lower valence for the outcome (42). Thus:

Hypothesis 4: Changes in task scope will have little, if any, direct impact on valence perceptions.

Valence of performance—Expectancy theory states that the valence of performance is a positive function of the sum of the valence times instrumentality of second-level (both task and externally-administered) outcomes. It follows from Hypotheses 3a, 3b, and 4 that:

Hypothesis 5: Increases in task scope will increase the valence of performance (solid line in Figure 3).

This impact of task scope is hypothesized to act solely through its impact on the instrumentality perceptions pertaining to task-administered outcomes (Hypothesis 3a). As a consequence, the curve drawn in Figure 3 will apply only to individuals who find task-administered outcomes to be positively valent. There is some evidence that a substantial proportion of workers do not view their work as particularly important beyond the externally-administered outcomes it provides (12, 20, 48). These employees may attach relatively low valence to the outcomes associated with behaving on a job or successfully performing a job.

This evidence suggests that increased task scope will not be uniformly successful in increasing the valence of performance and hence the motivation to perform among all workers. Hackman and Lawler (20) found that the relationship between task scope and quality of performance was significantly higher among workers placing high valence on task-administered outcomes than among workers placing a lower valence on them (although valence of task-administered outcomes was not found to moderate the relation between task scope and quantity of performance or an overall rating of performance effectiveness). Thus, individual differences in motivational responses to variations in task scope should be expected. In addition, responses to tasks of various scopes may change as an employee moves across phases of his or her life style. The absolute and relative deprivation of various needs probably will shift as a function of stage in life (e.g., single, married, children, middle years with spouse working, retirement). Such differences probably will occur across indiviuals at any one point in time and within individuals across time.

Discussion

These hypotheses outline the proposed model in its simplest form. A number of important implications and problems were ignored to highlight the basic issues. Several of these complicating factors are discussed in this section as they relate to an objective definition of task scope and to the use of expectancy theory for making predictions about the performance implications of variations in task scope.

Task Scope Definition

An objective definition of task scope allows for the unambiguous differentiation between variations in task scope and employee perceptions of it. If one is interested in psychological perceptions of task scope, they can be viewed as dependent on task scope.

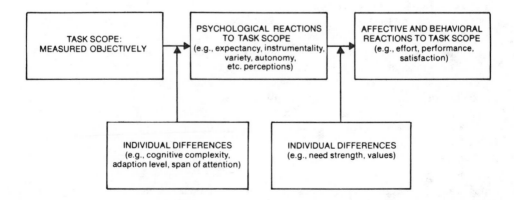

Figure 4. Psychological reactions to task scope as an intervening variable.

Indeed, it may be useful to view psychological reactions as intervening between the task and employee affective and behavioral reactions (see Figure 4).

Such a formulation suggests that future research be directed toward determining the conditions when variability in task scope leads to variability in perceptions of scope and the conditions when changes in these perceptions lead to changes in employee reactions. Both linkages are likely to be moderated by individual differences among employees. Research is just beginning on the second linkage and its moderators (2, 20, 47), but is nonexistent on the first. Yet attempts to change jobs involve manipulation of actual tasks, not perceptions of tasks. Questions of whether these manipulations result in shifts in employee perceptions and subsequent behaviors, and the causes of differences in these shifts, remain largely unanswered.

A second issue suggested by the objective formulation of task scope centers on the consequences of variations in the dimensions of the job that influence task scope. In this article, task scope has been treated as a unidimensional construct, recognizing that the relevant characteristics of the job are actually multidimensional. Some dimensions on which the job may vary probably will have relatively greater impacts on perceptions of task scope and hence motivation, than will others. Similarly, some may interact more strongly, or at least differently, with ability than will others. Research on this issue must await development of an acceptable multidimensional measure of task scope. Theorizing should begin on the probable characteristics of the dimensions as well as their probable relationships with employee ability and perceptions.

Task Scope and Performance

An analysis using expectancy theory suggests that task scope is likely to be related complexly to performance. In the first place, variation in task scope may not be monotonically related to a performance determinant over the whole range of scope variability. For example, some optimum combination of scope was hypothesized to exist for both relative ability (Hypotheses 1a, 1b, and 1c as depicted by X in Figure 2) and expectancy (Hypotheses 2a and 2b as depicted by Y in Figure 3).

Second, the impact of scope may have conflicting impacts on various performance determinants. For example, an increase in scope beyond the present task is likely to have a positive impact on instrumentality perceptions as in Hypothesis 3a (i.e., performance is seen as leading to task-administered outcomes), but a negative impact on expectancy perceptions as noted in Hypothesis 2a.

Third, variation in task scope may simply not appreciably influence certain motivational components. Such a situation was hypothesized regarding instrumentalities of externally-administered outcomes (Hypothesis 3b) which appeared to be heavily influenced by organizational reward systems (41). Similarly, valences of outcomes, both task and externally-administered, are probably largely determined by socialization experiences and reinforcement histories and not structural variables of the organization such as task scope.

Fourth, task scope can influence other organizational factors which, in turn, may influence performance. Variation in task scope (Hypothesis 3c) may influence the performer's ambiguity concerning performance standards. Increases in scope may generate uncertainty about the consequences of effort and the determinants of rewards. Alternatively, increases in task scope may lead to greater information about the organization and its implications for the performer. This increased cognitive content may influence both expectancy (knowing what intensity and direction of efforts lead to measured performances) and instrumentality (knowing what performances lead to rewards). Increased task scope also may increase the interpersonal contact experienced by the task performer. Such an increase may raise or lower the performer's expectancy and instrumentality perceptions depending on such things as: (a) whether the performer's task actually requires the contact and interaction, and (b) whether the other persons with whom contact is increased are involved in defining performance and administering rewards (as in the case of peer review). All of these possibilities suggest that future research efforts move in the direction of greater experimentation, so that controls can be established for these types of unintended consequences that serve to make interpretation of survey findings difficult.

Finally, the pervasive impact of individual differences must continually be kept in mind. Workers differ with respect to relative ability to perform a job. These differences persist even when the workers have been exposed to a common training program (35). Thus, the task scope leading to the highest relative ability may be unique for each worker. Such variability can also be expected regarding valence, instrumentality, and expectancy perceptions.

In summary, concepts and measures of task scope must be developed in terms of environmentally anchored, objectively measureable dimensions and units. There is a need to examine the impact of task scope, so conceived, on performer perceptions—both directly and as moderated by performer characteristics. Both scope and perceptions of scope must be related to the affective and behavioral reactions of performers. In pursuing these objectives, researchers should expect multidimensionality and multiple linkages, and search for individual differences. Environmentally anchored definitions of task scope and cognitive motivational models, like expectancy theory, should aid in these pursuits.

Notes

1. Task scope is here conceived of as incorporating both vertical (enrichment) and horizontal (enlargement) dimensions of the responsibilities and/or activities within a task.

References

1. Anastasi, A. *Differential Psychology*, 3rd ed. (New York: Macmillan, 1958).
2. Blood. M. R., and C. L. Hulin. "Alienation, Environmental Characteristics, and Worker Responses," *Journal of Applied Psychology,* Vol. 51 (1967), 284-290.
3. Brief, A. P., and R. J. Aldag. "Employee Reactions to Job Characteristics: A Constructive Replication," *Journal of Applied Psychology*, Vol. 60 (1975), 182-186.
4. Calder, B. J., and B. M. Staw. "Interaction of Intrinsic and Extrinsic Motivation: Some Methodological Notes," *Journal of Personality and Social Psychology,* Vol. 31 (1975), 76-80.
   Calder, B. J., and B. M. Staw, "Self-perception of Intrinsic and Extrinsic Motivation,"
5. *Journal of Personality and Social Psychology*, Vol. 31 (1975), 599-605.
6. Cummings, L. L., and D. P. Schwab. *Performance in Organizations: Determinants and Appraisal* (Glenview, Illinois: Scott Foresman, 1973).

7. Dachler, H. P., and W. H. Mobley. "Construct Validation of an Instrumentality-Expectancy-Task-Goal Model of Work Motivation: Some Theoretical Boundary Conditions," *Journal of Applies Psychology Monograph*, Vol. 58 (1973), 397-418.

8. Dawis, R. V., G. W. England, and L. H. Lofquist." A Theory of Work Adjustment: A Revision," *Minnesota Studies in Vocational Rehabilitation, Bulletin 47* (Minneapolis, 1968).

9. Deci, E. L. "The Effects of Externally Mediated Rewards on Intrinsic Motivation," *Journal of Personality and Social Psychology,* Vol. 18 (1971), 105-115.

10. Deci, E. L. "The Effects of Contingent and Noncontingent Rewards and Controls on Intrinsic Motivation," *Organizational Behavior and Human Performance*, Vol. 8 (1972), 217-229.

11. Deci, E. L. "Intrinsic Motivation, Extrinsic Reinforcement, and Inequity," *Journal of Personality and Social Psychology,* Vol. 22 (1072), 113-120.

12. Dubin, R., and D. R. Goldman. "Central Life Interests of American Middle Managers and Specialists," *Journal of Vocational Behavior*, Vol. 2 (1972), 133-141.

13. Evans, M. G. "The Effects of Supervisory Behavior on the Path-Goal Relationship," *Organizational Behavior and Human Performance,* Vol. 5 (1970), 277-298.

14. Ford, R. N. *Motivation Through the Work Itself* (New York: American Management Association, 1969).

15. Frieling, E., W. K nnheiser, and R. Lindberg. "Some Results with the German Form of the Position Analysis Questionnaire (PAQ)," *Journal of Applied Psychology,* Vol. 59 (1974), 741-747.

16. Grote, R. C. "Implementing Job Enrichment," *California Management Review,* Vol. 15 (1972), 16-21.

17. Guion, R. M. *Personnel Testing* (New York: McGraw-Hill, 1965).

18. Hackman, J. R. "Nature of the Task as a Determiner of Job Behavior," *Personnel Psychology,* Vol. 22 (1969), 435-444.

19. Hackman, J. R. "On the Coming Demise of Job Enrichment," *Technical Report No. 9* (Department of Administrative Sciences, Yale University, 1974).

20. Hackman, J. R., and E. E. Lawler, Ill. "Employee Reactions to Job Characteristics," *Journal of Applied Psychology Monograph,* Vol. 55 (1971), 259-286.

21. Hackman, J. R., and G. R. Oldham. "Development of the Job Diagnostic Survey," *Journal of Applied Psychology,* Vol. 60 (1975), 159-170.

22. Hamner, W. C., and L. W. Foster. "Are Intrinsic and Extrinsic Rewards Additive? A Test of Deci's Cognitive Theory of Task Motivation," *Academy of Management Proceedings,* 34th Annual Meeting, 1974.

23. Heneman, H. G., III, and D. P. Schwab. "Evaluation of Research on Expectancy Theory Predictions of Employee Performance," *Psychological Bulletin,* Vol. 78 (1972), 1-9.

24. Herzberg, F. "One More Time: How Do You Motivate Employees?" *Harvard Business Review,* Vol. 46 (1968), 53-62.

25. House, R. J. "A Path Goal Theory of Leader Effectiveness," *Administrative Science Quarterly,* Vol. 16, (1971), 321-338.

26. House, R. J., H. J. Shapiro, and M. A. Wahba. "Expectancy Theory as a Predictor of Work Behavior and Attitude: A Re-evaluation of Empirical Evidence," *Decision Sciences,* Vol. 5 (1974), 481-506.

27. Hulin, C. L., and M. R. Blood. "Job Enlargement, Individual Differences and Worker Responses," *Psychological Bulletin,* Vol. 69 (1968), 41-55.

28. Jaques, E. *Equitable Payment* (New York: Wiley, 1961).

29. Jenkins, G. D., Jr., D. A. Nadler, E. E. Lawler, III, and C. Cammann. "Standardized Observations: An Approach to Measuring the Nature of Jobs," *Journal of Applied Psychology,* Vol. 60 (1975), 171-181.

30. Kruglanski, A. W., A. Riter, A. Amitai, B. S. Margolin, L. Shabtai, and D. Zaksh. "Can Money Enhance Intrinsic Motivation? A Test of the Content-Consequence Hypothesis, *Journal of Personality and Social Psychology,* Vol. 31 (1975), 744-750.

31. Kruglanski, A. W., A. Riter, D. Arazi, R. Agassi, J. Montegio, I. Peri, and M. Peretz. "Effects of Task-Intrinsic Rewards upon Extrinsic and Intrinsic Motivation, *Journal of Personality and Social Psychology*, Vol. 31 (1975), 699-705.

32. Lawler, E. E., III. "Effects of Task Factors on Job Attitudes and Behavior (A Symposium), 3. Job Design and Employee Motivation," *Personnel Psychology*, Vol. 22 (1969), 426-435.

33. Lawler, E. E., III, and J. L. Suttle. "Expectancy Theory and Job Behavior," *Organizational Behavior and Human Performance*, Vol. 9, (1973), 482-503.

34. McCormick, E. J., P. R. Jeanneret, and R. C. Mecham. "A Study of Job Characteristics and Job Dimensions as Based on the Position Analysis Questionnaire (PAQ)," *Journal of Applied Psychology,* Vol. 56 (1972), 347-368.

35. McGehee, W., and P. W. Thayer. *Training in Business and Industry* (New York: Wiley, 1961).

36. Mitchell, T. R. "Expectancy Models of Job Satisfaction, Occupational Preference and Effort: A Theoretical, Methodological and Empirical Appraisal," *Psychological Bulletin*, Vol. 81 (1974), 1053-1077.

37. Mitchell, T. R., and A. Biglan. "Instrumentality Theories: Current Uses in Psychology," *Psychological Bulletin,* Vol. 76 (1971), 432-454.

38. Myers, M. S. *Every Employee a Manager: More Meaningful Work Through Job Enrichment* (New York: McGraw-Hill, 1970).

39. Porter, L. W., and E. E. Lawler, III. *Managerial Attitudes and Performance* (Homewood, Illinois: Irwin, 1968).

40. Schwab, D. P. *The Role of Compensation in Motivating High Employee Performance* (Berea, Ohio: American Society for Personnel Administration Foundation, Technical Report, January 1972).

41. Schwab, D. P. "Impact of Alternative Compensation Systems on Pay Valence and Instrumentality Perceptions," *Journal of Applied Psychology,* Vol. 88 (1973), 308-312.

42. Schwab, D. P., and L. L. Cummings. "Employee Performance and Satisfaction with Work Roles: A Review and Interpretation of Theory," *Industrial Relations*, Vol. 9 (1970), 408-430.

43. Scott, W. E., Jr. "Activation Theory and Task Design," *Organizational Behavior and Human Performance,* Vol. 1 (1966), 3-30.

44. Turner, A. N., and P. R. Lawrence. *Industrial Jobs and the Worker* (Boston: Harvard University, Division of Research, Graduate School of Business Administration, 1965).

45. United States Employment Service. *Dictionary of Occupational Titles: Vol. 1. Definition of Titles, Vol. II. Occupational Classification,* 3rd ed. (Washington, D. C.: U. S. Government Printing Office, 1965).

46. Vroom, V. H. *Work and Motivation* (New York: Wiley, 1964).

47. Wanous, J. P. "Individual Differences and Reactions to Job Characteristics," *Journal of Applied Psychology* Vol. 59 (1974), 616-622.

48. Wilensky, H. L. "Varieties of Work Experience," in E. Borow (Ed.), *Man in a World at Work* (Boston: Houghton Mifflin, 1964), 125-154.

TECHNOLOGY AND JOB SATISFACTION

LEONARD R. SAYLES
GEORGE STRAUSS

Automation and Continuous-process Technology

Perhaps a definition of automation is in order since the term has come into such widespread use. Although there is no single definition, most authors stress the following components: (1) use of high-speed computers for data processing or control, (2) use of "closed-loop feedback" techniques to facilitate self-control by machines themselves, (3) mechanization of transfer operations, (4) increased use of multiple-purpose equipment, and (5) the combination of jobs and work units in larger self-contained processes.[1]

Detroit Automation

Much "automation" leaves the intrinsic characteristics of jobs unchanged. Workers merely operate more productive machinery that positions the work, checks its accuracy, and transports materials from stage to stage automatically. But the operator continues to be a machine-tender, and a sharp status line continues to separate him from the engineers who install and maintain the equipment and the managers who supervise it. For the most part, this is what is called "Detroit Automation." Jobs may be somewhat less physically demanding, but there is also more pressure associated with the complicated, expensive and potentially very vulnerable processing techniques.[2] Should something go wrong, a great deal of production is lost. As a consequence, supervision may be even closer than before the changes.

Continuous-Process Technology

Something close to true automation does, however, exist today in some plants in the chemical and petroleum industries and in electrical power generation and steel manufacturing. Automation of this sort is most easily adapted to industries in which the product can flow continuously (particularly as a liquid or gas) from entering raw material to finished product through a number of interlinked stages. Continuous steel strip mills and electrical generating plants, where fuel or water power is used to make steam or is applied directly to power turbines, approximate the continuous flows of a chemical plant. In all such factories an employee spends much of his time monitoring gauges and control instruments, and his major work activities come only during breakdowns, and start-up and change-over periods.

Such work contrasts sharply with that of craftsmen and machine operators. As we have seen, a craftsman utilizes manual, motor, perceptual and conceptual skills. He manipulates materials, his own body, and ideas. Engineers have eliminated the conceptual and perceptual element from the job of the semiskilled machine-tender and the assembly-line worker, though they must still develop some manual dexterity and motor skill, but far less than the craftsmen. Automated employees, however, need few physical skills, but they are expected to use their "heads."[3]

Type of Worker		Skills Required		
Craftsman	Manual	Motor	Conceptual	Perceptual
Machine-tender and assembly-line worker	Manual	Motor		
Automation worker			Conceptual	Perceptual

Interest, Variety, and Movement

Most jobs in continuous-process plants require an irregular combination of surface attention and depth attention. The *job cycle* is a relatively long one. Dials have to be checked and adjustments made when readings are "off standard." In one case in a chemical plant, 50 different instruments are monitored every two hours.[4]

The pace of work is uneven, but in part it can be adjusted to the comfort, convenience, and natural "rhythms" of the employees. Although the checking operations must be periodic, they need not be done precisely on time:

Sometimes when it's close to the time for 2 o'clock readings, we might have soup on the stove. You can eat the soup first and do the work later or take the readings at 1:45 and then eat your soup.[5]

In utility generating stations and in some parts of a refinery, the operators may be confined to a control room. In a chemical plant, however, they must take lengthy walks through widely dispersed equipment.

Aside from monitoring operations, the other part of automated jobs consists of handling unexpected breakdowns (and sometimes assisting in regular starting-up and shutting-down activities). In this phase depth attention is called for, and time is of utmost importance. Because of the enormous costs involved in idle equipment, management expects everyone to pitch in energetically when there is trouble. But if there are going to be sufficient personnel available for such emergencies, when things are going smooth, there is of necessity going to be a good deal of idle time.

Unlike a typical mass-production plant where a breakdown is a welcome relief, here a stoppage is a sign of failure. It is also a period of excitement, even drama. The unexpected breaks up the monotony. Locating, diagnosing, and fixing troubles can be absorbing, even though breakdowns also call for very hard work.

Accomplishment, Autonomy, and Identification

"Continuous-processing technology may serve to reverse the historic trend toward the greater division of labor and specialization."[6] It is this involvement in a tangible, complete activity (refining oil, producing electric power) that produces job interest and the satisfaction which grows out of meaningful activity. Employees feel *responsible* for keeping highly expensive technology going. Rather than concentrate on a small, essentially meaningless task, the employee develops a sense of commitment to the total process. Thus, he gains the satisfaction of knowing that in some measure he contributes to an observable, finished product:

> The worker's role changes from providing skills to accepting responsibility . . . the very definition of responsibility as a job requirement involves a meaningful connection between the worker's own function and the goals of entire enterprise.[7]

In contrast to the mass-production factory, there are not endless, impersonal rows of people repeating small tasks. Instead, relatively few men patrol and control a vast array of massive equipment, or they oversee a control room which is like a command post. Here employees accept some of the functions that supervisors exercise in other technologies.

Their sense of growth and development and importance is further enhanced by the career ladders that develop naturally. A refinery still or a production unit in a chemical plant is handled by a small crew which is differentiated in skill and experience; the lowest-ranking employee is usually called a helper and the top-skilled person can be a head operator stillman or crew chief. Because of the close interdependence of their jobs and the need to be familiar with a variety of complex tasks, new employees are brought in as part of general labor gangs and progress through a series of jobs as their experience increases and they evidence willingness to accept responsibility. Each successive job enables them to get a broader view of operations.

And here management, far more than in craft or mass-production industries, is willing to invest in continuing training. Hence, most employees experience a sense of steady progress in status and earnings. Highly important by-products are, for the employee, substantial job security and, for management, a workforce showing unusually high identification with the company. Evidence of this opportunity to enjoy a real career and to progress is provided by wage differentials. In continuous-processing plants, unlike mass-production with its inherent limitations, jobs are arrayed in ascending ladders and there are considerable opportunities for promotions and steps upward in earnings.

The top skilled crew-chief positions involve enormous responsibility and challenge in these industries. As an example, let us look at the chief melter in a newly computerized oxygen-furnace steel plant. Premixed, preweighted ingredients are transported to a huge pressure cooker (the furnace's converter), which heats them for about an hour and is then tapped. Here is a description of the work of the employee who handles the operation, Mr. Peral:

> Mr. Peral directs operations with the computer from a control room several feet from the vessel. He is in touch with his eight men through a loudspeaker system. . . . To make a batch of steel, called a heat, Mr. Peral first has his computer figure out the ingredients, based on orders for specific grades of steel. Then the vessel is tilted to the "charging" side. The press of a button sets off 75 to 80 tons of scrap—. . . . How does Mr. Peral know when it's time to tap? "You've got to know your end points," he says. "You notice how the carbon flame above the vessel is dying? It's about ready." . . . Mr. Peral

orders the vessel tilted again toward the charging side. Protected by a metal shield, two of his assistants insert a long pole called a thermocouple into the vessel. . . . If the mixture is not hot enough, the vessel is turned upright again and heated some more. If it is too hot, Mr. Peral will have to have a look at it. . . . There is no device yet that will tell the melter about the heat that Mr. Peral can discover merely by peering into it through purple-tinted cobalt glasses. To Mr. Peral the process is "fascinating." . . . "On this process," he says, "I learn something new about steelmaking every day."[8]

Here, as elsewhere, machines do not completely displace employees; a number of critical jobs can still be performed more effectively by human beings.

The psychological satisfactions associated with these jobs has been highlighted by a recent study of an automated electricity-generating plant:

It would appear that company managements through their design engineers are now in a position to restore to our working population some of the pride and satisfaction that stems from performing interesting and challenging jobs. Rather than making men adjuncts to machines, automation seems to be capable of utilizing workers as human beings with a capacity for intellectual understanding.[9]

Job Pressures and Relations to Management

Under automation the speed-up that occurs during breakdowns or changeover periods is not resented as efforts by management to get more work done. Here the employees can see for themselves when hard work is required and the supervisor doesn't have to push them. Also, as we have seen, the technical leadership in these situations often is provided by the top-ranking member of the crew, the chief operator. Since he works right alongside the other members of the gang and shares their values and difficulties, his demands are likely to be interpreted as reasonable.[10]

Mistakes can be terribly expensive, so employees cannot be rushed or excessively pressured by management. Although a craft worker can redo poor-quality work and an assembler's mistakes can be remedied by a repairman farther down the line, an error by a continuous-process employee may cost thousands of dollars before it can be rectified. Checking and repairing involve mental processes which cannot be coordinated by stop watch.

In many circumstances, management is pleased when employees are not working hard—this indicates that things are going well. If the employees work wisely and effectively, there are few or no breakdowns. Under these conditions both employee relaxation and company product are maximized! One company considered developing an incentive payment plan under which employees would receive bonuses in proportion to how *little* time they had to work. Their work time was almost directly proportional to the amount of breakdown and loss of production, much of which reflected lack of employee foresight.

There are other reasons why management seldom appears oppressive to employees under this type of technology. Since at least the top-ranking workers are highly experienced and well informed, their opinions are often sought out by supervisors and by engineers. Particularly when pilot-plant operations are conducted, employees are likely to have contact with levels of management above their immediate supervisor and with staff engineers. Thus, in a modern continuous-process steel mill, there is less status distinction between skilled hourly workers and management and more personal relationships than are found in an automobile assembly plant, where relationships are highly formal and primarily limited to order-giving by the immediate manager.

Continuous-process industry is characterized by better human relations between management and employees over-all than those that prevail in other technologies. Since workers only indirectly control output, pressure on people is at a minimum. "The process foreman's job was to arrange things within limits, set by the plant, which both he and the operators understood and accepted."[11] And the small number of subordinates per manager helps improve human relations.

Since labor costs make up a much smaller percentage of total costs in automated plants than in nonautomated plants, management can provide more generous wages and fringe benefits. More important, since these plants are designed to operate with a minimum of employees, nearly all of whom are required no matter what the scale of operations, employees are less expendable during periods of recession. Furthermore, management as we have noted has a major investment in the career training of its workforce. The employees sense that they are not dealt with as a "variable cost," something that can be let go if business activity declines. Instead, they see themselves as having careers that will last their working life.[12]

Hours of Work

Many automated jobs require shift work and this is a source of dissatisfaction. To get maximum use of expensive equipment, it must be used round-the-clock. And, chemical plants and utilities operate day and night because their processes can't be turned "on" and "off" except at great cost.

Though a few employees like shift work, because it enables them to make alternative use of the daytime, most find that late hours interfere with normal family and social life. Many firms rotate shifts. This procedure avoids charges of discrimination and prevents jockeying for favorable schedules, but it requires employees to get used to constantly changing sleeping and waking hours, not an easy thing to do as anyone knows who has flown across a number of time zones.[13]

Social Relations

Most employees in automated industries work in teams. On some chemical operations there may be only two or three employees per shift; on others ten or so. The employees work closely together and must develop the ability to coordinate their efforts and help each other. In turn, close social relations develop on the team which may carry over into the community.

Whereas social-group boundaries are often ambiguous and vague in traditional industrial plants, they are more clear-cut here. Where hundreds of employees do similar operations under one roof or where an assembly line snakes for a mile or two past thousands working side by side, it is difficult for employees to identify with a specific group of fellow workers. The limited number of employees under automation and their specific relationship to a given process serves to unite a social group which has the same boundaries as the work unit.[14]

We should not exaggerate the beneficial effects of automation on social relations, however. Some automated plants have only a small number of employees, widely dispersed, who rarely see each other. Isolated locations plus noise may make difficult all but limited conversation.

Summary: Automation and Job Satisfaction

It would be a mistake to assume that all job-satisfaction problems are solved by the introduction of continuous-process automation. For there is substantial monotony associated with watching and waiting. Future research will likely emphasize the psychological reactions to this *surface-attention problem* since many military (for instance, missile bases and space ships) as well as civilian activities require "dial-watching" tasks to be performed over long periods of time.

> Automation often requires a very high-level person for one hour a week and somebody who is capable of doing nothing for the other 39 hours. . . . You are going to have trouble keeping people from getting a kind of "turnpike fatigue" running one of these machines.[15]

In addition employees are likely to feel substantial anxiety about making costly errors.

More than balancing these dissatisfactions, however, are the through-the-job satisfactions derived from the relatively long work cycles, flexible work rhythms, and the opportunities to work as a team in emergencies. In fact, the entire relationship between management and workers is improved over what obtained in traditional manufacturing: There is more two-way communication and mutual understanding. People handle problems as they arise and there is little need for management to impose quotas and work standards. Employees can see themselves progressing over time on a career through a series of graded job steps. Relatively small numbers and management's investment in training give a sense of individualism which contrasts sharply with the impersonality of the traditional sprawling factory.

True automation is really the opposite of Taylorism and scientific management's mass-production methods. The former involves looking at work processes as a whole and giving employees a broader view and wider responsibilities. Mechanization and mass production foster a piecemeal approach: speeding up a machine here, eliminating an arm motion there, saving an operation some place else. It is hardly any wonder that employee reactions to these widely different technologies vary so dramatically.

A Note: Unskilled Work and Floating Labor

Automation is having one of its most profound effects in helping to eliminate some of those jobs that used to be filled by completely unskilled, often temporary, employees. Jobs such as those of yard gangs, sweepers, and loaders used to be reserved for "floating labor" who move endlessly from job to job and sometime from region to region. Lacking education, or handicapped by membership in a minority group, they are disqualified from the better jobs. Experience has "taught" them that they have little chance to get ahead, that there is no point even in trying. Just to hold on to what they have is hard enough. When they find a job they work until they get enough to meet their minimum needs, and when they are unemployed their friends support them. Immediate pleasures are their only goal. They show little "drive" or "ambition."

> [Indeed,] only when one knows where his next week's or next month's shelter will come from, can he and his children afford to go in for long-term education and training, the endless search for opportunities, and the tedious apple polishing that the attainment of higher skills and occupational status requires.[16]

Since security and economic advancement mean little to these workers, they look for jobs that provide independence and a feeling of being one's own boss. They may not amount to much by middle-class standards, but they retain the freedom of telling off the boss and quitting their job whenever they want to.[17] Thus, in terms of commitment they represent the antithesis of the employee attitudes that can be fostered by continuous-process automation and its career lines. . . .

Notes and References

1. James Bright, *Automation and Management* (Boston: Harvard Business School, Division of Research, 1958); Floyd Mann and L. Richard Hoffman, *Automation and the Worker* (New York: Holt, Rinehart and Winston, 1960), p. 3; Charles R. Walker, *Toward the Automatic Factory* (New Haven, Conn.: Yale University Press, 1957).
2. *Cf.* William Faunce, "Automation in the Automobile Industry," *American Sociological Review*, Vol. 23, No. 4 (August 1958), pp. 401-407.
3. The table is adapted from Joan Woodward, *Industrial Organization: Theory and Practice* (London: Oxford University Press, 1965), pp. 63-64.
4. Robert Blauner, *Alienation and Freedom* (Chicago: University of Chicago Press, 1964), p. 134.
5. *Ibid.*, p. 138.
6. *Ibid.*, p. 143.
7. *Ibid.*
8. *The New York Times*, March 18, 1965, p. 43 and p. 50.
9. Mann and Hoffman, *op. cit.*, pp. 205-206.
10. One article suggests that leadership exercised by working, "inside" leaders was characteristic of man's earliest work groups: F. L. W Richardson, "Managing Man's Animal Nature," *Pittsburgh Business Review*, Vol. 34, No. 11 (December 1964), p. 4.
11. Joan Woodward, *Management and Technology* (London: HMSO, 1960), p. 30.
12. Of course, this assumes that the employee exhibits reasonable energy and learning ability. In recent years some oil refineries have had to cope with what they termed "obsolete" employees, often through early retirement.
13. For a more complete treatment of the total subject of working hours see Clyde Dankert, Floyd Mann, and Herbert Northrop, eds., *Hours of Work* (New York: Harper and Row, 1965).
14. In Chapter 16 we shall see that many work frictions are caused by work environments in which the social group contains other members than the work group which must coordinate itself.
15. P. L. Cook, Jr., "Social and Economic Effects of Automation," *Twenty First Annual*

Midwest Conference on Industrial Relations (Chicago: Graduate School of Business, University of Chicago, 1955), p. 10.

16. Allison Davis, "The Motivation of Underprivileged Workers," in William F. Whyte, ed., *Industry and Society* (New York: McGraw-Hill, 1946), p. 89.

17. See Richard Centers, "Motivation Aspects of Occupational Stratification," *Journal of Social Psychology*, Vol. 28 (November 1948), pp. 187-217.

THE HUMAN EFFECTS OF BUDGETING SYSTEMS ON MANAGEMENT

HENRY L. TOSI

If there is any single factor which makes the presence of accountants felt in organizations it is the budget. Every manager lives with a budget. Budgets represent the intensely impersonal character of bureaucratic controls and are the target of criticism by those who must live with them. Basically, the negative connotations associated with budgets probably stem from the fact that they tell a manager what he can do and what he cannot do. They tell him how many dollars he is allowed to spend. In short, the budget represents a constraint on decision making imposed by others. This constraint serves the specific function of managerial control. The manager who is authorized to spend a particular amount of funds is expected to do so in the fashion specified in the budget: X dollars can be spent for advertising, Y dollars may be spent for personnel, and Z dollars can be spent for equipment. The budget is a device by which managers at higher levels, carrying out the managerial planning function, can translate objectives into quantified dimensions of dollars and time and communicate them to lower organizational levels.

A budget, then, may be defined as a specification of how and at what rate a manager may expend resources to meet the responsibilities associated with his job. The determination of these expenditure levels and rates are, for the most part, influenced strongly by the desires of managers at higher levels of the organization to ensure that the expenditures fall within desired and specified limits so the resources expended do not exceed limits that result ultimately in ineffectiveness.

The budget is a systemic factor. A systemic factor, as used here, refers to a part of the formal structural system of the organization which affects and conditions behavior. It is impersonal and, in general, applies to all members of an organizational unit in a fairly even-handed way. Rules and policies, the nature of formal authority, and job design are specifications of behavior which become embodied in a system to affect behavior

Henry L. Tosi, "The Human Effects of Budgeting Systems on Management," pp. 53-63, *MSU Business Topics*, Autumn 1974. Reprinted by permission of the publisher, Division of Research, Graduate School of Business Administration, Michigan State University.

independent of differences in human beings. As a systemic factor, the budget is part of the formal system of organizations which expends large amounts of resources. It is an instrument used by managers. In order to understand its effects, the nature of the instrument must be considered as well as the manner in which human beings devise and use it.

The budget is an inanimate factor brought to life by human use. But, it has major significance—it is a critical vehicle in the general systemic structure of the organization. This vehicle, the budget, takes on this significance because it is: a planning and control device which is relatively easy to alter; a mechanism through which authority may be increased, decreased, delegated, or recentralized; a document which is seductively appealing as a basis for evaluation since it is quantified; and an ever-present factor in the life of a manager.

As *a planning and control device*, the budget is well known. However, it is a device which is relatively easy to alter, at least on the surface. Operating budgets may be cut back, expanded, or otherwise redirected during operating periods. Many times these budget changes occur at the stroke of a pen as a response to pressures for efficiency. Cuts are merely communicated to lower levels with the requirement: "Live with it!" In this way executives at higher levels at least have the illusion that they are managing the organization below them.

This characteristic, the flexibility of the budget, is related to another of its important attributes. It can be a powerful mechanism for the redistribution of power in an organization. Managers are always prodded to delegate more, to participate, to involve lower levels, and so on. The budget can be used to accomplish these goals. By simply increasing both the amount of funds and the discretion over them, power of lower-level managers can be increased. Recentralization of power occurs when a manager no longer has discretion to expend funds—when that decision is made at a higher level.

Perhaps the most important attribute of the budget is that it is a numerical presentation of the expenditure plans of an organization. This is both advantageous and insidious. It is advantageous because it provides a guideline for assessing how well an individual manager performs against a set of targets. At the same time, it is insidious in that all too often evaluators lose sight of the significance of other factors and merely assess how well the manager met his budget, as if it were created initially with such precision as to be a perfect measure.

Finally, like the poor, the budget is always with us. Managers are constantly bombarded with information about "expenditures as a percent of budget to-date," "excesses," and so on. Monthly, weekly, and perhaps even daily reports emanate from the comptroller's office with such regularity that they may begin to lose utility as a management tool.

The Budget and Motivation

There is no need to belabor the issue of the budget as a control mechanism and, more specifically, how it ties into the managerial function of motivation. Rather, the focus here is on how the budget is related to the psychological *concept* of motivation, as opposed to the *managerial process* of motivation. Since it is used by most managers, the budget will have different effects. These will arise from the nature, content, and use of the budget itself, as well as individual differences—personalities and needs of managers, for example.

The *use* of the budget has an impact on people. It affects both what they do and how they feel. It can be used by a manager to provide either rigid or loose constraints for his subordinates. It can provide a manager with a specific, rather than a less precise, set of goals. It can provide relatively objective criteria for evaluation of performance. It is generally because of this that the argument is made that the budget can have motivational effects.

Let us examine, however, the typical meaning behind the term *motivation* when used in this sense. In general, I would argue that to say the purpose of a budget is to motivate behavior (to achieve goals) is equivalent to the notion of control expressed earlier. The managerial function of motivation is manipulative in nature. It requires that the manager define the environment in such a way as to ensure that people do what he wants them to do. In short, he would like to have a reasonably high level of predictive accuracy that his subordinates will act in a way most likely to achieve their goals. And what devices does he use? Job descriptions, procedures, rules, policies, persuasion, and budgets. As such, the manager attempts to provide a series of contraints, pressures, or what otherwise might be regarded as conditions to obtain *desired* performance.

Before proceeding further, an important point must be made. Manipulative strategies, as defined here, should not be regarded as good or bad in themselves. Their goodness or badness depends upon whether the person ultimately is placed in a position in which he would not have chosen to be if he had some relative degree of autonomy in the situation. To be motivated by an attractive woman to ask her to dinner may be entirely pleasant and consistent with one's own desires. To be motivated by one's superior to perform a potentially illegal and unethical act is certainly another question.

Psychological View of Motivation

The term *motivation* has a different meaning psychologically. It means an "inner state that energizes, activates, or moves . . . directs or channels behavior toward goals. In short, a motive results in and hence can be inferred from purposive means end behavior."[1] Essentially, the individual behaves or thinks in such a way as to reduce a tension that is created when there is some discrepancy between a condition that he believes should be and a state that either exists or potentially may exist.

Psychologically, then, motivation is inferred from the case when an organism behaves in a fashion to minimize the discrepancy, or reduce the tension. But, what causes the tension to exist? It could be a result of extreme pressures or changes in the "objective" world that induce tension or anxiety, such as a commitment from a superior that outstanding performance will result in a promotion, which is perhaps a highly desired end state a person might want. Or the tension might arise from the internal motives of the individual, over which an external agent may have little influence, such as a case where a promotion is offered, but the individual does not value it highly since it would require a change in the life style he desires to maintain.

It is precisely this problem which makes it difficult to motivate others. It is difficult, if not impossible, to get into the heads of other human beings and change their motive, or needs, in such a way as to induce precisely the amount and kind of anxiety or tension that would result in the behavior that a manager deems desirable.

A Basic Assumption

Budgets are continuous factors in organizational life. They have a life cycle that is regenerated on a regular basis, usually annually. This article will analyze how managers live with budgets. The kind of budget which exists, it will be assumed here, contains two general item sets:

1) *Recurrent items*. Ongoing activities of an organizational unit will be refunded periodically. It is unlikely that the basic functions of a unit will change from period to period. Activities in the future will be similar to those that have been conducted in the past. Perhaps the most important facet of these types of activities is the *level* of funding. Increases or decreases in dollars allocated for manpower or materials require an adjustment of previous behavior patterns, but not the development of new ones. For example, reducing the number of allowable man-hours for a given activity means that a more efficient way must be discovered to do what an organizational unit already has a great deal of experience in doing.

2) *New Projects*. When a budget contains appropriations for new functions another problem exists. In this case, the specific level of expenditure is important, but also the particular type of expenditure. If, for instance, a unit is given additional responsibility for data-processing functions, then budget allocation levels affect not only the nature of the equipment, but also the type of personnel and other resources which may be needed.

Human Effects of Budgeting

In order to examine the behavioral consequences of the budgeting process, the sequence of activities which produces the budget, the budget itself (as an instrument), and the use of that device must be considered.

In the first stage, *budget development*, are those activities which take place to produce the final document. Managers meet with subordinates, projections of expenditures are formulated, evaluated, consolidated, and coordinated. Competition occurs between units for a given quantity of resource commitments. Finally, from this process the budget emerges. The *budget*, in a second stage, is a set of quantified goals. It is used to provide guidance to subordinate units. The goals may be specifically stated. The amount of latitude the manager has over resource allocations may be narrow or broad. Finally, the budget can be *used* as a standard of comparison to evaluate performance as a basis for rewarding managers. A consideration of the effects of these three stages in the budgeting process follows.

Budget Development

A budget is, after all, a document which allocates resources among different units in an organization. It is a reasonable stand to take here that the resources are scarce, and hence there is likely to be some competition among units for increased amounts both relative to their past funding levels and relative to other units. J. Pfeffer and G. Salancik examined the budgeting process at the University of Illinois to find predictors of "the proportional allocation of discretionary resources to the various departments of the University."[2] They examined several dependent variables such as the power of departments, the work load, and the national reputation of departments. The general hypothesis was that to the extent that a department had power, measured by presence in university committees, it would have an advantage in the budgetary process regardless of its work load. In general, they found support for this hypothesis and concluded that subunit power affects the allocation of resources within the organization.

While this is an extremely plausible hypothesis, *a priori*, there are other characteristics of the budgeting process which give rise to problems. If one assumes that allocations of compensation are representative forms of budgeting decisions, then some inferences might be drawn from the extensive pay research reported by E. Lawler, who states that:

> One of the findings that has consistently appeared in the research on pay secrecy is that managers tend to have incorrect information about the pay of other managers in the organization. Specifically, there is a general tendency for them to overestimate the pay of managers around them. For example, in one organization the average raise given was 6 percent, yet the managers believe it was 8 percent, and the larger their raise was, the larger they believed the other people's raises were. This had the effect of wiping out much of the motivational force of the differential reward system that was actually operating in the company. Almost regardless of how well the manager was performing, he felt he was getting less than the average raise. This problem was particularly severe among the high performers . . . they did not believe that pay was in fact based upon merit.[3]

In the paragraph above, substitute *budget allocation* for *pay*. The effects are probably the same. The argument that one can draw from the work of Lawler and from Pfeffer and Salancik is that since the budgeting process is very likely to be relatively closed and secret, allocations are likely to be based on power as well as the amount of work to be done, and that these factors give rise to a high level of anxiety for those managers who are involved. This is especially so since the successful achievement of organizational goals, and perhaps individual goals as well, depends upon one having adequate resources.

Results of Anxiety

The nature of the anxiety experienced in the budgeting process consists of a fear that there will be inequitable or inadequate distribution of resources.

This will lead to one or more of the following reactions by managers: political behavior to increase power, dysfunctional reactions toward budget units, overstatement of needs, and development of covert information systems.

Political behavior. Managers may attempt to increase their power in an organization by increased political behavior. This may take the form of withholding important information until the last minute to indicate its significance. It may lead to excessively ingratiating behavior toward superiors or those in positions of influence. Providing favors beyond the normal courtesies and requirements of the work assignment also may be a frequent strategy.

According to Pfeffer and Salancik however, political power is represented by influence to change resource allocations. This means that managers may need somehow to obtain a substantial increase in credibility with decision makers. It may be much more difficult in a business organization, which is less democratic than a university, which was the object of their study.[4]

Dysfunctional reactions toward budget units. Perceived inequity in the allocation of resources may trigger negative reactions toward those units responsible for the collection of budget data and budget preparation. The controller's office, probably consisting of a group of staff specialists, is likely to have the major responsibility for putting together the final figures. These specialists may end up bearing the brunt of criticism since they are more convenient targets than line managers. After all, an individual's superior will be responsible for promotion decisions. It may be unwise, therefore, to alienate him by directing aggression toward him.

If this mode of adaptation becomes at all widespread, it will hinder the effectiveness of the budgeting group's operation. It will become increasingly difficult for it to interact with other units so that the budget makers may obtain accurate and timely information.

Overstatement of needs. In order to protect his perceived equitable share of future resources, the manager will pad his budget estimates. He learns quickly that cuts are made in requested amounts and, as a need to be equitable, all units will suffer relatively similar cuts in their budgets. Therefore, the honest manager, estimating his needs with some degree of accuracy, is punished for his honesty. He quickly learns that an overstatement of requirements helps him secure his fair share.

Covert information systems. If there is a high degree of secrecy regarding budget allocations to other units, managers will seek to make some estimate of how they fare in relation to the others. As Lawler concluded, they are likely to overestimate these amounts. Nevertheless, because the allocations may represent something other than need—that is, the power one has—information will be sought. Secretaries, staff members from the budget offices, and peers will be prodded for information. A network may develop which provides some information. The danger here is that there is likely to be relatively inaccurate information on this network, magnifying instead of minimizing the problem.

Use of participation for anxiety reduction. It has been generally accepted that acceptance of budget requirements may be substantially increased through participative management strategies. J. March and H. Simon have concluded that participation may minimize problems when there is a "felt need for joint decision-making."[5] Certainly if power is a major factor in determining budget allocations, then a participative strategy is warranted.

Participation, in the sense used here, refers to a process in which an individual or group can influence or change decisions. Of course, by moving toward more participation in budget development and away from unilateral, or relatively unilateral, determination of budget levels there is likely to be a *redistribution* of power among those groups involved.

Effects of participation are perhaps among the most widely examined in the psychological literature. They are fairly strongly based empirically, so that they can be imputed with respect to budgets. Basically, the empirical literature shows that there is a strong positive relationship between participation and job satisfaction.[6] But, more specifically with regard to budgets, D. Searfoss and R. Monczka examined how participation affects perceived commitment. They found a highly significant positive relationship between perceived participation and the goal-directing effort element of motivation. Their research also found that involvement in the decision-making and goal setting processes will result in greater personal commitment to the organization and its goals.[7]

However, this author and S. Carroll suggest that participative strategies should be a more general managerial activity rather than limited to budgeting alone. In their study of management by objectives they found that *subordinate participation in setting goals* did not result in higher levels of perceived goal success or effort nor in more favorable attitudes toward the program or superior.[8] However, general influence over other aspects of the job seemed to have positive effects. This suggests that it may be difficult to ask managers to participate in budgeting and then to act unilaterally in other areas.

John M. Ivancevich indirectly speaks to this point and has examined how management by objectives was implemented in two companies with different strategies, one by external consultants and the other by the managers themselves. He concluded that there was more improvement in need satisfaction scores where top-level managers were actively involved in the implementation program.[9]

The conclusion, therefore, is to increase involvement, participation, and influence of managers in goal-setting or budgeting activities. As stated earlier, the results are likely to be positive, but some very practical problems present themselves. These are: individual reactions to participation, difference in competence of managers, and organizational levels.

Individual reactions to participation. Vroom found that highly authoritarian managers reacted less positively to high participation than did low authoritarians, although this author found there were no moderating effects attributable to authoritarianism. However, the relationship between participation and commitment is not a simple one. Indeed, it has been found that self-esteem can moderate the relationship between subordinate influence over goals and increased effort; also, self-assurance can affect the relationship between the level of goal difficulty and effort increases. Therefore, even though the results are somewhat scattered, it seems clear that individuals may react differently to different degrees of participation.[10]

Differences in subordinate competences. If participation is influence, and influence means the ability to change decisions, then, one factor which may limit the amount of influence is the competence of the subordinate. More competent individuals will likely have greater credibility and trust with superiors, leading very likely to more decision-making discretion.

Organizational levels. It has been concluded theoretically and demonstrated empirically that one determinant of the amount of influence is organizational level. The amount of influence in goal setting is higher for the higher levels of management.[11] Searfoss and Monczka found that the level of perceived participation in the budget process increases significantly as a person rises in the management hierarchy from foreman to general foreman. They wrote ''it appears that at the lower level of supervision in the sample studied, foremen are allowed only a minimal level of participation.''[12] This led these authors to the conclusion that it would be extremely doubtful that foreman would accept, and internalize, the budget as a meaningful goal.

Thus, organizational level is a constraint limiting participation. Job and organization redesign strategies, rather than simply exhorting more participation, might be the order of the day to increase participation and involvement.

Summary. In any event, it seems clear that participation in the budgeting process can be a promising method for anxiety reduction and increased involvement. The document that emerges will likely be more generally accepted if it developed through a process in which line managers are involved, and with apparent activity support by top management.

The Budget

The outcome of the *preparation* stage, with its attendant anxiety, is a budget. Basically, a budget is simply a listing of physical and human resources with authorized expenditure levels, which a manager uses in performing his job. It is a formal document which constrains or regulates an individual manager's behavior in such a way as to increase the predictability that a subordinate will act in a particular way. The assumption is that if resources are expended as allocated, satisfactory performance will result.

The Budget as "Structure".

R. M. Stogdill defines *structure in interaction* in terms of the

differential regularities of action and reaction exhibited in the positions in a system. The *position* of a group member becomes differentiated from other positions by virtue of the fact that the member exhibits predictable patterns of performance which elicit predictable responses from other members.[13]

A budget may be viewed as an attempt to structure the behavior system to obtain a predictable response. It is one factor which contributes to the total group structure of an organization. Stogdill formulates some hypotheses about the effects of various levels of structure on attitudes and performance. These ideas can be useful in understanding the general effects of budgets which provide different levels of freedom and discretion in the managerial environment. He concludes that structured groups tend to be more productive than unstructured ones, but he argues that high levels of structure may have negative motivational effects.

Little is gained from increasing the motivation of members if their roles are so closely structured as to deny them the right to initiate action. Granting freedom of action cannot be effective if roles are so poorly defined that members do not know what they are expected to do. Intermediate degrees of structure and control permit member motivation to be released in the form of group morale.[14]

From this one can conclude that a budget can have positive effects, providing a manager with some degree of role clarity, but that if it is too restrictive or too loose it may be counterproductive motivationally.

The Budget as a Set of Goals

What is the manner in which budgets affect performance? If it is argued that budget allocations are goals for which a manager will work, then an abundance of empirical literature on the subject of goals can provide some extremely useful insights into how budgets can affect performance.

The effects of goals. Some of the most extensive work on the relationship between goals and performance has been reported by E. Locke, who reasoned that if goals regulate performance, then hard goals should produce high performance. The results of several studies he conducted, as well as other research he cites, leads him to conclude that: "The results are unequivocal: The harder the goal the higher the level of performance."[15]

However, and perhaps more relevant to the problem of the budget, he also found that when subjects had specific goals, as would be the case with budget allocations, they were more likely to do better than when they had general or nonspecific goals.

In their management by objectives research, Carroll and Tosi also examined the effects of goals. They found:

> The results indicate that for all types of subordinates, the superior should make sure that the goals established focus on significant and important areas of departmental need . . . are clearly stated, and that the relative importance of the various goals is pointed out.
>
> The difficulty of goals, however, was not always related to positive reactions to the program. For example, difficult goals were related to decreased effort in managers with low self-assurance and among less mature and experienced managers. However, difficult goals were associated with increased effort among managers with high self-assurance, managers who associated their performance with the reward system, and mature managers.[16]

W. Turcotte conducted research comparing

> two large state agencies with homogeneous output measures, one . . . more effective than the other . . . over a two-year period, economic measures, goal setting, particularly budget goal setting . . . the type and emphasis of formal control systems were studied.[17]

His results are consistent with that of Locke and with Carroll and Tosi (1973) with regard to difficult goals. Turcotte concluded that

> demanding objectives, quantitatively expressed and understood by the executive branch, legislature, and the agency were essential foundations of the effectiveness of the high performing agency.[18]

From these studies, and an abundance of other data on target setting, goal clarity, and similar concepts, it can be concluded that the motivating effect of the budget derives from simply the fact that it is a statement of explicit goals.

Budget Implementation

Now let us examine some questions which focus on how the budget is used by the manager. It is in this phase that the budget comes to life. But, it should be clear that the effects previously noted, that is, anxiety in the preparation, the effects of goals, and so forth, have taken place and are likely to form the perceptual base from which individual reactions will develop. This section will focus on two theoretical formulations. The first deals specifically with the problem of how a superior's behavior potentially can interact with the budget to affect motivation and performance. The second considers the use of the budget as a basis for performance evaluation.

Managerial Use of the Budget

In the previous section the budget was characterized as a structure, or a device which constrained behavior by specifying authorized expenditure levels. Budget allocations may be viewed as specific goals, and in the previous section the effects of structure and goals on performance were noted. In essence, then, a budget may be viewed as a device which specifies, at least partially, certain actions that a manager must take to achieve his goals. If this is so, then path-goal theory has some implications for understanding the impact of budgets. M. Evans has described the basic notion rather succinctly in his statement that a particular activity set (a path) is likely to be seen as instrumental to goal achievement as a function of the degree to which the individual believes it will lead to a specific outcome.[19] Clearly, the budget may be viewed in these terms. One can strongly argue that those who prepare a final budget believe that if managers live with it and meet the requirements set forth, then success, defined in terms of organization effectiveness, will be achieved. Therefore, the budget specifies at least one aspect of the path (what resources can be used and how much) to the goal (profitable and/or effective performance).

The way the superior manages with the budget, we have said, can affect performance and motivation of subordinates. R. J. House argues that

> the motivational functions of the leader consist of increasing personal payoffs to subordinates for work-goal attainment, and making the path to these payoffs easier to travel by clarifying it, reducing roadblocks and pitfalls, and increasing the opportunities for personal satisfaction en route.[20]

But, since the budget is already a device which specifies and clarifies goals, certain types of leader behavior may have negative effects on motivation and ultimately, perhaps, on performance. If performance is directly affected by motivation and ability, then changes in motivation, with ability held constant, will result in changes in performance. Motivation to behave in a certain way (for example, to meet a budget) is affected by the attractiveness of the results (goals) of that behavior, and the probability that these results will in fact occur.[21]

Valences are defined as an affective orientation toward outcomes, or the desirability of the outcome to the individual. Outcomes will be valued when they satisfy individual needs or are consistent with values.

House's path-goal theory suggests that leader behavior may affect the valences employees attach to goals depending on whether or not paths to goals are clear or ambiguous. The budget and other control devices represent goals. The valence of these goals may vary from person to person, and the paths to these goals could be clear or ambiguous. According to House, the leader can affect motivation in the following ways:

1) He may be able to determine what extrinsic rewards are given for goal accomplishment.

2) He can affect the subordinate's perception that rewards are associated with work performance.

3) He can support, coach, or otherwise help the subordinate achieve the work goal.

4) He may be able to affect intrinsic valences employees attach to certain goals by increasing participation or otherwise creating satisfying work situations for the subordinate, giving more resources, and so forth.

5) He may aid goal attainment by eliminating frustrating barriers and being generally considerate of subordinate needs.[22]

The first two managerial strategies listed are more relevant to the question of how the budget is used as a part of the reward system. The last three leader behaviors are likely to be most significant in the use of the budget by a manager with his subordinates in the daily operations of a unit. Specifically, House draws four general propositions regarding the effects of leadership:

1) The motivational functions of a leader consist of increasing personal pay-offs for work-goal attainment, and making the paths to these pay-offs easier by clarifying it.

2) In increasing path instrumentality by clarifying path-goal relationships, the leader's behavior will have positive motivational effects to the extent that it reduces role ambiguity or makes possible the exercise of externally imposed controls. . . . Externally imposed controls result in improved performance (when) rewards under control of leader are positively valent; punishments under (leader control) are negatively valent . . . ; rewards and punishments are contingent on performance; and the contingency is clearly perceived by the subordinates.

3) Where leader attempts to clarify path-goal relationships are redundant with existing conditions, that is, . . . are apparent because of the routine of the tasks or objective system-fixed controls, attempts . . . to clarify path-goal relationship, will result in increased externally imposed control and will be seen by the subordinates as redundant. Although such control may increase performance, it will also result in decreased satisfaction.[23]

4) Leader behavior directed at need satisfaction will result in increased performance to the extent that such satisfaction increases the net positive valence associated with goal-directed effort.

We can now draw some general propositions about the relationship of managerial behavior, performance and satisfaction, and the budget.

If the subordinate does not know how budget allocations are intended to relate to performance, or is unclear about how to use resources, then increased direction from the superior will have positive effects on satisfaction and performance.

Under what conditions is this situation likely? First, when there is a relatively new incumbent in a position he may have had little opportunity to learn his job well. The direction from the superior is likely to be seen as coaching and support. It should increase the subordinate's understanding of how and what to do and should, therefore, have a positive effect.

Second, when a new activity is introduced into a unit, managers within may be unclear about how, at what rate, and what level expenditures are appropriate. Directive superior behavior which spells out his expectations, communicates to subordinates what he knows about the project, or otherwise acts to reduce ambiguity will have positive effects on both motivation and performance.

When the budget consists of allocations to accomplish functions that have been performed in the past, or new programs and plans are very specifically detailed in it, or elsewhere, then leader behavior which is path-goal directed is likely to have negative effects on motivation, and likely to have long-run, negative effects on performance.

Basically, this is consistent with House's redundancy argument.[24] Specific budgets, forced continually upon managers by their superiors, even though they clarify the job, are likely to generate negative feelings. While this pressure may increase short-run performance, it is likely to result in lower satisfaction leading to increases in turnover and absenteeism, both important components of general effectiveness.

The Budget as a Basis for Performance Evaluation

The seductive nature of a budget is that it is objective. Goals are quantified in a way that makes sense to the pragmatic manager—*dollars and cents*. The budget, then, is likely to be a significant component for the evaluation of a subordinate's performance. How the manager uses it is crucial since he may reinforce behavior which is likely to have negative effects on performance.

Learning theory postulates that when a behavior is reinforced, that is, rewards or punishments are seen as its consequences, the probability that an individual behaves similarly in later periods changes. Therefore, when a person is rewarded for, say, meeting a budget requirement, it can be predicted that later he will work to meet other budget requirements.

Disregarding the question of whether or not—or how—one finds a particular event associated with a behavior as rewarding, it is important to ask the question, "What are we reinforcing when we use the budget as a basis for evaluation?"

The answer is, of course, "It all depends."

Suppose the superior rewards or sanctions a subordinate based solely upon whether or not a budget requirement is met; for example, a subordinate who exceeds expenditures levels is not given a salary increase, while one who stays below budget is given a substantial one. In this case, the behavior which is reinforced is achievement at a particular level. Subordinate managers recognize the criterion and work toward it. It is possible that the methods that are used to achieve the goal may be organizationally suboptimal. For example, a manager may meet a budgeted maintenance expenditure level for a period by either foregoing the maintenance or having the work done but arranging for billing the next fiscal period. In both of these cases, the budget itself and what it is intended to accomplish had little effect. When the concern is on the budgeted level and this is the primary way that it is used as managerial tool, those who have to live with the budget learn the ropes of manipulating outcomes with little regard for what is intended to be the purpose of the activity.

This is true because budgets and most managerial controls do not offer any guidance on how to do something. Rather, they simply specify the approved level of resources to be used. Effectiveness depends both on the quantity of resources and how they are used.

To use a budget effectively, then, a manager must go beyond it. He should, of course, communicate to his subordinates the intended level of achievement. But, he must also ensure that he monitors the way they go about achieving that level. The manager may have to coach his subordinates extensively regarding how to achieve goals. This means that the evaluation should focus on both budget requirements and behavior so that, from a reinforcement point of view, the subordinate not only learns how much is expected, but how to do it.

Other factors in evaluation. It could be that the utility of the budget as an evaluation device is diluted by a number of other factors. Some of these can be briefly noted here. First, the rewards for achievement of performance goals may not be valued as highly by the subordinate as by the superior. Second, the budget contains only one type of performance criterion, while overall performance may include more subjective facets. Third, the frequency of performance reviews is not great, generally once or twice a year. This probably does not allow sufficient opportunities to link rewards strongly to performance against the budget. And, finally, some superiors simply may not regard the budget as a useful enough evaluative device to give it prominence in assessment.

In summary, the question addressed in this article is simply, "How and why do budgets affect managers?" The answer is that the budget itself, and the way it is used, affects both attitudes and behavior. Compliance, or attempted compliance, with a budget is not a difficult phenomenon to explain. The *psychological contract* is an adequate concept. Managers seek to comply with budget constraints because they see them as part of their job. But it is not quite that simple. Anxiety is created by budgets, managers sub-optimize in the name of the budget, and negative feelings of hostility occur.

Notes

The author is grateful to Douglas T. Hall, Northwestern University, for his assistance.

1. B. Berelson and G. Steiner, *Human Behavior: An Inventory of Scientific Findings* (New York: Harcourt Brace and World, 1964), p. 240.
2. J. Pfeffer and G. R. Salancik, "Organizational Decision Making as a Political Process: The Case of the University Budget," *Administrative Science Quarterly*, 19 June 1974, pp. 135-51.
3. E. Lawler, *Pay and Organizational Effectiveness: A Psychological View* (New York: McGraw Hill Book Company, 1971), p. 174.
4. Pfeffer and Salancik, "Organizational Decision Making."
5. J. March and H. Simon, *Organizations* (New York: John Wiley and Sons, Inc., 1958), pp. 54; 121-25.
6. See V. Vroom, *Work and Motivation* (New York: John Wiley and Sons, Inc., 1964), also Henry Tosi, "A Reexamination of Personality as a Determinant of the Effects of Participation," *Personnel Psychology* 23 (1970): 91-99; also Stephen Carroll and Henry J. Tosi, Jr., *Management by Objectives: Applications and Research* (New York: The Macmillan Company, 1973).
7. D. Searfoss and R. Monczka, "Perceived Participation in the Budget Process and Motivation to Achieve the Budget," *Academy of Management Journal*, December 1973, pp. 541-54.
8. Carroll and Tosi, *Management by Objectives*, p. 172.
9. John M. Ivancevich, "A Longitudinal Assessment of Management by Objectives," *Administrative Science Quarterly*, March 1972, pp. 126-35.
10. V. Vroom, *Some Personality Determinants of the Effects of Participation* (Englewood Cliffs, New Jersey: Prentice-Hall, Inc., 1960).

11. Henry L. Tosi, Jr., and Stephen J. Carroll, "Some Structural Factors Related to Goal Influence in the Management by Objectives Process," *MSU Business Topics*, Spring 1969, pp. 45-51.

12. Searfoss and Monczka, "Perceived Particiation in the Budget Process," p. 552.

12. R. M. Stogdill, *Individual Behavior and Group Achievement* (New York: Oxford University Press, 1959), p. 122.

14. Ibid., p. 242.

15. E. Locke, "Toward a Theory of Task Motivation and Incentives," *Organizational Behavior and Human Performance* 3 (1968): 162.

16. Carroll and Tosi, *Management by Objectives*, p. 171.

17. W. Turcotte, "Control Systems, Performance, and Satisfaction in Two State Agencies," *Administrative Science Quarterly*, March 1974, pp. 60-73.

18. Ibid., p. 71.

19. M. Evans, "The Effects of Supervisory Behavior upon Worker Perception of Their Path Goal Relationship" (Ph.D. diss., Yale University, 1968).

20. R. J. House, "A Path Goal Theory of Leader Effectiveness," *Administrative Science Quarterly*, September 1971, p. 324.

21. Ibid.

22. Ibid., p. 323.

23. Ibid., p. 324.

24. Ibid., p. 323.

SYSTEMS REWARDS
AND INDIVIDUAL REWARDS

DANIEL KATZ
ROBERT L. KAHN

Instrumental Satisfaction

. . . The first extension of machine theory beyond the rules is the addition of rewards to motivate performance. It is important to distinguish between rewards administered in relation to individual effort and performance and the system rewards which accrue to people by virtue of their membership in the system. In the former category are piece-rate incentives, promotion for outstanding performance, or any special recognition bestowed in acknowledgement of differential contributions to organizational functioning. The category of system rewards includes fringe benefits, recreational facilities, cost-of-living raises, across-the-board upgrading, job security, and pleasant working conditions.

Individual rewards properly administered help attract people to the system and hold them in it. A major factor in their effectiveness is the extent to which they are competitive with individual reward systems in other organizations. Individual rewards can also be effective in motivating people to meet and exceed the quantitative and qualitative standards of role performance. This effectiveness is limited, however, when large numbers of people are performing identical tasks, so that superior individual performance threatens the rewards and security of the majority. In other words, differential individual rewards are difficult to apply effectively to masses of people doing the same work and sharing a common fate in a mass production organization. It is no accident that large organizations have moved in the direction of converting individual rewards into system rewards.

Individual rewards are also difficult to apply to contributions that go beyond the formal requirements of role. Spectacular instances of innovative behavior can be singled out for recognition, of course, and heroism beyond the call of duty can be decorated. But the everyday cooperative activities which keep an organization from falling apart are more difficult to recognize and reward. Creative suggestions for organizational improvement are sometimes encouraged through financial rewards. In general, however, singling out of individuals for their extra contributions to the cause is not the most effective and reliable means of evoking high motivation for the accomplishment of organizational objectives.

Conditions Conducive to Effective Individual Instrumental Rewards

If rewards such as pay incentives are to work as they are intended, they must meet three primary conditions. (1) They must be clearly perceived as large enough in amount to justify the additional effort required to obtain them. (2) They must be perceived as directly related to the required performance and follow directly on its accomplishment. (3) They must be perceived as equitable by the majority of system members, many of whom will not receive them. These conditions suggest some of the reasons why individual rewards can work so well in some situations and yet be so difficult of application in large organizations. The facts are that most enterprises have not been able to use incentive pay, or piece rates, as reliable methods for raising the quality and quantity of production (McGregor, 1960; Marriott, 1957).

In terms of the first criterion many companies have attempted incentive pay without making the differential between increased effort and increased reward proportional from the point of view of the worker. If he can double his pay by working at a considerably increased tempo, that is one thing. But if such increased expenditure means a possible 10 per cent increase, that is another. Moreover, there is the tradition among workers, and it is not without some factual basis, that management cannot be relied upon to maintain a high rate of pay for those making considerably more than the standard and that their increased efforts will only result in their "being sweated." There is, then, the temporal dimension of whether the piece rates which seem attractive today will be maintained tomorrow.

More significant, however, is the fact that a large-scale organization consists of many people engaging in similar and interdependent tasks. The work of any one man is highly dependent upon what his colleagues are doing. Hence individual piece rates are difficult to apply on any equitable basis. Group incentives are more logical, but as the size of the interdependent group grows, we move toward system rather

TABLE 1. Conditions Affecting the Use of Individual Monetary Rewards

Objective Conditions	Mediated by Psychological Variables	Outcome
1. Amount of reward for individual effort	1. Frame of reference in evaluating reward: what standards are used for comparison purposes	Possible reduction in turnover
2. Immediacy of reward	2. Temporal frame of reference of individual	Some reduction in absenteeism
3. Constancy of reward	3. Perception of dependability and no cutting back of rates;	Possible increases in productivity
	Other consequences of reward striving such as disapproval of peers	No necessary increase in cooperative or protective behavior
		Possible increases in creative suggestions

than toward individual rewards. Moreover, in large-scale production enterprises the role performance is controlled by the tempo of the machines and their coordination. The speed of the worker on the assembly line is not determined by his decision but by the speed of the assembly line. An individual piece-rate just does not accord with the systemic nature of the coordinated collectivity. Motivational factors about the amount of effort to be expended on the job enter the picture not on the floor of the factory but during the negotiations of the union and management about the manning of a particular assembly line. Heads of corporations may believe in the philosophy of individual enterprise, but when they deal with reward systems in their own organizations they become realists and accept the pragmatic notion of collective rewards.

Since there is such a high degree of collective interdependence among rank-and-file workers the attempts to use individual rewards are often perceived as inequitable. Informal norms develop to protect the group against efforts which are seen as divisive or exploitive. Differential rates for subsystems within the organization will be accepted much more than invidious distinctions within the same subgrouping. Hence promotion or upgrading may be the most potent type of individual reward. The employee is rewarded by being moved to a different category of workers on a better pay schedule. Some of the same problems apply, of course, to this type of reward. Since differential performance is difficult to assess in assembly-type operations, promotion is often based upon such criteria as conformity to company requirements with respect to attendance and absenteeism, observance of rules, and seniority. None of these criteria is related to individual performance on the job. Moreover, promotion is greatly limited by the technical and professional education of the worker.

It is true, of course, that many organizations are not assembly-line operations, and even for those which are, the conditions described here do not apply to the upper echelons. Thus General Motors can follow a policy of high individual rewards to division managers based upon the profits achieved by a given division. A university can increase the amount of research productivity of its staff by making publication the essential criterion for promotion. In general, where assessment of individual performance is feasible and where the basis of the reward system is clear, instrumental individual rewards can play an important part in raising productivity.

System rewards differ from individual rewards in that they are not allocated on the basis of differential effort and performance but on the basis of membership in the system. The major basis for differential allocation of system rewards is seniority in the system. A higher pension for thirty years of service than for twenty years does not violate the principle of rewarding membership. Management often overlooks the distinction between individual and system rewards, and operates as if rewards administered across the board would produce the same effects as individual rewards.

System rewards are most effective for holding members within the organization. Since these rewards are often distributed on the basis of length of service, people will want to stay on to receive them. The limiting factor is competition with attractions in other systems. As the system increases its attractions, other things being equal, it should reduce its problems of turnover. In fact, it may sometimes have the problem of too little turnover, with many poorly motivated people staying on until retirement.

TABLE 2. Conditions Affecting the Use of System Rewards

Objective Conditions	*Mediated by Psychological Variables*	*Outcome*
1. Alternative system available to the individual	1. Perception of alternatives and law of least effort	Reduction in turnover
2. Relative advantages of system rewards in other available organizations	2. Perception and meaning to the individual of the differences	Some reduction in absenteeism Minimal quantity and quality of role performance
3. Uniformity of system rewards for all members or for major categories	3. Perception of equity	No creative contribution but some degree of cooperative and protective behavior and creation of favorable external environmental climate

System rewards will not lead to work of higher quality or greater quantity than is required to stay in the organization. Since rewards are given equally to all members or differentially in terms of seniority, people are not motivated to do more than meet the standards for remaining in the system. It is sometimes assumed that the liking for the organization created by system rewards will generalize to greater productive effort. Such generalization of motivation may occur to a very limited extent, but it is not a reliable basis for the expectation of higher productivity. Management may expect gratitude from workers because it has added some special fringe benefit or some new recreational facility. Employees will be motivated to remain in an enterprise with such advantages, but are unlikely to express gratitude by working harder for the company.

System rewards do little to motivate performance beyond the line of duty, with two possible exceptions. As people develop a liking for the attractions of the organization, they may be more likely to engage in cooperative relations with their fellows toward organizational goals. They may be more likely also to contribute to a favorable climate of opinion for the system in the external environment. It may be easier for a company to recruit personnel when employees have described it as a good place to work.

The effective use of system rewards requires their uniform application for all members of the system or for plausible major groupings within the system. If rewards are to be given by virtue of membership in the system, any allocation favoring some individuals over others is suspect. Management is frequently surprised by resentment over differential system rewards when there has been no resentment of differential individual rewards.

One public utility, for example, inaugurated an attractive retirement system for its employees before such fringe benefits were common. Its employees were objectively much better off because of the new benefits, and yet the most hated feature of the whole company was the retirement system. Employee complaints centered on two issues: years of employment in the company before the age of thirty did not count toward retirement pensions; and company officials, because of their higher salaries and correspondingly higher pensions, could retire on livable incomes. The employees felt intensely that, if they were being rewarded for service to the company, it was unfair to rule out years of service before age thirty. The service of a man who started to work for the company immediately after high school graduation was unrecognized for a dozen years. Moreover, workers felt that a lifetime of service to the company should enable them to retire on a livable income just as it enabled company officials to do so. The company house organ devoted considerable space over a few years to showing how much the workers actually benefited from the plan, as in fact was the case. On the occasion of a companywide survey, this campaign was found to have had little effect. The most common complaint was still the patent unfairness of the retirement system.

The critical point then is that system rewards have a logic of their own. Since they accrue to people by virtue of their membership or length of service in an organization, they will be perceived as inequitable if they are not uniformly administered. The perception of the organization member is that all members are equal in their access to organizational benefits. Office employees will not be upset by differences in individual rewards that recognize differences in responsibility. However, if their organization gives them free meals in a cafeteria and sets aside a special dining room for executives, many of them will be upset. In our culture we accept individual differences in income but we do not readily accept differences in classes of citizenship. To be a member of an organization is to be a citizen in that community, and all citizens are equal in their membership rights. Universities which do not extend to research workers the same tenure rights and fringe benefits accorded to the teaching staff have a morale problem on their hands.

The Citizenship Meaning of Membership in an Organization. There has been little systematic inquiry as to what it means for an individual to be a member of an organization or social system. By membership we do not necessarily mean that the individual pays or carries a card. We only mean that he is part of the system's operations, that he fulfills certain role obligations. Membership in this sense can be discussed in terms of the input a person regards as his due as a member of the system, and the output or behavior required of him to support the organization.

We have described the input side of this exchange in discussing system rewards. People in a democratic society feel that any system in which they are involved should accord them certain citizenship rights by virtue of their membership in the system. One such right is uniformity and equity in the distribution of system rewards. Another is equality of opportunity to earn the differential individual rewards available in the system. There should not be arbitrary discrimination against a worker because of race, religion, or social origin. Another right is that of due process of law, the right of the individual to be dealt with through established legal procedures and not through arbitrary, whimsical actions. Even though people are working for industrial organizations in which the power structure is oligarchical, they increasingly expect that their citizen rights in those organizations will be handled on the basis of democratic principles. Management in general also recognizes these citizen rights, and flagrant departures from them are not condoned. In fact, management goes even further in some instances and avoids the language of authority even though the citizen expectations of members do not demand a democratic authority structure.

There are many implications for organizations in the citizenship demands of members. The basic problem is the distribution of system rewards and privileges to different levels of workers, to different functional groups, and to the incumbents of different hierarchical positions.

The simple solution of uniform privileges and rewards for all organizational members regardless of position, type of work, or function would horrify the upper echelons. It would mean in a university, for example, that faculty members, research workers, clerks, and custodians would be entitled to the same provisions of tenure, retirement benefits, and vacations. When research workers and faculty members take ten days of vacation at Christmas, secretarial and administrative staffs would not be required to stay on the job. Though many would find this simple solution upsetting, the general trend is in this direction. Cost-of-living increases, which in many institutions are an important part of system rewards, are applied in a uniform fashion. Recreational facilities may be open to all members, and even parking permits, those coveted symbols of utility and prestige, are sometimes accorded to all.

A second solution is to translate inequitable system rewards into individual rewards. Instead of giving officials one plan of retirement and workers another, the retirement system can be the same for all, but the officials, by virtue of their individual positions and their unusual effort and achievement in those positions, can be given individual bonuses.

Another solution would be to find some acceptable rationale for distinguishing between functions and classes of citizens within an organization. In the university, the faculty perform a different function than clerical and custodial staff. Apart from meeting classes and conforming to other institutional requirements, faculty members can decide for themselves whether to work a thirty or a seventy hour week. Their Christmas vacation may in reality mean that they take less time from their professional duties than do their secretaries. In general, this distinction of functions is the major solution followed by most organizations in allocating system rewards. It has the merit of recognizing some of the realities of the situation, and encouraging a clear formulation of visible differences in functions, responsibilities, and obligations of different groups within the organization. On the other hand, this solution works against unification of all groups around the common goals of the organization, and it often encourages in-group loyalties and identifications at the expense of the total organization.

The problem of allocating system rewards is complicated by the functional subdivisions of the organization and the division of the total structure into sectors of organizational space. If system rewards are distributed differentially according to the status, responsibility, and power of subgroups, the identity of these subgroups will be reinforced and their goals will tend to become more important than organizational goals. If system rewards are distributed uniformly, the people whose positions carry more responsibility and require more effort and more investment in preliminary training will say that numerical equality is not genuine equality. Equal pay for equal work has the corollary that unequal pay should go with unequal work. The terms of the relations should not be lost.

The tendency of differential allocation of system rewards to intensify subgroup identification is greatest in an organization where the subgroup functions are in fundamental opposition. A university needs scientists who can pursue the search for knowledge with maximum freedom. It also needs security police to protect its laboratories from theft and destruction. The conventional arrangement makes the security police a subsystem of the university which ties directly to the top administrative structure and has no direct organizational tie to the functional units of the university whose premises the police are "protecting." As a result, none of the system rewards which accrue to the individual policeman—pay, promotion, timing and duration of vacation, and the like—are determined by the university units in which he physically performs his job. He patrols the premises at times when members of these subunits are for the most part not present and he is in the odd position of having physical occupancy without membership. Thus, he has little knowledge of the mission of the research group and little commitment to it. He may be just as suspicious of those he is protecting as he is of malicious intruders. An alternative arrangement would locate the security police in the subunit which they were protecting or at least woud allocate some of the system rewards on the basis of their performance as evaluated by the members of those subunits. This could lead to an embracing of the subsystem's mission by the security unit.

System rewards uniformly distributed will lead some people to identify with the larger organization, but more fundamental changes in organizational structure and roles make identification with the larger organization more likely. Specifically, this means broadening the role of members of the subgroup and giving them membership in some subsystem which is central to the mission of the organization. This could mean complete reorganization on the basis of teams concerned with problems rather than on the basis of functional specialization; it could mean assignment of a specialist to a team for limited periods, or it could mean maintaining the old groupings of functional specialists with additional organization along task lines.

Hospital administrators have attempted reforms exemplifying the last of the above-mentioned alternatives. Attendants and nurses in mental hospitals tend to become more concerned with their custodial duties than with the major objective of improving the health of patients. The creation of teams involving doctors, administrators, nurses, and attendants to discuss individual cases and alternative methods of dealing with them can help immeasurably in changing the conception of the job of the attendant and the nurse. One cannot make the security policeman a member of the scientific research team in the same sense, but he can be assigned to a particular laboratory and placed under the supervision of its director for the discharge of many of his duties. Thus he can learn that one of his functions is not to throw the scientist who has forgotten his identification card out of the laboratory, but to issue a new card for him. He can be given more responsibility rather than less in contributing to the mission of the organization.

The revision of organizational arrangements to involve peripheral and low-status groups in organizational goals has implications for system rewards. To the extent that the lowly member is now part of the team, it becomes more difficult to treat him as a third-class citizen in the distribution of organizational rewards. Professional baseball teams recognize this principle when they vote shares of the World Series bonus to players who have spent most of the season on the bench, to trainers, and to other nonplaying personnel. Football coaches follow the same principle by getting many of their first-squad members into a minute or more of playing in criterion games so that they can earn their varsity letters. Joint authorship, in which the names of all research workers are listed as responsible for a research report, is becoming a common practice. Where an obvious differentiation of individual contribution to the group product can be ascertained, it is feasible to set up individual rewards for differential effectiveness and effort. Where there are no palpable criteria for the determination of individual effort and where the emphasis is upon teamwork, system rewards are more feasible and lead to higher identification with the organization.

Though system rewards maintain the level of productivity not much above the minimum required to stay in the system, there still may be large differences *between* systems with respect to the quantity and quality of production as a function of system rewards. An organization with substantially better wage rates and fringe benefits than its competitors may be able to set a higher level of performance as a minimal requirement for its workers and still hold its employees. System rewards can be related to the differential productivity of organizations as a whole though they are not effective in maximizing the potential contributions of the majority of individuals within an organization. They may account for differences in motivation between systems rather than for differences in motivation between individuals in the same system. They operate through their effects upon the minimal standards for all people in the system. They act indirectly in that their effect is to make people want to stay in the organization; to do so people must be willing to accept the legitimately derived standards of role performance in that system. The direct mechanism for insuring performance is legal compliance, but the legal requirements of the organization will not hold members if demands are too great or rewards too meager in comparison to other organizations. The mediating variable in accounting for organizational differences based upon system rewards is the relative attractiveness of the system for the individual compared to other systems accessible to him.

The Rewards of Approval. Another instrumental satisfaction for group members derives, as we have mentioned earlier, from the approval and support of their leaders. This category has to do with the psychological rewards of leader approval and is distinct from the leader's use of more tangible rewards. The use of approval by organizational leaders is nevertheless subject to the same limitation as is use of other reward forms. He can avoid inequity and make his approval part of the system reward by speaking words of encouragement to every member meeting standards. Or he can single out for special approval the very few who perform above standard. In the former case, he may merely contribute to the feeling that this is a pleasant place to work. In the latter case, he may strengthen the motivation of a few "company" men and add to the resistance of the majority.

The actions of the superior in ministering to the dependency needs of his followers, moreover, may develop a satisfying interpersonal relationship which has, if anything, a negative effect upon organizational performance. The dependent employee may gravitate to the officer who can give him some psychological assurance in coping with personal problems. The support of the father figure, understandably enough, may not be given to the person who does the job well but to the dependent person on the basis of his needs. In turn, the superior may derive gratification from playing this supportive role. Though both individuals profit from the relationship, it may be so unrelated to the tasks to be performed that it merely subtracts from the productive time of both people. Kaye (1958) has provided data consistent with this interpretation.

Another type of reward is the approval of peers in the organization. Social support from peers can add to the attractiveness of the subsystem and can be a factor in the reduction of absenteeism and turnover. It will lead to increased productivity and quality of work, however, only if the norms of the peer group sanction such performance. In many industrial organizations, the norms of the peer group set informal standards for production which are not optimal from the company's point of view. In voluntary organizations, however, the norms of the group are often an important source of increased individual activity.

TABLE 3. Conditions Affecting the Use of Peer-Group Approval

Objective Conditions	Mediated by Psychological Variables	Outcome
1. Group cohesion	1. Individual's own attraction to group	Decreased turnover and absenteeism
	2. The relevance of group norms with respect to organizational objectives	Possible increases or decreases in productivity
		No necessary relations with behavior beyond the call of duty

Behavior beyond the formal requirements of role may be fostered or discouraged by the need for approval from peers. The norms of the local group generally sanction productive cooperation and support actions which protect the organization against disaster. The values of the work group seldom approve, however, of the eager member who wants to save the company money through some brilliant suggestion, or of the ambitious employees who seek to train themselves for better jobs. The work group tends to value seniority as the best principle for allocating privileges and benefits, and to be protective of the group rather than the organization.

References

Kaye, Carol. 1958. Some Effects of Organizational Change on the Personality of Key Role Occupants. Unpublished Doctoral Dissertation, University of Michigan.

McGregor, D. 1960. *The Human Side of Enterprise*. New York: McGraw-Hill.

Marriott, R. 1957. *Incentive Payment Plans*. London: Staple Press.

PART SIX

The Effects of Leadership on Individual and Group Behavior

Leadership is the process by which an individual influences the behavior of another person or group. Compliance with this influence is important. If it can be assured, direction and guidance are likely to be followed, and administration is minimized. But compliance is not a unitary concept. Schein, in discussing the "psychological contract," pointed out that a large number of individual responses in organizations can be accounted for simply by the fact of membership. A person is there to do a job, and within reason, he will not disregard directives, suggestions, or policies. Behavior which falls within the boundaries of the psychological contract should not be considered a response to leadership. Compliance with directives falling within the psychological contract is *administration*. To move an individual *beyond* those boundaries is leadership.

A basic assumption is that leadership is based on interpersonal relationships rather than on formal authority or position power. Position power gives an incumbent discretion over such matters as budgets or expenditures, and grants him the right of decision making. Using this discretion, or administrative prerogative, any incumbent can extract the necessary compliance required for an acceptable level of performance. The effective use of organization structure—budgeting, job descriptions, policies, and so forth—can be taught. Leadership as an interpersonal skill may be more difficult, if not impossible, to teach.

When performance problems occur, there is a tendency to feel that they are a result of leadership deficiencies. Yet failure is often due to the fact that a manager may not *administer* as well as he could. Managers are unwilling, in most circumstances, to make use of the formal sanctions at their disposal. They are unwilling to criticize. They are shy about discussing performance deficiences. They cannot bring themselves to demote poor performers. They expect instead response to their "charismatic" appeals for better performance and commitment.

Given the concept of leadership as an interpersonal relationship, it is necessary to examine what factors are related to the ability to influence another interpersonally. If leadership is influence, and influence is the ability to extract compliance, then power is the force upon which influence is based. Power results from some type of dependence relationship, and may arise for a number of reasons.

An individual may comply with influence attempts simply because another person has the perceived capacity to reward or sanction. Power, as French and Raven note, can be based upon the degree of individual control over the reward structure. Thus, a member may comply because he does not wish to incur negative effects, or because he hopes to be positively rewarded. Some rewards may be organizationally based; for example, promotion opportunities, pay increases, increased status, or any other factor which a manager has discretion to distribute among those who work for him. Rewards may also be socially or interpersonally based. For instance, there may be a high degree of personal attraction to another, so that one complies in order to be socially desirable to him.

When power is viewed as legitimate, the holder is viewed by others as having a right to expect compliance. Legitimate power may be organizationally based when certain rights and prerogatives are associated with certain positions. Under these circumstances, the holder has internalized the right to demand and expect compliance of others. To the extent that organizational definitions of jobs and positions are generally accepted, requests from individuals in those positions may be regarded as legitimate, increasing the likelihood of compliance.

A more complex problem in the consideration of leadership and administration is that it is easy to confuse these concepts. A leader is someone who is able to influence others. A manager is an individual in a particular organization position. While it certainly is true that most managers have discretion to make decisions about resource allocation and distribution which affect and influence subordinates, it is also possible that managers may not exert *leadership* influence.

The relationships of leadership, managerial behavior, and performance have always been of interest to those concerned with improving results. However, extensive research has produced inconsistent conclusions about the relationship between leadership style and performance. Some research has found, for instance, that considerate leader behavior, an activity characterized by close relationships and concern for subordinates, is related to high performance by work groups. Other research has found a negative relationship between considerate leader behavior and performance. The selections by Fiedler and House attempt to shed some light on this apparent inconsistency.

It is widely acknowledged that effective leadership style is a function of the leader, the characteristics of the work group, and the situation. Fiedler's article describes situational characteristics which seem to be related to leadership effectiveness. While there is some criticism of his approach, it does force thinking about the leadership process in the direction of specification of what situational variables are important, and how they may be changed in order to improve effectiveness. Essentially, Fiedler's argument is that it is likely to be more productive to change situational characteristics to improve interpersonal interaction than to try to change the leadership style of an individual. Fiedler argues that the situation in which the leader operates determines his effectiveness as much as his own interpersonal skills and abilities do. When the situation and his behavioral style are incongruent, he is likely to be ineffective.

House takes a slightly different approach to integrating inconsistent findings in the leadership literature. He uses the path-goal motivation theory as a foundation for understanding why different leadership styles are likely to be more or less effective in different circumstances. When the job is highly structured, directive leader behavior may have negative effects on employees. When the job is more ambiguous, or involves a good deal of managerial discretion, a directiove style may clarify the relationship between individual activity and the objectives of the job.

Vroom and Yetton discuss leadership and group member participation in decision making. They posit a continuum on which at one extreme the leader makes the decision alone and at the other involves the group in the decision process from beginning to end. The leader makes the decision about involvement of subordinates based on his or her diagnosis of the relative importance of quality and/or acceptance to the solution of the problem calling for a decision.

By no means has the last word on leadership been spoken. New approaches and theories will be advanced as better measures and new theoretical constructs develop. We have provided in this part a set of concepts which have some practical value. There are, indeed, ways to restructure the work situation and to make assignments more clear. It is a simple matter, if a manager wishes, to change the power assigned to an individual. This can be done by simply delegating more responsibility or discretion to make decisions. A manager can also change the characteristics of the situation to improve leadership effectiveness. Rather than worry about inducing highly charismatic individuals to join an organization, or changing the leadership style of an individual, it may be more effective to restructure the environment to improve interpersonal interaction. Fiedler has suggested some of the ways that the job can be "engineered to fit the manager."

THE BASES OF SOCIAL POWER

JOHN R. P. FRENCH, JR.
BERTRAM RAVEN

The processes of power are pervasive, complex, and often disguised in our society. Accordingly one finds in political science, in sociology, and in social psychology a variety of distinctions among different types of social power or among qualitatively different processes of social influence (1, 6, 14, 20, 23, 29, 30, 38, 41). Our main purpose is to identify the major types of power and to define them systematically so that we may compare them according to the changes which they produce and the other effects which accompany the use of power. The phenomena of power and influence involve a dyadic relation between two agents which may be viewed from two points of view: (a) What determines the behavior of the agent who exerts power? (b) What determines the reactions of the recipient of this behavior? We take this second point of view and formulate our theory in terms of the life space of P, the

Reprinted by permission of the authors and the publisher, Institute for Social Research, from *Studies in Social Power* (1959).

person upon whom the power is exerted. In this way we hope to define basic concepts of power which will be adequate to explain many of the phenomena of social influence, including some which have been described in other less genotypic terms.

Recent empirical work, especially on small groups, has demonstrated the necessity of distinguishing different types of power in order to account for the different effects found in studies of social influence. Yet there is no doubt that more empirical knowledge will be needed to make final decisions concerning the necessary differentiations, but this knowledge will be obtained only by research based on some preliminary theoretical distinctions. We present such preliminary concepts and some of the hypotheses they suggest.

Power, Influence, and Change

Psychological Change

Since we shall define power in terms of influence, and influence in terms of psychological change, we begin with a discussion of change. We want to define change at a level of generality which includes changes in behavior, opinions, attitudes, goals, needs, values and all other aspects of the person's psychological field. We shall use the word "system" to refer to any such part of the life space.[1] Following Lewin (26, p. 305) the state of a system at time 1 will be denoted s_1 (a).

Psychological change is defined as any alteration of the state of some system a over time. The amount of change is measured by the size of the difference between the states of the system a at time 1 and at time 2: $ch(a) = s_2(a) - s_1(a)$.

Change in any psychological system may be conceptualized in terms of psychological forces. But it is important to note that the change must be coordinated to the resultant force of all the forces operating at the moment. Change in an opinion, for example, may be determined jointly by a driving force induced by another person, a restraining force corresponding to anchorage in a group opinion, and an own force stemming from the person's needs.

Social Influence

Our theory of social influence and power is limited to influence on the person, P, produced by a social agent, O, where O can be either another person, a role, a norm, a group or a part of a group. We do not consider social influence exerted on a group.

The influence of O on a system a in the life space of P is defined as the resultant force on system a which has its source in an act of O. This resultant force induced by O consists of two components: a force to change the system in the direction induced by O and an opposing resistance set up by the same act of O.

By this definition the influence of O does not include P's own forces nor the forces induced by other social agents. Accordingly the "influence" of O must be clearly distinguished from O's "control" of P. O may be able to induce strong forces on P to carry out an activity (i.e., O exerts strong influence on P); but if the opposing forces induced by another person or by P's own needs are stronger, then P will locomote in an opposite direction (i.e., O does not have control over

P). Thus psychological change in P can be taken as an operational definition of the social influence of O on P only when the effects of other forces have been eliminated.

It is assumed that any system is interdependent with other parts of the life space so that a change in one may produce changes in others. However, this theory focuses on the primary changes in a system which are produced directly by social influence; it is less concerned with secondary changes which are indirectly effected in the other systems or with primary changes produced by nonsocial influences.

Commonly social influence takes place through an intentional act on the part of O. However, we do not want to limit our definition of "act" to such conscious behavior. Indeed, influence might result from the passive presence of O, with no evidence of speech or overt movement. A policeman's standing on a corner may be considered an act of an agent for the speeding motorist. Such acts of the inducing agent will vary in strength, for O may not always utilize all of his power. The policeman, for example, may merely stand and watch or act more strongly by blowing his whistle at the motorist.

The influence exerted by an act need not be in the direction intended by O. The direction of the resultant force on P will depend on the relative magnitude of the induced force set up by the act of O and the resisting force in the opposite direction which is generated by that same act. In cases where O intends to influence P in a given direction, a resultant force in the same direction may be termed positive influence whereas a resultant force in the opposite direction may be termed negative influence.

If O produces the intended change, he has exerted positive control; but if he produces a change in the opposite direction, as for example in the negativism of young children or in the phenomena of negative reference groups, he has exerted negative control.

Social Power

The *strength of power* of O/P in some system a is defined as the maximum potential ability of O to influence P in a.

By this definition influence is kinetic power, just as power is potential influence. It is assumed that O is capable of various acts which, because of some more or less enduring relation to P, are able to exert influence on P.[2] O's power is measured by his maximum possible influence, though he may often choose to exert less than his full power.

An equivalent definition of power may be stated in terms of the resultant of two forces set up by the act of O: one in the direction of O's influence attempt and another resisting force in the opposite direction. Power is the maximum resultant of these two forces:

$$\text{Power of O/P(a)} = (f_{a,x} - f_{\overline{a,x}}) \text{ max}$$

where the source of both forces is an act of O.

Thus the power of O with respect to system a of P is equal to the maximum resultant force of two forces set up by any possible act of O: (a) the force which O can set up on the system a to change in the direction x, (b) the resisting force[3] in the opposite direction. Whenever the first component force is greater than the second, positive power exists; but if the second component force is greater than the first, then O has negative power over P.

It is necessary to define power with respect to a specified system because the power of O/P may vary greatly from one system to another. O may have great power to control the behavior of P but little power to control his opinions. Of course a high power of O/P does not imply a low power of P/O; the two variables are conceptually independent.

For certain purposes it is convenient to define the range of power as the set of all systems within which O has power of strength greater than zero. A husband may have a broad range of power over his wife, but a narrow range of power over his employer. We shall use the term "magnitude of power" to denote the summation of O's power over P in all systems of his range.

The Dependence of s (a) on O.

Several investigators have been concerned with differences between superficial conformity and "deeper" changes produced by social influence (1, 5, 6, 11, 12, 20, 21, 22, 23, 26, 36, 37). The kinds of systems which are changed and the stability of these changes have been handled by distinctions such as "public vs. private attitudes," "overt vs. covert behavior," "compliance vs. internalization," and "own vs. induced forces." Though stated as dichotomies, all of these distinctions suggest an underlying dimension of the degree of dependence of the state of a system on O.

We assume that any change in the state of a system is produced by a change in some factor upon which it is functionally dependent. The state of an opinion, for example, may change because of a change either in some internal factor such as a need or in some external factor such as the arguments of O. Likewise the maintenance of the same state of a system is produced by the stability or lack of change in the internal and external factors. In general, then, psychological change and stability can be conceptualized in terms of dynamic dependence. Our interest is focused on the special case of dependence on an external agent, O (31).

In many cases the initial state of the system has the character of a quasi-stationary equilibrium with a central force field around $s_1(a)$ (26, p. 106). In such cases we may derive a tendency toward retrogression to the original state as soon as the force induced by O is removed.[4] Let us suppose that O exerts influence producing a new state of the system, $s_2(a)$. Is $s_2(a)$ now dependent on the continued presence of O? In principle we could answer this question by removing any traces of O from the life space of P and by observing the consequent state of the system at time 3. If $s_3(a)$ retrogresses completely back to $s_1(a)$, then we may conclude that maintenance of $s_2(a)$ was completely dependent on O; but if $s_3(a)$ equals $s_2(a)$, this lack of change shows that $s_2(a)$ has become completely independent of O. In general the degree of dependence of $s_2(a)$ on O, following O's influence, may be defined as equal to the amount of retrogression following the removal of O from the life space of P:

$$\text{Degree of dependence of } s_2(a) \text{ on } 0 = s_2(a) - s_3(a)$$

A given degree of dependence at time 2 may later change, for example, through the gradual weakening of O's influence. At this later time, the degree of dependence of $s_4(a)$ on O, would still be equal to the amount of retrogression toward the initial state of equilibrium $s_1(a)$. Operational measures of the degree of dependence on O will, of course, have to be taken under conditions where all other factors are held constant.

Consider the example of three separated employees who have been working at the same steady level of production despite normal, small fluctuations in the work environment. The supervisor orders each to increase his production, and the level of each goes up from 100 to 115 pieces per day. After a week of producing at the new rate of 115 pieces per day, the supervisor is removed for a week. The production of employee A immediately returns to 100 but B and C return to only 110 pieces per day. Other things being equal, we can infer that A's new rate was completely dependent on his supervisor whereas the new rate of B and C was dependent on the supervisor only to the extent of 5 pieces. Let us further assume that when the supervisor returned, the production of B and C returned to 115 without further orders from the supervisor. Now another month goes by during which B and C maintain a steady 115 pieces per day. However, there is a difference between them: B's level of production still depends on O to the extent of 5 pieces whereas C has come to rely on his own sense of obligation to obey the order of his legitimate supervisors rather than on the supervisor's external pressure for the maintenance of his 115 pieces per day. Accordingly the next time the supervisor departs, B's production again drops to 110 but C's remains at 115 pieces per day. In cases like employee B, the degree of dependence is contingent on the perceived probability that O will observe the state of the system and note P's conformity (5, 6, 11, 12, 23). The level of observability will in turn depend on both the nature of the system (e.g., the difference between a covert opinion and overt behavior) and on the environmental barriers to observation (e.g., O is too far away from P). In other cases, for example that of employee C, the new behavior pattern is highly dependent on his supervisor, but the degree of dependence of the new state will be related not to the level of observability but rather to factors inside P, in this case a sense of duty to perform an act legitimately prescribed by O. The internalization of social norms is a related process of decreasing degree of dependence of behavior on an external O and increasing dependence on an internal value; it is usually assumed that internalization is accompanied by a decrease in the effects of level of observability (37).

The concepts "dependence of a system on O" and "observability as a basis for dependence" will be useful in understanding the stability of conformity. In the next section we shall discuss various types of power and the types of conformity which they are likely to produce.

The Bases of Power

By the basis of power we mean the relationship between O and P which is the source of that power. It is rare that we can say with certainty that a given empirical case of power is limited to one source. Normally, the relation between O and P will be characterized by several qualitatively different variables which are bases of power (30). Although there are undoubtedly many possible bases of power which may be distinguished, we shall here define five which seem especially common and important. These five bases of O's power are:

1. reward power, based on P's perception that O has the ability to mediate rewards for him;
2. coercive power, based on P's perception that O has the ability to mediate punishments for him;
3. legitimate power, based on the perception by P that O has a legitimate right to prescribe behavior for him;
4. referent power, based on P's identification with O;
5. expert power, based on the perception that O has some special knowledge or expertness.

Our first concern is to define the bases which give rise to a given type of power. Next, we describe each type of power according to its strength, range, and the degree of dependence of the new state of the system which is most likely to occur with each type of power. We shall also examine the other effects which the exercise of a given type of power may have upon P and his relationship to O. Finally, we shall point out the interrelationships between different types of power, and the effects of use of one type of power by O upon other bases of power which he might have over P. Thus we shall both define a set of concepts and propose a series of hypotheses. Most of these hypotheses have not been systematically tested, although there is a good deal of evidence in favor of several. No attempt will be made to summarize that evidence here.

Reward Power

Reward power is defined as power whose basis is the ability to reward. The strength of the reward power of O/P increases with the magnitude of the rewards which P perceives that O can mediate for him. Reward power depends on O's ability to administer positive valences and to remove or decrease negative valences. The strength of reward power also depends upon the probability that O can mediate the reward, as perceived by P. A common example of reward power is the addition of a piece-work rate in the factory as an incentive to increase production.

The new state of the system induced by a promise of reward (for example the factory worker's increased level of production) will be highly dependent on O. Since O mediates the reward, he controls the probability that P will receive it. Thus P's new rate of production will be dependent on his subjective probability that O will reward him for conformity minus his subjective probability that O will reward him even if he returns to his old level. Both probabilities will be greatly affected by the level of observability of P's behavior. Incidentally, a piece rate often seems to have more effect on production than a merit rating system because it yields a higher probability of reward for conformity and a much lower probability of reward for nonconformity.

The utilization of actual rewards (instead of promises) by O will tend over time to increase the attraction of P toward O and therefore the referent power of O over P. As we shall note later, such referent power will permit O to induce changes which are relatively independent. Neither rewards nor promises will arouse resistance in P, provided P considers it legitimate for O to offer rewards.

The range of reward power is specific to those regions within which O can reward P for conforming. The use of rewards to change systems within the range of reward power tends to increase reward power by increasing the probability attached to future promises. However, unsuccessful attempts to exert reward power outside the range of power would tend to decrease the power; for example if O offers to reward P for performing an impossible act, this will reduce for P the probability of receiving future rewards promised by O.

Coercive Power

Coercive power is similar to reward power in that it also involves O's ability to manipulate the attainment of valences. Coercive power of O/P stems from the expectation on the part of P that he will be punished by O if he fails to conform to the influence attempt. Thus negative valences will exist in given regions of P's life space, corresponding to the threatened punishment by O. The strength of coercive power depends on the magnitude of the negative valence of the threatened punishment multiplied by the perceived probability that P can avoid the punishment by conformity, i.e., the probability of punishment for nonconformity minus the probability of punishment for conformity (11). Just as an offer of a piece-rate bonus in a factory can serve as a basis for reward power, so the ability to fire a worker if he falls below a given level of production will result in coercive power.

Coercive power leads to dependent change also; and the degree of dependence varies with the level of observability of P's conformity. An excellent illustration of coercive power leading to dependent change is provided by a clothes presser in a factory observed by Coch and French (3). As her efficiency rating climbed above average for the group the other workers began to "scapegoat" her. That the resulting plateau in her production was not independent of the group was evident once she was removed from the presence of the other workers. Her production immediately climbed to new heights.[5]

At times, there is some difficulty in distinguishing between reward power and coercive power. Is the withholding of a reward really equivalent to a punishment? Is the withdrawal of punishment equivalent to a reward? The answer must be a psychological one—it depends upon the situation as it exists for P. But ordinarily we would answer these questions in the affirmative; for P, receiving a reward is a positive valence as is the relief of suffering. There is some evidence that conformity to group norms in order to gain acceptance (reward power) should be distinguished from conformity as a means of forestalling rejection (coercive power) (5).

The distinction between these two types of power is important because the dynamics are different. The concept of "sanctions" sometimes lumps the two together despite their opposite effects. While reward power may eventually result in an independent system, the effects of coercive power will continue to be dependent. Reward power will tend to increase the attraction of P toward Q; coercive power will decrease this attraction (11, 12). The valence of the region of behavior will become more negative, acquiring some negative valence from the threatened punishment. The negative valence of punishment would also spread to other regions of the life space. Lewin (25) has pointed out this distinction between the effects of rewards and punishment. In the case of threatened punishment, there will be a resultant force on P to leave the field entirely. Thus, to achieve conformity, O must not only place a strong negative valence in certain regions through threat of punishment, but O must also introduce restraining forces, or other strong valences, so as to prevent P from withdrawing completely from O's range of coercive power. Otherwise the probability of receiving the punishment, if P does not conform, will be too low to be effective.

Legitimate Power

Legitimate power is probably the most complex of those treated here, embodying notions from the structural sociologist, the group-norm and role oriented social psychologist, and the clinical psychologist.

There has been considerable investigation and speculation about socially prescribed behavior, particularly that which is specific to a given role or position. Linton (29) distinguishes group norms according to whether they are universals for everyone in the culture, alternatives (the individual having a choice as to whether or not to accept them), or specialties (specific to given positions). Whether we speak of internalized norms, role prescriptions and expectations (34), or internalized pressures (15), the fact remains that each individual sees certain regions toward which he should locomote, some regions toward which he should not locomote, and some regions toward which he may locomote if they are generally attractive for him. This applies to specific behaviors in which he may, should, or should not engage; it applies to certain attitudes or beliefs which he may, should, or should not hold. The feeling of "oughtness" may be an internalization from his parents, from his teachers, from his religion, or may have been logically developed from some idiosyncratic system of ethics. He will speak of such behaviors with expressions like "should," "ought to," or "has a right to." In many cases, the original source of the requirement is not recalled.

Though we have oversimplified such evaluations of behavior with a positive-neutral-negative trichotomy, the evaluation of behaviors by the person is really more one of degree. This dimension of evaluation, we shall call "legitimacy." Conceptually, we may think of legitimacy as a valence in a region which is induced by some internalized norm or value. This value has the same conceptual property as power, namely an ability to induce force fields (26, p. 40-41). It may or may not be correct that values (or the superego) are internalized parents, but at least they can set up force fields which have a phenomenal "oughtness" similar to a parent's prescription. Like a value, a need can also induce valences (i.e., force fields) in P's psychological environment, but these valences have more the phenomenal character of noxious or attractive properties of the object or activity. When a need induces a valence in P, for example, when a need makes an object attractive to P, this attraction applies to P but not to other persons. When a value induces a valence, on the other hand, it not only sets up forces on P to engage in the activity, but P may feel that all others ought to behave in the same way. Among other things, this evaluation applies to the legitimate right of some other individual or group to prescribe behavior or beliefs for a person even though the other cannot apply sanctions.

Legitimate power of O/P is here defined as that power which stems from internalized values in P which dictate that O has a legitimate right to influence P and that P has an obligation to accept this influence. We note that legitimate power is very similar to the notion of legitimacy of authority which has long been explored by sociologists, particularly by Weber (42), and more recently by Goldhammer and Shils (14). However, legitimate power is not always a role relation: P may accept an induction from O simply because he had previously promised to help O and he values his word too much to break the promise. In all cases, the notion of legitimacy involves some sort of code or standard, accepted by the individual, by virtue of which the external agent can assert his power. We shall attempt to describe a few of these values here.

Bases for legitimate power. Cultural values constitute one common basis for the legitimate power of one individual over another. O has characteristics which are specified by the culture as giving him the right to prescribe behavior for P, who may not have these characteristics. These bases, which Weber (42) has called the authority of the "eternal yesterday," include such things as age, intelligence, caste, and physical characteristics. In some cultures, the aged are granted the right to prescribe behavior for others in practically all behavior areas. In most cultures, there are certain areas of behavior in which a person of one sex is granted the right to prescribe behavior for the other sex.

Acceptance of the social structure is another basis for legitimate power. If P accepts as right the social structure of his group, organization, or society, especially the social structure involving a hierarchy of authority, P will accept the legitimate authority of O who occupies a superior office in the hierarchy. Thus legitimate power in a formal organization is largely a relationship between offices rather than between persons. And the acceptance of an office as *right* is a basis for legitimate power—a judge has a right to levy fines, a foreman should assign work, a priest is justified in prescribing religious beliefs, and it is the management's prerogative to make certain decisions (10). However, legitimate power also involves the perceived right of the person to hold the office.

Designation by a legitimizing agent is a third basis for legitimate power. An influencer O may be seen as legitimate in prescribing behavior for P because he has been granted such power by a legitimizing agent whom P accepts. Thus a department head may accept the authority of his vice-president in a certain area because that authority has been specifically delegated by the president. An election is perhaps the most common example of a group's serving to legitimize the authority of one individual or office for other individuals in the group. The success of such legitimizing depends upon the acceptance of the legitimizing agent and procedure. In this case it depends ultimately on certain democratic values concerning election procedures. The election process is one of legitimizing a person's right to an office which already has legitimate range of power associated with it.

Range of legitimate power of O/P. The areas in which legitimate power may be exercised are generally specified along with the designation of that power. A job description, for example, usually specifies supervisory activities and also designates the person to whom the job-holder is responsible for the duties described. Some bases for legitimate authority carry with them a very broad range. Culturally derived bases for legitimate power are often especially broad. It is not uncommon to find cultures in which a member of a given caste can legitimately prescribe behavior for all members of lower castes in practically all regions. More common, however, are instances of legitimate power where the range is specifically and narrowly prescribed. A sergeant in the army is given a specific set of regions within which he can legitimately prescribe behavior for his men.

The attempted use of legitimate power which is outside of the range of legitimate power will decrease the legitimate power of the authority figure. Such use of power which is not legitimate will also decrease the attractiveness of O (11, 12, 36).

Legitimate power and influence. The new state of the system which results from legitimate power usually has high dependence on O though it may become independent. Here, however, the degree of dependence is not related to the level of observability. Since legitimate power is based on P's values, the source of the forces induced by O include both these internal values and O. O's induction serves to activate the values and to relate them to the system which is influenced, but thereafter the new state of the system may become directly dependent on the values with no mediation by O. Accordingly this new state will be relatively stable and consistent across varying environmental situations since P's values are more stable than his psychological environment.

We have used the term legitimate not only as a basis for the power of an agent, but also to describe the general behaviors of a person. Thus, the individual P may also consider the legitimacy of the attempts to use other types of power by O. In certain cases, P will consider that O has a legitimate right to threaten punishment for nonconformity; in other cases, such use of coercion would not be seen as legitimate. P might change in response to coercive power of O, but it will make a considerable difference in his attitude and conformity if O is not seen as having a legitimate right to use such coercion. In such cases, the attraction of P for O will be particularly diminished, and the influence attempt will arouse more resistance (11). Similarly the utilization of reward power may vary in legitimacy; the word "bribe" for example, denotes an illegitimate reward.

Referent Power

The referent power of O/P has its basis in the identification of P with O. By identification, we mean a feeling of oneness of P with O, or a desire for such an identity. If O is a person toward whom P is highly attracted, P will have a desire to become closely associated with O. If O is an attractive group, P will have a feeling of membership or a desire to join. If P is already closely associated with O he will want to maintain this relationship (39, 41). P's identification with O can be established or maintained if P behaves, believes, and perceives as O does. Accordingly O has the ability to influence P, even though P may be unaware of this referent power. A verbalization of such power by P might be, "I am like O, and therefore I shall behave or believe as O does," or "I want to be like O, and I will be more like O if I behave or believe as O does." The stronger the identification of P with O the greater the referent power of O/P.

Similar types of power have already been investigated under a number of different formulations. Festinger (7) points out that in an ambiguous situation, the individual seeks some sort of "social reality" and may adopt the cognitive structure of the individual or group with which he identifies. In such a case, the lack of clear structure may be threatening to the individual and the agreement of his beliefs with those of a reference group will both satisfy his need for structure and give him added security through increased identification with his group (16, 19).

We must try to distinguish between referent power and other types of power which might be operative at the same time. If a member is attracted to a group and he conforms to its norms only because he fears ridicule or expulsion from the group for nonconformity, we would call this coercive power. On the other hand if he conforms in order to obtain praise for conformity, it is a case of reward power. The basic criterion for distinguishing referent power from both coercive and reward power is the mediation of the punishment and the reward by O: to the extent that O mediates the sanctions (i.e., has means control over P) we are dealing with coercive and reward power; but to the extent that P avoids discomfort or gains satisfaction by conformity based on identification, regardless of O's responses, we are dealing with referent power. Conformity with majority opinion is sometimes based on a respect for the collective wisdom of the group, in which case it is expert power. It is important to distinguish these phenomena, all grouped together elsewhere as "pressures toward uniformity," since the type of change which occurs will be different for different bases of power.

The concepts of "reference group" (40) and "prestige suggestion" may be treated as instances of referent power. In this case, O, the prestigeful person or group, is valued by P; because P desires to be associated or identified with O, he will assume attitudes or beliefs held by O. Similarly a negative reference group which O dislikes and evaluates negatively may exert negative influence on P as a result of negative referent power.

It has been demonstrated that the power which we designate as referent power is especially great when P is attracted to O (2, 7, 8, 9, 13, 23, 30). In our terms, this would mean that the greater the attraction, the greater the identification, and consequently the greater the referent power. In some cases, attraction or prestige may have a specific basis, and the range of referent power will be limited accordingly: a group of campers may have great referent power over a member regarding campcraft, but considerably less effect on other regions (30). However, we hypothesize that the greater the attraction of P toward O, the broader the range of referent power of O/P.

The new state of a system produced by referent power may be dependent on or independent of O; but the degree of dependence is not affected by the level of observability to O (6, 23). In fact, P is often not consciously aware of the referent power which O exerts over him. There is probably a tendency for some of these dependent changes to become independent of O quite rapidly.

Expert Power

The strength of the expert power of O/P varies with the extent of the knowledge or perception which P attributes to O within a given area. Probably P evaluates O's expertness in relation to his own knowledge as well as against an absolute standard. In any case expert power results in primary social influence on P's cognitive structure and probably not on other types of systems. Of course changes in the cognitive structure can change the direction of forces and hence of locomotion, but such a change of behavior is secondary social influence. Expert power has been demonstrated experimentally (8, 33). Accepting an attorney's advice in legal matters is a common example of expert influence; but there are many instances based on much less knowledge, such as the acceptance by a stranger of directions given by a native villager.

Expert power, where O need not be a member of P's group, is called "informational power" by Deutsch and Gerard (4). This type of expert power must be distinguished from influence based on the content of communication as described by Hovland et al. (17, 18, 23, 24). The influence of the content of a communication upon an opinion is presumably a secondary influence produced after the *primary* influence (i.e., the acceptance of the information). Since power is here defined in terms of the primary changes, the influence of the content on a related opinion is not a case of expert power as we have defined it, but the initial acceptance of the validity of the content does seem to be based on expert power or referent power. In other cases, however, so-called facts may be accepted as self-evident because they fit into P's cognitive structure; if this impersonal acceptance of the truth of the fact is independent of the more or less enduring relationship between O and P, then P's acceptance of the fact is not an actualization of expert power. Thus we distinguish between expert power based on the credibility of O and informational influence which is based on characteristics of the stimulus such as the logic of the argument or the "self-evident facts."

Wherever expert influence occurs it seems to be necessary both for P to think that O knows and for P to trust that O is telling the truth (rather than trying to deceive him).

Expert power will produce a new cognitive structure which is initially relatively dependent on O, but informational influence will produce a more independent structure. The former is likely to become more independent with the passage of time. In both cases the degree of dependence on O is not affected by the level of observability.

The "sleeper effect" (18, 24) is an interesting case of a change in the degree of dependence of an opinion on O. An unreliable O (who probably had negative referent power but some positive expert power) presented "facts" which were accepted by the subjects and which would normally produce secondary influence on their opinions and beliefs. However, the negative referent power aroused resistance and resulted in negative social influence on their beliefs (i.e., set up a force in the direction opposite to the influence attempt), so that there was little change in the subjects' opinions. With the passage of time, however, the subjects tended to forget the identity of the negative communicator faster than they forgot the contents of his communication, so there was a weakening of the negative referent influence and a consequent delayed positive change in the subjects' beliefs in the direction of the influence attempt ("sleeper effect"). Later, when the identity of the negative communicator was experimentally reinstated, these resisting forces were reinstated, and there was another negative change in belief in a direction opposite to the influence attempt (24).

The range of expert power, we assume, is more delimited than that of referent power. Not only is it restricted to cognitive systems but the expert is seen as having superior knowledge or ability in very specific areas, and his power will be limited to these areas, though some "halo effect" might occur. Recently, some of our renowned physical scientists have found quite painfully that their expert power in physical sciences does not extend to regions involving international politics. Indeed, there is some evidence that the attempted exertion of expert power outside of the range of expert power will reduce that expert power. An undermining of confidence seems to take place.

Summary

We have distinguished five types of power: referent power, expert power, reward power, coercive power, and legitimate power. These distinctions led to the following hypotheses.

1. For all five types, the stronger the basis of power the greater the power.
2. For any type of power the size of the range may vary greatly, but in general referent power will have the broadest range.
3. Any attempt to utilize power outside the range of power will tend to reduce the power.
4. A new state of a system produced by reward power or coercive power will be highly dependent on O, and the more observable P's conformity the more dependent the state. For the other three types of power, the new state is usually dependent, at least in the beginning, but in any case the level of observability has no effect on the degree of dependence.
5. Coercion results in decreased attraction of P toward O and high resistance; reward power results in increased attraction and low resistance.
6. The more legitimate the coercion the less it will produce resistance and decreased attraction.

Notes

1. The word "system" is here used to refer to a whole or to a part of the whole.
2. The concept of power has the conceptual property of *potentiality;* but it seems useful to restrict this potential influence to more or less enduring power relations between O and P by excluding from the definition of power those cases where the potential influence is so momentary or so changing that it cannot be predicted from the existing relationship. Power is a useful concept for describing social structure only if it has a certain stability over time: it is useless if every momentary social stimulus is viewed as actualizing social power.
3. We define resistance to an attempted induction as a force in the opposite direction which is set up by the same act of O. It must be distinguished from opposition, which is defined as existing opposing forces which do not have their source in the same act of O. For example, a boy might resist his mother's order to eat spinach because of the manner of the induction attempt, and at the same time he might oppose it because he didn't like spinach.
4. Miller (33) assumes that all living systems have this character. However, it may be that some systems in the life space do not have this elasticity.
5. Though the primary influence of coercive power is dependent, it often produces secon-

dary changes which are independent. Brainwashing for example, utilizes coercive power to produce many primary changes in the life space of the prisoner, but these dependent changes can lead to identification with the aggressor and hence to secondary changes in ideology which are independent.

References

1. Asch, S. E. *Social psychology*, New York: Prentice-Hall, Inc., 1952.
2. Back, K. W. Influence through social communication. *J. abnorm. soc. Psychol.* 46 (1951): 9-23.
3. Coch, L., and French, J. R. P., Jr. Overcoming resistance to change. *Hum. Relat.* 1 (1948): 512-32.
4. Deutsch, M., and Gerard, H. B. A study of normative and informational influences upon individual judgment. *J. abnorm. soc. Psychol.* 51 (1955) 629-36.
5. Dittes, J. E., and Kelley, H. H. Effects of different conditions of acceptance upon conformity to group norms. *J. abnorm. soc. Psychol.* 53 (1956): 100-107.
6. Festinger, L. An analysis of compliant behavior. In Sherif, M, and Wilson, M. O., (Eds.). *Group relations at the crossroads.* New York: Harper & Row, Publishers, 1953, 232-56.
7. Festinger, L. Informal social communication. *Psychol. Rev.* 57 (1950): 271-82.
8. Festinger, L.; Gerard, H. B.; Hymovitch, B.; Kelley, H. H.; and Raven, B. H. The influence process in the presence of extreme deviates. *Hum. Relat.* 5 (1952): 327-46.
9. Festinger, L.; Schachter, S.; and Back, K. The operation of group standards. In Cartwright, D., & Zander, A. *Group dynamics: research and theory.* Evanston: Row, Peterson, 1953, 204-23.
10. French, J. R. P., Jr.; Israel; Joachim: and As, Dagfinn "Arbeidernes medvirkning i industribedriften. En eksperimentell undersokelse." Institute for Social Research, Oslo, Norway, 1957.
11. French, J. R. P., Jr.; Levinger, G.; and Morrison, H. W. The legitimacy of coercive power. In preparation.
12. French, J. R. P., Jr., and Raven, B. H. An experiment in legitimate and coercive power. In preparation.
13. Gerard, H. B. The anchorage of opinions in face-to-face groups. *Hum. Relat.* 7 (1954): 313-25.
14. Goldhammer, H., and Shils, E. A. Types of power and status. *Amer. J. Sociol* 45 (1939) 171-78.
15. Herbst, P. G. Analysis and measurement of a situation. *Hum. Relat.* 2 (1953): 113-40.
16. Hochbaum, G. M. Self-confidence and reactions to group pressures. *Amer. soc. Rev.,* 19 (1954) 678-87.
17. Hovland, C. I., Lumsdaine, A. A., and Sheffield, F. D. *Experiments on mass communication.* Princeton: Princeton Univer. Press, 1949.
18. Hovland, C. I., and Weiss, W. The influence of source credibility on communication effectiveness. *Publ. Opin. Quart.* 15 (1951): 635-50.
19. Jackson, J. M., and Saltzstein, H. D. The effect of person-group relationships on conformity processes. *J. abnorm. soc. Psychol.* 57 (1958): 17-24.
20. Jahoda, M. Psychological issues in civil liberties. *Amer. Psychologist* 11 (1956): 234-40.

21. Katz, D., and Schank, R. L. *Social psychology.* New York: John Wiley & Sons, 1938.
22. Kelley, H. H., and Volkart, E. H. The resistance to change of group-anchored attitudes. *Amer. soc. Rev.,* 17 (1952): 453-65.
23. Kelman, H. Three processes of acceptance of social influence: compliance, identification and internalization. Paper read at the meetings of the American Psychological Association, August 1956.
24. Kelman, H., and Hovland, C. I. "Reinstatement" of the communicator in delayed measurement of opinion change. *J. abnorm. soc. Psychol.* 48 (1953): 327-35.
25. Lewin, K. *Dynamic theory of personality.* New York: McGraw-Hill Book Company, 1935, 114-70.
26. Lewin, K. *Field theory in social science.* New York: Harper & Row, Publishers, 1951.
27. Lewin, K., Lippitt, R., and White, R. K. Patterns of aggressive behavior in experimentally created social climates. *J. soc. Psychol.* 10 (1939): 271-301.
28. Lasswell, H. D., and Kaplan, A. *Power and society: A framework for political inquiry.* New Haven: Yale Univer. Press, 1950.
29. Linton, R. *The cultural background of personality.* New York: Appleton-Century-Crofts, 1945.
30. Lippitt, R.; Polansky, N.; Redl, F.; and Rosen, S. The dynamics of power. *Hum. Relat.* 5 (1952): 37-64.
31. March, J. G. An introduction to the theory and measurement of influence. *Amer. polit. Sci. Rev.* 49 (1955): 431-51.
32. Miller, J. G. Toward a general theory for the behavioral sciences. *Amer. Psychologist* 10 (1955): 513-31.
33. Moore, H. T. The comparative influence of majority and expert opinion. *Amer. J. Psychol.* 32 (1921): 16-20.
34. Newcomb, T. M. *Social psychology.* New York: Dryden, 1950.
35. Raven, B. H. The effect of group pressures on opinion, perception, and communication. Unpublished doctoral dissertation, University of Michigan, 1953.
36. Raven, B. H., and French, J. R. P., Jr. Group support, legitimate power, and social influence. *J. Person.,* 26, 1958, 400-09.
37. Rommetveit, R. *Social norms and roles.* Minneapolis: Univer. Minnesota Press, 1953.
38. Russell, B. *Power: A new social analysis.* New York: Norton, 1938.
39. Stotland, E., Zander, A., Burnstein, E., Wolfe, D., and Natsoulas, T. Studies on the effects of identification. University of Michigan, Institute for Social Research. Forthcoming.
40. Swanson, G. E., Newcomb, T. M., and Hartley, E. L. *Readings in social psychology.* New York: Holt, Rinehart and Winston, 1952.
41. Torrance, E. P., and Mason, R. Instructor effort to influence: an experimental evaluation of six approaches. Paper presented at USAF-NRC Symposium on Personnel, Training, and Human Engineering. Washington, D.C., 1956.
42. Weber, M. *The theory of social and economic organization.* Oxford: Oxford Univer. Press, 1947.

ENGINEER THE JOB TO
FIT THE MANAGER

FRED E. FIEDLER

What kind of leadership style does business need? Should company executives be decisive, directive, willing to give orders, and eager to assume responsibility? Should they be human relations-oriented, nondirective, willing to share leadership with the men in their group? Or should we perhaps start paying attention to the more important problem of defining under what conditions each of these leadership styles works best and what to do about it?

The success or failure of an organization depends on the quality of its management. How to get the best possible management is a question of vital importance; but it is perhaps even more important to ask how we can make better use of the management talent which *we already have*.

To get good business executives we have relied primarily on recruitment, selection, and training. It is time for businessmen to ask whether this is the only way or the best way for getting the best possible management. Fitting the man to the leadership job by selection and training has not been spectacularly successful. It is surely easier to change almost anything in the job situation than a man's personality and his leadership style. Why not try, then, to fit the leadership job to the man?

Executive jobs are surprisingly pliable, and the executive manpower pool is becoming increasingly small. The luxury of picking a "natural leader" from among a number of equally promising or equally qualified specialists is rapidly fading into the past. Business must learn how to utilize the available executive talent as effectively as it now utilizes physical plant and machine tools. Your financial expert, your top research scientist, or your production genius may be practically irreplaceable. Their jobs call for positions of leadership and responsibility. Replacements for these men can be neither recruited nor trained overnight, and they may not be willing to play second fiddle in their departments. If their leadership style does not fit the job, *we must learn how to engineer the job to fit their leadership style*.

In this article I shall describe some studies that illuminate this task of job engineering and adaptation. It will be seen that there are situations where the authoritarian, highly directive leader works best, and other situations where the egalitarian, more permissive, human relations-oriented leader works best; but almost always there are possibilities for changing the situation around somewhat to match the needs of the particular managers who happen to be available. The executive who appreciates these differences and possibilities has knowledge that can be valuable to him in running his organization.

To understand the problems that a new approach would involve, let us look first at some of the basic issues in organizational and group leadership.

From "Engineer the Job to Fit the Manager," by Fred E. Fiedler, *Harvard Business Review*, vol. 43, no. 5 (1965), © 1965 by the President and Fellows of Harvard College; all rights reserved.

Styles of Leadership

Leadership is a personal relationship in which one person directs, coordinates, and supervises others in the performance of a common task. This is especially so in "interacting groups," where men must work together cooperatively in achieving organizational goals.

In oversimplified terms, it can be said that the leader manages the group in either of two ways. He can:

- Tell people what to do and how to do it.
- Or share his leadership responsibilities with his group members and involve them in the planning and execution of the task.

There are, of course, all shades of leadership styles in between these two polar positions, but the basic issue is this: the work of motivating and coordinating group members has to be done either by brandishing the proverbial stick or by dangling the equally proverbial carrot. The former is the more orthodox job-centered, auto-cratic style. The latter is the more nondirective, group-centered procedure.

Research evidence exists to support both approaches to leadership. Which, then, should be judged more appropriate? On the face of it, the first style of leadership is best under some conditions, while the second works better under others. Accepting this proposition immediately opens two avenues of approach. Management can:

- Determine the specific situation in which the directive or the nondirective leadership style works best, and then select or train men so that their leadership style fits the particular job.
- Or determine the type of leadership style which is most natural for the man in the executive position, and then change the job to fit the man.

The first alternative has been discussed many times before; the second has not. We have never seriously considered whether it would be easier to fit the executive's job to the man.

Needed Style?

How might this be done? Some answers have been suggested by a research program on leadership effectiveness that I have directed under Office of Naval Research auspices since 1951. This program has dealt with a wide variety of different groups, including basketball teams, surveying parties, various military combat crews, and men in open-hearth steel shops, as well as members of management and boards of directors. When possible, performance was measured in terms of objective criteria—for instance, percentage of games won by high school basketball teams; tap-to-tap time of open-hearth shops (roughly equivalent to the tonnage of steel output per unit of time); and company net income over a three-year period. Our measure of leadership style was based on a simple scale indicating the degree to which a man described, favorably or unfavorably, his least-preferred co-worker (LPC). This co-worker did not need to be someone he actually worked with at the time, but could be someone the respondent had known in the past. Whenever possible, the score was obtained before the leader was assigned to his group.

The study indicates that a person who describes his least-preferred co-worker in a relatively favorable manner tends to be permissive, human relations-oriented, and considerate of the feelings of his men. But a person who describes his least-preferred co-worker in an unfavorable manner—who has what we have come to call a low LPC rating—tends to be managing, task-controlling, and less concerned with the human relations aspects of the job. It also appears that the directive, managing, and controlling leaders tend to perform best in basketball and surveying teams, in open-hearth shops, and (provided the leader is accepted by his group) in military combat crews and company managements. On the other hand, the nondirective, permissive, and human relations-oriented leaders tend to perform best in decision- and policy-making teams and in groups that have a creative task—provided that the group likes the leader or the leader feels that the group is pleasant and free of tension.

Critical Dimensions

But in order to tell which style fits which situation, we need to categorize groups. Our research has shown that "it all depends" on the situation. After reviewing the results of all our work and the findings of other investigators, we have been able to isolate three major dimensions that seem to determine, to a large part, the kind of leadership style called for by different situations.

It is obviously a mistake to think that groups and teams are all alike and that each requires the same kind of leadership. We need some way of categorizing the group-task situation, or the job environment within which the leader has to operate. If leadership is indeed a process of influencing other people to work together effectively in a common task, then it surely matters how easy or difficult it is for the leader to exert his influence in a particular situation.

Leader-Member Relations. The factor that would seem most important in determining a man's leadership influence is the degree to which his group members trust and like him, and are willing to follow his guidance. The trusted and well-liked leader obviously does not require special rank or power in order to get things done. We can measure the leader-member relationship by the so-called sociometric nomination techniques that ask group members to name in their group the most influential person, or the man they would most like to have as a leader. It can also be measured by a group-atmosphere scale indicating the degree to which the leader feels accepted and comfortable in the group.

The Task Structure. The second important factor is the "task structure." By this term I mean the degree to which the task (a) is spelled out step by step for the group and, if so, the extent to which it can be done "by the numbers" or according to a detailed set of standard operating instructions, or (b) must be left nebulous and undefined. Vague and ambiguous or unstructured tasks make it difficult to exert leadership influence, because neither the leader nor his members know exactly what has to be done or how it is to be accomplished.

Why single out this aspect of the task rather than the innumerable other possible ways of describing it? Task groups are almost invariably components of a larger organization that assigns the task and has, therefore, a big stake in seeing it performed properly. However, the organization can control the quality of a group's performance only if the task is clearly spelled out and programmed or structured.

When the task can be programmed or performed "by the numbers," the organization is able to back up the authority of the leader to the fullest; the man who fails to perform each step can be disciplined or fired. But in the case of ill-defined, vague, or unstructured tasks, the organization and the leader have very little control and direct power. By close supervision one can ensure, let us say, that a man will correctly operate a machine, but one cannot ensure that he will be creative.

It is therefore easier to be a leader in a structured task situation in which the work is spelled out than in an unstructured one which presents the leader and his group with a nebulous, poorly defined problem.

Position Power. Thirdly, there is the power of the leadership position, as distinct from any personal power the leader might have. Can he hire or fire and promote or demote? Is his appointment for life, or will it terminate at the pleasure of his group? It is obviously easier to be a leader when the position power is strong than when it is weak.

Model for Analysis

When we now classify groups on the basis of these three dimensions, we get a classification system that can be represented as a cube; see Exhibit 1. As each group is high or low in each of the three dimensions, it will fall into one of the eight cells.

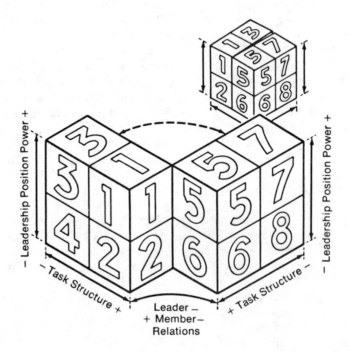

Exhibit 1. A model for classifying group-task situations.

From examination of the cube, it seems clear that exerting leadership influence will be easier in a group in which the members like a powerful leader with a clearly defined job and where the job to be done is clearly laid out (Cell 1); it will be difficult in a group where a leader is disliked, has little power, and has a highly ambiguous job (Cell 8).

In other words, it is easier to be the well-esteemed foreman of a construction crew working from a blueprint than it is to be the disliked chairman of a volunteer committee preparing a new policy.

I consider the leader-member relations the most important dimension, and the position-power dimension the least important, of the three. It is, for instance, quite possible for a man of low rank to lead a group of higher-ranking men in a structured task—as is done when enlisted men or junior officers conduct some standardized parts of the training programs for medical officers who enter the Army. But it is not so easy for a disrespected manager to lead a creative, policy-formulating session well, even if he is the senior executive present.

Varying Requirements

By first sorting the eight cells according to leader-member relations, then task structure, and finally leader position power, we can now arrange them in order according to the favorableness of the environment for the leader. This sorting leads to an eight-step scale, as in Exhibit 2. This exhibit portrays the results of a series of studies of groups performing well but (a) in different situations and conditions, and (b) with leaders using different leadership styles. In explanation:

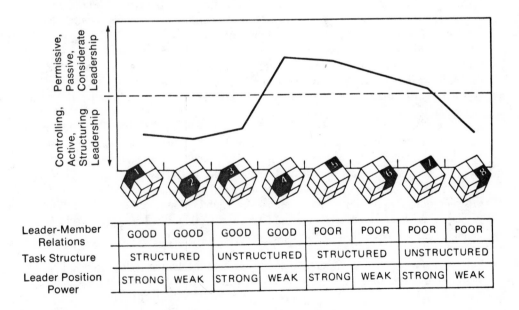

Leader-Member Relations	GOOD	GOOD	GOOD	GOOD	POOR	POOR	POOR	POOR
Task Structure	STRUCTURED		UNSTRUCTURED		STRUCTURED		UNSTRUCTURED	
Leader Position Power	STRONG	WEAK	STRONG	WEAK	STRONG	WEAK	STRONG	WEAK

Exhibit 2. How the style of effective leadership varies with the situation.

The *horizontal* axis shows the range of situations that the groups worked in, as described by the classification scheme used in Exhibit 1.

The *vertical* axis indicates the leadership style which was best in a certain situation, as shown by the correlation coefficient between the leader's LPC and his group's performance.

A positive correlation (falling above the midline) shows that the permissive, nondirective, and human relations-oriented leaders performed best; a negative correlation (below the midline) shows that the task-controlling, managing leader performed best. For instance, leaders of effective groups in situation categories 1 and 2 had LPC-group performance correlations of —.40 to —.80, with the average between —.50 and —.60; whereas leaders of effective groups in situation categories 4 and 5 had LPC-group performance correlations of .20 to .80, with the average between .40 and .50.

Exhibit 2 shows that both the directive, managing, task-oriented leaders and the nondirective, human relations-oriented leaders are successful under some conditions. Which leadership style is the best depends on the favorableness of the particular situation for the leader. In very favorable or in very unfavorable situations for getting a task accomplished by group effort, the autocratic, task-controlling, managing leadership works best. In situations intermediate in difficulty, the nondirective, permissive leader is more successful.

This corresponds well with our everyday experience. For instance:

• Where the situation is very favorable, the group expects and wants the leader to give directions. We neither expect nor want the trusted airline pilot to turn to his crew and ask, "What do you think we ought to check before takeoff?"

• If the disliked chairman of a volunteer committee asks his group what to do, he may be told that everybody ought to go home.

• The well-liked chairman of a planning group or research team must be nondirective and permissive in order to get full participation from his members. The directive, managing leader will tend to be more critical and to cut discussion short; hence he will not get the full benefit of the potential contributions by his group members.

The varying requirements of leadership styles are readily apparent in organizations experiencing dramatic changes in operating procedures. For example:

• The manager or supervisor of a routinely operating organization is expected to provide direction and supervision that the subordinates should follow. However, in a crisis the routine is no longer adequate, and the task becomes ambiguous and unstructured. The typical manager tends to respond in such instances by calling his principal assistants together for a conference. In other words, the effective leader changes his behavior from a directive to a permissive, nondirective style until the operation again reverts to routine conditions.

• In the case of a research planning group, the human relations-oriented and permissive leader provides a climate in which everybody is free to speak up, to suggest, and to criticize. Osborn's brainstorming method in fact institutionalizes these procedures. However, after the research plan has been completed, the situation becomes highly structured. The director now prescribes the task in detail, and he specifies the means of accomplishing it. Woe betide the assistant who decides to be creative by changing the research instructions!

Practical Tests

Remember that the ideas I have been describing emanate from studies of real-life situations; accordingly, as might be expected, they can be validated by organizational experience. Take, for instance, the dimension of leader-member relations described earlier. We have made three studies of situations in which the leader's position power was strong and the task relatively structured with clear-cut goals and standard operating procedures. In such groups as these the situation will be very favorable for the leader if he is accepted; it will be progressively unfavorable in proportion to how much a leader is disliked. What leadership styles succeed in these varying conditions? The studies confirm what our theory would lead us to expect:

• The first set of data come from a study of B-29 bomber crews in which the criterion was the accuracy of radar bombing. Six degrees of leader-member relations were identified, ranging from those in which the aircraft commander was the first choice of crew members and highly endorsed his radar observer and navigator (the key men in radar bombing), to those in which he was chosen by his crew but did not endorse his key men, and finally to crews in which the commander was rejected by his crew and rejected his key crew members. What leadership styles were effective? The results are plotted in Exhibit 3.

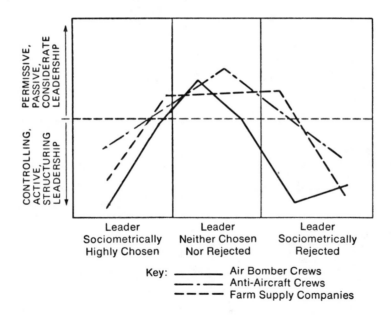

Exhibit 3. How effective leadership styles vary depending on group acceptance.

• A study of anti-aircraft crews compares the 10 most chosen crew commanders, the 10 most rejected ones, and 10 of intermediate popularity. The criterion is the identification and "acquisition" of unidentified aircraft by the crew. The results shown in Exhibit 3 are similar to those for bomber crew commanders.

• Exhibit 3 also summarized data for 32 small-farm supply companies. These were member companies of the same distribution system, each with its own board of directors and its own management. The performance of these highly comparable companies was measured in terms of percentage of company net income over a three-year period. The first quarter of the line (going from left to right) depicts endorsement of the general manager by his board of directors and his staff of assistant managers; the second quarter, endorsement by his board but not his staff; the third quarter, endorsement by his staff but not his board; the fourth quarter, endorsement by neither.

As can be seen from the results of all three studies, the highly accepted and strongly rejected leaders perform best if they are controlling and managing, while the leaders in the intermediate acceptance range, who are neither rejected nor accepted, perform best if they are permissive and nondirective.

Now let us look at some research on organizations in another country:

Recently in Belgium a study was made of groups of mixed language and cultural composition. Such teams, which are becoming increasingly frequent as international business and governmental activities multiply, obviously present a difficult situation for the leader. He must not only deal with men who do not fully comprehend one another's language and meanings, but also cope with the typical antipathies, suspicions, and antagonisms dividing individuals of different cultures and nationalities.

At a Belgian naval training center we tested 96 three-man groups, half of which were homogeneous in composition (all Flemish or all Walloon) and half heterogeneous (the leader differing from his men). Half of each of these had powerful leader positions (petty officers), and half had recruit leaders. Each group performed three tasks: one unstructured task (writing a recruiting letter); and two parallel structured tasks (finding the shortest route for ships through 10 ports, and doing the same for

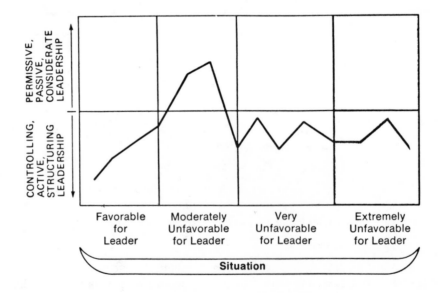

Exhibit 4. Effective leadership styles at the Belgian Naval Training Center.

12 ports). After each task, leaders and group members described their reactions—including group-atmosphere ratings and the indication of leader-member relations.

The various task situations were then arranged in order, according to their favorableness for the leader. The most favorable situation was a homogeneous group, led by a well-liked and accepted petty officer, which worked on the structured task of routing a ship. The situation would be especially favorable toward the end of the experiment, after the leader had had time to get to know his members. The least favorable situation was that of an unpopular recruit leader of a heterogeneous group where the relatively unstructured task of writing a letter came up as soon as the group was formed.

There were six groups that fell into each of these situations or cells. A correlation was then computed for each set of six groups to determine which type of leadership style led to best team performance. The results, indicated in Exhibit 4, support the conclusions earlier described.

Of particular interest is the fact that the difficult heterogeneous groups generally required controlling, task-oriented leadership for good performance. This fits the descriptions of successful leader behavior obtained from executives who have worked in international business organizations.

Conclusion

Provided our findings continue to be supported in the future, what do these results and the theory mean for executive selection and training? What implications do they have for the management of large organizations?

Selection and Training

Business and industry are now trying to attract an increasingly large share of exceptionally intelligent and technically well-trained men. Many of these are specialists whose talents are in critically short supply. Can industry really afford to select only those men who have a certain style of leadership in addition to their technical qualifications? The answer is likely to be negative, at least in the near future.

This being the case, can we then train the men selected in one leadership style or the other? This approach is always offered as a solution, and it does have merit. But we must recognize that training people is at best difficult, costly, and time-consuming. It is certainly easier to place people in a situation compatible with their natural leadership style than to force them to adapt to the demands of the job.

As another alternative, should executives learn to recognize or diagnose group-task situations so that they can place their subordinates, managers, and department heads in the jobs best suited to their leadership styles? Even this procedure has serious disadvantages. The organization may not always happen to have the place that fits the bright young man. The experienced executive may not want to be moved, or it may not be possible to transfer him.

Should the organization try to "engineer" the job to fit the man? This alternative is potentially the most feasible for management. As has been shown already, the type of leadership called for depends on the favorableness of the situation. The favorableness, in turn, is a product of several factors. These include leader-member relations, the homogeneity of the group, and the position power and degree to which the task is structured, as well as other, more obvious factors such as the leader's knowledge of his group, his familiarity with the task, and so forth.

It is clear that management can change the characteristic favorableness of the leadership situation; it can do so in most cases more easily than it can transfer the subordinate leader from one job to another or train him in a different style of interacting with his members.

Possibilities of Change

Although this type of organizational engineering has not been done systematically up to now, we can choose from several good possibilities for getting the job done:

1. *We can change the leader's position power.* We can either give him subordinates of equal or nearly equal rank or we can give him men who are two or three ranks below him. We can either give him sole authority for the job or require that he consult with this group, or even obtain unanimous consent for all decisions. We can either punctiliously observe the channels of the organization to increase the leader's prestige or communicate directly with the men of his group as well as with him in person.

2. *We can change the task structure.* The tasks given to one leader may have to be clarified in detail, and he may have to be given precise operating instructions; another leader may have to be given more general problems that are only vaguely elucidated.

3. *We can change the leader-member relations.* The Belgian study, referred to earlier, demonstrates that changing the group composition changes the leader's relations with his men. We can increase or decrease the group's heterogeneity by introducing men with similar attitudes, beliefs, and backgrounds, or by bringing in men different in training, culture, and language.

The foregoing are, of course, only examples of what could be done. The important point is that we now have a model and a set of principles that permit predictions of leadership effectiveness in interacting groups and allow us to take a look at the factors affecting team performance. This approach goes beyond the traditional notions of selection and training. It focuses on the more fruitful possibility of organizational engineering as a means of using leadership potentials in the management ranks.

A PATH GOAL THEORY
OF LEADER EFFECTIVENESS

ROBERT J. HOUSE

Introduction

Two major behavioral dimensions that have emerged from leadership research are those which sociologists have termed instrumental and social-emotional, or expressive, leadership behavior. Psychologists who have studied leadership have independently discovered these dimensions (Korman, 1966). The terms most frequently used to describe these behaviors are initiating structure and consideration. Leader initiating structure is used to describe the degree to which the leader initiates psychological structure for subordinates by doing such things as assigning particular tasks, specifying procedures to be followed, clarifying his expectations of subordinates, and scheduling work to be done. This dimension of leader behavior describes leaders who are similar to those prescribed by classical management theorists, that is, leaders who plan, organize, direct, and control. Leader consideration is used to describe the degree to which the leader creates a supportive environment of psychological support, warmth, friendliness, and helpfulness by doing such things as being friendly and approachable, looking out for the personal welfare of the group, doing little things for subordinates, and giving advance notice of change.

Research has indicated that leaders who initiate structure for subordinates are generally rated highly by superiors and have higher producing work groups than leaders who are low on initiating structure; and that leaders who are considerate of subordinates have more satisfied employees (Filley and House, 1969); however the evidence with respect to the relationship between initiating structure and satisfaction of subordinates is very mixed. Several studies have shown that initiating structure is frequently resented by unskilled and semiskilled employees and is a source of dissatisfaction (Filley and House, 1969), grievances, and turnover (Fleishman and Harris, 1962). However, employees in large groups have been found either to prefer initiating structure more or to dislike it less than employees in smaller groups (Hemphill, 1950; Mass, 1950; Vroom and Mann, 1960). And, Oaklander and Fleishman (1964) found initiating structure to be negatively correlated with intergroup conflict. Recent studies have shown that among high-level employees, initiating structure is positively related to satisfaction (House *et al.*, 1971a, 1971b), performance (House *et al.*, 1971b), and perceptions of organizational effectiveness, but negatively related to role conflict and ambiguity (Rizzo *et al.*, 1970).

This paper presents a theory of leader behavior that attempts to reconcile and integrate the conflicting results of previous studies under a set of general propositions from which they could have been deduced, and reports three studies designed to test eight hypotheses derived from the theory.

Reprinted by permission of the author and the publisher from *Administrative Science Quarterly*, vol. 16, no. 3 (Sept. 1971).

Theoretical Background

The theory advanced here is derived from the path-goal hypothesis advanced by Georgopoulos *et al.* (1957), and from previous research supporting the broad class of expectancy theory of motivation (Atkinson, 1958; Vroom, 1964; Porter and Lawler, 1967; Galbraith and Cummings, 1967; Graen, 1969; Lawler, 1968). The central concept of expectancy theories is that the force on an individual to engage in a specific behavior is a function of (*1*) his expectations that the behavior will result in a specific outcome; and (*2*) the sum of the valences, that is, personal utilities or satisfactions, that he derives from the outcome. The research findings indicate that the function is a nonlinear, monotonically increasing product of expectations and valences. Thus, according to this theory of motivation, an individual chooses the behaviors he engages in on the basis of (*1*) the valences he perceives to be associated with the outcomes of the behavior under consideration; and (*2*) his subjective estimate of the probability that his behavior will indeed result in the outcomes. Vroom (1964) formalized one perspective of expectancy motivation theory mathematically, and Galbraith and Cummings (1967) extended his formulation by pointing out that some of the valences associated with a specific behavior are intrinsic to the behavior itself and some are the extrinsic consequences of that behavior. To the extent that behavior is intrinsically valent it is also intrinsically motivational because the behavior is highly instrumental to the outcome of satisfaction. A person will be motivated to engage in such behavior because his expectancy that satisfaction will follow is nearly unity. That is, if the outcomes were contingent on an external rewarder—any significant other—the expectancy would be less than unity because the behavior might not be observed or recognized by the rewarder. However, when the reward is essentially self-administering, expectancy approaches unity.

The theory may be further extended and broken down into parts that have specific relevance for leadership using the concept of path instrumentality advanced by Evans (1968: 14): "This is the cognition of the degree to which following a particular path (behavior) will lead to a particular outcome, it is akin to (but not identical to) the concept of 'expectancy' introduced by Vroom." Evans (1968) has also advanced an extension of Vroom's (1964) theory and a path-goal theory of leadership. His theory is different from the one presented here in that its predictions are not contingent on situational variables, and it is not an attempt to account for the conflicting findings just revieweed.

According to the formulation advanced here, the individual makes probability estimates with respect to two linking points connecting behavior with its outcomes, and subjectively places values on the outcomes. The magnitude of these probability estimates indicates the degree of path instrumentality of his behavior for work-goal accomplishment and valence. This formulation can be expressed as the following formula:

$$M = IV_b + P_1 \left[IV_a + \sum_{i=1}^{n} (P_2 \, EV_i) \right]$$
$$i = 1, \ldots, n,$$

where:

M = motivation to work;
IV_b = intrinsic valence associated with goal-directed behavior;
IV_a = intrinsic valence associated with work-goal accomplishment;
EV_i = extrinsic valences associated with work-goal accomplishment;
P_1 = path instrumentality of behavior for work-goal attainment;
P_2 = path instrumentalities of work goal for extrinsic valences.

In work situations the individual estimates the path instrumentality, P_1, of his behavior for the accomplishment of some work goal. Here he considers such factors as his ability to behave in an appropriate and effective manner as well as the barriers to work-goal accomplishment in the environment, and the support he will receive from others to accomplish the work goal. In addition, he estimates the path instrumentality, P_2, of the work goal for attaining personal outcomes that have valence for him. For example, he estimates the probability that his superiors will recognize his goal accomplishment and reward him accordingly. He also considers, and places subjective values on the intrinsic valence associated with the behavior required to achieve the work goal, IV_b, the intrinsic valence associated with the achievement of the work goal, IV_a, and the extrinsic valences associated with the personal outcomes that he accrues as a result of achieving the work goal, EV_i.

The behavior of the leader is clearly relevant to all of the independent variables in this formulation. The leader, at least in part, determines what extrinsic rewards should be associated with work-goal accomplishment, EV_i. For example, he has some influence over the extent to which work-goal accomplishment will be recognized as a contribution and whether it will be rewarded with financial increases, promotion, assignment of more interesting tasks or opportunities for personal growth and development. Consequently, he influences the magnitude of the sum of the personal outcomes available. Second, the leader, through his interaction with the subordinate, can increase the subordinate's path instrumentality concerning the rewards forthcoming as a result of work-goal accomplishment, P_2. If he is consistent in his decision making with respect to recognizing and rewarding work-goal achievement, he will clarify the linkage between work-goal achievement and rewards. Thus, if he consistently rewards achievement, this will most probably increase the subordinate's path instrumentality, P_2, for valent personal outcomes. Third, through his own behavior he can provide support for the subordinate's efforts and thereby influence the probability that this effort will result in work-goal achievement, that is P_1. Fourth, the leader influences the intrinsic valences associated with goal accomplishment, IV_a, by the way he delegates and assigns tasks to subordinates, which determines the amount of influence the subordinate has in goal setting and the amount of control he is allowed in the task-directed effort. The greater the subordinate's opportunity to influence the goal and exercise control, the more intrinsically valent the work-goal accomplishment. Finally, the leader can increase the net intrinsic valence associated with goal-directed behavior, IV_b, by reducing frustrating barriers, being supportive in times of stress, permitting involvement in a wide variety of tasks, and being considerate of subordinate's needs.

Propositions

The above interpretation of motivation theory as applied to leadership suggests the following general propositions:

1. The motivation functions of a leader are to increase the net positive valences associated with work-goal attainment, increase the net positive valences associated with the path—behavior—to work-goal attainment, and increase the subordinate's path instrumentality with respect to work-goal attainment for personal outcomes and the behavior required for work-goal attainment. This statement assumes that when the subordinate is working under ambiguous path-goal relationships, his subjective probability estimates that his behavior will affect the valences he receives are less than the objective probabilities that his behavior will affect the valences he receives. When this assumption does not hold, that is, when under conditions of role ambiguity, his subjective probability estimates exceed the objective probabilities, then clarification of path-goal relationships will result in reduced motivation.

Stated less formally, the motivational functions of the leader consist of increasing personal pay-offs to subordinates for work-goal attainment, and making the path to these pay-offs easier to travel by clarifying it, reducing road blocks and pitfalls, and increasing the opportunities for personal satisfaction en route. The function of making the path easier and more satisfying to follow has been dealt with only implicitly in the leadership literature and, as will be shown, has significant implications for leader's behavior.

2. In increasing path instrumentality by clarifying path-goal relationships, the leader's behavior will have positive motivational effects to the extent that it reduces role ambiguity or makes possible the exercise of externally imposed controls. Reduction of role ambiguity results in increased motivation because role ambiguity is both negatively valent to subordinates (Rizzo *et al.*, 1970), and because it is usually associated with low path instrumentality. Externally imposed controls are motivational because they make possible the allocation of valences contingent on desirable behavior. Externally imposed control results in improved performance only to the extent that the rewards that are under the control of the leader are positively valent to the subordinates; punishments that are under the control of the leader are negatively valent to the subordinates; rewards and punishments are contingent on performance; and the contingency is clearly perceived by the subordinates. Whether performance motivated by external controls is satisfying to the subordinate, depends on his unconscious needs, conscious values, and perceptions of equity in the exchange of effort for rewards.

3. Where leader attempts to clarify path-goal relationships are redundant with existing conditions, that is, where path-goal relationships are apparent because of the routine of the tasks or objective system-fixed controls, attempts by the leader to clarify path-goal relationships will result in increased externally imposed control and will be seen by subordinates as redundant. Although such control may increase performance, it will also result in decreased satisfaction.

4. Leader behavior directed at need satisfaction of subordinates will result in increased performance to the extent that such satisfaction increases the net positive valence associated with goal-directed effort.

Hypotheses

From the above general propositions, several specific hypotheses concerning leader consideration, initiating structure, closeness of supervision, hierarchical influence, and authoritarianism can be derived. These hypotheses are consistent with empirical findings and thus illustrate how these prior findings could have been deduced from the general propositions of the theory. These hypotheses do not constitute an exhaustive list of relationships between the variables, but rather, serve to illustrate how the general propositions can be operationalized.

1. Leader initiating structure increases the path instrumentality for subordinates whose roles have nonroutine task demands by decreasing role ambiguity (Rizzo et al., 1970).

2. Informal leaders high in structure influence positively the subjective probabilities other group members assign to positively valent outcomes (Rim, 1965).

3. Leader initiating structure and consideration will have differential effects, depending on whether the task is satisfying or unsatisfying to the subordinate, and whether the task-role demands are clear or ambiguous.

The more satisfying the task, the less positive the relationship between consideration and subordinate satisfaction and performance (Fleishman, 1971: 13-14). These correlations will vary from insignificant to positive, depending on task satisfaction. For unsatisfying tasks, consideration will tend to offset dissatisfaction associated with the task; for satisfying tasks, consideration will be less important.

The less satisfying the task the more negative will be the relationship between structure and performance (Fleishman, 1971: 19-20). For unsatisfying tasks, structure will be viewed as an imposition of external control and, therefore dissatisfying, but will also be required to motivate subordinate effort toward goal achievement (Fleishman, 1971: 19-20).

The more ambiguous the task the more positive the relationship between leader initiating structure and subordinate satisfaction and performance. Structure serves to reduce role ambiguity and clarify path-goal relationships for ambiguous tasks but is viewed as unnecessary and redundant for nonambiguous tasks.

When task demands are self-evident due to a high degree of routinization, or where roles are clearly defined by such factors as mechanization, legal constraints, contracts, professional ethics, or group norms, initiating structure will not result in role clarification and will be unsatisfying to subordinates.

4. Where the follower's tasks are varied and interdependent and where teamwork norms are not developed within the group, initiating structure and close supervision will regulate and clarify path-goal relationships. Therefore, structure and close supervision will result in increased coordination, satisfaction, and performance (Patchen, 1962; Mass, 1950; Hemphill, 1950; Fleishman, 1971: 26).

5. Where tasks are interdependent, varied, and ambiguous, consideration will result in social support, friendliness among group members, increased cohesiveness, and team effort. These social outcomes will be positively valent to the members and thus increase the net sum of the positive valences associated with interdependent jobs requiring cooperation and team spirit (Oaklander and Fleishman, 1964; Fleishman, 1971: 13-14).

6. Where tasks and/or environment are frustrating and stress inducing, consideration will result in increased social support for followers and thus reduce negative valence associated with task-oriented behavior (Fiedler, 1967; Rim, 1965; Fleishman, 1971; 12-13.

7. Where stress is from sources external to the work unit and tasks are ambiguous, structure will result in increased ego protection, security, and satisfaction (Oaklander and Fleishman, 1964). In this instance, structure serves as an umbrella which protects followers from externally imposed stress.

8. Among hierarchically dependent employees under leaders with high upward influence, consideration will be positively related to satisfaction and performance of subordinates (Pelz, 1952). Among independent employees, or under leaders with low upward influence, consideration will have a lower positive relationship to subordinate satisfaction and performance (Wager, 1965; House *et al.*, 1971a; 1971b). Leader influence permits the leader to have more control over rewards for subordinates and thereby permits the leader to make subordinate valences contingent on performance and to make the outcomes of work-goal attainment more valent or less valent.

9. Under conditions of authoritarian or punitive leadership, both leader initiating structure and leader hierarchical influence will be negatively related to subordinate satisfaction. Under such conditions, both structure and influence will be seen as bases of authoritarian power by subordinates.

Reconciliation of Prior Findings

The usefulness of the theory can be illustrated by showing how it can be applied to reconcile what appear to be conflicting results of prior research cited earlier.

Fleishman and Harris (1962) found that when the leader's consideration toward subordinates' needs was used as a moderating variable—that is, when separate correlations are computed for high-considerate, medium-considerate, and low-considerate leaders—the relationship between leader structure and grievances and turnover varied. Specifically they found that there was no relationship between structure and grievances or turnover for highly considerate leaders; but for leaders with low consideration, the relationship was positive and significant.

House *et al.* (1971b) attempted to conduct a replication of the findings of Fleishman and Harris (1962), using the same scales for the predictor and moderator variables and eight measures of satisfaction with subordinate role expectations as criterion variables. The populations studied were salaried engineers, scientists, and technicians in three large research, design and development organizations. Unexpectedly, the data not only failed to replicate Fleishman and Harris' (1962) findings but suggested their opposite. Specifically it was found that leader initiating structure had a significant linear—unmoderated—positive relationship to half the satisfaction measures in two of the three companies, and significant positive correlations, .36, p«05, with satisfaction with the company management in all three companies studied. Furthermore, in one company under conditions of high leader consideration, leader initiating structure had significant positive curvilinear relationships to measures of satisfaction with job freedom, advancement, security, and family attitudes toward the respondent's job, with the eta correlation ranging from .36 to .50.

In a subsequent study of 192 nontechnical corporate office employees of a chemical manufacturing company, House *et al.* (1970) failed to replicate the findings of Fleishman and Harris (1962) and showed significant positive relationships between leader initiating structure and six measures of satisfaction.

The following three hypotheses derived from the theory serve to reconcile these findings.

Leader initiating structure can be hypothesized to clarify path-goal relationships for higher occupational level jobs which are frequently ambiguously defined. Such clarification reduces role ambiguity and increases the employee's perceived instrumentality of effort toward goal attainment. That is, it increases his subjective probability estimates that his efforts will result in goal attainment. Thus, the path-goal theory advanced here offers an explanation for the positive correlations between leader initiating structure and satisfaction among the high occupational level groups studied by House *et al.* (1970, 1971a, 1971b). The theory also explains the negative relationships found at lower occupational levels by Fleishman and Harris (1962). If it can be assumed that lower level jobs are generally more routine, that their path-goal relationships are usually self-evident, and that the job itself is frequently not intrinsically satisfying, then it can be hypothesized that leader initiating structure would be viewed by subordinates as an imposition of external control that does little to clarify path-goal relationships and is viewed by subordinates as being directed at keeping them working at unsatisfying activities. Although such control is likely to increase productivity by preventing soldiering, work restriction, or slowdowns, it is also a source of dissatisfaction to employees.

Another hypothesis derived from path-goal theory explains the findings concerning the moderating effect of consideration in some studies and not in others. Where the path is not viewed as satisfying, that is, for lower level jobs, it can be hypothesized that consideration serves as a source of extrinsic social satisfaction and support to the employee, thus making the path easier to travel. Consequently, for Fleishman and Harris' (1962) blue-collar workers, leader consideration moderated the unsatisfying effects of leader structure; whereas, for higher level jobs, where the path was intrinsically satisfying, the need for such support was lower and consequently consideration would be expected to have little or no moderating effect on the relationship between initiating structure and satisfaction.

Similarly in the International Harvester study reviewed by Fleishman (1971: 19-20), high leader initiating structure was found to be related to foremen ratings of proficiency, but also higher grievances; high leader consideration was found to be related to lower proficiency ratings, a tendency more pronounced in production than in other departments. The specific variable that was subsequently discovered to account for the differential relations across departments was pressure for output. If it can be assumed that the tasks in the production departments were less satisfying, then it follows that under conditions of high pressure for output, leader initiating structure would be viewed as an externally imposed form of control. Such control would be more acceptable to higher managers, but resented by the subordinates on whom it was imposed. Leader consideration is more likely to serve as a stress reducer as tasks become more unsatisfying and pressure for output increases. Thus the differential relationship found across types of departments can be explained in terms of differences in task satisfaction, that is, path valence and pressure for production differences. This explanation is directly deducible from the path-goal theory presented here and again illustrates the ability of the theory to accommodate and explain otherwise confusing empiric findings.

Three studies were conducted in which eight hypotheses specifically derived from the theory were tested, and three of these hypotheses were retested. . . .*

Conclusion

The theory advanced here has been shown to reconcile apparently conflicting findings from previous research. It has also been shown to provide an integrated explanation of the results of findings about authoritarianism in leader hierarchical influence, closeness of supervision, initiating structure, and consideration.

The theory was tested by correlational tests of 8 hypotheses derived from general propositions. The tests are somewhat weak in that the theoretical constructs, such as intrinsic task satisfaction and ambiguity of task-role demands, were inferred from situational measures of task autonomy and job scope and from occupational characteristics of the populations studied. These inferences make the tests susceptible to the error of rejecting a valid hypothesis, so that the tests are conservative ones. A further limitation is inherent in cross-sectional survey research, which can rule out invalid hypotheses, but cannot establish causal relationships among the variables.

The findings, when viewed collectively, generally support the theory. Among high-occupational groups, leader initiating structure was generally positively related to subordinate satisfaction and performance. This relationship was accounted for in terms of variance in subordinate role ambiguity, which was shown to have a negative correlation with initiating structure. The relationships between leader structure and subordinate role ambiguity, and satisfaction, although significant and in the theoretically predicted direction, were quite low, probably because it was not possible to control for contaminating variables that would be expected to suppress these relationships. The relationships between initiating structure and consideration, and subordinate satisfaction and performance varied significantly and widely in the directions predicted when moderated by job scope. When moderated by task autonomy the theoretical predictions were supported by one sample and not supported by another which raised a question about the appropriateness of task autonomy as an indicator of ambiguity of task-role demands and satisfaction among blue-collar workers as well as a question about the validity of the general proposition from which the hypothesis was derived.

On balance, the ability of the theory to reconcile and integrate earlier findings, together with moderate-to-strong support, for seven of the eight hypotheses tested, two of which were replicated in a second study, suggests that the theory shows promise and warrants further testing with more direct measurement of the theoretical constructs using experimental as well as correlational methods.

---

*Editor's Note: The results of the research studies, which generally support the hypotheses presented by House, are not included here. They are likely to be of great interest to students of leadership or to those who would like to see how theoretical formulations may be supported by empirical research evidence.

References

Atkinson, J. W. "Towards experimental analysis of human motivation in terms of motives, expectancies, and incentives." In J. W. Atkinson (ed.), Motives in Fantasy, Action and Society. New York: Van Nostrand. 1958.

Bescoe, Robert O., and C. H. Lawshe. "Foreman leadership as perceived by superiors and subordinates." Personnel Psychology, 12: 573-582. 1959.

Campbell, Donald T., and Donald W. Fiske. "Convergent and discriminant validation by the multitrait, multimethod matrix." Psychological Bulletin, 56: 81-105. 1959.

Evans, Martin G. The Effects of Supervisory Behavior upon Worker Perception of Their Path-Goal Relationships. Doctoral dissertation, Yale University. 1968.

———. "Convergent and discriminant validites of the Cornell job descriptive index and a measure of goal attainment." Journal of Applied Psychology, 55: 102-106. 1969.

Fiedler, Fred E. A Theory of Leadership Effectiveness. New York: McGraw-Hill. 1967.

Filley, Alan C., and Robert J. House. Managerial Process and Organizational Behavior. Glenview, Ill.: Scott Foresman. 1969.

Fleishman, Edwin A. "Twenty years of consideration and structure." In Symposium on Contemporary Development in the Study of Leadership. Carbondale: Southern Illinois University, in press. 1971.

Fleishman, Edwin A., and Edwin F. Harris. "Patterns of leadership behavior related to employee grievances and turnover." Personnel Psychology, 15: 43-56. 1962.

Galbraith, Jay, and Larry L. Cummings. "An empirical investigation of the motivational determinants of past performance: interactive effects between instrumentality, valence, motivation and ability." Organizational Behavior and Human Performance 2: 237-257. 1967.

Georgopoulous, Basil S., Gerald M. Mahoney, and Nyle W. Jones, Jr. "A path-goal approach to productivity." Journal of Applied Psychology, 41: 345-353. 1957.

Graen, George. "Instrumental theory of work motivation: some empirical results and suggested modifications." Journal of Applied Psychology, 53: 1-25. 1969.

Halpin, Andrew W. "The leader behavior and effectiveness of aircraft commanders." In Ralph H. Stogdill and A. E. Coons (eds.), Leader Behavior: Its Description and Measurement. Ohio State University, Bureau of Business Research. 1957.

Hemphill, John K. "Relations between the size of the group and the behavior of superior leaders." Journal of Abnormal and Social Psychology, 32: 11-12. 1950.

House, Robert J., Alan C. Filley, and Domo N. Gujarati. "Leadership style, hierarchical influence and the satisfaction of subordinate role expectations: a test of Likert's influence proposition." Journal of Applied Psychology, in press. 1971.

House, Robert J., Alan C. Filley, and Steven Kerr. "Relation of leader consideration and initiating structure to R and D subordinate satisfaction." Administrative Science Quarterly, 16: 19-30. 1971b.

House, Robert J., Lawrence A. Wigdor, and Kenneth Shulz. "Leader behavior, psychological participation, employee satisfaction and performance: an extension of prior investigations and a motivation theory interpretation." In W. M. Frey (ed.), Proceedings Seventh Annual Conference of Eastern Academy of Management: 179-195. Amherst: University of Massachusetts. 1970.

Korman, Abraham K. "Consideration, initiating structure and organizational criteria—a review." Personnel Psychology, 19: 349-361. 1966.

Lawler, Edward E. III. "Ability as a moderator of the relationship between job attitudes and job performance." Personnel Psychology, 19: 153-164. 1966.

——. "A correlation-causal analysis of the relationship between expectancy attitudes and job performance." Journal of Applied Psychology, 52: 462-468. 1966.

Mass, H. S. "Personal and group factors in leader's social perception." Journal of Abnormal and Social Psychology, 45: 54-63. 1950.

Oaklander, Harold, and Edwin A. Fleishman. "Patterns of leadership related to organizational stress in hospital settings." Administrative Science Quarterly, 8: 520-532. 1964.

Patchen, Marvin. "Supervisory methods and group performance norms." Administrative Science Quarterly, 7: 275-294. 1962.

Pelz, Donald C. "Influence: a key to effective leadership in the first-line supervisor." Personnel 29: 209-221. 1952.

Porter, Lyman, and Edward E. Lawler, III. Managerial Attitudes and Performance. Homewood, Ill.: Irwin Dorsey. 1967.

Rim, Y. "Leadership attitudes and decisions involving risk." Personnel Psychology, 18: 423-430. 1965.

Rizzo, John R., Robert J. House, and Sidney E. Lirtzman. "Role conflict and ambiguity in complex organizations." Administrative Science Quarterly, 15: 150-153. 1970.

Siegel, Sidney. Nonparametric Statistics. New York: McGraw-Hill. 1956.

Stogdill, Ralph M. Manual for the Leader Behavior Description Questionnaire. Columbus: Ohio State University of Business Research. 1965.

Vroom, Victor H. Work and Motivation. New York: Wiley. 1964.

Vroom, Victor, and Floyd Mann. "Leader authoritarianism and employee attitudes." Personnel Psychology, 13: 125-139. 1960.

Wager, Wesley L. "Leadership style, influence and supervisory role obligations." Administrative Science Quarterly, 9: 391-420. 1965.

Wigdor, Larry. "Effectiveness of Various Management and Organization Characteristics on Employee Satisfaction and Performance as a Function of Employees Need for Independence. Doctoral dissertation, Bernard M. Baruch College, City University of New York. 1969.

A NEW LOOK AT MANAGERIAL DECISION MAKING

VICTOR H. VROOM

While there are many differences in the roles that managers are called upon to play in organizations, all managers are decision-makers. Furthermore, there is little doubt that their effectiveness as managers is largely reflected in their "track record" in making the "right decisions."

Several scholarly disciplines share an interest in the decision-making process. On one hand, we have the fields of operations research and management science, both concerned with how to improve the decisions which are made. Their models of decision-making, which are aimed at providing a rational basis for selecting among alternative courses of action, are termed normative or prescriptive models. On the other hand, we have, in the efforts of psychologists, sociologists, and political scientists, attempts to understand the decisions and choices that people do make. March and Simon were among the first to suggest that an understanding of the decision-making process could be central to an understanding of the behavior of organizations—a point of view that was later amplified by Cyert and March in their behavioral theory of the firm. In this tradition, the goal is understanding rather than improvement, and the models descriptive rather than normative.

Whether the models are normative or descriptive, the common ingredient is a conception of decision-making as an information-processing activity, frequently one which takes place within a single manager. Both sets of models focus on the set of alternative decisions or problem solutions from which the choice is, or should be, made. The normative models are based on the consequences of choices among these alternatives; the descriptive models on the determinants of these choices. Alternatively, one could view the decision-making which occurs in organizations as a social or interpersonal process rather than a cognitive one. A major aspect of the manager's role in the decision-making process is to determine which person or persons should take part in the solution of the problem—or to put it more broadly—which social process should be engaged in the solution of the problem or the making of the decision.

. . . Underlying traditional approaches to leadership is the conviction that the manager is *the* problem-solver or decision-maker—that the task of translating problems into solutions is inevitably his task. In the alternative view of decision-making as a social process, we see the manager's task as determining how the problem is to be solved, not the solution to be adopted. . . .

Toward a Normative Model

[Let us begin] with [a] normative question. What would be a rational way of deciding on the form and amount of participation in decision-making that should be used

Reprinted by permission of the publisher from *Organizational Dynamics*, Spring 1973. © 1973 by AMACOM, a division of American Management Associations.

in different situations? We [are] tired of debates over the relative merits of theory X and theory Y and of the triusm that leadership depends upon the situation. We [feel] that it [is] time for the behavioral sciences to move beyond such generalities and to attempt to come to grips with the complexities of the phenomena with which they intended to deal.

TABLE 1. Types of Management Decision Styles

AI: You solve the problem or make the decision yourself, using information available to you at that time.

AII: You obtain the necessary information from your subordinate(s), then decide on the solution to the problem yourself. You may or may not tell your subordinates what the problem is in getting the information from them. The role played by your subordinates in making the decision is clearly one of providing the necessary information to you, rather than generating or evaluating alternative solutions.

CI: You share the problem with relevant subordinates individually, getting their ideas and suggestions without bringing them together as a group. Then *you* make the decision which may or may not reflect your subordinates' influence.

CII: You share the problem with your subordinates as a group, collectively obtaining their ideas and suggestions. Then *you* make the decision which may or may not reflect your subordinates' influence.

GII: You share a problem with your subordinates as a group. Together you generate and evaluate alternatives and attempt to reach agreement (consensus) on a solution. Your role is much like that of chairman. You do not try to influence the group to adopt "your" solution and you are willing to accept and implement any solution which has the support of the entire group.

Table 1 shows a set of alternative decision processes which we have employed in our research. Each process is represented by a symbol (e.g., AI, CI, GII) which will be used as a convenient method of referring to each process. The first letter in this symbol signifies the basic properties of the process (A stands for autocratic, C for consultative, and G for group). The roman numerals which follow the first letter constitute variants on that process. Thus, AI represents the first variant on an autocratic process, and AII the second variant, etc.[1]

Conceptual and Empirical Basis of the Model

A Model designed to regulate, in some rational way, choices among the decision processes shown in table 1 should be based on sound empirical evidence concerning the likely consequences of the styles. The more complete the empirical base of knowledge, the greater the certainty with which one can develop the model and the greater will be its usefulness. To aid in understanding the conceptual basis of the model, it is important to distinguish three classes of outcomes which bear on the ultimate effectiveness of decisions. These are:

1. The quality or rationality of the decision.

2. The acceptance or commitment on the part of subordinates to execute the decision effectively.

3. The amount of time required to make the decision.

The evidence regarding the effects of participation on each of these outcomes of consequences has been reviewed in a chapter written by the author for *The Handbook of Social Psychology*. It was concluded that:

> The results suggest that allocating problem solving and decision-making tasks to entire groups, requires a greater investment of man hours but produces higher acceptance of decisions and a higher probability that the decision will be executed efficiently. Differences between these two methods in quality of decisions and in elapsed time are inconclusive and probably highly variable. . . . It would be naive to think that group decision-making is always more "effective" than autocratic decision-making, or vice versa; the relative effectiveness of these two extreme methods depends both on the weights attached to quality, acceptance, and time variables, and on differences in amounts of these outcomes resulting from these methods, neither of which is invariant from one situation to another. The critics and proponents of participative management would do well to direct their efforts toward identifying the properties of situations in which different decision-making approaches are effective rather than wholesale condemnation or deification of one approach (Vroom, 1970, pp. 239-40).

Stemming from this review, an attempt has been made to identify these properties of the situation or problem which will be the basic elements in the model. These problem attributes are of two types: (1) those which specify the importance for a particular problem of quality and acceptance, and (2) those which, on the basis of available evidence have a high probability of moderating the effects of participation on each of these outcomes. Table 2 shows the problem attributes used in the present form of the model. For each attribute a question is provided which might be used by a leader in diagnosing a particular problem prior to choosing his leadership style.

In phrasing the questions, technical language has been held to a minimum. Furthermore, the questions have been phrased in Yes-No form, translating the continuous variable defined above into dichotomous variables. For example, instead of attempting to determine how important the decision quality is to the effectiveness of the decision (attribute A), the leader is asked in the first question to judge whether there is any quality component to the problem. Similarly, the difficult task of specifying exactly how much information the leader possesses that is relevant to the decision (attribute B) is reduced to a simple judgment by the leader concerning whether he has sufficient information to make a high-quality decision.

It has been found that managers can diagnose a situation quite quickly and accurately by answering this set of seven questions concerning it. But how can such responses generate a prescription concerning the most effective leadership style or decision process? What kind of normative model of participation in decision-making can be built from this set of problem attributes?

TABLE 2. Problem Attributes Used in the Model

Problem Attributes	*Diagnostic Questions*
A. The importance of the quality of the decision.	Is there a quality requirement such that one solution is likely to be more rational than another?
B. The extent to which the leader possesses sufficient information/expertise to make a high-quality decision by himself.	Do I have sufficient information to make a high-quality decision?
C. The extent to which the problem is structured.	Is the problem structured?
D. The extent to which acceptance or commitment on the part of subordinates is critical to the effective implementation of the decision.	Is acceptance of decision by subordinates critical to effective implementation?
E. The prior probability that the leader's autocratic decision will receive acceptance by subordinates.	If you were to make the decision by yourself, is it reasonably certain that it would be accepted by your subordinates?
F. The extent to which the subordinates are motivated to attain the organizational goals as represented in the objectives explicit in the statement of the problem.	Do subordinates share the organizational goals to be obtained in solving this problem?
G. The extent to which subordinates are likely to be in conflict over preferred solutions.	Is conflict among subordinates likely in preferred solutions!

Figure 1 shows one such model expressed in the form of a decision tree. It is the seventh version of such a model which we have developed over the last three years. The problem attributes, expressed in question form are arranged along the top of the figure. To use the model for a particular decision-making situation, one starts at the left-hand side and works toward the right, asking oneself the question immediately above any box' that is encountered. When a terminal node is reached, a number will be found designating the problem type[2] and one of the decision-making processes appearing in table 1. AI is prescribed for four problem types (1, 2, 4, and 5): AII is prescribed for two problem types (9 and 10); CI is prescribed for only one problem type (8); CII is prescribed for four problem types (7, 11, 13, and 14); and GII is prescribed for three problem types (3, 6,

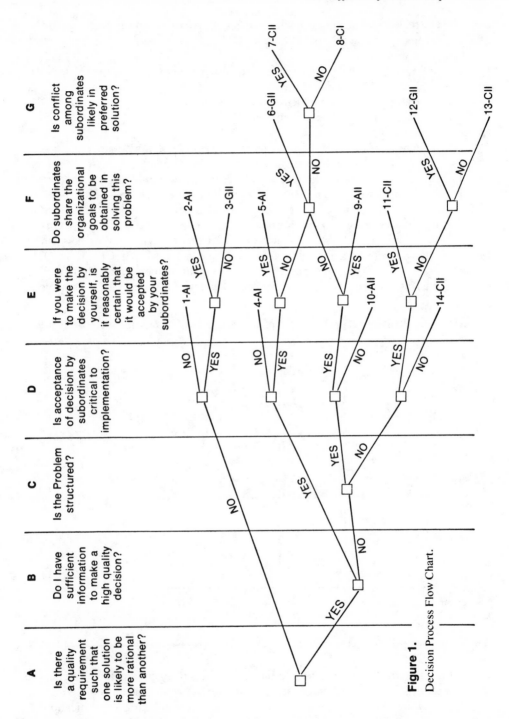

A	B	C	D	E	F	G
Is there a quality requirement such that one solution is likely to be more rational than another?	Do I have sufficient information to make a high quality decision?	Is the Problem structured?	Is acceptance of decision by subordinates critical to implementation?	If you were to make the decision by yourself, is it reasonably certain that it would be accepted by your subordinates?	Do subordinates share the organizational goals to be obtained in solving this problem?	Is conflict among subordinates likely in preferred solution?

Figure 1.
Decision Process Flow Chart.

and 12). The relative frequency with which each of the five decision processes would be prescribed for any manager would, of course, be dependent on the distribution of problem types in his role.

Once all seven rules have been applied to a given problem, a feasible set of decision processes is given. The feasible set for each of the 14 problem types is shown in table 3. It can be seen that there are some problem types for which only one method remains in the feasible set, others for which two remain feasible, and still others for which five methods remain feasible.

When more than one method remains in the feasible set, there are a number of alternative decision rules which might dictate the choice among them. One, which underlies the prescriptions of the model shown in figure 1, utilizes the number of manhours used in solving the problem as the basis for choice. Given a set of methods with equal likelihood of meeting both quality and acceptance requirements for the decision, it chooses that method which requires the least investment in manhours. On the basis of the empirical evidence summarized earlier, this is deemed to be the method furthest to the left within the feasible set. For example, since AI, AII, CI, CII, and GII are all feasible as in Problem Types 1 and 2, AI would be the method chosen. This decision rule acts to minimize manhours subject to quality and acceptance constraints.

TABLE 3. Problem Types and the Feasible Set of Decision Processes

Problem Type	Acceptable Methods
1	AI, AII, CI, CII, GII
2	AI, AII, CI, CII, GII
3	GII
4	AI, AII, CI, CII, GII*
5	AI, AII, CI, CII, GII*
6	GII
7	CII
8	CI, CII
9	AII, CI, CII, GII*
10	AII, CI, CII, GII*
11	CII, GII*
12	GII
13	CII
14	CII, GII*

*Within the feasible set only when the answer to question F is Yes

Application of the Model

To illustrate how the model might be applied in actual administrative situations, a . . . case will be presented and analyzed with the use of the model. Following the description of the case, the author's analysis will be given including a specification of problem type, feasible set, and solution indicated by the model. While an attempt has been made to describe [this] case as completely as is necessary to permit the reader to make the judgments required by the model, there may remain some room for subjectivity. The reader may wish after reading the case to analyze it himself using the model and then to compare his analysis with that of the authors.

. . . You are manufacturing manager in a large electronics plant. The company's management has always been searching for ways of increasing efficiency. They have recently installed new machines and put in a new simplified work system, but to the surprise of everyone, including yourself, the expected increase in productivity was not realized. In fact, production has begun to drop; quality has fallen off, and the number of employee separations has risen.

You do not believe that there is anything wrong with the machines. You have had reports from other companies who are using them and they confirm this opinion. You have also had representatives from the firm that built the machines go over them and they report that they are operating at peak efficiency.

You suspect that some parts of the new work system may be responsible for the change, but this view is not widely shared among your immediate subordinates, who are four first-line supervisors, each in charge of a section, and your supply manager. The drop in production has been variously attributed to poor training of the operators, lack of an adequate system of financial incentives, and poor morale. Clearly, this is an issue about which there is considerable depth of feeling within individuals and potential disagreement between your subordinates.

This morning you received a phone call from your division manager. He had just received your production figures for the last six months and was calling to express his concern. He indicated that the problem was yours to solve in any way that you think best, but that he would like to know within a week what steps you plan to take.

You share your division manager's concern with the falling productivity and know that your men are also concerned. The problem is to decide what steps to take to rectify the situation.

Analysis

Questions A (Quality?) = Yes
         B (Manager's Information?) = No
         C (Structured?) = No
         D (Acceptance?) = Yes
         E (Prior Probability of Acceptance?) = No
         F (Goal Congruence?) = Yes
         G (Conflict?) = Yes
Problem Type: 12
Feasible Set: GII
Minimum Man-Hours Solution (from Figure 1): GII
Rule Violations: AI violates Rules 1, 3, 4, 5, 7
                AII violates Rules 3, 4, 5, 7
                CI violates Rules 3, 5, 7
                CII violates Rule 7

Therefore, in the example, the appropriate decision process would be GII: you share the problem with your subordinates and arrive at a decision as a group.

Reference

Vroom, V., and Yetton, P., *Leadership and Decision-Making* (Pittsburgh: University of Pittsburgh Press, 1973).

Notes

1. The absence of GI from the code is attributable to the fact that the list of decision processes used in this paper is a part of a larger set of such processes used in broader and more comprehensive models. A complete explication of the entire set of processes and of the models which use them may be found in Vroom and Yetton [1973].
2. Problem type is a nominal variable designating classes of problems generated by the paths which lead to the terminal nodes.

PART SEVEN

Organizational Change and Development

Organization change can be treated at both the organizational and the individual level. At the organizational level, change is involved with how organizations adjust or adapt their structure to be consistent with the organization's environment. Organization change is externally induced: when the environment changes from turbulent to stable, organic organizations will become more mechanistic—and vice versa. Structural change of this type is an evolutionary process. The manager can do little but react to it. Awareness of alternative structural forms should facilitate adaptation rather than resistance. Under changing conditions, resisting a change in organization structure to a more appropriate form is certainly likely to restrict the effectiveness of the system.

Individual change is generally of greater concern to managers. Change at the individual level means changing people, singly or in groups, to improve the effectiveness of the organization. The focus is on changing knowledge, attitudes, skills, and/or the capability to perform a job.

A different strategy of change can be applied, at both the individual and organizational level, for each of the following sets of conditions:

1. The organization structure may be appropriate to the environment, and the individuals within the system may have effectively adapted. This, of course, means that the system is functioning relatively well and surviving. Under these conditions, there is little need to attempt any change of a major nature. Introducing such efforts would be self-defeating, disturbing the equilibrium of the organization-environment-individual relationship.

2. The structure may not be appropriate for the environmental conditions, and the individuals may not possess required skills and attitudes. For instance, a mechanistic structure in a dynamic environment, staffed largely by people who function reasonably well in a fairly structured setting, is a situation which needs major change. Under such conditions major structural change, along with personnel changes, may be requried.

It is unlikely that this problem will exist for a total organization, since a whole organization so incongruent with the environment is not likely to survive long. Rather, this may be a problem for a particular subunit; for instance, a shift in the technological environment may alter the kind of work done by a research and development group. If the nature of the shift is dynamic to stable, more routine policies and procedures may be required in the lab. Personnel changes might be required, such as replacing research chemists with chemical engineers.

3. It is possible that the organization structure is inappropriate for effective environmental adaptation, but the members have the capacity to perform effectively if it were changed. There is no people problem here—the system itself is inappropriate. This might occur when an organization structure is imposed without regard to external conditions. For example, a director of manufacturing might be assigned control of the R and D lab and impose relatively rigid rules and policies which could seriously hamper its effectiveness. The solution seems to be the revision of the structural system. Of course, structural alteration may be possible only by putting someone else in charge, but within the unit the prescription for change is structural.

4. The structure may be appropriate, but the attitudes, values, and/or skills of the members are inconsistent or incongruent. In this case, it is clear that some sort of *organizational development* is necessary. The need for major structural alterations is less likely. Although some minor policy adjustments may be necessary, the major thrust must be on changing individuals or groups.

One strategy for change is the selection approach. An attempt can be made to replace current employees with new ones who possess attributes compatible with the system. A second, more likely, alternative, would be training and development.

The fourth condition, involving organizational development, is the one treated in the readings in this part of the book.

In a set of three articles, Hersey and Blanchard provide an overview of organizational change problems. In the first selection they define four levels or types of change: knowledge change, attitude change, individual-behavior change, and group behavior change. Each type along the line involves a substantial increase over the previous one in both time and difficulty. This is so because more factors must be dealt with at each level in order to induce and maintain new performance patterns. It may be necessary, for instance, to alter leadership relationships *and* a complex set of structural factors to induce *major* individual and group change.

Hersey and Blanchard describe how positive and negative reinforcement may affect the behavior and attitudes of individuals, and go on to consider some of the general problems of implementing organizational change. They note that there are forces which drive an organization toward an equilibrium state, and that to induce change, these forces must be altered.

The methods described by Hersey and Blanchard attempt to change the behavior or attitudes of individuals. Too often, however, change programs have not taken into account the environment within which an individual works or the initial values and beliefs of those who are subjects of the environment. Organizational Development (OD) aims not only at individuals, but at the organization as a whole. The objective is a coordinated, planned change of all factors which may cause interpersonal problems in the organization. OD solutions may range from intervention methods, such as T-groups, to changing the nature of the structural characteristics, such as the compensation system, accounting system, or production system. A review of part 5 will suggest once more how these structual factors can affect performance and attitudes.

A broad overview of organizational development is given by French. He details the necessary conditions for OD to be successful. He clearly stresses the underlying humanistic orientation of OD as one of its fundamental premises. Basically, OD is a general approach to dealing with the problem of changing the effectiveness of organizations. It may be any one or a combination of a number of techniques and methods designed to induce more effective interaction among individuals. The techniques range from lectures, to sensitivity-training, to the redesign of organization structure.

The most important aspect of OD may well be the *diagnostic effort* to determine problem areas. Organization diagnosis may uncover problems otherwise left untouched. Effective diagnosis will focus problem-solving where it can have the most impact.

OD efforts are likely to work best when there is top-management commitment to change. But commitment means more than a statement of support. It must be exhibited in practice, which means that top managers must operate in ways consistent with what they expect subordinates to do. "Do as I say, not as I do," does not work with OD, or any other change effort.

We have argued earlier that systemic factors, one of which is the characteristics of the work itself, affect behavior patterns. When a work setting is a performance deterrent, trying to change people may have little impact; therefore, the job itself must be changed. Yet not all jobs can be altered. When such is the case, the manager must be prepared to live with the problem created by the job environment, or eliminate the job through automation.

Beer and Huse describe a broadly-based OD effort. They show how several strategies were brought together in a change program. Their study shows the incredibly interactive nature of OD. It is not reasonable to undertake change effort without attempting to assess the problems emanating from such interactive effects.

The development of stable, predictable performance patterns is a major part of a manager's job. This can be regarded as a form of behavioral manipulation. Motivation strategies, the design of organization structure, and the implementation of change programs, especially those which use positive reinforcement methods, represent forms of behavior modification. These methods can be powerful, and yet they may be applied without the awareness of those they affect. In the closing article of the book, Kanfer analyzes the ethical questions involved in this issue and discusses safeguards against misapplication of change efforts.

ORGANIZATION DEVELOPMENT:
OBJECTIVES, ASSUMPTIONS, AND STRATEGIES

WENDELL FRENCH

Organization development refers to a long-range effort to improve an organization's problem solving capabilities and its ability to cope with changes in its external environment with the help of external or internal behavioral-scientist consultants, or change agents, as they are sometimes called. Such efforts are relatively new but are becoming increasingly visible within the United States, England, Japan, Holland, Norway, Sweden, and perhaps in other countries. A few of the growing number of organizations which have embarked on organization development (OD) efforts to some degree are Union Carbide, Esso, TRW Systems, Humble Oil, Weyerhaeuser, and Imperial Chemical Industries Limited. Other kinds of institutions, including public school systems, churches, and hospitals, have also become involved.

Organization development activities appear to have originated about 1957 as an attempt to apply some of the values and insights of laboratory training to total organizations. The late Douglas McGregor, working with Union Carbide, is considered to have been one of the first behavioral scientists to talk systematically about and to implement an organization development program[1] Other names associated with such early efforts are Herbert Shepard and Robert Blake who, in collaboration with the Employee Relations Department of the Esso Company, launched a program of laboratory training (sensitivity training) in the company's various refineries. This program emerged in 1957 after a headquarters human relations research division began to view itself as an internal consulting group offering services to field managers rather than as a research group developing reports for top management.[2]

Objectives of Typical OD Programs

Although the specific interpersonal and task objectives of organization development programs will vary according to each diagnosis of organization problems, a number of objectives typically emerge. These objectives reflect problems which are very common in organizations:

1. To increase the level of trust and support among organization members.

2. To increase the incidence of confrontation of organization problems, both within groups and among groups, in contrast to "sweeping problems under the rug."

3. To create an environment in which authority of assigned role is augmented by authority based on knowledge and skill.

4. To increase the openness of communications laterally, vertically, and diagonally.

5. To increase the level of personal enthusiasm and satisfaction in the organization.

6. To find synergistic solutions[3] to problems with greater frequency. (Synergistic

Reprinted from *California Management Review*, vol. 12, no. 2, pp. 23-46, by permission of The Regents; © 1969, by The Regents of the University of California.

solutions are creative solutions in which 2+2 equals more than 4, and through which all parties gain more through cooperation than through conflict.)

7. To increase the level of self and group responsibility in planning and implementation.[4]

Difficulties in Categorizing

Before describing some of the basic assumptions and strategies of organization development, it would be well to point out that one of the difficulties in writing about such a "movement" is that a wide variety of activities can be and are subsumed under this label. These activities have varied all the way from inappropriate application of some "canned" management development program to highly responsible and skillful joint efforts between behavioral scientists and client systems.

Thus, while labels are useful, they may gloss over a wide range of phenomena. The "human relations movement," for example, has been widely written about as though it were all bad or all good. To illustrate, some of the critics of the movement have accused it of being "soft" and a "hand-maiden of the Establishment," of ignoring the technical and power systems of organizations, and of being too naively participative. Such criticisms were no doubt warranted in some circumstances, but in other situations may not have been at all appropriate. Paradoxically, some of the major insights of the human relations movement, e.g., that the organization can be viewed as a social system and that subordinates have substantial control over productivity have been assimilated by its critics.

In short, the problem is to distinguish between appropriate and inappropriate programs, between effectiveness and ineffectiveness, and between relevancy and irrelevancy. The discussion which follows will attempt to describe the "ideal" circumstances for organization development programs, as well as to point out some pitfalls and common mistakes in organization change efforts.

Relevancy to Different Technologies and Organization Subunits

Research by Joan Woodward[5] suggests that organization development efforts *might be more relevant to certain kinds of technologies and organizational levels, and perhaps to certain workforce characteristics, than to others.* For example, OD efforts may be more appropriate for an organization devoted to prototype manufacturing than for an automobile assembly plant. However, experiments in an organization like Texas Instruments suggest that some manufacturing efforts which appear to be inherently mechanistic may lend themselves to a more participative, open management style than is often assumed possible.[6]

However, assuming the constraints of a fairly narrow job structure at the rank-and-file level, organization development efforts may inherently be more productive and relevant at the managerial levels of the organization. Certainly OD efforts are most effective when they start at the top. Research and development units—particularly those involving a high degree of interdependency and joint creativity among group members—also appear to be appropriate for organization development activities, if group members are currently experiencing problems in communicating or interpersonal relationships.

Basic Assumptions

Some of the basic assumptions about people which underlie organization development programs are similar to "Theory Y" assumptions[7] and will be repeated only briefly here. However some of the assumptions about groups and total systems will be treated more extensively. The following assumptions appear to underlie organization development efforts.[8]

About People

● Most individuals have drives toward personal growth and development, and these are most likely to be actualized in an environment which is both supportive and challenging.

● Most people desire to make, and are capable of making, a much higher level of contribution to the attainment of organization goals than most organizational environments will permit.

About People in Groups

● Most people wish to be accepted and to interact cooperatively with at least one small reference group, and usually with more than one group, e.g., the work group, the family group.

● One of the most psychologically relevant reference groups for most people is the work group, including peers and the superior.

● Most people are capable of greatly increasing their effectiveness in helping their reference groups solve problems and in working effectively together.

● For a group to optimize its effectiveness, the formal leader cannot perform all of the leadership functions in all circumstances at all times, and all group members must assist each other with effective leadership and member behavior.

About People in Organizational Systems

● Organizations tend to be characterized by overlapping, interdependent work groups, and the "linking pin" function of supervisors and others needs to be understood and facilitated.[9]

● What happens in the broader organization affects the small work group and vice versa.

● What happens to one subsystem (social, technological, or administrative) will affect and be influenced by other parts of the system.

● The culture in most organizations tends to suppress the expression of feelings which people have about each other and about where they and their organizations are heading.

● Suppressed feelings adversely affect problem solving, personal growth, and job satisfaction.

● The level of interpersonal trust, support, and cooperation is much lower in most organizations than is either necessary or desirable.

● "Win-lose" strategies between people and groups, while realistic and appropriate in some situations, are not optimal in the long run to the solution of most organizational problems.

- Synergistic solutions can be achieved with a much higher frequency than is acutally the case in most organizations.
- Viewing feelings as data important to the organization tends to open up many avenues for improved goal setting, leadership, communications, problem solving, intergroup collaboration, and morale.
- Improved performance stemming from organizational development efforts needs to be sustained by appropriate changes in the appraisal, compensation, training, staffing, and task-specialization subsystem—in short, in the total personnel system.

Value and Belief Systems of Behavioral Scientist-change Agents

While scientific inquiry, ideally, is value-free, the applications of science are not value-free. Applied behavioral scientist-organization development consultants tend to subscribe to a comparable set of values, although we should avoid the trap of assuming that they constitute a completely homogenous group. They do not.

One value, to which many behavioral scientist-change agents tend to give high priority, is that the needs and aspirations of human beings are the reasons for organized effort in society. They tend, therefore, to be developmental in their outlook and concerned with the long-range opportunities for the personal growth of people in organizations.

A second value is that work and life can become richer and more meaningful, and organized effort more effective and enjoyable, if feelings and sentiments are permitted to be a more legitimate part of the culture. A third value is a commitment to an action role, along with a commitment to research, in an effort to improve the effectiveness of organizations.[10] A fourth value—or perhaps a belief—is that improved competency in interpersonal and intergroup relationship will result in more effective organizations.[11] A fifth value is that behavioral science research and an examination of behavioral science assumptions and values are relevant and important in considering organizational effectiveness. While many change agents are perhaps overly action-oriented in terms of the utilization of their time, nevertheless, as a group they are paying more and more attention to research and to the examination of ideas.[12]

The value placed on research and inquiry raises the question as to whether the assumptions stated earlier are values, theory, or "facts." In my judgment, a substantial body of knowledge, including research on leadership, suggests that there is considerable evidence for these assumptions. However, to conclude that these assumptions are facts, laws, or principles would be to contradict the value placed by behavioral scientists on continuous research and inquiry. Thus, I feel that they should be considered theoretical statements which are based on provisional data.

This also raises the paradox that the belief that people are important tends to result in their being important. The belief that people can grow and develop in terms of personal and organizational competency tends to produce this result. Thus, values and beliefs tend to be self-fulfilling, and the question becomes "What do you choose to want to believe?" While this position can become Pollyannaish in the sense of not seeing the real world, nevertheless, behavioral scientist-change agents, at least this one, tend to place a value on optimism. It is a kind of optimism that says people can do a better job of goal setting and facing up to and solving problems, not an optimism that says the number of problems is diminishing.

It should be added that it is important that the values and beliefs of each behavioral science-change agent be made visible both to himself and to the client. In the first place, neither can learn to adequately trust the other without exposure—a hidden agenda handicaps both trust building and mutual learning. Second, and perhaps more pragmatically, organizational change efforts tend to fail if a prescription is applied unilaterally and without proper diagnosis.

Strategy in Organization Development: an Action Research Model

A frequent strategy in organization development programs is based on what

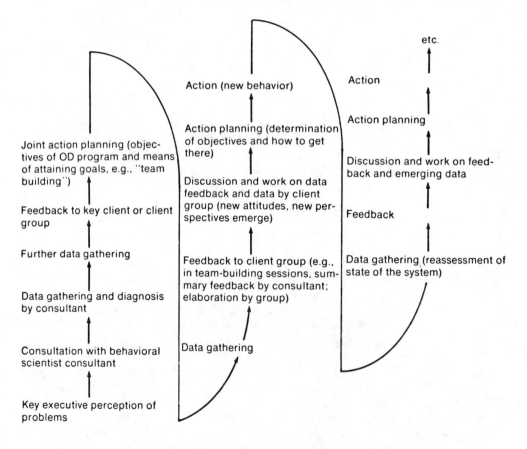

Figure 1. An action research model for organization development.

behavioral scientists refer to as an "action research model." This model involves extensive collaboration between the consultant (whether an external or an internal change agent) and the client group, data gathering, data discussion, and planning. While descriptions of this model vary in detail and terminology from author to author, the dynamics are essentially the same.[13]

Figure 1 summarizes some of the essential phases of the action research model, using an emerging organization development program as an example. The key aspects of the model are *diagnosis, data gathering, feedback to the client group, data discussion and work by the client group, action planning,* and *action.* The sequence tends to be cyclical, with the focus on new or advanced problems as the client group learns to work more effectively together. Action research should also be considered a process, since, as William Foote Whyte says, it involves ". . . a continuous gathering and analysis of human relations research data and the feeding of the findings into the organization in such a manner as to change behavior."[14] (Feedback we will define as nonjudgmental observations of behavior.)

Ideally, initial objectives and strategies of organization development efforts stem from a careful diagnosis of such matters as interpersonal and intergroup problems, decision-making processes, and communication flow which are currently being experienced by the client organization. As a preliminary step, the behavioral scientist and the key client (the president of a company, the vice president in charge of a division, the works manager or superintendent of a plant, a superintendent of schools, etc.), will make a joint initial assessment of the critical problems which need working on. Subordinates may also be interviewed in order to provide supplemental data. The diagnosis may very well indicate that the central problem is technological or that the key client is not at all willing or ready to examine the organization's problem-solving ability or his own managerial behavior.[15] Either could be a reason for postponing or moving slowly in the direction of organization development activities, although the technological problem may easily be related to deficiencies in interpersonal relationships or decision making. The diagnosis might also indicate the desirability of one or more additional specialists (in engineering, finance, or electronic data processing, for example) to simultaneously work with the organization.

This initial diagnosis, which focuses on the expressed needs of the client, is extremely critical. As discussed earlier, in the absence of a skilled diagnosis, the behavioral scientist-change agent would be imposing a set of assumptions and a set of objectives which may be hopelessly out of joint with either the current problems of the people in the organization or their willingness to learn new modes of behavior. In this regard, it is extremely important that the consultant *hear and understand* what the client is trying to tell him. This requires a high order of skill.[16]

Interviews are frequently used for *data gathering* in OD work for both initial diagnosis and subsequent planning sessions, since personal contact is important for building a cooperative relationship between the consultant and the client group. The interview is also important since the behavioral scientist-consultant is interested in spontaneity and in feelings that are expressed as well as cognitive matters. However, questionnaires are sometimes successfully used in the context of what is sometimes referred to as survey feedback, to supplement interview data.[17]

Data gathering typically goes through several phases. The first phase is related to diagnosing the state of the system and to making plans for organizational change.

This phase may utilize a series of interviews between the consultant and the key client, or between a few key executives and the consultant. Subsequent phases focus on problems specific to the top executive team and to subordinate teams. (See Figure 2.)

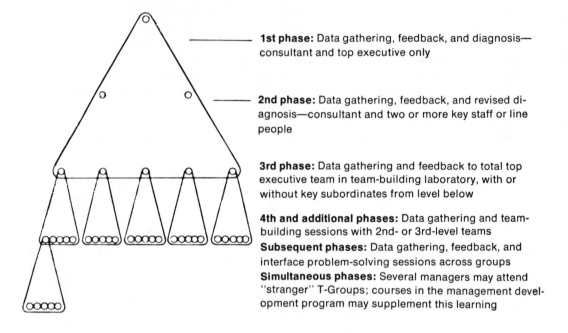

1st phase: Data gathering, feedback, and diagnosis—consultant and top executive only

2nd phase: Data gathering, feedback, and revised diagnosis—consultant and two or more key staff or line people

3rd phase: Data gathering and feedback to total top executive team in team-building laboratory, with or without key subordinates from level below

4th and additional phases: Data gathering and team-building sessions with 2nd- or 3rd-level teams

Subsequent phases: Data gathering, feedback, and interface problem-solving sessions across groups

Simultaneous phases: Several managers may attend "stranger" T-Groups; courses in the management development program may supplement this learning

Figure 2. Organization development phases in a hypothetical organization.

Typical questions in data gathering or "problem sensing" would include: What problems do you see in your group, including problems between people, that are interfering with getting the job done the way you would like to see it done?; and what problems do you see in the broader organization? Such open-ended questions provide wide latitude on the part of the respondents and encourage a reporting of problems *as the individual sees them.* Such interviewing is usually conducted privately, with a commitment on the part of the consultant that the information will be used in such a way as to avoid unduly embarrassing anyone. The intent is to find out what common problems or themes emerge, with the data to be used constructively for both diagnostic and feedback purposes.

Two- or three-day offsite *team-building or group problem-solving sessions* typically become a major focal point in organization development programs. During these meetings the behavioral scientist frequently provides *feedback* to the group in terms of themes which emerged in the problem-sensing interviews.[18] He may also encourage the group to determine which items or themes should have priority in terms of maximum utilization of time. These themes usually provide substantial and meaningful data for the group to begin work on. One-to-one interpersonal matters, both positive and negative, tend to emerge spontaneously as the participants gain confidence from the level of support sensed in the group.

Different consultants will vary in their mode of behavior in such sessions, but will typically serve as *"process" observers and as interpreters of the dynamics of the group interaction* to the degree that the group expresses a readiness for such intervention. They also typically encourage people to take risks, a step at a time, and to experiment with new behavior in the context of the level of support in the group. Thus, the trainer-consultant(s) serves as a stimulant to new behavior but also as a protector. The climate which I try to build, for example is "Let's not tear down any more than we can build back together."[19] Further, the trainer-consultant typically works with the group to assist team members in improving their skills in diagnosing and facilitating group progress.[20]

It should be noted, however, that different groups will have different needs along a task-process continuum. For example, some groups have a need for intensive work on clarifying objectives; others may have the greatest need in the area of personal relationships. Further, the consultant or the chief consultant in a team of consultants involved in an organization development program will play a much broader role than serving as a T-group or team-building trainer. He will also play an important role in periodic data gathering and diagnosis and in joint long-range planning of the change efforts.[21]

Laboratory Training and Organization Development

Since organization development programs have largely emerged from T-group experience, theory, and research, and since laboratory training in one form or another tends to be an integral part of most such programs, it is important to focus on laboratory training per se. As stated earlier, OD programs grew out of a perceived need to relate laboratory training to the problems of on-going organizations and a recognition that optimum results could only occur if major parts of the total social system of an organization were involved.

Laboratory training essentially emerged around 1946, largely through a growing recognition by Leland Bradford, Ronald Lippitt, Kenneth Benne, and others, that human relations training which focused on the feelings and concerns of the participants was frequently a much more powerful and viable form of education than the lecture method. Some of the theoretical constructs and insights from which these laboratory training pioneers drew stemmed from earlier research by Lippitt, Kurt Lewin, and Ralph White. The term "T-Group" emerged by 1949 as a shortened label for "Basic Skill Training Group", these terms were used to identify the programs which began to emerge in the newly formed National Training Laboratory in Group Development (now NTL Institute for Applied Behavioral Science).[22] "Sensitivity Training" is also a term frequently applied to such training.

Ordinarily, laboratory training sessions have certain objectives in common. The following list, by two internationally known behavioral scientists,[23] is probably highly consistent with the objectives of most programs:

Self-objectives
- Increased *awareness* of own feelings and reactions, and own impact on others.
- Increased *awareness* of feelings and reactions of others, and their impact on self.
- Increased *awareness* of dynamics of group action.
- *Changed attitudes* toward self, others, and groups, i.e., more respect for, tolerance for, and faith in self, others, and groups.
- Increased *interpersonal competence*, i.e., skill in handling interpersonal and group relationships toward more productive and satisfying relationships.

Role Objectives
- Increased *awareness* of own organizational role, organizational dynamics, dynamics of larger social systems, and dynamics of the change process in self, small groups, and organizations.
- *Changed attitudes* toward own role, role of others, and organizational relationships, i.e., more respect for and willingness to deal with others with whom one is interdependent, greater willingness to achieve collaborative relationships with others based on mutual trust.
- Increased *interpersonal competence* in handling organizational role relationships with superiors, peers, and subordinates.

Organizational Objectives
- Increased *awareness* of, *changed attitudes* toward, and increased *interpersonal competence* about specific organizational problems existing in groups or units which are interdependent.
- *Organizational improvement* through the training of relationships of groups rather than isolated individuals.

Over the years, experimentation with different laboratory designs has led to diverse criteria for the selection of laboratory participants. Probably a majority of NTL-IABS human relations laboratories are "stranger groups," i.e., involving participants who come from different organizations and who are not likely to have met earlier. However, as indicated by the organizational objectives above, the incidence of special labs designed to increase the effectiveness of persons already working together appears to be growing. Thus terms like "cousin labs," i.e., labs involving people from the same organization but not the same subunit, and "family labs" or "team-building" sessions, i.e., involving a manager and all of his subordinates, are becoming familiar. Participants in labs designed for organizational members not of the same unit may be selected so as to constitute a heterogeneous grouping by rank ("diagonal slice"). Further, NTL-IABS is now encouraging at least two members from the same organization to attend NTL Management Work Conferences and Key Executive Conferences in order to maximize the impact of the learning in the backhome situation.[24]

In general, experienced trainers recommend that persons with severe emotional illness should not participate in laboratory training, with the exception of programs designed specifically for group therapy. Designers of programs make the assumptions, as Argyris states them,[25] that T-Group participants should have:

1. A relatively strong ego that is not overwhelmed by internal conflicts.

2. Defenses which are sufficiently low to allow the individual to hear what others say to him.

3. The ability to communicate thought and feelings with minimal distortion.

As a result of such screening, the incidence of breakdown during laboratory training is substantially less than that reported for organizations in general,[26] However, since the borderline between "normalcy" and illness is very indistinct, most professionally trained staff members are equipped to diagnose severe problems and to make referrals to psychiatrists and clinical psychologists when appropriate. Further, most are equipped to give adequate support and protection to participants whose ability to assimilate and learn from feedback is low. In addition, group members in T-Group situations tend to be sensitive to the emotional needs of the members and to be supportive when they sense a person experiencing pain. Such support is explicitly fostered in laboratory training.

The duration of laboratory training programs varies widely. "Micro-Labs," designed to give people a brief experience with sensitivity training, may last only one hour. Some labs are designed for a long weekend. Typically, however, basic human relations labs are of two weeks duration, with participants expected to meet mornings, afternoons, and evenings, with some time off for recreation. While NTL Management Work Conferences for middle managers and Key Executive Conferences run for one week, team-building labs, from my experience, typically are about three days in length. However, the latter are usually only a part of a broader organization development program involving problem sensing and diagnosis, and the planning of action steps and subsequent sessions. In addition, attendance at stranger labs for key managers is frequently a part of the total organization development effort.

Sensitivity training sessions typically start with the trainer making a few comments about his role—that he is there to be of help, that the group will have control of the agenda, that he will deliberately avoid a leadership role, but that he might become involved as both a leader and a member from time to time, etc. The following is an example of what the trainer might say:

> This group will meet for many hours and will serve as a kind of laboratory where each individual can increase his understanding of the forces which influence individual behavior and the performance of groups and organizations. The data for learning will be our own behavior, feelings, and reactions. We begin with no definite structure or organization, no agreed-upon procedures, and no specific agenda. It will be up to us to fill the vacuum created by the lack of these familiar elements and to study our group as we evolve. My role will be to help the group to learn from its own experience, but not to act as a traditional chairman nor to suggest how we should organize, what our procedure should be, or exactly what our agenda will include. With these few comments, I think we are ready to begin in whatever way you feel will be most helpful.[27]

The trainer then lapses into silence. Group discomfort then precipitates a dialogue which, with skilled trainer assistance, is typically an intense but generally highly rewarding experience for group members. What goes on in the group becomes the data for the learning experience.

Interventions by the trainer will vary greatly depending upon the purpose of the lab and the state of learning on the part of the participants. A common intervention, however, is to encourage people to focus on and own up to their own feelings about what is going on in the group, rather than to make judgments about others. In this way, the participants begin to have more insight into their own feelings and to understand how their behavior affects the feelings of others.

While T-Group work tends to be the focal point in human relations laboratories, laboratory training typically includes theory sessions and frequently includes exercises such as role playing or management games.[28] Further, family labs of subunits of organizations will ordinarily devote more time to planning action steps for back on the job than will stranger labs.

Robert J. House has carefully reviewed the research literature on the impact of T-Group training and has concluded that the research shows mixed results. In particular, research on changes as reflected in personality inventories is seen as inconclusive. However, studies which examine the behavior of participants upon returning to the job are generally more positive.[29] House cites six studies, all of which utilized control groups, and concludes:

> All six studies revealed what appear to be important positive effects of T-Group training. Two of the studies report negative effects as well . . . all of the evidence is based on observations of the behavior of the participants in the actual job situations. No reliance is placed on participant response; rather, evidence is collected in his normal work activities.[30]

John P. Campbell and Marvin D. Dunnette,[31] on the other hand, while conceding that the research shows that T-Group training produces *changes in behavior*, point out that the usefulness of such training in terms of *job performance* has yet to be demonstrated. They urge research toward "forging the link between training-induced behavior changes and changes in job-performance effectiveness."[32] As a summary comment they state:

> . . . the assumption that T-Group training has positive utility for organizations must necessarily rest on shaky ground. It has been neither confirmed nor disconfirmed. The authors wish to emphasize . . . that utility for the organization is not necessarily the same as utility for the individual.[33]

At least two major reasons may account for the inconclusiveness of research on the impact of T-Group training on job performance. One reason is simply that little research has been done. The other reason may center around a factor of cultural isolation. To oversimplify, a major part of what one learns in laboratory training, in my opinion, is how to work more effectively with others in group situations, *particularly with others who have developed comparable skills*. Unfortunately, most participants return from T-Group experiences to environments including colleagues and superiors who have not had the same affective (emotional, feeling) experiences, who are not familiar with the terminology and underlying theory, and who may have anxieties (usually unwarranted) about what might happen to them in a T-Group situation.

This cultural distance which laboratory training can produce is one of the reasons why many behavioral scientists are currently encouraging more than one person from the same organization to undergo T-Group training and, ideally, all of the members of a team and their superior to participate in some kind of laboratory training together. The latter assumes that a diagnosis of the organization indicates that the group is ready for such training and assumes such training is reasonably compatible with the broader culture of the total system.

Conditions and Techniques for Successful Organization Development Programs

Theory, research, and experience to date suggest to me that *successful* OD programs tend to evolve in the following way and that they have some of these characteristics (these statements should be considered highly tentative, however):

 ● There is a strong pressure for improvement from both outside the organization and from within.[34]

 ● An outside behavioral scientist-consultant is brought in for consultation with the top executives and to diagnose organizational problems.

 ● A preliminary diagnosis suggests that organization development efforts, designed in response to the expressed needs of the key executives, are warranted.

 ● A collaborative decision is made between the key client group and the consultant to try to change the culture of the organization, at least at the top initially. The specific goals may be to improve communications, to secure more effective participation from subordinates in problem solving, and to move in the direction of more openness, more feedback, and more support. In short, a decision is made to change the culture to help the company meet its organizational goals and to provide better avenues for initiative, creativity, and self-actualization on the part of organization members.

 ● Two or more top executives, including the chief executive, to to laboratory training sessions. (Frequently, attendance at labs is one of the facts which precipitates interest in bringing in the outside consultant.)

 ● Attendance in T-Group program is voluntary. While it is difficult to draw a line between persuasion and coercion, OD consultants and top management should be aware of the dysfunctional consequences of coercion (see the comments on authentic behavior below). While a major emphasis is on team-building laboratories, stranger labs are utilized both to supplement the training going on in the organization and to train managers new to the organization or those who are newly promoted.

 ● Team-building sessions are held with the top executive group (or at the highest point where the program is started). Ideally, the program is started at the top of the organization, but it can start at levels below the president as long as there is significant support from the chief executive, and preferably from other members of the top power structure as well.

 ● In a firm large enough to have a personnel executive, the personnel-industrial relations vice president becomes heavily involved at the outset.

 ● One of two organizational forms emerges to coordinate organization development efforts, either (a) a coordinator reporting to the personnel executive (the personnel executive himself may fill this role), or (b) a coordinator reporting to the chief executive. The management development director is frequently in an ideal position to coordinate OD activities with other management development activities.

● Ultimately, it is essential that the personnel-industrial relations group, including people in salary administration, be an integral part of the organization development program. Since OD groups have such potential for acting as catalysts in rapid organizational change, the temptation is great to see themselves as "good guys" and the other personnel people as "bad guys" or simply ineffective. Any conflicts between a separate organization development group and the personnel and industrial relations groups should be faced and resolved. Such tensions can be the "Achilles heel" for either program. In particular, however, the change agents in the organization development program need the support of the other people who are heavily involved in human resources administration and vice versa; what is done in the OD program needs to be compatible with what is done in selection, promotion, salary administration, appraisal, and vice versa. In terms of systems theory, it would seem imperative that one aspect of the human resources function such as any organization development program must be highly interdependent with the other human resources activities including selection, salary administration, etc. (TRW Systems is an example of an organization which involves top executives plus making the total personnel and industrial relations group an integral part of the OD program.[35])

● Team-building labs, at the request of the various respective executives, with laboratory designs based on careful data gathering and problem diagnosis, are conducted at successively lower levels of the organization with the help of outside consultants, plus the help of internal consultants whose expertise is gradually developed.

● Ideally, as the program matures, both members of the personnel staff and a few line executives are trained to do some organization development work in conjunction with the external and internal professionally trained behavioral scientists. In a sense, then, the external change agent tries to work himself out of a job by developing internal resources.

● The outside consultant(s) and the internal coordinator work very carefully together and periodically check on fears, threats, and anxieties which may be developing as the effort progresses. Issues need to be confronted as they emerge. Not only is the outside change agent needed for his skills, but the organization will need someone to act as a "governor"—to keep the program focused on real problems and to urge authenticity in contrast to gamesmanship. The danger always exists that the organization will begin to punish or reward involvement in T-Group kinds of activities per se, rather than focus on performance.

● The OD consultants constantly work on their own effectiveness in interpersonal relationships and their diagnostic skills so they are not in a position of "do as I say, but not as I do." Further, both consultant and client work together to optimize the consultant's knowledge of the organization's unique and evolving culture structure, and web of interpersonal relationships.

● There needs to be continuous audit of the results, both in terms of checking on the evolution of attitudes about what is going on and in terms of the extent to which problems which were identified at the outset by the key clients are being solved through the program.

• As implied above, the reward system and other personnel systems need to be readjusted to accommodate emerging changes in performance in the organization. Substantially improved performance on the part of individuals and groups is not likely to be sustained if financial and promotional rewards are not forthcoming. In short, management needs to have a "systems" point of view and to think through the interrelationships of the OD effort with the reward and staffing systems and the other aspects of the total human resources subsystem.

In the last analysis, the president and the "line" executives of the organization will evaluate the success of the OD effort in terms of the extent to which it assists the organization in meeting its human and economic objectives. For example, marked improvements on various indices from one plant, one division, one department, etc., will be important indicators of program success. While human resources administration indices are not yet perfected, some of the measuring devices being developed by Likert, Mann, and others show some promise.[36]

Summary Comments

Organization development efforts have emerged through attempts to apply laboratory training values and assumptions to total systems. Such efforts are organic in the sense that they emerge from and are guided by the problems being experienced by the people in the organization. The key to their viability (in contrast to becoming a passing fad) lies in an authentic focus on problems and concerns of the members of the organization and in their confrontation of issues and problems.

Organization development is based on assumptions and values similar to "Theory Y" assumptions and values but includes additional assumptions about total systems and the nature of the client-consultant relationship. Intervention strategies of the behavioral scientist-change agent tend to be based on an action-research model and tend to be focused more on helping the people in an organization learn to solve problems rather than on prescriptions of how things should be done differently.

Laboratory training (or "sensitivity training") or modifications of T-Group seminars typically are a part of the organizational change efforts, but the extent and format of such training will depend upon the evolving needs of the organization. Team-building seminars involving a superior and subordinates are being utilized more and more as a way of changing social systems rapidly and avoiding the cultural-distance problems which frequently emerge when individuals return from stranger labs. However, stranger labs can play a key role in change efforts when they are used as part of a broader organization development effort.

Research has indicated that sensitivity training generally produces positive results in terms of changed behavior on the job, but has not demonstrated the link between behavior changes and improved performance. Maximum benefits are probably derived from laboratory training when the organizational culture supports and reinforces the use of new skills in ongoing team situations.

Successful organization development efforts require skillful behavioral scientist interventions, a systems view, and top management support and involvement. In addition, changes stemming from organization development must be linked to changes in the total personnel subsystem. The viability of organization development efforts lies in the degree to which they accurately reflect the aspirations and concerns of the participating members.

In conclusion, *successful organization development tends to be a total system effort; a process of planned change—not a program with a temporary quality; and aimed at developing the organization's internal resources for effective change in the future.*

Notes and References

This article is largely based on the . . . second edition of my *The Personnel Management Process: Human Resources Administration* (Boston: Houghton Mifflin Company, 1970), chap. 28.

1. Richard Beckhard, W. Warner Burke, and Fred I. Steele, "the Program for Specialists in Organization Training and Development," mimeographed, NTL Institute for Applied Behavioral Science, Dec. 1967, p. ii; and John Paul Jones, "What's Wrong With Work?" in *What's Wrong With Work?* (New York: National Association of Manufacturers, 1967), p. 8. For a history of NTL Institute for Applied Behavioral Science, with which Douglas McGregor was long associated in addition to his professorial appointment at M.I.T. and which has been a major factor in the history of organization development, see Leland P. Bradford, "Biography of an Institution," *Journal of Applied Behavioral Science*, III:2 (1967), 127-143. While we will use the word "program" from time to time, ideally organization development is a "process," not just another new program of temporary quality.

2. Harry D. Kolb, Introduction to *An Action Research Program for Organization Improvement* (Ann Arbor: Foundation for Research in Human Behavior, 1960), p. i.

3. Cattell defines synergy as "the sum total of the energy which a group can command." Daniel Katz and Robert L. Kahn, *The Social Psychology of Organizations* (New York: John Wiley and Sons, 1966), p. 33.

4. For a similar statement of objectives, see "What is OD?" *NTL Institute: News and Reports from NTL Institute for Applied Behavioral Science*, II (June 1968), 1-2. Whether OD programs increase the overall level of authority in contrast to redistributing authority is a debatable point. My hypothesis is that both a redistribution and an overall increase occur.

5. Joan Woodward, *Industrial Organization: Theory and Practice* (London: Oxford University Press, 1965).

6. See M. Scott Myers, "Every Employee a Manager," *California Mangement Review*, X (Spring 1968), 9-20.

7. See Douglas McGregor, *The Human Side of Enterprise* (New York: McGraw-Hill Book Company, 1960), pp. 47-48.

8. In addition to influence from the writings of McGregor, Likert, Argyris, and others, this discussion has been influenced by "Some Assumptions About Change in Organizations," in notebook "Program for Specialists in Organization Training and Development," NTL Institute for Applied Behavioral Science, 1967; and by staff members who participated in that program.

9. For a discussion of the "linking pin" concept, see Rensis Likert, *New Patterns of Management* (New York: McGraw-Hill Book Company, 1961).

10. Warren G. Bennis sees three major approaches to planned organizational change, with the behavioral scientists associated with each all having "a deep concern with applying social

science knowledge to create more viable social systems; a commitment to action, as well as to research . . . and a belief that improved interpersonal and group relationships will ultimately lead to better organizational performance.'' Bennis, ''A New Role for the Behavioral Sciences: Effecting Organizational Change,'' *Administrative Science Quarterly* VIII (Step. 1963), 157-158; and Herbert A. Shepard, ''An Action Research Model,'' in *An Action Research Program for Organization Improvement*, pp. 31-35.

11. Bennis, ''A New Role for the Behavioral Sciences,'' 158.

12. For a discussion of some of the problems and dilemmas in behavioral science research, see Chris Argyris, ''Creating Effective Relationships in Organizations,'' in Richard N. Adams and Jack J. Preiss, eds., *Human Organization Research* (Homewood, Ill.: The Dorsey Press, 1960), pp. 109-123; and Barbara A. Benedict. et al., ''The Clinical Experimental Approach to Assessing Organizational Change Efforts,'' *Journal of Applied Behavioral Science*, (Nov. 1967), 347-380.

13. For further discussion of action research, see Edgar H. Schein and Warren G. Bennis, *Personal and Organizational Change Through Group Methods* (New York: John Wiley and Sons, 1966), pp. 272-274.

14. William Foote Whyte and Edith Lentz Hamilton, *Action Research for Mangement* (Homewood, Ill.: Richard D. Irwin, 1964), p. 2.

15. Jeremiah J. O'Connell appropriately challenges the notion that there is ''one best way'' of organizational change and stresses that the consultant should choose his role and intervention strategies on the basis of ''the conditions existing when he enters the client system'' (*Managing Organization Innovation* [Homewood, Ill.: Richard D. Irwin, 1968], pp. 10-11).

16. For further discussion of organization diagnosis, see Richard Beckhard, ''An Organization Improvement Program in a Decentralised Organization,'' *Journal of Applied Behavioral Science*, 1 (Jan.—March 1966), 3-4, ''OD as a Process,'' in *What's Wrong with Work?*, pp. 12-13.

17. For example, see Floyd C. Mann, ''Studying and Creating Change,'' in Timothy W. Costello and Sheldon S. Zalkind, eds., *Psychology in Administration—A Research Orientation* (Englewood Cliffs: Prentice-Hall, 1963), pp. 321-324, See also Delbert C. Miller, ''Using Behavioral Science to Solve Organization Problems,'' *Personnel Administration*, XXXI (Jan.—Feb. 1968), 21-29.

18. For a description of feedback procedures used by the Survey Research Center, Univ. of Michigan, see Mann and Likert, ''The Need for Research on the Communication of Research Results,'' in *Human Organization Research*, pp. 57-66.

19. This phrase probably came from a management workshop sponsored by NTL Institute for Applied Behavioral Science.

20. For a description of what goes on in team-building sessions, see Beckhard, ''An Organizational Improvement Program,'' 9-13; and Newton Margulies and Anthony P. Raia, ''People in Organizations—A Case for Team Training,'' *Training and Development Journal*, XXII (August 1968), 2-11. For a description of problem-solving sessions involving the total management group (about 70) of a company, see Beckhard, ''The Confrontation Meeting,'' *Harvard Business Review*, XLV (March—April 1967), 149-155.

21. For a description of actual organization development programs, see Paul C. Buchanan, ''Innovative Organizations—A Study in Organization Development,'' in *Applying Behavioral Science Research in Industry* (New York: Industrial Relations Counselors, (1964), pp. 87-107; Sheldon A. Davis, ''An Organic Problem-Solving Method of Organizational Change,'' *Journal of Applied Behavioral Science*, III:1 (1967), 3-21; Cyril Sofer, *The Organization from Within* (Chicago: Quadrangle Books, 1961); Alfred J. Marrow, David G. Bowers, and Stanley E. Seashore, *Management by Participation* (New York: Harper and Row, 1967); Robert R. Blake, Jane S. Mouton, Louis B. Barnes, and Larry E. Greiner, ''Breakthrough in Organiza-

tion Development," *Harvard Business Review*, XLII (Nov.—Dec. 1964), 133-155; Alton C. Bartlett, "Changing Behavior as a Means to Increased Efficiency," *Journal of Applied Behavioral Science*, III:3 (1967), 381-403; Larry E. Greiner, "Antecedents of Planned Organization Change," *ibid.*, III:1 (1967), 51-85; and Robert R. Blake and Jane Mouton, *Corporate Excellence Through Grid Organization Development* (Houston, Texas: Gulf Publishing Company, 1968).

22. From Bradford, "Biography of an Institution." See also Kenneth D. Benne, "History of the T-Group in the Laboratory Setting," in Bradford, Jack R. Gibb, and Benne, eds., *T/Group Theory and Laboratory Method* (New York: John Wiley and Sons, 1964), pp. 80-135.

23. Schein and Bennis, p. 37.

24. For further discussion of group composition in laboratory training, see Schein and Bennis, pp. 63-69. NTL-LABS now include the Center for Organization Studies, the Center for the Development of Educational Leadership, the Center for Community Affairs, and the Center for International Training to serve a wide range of client populations and groups.

25. Chris Argyris, "T-Groups for Organizational Effectiveness," *Harvard Business Review*, XLII (March—April 1964), 60-74.

26. Based on discussions with NTL staff members. One estimate is that the incidence of "serious stress and mental disturbance" during laboratory training is less than one percent of participants and in almost all cases occurs in persons with a history of prior disturbance (Charles Seashore, "What is Sensitivity Training," *NTL Institute News and Reports*, II [April 1968], 2).

27 *Ibid.*, 1.

28. For a description of what goes on in T-groups, see Schein and Bennis, pp. 10-27; Bradford, Gibb, and Benne, pp. 55-67; Dorothy S. Whitaker, "A Case Study of a T-Group," in Galvin Witaker, ed., *T-Group Training: Group Dynamics in Mangement Education*, A.T.M. Occasional Papers, (Oxford: Basil Blackwell, 1965), pp. 14-22; Irving R. Weschler and Jerome Reisel, *Inside a Sensitivity Training Group* (Berkeley: University of California, Institute of Industrial Relations, 1959); and William F. Glueck, "Reflections on a T-Group Experience," *Personnel Journal*, XLVII (July 1968), 501-504. For use of cases or exercises based on research results ("instrumented training") see Robert R. Blake and Jane S. Mouton, "The Instrumented Training Laboratory," in Irving R. Weschler and Edgar H. Schein, eds., *Five Issues in Training* (Washington: National Training Laboratories, 1962), pp. 61-76; and W. Warner Burke and Harvey A. Hornstein, "Conceptual vs. Experimental Mangement Training," *Training and Development Journal*, XXI (Dec. 1967), 12-17.

29. Robert J. House, "T-Group Education and Leadership Effectiveness: A Review of the Empiric Literature and a Critical Evaluation." *Personnel Psychology*, XX (Spring 1967), 1-32. See also Dorothy Stock, "A Survey of Research on T-Groups," in Bradford, Gibb, and Benne, pp. 395-441.

30. House, *ibid.*, pp. 18-19.

31. John P. Campbell and Marvin D. Dunnette, "Effectiveness of T-Group Experiences in Managerial Training and Development," *Psychological Bulletin*, LXX (August 1968), 73-104.

32. *Ibid.*, 100.

33. *Ibid.*, 101. See also the essays by Dunnette and Campbell and Chris Argyris in *Industrial Relations*, VIII (Oct. 1968), 1-45.

34. On this point, see Larry E. Greiner, "Patterns of Organization Change," *Harvard Business Review*, XLV (May—June 1967), 119-130.

35. See Sheldon A. Davis, "An Organic Problem-Solving Method."

36. See Rensis Likert, *The Human Organization: Its Mangement and Value* (New York: McGraw-Hill Book Company, 1967).

THE MANAGEMENT OF CHANGE

PAUL HERSEY
KENNETH H. BLANCHARD

In the dynamic society in which today's organizations exist, the question of whether change will occur is no longer relevant. Instead, the issue now is how do managers cope with the inevitable barrage of changes which confront them daily in attempting to keep their organizations viable and current. While change is a fact of life, effective managers (if they are to be effective), can no longer be content to let change occur as it will, they must be able to develop strategies to plan, direct and control change. The purpose of [this three-part] article on "The Management of Change" is to provide practitioners with a general framework of change theory, hopefully with some strategies that can be used in planning and implementing change in their own environments.

In the first [part], "Change and the Use of Power," we will discuss two kinds of power, position power and personal power, then examine the use of both in varying situations. We will examine various levels of change from knowledge and attitude to individual behavior and organizational performance. These levels of change will then be analyzed in terms of two change cycles—participative and coerced.

In the second [part], "Change Through Behavior Modification," we will look at how managers can create an environment to move people from one level of maturity and responsibility to a higher level. Behavior modification will be examined as a tool for making changes at the operational level for both individuals and groups and we will discuss what implications reinforcement theory can have for the practitioner or change agent.

In the final [part], "Planning and Implementing Change," we will attempt to integrate much that we discussed in the first two articles into some theoretical frameworks that can be used to develop specific change strategies in various situations. In particular, we will examine force field analysis and the process of change and then look at the impact of change on the total system.

Part One: Change and the Use of Power

In developing a change strategy, the practitioner must be conscious of whatever power he has and be able to determine how this power might be appropriately used.

Reproduced by special permission from the January, February, and March, 1972, *Training and Development Journal*, copyright by the American Society for Training and Development, Inc., and the authors, Paul Hersey and Kenneth H. Blanchard.

Sources of Power

Amitai Etzioni discusses the difference between *position power* and *personal power*.[1] His distinction springs from his concept of power as the ability to induce or influence behavior. He claims that power is derived from an organizational office, personal influence or both. An individual who is able to induce another individual to do a certain job because of his position in the organization is considered to have position power, while an individual who derives his power from his followers is considered to have personal power. Some individuals can have both position and personal power.

Etzioni postulates that the best situation for a leader is when he has both personal and position power. But in some cases it is not possible to build a relationship on both. Then the question becomes whether it is more important to have personal power or position power. Happiness and human relations have been culturally reinforced over the past several decades. With this emphasis, most people would pick personal power as being the most important, but there may be another side of the coin.

Machiavelli in the fifteenth century in his treatise *The Prince* presents an interesting viewpoint when he raises the question—whether it is better to have a relationship based upon love (personal power) or fear (position power).[2] Machiavelli, as Etzioni, contends it is best to be both loved and feared. If, however, you cannot have both, he suggest a relationship based on love alone tends to be volatile, short run and easily terminated when there is no fear of retaliation. On the other hand, Machiavelli contends a relationship based upon fear tends to be longer lasting since the individual must be willing to incur the sanction (pay the price) before terminating the relationship. This is a difficult concept for many people to accept; and yet one of the most difficult roles for a leader, whether he be a boss, teacher or parent, to engage in is disciplining someone about whom he cares. Yet to be effective we sometimes have to sacrifice short-term friendship for long-term respect if we are interested in the growth and development of the people with whom we are working. Machiavelli warns, however, that one should be careful that fear does not lead to hatred. For hatred often evokes overt behavior in terms of retaliation, undermining and attempts to overthrow.

Successful Leadership versus Effective Leadership

If an individual attempts to have some effect on the behavior of another, we call this stimulus attempted leadership. The response to this leadership attempt can be successful or unsuccessful. Since a manager's basic responsibility in any type of organization is to get work done with and through people, his success is measured by the output or productivity of the group he leads. With this thought in mind, Bernard M. Bass suggests a clear distinction between *successful* and *effective* leadership or management.[3]

Suppose manager A attempts to influence individual B to do a certain job. It is not really an either/or situation. A's success could be depicted on a continuum (Figure 1) ranging from very successful to very unsuccessful with gray areas in between which would be difficult to ascertain as either.

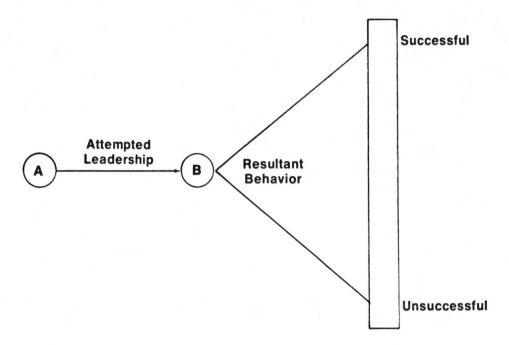

Figure 1. Successful-unsuccessful leadership continuum.

Let us assume that A's leadership is successful. In other words, B's response to A's leadership stimulus falls on the successful side of the continuum. This still does not tell the whole story of effectiveness.

If A's leadership style is not compatible with the expectations of B and, if B is antagonized and does the job only because of A's position power, then we can say that A has been successful but not effective. B has responded as A intended because A has control of rewards and punishment, and not because B sees his own needs being accomplished by satisfying the goals of the manager or organization.

On the other hand, if A's attempted leadership leads to a successful response, and B does the job because he wants to do it and finds it rewarding, then we consider A as having not only position power but also personal power. B respects A and is willing to cooperate with him realizing that A's request is consistent with his own personal goals. In fact, B sees his own goals as being accomplished by this activity. This is the meaning of effective leadership, keeping in mind that effectiveness also appears as a continuum which can range from very effective to very ineffective as illustrated in Figure 2.

Success has to do with how the individual or group behaves. On the other hand, effectiveness describes the internal state or predisposition of an individual or group and thus is attitudinal in nature. If an individual is interested only in success, he tends to emphasize his position power and uses close supervision.

However, if he is effective he will depend also on personal power and be characterized by more general supervision. Position power tends to be delegated down

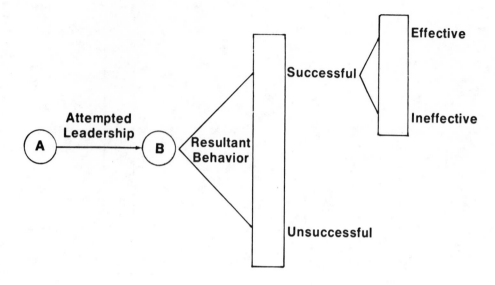

Figure 2. Successful and effective leadership continuums.

from the organization, while personal power is generated from below through follower acceptance.

In the management of organizations, the difference between successful and effective often explains why many supervisors can get a satisfactory level of output only when they are right there, looking over the worker's shoulder. But as soon as they leave output declines and often such things as horseplay and scrap loss increase.

The phenomenon described applies not only to business organizations but also to less formal organizations like the family. If parents are successful and effective, have both position and personal power, their children accept family goals as their own. Consequently, if the husband and wife leave for the weekend, the children behave no differently than if their parents were there. If, on the other hand, the parents continually use close supervision and the children view their own goals as being stifled by their parents' goals, the parents have only position power. They maintain order because of the rewards and punishments they control. If these parents went away on a trip leaving the children behind, upon returning they might be greeted by havoc and chaos.

In summary, a manager could be successful, but ineffective, having only short-run influence over the behavior of others. On the other hand if a manager is both successful and effective, his influence tends to lead to long-run productivity and organizational development.

Levels of Change

We have to look at changes from more than just a behavioral viewpoint because often changes in behavior are a result of changes in knowledge and attitude. In fact, there are four levels of change in people: (1) knowledge changes, (2) attitudinal changes, (3) behavior changes and (4) group or organizational performance changes.[4] The time relationship and relative difficulty involved in making each of these levels of change are illustrated in Figure 3.

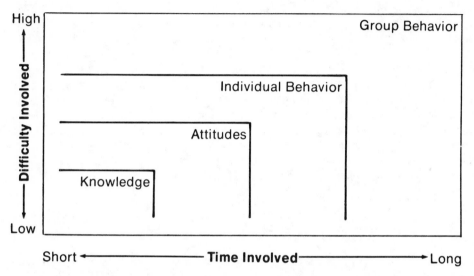

Figure 3. Time and difficulty involved in making various changes.

Changes in knowledge tend to be easiest to make; all one has to do is give a person a book or article to read, or have someone whom he respects tell him something new. Attitude structures differ from knowledge structures in that they are emotionally charged in a positive or negative way. The addition of emotion often makes attitudes more difficult to change than knowledge.

Changes in individual behavior seem to be significantly more difficult and time consuming than either of the two previous levels. For example, a person may have knowledge about the potential dangers of smoking, even actually feel that smoking is a bad habit he would like to change and still be unable to stop smoking because a habit pattern has been reinforced over a long period of time. It is important to point out that we are talking about change in patterned behavior and not a single event. In our example, anyone can quit smoking for a short period of time; the real test comes months later to see if a new long term pattern has evolved.

While individual behavior is difficult enough to change, when we get to the implementation of group or organizational performance, it is compounded because at this level we are concerned with changing customs, mores and traditions. Being a group, it tends to be a self-reinforcing unit and therefore a person's behavior as a member of a group is more difficult to modify without first changing the group norms.[5]

The Change Cycles

The levels of change become very significant when we examine two different change cycles—the participative change cycle and the coerced change cycle.

Participative Change

A participative change cycle is implemented when new knowledge is made available to the individual or group. It is hoped that the group will accept the data and will develop a positive attitude and commitment in the direction of the desired change. At this level the strategy may be direct participation by the individual or group in helping to select or formalize the goals or new methods for obtaining the goals. This is group participation in problem-solving. The next step is to attempt to translate this commitment into actual behavior. This tends to be the real tough barrier to overcome. For example, it is one thing to be concerned (attitude) about a social problem but another thing to be willing to actually get involved in doing something (behavior) about the problem. One strategy that is often useful is to attempt to identify informal as well as formal leaders within the group and concentrate on gaining their acceptance and behavior. Once this is accomplished you have moved a long way in getting others in the group to begin to pattern their behavior after those persons whom they respect and perceive in leadership roles. This participative change cycle is illustrated in Figure 4.

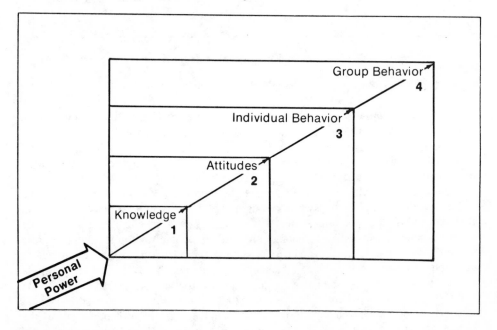

Figure 4. Participative change cycle.

Coerced Change

We've all probably been faced with a situation similar to one in which there is an announcement on Monday morning that "as of today all members of this organization shall begin to operate in accordance with Form 10125." This is an example of a coerced change cycle. This cycle begins by imposing change on the total organization. This will tend to affect the interaction—influence system at the individual level. The new contacts and modes of behavior create new knowledge which tend to develop predispositions toward or against the change. The coerced change cycle is illustrated in Figure 5.

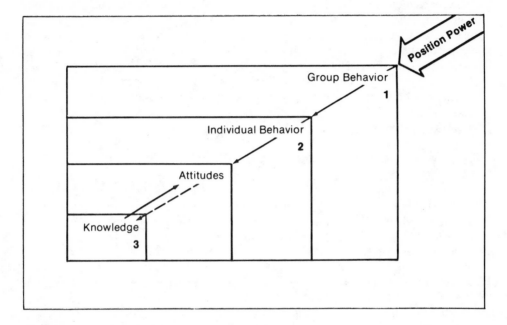

Figure 5. Coerced change cycle.

The intention of this coerced change cycle is that the new behavior creates the kind of knowledge which creates commitment to the change and therefore approximates a participative change cycle as it reinforces the individual and group behavior.

Differences Between Change Cycles

The participative change cycle tends to be more appropriate for working with mature groups since they tend to be achievement-motivated and have a degree of knowledge and experience that may be useful in developing new strategies for accomplishing goals.[6] Once the change starts, mature people are much more capable of assuming responsibilities for implementation. On the other hand, with immature people the coerced change cycle might be more productive because they are often dependent and not willing to take new responsibilities unless forced to do so. In fact, by their very nature, these people might prefer direction and structure to being faced with decisions that might be frightening to them.

There are some other significant differences between these two change cycles. The participative change cycle tends to be effective when induced by leaders with personal power, while the coerced cycle necessitates significant position power—rewards, punishments and sanctions.

With the participative cycle, the main advantage is that once accepted it tends to be long-lasting, since the people are highly committed to the change. Its disadvantage is that it tends to be slow and evolutionary. On the other hand, the advantage of the coerced cycle is speed. Using his position power, the leader can often impose change immediately. The disadvantage of this cycle is that it tends to be volatile. It can only be maintained as long as the leader has position power to make it stick. It often results in animosity, hostility and in some cases overt and covert behavior to undermine and overthrow.

These cycles have been described as if they were either/or positions. In reality, it is more a question of the proper blend of each, depending upon the situation.

Part Two: Change Through Behavior Modification

Rensis Likert found that employee-centered supervisors who use general supervision tend to have higher producing sections than job-centered supervisors who use close supervision.[7] We underline the word "tend" because this seems to be high probability in our society, yet we also must realize there are exceptions to this tendency which are even evident in Likert's data. What Likert found was that a subordinate generally responds well to a superior's high expectations and genuine confidence in him and tries to justify his boss's expectations of him. His resulting high performance will reinforce his superior's high trust for him, for it is easy to trust and respect the man who meets or exceeds your expectations. This occurrence could be called the effective cycle.

Yet, since top management often promotes on the basis of short run output alone, managers tend to overemphasize task accomplishment, placing extreme pressure on everyone to achieve high levels of productivity. This task-oriented leader behavior style, in some cases, does not allow much room for a trusting relationship with employees. Instead, subordinates are told what to do and how to do it. With little consideration, subordinates respond with minimal effort and resentment; low performance results in these instances. Reinforced by low expectations, it becomes a vicious cycle. Many other examples could be given which result in this all too common problem in organizations as shown in Figure 2.

These cycles are depicted as static but in reality they are very dynamic. The situation tends to get better or worse. For example, high expectations result in high performance, which reinforces the high expectations and produces even higher productivity. It almost becomes a spiral effect as illustrated in Figure 3.

In many cases, this spiraling effect is caused by an increase in leverage created through the use of what Frederick Herzberg calls "motivators."[8] In analyzing the data from his research, Herzberg concluded that man has two different categories of needs which are essentially independent of each other and affect behavior in differ-

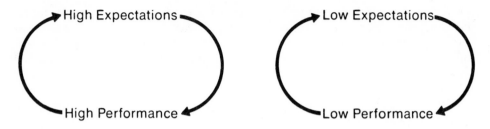

Figure 1. Effective cycle.   **Figure 2.** Ineffective cycle.

ent ways. He found that when people felt dissatisfied about their jobs, they were concerned about the environment in which they were working. On the other hand, when people felt good about their jobs, this had to do with the work itself. Herzberg called the first category of needs *hygiene factors* because they describe man's environment and serve the primary function of preventing job dissatisfaction. He called the second category of needs *motivators* since they seemed to be effective in motivating people to superior performance.

Company policies and administration, supervision, working conditions, interpersonal relations, money, status and security may be thought of as hygiene factors. There are not an intrinsic part of a job, but are related to the conditions under which a job is performed. Herzberg relates his use of the word "hygiene" to its medical meaning (preventative and environmental). Hygiene factors produce no growth in worker output capacity; they only prevent losses in worker performance due to work restriction.

Satisfying factors that involve feelings of achievement, professional growth and recognition that one can experience in a job which offers challenge and scope are referred to as motivators. Herzberg used this term because these factors seem capable of having a positive effect on job satisfaction often resulting in an increase in one's

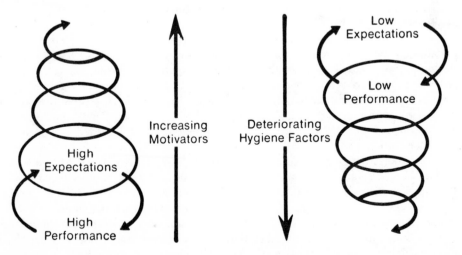

Figure 3. Spiraling effect of effective cycle.   **Figure 4.** Spiraling effect of ineffective cycle.

total output capacity. In terms of the upward spiraling effect, as people perform they are given more responsibility and opportunities for achievement and growth and development, which results in higher productivity and continued high expectations.

Ineffective Cycle

This spiraling effect can also occur in a downward direction as shown in Figure 4. Low expectations result in low performance, which reinforces the low expectations and produces even lower productivity. It becomes a spiral effect like a whirlpool as shown in Figure 4.

If this downward spiraling continues long enough, the cycle may reach a point where it cannot be turned around in a short period of time because of the large reservoir of negative past experience which has built up in the organization. Much of the focus and energy is directed toward the perceived problems with hygiene factors rather than the work itself. This takes such form as hostility, undermining and slow-down in work performance. When this happens, even if a manager actually changes his behavior, the credibility gap based on long-term experience is such that the response is still distrust and skepticism rather than change.

Style Change

One alternative that is sometimes necessary at this juncture is to bring in a new manager from the outside. The reason this has a higher probability of success is that the sum of the past experience of the people involved with the new manager is likened to a "clean slate," and thus different behaviors are on a much more believable basis. This was vividly illustrated by Robert H. Guest in a case analysis of organizational change.[9] He examined a large assemply plant of an automobile company, Plant Y, and contrasts the situation under two different leaders.

Under Mr. Stewart, plant manager, working relationships at Plant Y were dominated by hostility and mistrust. His high task style was characterized by a continual attempt to increase the driving forces pushing for productivity. As a result, the prevailing atmosphere was that of one emergency following on the heels of another, and the governing motivation for employee activity was fear—fear of being "chewed out" right on the assembly line, fear of being held responsible for happenings in which one had no clear authority, fear of losing one's job. Consequently, of the six plants in this division of the corporation, Plant Y had the poorest performance record, and it was getting worse.

Mr. Stewart was replaced by Mr. Cooley, who seemed like a truly effective leader. Three years later, dramatic changes had occurred. In various cost and performance measures used to rate the six plants, Plant Y was now truly the leader; and the atmosphere of interpersonal cooperation and personal satisfaction had improved impressively over the situation under Stewart. These changes, moreover, were effected through an insignificant number of dismissals and reassignments. Using a much higher relationships style, Cooley succeeded in "turning Plant Y around."

Expectations Change

On the surface, the big difference was style of leadership. Cooley was a good leader. Stewart wasn't. But Guest points out clearly in his analysis that leadership style was only one of two important factors. "The other was that while Stewart received daily orders from division headquarters to correct specific situations, Cooley was left alone. Cooley was allowed to lead; Stewart was told how to lead."[10] In other words, when productivity in Plant Y began to decline during changeover from wartime to peacetime operations. Stewart's superiors expected him to get productivity back on the upswing by taking control of the reins and they put tremendous pressure on him to do just that. Guest suggests that these expectations forced Stewart to operate in a very crisis-oriented, autocratic way. However, when Cooley was given charge as plant manager, a "hands off" policy was initiated by his superiors. The fact that the expectations of top management had changed enough to put a moratorium on random, troublesome outside stimuli from headquarters gave Cooley an opportunity to operate in a completely different style. One could raise the question, what might have happened if instead of hiring Cooley, top management had given Stewart this same kind of support and "free hand"? Could he have turned the plant around like Cooley did? Probably not. The ineffective cycle seemed to have been in a downward spiral far past the point where Stewart would have had a good opportunity to make significant change. But with the introduction of a new manager with whom the employees had no past experience, now-significant changes were possible.

While a new manager may be in a better position to initiate change in a situation which has been spiraling downward, he still does not have an easy task. Essentially, he has to break the ineffective cycle. There are at least two alternatives available to him. He can either fire the low performing personnel and hire people who he expects to perform well or respond to low performance with high expectations and trust.

The latter choice for the manager is difficult. In effect, the attempt is to change the expectations or behavior of his subordinates. It is especially difficult for a manager to have high expectations about people who have shown no indication that they deserve to be trusted. The key, then, is to change appropriately. This is where the concepts of behavior modification might be helpful.

Behavior Modification

In the normal work environment, managers feel that either close supervision and pressure (task-oriented behavior) or consideration and trust (relationship-oriented behavior) are the only ways to focus a subordinate on his task or change patterns of behavior. They use these methods even when they prove unsuccessful, because they are often unaware of better techniques. At one time, managers were too structured, rigid and punishing. Now there seems to be a swing to the overly trusting, unstructured manager. Both these strategies when inappropriate have created problems. Another alternative is behavior modification,[11] which can provide a strategy for shifting leadership style appropriately to stimulate changes in maturity. In order

TABLE 1
DIFFERENT APPROACHES USED IN DEALING WITH A DISRUPTIVE WORKER

	HIGH TASK MANAGER	HIGH RELATIONSHIPS MANAGER	BEHAVIOR MODIFICATION MANAGER
Manager Reaction	"This worker is going to be a trouble-maker. This behavior must be stopped!"	"Oh dear, I hope I can get them interacting and happy."	"Feels Tony needs to learn to cope in positive ways to replace aggressive behavior!" Separates conflicting workers without hostility or comment.
Supervisor Subordinate Interaction	"Hey, you. Knock it off! We don't allow fighting around here," said with coldness or anger.	"How would you both like to give me a hand on a job over here."	Manager watches for any positive behavior he can immediately reinforce. Supervisor sets limits on some behavior and carefully ignores others.
Worker Reaction	Tony builds resentment and hostility. Next few days, behavior becomes more aggressive.	Tony finds he can get attention of supervisor by being disruptive because the supervisor wants to be "understanding." He causes trouble and watches supervisor's reaction. Supervisor pays more and more attention as his behavior gets worse. Disruptive behavior reinforced.	Tony finds the supervisor appreciates good things about him. Wants to gain his respect. Supervisor Strategy: 1. Watches for any occurrences of positive behavior to reinforce. 2. Decides which new behaviors Tony needs to learn first. 3. Plans strategy to get desired behavior. 4. Attempts to better understand Tony in an effort to use incentives appropriate for his need structure. 5. Uses the incentives to reinforce behavior Tony needs to learn. 6. Continues to evaluate to make sure incentives are still appropriate since these tend to change with time.
Outcome	Tony feels disliked by supervisor. Self-image deteriorates as he attempts to defend ego from assaults. Becomes more hostile and aggressive or withdrawn. Avoids supervisor and learning tasks.	Aggressiveness remains. Becomes more obnoxious as other workers withdraw. Creates incidents to get attention and assigned to those jobs he wants. Does not learn. No friends. Low self-image covered by bravado.	Outcome in two or three weeks. Tony's work and acceptance by other members of his work group continue to improve. Builds new self-image on basis of new behavior he has learned. Hostile and aggressive behavior toward other employees stops. Begins to have a sense of accomplishment. Inner needs and feelings start to change. Aggressiveness used in constructive ways. Has friends and becomes a positive rather than a disruptive influence on his work group.

to illustrate the differences between these three strategies—task behavior, relationships behavior and behavior modifications—we can compare how a manager using each might handle a potential problem-worker.

Tony, a new employee right out of high school, is a very aggressive, competitive individual. During his first day on the job, he argues over tools with another young employee. Table I attempts to illustrate the possible reactions of a high task manager, a high relationships manager and a manager using behavior modification techniques.

Behavior modification (often referred to as operant conditioning or reinforcement theory) is based upon *deserved* behavior and not internal psychological feelings or attitudes.[12] Its basic premise is that *behavior is controlled by its immediate consequences*. Any behavior will be made stronger or weaker by what happens immediately after it occurs. If what happens is positive, it tends to increase the frequency of that behavior occurring again. Positive reinforcement is anything that is rewarding to the individual being reinforced. Reinforcement, therefore, depends on the individual. What is reinforcing to one person may not be reinforcing to another. Money might motivate some people to work harder, but to others money is not a high strength need; the challenge of the job might be the most rewarding incentive. Managers must look for unique differences in their people and recognize the dangers of generalizing.

Positive Reinforcement

In order for a desirable behavior to be obtained, the slightest positive behavior exhibited by the individual in that direction must be rewarded as soon as possible. This is called reinforcing positively successive approximations toward a goal. For example, when an individual's performance is low, one cannot expect drastic changes over night, regardless of changes in expectations or other incentives. Similar to the child learning some new behavior, we do not expect high levels of performance at the outset. So, as a parent or teacher, we would use *positive reinforcement* as the child's behavior approaches the desired level of performance. Therefore, the manager must be aware of any progress of his subordinate, so he is in a position to reinforce appropriately this change.

This is compatible with the concept of setting interim rather than final goals and then reinforcing appropriate progress toward the final goal as interim goals are accomplished. In this process, the role of a manager is not always setting goals for his followers. Instead, effectiveness may be increased by providing an environment where subordinates can play a role in setting their own goals. Research indicates that commitment increases when a person is involved in his own goal setting. If an individual is involved, he will tend to engage in much more goal-directed activity before he becomes frustrated and gives up. On the other hand, if the boss sets the goal for him, he is apt to give up more easily because he perceives these as his boss's goals and not as his own. Goals should be set high enough so a person has to stretch to reach them but low enough so that they can be attained.

So often final goals are set and the person is judged only in terms of success in relation to this terminal goal. Suppose, in our example, the manager had expected

Tony to become a "perfect" employee overnight. Suppose after the first week Tony is better but still causes some problems. The result is usually the manager reprimanding him (punishment) even though he has shown improvement. If this reprimanding continues to occur, there is a high probability that Tony may stop trying. His behavior, rather than improving, may become worse. An alternative for the manager is setting interim realistic goals which move in the direction of the final goals as they are attained. Then with a change in the desired direction, even though only moderate, positive reinforcement may be used rather than some form of punishment.

Negative Reinforcement

While positive reinforcement tends to be more effective in working with people, experiencing some unpleasant consequences or *negative reinforcement* can sometimes strengthen a particular behavior. For example, suppose a manager reprimands Al, one of his subordinates, for sloppy work, rather than giving him his usual "praise." If Al becomes just anxious enough, finds out what he did wrong, then does it right and gets his boss's praise, the unpleasantness of the reprimand becomes a negative "reinforcer." In this case, the manager was not just trying to punish Al because he wanted to make him feel badly but was giving him negative feedback because he wanted him to do better. Al responded as he had hoped he would, giving the manager a chance to use positive reinforcement with him again.

A leader or manager has to be careful in using negative reinforcement or punishment because he does not always know what he is reinforcing in a person when he uses these methods. He might be reinforcing lying, manipulation or all kinds of undesirable behavior because the individuals involved may use these behaviors, rather than improved performance, to eliminate punishment or further negative reinforcement. Another possible reaction to punishment is that the individual may begin to use avoidance behaviors such as attempting to eliminate communications and interactions between himself and the person who makes him feel threatened.

Extinction

Another way to respond to behavior besides positive or negative reinforcement is to not reinforce it at all. This is called *extinction* because it tends to get rid of a behavior. For example, suppose a worker is disruptive to get the attention of his supervisor. What would happen if his supervisor paid no attention to him? After engaging in this behavior on several occasions without accomplishing anything, he soon would be trying other behaviors.

People do not tend to continue doing things that do not provide positive reinforcement. This is even true sometimes when they are behaving well. Parents often get into this situation when they tend to pay attention to their children only when they are behaving poorly. When children are behaving appropriately adults may pay little or no attention to them, which in a sense could put that behavior on extinction. If a child wants attention from his parents (it is rewarding to him), he may be willing to endure what the parent thinks is punishment for that attention. In the long run the parents might be reinforcing the very behavior they don't want and extinguishing more appropriate behavior.

Psychotherapy Not Appropriate

Behavior modification seems like a useful tool for practitioners since it can be applied, to some extent, in most environments. Therefore, it has relevance for most people interested in accomplishing goals through others. This was not the case with psychotherapy. This process was based upon the assumption that to change behavior one had to first start with the feelings and attitudes within an individual.

The problem with psychotherapy from a practitioner's viewpoint is that it is too expensive and is appropriate for use only by trained professionals. This is true because the emphasis in psychotherapy is on analyzing the reasons underlying behavior which often requires extensive probing into the early experiences in the life of an individual. Behavior modification, on the other hand, is not as complex since it concentrates on observed behavior using goals or rewards outside the individual to modify behavior.

Part Three: Planning and Implementing Change

In evaluating effectiveness, perhaps more than 90 per cent of managers in organizations look at measures of output alone. Thus, the effectiveness of a business manager is often determined by net profits, the effectiveness of a college professor may be determined by the number of articles and books he has published, and the effectiveness of an athletic coach may be determined by his won-lost record.

Others feel that it is unrealistic to think only in terms of productivity or output in evaluating effectiveness. According to Rensis Likert,[13] another set of variables should be taken into consideration in determining effectiveness. These are *intervening variables* which reflect the current condition of the human resources in an organization and are represented in its skills, loyalty, commitment to objectives, motivations, communications, decision-making and capacity for effective interaction. These intervening variables are concerned with building and developing the organization and tend to be long-term considerations. Managers are often promoted, however, on the basis of short-run output variables such as increased production and earnings, without concern for the long-run and organizational development. This creates a dilemma.

Organizational Dilemma

One of the major problems in industry today is that there is a shortage of successful managers. Therefore, it is not uncommon for a manager to be promoted in six months or a year if he is a "producer." Let's look at the example of Mr. X, a manager who realizes that the basis on which top management promotes is often short-run output, and therefore attempts to achieve high levels of productivity by over-emphasizing task accomplishment and placing extreme pressure on everyone, even when it is inappropriate.

The immediate or short-run effect of Mr. X's behavior will probably be increased productivity. Yet if his task-oriented style is inappropriate for those involved, and if it continues over a long period, the morale and climate of the organization will deteriorate. Some indications of deterioration resulting from these intervening variables may be turnover, absenteeism, increased accidents, scrap loss and numerous grievances. Not only the number of grievances, but the nature of grievances is important. Are grievances really significant problems or do they reflect pent-up emotions due to anxieties and frustration? Are they settled at the complaint stage between the employee and supervisor or are they pushed up the hierarchy to be settled at higher levels or by arbitration? The organizational dilemma is that in many instances a manager like Mr. X, who places pressure on everyone and produces in the short run, is promoted out of this situation before the disruptive aspects of the intervening variables catch up.

Time Lag

There tends to be a time lag between declining intervening variables and significant restriction of output by employees under such management climate. Employees tend to feel "things will get better." Thus, when Mr. X is promoted rapidly, he often stays "one step ahead of the wolf."

The real problem is faced by the next manager, Mr. Y. Although productivity records are high, he has inherited many problems. Merely the introduction of a new manager may be enough to collapse the slowly deteriorating intervening variables. A tremendous drop in morale and motivation leading almost immediately to significant decrease in output can occur. Change by its very nature is frightening; to a group whose intervening variables are declining, it can be devastating.

Regardless of Mr. Y's style, the present expectations of the followers may be so distorted, that much time and patience will be needed to close the now apparent "credibility gap" between the goals of the organization and the personal goals of the group. No matter how effective Mr. Y might be in the long run, his superiors, in reviewing a productivity drop, may give him only a few months to improve performance. But as Likert's studies indicate, rebuilding a group's intervening variables in a small organization may take one to three years, and in a large organization, may extend to seven years.

Short and Long Term

It should be made clear that the choice for a manager is not whether to concentrate on output or intervening variables but often a matter of how much emphasis to place on each. The decision is between short- and long-range goals. If the accepted goal is building and developing an organization for the future, then the manager should be evaluated on these terms and not entirely on his present productivity.

While intervening variables do not appear on balance sheets, sales reports or accounting ledgers, we feel that these long-term considerations can be just as important to an organization as short-term output variables. Therefore, although difficult to measure, intervening variables should not be overlooked in determining organizational effectiveness.

In summary, we feel that effectiveness is actually determined by whatever the manager and the organization decide are their goals and objectives, but should consider these factors: output variables, intervening variables, short-range goals and long-range goals.

Force Field Analysis

Force field analysis, a technique for diagnosing situations developed by Kurt Lewin, may be useful in looking at the variables involved in determining effectiveness and in developing strategies for changing in particular the condition of the output or intervening variables.[14]

Lewin assumes that in any situation there are both driving and restraining forces which influence any change which may occur. *Driving forces* are those forces affecting a situation which are "pushing" in a particular direction; they tend to initiate a change and keep it going. In terms of improving productivity in a work group, pressure from a supervisor, incentive earnings and competition may be examples of driving forces. *Restraining forces* are forces acting to restrain or decrease the

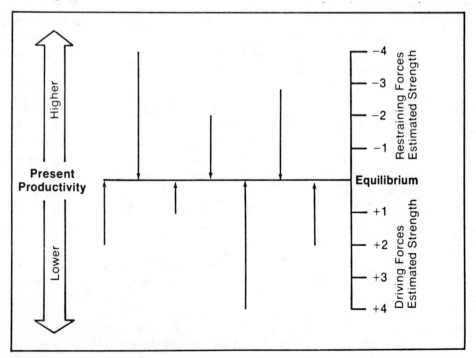

Figure 1. Driving and restraining forces in equilibrium.

driving forces. Apathy, hostility and poor maintenance of equipment may be examples of restraining forces against increased production. Equilibrium is reached when the sum of the driving forces equals the sum of the restraining forces. In our example, equilibrium represents the present level of productivity as shown in Figure 1.

This equilibrium or present level of productivity can be raised or lowered by changes in the relationship between the driving and restraining forces. For illustrations, let us look again at the dilemma of Mr. Y, the new manager who takes over a work group where productivity is high but Mr. X, his predecessor, drained the human resources (intervening variables). Mr. X had upset the equilibrium by increasing the driving forces (i.e., being autocratic and keeping continual pressure on his men) and thus achieving increases in output in the short run. By doing this though, new restraining forces developed, such as increased hostility and antagonism, and at the time of his departure the restraining forces were beginning to increase and the results manifested themselves in turnover, absenteeism and other restraining forces which lowered productivity shortly after Mr. Y arrived. Now a new equilibrium at a significantly lowered productivity is faced by the new manager.

Now just assume that Mr. Y decides not to increase the driving forces, but to reduce the restraining forces. He may do this by taking time away from the usual production operation and engaging in problem-solving and training and development. In the short run, output will tend to be lowered still further. However, if commitment to objectives and technical know-how of his group are increased in the long run, they may become new driving forces, and that, along with the elimination of the hostility and apathy which were restraining forces, will now tend to move the balance to a higher level of output.

A manager, in attempting to implement change, is often in a position where he must consider not only output but also intervening variables, not only short-term but also long-term goals, and a framework which is useful in diagnosing these interrelationships is available through force field analysis.

Process of Change

In developing a change strategy, another important aspect that must be taken into consideration is the process of change. Kurt Lewin, in his pioneer work in change, identified three phases of the change process.[15] These are unfreezing, changing and refreezing.

Unfreezing

The aim of unfreezing is to motivate and make the individual or group ready to change. It is a "thawing out" process where the forces acting on an individual are rearranged so now he sees the need for change. According to Edgar H. Schein, some elements that unfreezing situations seem to have in common are: (1) the physical removal of the individual being changed from his accustomed routines, sources of information and social relationships; (2) the undermining and destruction of all social supports; (3) demeaning and humiliating experience to help the individual being changed to see his old self as unworthy and thus to be motivated to change; (4) the consistent linking of reward with willingness to change and of punishment with unwillingness to change.[16]

In brief, unfreezing is the breaking down of the mores, customs, and traditions of an individual—the old ways of doing things—so he is ready to accept new alternatives. In terms of force field analysis, unfreezing may occur when either the driving forces are increased or the restraining forces that are resisting change are reduced.

Changing

Once the individual has become motivated to change, he is now ready to be provided with new patterns of behavior. This process is most likely to occur by one of two mechanisms: identification and internalization.[17] *Identification* occurs when one or more models are provided in the environment from whom an individual can learn new behavior patterns by identifying with them and trying to become like them. *Internalization* occurs when an individual is placed in a situation where new behaviors are demanded of him if he is to operate successfully in that situation. He learns these new behavior patterns not only because they are necessary to survive but as a result of new high strength needs induced by coping behavior.

> Internalization is a more common outcome in those influence settings where the direction of change is left more to the individual. The influence which occurs in programs such as Alcoholics Anonymous, in psychotherapy or counseling for hospitalized or incarcerated populations, in religious retreats, in human relations training of the kind pursued by the National Training Laboratories (1953), and in certain kinds of progressive education programs is more likely to occur through internalization or, at least, to lead ultimately to more internalization.[18]

Identification and internalization are not either/or courses of action and effective change is often the result of combining the two into a strategy for change.

Force or compliance is sometimes discussed as another mechanism for inducing change.[19] It occurs when an individual is forced to change by the direct manipulation of rewards and punishment by someone in a power position. In this case, behavior appears to have changed when the change agent is present, but often is dropped when supervision is removed. Thus, rather than discussing force as a mechanism of changing, we would rather think of it as a tool for unfreezing.

Refreezing

The process by which the newly-acquire behavior comes to be integrated as patterned behavior into the individual's personality and/or ongoing significant emotional relationships is referred to as *refreezing*. As Schein contends, if the new behavior has been internalized while being learned, "this has automatically facilitated refreezing because it has been fitted naturally into the individual's personality. If it has been learned through identification, it will persist only so long as the target's relationship with the original influence model persists unless new surrogate models are found or social support and reinforcement is obtained for expressions of the new attitudes.''[20]

This highlights how important it is for an individual engaged in a change process to be in an environment which is continually reinforcing the desired change. The effect of many a training program has been short-lived when the person returns to an environment that does not reinforce the new patterns or, even worse, is hostile toward them.

What we are concerned about in refreezing is that the new behavior does not get extinguished over time. To insure this not happening, reinforcement (rewards and incentives) must be scheduled in an effective way. There seem to be two main reinforcement schedules: continuous and intermittent.[21] Continuous reinforcement means that the individual being changed is rewarded every time he engages in the desired new pattern. With intermittent reinforcement on the other hand, not every desired response is reinforced. Reinforcement can be either completely random or scheduled according to a prescribed number of responses occurring or a particular interval of time elapsing before reinforcement is given.

With continuous reinforcement, the individual learns the new behavior quickly, but if his environment changes to one of nonreinforcement, extinction (elimination of the behavior) can be expected to take place relatively soon. With intermittent reinforcement, extinction is much slower because the individual has been conditioned to go for periods of time without any reinforcement. Thus for fast learning, a continuous reinforcement schedule should be used. But once the individual has learned the new pattern, a switch to intermittent reinforcement should insure a long lasting change.

Change Process—Some Examples

To see the change process in operation, several examples could be cited.

A college basketball coach recruited for his team Bob Anderson, a 6' 4'' center from a small town in a rural area. In his district, 6' 4'' was good height for a center. This fact, combined with his deadly turn-around-jump shot, made Anderson the rage of his league and enabled him to average close to 30 points a game.

Recognizing that 6' 4'' is small for a college center, the coach hoped that he could make Anderson a forward, moving him inside only when they were playing a double pivot. One of the things the coach was concerned about, however, was when Anderson would be used in the pivot, how he could get his jump shot off when he came up against other players ranging in height from 6' 8'' to 7'. He felt that Anderson would have to learn to shoot a hook shot, which is much harder to block, if he was going to have scoring potential against this kind of competition.

The approach that many coaches use to solve this problem would probably be as follows: The first day of practice when Anderson arrived, the coach would welcome Anderson and then explain the problem to him as he had analyzed it. As a solution he would probably ask Anderson to start to work with the varsity center, Steve Cram, who was 6' 10'' and had an excellent hook. "Steve can help you start working on that new shot, Bob," the coach would say. Anderson's reaction to this interchange might be one of resentment and he would go over and work with Cram only because of the coach's position power. After all, he might think to himself, "Who does he think he is? I've been averaging close to 30 points a game for three years now and the first day I show up here the coach wants me to learn a new shot." So he may start to work with Cram reluctantly, concentrating on the hook shot only when the coach is looking but taking his favorite jump shot when he wasn't being observed. Anderson is by no means unfrozen or ready to learn to shoot another way.

Another Approach

Let's look at another approach the coach could have used to solve this problem. Suppose on the first day of practice he sets up a scrimmage between the varsity and freshmen. Before he starts the scrimmage he gets big Steve Cram, the varsity center, aside and tells him, "Steve, we have this new freshman named Anderson who has real potential to be a fine ball player. What I'd like you to do today though, is not to worry about scoring or rebounding, just make sure every time Anderson goes up for a shot you make him eat it. I want him to see that he will have to learn to shoot some other shots if he is to survive against guys like you."

So when the scrimmage starts, the first time Anderson gets the ball and turns around to shoot Cram leaps up and "stuffs the ball right down his throat." Time after time this occurs. Soon Anderson starts to engage in some coping behavior, trying to fall away from the basket, shooting from the side of his head rather than the front, in an attempt to get his shot off.

After the scrimmage, Anderson comes off the court dejected. The coach says, "What's wrong Bob?" He replies, "I don't know, Coach, I just can't seem to get my shot off against a man as big as Cram. What do you think I should do, Coach?" he asks. "Well, Bob, why don't you go over and start working with Steve on a hook shot. I think you'll find it much harder to block. And with your shooting eye I don't think it will take long for you to learn." How do you think Anderson feels about working with Cram now? He's enthusiastic and ready to learn. Having been placed in a situation where he learns for himself that he has a problem, Anderson is already in the process of unfreezing his past patterns of behavior. Now he's ready for identification. He has had an opportunity to internalize his problem and is ready to work with Steve Cram.

So often the leader who has knowledge of an existing problem forgets that until the people involved recognize the problem as their own, it is going to be much more difficult to produce change in their behavior. Internalization and identification are not either/or alternatives but can be parts of developing specific change strategies appropriate to the situation.

The Military Example

Another example of the change processes in operation can be seen in the military, particularly in the induction phase. There are probably few organizations that have entering their ranks people who are less motivated and committed to the organization than the recruits the military gets. Yet in a few short months, they are able to mold these men into a relatively effective combat team. This is not an accident. Let's look at some of the processes that help accomplish this.

The most dramatic and harsh aspects of the training are the unfreezing phase. All four of the elements that Schein claims unfreezing situations have in common are present. A specific example follows.

(1) The recruits are *physically removed from their accustomed routines, sources of information and social relationships* in the isolation of a place such as Parris Island.

> During this first week of training at Parris Island, the recruit is . . . hermetically sealed in a hostile environment, required to rise at 4:55 a.m., do exhausting exercises, attend classes on strange subjects, drill for hours in the hot sun, eat meals in silence and stand at rigid attention the rest of the time; he has no television, no radio, no candy, no coke, no beer, no telephone—and can write letters only during one hour of free time a day.[22]

(2) *The undermining and destruction of social supports* is one of the DI's (Drill Instructor) tasks. "Using their voices and the threat of extra PT (physical training), the DI . . . must shock the recruit out of the emotional stability of home, pool hall, street corner, girl friend or school."[23]

(3) *Demeaning and humiliating experiences* are commonplace during the first two weeks of the training as the DI's help the recruits *see themselves as unworthy and thus motivated to change* into what they want a Marine to be. "It's a total shock . . . Carrying full seabags, 80 terrified privates are herded into their 'barn,' a barracks floor with 40 double-decker bunks. Sixteen hours a day, for two weeks, they will do nothing right."[24]

(4) Throughout the training there is *consistent linking of reward with willingness to change and punishment with unwillingness to change.*

> Rebels or laggards are sent to the Motivation Platoon to get "squared away." A day at Motivation combines constant harrassment and PT (physical training), ending the day with the infiltration course. This hot, 225-yard ordeal of crawling, jumping and screaming through ditches and obstacles is climaxed by the recruits dragging two 30-pound ammo boxes 60 yards in mud and water. If he falters he starts again. At the end, the privates are lined up and asked if they are ready to go back to their home platoons . . . almost all go back for good.[25]

While the recruits go through a severe unfreezing process, they quickly move to the changing phase, first identifying with the DI and then emulating informal leaders, as they develop. "Toward the end of the third week a break occurs. What one DI calls 'that five per cent—the slow fat, dumb or difficult' have been dropped. The remaining recruits have emerged from their first-week vacuum with one passionate desire—to stay with their platoon at all costs."[26]

Internalization takes place when the recruits through their forced interactions develop different high strength needs. "Fear of the DI gives way to respect, and survival evolves into achievement toward the end of training." "I learned I had more guts than I imagined" is a typical comment.[27]

Since the group tends to stay together throughout the entire program, it serves as a positive reinforcer which can help refreeze the new behavior.

Impact of Change on Total System

The focus in [this three-part] article has been on the management of human resources and as a result we have spent little time on how technical change can have an impact on the total system. And yet, the importance of combining the social and technical into a unified social systems concept is stressed by Robert Guest.

> On his part the social scientist often makes the error of concentrating on human motivation and group behavior without fully accounting for the technical environment which circumscribes, even determines, the roles which the actors play. Motivation, group structure, interaction processes, authority—none of these abstractions of behavior take place in a technological vacuum.[28]

A dramatic example of the consequences of introducing technical change and ignoring its consequences on the social system is the case of the introduction of the steel axe to a group of Australian aborigines.[29]

This tribe remained considerably isolated, both geographically and socially, from the influence of Western cultures. In fact, their only contact was an Anglican mission established in the adjacent territory.

The polished stone axe was a traditionally basic part of the tribe's technology. Used by men, women and children, the stone axe was vital to the subsistence economy. But more than that, it was actually a key to the smooth running of the social system; it defined interpersonal relationships and was a symbol of masculinity and male superiority. "Only an adult male could make and own a stone axe; a woman or a child had to ask his permission to obtain one."[30]

The Anglican mission in an effort to help improve the situation of the aborigines introduced the steel axe, a product of European technology. It was given indiscriminately to men, women and children. Because the tool was more efficient than the stone axe, it was readily accepted but it produced severe repercussions unforeseen by the missionaries or the tribe. As Stephan R. Cain reports:

> The adult male was unable to make the steel axe and no longer had to make the stone axe. Consequently, his exclusive axe-making ability was no longer a necessary or desirable skill, and his status as sole possessor and dispenser of a vital element of technology was lost. The most drastic overall result was that traditional values, beliefs, and attitudes were unintentionally undermined.[30]

This example illustrates that an organization is an "open social system," that is, all aspects of an organization may have an impact on other parts or the organization itself. Thus a proposed change in one part of an organization must be carefully assessed in terms of its likely impact on the rest of the organization.

Notes and References

1. Etzioni, Amitai, *A Comparative Analysis of Complex Organizations*, The Free Press of Glencoe, New York, 1961.
2. Machiavelli, Niccolo, *The Prince and the Discources*, Chapter XVII, "Of Cruelty and Clemency, Whether It Is Better to be Loved or Feared," Random House, New York, 1950.
3. Suggested by Bernard M. Bass in *Leadership, Psychology, and Organizational Behavior*, Harper & Bros., New York, 1960.
4. R. J. House discusses similar concepts in *Management Development: Design, Implementation and Evaluation*, Bureau of Industrial Relations, University of Michigan, Ann Arbor, Mich., 1967.
5. Brown, J.A.C., *The Social Psychology of Industry*, Penguin Books, Baltimore, Md., 1954, p. 249.
6. For a definition of maturity and a discussion of the relationship between leadership style and the maturity of one's followers see Paul Hersey and Kenneth H. Blanchard "Life Cycle Theory of Leadership," *Training and Development Journal*, May, 1969.
7. Likert, Rensis, *New Patterns of Management* McGraw-Hill, New York, 1961, p. 7.
8. Frederick, Herzberg, Bernard Mausner and Barbara Synderman, *The Motivation to Work*, John Wiley, New York, 1959 and Herzberg, *Work and the Nature of Man*, World Publishing Co., New York, 1966.
9. Guest, Robert H., *Organizational Change: The Effect of Successful Leadership*, Dorsey Press and Irwin Inc, Homewood, Ill., 1964.
10. Perrow, Charles, *Organizational Analysis: A Sociological View*, Wadsworth Publishing Co., Inc., Belmont, Calif., 1970, p. 12.
11. A discussion of behavior modification by Glema G. Holsinger in *Motivating the Reluctant Learner*, Motivity, Inc., Lexington, Mass., 1970, was very helpful in developing this section.
12. The most classic discussions of behavior modification or operant conditioning have been done by B. F. Skinner. See Skinner, *Science and Human Behavior*, Macmillan, New York, 1953, and *Analysis of Behavior*, McGraw-Hill, New York, 1961.
13. Likert, *op. cit.*, p. 2.
14. Lewin, Kurt, "Frontiers in Group Dynamics: Concept, Method and Reality in Social Science; Social Equilibria and Social Change," *Human Relations*, Vol. 1, No. 1, June, 1947, pp. 5-41.
15. *Ibid.*
16. Schein, Edgar H., "Management Development as a Process of Influence" in David R. Hampton, *Behavioral Concepts in Management*, Dickinson publishing Co., Belmont, Cal., 1968, p. 110. Reprinted from the *Industrial Management Review*, Vol. II, No. 2, May, 1961, pp. 59-77.
17. The mechanisms are taken from H. C. Kelman "Compliance, Identification and Internalization: Three Processes of Attitude Change," *Conflict Resolution*, 1958, II, pp. 51-60.
18. Schein, *op. cit.*, p. 112.
19. Kelman discussed compliance as a third mechanism for attitude change.
20. Schein, *op cit.*, p. 112.
21. See C. B. Ferster and B. F. Skinner, *Schedules of Reinforcement*, Appleton-Century Crofts, New York, 1957.
22. "Marine Machine," *Look Magazine*, Aug. 12, 1969.

23. *Ibid.*
24. *Ibid.*
25. *Ibid.*
26. *Ibid.*
27. *Ibid.*
28. Guest, *op. cit.* p. 4.
29. Sharp, Lauriston, "Steel Axes for Stone Age Australians," in *Human Problems in Technological Change*, ed. Edward H. Spicer, Russell Sage Foundation, New York, 1952, pp. 69-94.
30. Cain, Stephen R., "Anthropology and Change" taken from *Growth and Change*, Vol. 1, No. 3, July, 1970, University of Kentucky.
31. *Ibid.*

A SYSTEMS APPROACH TO ORGANIZATION DEVELOPMENT

MICHAEL BEER
EDGAR F. HUSE

Introduction and Historical Perspective

Although the plant has since grown considerably, at the beginning of the change effort there were approximately 35 hourly employees, mostly women; some 15 weekly-salaried technical and clerical personnel; and approximately eight professional and managerial personnel, who were paid monthly.

Some particulars about this plant which need to be considered in generalizing the results obtained in this study[1] to other organizations follow: (1) the products are complex; (2) the operation is primarily assembly, as opposed to fabrication; (3) a majority of factory workers are women; (4) the organization is nonunion; and (5) the organization is relatively small. In other words, approaches which might work with female assembly workers in a nonunion plant might not have the same impact with male union workers in a plant utilizing a different technology.

Because the organization was relatively new when this organization development effort started, it did not have a well-established historical culture and set of norms. It was in its formative stages, and crucial decisions were in the making concerning the technology in the plant (means of production), methods of setting production standards and controls, personnel practices and policies, managerial practices and philosophy, and the like. For example, at the time of our entry this was one of the relatively few nonunionized plants in an organization having about fifty geographically separate

Reproduced by special permission from *The Journal of Applied Behavioral Science*, "A Systems Approach to Organization Development," by Michael Beer and Edgar F. Huse. Volume 8, Number 1, pp. 79-101. Copyright 1972 NTL Institute for Applied Behavioral Science.

plants. Thus, an opportunity existed to do work in a plant which had not yet completely internalized the practice and traditions of older plants and of the corporation as a whole.

Since I've been working here, my husband is a much better supervisor in *his* plant. I tell him what he should do to make his people more interested in what they are doing—based on what *our* supervisors do here. (*Assembly Worker*)

I hate to say it, but I think that I could be off the manufacturing floor for a month and my girls would still make the manufacturing schedule. (*First-Line Supervisor*)

The comments above were gathered in one plant of a large company which, for several years, has been the focus of a successful systems approach to organizational development (OD) at all levels. It is important to point out at the outset that no single OD approach was used with this plant. Rather, in the systems approach, a wide variety of behavioral science concepts concerning organizational change and effective management were operationalized.

This article is written to provide the reader with an understanding of the systems organizational model that guided our efforts as change agents; to describe the varied approaches used for organizational change; and to describe the results and what we have learned about the process of change and its prospects in large, complex organizations. Rather than consigning the conclusions to the end, we shall underscore our major findings as we proceed through the sections of the case study.

The organizational development program took place in a plant designing and manufacturing complex instruments for medical and laboratory use.

Through the efforts of the personnel supervisor, enough interest existed initially for our holding a series of seminars which contrasted traditional approaches with newer approaches based on behavioral research findings and theory. Although these seminars never succeeded in getting an explicit decision on the pattern of management that would prevail in the plant (indeed, as will be discussed later, there was considerable resistance to "theory"), they did start to unfreeze the managerial group (which was steeped in the tradition of the parent organization) sufficiently to commit themselves to "trying" some new approaches on a very limited basis. This constituted much less than commitment to a new pattern of management, but it did open the door to experimentation and examination.

Overworked Theories

A number of practitioners of OD stress the importance of top management commitment to OD if such a program is to be successful. As one author puts it, "Without such support, we have found no program of this kind can ever succeed. . . . First, we worked with top managers to help them fully understand. . . . This proved vital, not only in helping their understanding of the concepts but also in earning their commitment to the program" (Roche and MacKinnon, 1970). In the same vein. Beckhard (1969) and Blake and Mouton (1969) stress that OD must be planned and managed from the top down.

Certainly no one would dispute the proposition that top management commitment to OD is highly valuable and helpful. However, our experience in this study [*Finding 1*] indicates that *a clear-cut commitment at the top of the organizational unit to a particular OD approach is not necessary for a development program to succeed*. Indeed, an attempt to obtain too strong a commitment from top management in the early stages may be threatening enough to cause the withdrawal of any commitment to planned change, especially since the concept of OD and its technologies (e.g., Theory Y, job enrichment, sensitivity training, and the like) are foreign and threatening to the established beliefs of many managers.

Moreover, we found [*Finding 2*] that *total top management understanding of where the OD process will lead and the state of the organization at the end is not necessary for successful programs to take place*. Indeed, given the current state of the art, the OD practitioner himself may not have a clear view of the road ahead, except in very general terms.

What *is* necessary is that someone in a strategic position feel the need for change and improvement. In our plant, that person was the personnel supervisor. Although the plant manager was mildly interested in the initial stages, he was mainly submitting to pressures from the personnel man. Throughout his tenure in the plant, the plant manager's commitment and interest mildly increased, but he was never a strong proponent nor the most skilled manager in some of the new approaches. Furthermore, the plant manager's "boss" never fully knew what was going on in the plant nor did he ever commit himself in any way to the OD program. We now believe that it is possible to change a relatively autonomous unit of a larger organization without the total commitment or understanding of top management in that unit and, in larger and more complex organizations, even without their knowledge.

Initial Commitment to New Approaches

In addition to felt need, the second essential condition is that there be, somewhere in the organization, some initial commitment to experimentation, application, and evaluation of new approaches to present problems. A case study report by the second author (Huse, 1965) describes a successful OD program that took place because a middle manager in a large organization felt the need for change and requested help. He could not have cared less about specific OD principles. He simply wanted help in improving his organization. Davis (1967) points out, in his now classic case study, that top management was not really involved at the beginning and that a majority of the effort was expended in "on-the-job" situations, working out real problems with the people who are involved with them."

Of course, it is obvious that top management support of both theory and practice makes it easier for the change agent; conversely, the lack of such support increases the risk involved for consultants and managers, and causes other systems problems, as we shall discuss later in this article. Furthermore, the conditions of a felt need, a strong and self-sufficient commitment to change, and relative unit autonomy are needed. What we *are* saying is that the commonly heard dicta that one must start at the top and that top management must be committed to a set of normative principles are overworked. *Change can and does begin at lower levels in an organization[Finding 3].*

A Conceptual Model

If the client system and its management in this case did not (need to) have specific OD concepts in mind, who did? The change agents did.

It is important that the change agent have in mind an organizational model and a flexible set of normative concepts about management with a systems orientation. The organization model should be general and reflect the complex *interactive* nature of systems variables. The concepts must be updated and changed as new research findings become available and as more is learned about the functioning of the client system, the environment in which the client system operates, and the effects of changes made in the client system. That is, of course, an iterative procedure.

Figure 1 represents the model of organizational change which guided our efforts. This model has some basic characteristics which must be understood if we are to see how it can shape the planning of a change effort. It represents an organization as an open system engaged in a conversion process. Employee needs, expecations, and abilities are among the raw materials (inputs) with which a manager must work to achieve his objectives.

Organizations have many processes. Figure 1 includes only the more important ones in general terms, and these exist at both the structural and interpersonal levels. Leadership and communication, for example, are two of the interpersonal dimensions which serve to pull together, integrate, and shape the behavior of organizational members. They convert into effort and attitudes the potential brought to the organization in the form of needs and abilities of individuals. The structure or formalized dimensions of the organization obviously cannot exist independently of the interpersonal variables, but they are different from the interpersonal variables in terms of their susceptibility to managerial control, the means by which they might be changed, and the timing of their change. Previous literature on organizational change has emphasized interpersonal variables; more recent literature (Lawrence and Lorsch, 1969) has emphasized structural variables. It is our opinion, based upon experience, that both interpersonal and structural variables are crucial to effective organizational change. The effects of organizational design or managerial control systems on employees have been researched and documented but are still insufficiently understood. For example, we are convinced that an operant conditioning model can be used to understand the behavior of managers with respect to controls. "Beating" goals and looking good on standard measures are like food pellets to the manager.

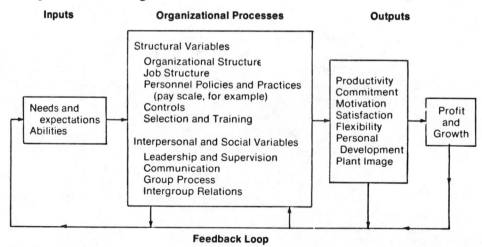

Figure 1. Systems model of an organization.

In the outputs column, we have listed multiple outcomes. These are not completely independent, but they are conceptually distinctive enough in their relationship to the organizational process variables that it is useful to think of them individually. It is the optimization of the organizational outputs that leads to long-term profitability and growth for employees and the organization. Other final outcomes could be listed if we were discussing organizations with different objectives.

Inherent in this model are several basic notions: An organization is an open system which, from the human point of view, converts individual needs and expectations into outputs. Organizational outputs can be increased by improving the quality of the input. An example of this would be the selection of people with higher levels of ability and needs. However, because there are costs associated with selecting personnel of higher quality, we might say that efficiency has not increased. The organization may improve its performance, but this gain has been obtained only because the input, i.e., the quality of personnel has improved, not because there has been a change in the manner in which the organization *utilizes* its human resources.

Since organizations are open systems, organizational performance can also improve by unleashing more of the potential inherent in the human resources. If you will, outputs will increase because we have made the conversion process more efficient. This can be done, for example, by designing organizational processes which better fit the organization's environment or by changing organizational processes so that human resources can be fully unleashed and brought to bear on the task and objectives of the organization. The adjustment of organizational processes to reflect more accurately the needs of the environment and of the persons in it is one of the key objectives of our organizational development program.

Figure 1[2] does not cover some of the more traditional but vitally important concepts of an organization as a total system. For example, capital budgets, the R & D thrust of an organization, overhead or indirect budgets, and the marketing direction of an organization are extremely important aspects which need to be considered. Blake and Mouton (1969) have developed the Corporate Excellence Rubric as a means of assessing the health of the organization through a traditional functional framework. Furthermore, current research (Lawrence and Lorsch, 1969) points up the fact that the differentiation of functional units has a tremendous influence upon the effectiveness of an organization. However, for purposes of brevity, these aspects are not covered in this article.

Mechanisms of Change

We chose an eclectic approach to create change in the organizational processes listed in Figure 1, with the basic belief that a variety of approaches to change should be used with the plant in question. The primary mechanism was consulting, counseling, and feedback by a team of four. The primary change agents were the personnel man within the organization (there have been four different ones since the OD effort began); Beer as an external-to-the-plant agent but internal to the organization, and Huse as the outside change agent. The fourth member of the team was a research assistant whose responsibility it was to interview and gather data in the client system for diagnostic and feedback uses by the change agents.[3]

We began a basic strategy of establishing working relationships with individuals at all levels of the organization. We operated as resource persons who could be used to solve specific problems or initiate small experiments in management; we tried to encourage someone or some organizational component to start implementing the concepts inherent in our model of an organization. Managers gained familiarity with these ideas through consultation and, to a much lesser extent and without full understanding, from the initial few seminars that we held. The main ingredients were a problem or a desire to change and improve, combined with action recommendations from the change agents. Soon there were a few individuals throughout the organization who began, with our help, to apply some new approaches. Because most of these approaches were successful, the result was increased motivation to change. To a degree, nothing succeeds like success!

Models for Learning

There are at least two basic models for learning. The traditional method, that of the classroom and seminar, stresses theory and cognitive concepts before action. As Argyris (1967) points out, "The traditional educational models emphasize substance, rationality. . . ." However, a number of authors (Bartlett, 1967; Bradford, 1964; Schein and Bennis, 1965) make the point that behavior is another place to start. For example, Huse (1966) has shown that one's own facts are "much more powerful instruments of change than facts or principles generated and presented by an outside 'expert.' " The process of change in this OD effort started with behavioral recommendations, was followed by appropriate reinforcement and feedback, and then proceeded to attitudinal and cognitive changes.

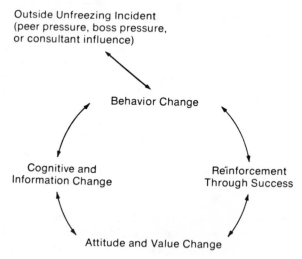

Figure 2. The learning process.

Figure 2 summarizes the basic concept from our experience. *Effective and permanent adult learning [Finding 4] comes after the individual has experimented with new approaches and received appropriate feedback in the on-the-job situation.* This approach is analogous to, but somewhat different from, the here-and-now learning in the T-group.

In other words, a manager might have a problem. Without discussing theory, the change agent might make some recommendations relating to the specific situation at hand. If, in the here-and-now, the manager was successful in the attempt to solve the problem, this would lead to another try, as well as a change in his attitude toward OD. This approach capitalizes upon the powerful here-and-now influence which the job and the organizational climate can have upon the individual. Indeed, such changes can occur without *any* knowledge of theory.

Either model of learning can probably work to produce change in the individual. However, if one starts with cognitive facts and theory (as in seminars), this may be less effective and less authentic than starting with the individual's own here-and-now behavior in the ongoing job situation. In any case, the process is a cyclic one, involving behavior, attitudes, and cognition, each reinforcing the other. In our case, there was an early resistance to seminars and the presentation of "Theory." However, after behavior and attitude changes occurred, there began to be more and more requests for cognitive inputs through reading, seminars, and the like. It is at this later stage that seminars and "theory inputs" would seem to be of most value.

That learning starts with behavior and personal experience has been one of the most important things we have learned as we have worked to effect organizational change. The process is quite similar to what is intended to happen in laboratory training. What we have found [*Finding 5*] is that *the operating, ongoing organization may, indeed, be the best "laboratory" for learning*. This knowledge may save us from an overreliance upon sensitivity training described by Bennis (1968) when he states that "when you read the pages of this Journal, you cannot but think that we're a one-product outfit with a 100 percent foolproof patent medicine." This finding may also be the answer in dealing with Campbell and Dunnette's (1968) conclusions that "while T-group training seems to produce observable changes in behavior, the utility of these changes for the performance of individuals in their organizational roles remains to be demonstrated."

The unfreezing process. What triggers an individual to unfreeze and to allow the process to begin, if it is not "theory"? First, there are some individuals who are ready to change behavior as soon as the opportunity presents itself in the form of an outside change agent. These are people who seem to be aware of problems and have a desire to work on them. Sometimes all that they need are some suggestions or recommendations as to different approaches or methods they may try. If their experiences are successful, they become change leaders in their own right. *They then [Finding 6] are natural targets for the change agent, since they become opinion leaders that help shape a culture that influences others in the organization to begin to experiment and try out new behaviors.* As Davis (1967) points out, it is necessary to "provide a situation which could initiate the process of freeing up these potential multipliers from the organizational and personal constraints which . . . kept them from responding effectively to their awareness of the problems." Davis used "strangers" and "cousins" laboratories. In our case, the unfreezing process was done almost exclusively in the immediate job context.

An early example of the development of change leaders in our work with this company was the successful joint effort of an engineer and a supervisor to redesign a hotplate assembly operation which would eliminate an assembly line and give each worker total responsibility for the assembly of a particular product. It resulted in a productivity increase of close to 50 per cent, a drop in rejects from 23 per cent, controllable rejects to close to 1 per cent, and a reduction in absenteeism from about 8 per cent to less than 1 per cent in a few months. Not all the early experiments were successful, but mistakes were treated as part of the experiential learning process.

As some in the organization changed and moved ahead by trying out new behaviors, others watched and waited but were eventually influenced by the culture. An example of late changers so influenced was the supervisor of Materials Control, who watched for two years what was going on in the plant but basically disagreed with the concepts of OD. Then he began to feel pressure to change because his peers were trying new things and he was not. He began by experimenting with enriching his secretary's job and found, in his own words, that "she was doing three times as much, enjoying it more, and giving me more time to manage." When he found that this experiment in managerial behavior had "paid off," he began to take a more active interest in OD. His next step was to completely reorganize his department to push decision making down the ladder, to utilize a team approach, and to enrich jobs. He supervised four sections: purchasing, inventory control, plant scheduling, and expediting. Reorganization of Materials Control was around product line teams. Each group had total project responsibility for their own product lines, including the four functions described above. We moved slowly and discussed with him alternative ways of going about the structural change. When he made the change, his subordinates were prepared and ready. The results were clear: In a three-month period of time (with the volume of business remaining steady), the parts shortage list was reduced from 14 I.B.M. pages to less than a page. In other words, although he was a late-changer in terms of the developing culture, his later actions were highly successful.

The influence of the developing culture was also documented through interviews with new employees coming into the plant. The perception by production employees that this was a "different" place to work occurred almost immediately, and changes in behavior of management personnel were clear by the second month.

In other words, while seminars and survey feedback techniques were used in our work with this plant, the initial and most crucial changes were achieved through a work-centered, consulting-counseling approach, e.g., through discussion with managers and others about work-related problems, following the model of adult learning described earlier.

So much for the manner in which the unfreezing process occurred and some of our learning about this process. What were some of the normative concepts applied and why? A brief overview of our approaches and findings follows.

A Normative Model

Communications

In this phase we attempted to open up communications at all levels. We started monthly meetings at every level of the organization, as well as a weekly meeting between the plant manager and a sample of production and clerical employees. The aim was to institutionalize the meetings to serve as a means for exchanging information and ideas about what had happened and what needed to happen. The meetings, especially between first-line supervisors and production workers, began primarily as one-way communications downward. Little by little, qualitative changes occurred and the meetings shifted to two-way communications about quality, schedules and production problems. This effort to communicate (which was also extended through many other approaches) was an entire year in attaining success. It was an agonizingly slow process of change. In retrospect, this was a critical period during which trust was building and a culture conducive to further change was developing. Out of this, we concluded [*Finding 7*] that *organizational change occurs in stages: a stage of unfreezing and trust building, a take-off stage when observable change occurs, and a stabilization stage. Then the cycle iterates.* In addition to the communication type of meeting described above, confrontation meetings between departments were also held (Blake, Shepard, and Mouton, 1964). These, too, improved relationships between departments, over time.

Job Enrichment

A second area of change was in job structure, primarily through the use of job enrichment, or, as it has been called in the plant, "the total job concept." We have already discussed the importance of the job for psychological growth and develop-ment—our findings in this area parallel those of Ford (1969). Our first experience of tearing down a hotplate assembly line has already been discussed. This was followed by similar job enrichment efforts in other areas. In one department, girls individually assemble instruments containing thousands of parts and costing several thousand dol-lars. The change here allowed production workers to have greater responsibility for quality checks and calibration (instead of trained technicians). In another case, the changeover involved an instrument which had been produced for several years. Here, production was increased by 17 per cent with a corresponding increase in quality; absenteeism was reduced by more than 50 per cent.

The plant is presently engaged in completely removing quality control inspection from some departments, leaving final inspection to the workers themselves. In other departments, workers have been organized into autonomous workgroups with total responsibility for scheduling, assembly, training, and some quality control inspection (the source for the supervisor's laudatory quote at the beginning of this case study). Changes in these areas have evolved out of cohesive workgroups. However, like Ford (1969), we have found that not everyone in the assembly workforce responds positively to such changes, although a high majority do so over time.

Mutual goal setting has also been widely adopted. Instead of standards established by engineering (a direction in which the plant was heading when we started), goals for each department are derived from the plant goal, and individual goals for the week or month are developed in individual departments through discussions between the boss and subordinates. Our interview data clearly show that in this way workers understand how their individual goals fit into the plant goal structure and can work on their own without close supervision for long periods of time.

Changes toward a pay process more clearly based on merit (including appraisals for hourly and weekly salaried clerical and technical employees as well as for managerial and professional personnel) were made to reinforce and legitimate an escalating climate of work involvement. More and more employees are now involved in questions of production, quality, department layout, and methods. Assembly workers give depart-ment tours to visitors, including vice presidents. Organization-wide technical and product information sessions are held. Concerned more with strategy than with daily problems, the top team has for some time molded itself into a business team, meeting periodically to discuss future plans.

More recently, changes in organizational structure are taking place to move a functionally oriented organization to a matrix organization, using concepts derived directly from Lawrence and Lorsch (1969). This involves, among other approaches, the use of "integrators" at varying levels within the organization.

Systems Interaction

A systems approach requires that mutually consistent changes in *all* subsystems be made in affecting the organizational processes listed in our model. In other words, *[Finding 8] multiple changes in the subsystems are needed for the individual employee to change behavior and perceptions of his role.* For example, participative supervision should be accompanied by redesign of jobs to allow more responsibility, by a pay system that recognizes performance, by a communication system that is truly open, and by corresponding changes in other subsystems throughout the organization. Past attempts to change organizations through a nonsystems approach, e.g., through such single media as supervisory training or sensitivity training, have had limited success because other key leverage points have not been changed in the total system. Further, an attempt to change one subsystem too quickly or too drastically can have severely harmful results, as pointed out in the "Hovey and Beard Company" case (Lawrence, Bailey, Katz, Seiler, Orth, Clark, Barnes, and Turner, 1961). Whether structural *or* interpersonal changes should take precedence in a given period of time depends upon the readiness of the system to change and the key leverage points. The key concept *[Finding 9]* is that *structural and interpersonal systems changes must reinforce and legitimate each other.* Figure 3 presents this concept. The change can be in either direction in the model.

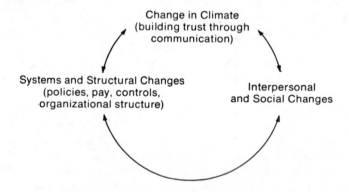

Figure 3. The sequence of organizational change.

We also learned *[Finding 10]* that *systems changes set off additional interactive processes in which changes in organizational functioning increase not only outputs but also develop the latent abilities of people.* We have concluded that the real potential in organizational development lies in setting in motion such a positive snowball of change, growth, and development. For example, as assembly workers took on additional responsibility they became more and more concerned about the total organization and product. "Mini-gripes" turned into "megagripes," indicating a change in the maturity of the assembly workers (Huse and Price, 1970). At the same time, this freed up management personnel to be less concerned about daily assignments and more concerned about long-range planning.

To illustrate this, at the beginning of the OD effort, the organization had a plant manager, a production superintendent, and three first-line supervisors, or a total of five supervisory personnel in the direct manufacturing line. As the assembly-line workers took on more responsibility, the five have been reduced to three (the plant manager and two first-line supervisors). The number of inspection and quality control personnel has also been reduced.

A Subsystem Within the Larger Organization

Up to this point in the case study we have been considering the plant as a system in its own right. However, changes set in motion here have also provided the first step in a larger plan for change and development to occur in the parent corporation (consisting of some 50 plants). As a subsystem within the larger system, this plant was to serve as a model for the rest of the corporation—as an example of how change should be planned and implemented. It was our hope that the systems approach to change would create such a clearly different culture in this plant that it would become visible to the rest of the corporation; that people from other segments of the larger organization would visit and become interested in trying similar models and mechanisms of change. Our hopes have been realized. Indeed, both authors are now applying OD concepts to other areas of the organization.

Influence is also exerted upward, with greater acceptance of these concepts by individuals at higher levels in the organization [Finding 11]. It is our perception that changes in organizational subsystems can have strong influences on the larger culture if the change is planned and publicized; if seed personnel are transferred to other parts of the system; if a network of change agents is clearly identified; and if careful planning goes into where and how change resources are to be used. Once again, top-management commitment is not a necessary commitment for evolutionary change in a complex, multidivision, multilocation organization. (*Sometimes*, the tail begins to wag the dog.)

Subsystem Difficulties

However, this change process may cause some difficulties in the area of interface between the smaller subsystem and the larger system. For example, the increased responsibilities, commitment, and involvement represented by job enrichment for assembly workers are not adequately represented in the normal job evaluation program for factory workers and are difficult to handle adequately within the larger system. So pay and pay system changes must be modified to fit modern OD concepts. Figure 4 is a model which shows the effects of change in climate on individual model perceptions of equity in pay.

In addition to the larger system difficulties over wage plans, there still exists a great deal of controversy as to the importance of pay as a motivator (or dissatisfier). For example, Walton (1967) takes a basically pessimistic approach about participation through the informal approach, as opposed to the more formal approaches embodied in the Scanlon Plan (Lesieur, 1958), which "stress the economic rewards which can come from [formal] participation." On the other hand, Paul, Robertson, and Herzberg (1969) review a number of job enrichment projects and report: "In no instance did management

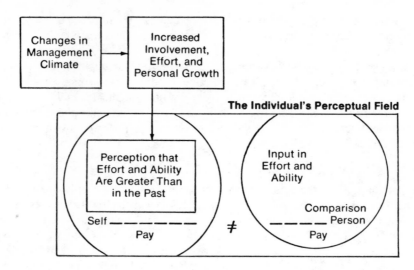

Figure 4. Equity model.

face a demand of this kind [higher pay or better conditions] as a result of changes made in the studies." In a recent review of the Scanlon Plan (Lesieur and Puckett, 1969), the authors point out that Scanlon's first application did not involve the use of financial incentives but, rather, a common sharing between management and employees of problems, goals, and ideas. Indeed, Ford (1969) reports on the results of a series of job enrichment studies without ever mentioning the words "pay" or "salary." In the plant described in this case, no significant pressures for higher pay have been felt to date. However, there has been sufficient opportunity for promotion of hourly employees to higher level jobs as the plant has grown.

It is certainly not within the scope of this article to handle the controversy regarding the place of pay as a motivator. We do want to make the point that standard corporate job evaluation plans are only one instance of the difficulties of interface between the client plant as a subsystem and the larger system. In our experience, these and other areas have been minor rather than major problems, but they have been problems.

Changes in Consumption of Research Findings

An important by-product of our experience has been [*Finding 12*] that *the client system eventually becomes a sophisticated consumer of new research findings in the behavioral sciences*. As mentioned earlier, there was early resistance to "theory"; but as the program progressed, there was increasing desire for "theory." We also found that a flexible and adaptable organization is more likely to translate theory into new policies and actions. Perhaps this is where behavioral scientists may have gone wrong in the past. We may have saturated our client systems with sophisticated research studies before the culture was ready to absorb them. This would suggest that a more effective approach may be carefully planned stages of evolution from an action orientation to an action-research orientation to a research orientation. This implies a long-range plan for change that we often talk about but rarely execute with respect to the changes in organizations that we seek as behavioral scientists.

Results of the Organizational Development Program

To a great extent we have tried to share with you our results and findings throughout the article. In addition, we are retesting these concepts in several other plants. In retrospect, how much change really occurred at the client plant, and how effective have been the new approaches introduced? We have only partial answers since a control plant did not exist and since the plant was relatively new; no historical data existed against which to compare performance. However, considerable data do exist to support the thesis that change has occurred and that new managerial approaches have created an effective organization. (In addition, the second author is conducting ongoing research in another plant in the organization which has historical data. Before- and after-measures have already shown dramatic change: e.g., reduction in manufacturing costs for the plant of 40 percent to 45 per cent.)

Extensive interviews by the researcher and detailed notes and observations by the change agents indicate considerable improvement after our work with this plant. Communication is open, workers feel informed, jobs are interesting and challenging, and goals are mutually set and accomplished.

In each of the output dimensions, positive changes have occurred which we think, but cannot always prove, would not have occurred without the OD effort. Turnover has been considerably reduced; specific changes in job structure, organizational change, or group process have resulted in measurable productivity changes of up to 50 per cent. Recent changes in the Instrument Department have resulted in productivity and quality improvements. We have witnessed the significant changes in maturity and motivation which have taken place among the assembly workers. A change to a project team structure in the Materials Control Department led to a reduction of the weekly parts shortages. Following the findings of Lawrence and Lorsch (1969), the use of "integrators" and project teams has significantly reduced the time necessary for new product development, introduction, and manufacture. A fuller evaluation of the integrator role and the project organization as it affects intergroup relations and new product development is reported elsewhere (Beer, Pieters, Marcus, and Hundert, 1971).

Several recent incidents in the plant are evidence of the effect of the changes and bear repeating. An order called for in seven days and requiring extraordinary cooperation on the part of a temporary team of production workers was completed in fewer than seven days. A threatened layoff was handled with candor and openness and resulted in volunteers among some of the secondary wage earners.

New employees and managers now transferred into the plant are immediately struck by the differences between the "climate" of this plant and other locations. They report more openness, greater involvement by employees, more communication, and more interesting jobs. Even visitors are struck immediately by the differences. For example, one of the authors has on several occasions taken graduate students on field trips to the plant. After the tour, the consensus is, "You've told us about it, but I had to see it for myself before I would believe it." Managers transferred or promoted out of the plant to other locations report "cultural shock."

Summary and Conclusions

The Medfield Project (as it can now be labeled) has been an experiment in a systems approach to organizational development at two systems levels. On the one hand, we have regarded the plant as a system in and of itself. On the other hand, we have regarded the plant as a subsystem within a larger organization. As such a subsystem, we wanted it to serve as a model for the rest of the organization. Indeed, as a result of this study, OD work is going forward elsewhere in the parent company and will be reported in forthcoming articles.

Although we have shared our findings with you throughout the article, it seems wise now to summarize them for your convenience, so that they may be generalized to other organizations and climates.

Findings

1. A clear-cut commitment to a particular OD approach is not necessary (although desirable) for a successful OD program to succeed.

2. Total top-management understanding of where the OD process will lead and the state of the organization at the end is not necessary for organizational change to occur.

3. Change can and does begin at lower levels in the organization.

4. Effective and permanent adult learning comes after the individual has experimented with new approaches and received appropriate feedback in the on-the-job situation.

5. Rather than the T-group, the operating, ongoing organization may be the best "laboratory" for learning, with fewer problems in transfer of training.

6. Internal change leaders are natural targets for the change agent, since they become influence leaders and help to shape the culture.

7. Organizational change occurs in stages: a stage of unfreezing and trust building, a take-off stage when observable change occurs, and a stabilization stage. Then the cycle iterates.

8. Multiple changes in the subsystems are needed for the individual employee to change behavior and perceptions of his role.

9. Structural and interpersonal systems changes must reinforce and legitimate each other.

10. Systems changes set off additional interactive processes in which changes in organizational functioning not only increase outputs but also develop the latent abilities of people.

11. Influence is also exerted upward, with greater acceptance of these concepts by individuals at higher levels in the organization.

12. The client system eventually becomes a sophisticated consumer of new research findings in the behavioral sciences.

Perhaps the most important and far-reaching conclusion is that as organizational psychologists we have viewed our role too narrowly and with an insufficient historical and change perspective. Our research studies tend to be static rather than dynamic. We need to do a better job of developing a theory and technology of changing and to develop a flexible set of concepts which will change as we experiment with and socially engineer organizations. We are suggesting a stronger action orientation for our field and less of a natural science orientation. We must be less timid about helping organizations to change themselves. We must create a positive snowball of organizational change followed by changes in needs and expectations of organizational members, followed again by further organizational change. The objective of change agents should be to develop an evolving system that maintains reasonable internal consistency while staying relevant to and anticipating changes and adaptation to the outside environment. As behavioral scientists and change agents, we must help organizations begin to "become."

Notes

1. Based on a paper presented as part of a symposium entitled "Organizational Change," at American Psychological Association convention, Washington, D.C., September 3, 1969. The authors would like to acknowledge the innovative and far-sighted approaches to management implemented by the managers and supervisors of the organization described. Particular thanks are due to J. G. Sabin, C. F. Wheatley, and J. Johnson. Many others were and are involved, and we thank them also.
2. Cf. the traditional aspects included in the conceptual model developed by Huse (1969).
3. We should like to acknowledge the help and participation of Mrs. Gloria Gery and Miss Joan Doolittle in the data-gathering phase.

References

Argyris, C. On the future of laboratory training, *Journal of Applied Behavioral Science*, 1967, 3 (2), 153-83.

Bartlett, A. C. Changing behavior as a means to increased efficiency. *Journal of Applied Behavioral Science*, 1967, 3 (3), 381-403.

Beckhard, R. *Organization development: Strategies and models*. Reading, Mass.: Addison-Wesley, 1969.

Beer, M., Pieters, G. R. Marcus, S. H., and Hundert, A.T. Improving integration between functional groups: A case in organization change and implications for theory and practice. Symposium presented at American Psychological Association convention, Washington, D.C., September 1971.

Bennis, W. G. The case study—I. Introduction. *Journal of Applied Behavioral Science*. 1968, 4 (2), 227-231.

Blake, R. R., and Mouton, J. S. *Building a dynamic corporation through grid organization development*. Reading, Mass.: Addison-Wesley, 1969.

Blake, R. R., Shepard. H. A., and Mouton, J. S. *Managing intergroup conflict in industry*. Houston, Tex.: Gulf, 1964.

Bradford, L. P. Membership and the learning process. In L. P. Bradford, J. R. Gibb, and K. D. Benne (Eds.), *T-group theory and laboratory method: Innovation in re-education*. New York: Wiley, 1964.

Campbell, J. P., and Dunnette, M. D. Effectiveness of T-group experiences in managerial training and development. *Psychological Bulletin*, 1968 (August), 70, (2), 73-104.

Davis, S. A. An organic problem-solving method of organizational change. *Journal of Applied Behavioral Science*, 1967, 3 (1), 3-21.

Ford, R. N. *Motivation through the work itself*. New York: American Management Association, 1969.

Huse, E. F. The behavioral scientist in the shop. *Personnel*, 1965 (May/June), 42 (3), 50-57.

Huse, E. F. Putting in a management development program that works. *California Management Review*, (Winter) 1966, 73-80.

Huse, E. F., and Price, P. S. The relationship between maturity and motivation in varied work groups. *Proceedings* of the Seventieth Annual Convention of the American Psychological Association September, 1970.

Lawrence, P. R., and Lorsch, J. W. *Organization and environment*. Homewood, Ill.: Irwin, 1969.

Lawrence, P. R., Bailey, J. C., Katz, R. L., Seiler, J. A., Orth, C. D. III, Clark, J. V., Barnes, L. B., and Turner, A. N. *Organizational behavior and administration*. Homewood, Ill,: Irwin-Dorsey, 1961.

Lesieur, F. G. (Ed.) *The Scanlon plan: A frontier in labor-management cooperation*. Cambridge, Mass.: M.I.T. Press, 1958.

Lesieur, F. G., and Puckett, E. S. The Scanlon plan has proved itself. *Harvard Business Review*, 1969 (September/October), 47, 109-18.

Paul, W. J., Robertson, K. B., and Herzberg, F. Job enrichment pays off. *Harvard Business Review*. 1969 (March/April), 47 (2) 61-78.

Roche, W. J., and MacKinnon, N. L. Motivating people with meaningful work. *Harvard Business Review*, 1970 (May/June), 48 (3), 97-110.

Schein, E. H., and Bennis, W. G. *Personal and organizational change through group methods. The laboratory approach*. New York: Wiley, 1965.

Walton, R. E. Contrasting designs for participative systems. *Personnel Administration*, 1967 (November/December), 30 (6), 35-41.

ISSUES AND ETHICS IN BEHAVIOR MANIPULATION

FREDERICK H. KANFER

Whenever a science is ready to apply its principles or methoas to the control of man's social and physical environment, public attention demands that the consequences of such application be carefully examined. This scrutiny often results in argumentative debates and emotional alignment of the public vis-a-vis the science, its contents and its practitioners. The merciless beam of the public spotlight has by no means been confined to psychology. In our own time chemistry, physics and biology have repeatedly provided discoveries which the public viewed and discussed with alarm. Public concern usually declined gradually as scientific contributions were absorbed into the social fabric. Nevertheless, the vigor of recent public reactions to progress in the study and control of human behavior has taken our academically-minded science by surprise Perhaps the sudden widespread concern with test makers, public opinion swayers, and adjustment manipulators simply indicates that

Reprinted with permission of author and publisher: Kanfer, F. H., "Issues and Ethics in Behavior Manipulation," from *Psychological Reports*, 1965, 16, 187-96.

psychology finally may have something to offer which has applicability to everyday life. The hope for eventual development of the psychology of behavioral control also raises the problem of the ethics of manipulating the behavior of another person. The most surprising aspect of the psychologist's dilemma posed by this problem is its recency. After all, the maniuplation of behavior reportedly first took place when Eve whetted Adam's appetite in the Garden of Eden. For centuries, the issues of morality and the control of one human being over another either have been kept separated or, in fact, combined in such absurd fashion that the most cruel methods of control were perpetrated under the guise of morality. The slaughter during the crusades, the elimination of witchcraft, the conquest of the American Indian, the "liberation" of Europe by the Nazis represent a few choice historical examples of human misbehavior and the use of the ultimate in behavior control through physical force and extermination. By comparison, the minor infraction committed currently when a psychotherapist subtly alters a neurotic patient's value system or his social behavior pattern seems rather mild. Nevertheless, numerous recent popular articles and books reflect the increasing public concern with the use of psychological methods in education, in industry, in the treatment of the mentally ill, and in politics.

The purpose of this paper is to discuss several issues concerning use of psychological principles in the manipulation of human behavior. These issues may arise in the context of psychology practiced in the clinic, in industry, by the military, or by governments. This paper will focus on behavior control by psychotherapy. The issues concern: (1) the methods of control, (2) the domain of controlled behavior, and (3) the selection of ends for which control is exercised.

Control by Reward versus Punishment

With regard to the "psychology of behavior control" (Krasner, 1962a) in a clinic, the current sensitivity to the ethical issues stems largely from an increased proficiency in the control of behavior, and especially from a fear of one special kind of manipulation.[1] In the past, efforts toward improving control over adult behavior have been mainly directed at finding better methods of aversive control, e.g., threat, coercion, or physical force. Currently, there is a tendency toward increasing use of control by positive reinforcement in all areas of life. This shift to promises, rewards, and seductions rather than coercion represents, in our opinion, the pith of public concern. In his discussion of methods used by controlling agencies, Skinner (1953) suggests that government, law, and religion mainly use practices of threat of punishment, withdrawal of positive reinforcers, or presentation of negative reinforcers to achieve obedience. Further, with use of these methods by social agencies the usual "effect of group control is in conflict with a strong primarily reinforced behavior of the individual" (Skinner, 1953, p. 327). In contrast, economic control, education, and psychotherapy rely more heavily on positive reinforcement. Recently, control by positive reinforcement has been used extensively in programs of "ideological totalism" (Lifton, 1961). In practice, such control is heightened when used only after achievement of complete control over the individual's environment and thought processes by force. As in laboratory animals, positive reinforcement is most effective following severe deprivation. If such deprivations can be created in human groups, success in behavior control should be markedly enhanced for the possessor of the positive reinforcers. The deliberate application of methods reserved earlier mostly for education, work achievement, child rearing and therapy, in politics and government represents a major innovation. Coupled with extension from control over individuals to control over groups, this advance in control techniques raises public concern. The shift in methods of control is illustrated in the history of psychotherapy by the progress from straitjackets, padded cells, and beatings to therapeutic communities, insight therapy, and counter-conditioning.

It is interesting to speculate why control by positive reinforcement might be more dangerous than control by coercion. Manipulation by aversive control creates its own hazards. The person under aversive control usually knows it. He suffers pain, experiences humiliation, anger, or other emotional discomfort. It is also likely that aversive control inevitably breeds attempts at counter-control. Even in the young child the first response to being slapped is to try to slap back. Aversive control thus motivates behavior aimed at reducing such control by annoying, teasing, or destroying the controller. Further, aversive control is difficult to maintain by a small group. To use force effectively you have to be bigger, stronger, or more numerous than your adversary. Thus aversive control by an individual over a large group, or by a small minority is doomed to failure in the long run. Finally, as Skinner (1953) has indicated, aversive control affects only public behavior. It is of limited use in "thought control" because a person can escape some aversive consequences by thinking silently or by nonconforming behavior in his private experiences.

In contrast, manipulation by positive control produces none of these disturbing by-products. By definition these methods use reinforcing stimuli which have the inherent potential for increasing or maintaining behaviors which procure these stimuli. People respond in blind faith to reward, to promises, and to reassurances. Large scale use of these methods, however, has not concerned people because the age-old deceptions of the Pied Piper have been assumed to be sufficiently transparent to allow most adults to recognize them as false promises and to resist temptation by persuasion. Recently, Browning's Pied Piper of Hamlin has become more sophisticated. He has put on the disguise of a gray flannel suit, of a human relationship expert, a psychotherapist, or a friendly interrogator in a prison camp. His pipe has turned into other instruments promising such sweet things as affection and happiness to a juvenile delinquent, money-back guaranteed satisfaction with soaps and cereals, or a political paradise for the masses, all without pain, coercion, or physical violence. This increased professionalism and sophistication in the application of psychological principles has caused uneasiness to the public because the methods have lost some of their transparency and amateurish quality. Although there is contradictory experimental evidence on the question of behavioral modification without awareness (Eriksen, 1962; Kanfer & Marston, 1961), these studies also clearly indicate that Ss cannot verbalize all aspects of the controlling stimuli which affect their behavior.

Certainly, the increase in psychological sophistication has also made it easier for the controller to disguise his own motives in order to mislead Ss of his controlling influence. In addition, he can manipulate conditions which would make his positive reinforcement more effective. Frank (1961) makes this point in discussing methods of thought reform: "the essence of the relationship is that the persuader invests great effort to bring about changes in the sufferer's bodily state or attitudes that he regards as beneficial . . . (and the setting) . . . occurs in the context of hope and potential support from the persuader and the group'' (1961, p. 95). Since our democratic principles also uphold the right of consent of the governed, any use of control resulting in a change of behavior without S's awareness of the methods of influence and the intent of his controllers would be ethically objectionable to our society. Even though these emphases placed upon self-control, self-government, and self-determination are accepted by our culture and its scientist members, a deterministic behavioral psychology cannot disavow its implication that behavior is controlled by an organism's previous history and its environment, regardless of its ability to describe verbally these controlling variables. Regardless of ethic or social interest the fiction of the complete Rational Man as the captain of his own destiny, is as naive to behavioristic psychology as it was to Freudian psychoanalysis (although for different reasons).

In psychotherapy, social pressures or other devices attempting to maniupulate the patient's behavior by coercion are rarely used as a primary method of control. Therapeutic operations are more likely to stress positive goals, to reduce tensions, to reinforce and strengthen new behaviors. The therapist is, of course, at an additional disadvantage in the use of aversive controls. When the therapist acts as a noxious stimulus the patient can counter by "resistance," by failing to keep his appointments, or by leaving the field altogether. Patients under strong aversive control by parental pressure or court order are notoriously poor risks for psychotherapy.

Control of Private Experiences

The invitability of mutual influence in a clinical relationship is well domumented by recent research and some of its implications have been discussed by Krasner (1962a).

What are some of the features then which make the psychotherapeutic interaction or other similar relationships especially suited for the manipulation or control of behavior?

One factor is the distress and discomfort of the patient. The social role of the patient has been described by Parsons (Parsons & Fox, 1958). In our society the sick person can claim certain privileges. It is assumed that he is not responsible for his incapacity, and his state of sickness exempts him from his normal social obligations. In turn, it is understood that he will attempt to get well and that he has an obligation to seek help and cooperate with others who treat him. As Parsons states, the latter implies a dependency of the sick person on the healer. The act of coming for help signifies the patient's realization that he cannot cope with the problem and that he wishes another person to take responsibility for treating it. This dependency status should tend to increase the effectiveness of the therapist's reinforcing operations (cf. research on the role of dependency, prestige, and other therapist-patient variables in verbal conditioning; Greenspoon, 1962, Krasner, 1962b).

A second feature concerns the *content* of the interactions. Most psychologists agree that the specific content of the patient's verbalizations in psychotherapy is far less important than was believed by earlier theorists. One common element in all therapeutic interactions is the therapist's insistence that the patient talk about those private experiences, fears, attitudes, and beliefs which are usually not shared with other people. Recent reviews by William Sargant (1957), Jerome Frank (1961) and Robert Lifton (1961) of methods of persuasion, thought reform, and therapy all suggest that the most successful methods of behavior manipulation, including magic, religion, and political coercion, share the requirement that the person publicly expose at least some of his privately held beliefs and attitudes. This accessibility to personal and private behavior, in turn, makes the person more vulnerable to control. The more behavior is exposed to the controlling agent the easier it is to set up conditions which modify behavior. Lifton (1961) points out that the admissions of guilt over minimal crimes against the state in Chinese "brainwashing" camps and universities provide the opportunity for the controller to reinforce such self-accusing behavior, to promise relief from guilt by self-punishing procedures and generally to weaken existing behavior and introduce new responses.

Privacy, the inaccessibility of much personal behavior in a democratic society, probably represents the bulwark of democracy because it allows for variability, and for divergence of attitudes and beliefs. What is jealously guarded as a right to privacy in everyday life is, in fact, surrendered in the psychotherapeutic hour. The consequences of this making accessible of the patient's private experiences have been discussed elsewhere (Kanfer, 1961). The potentials for controlling important behavioral sequences, usually not subject to control by direct social reinforcement, increase very much the extent of the therapist's influence.

Metavalues and Personal Values

Clinicians are beginning to accept the thesis that the therapist's value system tends to affect the direction of the patient's change in treatment (Rosenthal, 1955; Schrier, 1953). Among the many problems raised by this recognition are the methods of handling value material (e.g., Ellis, 1962; Meehl, 1959; Segal, 1959), and the ethical implications of the intrusion of personal values into psychotherapy (Williamson, 1958; Weisskopf-Joelson, 1953). Existential analysis (Weisskopf-Joelson, 1958) assumes that the purpose of treatment is the realization of creative and attitudinal values and this school frankly admits its value-orientation.

Although the term "value" is difficult to define, two separate aspects relating to the problem in psychotherapy are worthy of mention.

There are clear cut rules for many behaviors which are common to practically all members of a given culture. These rules are usually also accepted by the therapist and his client. We will call these *metavalues* (cultural values). In addition, there is a variety of situations in which several alternate behaviors and goal hierarchies are equally tolerated by society but which differ in the degree to which they lead to satisfaction in the individual. These alternatives are determined primarily by the individual's past experience. We shall call these alternatives *personal values*. Complications arise both in the patient's value system and in the psychotherapy relationship because of the inconsistencies between metavalues and personal values. Interpretation of the cultural metavalues further varies as a function of membership in a subgroup such as a socio-economic, religious, or geographic affiliation. The outcome of therapy should provide a wider choice of alternative behaviors for the patient with only the restriction that the new behaviors must also be compatible with the metavalues of the patient's cultural environment. The problem lies mainly in producing those changes which lead to socially acceptable behavior even while they result in sweeping changes in the life pattern of the patient. For example, therapists generally do not disagree whether to manipulate behavior which may avert a suicide, but they *do* disagree whether a client's vocational or marital choice should be modified. In complete absence of standards for such personal and private modes of behavior the therapist's judgments are based mainly on his theoretical orientation, on his own experiences, and on his own personal values. These therapist experiences then become the standards for selecting the goals for a particular patient in psychotherapy.[2]

In most cases the neurotic patient can be of little help in deciding what personal values need changing and what range of alternatives would be tolerated both by him and by his environment. When a patient *is* able to do this, the therapist's job does not involve the problem of values. The patient might indicate that he wishes to improve his study habits or seek technical help in making a vocational choice. In these cases technical skills by the psychologist may be applied directly to a problem with an outcome defined clearly by the client himself. Unfortunately, therapists sometimes become suspicious even in these cases and the desirability of the patient's stated goal is often questioned by therapists from the viewpoint of their own personal value systems. Endowed with a tradition of depth-probing, many a therapist is tempted to substitute his own goal for that of the patient. Instead of rendering technical assistance in a circumscribed area, the therapist may then attempt to change the patient's total pattern of living.

Rules for Control

The most heated arguments are generated by the question, "Who establishes the legitimacy of means and ends in behavioral control?" The writer does not presume to have a solution to this question, but wishes to present a few thoughts designed to stimulate further debate.

The APA attempted to indicate the limitations of appropriate means and ends for psychological practice in its early code of ethics (1953). Principle 1.12-1 (p. 7) reads in part: "the psychologists's ultimate allegience is to society, and his professional behavior should demonstrate awareness of his social responsibilities. The welfare of the profession and of the individual psychologist are clearly subordinate to the welfare of the public." Further, Principle 1.13-1 (p. 10): "The psychologist should express in his professional behavior a firm commitment to those values which lie at the foundation of a democratic society, such as freedom of speech, freedom of research, and respect for the integrity of the individual." While these statements arouse the unqualified support of all good psychologists, they do not help to resolve the conflict inherent in the problem of treating neurotic patients. On the one hand, as citizens in a democratic society, psychologists believe that every person has the right to make his own free choice about his way of life. On the other hand, as professionals they also recognize that people who are in difficulties should be helped and choices must often be made for them. The clinical psychologist is an expert in assessing and modifying human behavior by virtue of his training. Regardless of the limitations of psychological theories and methods, psychologists constitute a profession (some say the only profession) which offers extensive training in behavior theory and in methods used to assist people with psychological problems. Therefore, the psychologist is better prepared to apply his knowledge than the layman.[3] However, as noted above, there is a difference between competence in bringing about behavioral changes and in judging the desirability of the behavior and the value system to be substituted. The clinician cannot accept sole responsibility for judging the adequacy of the individual's value system, nor can he become the ultimate interpreter of cultural metavalues to the patient by psychotherapy or education. In clinical practice, the patient, social milieu and other significant persons in his life must all be considered in selecting appropriate goals for therapy.

Nor can psychology be held responsible for the application of its principles and methods by social agencies or industry in the fields of government, economics, or education. Decisions concerning the legitimacy of means and ends in use of behavioral control methods are no more the responsibility of the psychologist than is the question whether to use atomic weapons in a war in the area of competence of the physicist, or the decision to adopt sterilization procedures with some humans in the domain of the biologist. In the absence of any specific mandate from the social community through its legal, political, religious, or social agencies psychologists will continue to use methods of control which are sometimes not acceptable to the public and use these for purposes about which there is some debate.

There has already been some indication that psychological knowledge is gradually becoming incorporated into the legal system, providing some standards of behavior which are more consistent with our knowledge of man than many current laws. There is, however, a considerable lag between mores and their incorporation into the legal structure of a society. During this lag professional groups will have to provide leadership in working out rules which describe the goals for which individual human behavior may be manipulated, and the restrictions upon methods under which this purpose is to be accomplished.

When the psychologist leaves his immediate work setting, his conduct falls under the rules by which other social groups operate. A social scientist who publicly gives opinions about the implications of behavioral control techniques for international politics, education, or consumer behavior must expect the same treatment as other public figures who champion controversial issues. It is probably this change in the accustomed reaction from student or patient audiences which has made psychologists so reluctant to participate in public debate and to provide information and guidance to social groups. An additional problem, of course, lies in the thin line of distinction between fact and opinion, between researcher and reformer.

From these considerations, it seems that several specific contributions can be made by psychologists to further public recognition of the social implications of recent advances in psychology.

(1) In their roles as scientists, continuing research on behavioral control methods and on factors limiting their effects to special circumstances should provide clearer understanding of the extent of the problem in practical situations. Research findings already exist which tend to suggest that total behavioral control requires a totally

controlled environment; that verbal (and attitudinal) behavior can be influenced by a variety of variables toward maximal or minimal change; and that self-control training can modify the effect of incentives, thereby reducing greatly the utility of many conditioning procedures. Knowledge of these factors should permit a better estimate of the actual threat inherent in practical methods to which objections are currently raised. If recently described methods turn out to be no more effective than previous controlling devices, or if easy countermeasures are available, no further concern or action would be warranted.

(2) With no special prerogatives to dictate to society the rules by which its members should be educated, controlled, or changed, psychologists as educated citizens can make a contribution as resource persons to established social agencies. These activities demand of the consultant that he explicitly distinguish between facts, interpretation of facts, and his personal opinion.

(3) Our discussion suggests that continued public awareness of the growing effectiveness of psychological techniques may present the best safeguards against their misapplication. Ultimately, the products of any science become public property and only the informed public can wisely regulate their use.

(4) If psychologists have a service to perform in society's effort to evaluate itself, it is the scientific analysis of current psychological practices, embedded in our social matrix. Among those are many which appear to have relevance to the control of *individual* behavior, i.e., practices in education, in law-enforcement, in treatment of emotional adjustment, in consumer persuasion, and industrial personnel procedures. Contributions to each of these fields lie not only in suggestions for changes but also in a thorough analysis of the present practices and their consequences.

Notes

1. While skeptics can point to evidence of current ignorance of even the most common determinants of individual behavior, few will doubt that rapid progress has been made in the last decade. We assume here that modification of individual behavior is feasible, though all the necessary controlling variables are not yet known.
2. If all mental health workers were to share a single set of values their influence would carry with it the same dangers as any system of total control. A requirement of strict conformity to the norms and values set up by the therapist's model of behavior is also tantamount to the complete subservience imposed by totalistic control systems.
3. We recognize that personality variables as yet unexplored may be important determinants of therapist effectiveness. But no scientifically grounded professional can fail to assume that additional didactic training is a necessary, if not sufficient, condition for practice

References

Ellis, A., *Reason and emotion in psychotherapy*. New York: Lyle Stuart, 1962.

Eriksen, C. W., (Ed.) *Behavior and awareness*. Durham: Duke Univer. Press, 1962.

Frank, J. D., *Persuasion and healing: a comparative study of psychotherapy.* Baltimore: Johns Hopkins Press, 1961.

Greenspoon, J., Verbal conditioning and clinical psychology. In A. J. Bachrach (Ed.), *Experimental foundations of clinical psychology.* New York: Basic Books, 1962.

Kanfer, F. H., Comments on learning in psychotherapy. *Psychol. Rep.,* 1961, 9, 681-699.

Kanfer, F. H., & Marston, A. R., Verbal conditioning, ambiguity, and psychotherapy. *Psychol. Rep.,* 1961, 9, 461-475.

Krasner, L., Behavior control and social responsibility. *Amer. Psychologist,* 1962, 17, 199-204. (a)

Krasner, L., The therapist as a social reinforcement machine. In H. Strupp & L. Luborsky (Eds.), *Research in psychotherapy.* Washington: APA, 1962. Pp. 61-95.

Lifton, R. J., *Thought reform and the psychology of totalism.* New York: Norton, 1961.

Meehl, P. E. Some technical and axiological problems in the therapeutic handling of religious and valuational material. *J. counsel. Psychol.,* 1959, 6, 255-259.

Parsons, T. & Fox, R., Illness, therapy and the modern urban family. In E. G. Jaco (Ed.), *Patients, physicians, and illness.* Glencoe: Free Press, 1958. Pp. 234-245.

Rosenthal, D., Changes in some moral values following psychotherapy. *J. consulting Psychol.,* 1955, 19, 131-136.

Sargant, W., *Battle for the mind: a physiology of conversion and brainwashing.* New York: Doubleday 1957.

Schrier, H., The significance of identification in therapy. *Amer. J. Orthopsychiat.,* 1953, 23, 585-604.